Praise for *Austerity Britain, 1945–51*

'One of the most vividly imagined, brilliantly researched and hugely entertaining books of social history I have ever encountered and I can't wait for the next volume in the series'   Rupert Christiansen, *Spectator* Books of 2007

'Narrative history at its best – thoughtful, compassionate, quirky, with immense, rich quotations'
Richard Davenport-Hines, *Sunday Telegraph* Books of 2007

'Kynaston's improbably entertaining history made enterprising use of unusual sources and was an unexpected popular success'
Philip Hensher, *Spectator* Books of 2007

'Kynaston writes brilliantly and readably'
Mark Bostridge, *Independent on Sunday* Books of 2007

'Tuck into David Kynaston's *Austerity Britain*, a hugely enjoyable history of the Attlee years and definitely one to bring back memories both fond and wistful'
Dominic Sandbrook, *Daily Telegraph* Books of 2007

'This was a vintage year for history books, none better than Kynaston's *Austerity Britain*, a cracking read with powerful resonances for those of us born under the Attlee Junta'   Geoffrey Wheatcroft, *Spectator* Books of 2007

'Gloriously vivid . . . flavours its democratic vision of post-war Britain with tantalising foretastes of celebrity culture, by supplementing Mass Observation -style oral history with snippets from famous people's diaries'
Ben Thompson, *Independent on Sunday* Books of 2007

'A marvellous new book . . . Reading it, I found myself increasingly unable to answer a simple question about life in this country: why are we less human and less kind when prosperous than we managed to be when we were poor? No washing machines, no Starbucks, no computers, no television – but people evidently knew how to listen in a spirit of fairness'
Andrew O'Hagan, *Daily Telegraph*

'In this appealing slice of social history, Kynaston doesn't so much sprinkle his text with first-hand testimony as drench it. Mixing recollections from the famous (Fay Weldon, Joan Bakewell and Doris Lessing all chip in with memories) with extracts from Mass-Observation reports, his giant book summons up in vivid brushstrokes both the actuality of life in staple-starved post-war Britain and the state of the nation's morals and attitudes . . . a triumph'

Andrew Holgate, *Sunday Times*

'An object lesson for social historians in how to blend chronological flow and thematic attack into a single, seamless narrative'   D.J. Taylor, *TLS*

'This is a classic; buy at least three copies – one for yourself and two to give to friends and family. It is a classic because its portrayal of that unheroic, slightly shabby yet formative era that was Attlee's Britain is utterly convincing – and more than that, evocative. No one born in this country between 1939 and 1959 will fail to recognise what is being described . . . a plum-duff of a book for both the historian and the general reader'

John Charmley, *Guardian*

'This is a must-read history, an intimate picture of a country trying to pick itself up after the war . . . magnificent'

Sue Baker, Book of the Month, *Publishing News*

'A masterly account . . . *Austerity Britain* has a marvellous flowing sweep to it. Kynaston does not press his opinions on us, but they emerge sharply enough from the weight of evidence he marshals and the expertise he deploys as a leading historian . . . unfailingly evocative'

Ferdinand Mount, *Times Literary Supplement*

'A skilful blend of statistical data, personal testimony and obscure but entertaining detail, it is remarkable for the freshness of the materials on which it is based . . . This is social history fashioned into narrative on the grand scale . . . *Austerity Britain* is an outstanding portrait of an age'

Paul Addison, *Literary Review*

'This wonderful volume is only the first in a series that will take us to 1979 and the election of Margaret Thatcher. When complete, Kynaston's skill in mixing eyewitness accounts and political analysis will surely be one of the greatest and most enduring publishing ventures for generations. It is very hard to praise the author too highly. . . unputdownable'

Brian Thompson, *Observer*

'The book is a marvel . . . the level of detail is precise and fascinating . . . If the succeeding volumes can sustain this quality, Kynaston will have written the fullest, deepest and most balanced history of our times'

John Campbell, *Sunday Telegraph*

'Magnificently refulgent take on the immediate post-war years . . . A couple of months before the Attlee landslide, Evelyn Waugh published *Brideshead Revisited*, that bestselling high-Tory paean to a lost age. A couple of years after Margaret Thatcher took office, a TV adaptation made Waugh's vision of a sweet and innocent past more popular than ever. Nearly 700 pages long, *Austerity Britain* is only the first in a projected series of books that will take us all the way from *Brideshead* to *Brideshead*. I, for one, can't wait'

Chris Bray, *New Statesman*

'Kynaston's book is not only a blood-draining record of wide-scale misery but an absorbing history with surprises for young and old . . . Kynaston's achievement is great, and the facts and views and values here will give us much to think about' Rhoda Koenig, *Evening Standard*

'Truly brilliant social history of Britain in the immediate post-war years, Kynaston depicts a country battered but hopeful . . . Rarely has a book's title been more at odds with the sheer pleasure derived from reading it'

Elizabeth Jenkins, *London Paper*

'A moving read, not least for anyone whose parents came of age in the era' Greg Neale, *BBC History Magazine*

'The sheer ambition of the project is breathtaking . . . Peering through the grey pall that characterises the public imagination of these years, Kynaston sheds light on both the hardships and lighter moments . . . It will be a determined nostalgic who can get through this book without once thanking their lucky stars for the comforts of today. It will also be a rare social historian who will not be looking forward to the next instalment'

Sarah Warwick, *Family History Monthly*

'A glorious bran-tub of a book . . . full of miscellaneous information about the post-war habits of the British people . . . it is written with a wit and sparkle that makes it a pleasure to read' Vernon Bogdanor, *Financial Times*

'A wonderful evocation of post-war Britain . . . this is a convincing picture of the profound cultural conservatism of post-war Britain, an antidote to nostalgia accounts of the Attlee years' Pat Thane, *History Today*

'*Austerity Britain* calls on a dazzling array of contemporary voices, many of them writing in private diaries, to chart the emergence of today's Britain from VE day to 1979' Martin Waller, *The Times*

'A magnificent, rich and moving social history that grips as firmly as any great novel, with the mouth-watering promise of much, much more to come in the not too distant future'   *Manchester Evening News*

AUSTERITY BRITAIN

1945–51

David Kynaston

BLOOMSBURY

LONDON · BERLIN · NEW YORK

Bloomsbury Publishing Plc
36 Soho Square
London W1D 3QY

www.bloomsbury.com

Bloomsbury Publishing, London, New York and Berlin

A CIP catalogue record for this book
is available from the British Library

ISBN 978 0 7475 9923 4
10 9 8 7 6 5 4

Typeset by Hewer Text Ltd, Edinburgh
Printed in Great Britain by Clays Ltd, St Ives plc

The paper this book is printed on is certified independently in accordance with the
rules of the FSC. It is ancient-forest friendly. The printer holds chain of custody.

FSC

Mixed Sources

Product group from well-managed
forests and other controlled sources

Cert no. SGS-COC-2061
www.fsc.org
© 1996 Forest Stewardship Council

Contents

Preface   ix

A WORLD TO BUILD

PART ONE
1 Waiting for Something to Happen   5
2 Broad Vistas and All That   19
3 Oh Wonderful People of Britain!   60

PART TWO
4 We're So Short of Everything   93
5 Constructively Revolutionary   129
6 Farewell Squalor   143
7 Glad to Sit at Home   171

PART THREE
8 Christ It's Bleeding Cold   185
9 Our Prestige at Stake   206
10 The Whole World Is Full of Permits   222
11 Ain't She Lovely?   242
12 A Change in the Terms of Struggle   278

SMOKE IN THE VALLEY

PART ONE
1 What Do You Say?   291
2 Oh, for a Little Extra Butter!   296
3 Jolly Good as a Whole   325
4 A Decent Way of Life   352

PART TWO

5 A Negative of Snowflakes   397
6 Part of the Machinery   405
7 Stiff and Rigid and Unadaptable   431
8 Too High a Price   460
9 Proper Bloody Products   470

PART THREE

10 Andy Is Waving Goodbye   503
11 The Heaviest Burden   535
12 A Kind of Measuring-Rod   560
13 Their Own Private Domain   592
14 That Dump?   619

Afterword   633
Notes   634
Acknowledgements   671
Picture Credits   675
Index   677

Preface

Austerity Britain comprises *A World to Build* and *Smoke in the Valley* – the first two books of *Tales of a New Jerusalem*, a projected sequence about Britain between 1945 and 1979.

These dates are justly iconic. Within weeks of VE Day in May 1945, the general election produced a Labour landslide and then the implementation over the next three years of a broadly socialist, egalitarian programme of reforms, epitomised by the creation of the National Health Service and extensive nationalisation. The building blocks of the new Britain were in place. But barely three decades later, in May 1979, Margaret Thatcher came to power with a fierce determination to apply the precepts of market-based individualism and dismantle much of the post-war settlement. In the early twenty-first century, it is clear that her arrival in Downing Street marks the defining line in the sand of contemporary British history, and that therefore the years 1945 to 1979 have become a period – a story – in their own right.

It is this story that *Tales of a New Jerusalem* is intended to tell: a story of ordinary citizens as well as ministers and mandarins, of consumers as well as producers, of the provinces as well as London, of the everyday as well as the seismic, of the mute and inarticulate as well as the all too fluent opinion-formers, of the Singing Postman as well as John Lennon. It is a history that does not pursue the chimera of being 'definitive'; it does try to offer an intimate, multilayered, multivoiced, unsentimental portrait of a society that evolved in such a way during these 34 years as to make it possible for the certainties of '1945' to become the counter-certainties of '1979'.

Many of us grew up and were formed during that evolution. We live – and our children will continue to live – with the consequences.

———

'Unadjusted impressions have their value, and the road to a true philosophy of life seems to lie in humbly recording diverse readings of its phenomena as they are forced upon us by chance and change.'

Thomas Hardy
Preface to *Poems of the Past and Present*
1901

A WORLD TO BUILD

This book is dedicated to Lucy

PART ONE

I

Waiting for Something to Happen

Eleven a.m. on Tuesday, 8 May 1945, overheard by a Mass-Observation investigator at a newsagent's somewhere in central London:

First woman: They played us a dirty trick – a proper dirty trick.

First man: A muddle it was. Just a muddle.

Second woman: People waiting and waiting and nothing happening. No church bells or nothing.

Second man: Yes – what 'appened to them church bells, I'd like to know.

Third man: (ironically) Heard that thunderstorm in the night? God's wrath that was!

Fourth man: Telling us over and over the church bells would be the signal. And then there was *no* signal. Just hanging around.

Second man: Well, I'm sick and tired – browned off of them I am. The way they've behaved – why, it was an insult to the British people. Stood up to all wot we've stood up to, and then afraid to tell us it was peace, just as if we was a lot of kids. Just as if we couldn't be trusted to be'ave ourselves.

Third man: Do 'em no good in the general election – the way they've gone on over this. People won't forget it. Insult's just what it was. No more and no less.

Third woman: (placatingly) Oh, well, I expect people will get excited enough later in the day.

Second man: It's not the same. It should of been yesterday. When you think of it – peace signed at 2.40 in the morning, and then people wait and wait all day, and then nothing but it would be

VE Day tomorrow. No bells, no All Clear, nothing to start people off.

First woman: That's just what they were afraid of, I reckon.[1]

Over a week after Hitler's death, and following the tardy radio announcement at 7.40 the previous evening, two days of celebration and good cheer were at last under way.

It took a while for things to warm up. Many people, not having heard the news, had arrived for work only to be turned back; quite a few stockbrokers, who naturally had heard the news, journeyed to the City anyway, just to make sure that the Stock Exchange really was closed; outside food shops the inevitable queues were even worse than usual; and in the north of England it rained steadily until lunchtime. Anthony Heap, a middle-aged local-government officer from St Pancras, found himself (with his wife Marjorie) in Piccadilly. 'Had some lunch at the Kardomah Café followed by ice cream at a Milk Bar in Leicester Square.' They did themselves better in Liverpool, where Beryl Bainbridge's parents took her to a celebratory businessmen's luncheon: 'The man who earned his living by having boulders broken on his chest in Williamson Square was standing outside the restaurant belting out the song "It's a lovely day tomorrow/ Tomorrow is a lovely day". My Dad gave him a shilling and shook his hand . . . like they were equals. My mother made him go instantly to the Gents, to wash off the germs.'

By early afternoon, huge crowds were gathering in all the main city centres, especially London. Gladys Langford, a middle-aged school-teacher, caught a bus from Islington to Knightsbridge: 'Piccadilly was already a seething mass of people. The hoarding around Eros was overcrowded with young people of both sexes, mostly of the Forces. About 1/3 of the people were wearing paper-hats, many of them of very attractive design. People were everywhere – on shop-fronts, up lamp-standards, singing and shouting.' Harold Nicolson, walking through Trafalgar Square and down Whitehall after his lunch at the Beefsteak, was less enamoured of what he called 'paper caps' – 'horrible, being of the comic variety' – and regretfully observed 'three Guardsmen in full uniform wearing such hats'. At 2.20 a bus managed to get through Whitehall – 'HITLER MISSED THIS BUS' chalked across it – and soon afterwards, down at the jam-packed Parliament Square end, three middle-aged women were overheard uttering their thoughts: 'I bet Churchill's pleased with himself.' 'So he should. He's done a grand job of work for a man his age – never sparing himself.' 'Pity Roosevelt's dead.' A 50-year-old man butted in: 'It was just like this after the last war and twelve months later we was standing in dole queues.' But after cries of 'Shut up', another middle-aged woman had, for the moment, the final word: 'Nobody's going to make me miserable today. I've been waiting for it too long.'[2]

At 3.00 the flags stopped waving, the bells stopped ringing, and the tumult briefly died down as everyone paused to hear Winston Churchill's short speech, delivered from 10 Downing Street and heard across the land not only on radios but from innumerable loudspeakers, including in Whitehall itself. He announced that the war in Europe would formally end just after midnight but that hostilities had in effect ceased; declared with a characteristic flourish that 'the evil-doers now lie prostrate before us' (a gasp from the Whitehall crowds); and near the end almost barked out the words 'Advance Britannia!' 'There followed,' Nicolson recorded, 'the Last Post and *God Save the King* which we all sang very loud indeed. And then cheer upon cheer.' Gladys Langford, sitting on a chair just inside Green Park and hearing the speech 'broadcast thro' loudspeakers in the trees', was unsure whether it was the King or Churchill speaking, but few others had doubts. A notably unenthusiastic member of the dense throng around Westminster was Vera Brittain, a pacifist throughout the war and now returning to the spot where she had been on Armistice Day, 1918. She generally found the mood of the afternoon 'all so formal and "arranged"' in comparison with the 'spontaneity' 27 years earlier – but it was Churchill specifically whom she could not bear. She felt his appeal to crude nationalism all too 'typical'; condemned him for having in his speech 'introduced no phrase of constructive hope for a better society which renounces war'; and even 'caught a glimpse of him standing in his car as he went from Downing St. to the H. of Commons surrounded by cheering crowds, waving his hat, with the usual cigar & self-satisfied expression'.

As soon as his speech was over, the Heaps, who had joined the multitude in Parliament Square, managed to beat a temporary retreat home (a top-floor flat at Rashleigh House, near Judd Street) for 'a much needed wash and cool off' on what was becoming 'a sweltering hot day'. But for Langford, who had no intention of returning to the fray, escape was far more difficult:

> Queued for a bus but none came – contingents of marchers – officers, men, girls, lads in rough marching order. Walked back to Piccadilly but couldn't negotiate the Circus. Solid mass of people (St John's Ambulance men and nurses behind Swan and Edgar's). A policeman advised me to work my way along by the wall – but I couldn't get near the wall. Followed a tall American soldier and made my way to Wardour St. but Leicester Sq. was impassable. Dodged thro' Soho side streets and finally reached Tottenham Court Rd – a 19 bus and home.

Between 3.20 and 4.00, about a third of the adult population was tuned in to *Bells and Victory Celebrations*. Happily for BBC Audience Research, the 'great majority' of its listeners' panel 'found this broadcast exactly fitted their mood and taste – it was vivid, noisy and inspiring; it brought invalids, and those who lived in remote corners of the country, in touch with the spirit of festivity in the capital and other cities visited'. Even so, 'some wished that the noises – of merrymaking, bells and sirens – had been left to speak for themselves, without the constant flow of "patter"' – and 'the commentator at Cardiff who spoke through the Hallelujah Chorus was thought particularly tiresome.' Frank Lewis, a young man from Barry, might well have been in Cardiff that afternoon but in fact was in Manchester, where he had been studying at the university and had just started a job in a warehouse. At 3.15, having listened to the Prime Minister's address, he left his suburban lodgings and caught a tram to the city centre: 'Town was full of people, all lounging about doing nothing . . . I went in Lyons, by the Oxford cinema (where there was a queue) and got a cup of tea.' Lewis, definitely a glass-half-empty diarist, then went to the crowded Albert Square: 'Everybody seemed to be waiting for something to happen. I stayed for only 10 minutes, then came home; there was nothing doing. These so-called celebrations seem so useless, – people hanging about "doing nought".'[3]

Lewis was no doubt more curmudgeonly than most participants, or indeed non-participants. But it is clear from the findings of the pioneering sociological-cum-anthropological organisation Mass-Observation – which had begun in 1937 and relied largely on volunteer diarists and observers – that riotous abandon was the exception rather than the rule:

> Mostly, the crowds are concentrated in the few focal points of Central London. Away from these, people are restrained and orderly; the excitement seems to be almost entirely a result of the stimulus of crowds and group feeling . . . There was little gaiety in Central London away from the thickest of the crowds, and correspondingly little in the suburbs. People had put great efforts into decorating their houses, but seemed to anticipate little further in the way of celebrations . . . Bonfires, street tea-parties and fireworks, activities meant in the first place for children, were the chief features of provincial celebrations.

Adeline Vaughan Williams (the composer's first wife) was struck by how 'very sedate' Dorking in Surrey was, while Cecil Beaton found Kensington 'as quiet as a Sunday'. And he added, 'There is no general feeling of rejoicing. Victory does not bring with it a sense of triumph – rather a dull numbness of relief that the blood-letting is over.' Even young people could find it hard to celebrate with a full heart – 'I felt most depressed which I felt was very naughty considering how long we have worked and fought for this' was the downbeat diary entry of Joan Waley, who after school and a year's domestic-science course had joined the WRNS and worked near Bletchley on the Enigma code-breaking machines – while for those who had lost loved ones, a heavy tinge of sadness was inevitable.

Nevertheless, the probability is that *most* people were neither depressed nor ecstatic. Rather, they took the two days in their stride, reflected upon them to a greater or lesser extent, and above all tried to have a good time while enjoying the spectacle. '*V.E. Day*,' noted Alice (known to all as Judy) Haines, a youngish married woman living in Chingford, with a firm underlining in her diary, 'and we are due to go to the Westminster Theatre, Buckingham Gate (!) to see Cedric Hardwicke in "Yellow Sands". Decided to chance it by 38, which indicated "Victoria" as the destination anyway. Yes, but we dodged

Piccadilly, travelling via Oxford St.' The exclamation mark was a nod
to Buckingham Palace, where from soon after Churchill's speech the
Royal Family had started to make a series of balcony appearances to
the delight of the massed subjects below. But Haines's main concern,
especially as she was accompanying her husband to the show, was to
look the part on this special day: 'I wore my blue silk frock with red,
white and blue (mountain rose, edelweiss and gentian flowers) brooch
and red coat, and felt right in the fashion.'[4]

Many in the course of the evening went to thanksgiving services.
'In the quiet of that tiny country church we found the note we really
had been seeking,' the Cotton Board's Sir Raymond Streat, one of
whose sons had died in action the previous autumn, wrote to another
son about attending Nether Alderley Church. 'Manchester business
men and Cheshire farm labourers joined in a crowded service. References were made to those whose lives had gone into the purchase of
victory. Your lady mother took this stoically.' Ernest Loftus, headmaster of Barking Abbey School, attended the church in the village
near Tilbury where he lived: 'A full house – largest congregation I've
seen for years. I read lesson as usual. Villagers had bonfire & social
afterwards. We went home & listened to B.B.C.' He was probably in
time to hear the Home Service's *Tribute to the King*, running from
8.30 to 9.00 and listened to by 36 per cent of the adult population.
Representatives from different walks of life were lined up in Studio
8, Broadcasting House to pay their particular live tributes. 'I speak
for the men and women of the British Police,' an anonymous policeman
announced. 'The war brought us many new tasks: we've faced them
not only as officers of the law, but as the friends and protectors of
your Majesty's subjects.' The not yet unmistakable voice belonged to
John Arlott, still an acting patrol sergeant based in Southampton but
starting to get some radio work.

The royal tribute was the prelude to George VI's address to his
people, broadcast live at 9.00. The King's stammer made it a somewhat nerve-wracking occasion for all concerned, but in fact his
longest-ever broadcast (some 13 minutes) did not go too badly – the
ultra-royalist James Lees-Milne even describing it as 'perfect, well
phrased, well delivered in his rich, resonant voice' and 'expressed
with true feeling'. Just before it began, one of Mass-Observation's

investigators slipped into her local pub in Chelsea, where she joined three young Marxist neighbours ('two M22B, twin brothers, and F25B', in other words two 22-year-old middle-class men and a 25-year-old middle-class woman):

> They say the pub has sold out of everything but gin, so Inv. gets four gins, and a few minutes later – a little late for the start – the King's speech is turned on. Several women at the back of the lounge stand up, assuming reverent attitudes. There is a sense that people have been waiting all this time for something symbolic and now they have got it: the room is hushed as a church. M22B puts his feet on the table, leans back in his chair, and groans . . . At 'endured to your utmost' there are deep cries of 'Hear hear!'. Whenever the King pauses, M22B says loudly, Ts, Ts, and becomes the centre of looks of intense malevolence from all corners of the room . . . When the King says 'Of just (long pause) – of just triumph' several women's foreheads pucker and they wear a lacerated look. At 'strength and shield' Marxist unaccountably removes feet from table. When *God Save the King* is sung, the whole room rises to its feet and sings, with the exception of the Marxist twins, who remain sullenly seated. F25B, the wife of one, gets up.

Afterwards, the investigator asked her why she had stood up. 'Was it sheer politeness? She says yes, she supposes so – she felt like being in harmony with everyone else.'[5]

The news bulletin that accompanied the King's broadcast included the welcome return of the weather report (Stuart Hibberd referring jocularly to 'news of an old friend – the large depression'), though for Nella Last, a middle-aged, middle-class housewife living in Barrow-in-Furness, not even this made her 'fully realise things' as she continued to have 'that curious "flat" feeling' through the evening. Thirty-nine per cent of adults then stayed tuned to *Victory Parade*, though by the time the programme ended at 10.45 the audience had dropped by more than half as even the unadventurous left home to see the floodlights and the bonfires. 'A grand team of voices', as one grateful listener put it, included Stewart MacPherson describing the scene in Piccadilly, Richard Dimbleby in Whitehall and Howard Marshall outside Buckingham Palace. There was praise for 'the choice of Tommy

Trinder to give the running commentary from Lambeth', while 'listeners were much moved by the final sequence of Ralph Wightman [the countryman broadcaster] from Piddletrenthide', which was 'even described as "a stroke of genius"'. The programme also featured the recorded voices of Eisenhower, Montgomery, Air Chief Marshal Tedder and men of the fighting units, as well as descriptions of the celebrations in Dover, Birmingham and several American cities. 'Made me think,' ruminated Frank Lewis in his digs at 233 Upper Brook Street, Manchester 13. 'Pretty picturesque and patriotic picture as a whole; especially descriptive were the crowded scenes, Piccadilly etc, and Mr Churchill speaking to a crowd from a roof top in Whitehall, with his cabinet'. Even so, he ended his diary entry on a far from gruntled note: '"On this most memorable of all days," to quote the radio, I have spent the enormous sum, I don't think, of 1/11d.'[6]

Of course, the image we have of that warm Tuesday night is very different and predominantly takes its cue from the events in London's West End. 'There was wild excitement in Trafalgar Square, half London seemed to be floodlit – so much unexpected light was quite unreal,' wrote Joan Wyndham, having taken time off from her WAAF mess in the East Midlands. 'There were people dancing like crazy, jumping in the fountains and climbing lamp-posts.' Or take Noël Coward: 'I walked down the Mall and stood outside Buckingham Palace, which was floodlit. The crowd was stupendous. The King and Queen came out on the balcony, looking enchanting. We all roared ourselves hoarse . . . I suppose this is the greatest day in our history.' The iconography is understandably imperishable: of Churchill making the 'V' sign from a floodlit Ministry of Health balcony as the jubilant crowd below sang 'Land of Hope and Glory'; of the Old Etonian trumpeter (and young Guards officer) Humphrey Lyttelton playing 'Roll out the Barrel' as he lurched on a handcart from Buckingham Palace to Trafalgar Square and back followed by a long, swaying line of revellers doing the conga; of young women in confident groups on their own; of even the two princesses (Elizabeth and a 14-year-old Margaret Rose) being allowed to mingle with the crowds after midnight.

Certainly Anthony Heap had no complaints, or at least no complaints bar the absence of live music and 'the fact that the pubs, though allowed to keep open till midnight, were nearly all closed'.

He and his wife returned to the West End at 7.30, saw one of the Royal Family's 11 balcony appearances and made a typically painstaking tour of the main floodlit buildings. 'One small incident we witnessed in St James's Street – a dozen or so young revellers dancing "ring-a-ring-a-roses" round Philip Page, the gouty and arthritic dramatic critic of the *Daily Mail*, as he slowly hobbled across the road – was typical of the hundreds of smaller manifestations of high spirited gaiety that we saw tonight.' For many, Heap noted, that night was still young:

> No one seemed to bother much about getting home, for though the last trains to the suburbs had left the West End at the ridiculously early hour of 11.15 or thereabouts, there were still as many sightseers about when we started to walk home just before midnight as there were when we arrived on the scene in the early evening. While outside Leicester Square station was a queue extending all the way up to Cambridge Circus waiting for the first trams in the morning! A sight which made us truly thankful that we were able to walk home, footsore and weary though we were as we trudged through Bloomsbury, so dark and drear by comparison with the brightly illuminated West End.

The couple finally flopped into bed at 1 a.m. 'It had been a grand day and we'd savoured it to the full. We were, in fact, VE Day-drunk!'[7]

The West End, though, was not London, let alone Britain. 'Usually, crowds were too few and too thin to inspire much feeling,' reckoned Mass-Observation, 'and on V.E. night most people were either at home, at small private parties, at indoor dances or in public houses, or collected in small groups around the bonfires, where there was sometimes singing and dancing, but by no means riotously.' Most contemporary accounts confirm this rather low-key feel to proceedings. 'The town was thronged but the crowds were orderly' was how Colin Ferguson, a pattern-maker working for Babcock & Wilcox in Glasgow, found that city's George Square shortly before midnight. 'Most of those walking about evidently just out to see what was going on.' So, too, in the Birmingham suburb of Erdington, where after the King's broadcast 'the "bonfire" in Mr Swinnerton's field in Marsh

Lane' was the attraction for Mary King (a retired teacher), her husband and a group of friends: 'It was a tremendous scene. Many people gathered to enjoy the sight. Everything quiet and orderly & enjoyable.' Raymond Streat was at a big bonfire in Wilmslow, built by the Boy Scouts: 'What curious people are we English? There was no cheering or rowdying. About two thousand folk stood there silently watching flames lighting up the dark skies . . . We were all content, apparently, to stand still and to stare. One or two attempts to launch a song died away.' Judy Haines and her husband, meanwhile, had heard the King's speech relayed at the Westminster Theatre before setting out for home: 'Quite easy to get on the bus (though we changed at Leyton) and we had a front seat and good view of the bonfires and merriment. Met Mother H. waiting for Dad, at Chingford. Went in to spam and chips, etc. After that we were invited to a party at the Odeon, which we refused. Mrs Telford had thought we would have loved it, but I explained we had just done a show and had a meal.' She noted, as any sensible person would, 'It was twenty to twelve, by the way.'[8]

Not all the bonfires were quiet, meditative affairs. Certainly not in deepest Herefordshire, where the local paper described what it was pleased to call 'A Country Village Celebration':

Passing through the village of Stoke Lacy early on Tuesday afternoon one was startled to see the effigy of Hitler hanging from a gibbet in the car park of the Plough. That evening, a crowd began to gather, and word went round that Hitler was to be consumed in flames at 11 pm. At that hour excitement was intense, when Mr W R Symonds called upon Mr S J Parker, the Commander of No 12 Platoon, of the Home Guard, to set the effigy alight. In a few minutes the body of Hitler disintegrated as his 1,000-years Empire has done. First, his arm, poised in a Heil Hitler salute, dropped as smartly as it was ever raised in life. Quickly followed his German hat; then a leg fell off, and then the flames burnt fiercely to the strains of 'Rule Britannia', 'Land of Hope and Glory', 'There'll always be an England' and 'Roll out the Barrel'. Then the crowd spontaneously linked hands, and in a circle of 300 strong sang 'Auld Lang Syne'. Mr Parker then called for cheers for Mr Churchill, President Truman, Marshal Stalin, and our serving boys and girls.

The ceremony was followed by the singing of 'God Save the King'.

There were similar scenes elsewhere. In the West Midlands, where streets in the working-class districts of Wolverhampton 'vied with each other in the number of streamers and flags they could produce', Hitler was 'burned many times over'; in a Coventry suburb a self-appointed 'Mayor and Wife' – both men, with a builder, 'the fattest man in the street, and the jolliest', as the Mayoress – conducted a mock funeral for the effigy. 'Preparations for these affairs were elaborate and careful and they were well-organised,' the Mass-Observation survey found. 'The whole performance seems to have been charged with a deep satisfaction for most of the people who watched it.'[9]

But for Gladys Langford – 55 years old, married in 1913, deserted by her husband in 1914, living on her own at the Woodstock Hotel, N5 – the escape from central London on a number 19 bus did not presage a happy evening:

> Miss Sweeney invited me to the bar [ie at the hotel] and I said I would go after the King's Speech. When I arrived and saw a semi-circle of people all 'put' so to speak, I just fled. I remembered what Lil used to say at parties at home, 'They don't really want you – they are only being polite', so I fled! Miss Sweeney & Miss Gilman both followed me but I refused their welcome and decided to go to bed early. However, Miss Stevens, Mrs Polley and Mrs Mobbs came about 11 pm to call me from the drive, inviting me to go to Highbury Fields where there was a concert – of sorts – and flood-lit dancing spaces. Crowds there with dogs and children much in evidence. Came back to find everyone almost in the bar and was persuaded to join the throng. Peter Gurney bought me a light ale and Mr Burchell a double gin. People were dancing on a space the size of a handkerchief, sentimentalising and singing – all in different keys and often different songs. Mafoot [?] insisted on kissing me and holding my hand – and I detest him. 18 year old Gurney took me on his knee and put his arm round my neck and Burchell wanted me to do 'Boomps-a-daisy' with him. My inhibitions made me refrain from doing more than laugh at less restrained people.

Writing up her diary some hours later, she added with grim satisfaction, 'there are some sore heads here this morning.'

Henry St John was also on his own and living in a hotel, in his case the Westbourne in Bristol. In his mid-30s, he had been educated at Acton County School, and his parents had run a confectioner's in Chiswick High Street. He had joined the Civil Service straight from school and seems by the mid-1940s to have had a fairly itinerant role, going to different regions and auditing the accounts at their labour exchanges. For him, rather as for Philip Larkin, the war had essentially been a personal inconvenience, and his diary entry for VE Day was entirely in character. It read in toto: 'It was learned that the cook, who had been living at the Westbourne, went out yesterday and had not come back.' Nor did St John's next entry, recording the events of the Tuesday night, quite take the big view: 'A party in a nearby house went on until 2 a.m., with music, dancing, singing, and shouting, so that I could not sleep until well past that hour, and as I slept badly the previous night I felt good for nothing today.' St John seems to have been a man of virtually non-existent human sympathies but was not wholly exceptional in apparently having zero interest in this historic event. Another sleepless diarist was perhaps more typical. 'Far into the night there was the noise of singing and shouting at the pub and fireworks going off, and in the sky the glimmer of some huge bonfire, or was it the illumination of London?' The writer Denton Welch, living in Hadlow in Kent, then felt – as surely so many did – the discomfort of imminent change from a condition that, for all its inconveniences, had become familiar: 'There were awful thoughts and anxieties in the air – the breaking of something – the splitting apart of an atmosphere that had surrounded us for six years.'[10]

VE+1, the Wednesday, was inevitably a bit of a let-down, not helped by most pubs (in London anyway) having run out of beer. 'This VE business is getting me down with fatigue' was how Lees-Milne bluntly put it. A certain amount of normality returned – for example, the senior Labour politician Hugh Dalton took Michael Young from his party's research department to lunch at the Marsham Restaurant and found him 'not particularly sympathetic, but quite capable' – but there were still plenty of festivities, including a plethora of street parties for children. These were mainly jolly affairs, as innumerable photographs show, though not without their tensions. 'Half our road where all my friends lived had semi-detached houses and detached bungalows while at the bottom end the houses were small and terraced,'

Michael Burns later recalled about growing up in Tolworth just off the Kingston bypass. 'We had a street party that our parents were insistent should not include the children from the terraced houses, so there were two parties in Southwood Drive divided by about two hundred yards.' In Islington one of the children's street parties was organised by a maid from the Woodstock Hotel. 'She obtained a Nazi flag and took it into a pub and let people pay 6d a time to spit on it,' Gladys Langford recorded. 'She finally sold it for 10/-, having made a total of £2 15s 0d.' Frank Lewis once again tried the centre of Manchester and once again was unimpressed: 'Big crowds everywhere, especially Albert Square, still doing nothing, apparently just hanging about.'

As for Anthony Heap, he more or less repeated his 'programme' of the day before, this time on his first leg getting a glimpse of the Royal Family as they set out for their tour of the East End. In the evening it was 'once more unto the West End', where he found 'the same good humoured crowds, the same high spirited skylarking, the same awe inspiring floodlighting', though it 'wasn't perhaps *quite* so over-whelming an occasion'. He finished with 'a last enchanting eye-full of the floodlit splendour of St Paul's Cathedral, Houses of Parliament etc from Waterloo Bridge' before catching 'what must have been the last 68 bus to Euston Rd which was completely illuminated from end to end with its full pale-blue peace-time lighting'. After seemingly interminable blackouts and no street lighting, this did indeed 'seem the most amazing thing – this prodigality with light', as Alan Bennett would express it when describing his VE memories (improbably enough of Guildford, to where his parents had moved briefly from Leeds). Heap concluded his diary entry without ambiguity: 'And so we came to end of two perfect days. They couldn't have furnished a happier set of memories to look back on in my old age.'[11]

Kenneth Tynan might not have agreed. A precocious schoolboy in his last year at King Edward's, Birmingham, Tynan had spent VE night watching his girl (Joy Matthews) go off with someone else, only not coming to blows because he realised that his rival was stronger. 'But Wednesday night capped everything,' he wrote to a friend. 'I have never felt nearer to murder than I did then and do now.' Ken and Joy were among a party – of fifty to a hundred strong – that

spent most of the evening first at a 'Jazz Jamboree' at the Midland
Institute and then at the Birmingham University Students' Union,
before heading towards Moseley:

> We walked along in a colossal line spread out across Bristol Rd – all
> except Joy and Bernard, who walked ecstatically in front, embracing
> each other every few yards. Then I got mad. I went completely berserk
> and walked bang into the headlights of a car approaching along Priory
> Rd. I was utterly, utterly despondent . . . I dashed off after Joy, croaking
> in a reedy hoarse treble that I was taking her home and that I would
> slit both their throats if they didn't stop. Of course, they didn't. They
> stopped, *laughed at me* (O Christ) and proceeded to neck in front of
> me in the middle of the road.
>
> It took eight of them to stop me from strangling the filthy bitch and
> that low bastard.

A provincial wannabe being laughed at: a terrible moment, but he
would soon enough be on the fast track to exact cosmic revenge.

About the same time as Tynan's humiliation, the Chelsea-based
Mass-Observation investigator was returning home. She had spent the
evening in the West End, mainly outside Buckingham Palace watching
the crowds waiting for a balcony appearance and eventually getting
it at about 10 p.m.: '"Doesn't the Queen look lovely?" says F35C.
"The princesses were among the crowd last night, only nobody recognised them," says somebody else.' The gates were closed at both
Piccadilly Circus and Green Park stations, so she walked home. Her
report finished with a post-midnight vignette: 'On a piece of waste
ground in Flood Street ten or twelve children are silently gathered
round a bonfire. They look tired but happy and absorbed. One says
in a low voice, "It'll last a long time yet." A man at the end of the
street is striking matches and says he is looking for a shilling he has
dropped. Throws match away angrily, saying, "They don't last long
enough."'[12]

Broad Vistas and All That

Britain in 1945. No supermarkets, no motorways, no teabags, no sliced bread, no frozen food, no flavoured crisps, no lager, no microwaves, no dishwashers, no Formica, no vinyl, no CDs, no computers, no mobiles, no duvets, no Pill, no trainers, no hoodies, no Starbucks. Four Indian restaurants. Shops on every corner, pubs on every corner, cinemas in every high street, red telephone boxes, Lyons Corner Houses, trams, trolley-buses, steam trains. Woodbines, Craven 'A', Senior Service, smoke, smog, Vapex inhalant. No launderettes, no automatic washing machines, wash day every Monday, clothes boiled in a tub, scrubbed on the draining board, rinsed in the sink, put through a mangle, hung out to dry. Central heating rare, coke boilers, water geysers, the coal fire, the hearth, the home, chilblains common. Abortion illegal, homosexual relationships illegal, suicide illegal, capital punishment legal. White faces everywhere. Back-to-backs, narrow cobbled streets, Victorian terraces, no high-rises. Arterial roads, suburban semis, the march of the pylon. Austin Sevens, Ford Eights, no seat belts, Triumph motorcycles with sidecars. A Bakelite wireless in the home, *Housewives' Choice* or *Workers' Playtime* or *ITMA* on the air, televisions almost unknown, no programmes to watch, the family eating together. Milk of Magnesia, Vick Vapour Rub, Friar's Balsam, Fynnon Salts, Eno's, Germolene. Suits and hats, dresses and hats, cloth caps and mufflers, no leisurewear, no 'teenagers'. Heavy coins, heavy shoes, heavy suitcases, heavy tweed coats, heavy leather footballs, no unbearable lightness of being. Meat rationed, butter rationed, lard rationed, margarine rationed, sugar rationed, tea rationed, cheese rationed, jam rationed, eggs rationed, sweets rationed, soap rationed, clothes rationed. Make do and mend.

For the policy-makers, the planners, the intelligentsia, the readers of Penguin Specials, everyone with an occupational or emotional stake in 'the condition of the people', there was no shortage of problems to be tackled.[1] Some flowed directly from the war – three-quarters of a million houses destroyed or severely damaged, huge disruption to public services, Britain's debt a record £3.5 billion – but others were of longer standing. Life expectancy had increased from some 50 years in the Edwardian era to about 65, and classic killer diseases like tuber-culosis, scarlet fever and typhoid were almost under control; yet access to the medical services remained for many far from free or equitable, and considerable suffering resulted from an unwillingness or (more usually) financial inability to use them. Despite a reasonably energetic slum-clearance programme between the wars, there were still many appalling Victorian slums in the major cities and large pockets of overcrowded, inadequate-to-wretched housing almost everywhere. About seven million dwellings lacked a hot-water supply, some six million an inside WC, almost five million a fixed bath. Above all, there was the profound emotional as well as practical legacy of the economic slump between the wars – at its worst from the late 1920s to the mid-1930s, causing widespread poverty and destroying or at best stunting millions of lives. The resonance of 'Jarrow', the 'murdered' north-east shipyard town that famously marched against unemployment, or indeed 'the thirties', would last for half a century. Even a Prince of Wales had once murmured that something had to be done; it had become a less than revolutionary sentiment to agree.

Wartime developments had – at least in retrospect – a seemingly irresistible momentum. As early as January 1941, while the bombs were falling, *Picture Post* outlined in a celebrated special issue (complete with six naked, presumably impoverished small children on the cover) 'A Plan For Britain'. The magazine recalled the sudden end of the war in November 1918: 'The plan was not there. We got no new Britain . . . This time we can be better prepared. But we can only be better prepared if we think now.' Accordingly, a series of articles (including 'Work for All', 'Plan the Home', 'Social Security', 'A Plan for Education', 'Health for All' and 'The New Britain Must be Planned') offered an initial blueprint for 'a fairer, pleasanter, happier, more beautiful Britain than our own'.[2]

Over the next 18 months or so, the concept began to be accepted that the British people, in return for all their sufferings in a noble cause, deserved a new start after the war. December 1942 saw the publication of the Beveridge Report, drawn up by the eminent economist and civil servant Sir William Beveridge. In it he set out proposals for a comprehensive post-war system of social security, in effect laying the foundations for the 'classic' welfare state – an attack upon what he memorably depicted as 'the five giant evils' of want, disease, ignorance, squalor and idleness – and in so doing caused such a stir that an extraordinary 630,000 copies of the report (mainly the abridged, popular edition) were sold. Then, in 1944, as the war began to draw to a close, there were two major 'reconstruction' moments: in May the publication of a White Paper that committed the British govern-ment to the pursuit of full employment as the highest economic objective; and in August the arrival on the statute book of R. A. ('Rab') Butler's Education Act, which, among other things, created free, non-fee-paying grammar schools.

To all appearances the reforming, forward-looking tide was running fast. *Who Else Is Rank* was the symptomatic title of an unpublished novel co-written the following winter by a 22-year-old Kingsley Amis and a fellow Signals officer. 'We must see to it after we're demobilised,' the Amis figure (a sensitive young lieutenant) says at one point, 'that these common men, from whom we're separated only by a traditional barrier – we're no more than common men ourselves – benefit from the work that has been done, and if the system won't let that happen, well, we shall just have to change the system.'[3]

In April 1945, as Hitler made his last stand in Berlin, the Labour Party issued its manifesto for the election that was bound to follow the end of the war. Called *Let Us Face the Future*, it demanded decisive action by the state to ensure full employment, the nationalisation of several key industries, an urgent housing programme, the creation of a new national health service and (in a nod to Beveridge) 'social provision against rainy days'. The tone was admirably lacking in bombast but distinctly high-minded. 'The problems and pressures of the post-war world,' the fairly brief document declared, 'threaten our security and progress as surely as – though less dramatically than – the Germans threatened them in 1940. We need the spirit of Dunkirk and of the

Blitz sustained over a period of years. The Labour Party's programme is a practical expression of that spirit applied to the tasks of peace. It calls for hard work, energy and sound sense.' The manifesto's principal author was Michael Young, not long before his lunch with Hugh Dalton. Aged 29, he had been educated at the progressive Dartington Hall and been director of a newish organisation, Political and Economic Planning (PEP), before in February 1945 moving to the Labour Party's research department. Young in later life was self-deprecating about the manifesto: 'The mood was such that second-class documents were going to be thought first-class with a star.'[4]

Two crucial questions suggest themselves, however. How by 1945, at the apparent birth of a new world, did the 'activators' – politicians, planners, public intellectuals, opinion-formers – *really* see the future? And how did their vision of what lay ahead compare with that of 'ordinary people'? The overlaps and mismatches between these two sets of expectations would be fundamental to the playing out of the next three or more decades.

———

There would be no fly-pasts in its honour, but arguably 1940 was the British state's finest hour, as the nation – under the iron-willed direction of Ernest Bevin as Minister of Labour in Churchill's coalition government – mobilised for total war more quickly and effectively than either Germany or Russia. The state, in other words, proved that it could deliver, as it also did by introducing wide-scale rationing in a way generally seen as equitable. Simultaneously, the first half of the war saw the creation of a plethora of new ministries: not only Labour but Economic Warfare, Food, Home Security, Information, Shipping, Aircraft Production and Production. By 1943 there were, not surprisingly, well over a quarter of a million more civil servants than there had been before the war. It was soon clear, moreover, that all the work of these ministries, as well as of the traditional ones, was now predicated upon assumptions of co-ordinated central planning – an utterly different mindset from Whitehall's customary approach and propagated by some exceptionally talented temporary recruits there, often operating at a very high level.

How, if at all, might this translate into peacetime economic policy? Relatively early in the war, the great economist John Maynard Keynes had more or less won the battle within the Treasury to persuade that deeply conservative institution to accept at least a substantial measure of demand management as the principal way of regulating the economy in order to keep the level of unemployment down. Thereafter, the real intellectual conflict among radically minded 'activators' was between Keynesians and those whose ideal was wartime-style (and Soviet-style) direct physical planning. For the former, there was still a significant role – at least in theory – to be played by the price mechanism of the market; for the latter, that role was fairly surplus to requirements. By the end of the war, it seemed that the force was with the out-and-out planners, with their emphasis on investment planning and, through direct controls over labour, manpower planning.

Indeed, such was the temper of the times that even most Keynesians had, in a visceral sense, little real faith in, or any great intellectual curiosity about, the possible economic merits of the market or of supply-side reforms. Hence the largely stony academic-cum-intellectual reception accorded in 1944 to *The Road to Serfdom* (dedicated 'To the Socialists of All Parties') by the Austrian economist F. A. Hayek, who was based at the London School of Economics (LSE). 'His central argument was that a modern economy was a vast system of information flows which signal to everyone indispensable facts about scarcity and opportunity,' a latter-day follower, Kenneth Minogue, has helpfully summarised. 'The vitality of modern Western economies, and the best use of scarce resources, rested upon the workers and entrepreneurs having these signals available to them. No planning committee could possibly plug into them. Central direction could lead only to poverty and oppression.'[5] Such was the loss of confidence among economic liberals following the events of the previous 20 years – the inter-war slump, the lessons of the war (including the apparent Russian lessons) – that it would be a long time before a critical mass of politicians began to make a full-bloodedly coherent or attractive case on Hayek's behalf.

Unsurprisingly, then, the inescapable necessity of a substantial portion of the economy being in public ownership was hardly questioned for many years after 1945. Indeed, such had arguably become the prevailing activator consensus from well before the war. The BBC (1922), Central Electricity Board (1926) and BOAC (British Overseas Airways Corporation, 1939) were all examples of important new organisations being set up on a public rather than private basis, while Harold Macmillan, the rising force on the Tory left, called in *The Middle Way* (1938) for a programme of nationalisation at least as ambitious as that then being advocated by the Labour Party. To many, the arguments seemed unanswerable: not only were there the examples of major, palpably enfeebled industries like coal mining and the railways as clear proof that private enterprise had failed, but in economies of scale, especially as applied to utilities (the so-called natural monopolies), there was an even more powerful siren call, very much reflecting what the political economist John Vaizey would term the prevailing 'cult of giganticism'. During the last year of war, a quite sharp leftwards shift in the Labour Party – identifying public owner-ship with both economic efficiency and, in an ominously fundamen-talist way, socialist purity – resulted in a fairly ambitious shopping list in *Let Us Face the Future*, featuring the Bank of England, fuel and power, inland transport, and (most contentiously) iron and steel, though with the high-street banks, heavy industry and building all excluded.

What sort of nationalisation would it be? The key text was the 1933 treatise *Socialisation and Transport* by the leading Labour politician Herbert Morrison, creator of the London Passenger Transport Board and, in due course, grandfather of Peter Mandelson. Notably short of hard economic analysis, Morrison's paper nevertheless put forward a plausible enough public-corporation model that envisaged publicly appointed managers running monopoly industries in the public interest, though in a more or less autonomous way. Morrison did not have any truck with the notion of democratic control over these nationalised industries – certainly not democratic control as exercised from the shop floor. 'The majority of workmen are,' he insisted, 'more interested in the organisation, conditions, and life of their own work-shop than in those finer balances of financial and commercial policy which are discussed in the Board room.'[6] The assumption was that the managers of these public corporations would be exemplars of scrupulous, objective professionalism – and that the workers in them should know their place.

A similar faith in the beneficent, public-minded expert underlay the creation of the modern welfare state. There was in December 1942 no greater expert than Beveridge himself, who summarised his Report as 'first and foremost, a plan of insurance – of giving in return for contributions benefits up to subsistence level, as of right and without means test'. This last point was crucial, given the widespread detestation that had developed between the wars of the many forms of means testing. And this in practice meant that the social insurance provided – essentially against loss or interruption of earnings due to unemployment, sickness or old age – would be *universal*. Beveridge's proposals engendered serious consternation on the part of Churchill, most Conservative MPs and some top Whitehall officials. But by March 1943 it was clear, following a clutch of by-elections, that there was an unignorable head of steam behind them. That month, Churchill – in a broadcast called 'After the War' – solemnly promised 'national compulsory insurance for all classes for all purposes from the cradle to the grave' – not the first use of that striking phrase but the one that made it famous. There were still plenty of debates and committees to go through, but by the time the war in Europe ended, family allowances – the first of the Beveridge-inspired pieces of legislation, providing 5s a week (more than 5 per cent of the average male wage) for each child from the second onwards – were virtually on the statute book.

From the perspective of more than half a century later, three of Beveridge's central assumptions are especially striking, starting with what one might call the 'Nissen hut' assumption. Beveridge's insistence that contributions be levied at a flat rate, rather than in the earnings-related way that tended to be adopted in other advanced industrial economies, was perhaps appropriate in an age of austerity. But that would change in an age of affluence with its inflationary implications and, above all, financially onerous concept of *relative* poverty. Secondly, there was Beveridge's assumption that married women would – following their wartime experience – return to and stay at home, given that their prime task was to 'ensure the continuation of the British race', which at 'its present rate of reproduction . . . cannot continue'. In administrative terms this meant that a married woman would be subordinate to her husband, with benefits to her coming only as a result of his insurance. Beveridge's third, equally Victorian assumption, befitting a Liberal who was already in his teens when

Gladstone had been Prime Minister in the 1890s, was that in the post-war world enhanced rights would be matched by enhanced responsibilities. Not only did he insist that his social-security system be contribution-based rather than tax-based, but he was also determined that his ultimate safety net of means-tested national assistance would be pitched at such an unattractively minimalist level that it would 'leave the person assisted with an effective motive to avoid the need for assistance and to rely on earnings or insurance'. And he added sternly that 'an assistance scheme which makes those assisted unamenable to economic rewards and punishments while treating them as free citizens is inconsistent with the principles of a free community'.[7] Beveridge's welfare state – a term not yet invented but one that he would come to loathe – was not, in short, to be a soft touch.

Integral to the Beveridge vision of the future was a free and comprehensive national health service. The key propagandist, in terms of preparing the intellectual ground for such a development, was undoubtedly Richard Titmuss – a remarkable person who would become (in Edmund Leach's words) the 'high priest of the welfare state'. Titmuss was still a young man, the son of a failed farmer-turned-haulier, when he researched and wrote *Poverty and Population* (1938), which he somehow managed to do while holding down a full-time job as an insurance actuary. In it he examined the depressed areas of industrial Britain and showed in irrefutable detail the appalling human wastage resulting there from poverty and inequality. Other books followed, including (soon after Beveridge) *Birth, Poverty and Wealth* (1943), which put infant mortality under the microscope of social class and found that each week almost 2,000 lives were lost unnecessarily. 'The writings of Titmuss set a new standard,' the historian of the NHS has written. 'Their influence was extensive and immediate. His method of demonstrating inequalities found its way into popularisations aimed at various classes of reader.'

In February 1944 the Conservative Minister of Health in Churchill's coalition government, Henry Willink, issued a White Paper that spoke of 'the need to bring the country's full resources to bear upon reducing ill-health and promoting good health in all its citizens' – in effect making it clear that a post-war Conservative administration would bow to Beveridge's wishes and introduce a national health service.

Nevertheless, 'there is a certain danger in making personal health the subject of a national service at all,' the document added. 'It is the danger of over-organisation.' One way in which Willink intended to minimise that danger was through combining free, universal access on the one hand with diversity of provision on the other – above all through not nationalising the hospital stock as a whole, maintaining instead a mixture of voluntary and municipally run hospitals.

The attitude of the medical profession to all this was ambivalent. It broadly accepted the case for a free and universal health service, but it was understandably reluctant to abandon its profitable private work, feared political interference (whether at a local or at a national level) and – on the part of GPs, who usually operated solo – saw in the increasingly fashionable nostrum of the health centre a dastardly socialist plot. 'We have entered a new era of social consciousness,' the *Spectator* – hardly noted for left-wing views – observed in the spring of 1944. 'Some of the doctors seem not to have realised that fully, and it is desirable in everyone's interest that they should.'[8] A year later there was still a significant degree of consciousness-raising to be done.

If in health there was still much to play for by 1945, the same was rather less true in education, where in outline anyway the post-war settlement had already taken shape. In a flurry of wartime action, it had three main elements: the Norwood Report of 1943, which examined what should be emphasised in the curriculum at secondary schools and (to the private satisfaction of the President of the Board of Education, Rab Butler, in theory a reforming Conservative) plumped for the time-honoured virtues of PE, 'character' and the English language, as opposed to anything more technical or modern; the Butler Act of 1944, which vastly expanded access to free secondary education; and, from the same year, the Fleming Report on the public schools, which in retrospect represented the spurning of a realistic chance to seek the abolition of the independent sector.

Relatively few people at the time appreciated the negative significance of Norwood and Fleming, amid a general preference for concentrating on provision and numbers, whereas even at its outline stage the Butler legislation was widely seen as historic. 'A landmark has been set up in English education,' the *Times Educational*

Supplement declared. 'The Government's White Paper promises the greatest and grandest educational advance since 1870.' The paper's editor, the progressive-minded Harold Dent, claimed that the government now accepted two key principles – 'that there shall be equality of opportunity, and diversity of provision without impairment of the social unity' – and boldly prophesied that 'the throwing open of secondary education, of various types, to all' would 'result in a prodigious freeing of creative ability, and ensure to an extent yet incalculable that every child shall be prepared for the life he is best fitted to lead and the service he is best fitted to give'.

Did that innocuous phrase 'of various types' catch some eyes? Quite possibly, for although Butler's subsequent legislation would have nothing specific to say about different types of secondary school within the state sector, the fact was that at the very time of his White Paper the Norwood Report was not only enshrining as orthodoxy a tripartite system of grammar schools, technical schools and secondary moderns but explicitly avowing that 'in the Grammar School the pupil is offered, because he is capable of reaching towards it, a conception of knowledge which is different from that which can be and should be envisaged in other types of school'. A former headmaster of Bristol Grammar School, Marlborough College and Harrow School, Sir Cyril Norwood had no qualms about pecking orders. In fact, there was an incipient movement under way in favour of the comprehensive school (or the 'multilateral', as it was then usually called), a movement in which Dent cautiously participated; yet even in one of English society's more egalitarian phases, such a concept was far removed from practical politics. Significantly, when Dent in early 1944 wrote a pamphlet entitled *The New Educational Bill*, he neither questioned tripartism nor mentioned the comprehensive alternative.

There seems, moreover, to have been a similar lack of concern about the inevitable selection implications of a tripartite structure. 'The Government hold that there is nothing to be said in favour of a system which subjects children at the age of 11 to the strain of a competitive examination on which not only their future schooling but their future careers may depend,' wrote Dent about the White Paper in wholly sanguine mode. 'In the future, children at the age of 11 should be classified, not on the results of a competitive test, but on assessment of their individual aptitudes largely by such means as school records, supplemented, if necessary, by intelligence tests, due regard being had to their parents' wishes and the careers they have in mind.' Just in case anyone was worried, he added that there would be arrangements for children to transfer at 13 in the unlikely event of a mistake having been made two years earlier.[9]

If for Keynesians, social reformers and educationalists the war provided unimagined opportunities for influencing the shape of the future, this was even more true for architects and town planners and their cheerleaders. In their case a momentum for fundamental change had been building inexorably between the wars, and now the heady mixture of destruction and reconstruction gave them their chance. That gathering impetus was perfectly encapsulated as early as 1934 by a young architectural writer answering the question 'What Would Wren Have Built Today?' After diagnosing the City of London as overcrowded, badly lit and generally impossible to work in either efficiently or pleasantly, he went on:

> We must give up the building rule which restricts the height of buildings, and we must not only do that, but we must build office blocks twice as high as St Paul's, and have green spaces and wide roads in between the blocks ... Two dozen skyscrapers, though they would obviously dwarf St Paul's, would not take away from its beauty if they were beautiful themselves. They would alter the skyline, certainly, yet we should not sacrifice health, time, and comfort to one skyline because we have not the courage to create another.

The author of this confident, uncompromising clarion call? John Betjeman, that future doughty conservationist.

Crucially, this rapidly swelling appetite for the new embraced not only the horrors (real and perceived) of the unplanned Victorian city – above all, understandably enough, the horrors of the industrial slums. It also addressed the much more recent blight, as received 'activator' opinion had it, of the suburbs, sprawling outwards through the 1920s and 1930s, especially around London, in a spectacular and apparently unplanned way. They were, declared the Welsh architect Sir Clough Williams-Ellis in 1928, full of 'mean and perky little houses that surely none but mean and perky little souls should inhabit with satisfaction', while ten years later, according to Osbert Lancaster (cartoonist, architectural writer and coiner of the derogatory term 'Stockbroker Tudor'), the certainty that the streets and estates of the suburbs would 'eventually become the slums of the future' unless they were obliterated did much 'to reconcile one to the prospect of aerial bombardment'. Even George Orwell could not see their point. In his last pre-war novel, *Coming Up for Air*, he wrote contemptuously of 'long, long rows of little semi-detached houses', of 'the stucco front, the creosoted gate, the privet hedge, the green front door', of 'the Laurels, the Myrtles, the Hawthorns, Mon Abri, Mon Repos, Belle Vue', and of the 'respectable householders – that's to say Tories, yes-men, and bumsuckers who live in them'. To someone like Thomas Sharp, a planning consultant as well as a university lecturer in architecture and town planning, 'suburbia' – where by the end of the 1930s about a quarter of the population lived – was complete anathema; without compunction he condemned 'its social sterility, its aesthetic emptiness, its economic wastefulness'. In short: 'Suburbia is not a utility that can promote any proper measure of human happiness and fulfilment.'

Sharp had been implacably anti-suburb through the 1930s, but this particular broadside was published in *Town Planning*, an influential 1940 Pelican paperback. 'However little can be done in wartime towards the achievement of the ideals I have tried to set out, it is essential that we should get our minds clear *now* as to what we are going to do when the war is over,' he stressed. 'The thing is there for us to do if we will. We can continue to live in stale and shameful slum-towns. Or in sterile and disorderly suburbs. Or we can build clean proud towns of living and light. The choice is entirely our own.' Two years later, *When We Build Again* (a documentary focusing on Bournville Village in Birmingham) was even more ideal-istic. 'There must be no uncontrolled building, no more ugly houses and straggling roads, no stinting of effort before we build again,' declared the film's narrator, Dylan Thomas, who also wrote the script. 'Nothing is too good for the people.' The Beveridge Report did not concern itself specifically with town planning, but in February 1943 – the same year that a bespoke Ministry of Town and Country

Planning was set up – it was Beveridge who opened a notable exhibition, Rebuilding Britain, at the National Gallery. 'How can the war on Squalor be won?' asked the accompanying catalogue, referring to one of the five evil giants that Sir William's report hoped to slay. The answer was sublime in its certainty: 'The very first thing to win is the Battle of Planning. We shall need to have planning on a national scale, boldly overstepping the traditional boundaries of urban council, rural council, County Council. Boldly overstepping the interests described so often as vested.'

The following year's Town and Country Planning Act did indeed give far-reaching powers to local authorities for reconstruction and redevelopment, and by the time the war ended it was almost a truism that the future lay with the planners. Entirely characteristic was the plan published in March 1945 for the future of Glasgow, with the most stirring of mottoes on its front cover: 'The Voice of Time Cries out to Man – ADVANCE!' One old man, though, was unconvinced. 'Ah, yes,' said Churchill, as towards the end of the war he looked round the Cabinet and considered his minister's favourable assessment of the latest town and country planning reports. 'All this stuff about planning and compensation and betterment. Broad vistas and all that. But give to me the eighteenth-century alley, where foot-pads lurk, and the harlot plies her trade, and none of this new-fangled planning doctrine.'[10]

Among those actively seeking a new and better post-war environment for the British people there were two main camps: baldly put, those who did not believe that the future lay in the big cities, and those who, broadly embracing modernism, did believe just that. They were, with on the whole unfortunate results, almost diametrically opposed to each other.

To-morrow: A Peaceful Path to Real Reform was the title of Ebenezer Howard's influential 1898 treatise, a utopian vision (heavily influenced by William Morris) of dispersal of population from the huge industrial cities and the creation of new, self-supporting towns of some 30,000 residents of mixed social background, living in light, airy surroundings and surrounded by a 'green belt'. The first 'garden city' was established five years later at Letchworth, in Herfordshire, and it was followed in 1920 by Welwyn Garden City. During the war, the Howardian agenda entered the political mainstream, as a series of reports and plans, culminating in the *Greater London Plan* published in 1945, recommended a less populous inner core, a suburbia contained by a substantial green-belt ring and, beyond that ring, the building of environmentally favoured new towns.

Howard's direct successor, and a formidable but in many ways attractive figure in the planning world, was Frederic Osborn, kingpin by the 1940s of the Town and Country Planning Association and an indefatigable propagandist as well as administrator. 'It is not a passion for order, or even for harmony (desirable as they are in measure) that has produced the demand for town planning,' he wrote shortly before the end of the war. 'The thing that has produced the dynamic for planning – the really big and fundamental thing that is wrong with our cities – is congestion: too many buildings and too many people in too little space.'[11] Osborn, though just about willing to concede that suburbanites might actually enjoy living in the suburbs, never really faced foursquare the possibility that life in a high-density, imperfectly planned city might have its positive attractions. But unlike many planners, he was well aware that planning did not automatically fit the crooked timber of humanity.

The other camp comprised architects as much as town planners, with many (but not all) looking to the alternative utopia set out in the pronouncements and example of the charismatic French architect Le Corbusier. His *La Ville radieuse* had been translated in 1929 and *Vers une architecture* in 1931; in them he demonstrated his belief in the future of great cities – but great cities entirely transformed along ultra-modern lines. 'Men can be paltry,' he declared, 'but the thing we call Man is great . . . What gives our dreams their daring is that they can be realized.' There were also his four famous, increasingly verbless propositions: 'Architecture has for its first duty that of bringing about a revision of values. We must create the mass production spirit. The spirit of constructing mass production houses. The spirit of living in mass production houses.'

Le Corbusier's English followers had established the MARS (Modern Architectural Research) Group in 1933, with the young Maxwell Fry as one of its most active members. 'Courts and alleys are swept away' ran part of the caption to the visual plan of Fry's ideal city published in the *Picture Post* special issue in 1941. 'New flats stand in a park.' These high-minded, modern-minded, well-intentioned men – who for a mixture of pragmatic and more or less socialist reasons tended to look to public housing (as yet the Cinderella of the British housing stock) as the likeliest opportunity for making an impact – took few prisoners in either their drawings or their writings. Another such individual with high ambitions and limited tolerance was Ernö Goldfinger: born in Hungary in 1902, a student in Paris until moving to England in 1933, a larger-than-life presence with a frightening temper. Writing in 1942 in the *Architectural Review* (one of modernism's strongholds), he gave a hostile appraisal of a clutch of publications in Faber and Faber's 'Rebuilding Britain' series, masterminded by Osborn and including Osborn's own *Overture to Planning*. After noting that all the publications 'state as axiomatic truths the one-sided arguments of the Garden City Movement', Goldfinger went on: 'The problem before the re-planners of the country can be neatly and precisely defined by saying that *it is to create a frame for human life*, liberated as far as possible from the drudgery of material need. Modern technology enables this to be done. But this aim will not be furthered by the introduction of sentimentality.' Justifying this charge by picking out phrases from Osborn's pamphlet like 'values of our civilisation' and 'sacred fires', Goldfinger then put his modernist cards on the table:

In all these publications the problem of the size of cities is treated again and again with an unrealistic and sentimental bias. The tendency to industrial concentration is brushed aside as one of the evil consequences of modern ways and not as it should be treated, as one of the basic means of efficient production ... All the authors seem to be smitten by a kind of agoraphobia and a tendency to animize at the same time. The small, the child-like, seems to haunt them, they transpose their feelings for persons to geographical units.

He added, with a final put-down from a considerable height, that such infantilism was 'noticeable not only in Garden City circles, but in a large section of well-meaning, so-called progressives'.

Fundamental to Le Corbusier's vision was the high-rise, with his ideal city featuring at its centre towers of as many as 60 storeys. However, even though a fair number of new blocks of flats (rarely above four or five storeys) were built in the 1930s, that aspect of his vision elicited relatively little enthusiasm before the war, with even a modernist like Fry somewhat sceptical. The real flats versus houses (or, as they were often called, 'cottages') controversy only seriously flared up during the war. 'It is eventually undeniable,' insisted Sharp in his 1940 Pelican, 'that the flat, if its own particular problems of design are sufficiently studied, *can* afford the pleasantest possible conditions of living for a very considerable proportion of the inhabitants of our towns.' And although he conceded that flats were not ideal for everyone, there were 'hosts' of people who 'could live far more happily in a block of flats, among all the communal facilities and advantages which that form of dwelling can offer, than in the social isolation of the small house, burdened with a private garden which they have neither the time nor the inclination to cultivate'.[12]

Two key documents produced during the second half of the war tilted the balance towards flats. The first was the 1943 *County of London Plan*, the work of Patrick Abercrombie (the leading town planner of the day, with a foot in both camps) and J. H. Forshaw. They concluded that if even six out of ten former inhabitants of bombed-out inner London (above all of the East End) were to be rehoused in their own familiar districts, this would entail a density of 136 people per net residential acre – which in turn meant that only a third of these resettled residents would be in houses and almost two-thirds would be in flats of eight or ten storeys. A deeply disappointed Osborn was convinced that Abercrombie had been nobbled by the London County Council (LCC), to which Forshaw was Architect. He was probably right. The LCC, which unlike the subsequent Greater London Council did not include the new outer suburbs, was dominated by inner-London Labour boroughs; and their councillors were naturally fearful that excessive dispersal would not only play havoc with rateable values but significantly diminish their reliably loyal working-class electorates.

The other pivotal document appeared a year later, with the Dudley Committee's report *The Design of Dwellings*, which for 'large concentrated urban areas' recommended a maximum density of 120 per acre – again, in other words, with significant high-rise implications. Importantly, the submissions that seem to have pushed the committee towards this conclusion were not from zealous architects but from thoroughly 'sensible' organisations like the National Council of Social Service, which argued that most of the low-rise housing estates built between the wars by the LCC had lacked adequate communal facilities, something that well-designed blocks of flats could provide, thereby obviating social problems. Between them, with fateful consequences, the plan and the report went a long way towards making the flat officially acceptable as a standard form of housing, especially public housing.

What gave such matters a new urgency was the Luftwaffe. 'Hitler has at last brought us to our senses,' declared Max Lock, a young architect and planner. 'We, the British public, have suddenly seen our cities as they are! After experiencing the shock of familiar buildings disembowelled before our eyes – like an all too real surrealism – we find the cleared and cleaned up spaces a relief. In them we have hope for the future, opportunities to be taken or lost.'[13] It was apparent from soon after the worst of the Blitz that the government was broadly backing, albeit with considerable financial nervousness, major reconstruction in the most badly affected cities, so that by the end of the war a series of plans for the future of those cities had been published and/or exhibited.[14] Southampton was to have a wholly new road system and city centre; Portsmouth a rather more modest redevelopment; Bristol a heavily zoned new city centre, including an ambitious new shopping precinct in the Broadmead area; and Hull (through the joint efforts of Abercrombie and Lock) a fairly ambitious redevelopment that included segregated industrial zones and a new, semi-pedestrianised shopping area.

Abercrombie – in his mid-60s, exceedingly well connected, author of the hugely influential textbook *Town and Country Planning* (1933) that saw virtually no role for preservation, even in the most historic cities – was also persuaded, for a not especially generous fee of 250 guineas, to submit a plan for Plymouth. The doyen of town planning did not disappoint. 'The outworn street pattern was totally abandoned, the old Devonport shopping area was swallowed up, and the precinct principle was applied to the civic, business and shopping areas' is how the planning historian Gordon Cherry has aptly summed up

Abercrombie's 1943 vision for a city where less than a tenth of its pre-war housing stock was irrevocably beyond repair as a result of enemy action. 'Unified architectural treatment would be introduced. A new central area road system was decided. One monumental feature was provided: a garden parkway from the station to the Hoe constructing a backbone to the whole of central Plymouth.' It was, Abercrombie himself insisted, the only possible way 'out of the disasters of war to snatch a victory for the city of the future'. There was little or no local consultation, with all objections overruled.[15]

In one blitzed city, even more than Plymouth, the man and the hour came together. 'Every town should have in its architect's department a group of town planners . . . Building science is advancing so rapidly that we have no right to build for a thousand years . . . A house should be regarded as permanent only for about thirty years and should then be replaced by an up-to-date one . . . For the good of the community private interests must be subordinated to public ones.' The speaker was Donald Gibson, City Architect of Coventry, addressing the Royal Society of Arts in early December 1940, less than three weeks after a night's intense bombardment had destroyed or seriously damaged most of the medieval city centre. Since his appointment a year before the war, he had been working on radical, more or less modernist plans for the city's future, culminating in May 1940 in a MARS-influenced exhibition on the 'Coventry of Tomorrow'; but the devastation only six months later created a wholly new opportunity.

As early as February 1941, the city council was able to make the choice between two competing plans for the centre's redevelopment. One plan (by Ernest Ford, the City Engineer) emphasised continuity and traditional street patterns; the other, Gibson's, envisaged an entirely new centre that, set inside an inner ring road, would boast not only impressive – and culturally improving – municipal facilities (including library, civic hall, museum, adult educational institution, and school of art and art gallery) surrounded by large open spaces but also a largely pedestrianised shopping precinct of six- or seven-storey buildings. Perhaps emboldened by Gibson's appeal – 'Let it not be said by future generations that the people of Coventry failed them, when the ideal was within their reach' – the Labour-controlled council voted 43 to 6 in his favour.

The decision immediately attracted considerable national attention, and in a visit about a year later the King himself made approbatory noises and 'expressed the opinion that in all schemes of re-planning towns and cities which had been badly bombed, the future amenities for the citizens were of supreme importance'. During the rest of the war, despite concerns from Whitehall about cost and precedent, the City Council held firm to Gibson's plan. 'A cauldron in which experiments were taking place' was how the Bishop of Coventry proudly saw his city early in 1945. Speaking to the local Rotary, he added, 'England was watching to see if the city was going to do its job and allow a full life to the people.'[16] Given Coventry's unique pre-war place in the national psyche as the hub of the thriving British motor industry, the cutting edge of the second Industrial Revolution, this was perhaps not an absurd claim to make.

But would the new, rebuilt, reconstructed Britain enjoy – as Gibson in his plans clearly hoped it would – a new, more democratic, more socially concerned, more politically conscious culture? 'When Work is Over' was J. B. Priestley's contribution to *Picture Post*'s 1941 'Plan' for Britain and, apart from 'real holidays for all', his main vision of leisure in the post-war age seemed to involve more facilities to study the arts and the setting up of civic centres of music, drama, film and talk. Increased leisure as such, he emphasised, was not necessarily a boon: 'We do not want greyhound racing and dirt track performances to be given at all hours of the day and night, pin table establishments doing a roaring trade from dawn to midnight, and idiotic films being shown down every street.' Priestley himself kept his distance from the Labour Party, but during the war there was a comfortable, almost automatic assumption on the part of Labour politicians and activists that the conflict was producing a more egalitarian society and thus a more serious-minded, socialist people. Herbert Morrison, for example, was apparently convinced by the spring of 1944 that there now existed a 'genuine social idealism', reflecting the 'altered moral sense of the community', and that accordingly the British people were 'moving into an altogether different form of society, working in an altogether different atmosphere of ideas' – a revolution of outlook, shifting from the values of private enterprise to the values of socialism, that meant that the people would never again 'be content with limited and material aims'.[17]

These were not assumptions shared by Evan Durbin, the Labour Party's most interesting thinker of the 1940s and arguably of the twentieth century. Durbin – born in 1906, the son of a Baptist minister – was an attractively paradoxical figure. He once remarked that his three greatest pleasures were 'food, sleep and sex' but accused D. H. Lawrence of 'shallow abstractions' in relation to 'freedom in sexual relations'; politically, he defined himself as a 'militant Moderate'; and, as a trained economist who had lectured through the 1930s at the LSE, he combined a strong belief in economic planning with the conviction that the price mechanism was indispensable if the liberty of consumers in a modern democracy was to be ensured. During the 1930s, Durbin became close to the young psychiatrist John Bowlby, and the influence of Bowlby ran through much of his major work, *The Politics of Democratic Socialism*, published in 1940. As for economics itself, Durbin made a brave gesture towards the 'sound money' school – its citadel the City of London – that had wrecked Ramsay MacDonald's 1931 Labour government, by declaring that 'it is not wise in the long run to expect to live upon golden eggs and slowly to strangle the goose that lays them'.

Towards the end of his book, an arrestingly bleak passage shows how far removed Durbin was from the average political or economic thinker:

> Although wealth, physical health and social equality may all make their contributions to human happiness, they can all do little and cannot themselves be secured, without health in the individual mind. We are our own kingdoms and make for ourselves, in large measure, the world in which we live. We may be rich, and healthy, and liberal; but unless we are free from secret guilt, the agonies of inferiority and frustration, and the fire of unexpressed aggression, all other things are added to our lives in vain. The cruelty and irrationality of human society spring from these secret sources. The savagery of a Hitler, the brutality of a Stalin, the ruthlessness and refined bestiality that is rampant in the world today – persecution, cruelty and war – are nothing but the external expression, the institutional and rationalized form, of these dark forces in the human heart.

Among the many phrases that stand out is 'the brutality of a Stalin' – language not yet much heard (as George Orwell had already lamented) on the left.

In 1944, by this time seconded to Whitehall and contemplating standing as a candidate in the next general election, Durbin locked horns with Hayek after the latter's *The Road to Serfdom* was published. Planning, Durbin insisted, was used by socialists to 'indicate a principle of administration and not an inflexible budget of production'; and he emphasised anew that 'the centrally directed economy can be, and should be, instructed to adapt its programme to the changing wishes of the consuming public and the changing conditions of technical efficiency.'[18] It was the characteristically assured, with-the-grain response of a man seemingly poised for the most glittering prizes.

How in fact *did* all these noble aspirations for a better post-war world strike the much-invoked, less often consulted and still heavily (about 75 per cent) working-class British people?

Some observers as well as politicians were convinced that the plates had shifted not just in terms of the formation of an elite progressive consensus (though with hindsight one can see how the extent of that consensus was possible to exaggerate) but also in terms of opinion and sentiment at large. 'At every period,' reflected a Political and Economic Planning (PEP) broadsheet in the winter of 1941/2, 'there have been idealists who have wanted to reform the world; only at rare moments has the demand for the assertion of new principles and new liberties surged from the bottom of society upwards with such overwhelming force that serious opposition is not possible. Now is one of those moments.' The well-informed journalist and author James Lansdale Hodson, in the overall 'ledger of war' that he drew up in February 1945, might not have disagreed: 'Glancing, if one may, at the minds of our people, I think we have moved Leftwards, i.e. turned more progressive in the sense that not many would wish to go back to where we were in 1938–9. The love of books and good music has grown. Our A.B.C.A. [Army Bureau of Current Affairs] and other discussion groups in the Forces have encouraged a number, at all events, to enjoy arguments and the methods of democracy, and our production

committees have worked similarly in factories.' Such was also the
conviction of Richard Titmuss, who in 1942 was commissioned to
write an official history of the wartime work of the Ministry of Health.

The eventual magisterial account, *Problems of Social Policy* (1950),
would make canonical the interpretation that there had indeed been a
sea-change in the British outlook – first as the mass evacuation of
women and children from the main cities brought the social classes
into a far closer mutual understanding than there had ever been before,
then as the months of stark and dangerous isolation after Dunkirk
created an impatient, almost aggressive mood decrying privilege and
demanding 'fair shares' for all. Between them, according to the Titmuss
version, these two circumstances led to a widespread desire for major
social and other reforms of a universalist, egalitarian nature. The
Beveridge Report and the rest of the reconstruction package followed.
Tellingly, in his treatment of the Blitz, Titmuss noted that 'there was
nothing to be ashamed of in being "bombed out" by the enemy' and
that 'public sympathy with, and approval of, families who suffered in
the raids was in sharp contrast to the low social evaluation accorded
to those who lost material standards through being unemployed during
the 1930s'.[19] In the round, such a Whiggish, feel-good reading – unity
forged through adversity, irresistible pressure from below leading to
longed-for change, human nature actually improving – would, not
surprisingly, take some shifting.

And of course, there were plausible grounds for it. In August 1942,
a year and a half after Orwell in *The Lion and the Unicorn* had detected
a 'visible swing in public opinion' towards socialism and a planned
economy since the fall of France, Mass-Observation asked working-
class residents of Holborn and Paddington what changes they hoped
to see after the war. 'Well, I can't say I'm sure,' was the rather helpless
reply of one middle-aged woman, but others were more forthcoming.
'C' in M-O annotation referred to 'artisan and skilled workers', with
'D' being 'unskilled workers and the least economically or educationally
trained third of our people':

> There'll have to be more equalness. Things not fair now. Nobody can
> tell me they are. There's them with more money what they can ever
> use. This ain't right and it's got to be put right. (*M65C*)

I think the biggest change of all should be security for the ordinary people; I mean, nothing like the depression that followed the last war. I think a lot could be done to avoid that. (*Inv. asked how*). I'm afraid that's too big a question. (*M30C*)

I think I'd like a lot of changes. (*What particularly?*) I don't know. (*F50D*)

I do feel that the schooling of children should be a sort of pooled schooling; every child should be allowed to have the same chance; not because a mother has more money she should be allowed to send her child to one school – the class distinction in the schools, I think that should be wiped right out ... (*F30C*)

Oh, lots. (*asked what*) Much better living for the ordinary working man. (*Anything else?*) Better housing and everything. (*F25C*)

There'll have to be changes. Did you read about that old bitch Lady Astor? She's one that'll be changed, if I had my way. It's the likes of her that causes revolutions. (*M45C*)

Later that year, in early December, the publication of the Beveridge Report caused a sensation. One London diarist noted that it had 'set everybody talking', and Beveridge himself conceded that 'it's been a revelation to me how concerned people are with conditions after the war'. Among 'my friends and colleagues', stated an engineering draughtsman, 'the publication of the Report caused more discussion and interest than any war news for a long time,' and he added that 'the tone of *all* the discussions was favourable.' From Mass-Observation's national panel of some 1,500 regular correspondents (from 'all walks of life, living in all parts of the country', though in practice almost certainly with a middle-class bias), more than 300 wrote in to express their views, with only a handful against. Reconstruction hopes seemingly remained high and widespread later in the war. Debates in 1943/4 in the Forces 'Parliament' in Cairo saw strong support for bills to nationalise the retail trade and restrict inheritances; a poll by Gallup in July 1944 found 55 per cent welcoming the idea of a national health service (and 69 per cent preferring the prospect of health centres to the normal doctor's surgery); and shortly before Christmas that year almost one in four of the adult population listened to a series of eight Home Service programmes about full employment.[20]

One activator who had no doubt that things were going the right
way was Mrs Madge Waller, who in March 1942 chaired a meeting at
the Housing Centre in London. In her introductory remarks she assured
the audience that 'there seemed to her to be a fairly general opinion
that after the war everything was going to be better, especially among
young people'; remarked that 'she had come in contact with several
who were thinking and talking about planning for post-war Britain';
and declared that after 'an almost wasted quarter of a century – muddled
thinking and mere talking about planning, without any real plan – we
would probably not be allowed to "muddle through" again'. She then
introduced her main speaker, Tom Harrisson, co-founder five years
earlier of Mass-Observation.

Almost certainly the audience, including Mrs Waller, sat up in their
seats as Harrisson at the outset stated bluntly that the growing assumption 'that everyone wanted a better Britain in future' was 'rather a false
one':

> There was quite a striking number of people who were thinking not in
> terms of helping to make this country better to live in, but of getting
> out of the country after the war and going to America, Australia, etc.
> A strong feeling was growing up that people should have less planned
> and ordered lives and could be themselves more. Certain types of people
> were in favour of more co-operation in planning, but a very large number
> of people of the working-class population were so appalled by what
> would have to be done after the war that they felt rather hopeless about
> the task.

For elaboration, Harrisson then turned to the study that Mass-
Observation had been making of what people wanted after the war
compared with what they expected:

> What were most hoped for were equality of opportunity, better housing
> and education, socialism, security, abolition of unemployment, and a
> mass of other things which might be lumped together as town planning,
> but was not consciously thought of as such. Their expectations were far
> inferior to their hopes ... People had the right hopes, but the feeling
> that these hopes would not or could not materialise was very strong.

Overwhelming emphasis was laid on what had happened after the last war. Disappointment then had created a kind of neurosis that seemed unconquerable to a lot of people.

He ended this section of his talk with his killer facts: 'It had been found that five people were pessimistic to every one that was optimistic about reconstruction plans in general after the war, and that proportion increased to nine to one in certain heavily-raided areas.'[21]

The evidence suggests that Harrisson was broadly right – that although in 1940/41 there was at least some popular, largely positive engagement with post-war reconstruction issues, from 1942 the trend was (apart from a blip at the time of the Beveridge Report) the other way. Indeed, some qualifying remarks even need to be made about Beveridge. Before it appeared, a wide-ranging survey (supervised by G.D.H. Cole, a leading socialist intellectual) into popular attitudes to welfare found that, in the words of its Manchester investigator, 'some seemed to be quite satisfied in an inarticulate sort of way' and 'the majority just *did not know*'. At the time of the report's celebrated publication, there was a significant minority of dissenters ('If people here stand for the trades unions putting this bloody Beveridge scheme across they deserve to lose the sodding war' was how one middle-aged man, who called himself a 'Jack of All Trades', put it to an Mass-Observation observer in London), and it is far from clear how many outside the middle class were among those who bought the report in either of its forms. Moreover, from soon afterwards there was widespread cynicism about whether it would ever be implemented, typified by a 55-year-old woman of the 'artisan class' telling an interviewer that 'soon as it's over and they've no further use for you, they'll have a general election and apologise that they can't stand by the promise of the war government – it'll happen just as it did last time'.[22]

A Gallup poll taken in April 1943, asking people whether they would like to see 'any great changes' in their way of life after the war, probably captured accurately enough the popular political mood. Of the 57 per cent who agreed with that proposition, 35 per cent had 'no comment' on what changes these might be; 16 per cent hoped for 'better working conditions, better wages, work for everybody, no unemployment'; 15 per cent nominated a 'better standard of living all round, pension and security when old'; a bare 3 per cent mentioned 'socialism' or a 'changed economic system'; and only 1 per cent plumped even more idealistically for 'no more wars, better international understanding'. The widespread middle-class feeling that the focus on reconstruction was premature may well have been shared instinctively by at least some in the working class. 'Meeting many people in various occupations daily, I find, with my own opinion, too much is being broadcast by the BBC, and circulated in the newspapers, re post-war plans,' wrote a correspondent styling himself 'Commercial' to his local paper in Wolverhampton later that year. 'It is generally agreed that these plans could be arranged without all this prattle, because it definitely tends to make everyone certain that our Government know just when this war will finish, and encourages people to sit easy, instead of getting on with the job.'[23]

In the workplace there was (in the context of full employment in a wartime economy) an undeniable new self-assertiveness – Hodson in his 'ledger of war' complained that 'the working-classes, feeling their power, have often shown some ruthlessness, manifested by bus drivers refusing to stop at halts, transport workers striking on Christmas Day, coal-miners refusing sometimes to do a decent day's work' – but this was far from automatically translating into any enhanced political radicalism. *War Factory*, Mass-Observation's 1942/3 study of a Gloucestershire factory producing radar systems where the workers were mainly women, revealed resentment, boredom and alienation as the predominant sentiments, including predictably little interest in the progress of the war. Soon after Beveridge, an engineer from Dudley told M-O that, as far as his fellow-workers in an electrode factory were concerned, the prevailing atmosphere of each man for himself had 'dulled the mind to all except personal problems'. Nor were the armed forces quite the radical hotbed they have sometimes been depicted as. Analysis of the Army Bureau of Current Affairs suggests that their debates were seen more as an opportunity for a welcome respite from military duties than as an occasion to engage in serious political discussion; the future novelist Nicholas Monserrat wrote of the sailors under his command that 'there is no time and, in effect, no occasion for political interest'; or as Hodson heard an officer with the 79th Armoured Division in Germany put it just before the war's end, 'in fifteen months in the ranks I never heard politics mentioned'.[24]

Was there perhaps widespread popular anticipation of a future national health service? Those who have scoured wartime diaries report remarkably few sightings, and indeed the 1944 Gallup poll revealing 55 per cent approval also showed a not inconsiderable 32 per cent in favour of the status quo. Polling evidence demonstrated that approval towards the end of the war for Labour's nationalisation plans was reasonably broad (usually in the 40–60 per cent range) but invariably shallow, with few people seeing it as a high-priority issue. As for education, a poll in early 1945 found less than half those questioned had heard of the recent Education Act and a mere 13 per cent were aware of its provision to remove fees from grammar schools. Understandably, Orwell's earlier optimism about a newly radicalised people had by this time completely vanished. 'I overhear very little discussion of the wider issues of the war,' he told his American readers in autumn 1944. 'Everyone expects not only that there will be a ghastly muddle over demobilization, but that mass unemployment will promptly return.' And he added, 'Everyone wants, above all things, a rest.'[25]

There was plenty of further statistical underpinning available for these and similar assertions. In the autumn of 1943, for example, more than 500 interviews by Mass-Observation across the country found that 43 per cent expected heavy post-war unemployment, 46 per cent another war after the present one, 50 per cent uncertain or without an opinion as to whether the government was paying too much or too little attention to post-war reconstruction, and 49 per cent (up from 19 per cent a year earlier) saying that their main priority after the war was to 'relax or have a change'. But in the end, over and above the figures, we need to listen to the voices, as in the cynical, mistrustful, rather truculent tone of four young tradesmen in an army unit – reminiscent of Rudyard Kipling's 'Tommy' – describing their expectations of demobilisation:

It'll be the same old story, those who can pull the strings will be all right, the other poor buggers can look after themselves.

Just the same mess as last time.

Personally I don't trust the Government and I don't suppose they're likely to worry much about us. We're heroes while the war's on, but we can look after ourselves afterwards.

I can't see they can afford to unload everybody at once, or there'll be a lot of trouble. Chaps aren't going to stand for it.

In August 1944, with the long war clearly drawing to an end, an M-O team was in Gloucester. 'What do you feel the next ten years of your life will be like?' it asked a group of working-class mothers. 'Are you looking forward to them, or aren't you looking forward to them much?' The replies have a wonderful – and revealing – authenticity about a world where the big picture was infinitely more local and immediate than any of the activators ever imagined:

> Oh God! I'm not good at answering questions.
>
>   Well, yes and no. As long as I don't have any more kids I shall be all right.
>
>   Don't know. Really I don't.
>
>   Why, yes.
>
>   Well, I suppose I am – we like to think the future's going to be better.
>
>   Oh yes, I don't want to die yet!
>
>   Am I? I'll say I am. I want to buy my own house if I can. But it won't be in Alma Place – the row here is terrible, and they keep the kids up till 11 and 12 at night, yelling about the street.
>
>   Oh, well, of course I am, hoping for the war to end and things to improve.
>
>   Well, it's all according. It all depends on if it's any better than the last two or three.

One of the women was the 'worn and dirty' 43-year-old mother of fourteen 'filthy and ragged' offspring aged between twenty and eight months. 'Well,' she answered when she found a moment, 'I hope I live to see 'em all grow up to look arter theirselves.' She was also asked whether she was religious. 'Well, I believe in God but I can't say I'm religious. You get a bit hasty when you've so many children.'[26]

These were the sort of people whom Harrisson surely had in mind when in March 1942 he turned specifically to his lecture's title, 'Propaganda for Town Planning', and let rip:

> The idea that places really were going to be rebuilt and better new houses constructed had not penetrated down to the large masses of the population. While there had certainly been much talk and propaganda

about town planning, about 95 per cent of it had been quite above most people's heads. Mr Harrisson said that he was worried most by the way that planners and others associated with the matter talked as if they were winning over the general public when really they were only winning over each other. He had never met any group of people who 'scratched each other's backs' more than planners did.

For those in the audience bitten with the planning bug there was worse to come:

The planning conferences were only for those who knew about the subject; the talks on the wireless probably did not reach the people for whom they would be most use; the majority of the planning exhibitions seemed to mean little to any of the general public who saw them. The people needing planning propaganda are those who are used to thinking in concrete terms – who could talk for ages about things connected with their own house, but could not frame a single sentence about planning.

'Planning will have,' Harrisson concluded bluntly, 'either to find out what people want and design propaganda that will have an immediate appeal, or educate people to appreciate how their own lives could be improved by putting into practice the theories held by the planners.'[27] The record of the meeting does not, sadly, include any ensuing discussion.

Was Harrisson being unfair to the planners? Significantly, only a few months earlier, the editor of the *Architectural Review*, J. M. Richards, had strongly criticised organisations like Mass-Observation ('a phenomenon very typical of recent years') as tending to block properly visionary town planning. 'The needs of society are a fit subject for scientific study, but they cannot be elucidated by a gigantic piece of consumer research' was the Richards line. 'It is a fallacy that the needs of society are the aggregate of as many individual demands as can be ascertained.' In practice, many planners, exemplified by Max Lock at Middlesbrough, did try quite hard to initiate and then sustain a dialogue with public opinion at both a local and a national level, in order to try to keep that opinion broadly on side with their plans; any view that sees the planners (of the 1940s anyway) as crazed, tinpot dictators is simply a caricature. The fact that there were so few opportunities during the war, and indeed afterwards, for those being planned for to express an explicit democratic verdict on the plans was less the fault of the planners than of local (and arguably national) politicians.

Nevertheless, to read Thomas Sharp's presidential address in 1945 to the Town Planning Institute is still to be struck by his profession's ultimately top-down assumptions. He did not deny that people had 'the inalienable right to know fully what is being planned for them' – including 'the right to comment on the plans, to require alterations in them, and, if necessary, to reject them'. What Sharp explicitly repudiated, however, was 'actual participation in the act of planning', in other words before draft plans had been drawn up; the notion that the planner should essentially be the servant of the people, putting their wishes into technical form, he castigated as nothing other than 'sheer demagogy, rather than a manifestation of the working of a true democracy'.[28]

That the language of the Rebuilding Britain exhibition in 1943 was so notably circumspect and reassuring presumably reflected the lack of popular enthusiasm for town planning. 'Don't get the idea,' it insisted in almost hurt tones, 'that the planner is a robot of a man without sentiment or good manners, whose *idée fixe* is to tear out the ancient core of our towns in the cause of traffic-flow or Brave New Worldliness. The truth is the exact opposite. The move for planning in England has come largely from those who loved old buildings and could see no other way of saving them than by getting "building development" controlled. It is not the dream of the planner to recondition towns until nothing of their personality remains.' They did not see it quite that way in Bristol, where in the last two years of the war a sustained, unavailing campaign (mostly waged by traders but not entirely) sought to reverse the planners' decision to create a large new shopping centre in the 'off the beaten track' Broadmead area at the expense of the city's traditional shopping core. Nor did they in Wolverhampton, where in early 1945 what response there was to the plan for thoroughgoing redevelopment was typified by the view of one correspondent to the local paper: 'I think Wolverhampton people's best interests will be served in the preservation of much that is old in the town, rather than the sweeping away of familiar landmarks in a fetish or orgy of modernising that is almost an obsession today.'[29]

The same, crucially, may well also have been the case in Coventry, or at least on the part of the middle-aged and elderly suddenly finding themselves living in the middle of the new symbol of the new Britain. Barely a week after the decisive vote by the city council in February 1941 in favour of Gibson's radical plan, a local paper published a cry from the heart by 'An Old Citizen': 'It is to be hoped that the citizens as a whole will have the opportunity of expressing their views before any irretrievable step is taken, for the views of local government officials are not necessarily those of Coventry people who, after all, may want to live here after the war. We should like the new Coventry to be something of the old Coventry, and not merely a fourth-rate provincial city on futurist lines.' Over the next three years there seems to have been relatively little expression of popular feeling either way, as local traders tried unsuccessfully to persuade the City Reconstruction Committee that, in the words of the President of the local chamber of commerce, 'the old idea of street shopping was much better than "cloistered precincts"'. But in December 1944 the issue did briefly if obliquely break cover after the pro-plan *Coventry Evening Telegraph* reported Gibson's talk on 'The New Coventry' to a meeting of Armstrong Siddeley workers. After stressing the need for 20,000 new houses in the city, Gibson had 'pointed out the need for a departure from tradition in building methods' before remarking in conclusion that 'the people themselves would decide how they would be housed in the future'. This brought a double negative response: from 'Coventrian', arguing that 'the people will decide that it is bricks and mortar they require, and perhaps a few less planners,' and from 'Longview', who was 'certain that if a referendum could be taken there would be an overwhelming majority in favour of the orthodox brick and mortar house'.

But for most Coventrians in the years after their devastating Blitz, the top priority was not to take part in controversies about a nebulous future. Rather it was to regroup, to retrench and to try to get back as soon as possible to something like normality, which in essence meant life before the war. 'For the majority of the city's population,' the historians of this strong trend have noted, 'abstract ruminations were simply irrelevant.' By 1944 local cinemas were attracting record attendances, organised cricket and football were once again being played on Saturday afternoons, the Coventry Amateur Operatic Society was meeting for the first time since 1939, and the National Federation of Anglers was choosing Coventry as the venue for its AGM, reflecting the city's almost 7,000 members of that decidedly non-reconstructionist body. Perhaps most telling of all was the behaviour of Coventry's gardeners. Amid warnings from civic leaders that the proper business of horticulture was still the cultivation of vegetables, they quietly and privately during the last fifteen months of the war grew flowers and shrubs – potent, non-utilitarian reminders of a peaceful way of life that perhaps had not been irretrievably fractured.[30]

Above all, across the country, it was on the home that most people's hopes and concerns were really focused. 'Home means a place to go to when in trouble,' a female Mass-Observation panellist declared in 1943. 'A place where bygone days were happiest. A place sadly altered by the war. A place where you can do as you like without landladies to consider . . . A place to glorify when away and rely on always.' The same year M-O published *People's Homes*, a comprehensive survey of working-class attitudes to housing. 'One often hears planners argue that ordinary people have no idea of what they want in housing,' the survey's introduction noted. 'This is a satisfactory argument when you are planning for others without knowing their hearts and minds. The many verbatim remarks in this report put that tale out of court once and for all.' Among those quoted was a 50-year-old working woman who lived in an upper tenement flat 'with a husband, two children working and two children still at school'. She was asked about her dream home:

> I'd like a sitting-room-kitchen, so that you could have meals in it, and a nice garden at the back for vegetables and chickens, and a flower garden in front. A nice bathroom all done with lino . . . Coal fire in the living room and none in the bedrooms, I don't think fires in a bedroom are healthy. I'd like a sort of sunshine paper, if you know what I mean, with just a little beading round the top, flowers or fruit. That for the sitting room, and blue for the bedrooms. I like boards in the bedrooms, not polished or anything of that, but scrubbed, so that they come up lovely and white. Just scrub them with a bit of soap. The same in the kitchen unless we had a bit of lino there. I don't like the stone floor in the kitchen. It's so cold and damp.

On the basis of this and much other evidence, the survey concluded that 'the "dream home" of the majority is still the small modern suburban house, preferably possessing all modern conveniences, such as a labour-saving kitchen, hot and cold water laid on to a sink in the scullery, and a bathroom with a separate lavatory'. It would also have 'small but light windows, built-in cupboards, coal fires for warming, electric points in most rooms – these and a hundred other things would be appreciated'. Inevitably, 'the range of personal wants is immense – but happily the elasticity of true democratic planning can offer an almost infinite variety, and so satisfy the healthy, contradictory categories of human need and hope and hate.'

This was not good enough for one of the book's reviewers, the economist P. Sargant Florence. 'The most that can be deduced is that some people like one thing, some another' was his unenthusiastic response, and he argued that the book once again pointed 'to the moral that standards it is desirable to achieve cannot safely be left to house-wives who are not equipped with the necessary knowledge of what lies within the realm of possibility'. Accordingly, 'architects and planners must give the lead and the target must be placed higher than the inarticulate yearnings of the average working-class housewife, if the same ill-defined sense of dissatisfaction is not to be perpetuated'.[31]

Over and above 'all mod cons', what people wanted – and clearly, unambiguously wanted – was privacy in their homes. 'A garden that is overlooked, windows into which neighbours can see, balconies visible from the road or from houses opposite are all deplored,' the report noted. 'But above all, people dislike sharing a house with another family or even with one person, as many have to do.' The unashamedly unemancipated Mrs Michael Pleydell-Bouverie, who by 1944 had spent three and a half years on behalf of the *Daily Mail* talking to 'the Women of Britain' about present and putative homes, agreed: 'Speaking generally the people want to breathe and move, to be rid of neighbours' wireless, and the clatter of early-risers and late-bedders . . . The community life of which everyone has had experience to some degree or other in this war, has not endeared or recommended itself as a permanent state of affairs.' This strong desire for greater privacy was hardly a new phenomenon – historical demographers have shown that the 'privatised', home-centred domestic unit, founded on the nuclear family, goes back to pre-industrial England – but undoubtedly the war's more or less enforced communal sociability sharpened such instincts. 'Emphatically, no' and 'We prefer to wash our dirty linen in private' were two typical, highly symptomatic contributions to discussions in 1943 by almost 300 Townswomen's Guilds about the desirability of developing communal laundries.[32]

There is evidence, moreover, that if having to move some distance (usually out of a city centre) was the only way in which the desired mixture of greater privacy and more amenities-cum-space (including a garden) could be achieved, then most people were prepared to do that. A cross-class survey in 1943 of 2,000 women in their teens and 20s found that over half wanted to live in a suburb or small town and nearly a third in the country; while a study the same year by the Society for Women Housing Managers discovered that 'an overwhelming majority plumped for a suburban house' if given the choice between different types of modern housing. Nevertheless, the very understandable wish for modern conveniences far from implied an unambiguously positive attitude towards the modern as a whole. An official survey carried out in the closing weeks of the war saw a random sample of 1,727 housewives being shown four photographs of bedroom furniture. Number 1 was 'plain and fairly modern', number 2 'the most old fashioned', and numbers 3 and 4 'extremely modern'. The preferences respectively expressed were 27, 45, 13 and 12 per cent. Significantly, in terms of the breakdown of these preferences, 'the upper economic group tend towards modernity rather more than the lower economic groups' and 'the younger age groups like modern furniture more than the older age group'.[33]

It was the overwhelming desire for privacy that pervaded what was nothing less than a mass aversion towards the whole idea of flats – despite, as Frederic Osborn caustically put it in 1942, 'the most persistent propaganda by architectural playboys who want larger boxes of plasticine with which to indulge their creative fancy'. A year earlier, the *Picture Post* special (including Maxwell Fry's modernist vision) had prompted congratulatory letters (with a fair sprinkling from the great and the good), but Margaret Blundell dissented: 'Your Brave New World plan is all very well in some respects, but will "the workers" be satisfied even if it is put into practice?' asked this gasfitter's wife from Sirdar

Road, Wood Green, N22. 'I doubt it. Your flats would never be home to me. You can clear away whole towns of ugly old houses in one sweep, but you cannot change human nature so quickly. Slow change is better in the long run.'[34]

Over the rest of the war, a series of surveys showed how far from unusual Blundell's dislike of flats was – a dislike, it must be remembered, at a time when 'flats' meant in most people's minds a handful of storeys, not a high-rise in the modern sense of the term. Whereas 49 per cent of those asked in the *People's Homes* survey wanted ideally to 'live in a small house with a garden', only 5 per cent of the sample 'would by choice inhabit a flat, and even among flat dwellers only 28 per cent would not prefer to move to some sort of house, if they had the choice'. Soon afterwards, a submission made to the Dudley Committee by the Women's Advisory Housing Council similarly asserted that only 5.7 per cent of its respondents preferred flats to houses, with drawbacks of the former including not only lack of privacy but noise, fears over children's safety, 'gangsterism' and problems of coal deliveries and refuse disposal. And Pleydell-Bouverie confirmed that 90.2 per cent of the women she had polled had expressed a preference for a house or a bungalow, a preference partly explained by one of her more graphic chapter titles, '99% Want a Garden'. Still, as the *People's Homes* report had wryly concluded about working-class people and such apparently firm wishes, 'Happily for the planners, they will make the best of a bad lot or a good little.'[35]

What about 'community'? That bewitching, tantalising word would be the subject of many facile generalisations and much mental anguish in the years ahead but was not yet on the lips of every social investigator. Probably the closest to a 'community study' undertaken during the war was Dennis Chapman's survey of Middlesbrough (a town not short of slums and industrial pollution), based on interviews in the summer of 1944 with 1,387 'housewives', 971 'men workers' and 238 'women workers'.

Almost three-quarters expressed the wish to continue living in Middlesbrough after the war, with easily the most common reason being 'born here, used to it', followed by 'reasons connected with employment', 'friends and relatives here', and 'like it'. Predictably, it was younger people and higher earners who most frequently expressed the wish to live elsewhere. Asked about Middlesbrough's post-war problems, most people put unemployment and housing as their two main concerns; but although 'neither men nor women in Middlesbrough considered problems of physical planning to be of first importance', they were prepared to express views when asked what 'should be done after the war to make Middlesbrough a better place to live in', with 'improved roads and traffic circulation' seen as the top priority. Most people also wanted to see more libraries, theatres, playing fields, play centres, swimming pools and health clinics, but there was no majority support for more meeting places.

In answer to the question 'In what part of Middlesbrough and its neighbourhood would you prefer to live – why?', the most popular reason for choosing a particular district was 'healthier, better air, better for children', followed by 'like country, open', 'like the district' and 'better housing', with 'near relatives and friends' trailing badly behind. Asked if they wanted to move to a new house, in practice almost certainly in a suburb, more than two-thirds answered in the affirmative – with the desire for better amenities (including a garden) as the principal motive but with what Chapman called 'dissatisfaction caused by the social quality of the neighbourhood' also playing a part. He got closer to that factor by asking the pertinent question 'If you were entirely free to choose, would you want to live amongst the same kind of people that are in your neighbourhood now, or would you prefer to live amongst a different group of people?' In reply, 55 per cent said they did want to go on living among the same kind of people; 28 per cent would prefer to live among different people; and 17 per cent were 'unable or unwilling to express an opinion'. By far the most common reason given by the satisfied was 'like them, they are all right, etc', while among the dissatisfied a pervasive complaint was that 'people are noisy, rough, etc', though 'don't have much to do with neighbours – don't like people round here' was also popular.

Chapman further found that 'neighbourly relations are of considerable extent and play an important part in many fields of the daily life of the housewife', though he added the crucial qualifying point that 'the unit of neighbourly relations appears to be very small, a handful of families participating in each group'. Moreover, not only was it the case that 'the common social institution has so far been an insignificant source of "best friends" and even the common school is of very minor importance', but 'visits to common social institutions between neighbours who are friends are likewise seen to affect only a small number of people'. There were, accordingly, no strong grounds for 'centring a residential unit around a common social institution – a community centre or a school – from the point of view of creating social integration'. Put another way, 'the evidence is fairly conclusive that the idea of a neighbourhood unit [à la latest American town planning] which should be a microcosm of the social structure of the whole community is incorrect'.[36]

All in all, Chapman's report was sober, unsentimental stuff. It realistically portrayed people's strong desire for improvement in their personal conditions, preferably as part of a suburban lifestyle; their almost equally strong wish to live among those whom they perceived to be their own kind of people (whatever that kind might be); and their strictly limited appetite for the communal.

Was 'the Titmuss version' a complete myth, then? No, not quite. An official survey in late 1942 into public attitudes to plans for reconstruction located what it called a 'thinking minority' that was *actively* in favour of more state intervention in order to implement policies (in areas such as employment, welfare, housing and education) that would seek to benefit all – even if such policies involved higher taxation. The size of this 'thinking minority' was reckoned at between 5 and 20 per cent. Beyond that point it is difficult to salvage the myth. Indeed, the probability is that the size of this minority (inevitably disproportionately middle-class in composition) was actually shrinking towards the end of the war. Penguin Specials, originally launched in 1937, probably hit their peak in February 1942 with the publication of Archbishop William Temple's *Christianity and the Social Order*, which sought to marry faith with socialism and rapidly sold 140,000 copies. But by 1945 sales of the Specials had slumped to such an extent that the series was temporarily abandoned.

Fundamental social and cultural continuities remained – indeed, were arguably strengthened rather than lessened by the war. 'Class feeling and class resentment are very strong,' Harold Nicolson observed with foreboding soon after the European conflict ended. The Cutteslowe walls – built across and even along a north Oxford road in 1934 in order to separate private from council housing – stayed obstinately in place. The most-watched films during the war were Gainsborough melodramas, virtually without political or even social content, while the plots of the ever-popular Mills and Boon novels coursed along almost regardless of what was going on in the outside world. A culture that was still holding its own was that of the improving, intensely respectable, wanting-no-hand-outs working class. The gasfitter's wife Margaret Blundell spoke eloquently for it in her 1941 letter to *Picture Post:* 'What sort of men and women will the New World children turn out to be if they are to have no struggle? One must strive if one is to develop character. Your picture of Rich *v* Poor does not ring quite true. A considerable number of working-class manage a holiday every year, all the more enjoyable when one has struggled for it. You would make things too easy. Jealousy is the canker of our time. The rich will always be with us in one form or another and rightly so.' But within the working class the cultural future lay elsewhere – a future simultaneously epitomised and hastened by the startling rise in the *Daily Mirror*'s popularity (beginning in the mid-1930s but accelerating from 1943, with circulation rising from two million that year to three million by 1946). Drawing inspiration directly from America, it successfully relied on a threefold formula: a brash irreverence (not only in peacetime) towards the authorities; a Labour-supporting politics of a far more populist, less heavy-duty type than that ponderously upheld by the Trades Union Congress-backed *Daily Herald*; and a very professionally assembled tabloid blend of cartoons, comic strips (the legendary Jane), human interest, sport and (often Hollywood) celebrities. 'Catering for short tea-breaks and even shorter attention spans', in the regretful but probably accurate words of one historian, it was a formula whose time had come.[37]

A final survey. *Patterns of Marriage* by Eliot Slater (a psychologist) and Moya Woodside (a psychiatric social worker) was not published until 1951, but its richly suggestive fieldwork comprised a detailed survey conducted between 1943 and 1946 of 200 working-class soldiers and their wives, mainly from the London area. Slater and Woodside's central focus was on courtship, marriage and sex – revealing in the last area an extensive amount of what the authors called 'passive endurance' on the part of the wives, typified by one's remark: 'He's very good, he doesn't bother me much.' But there was much else. Both men and women, they found on the class front, 'were dominated by the distinction that is expressed in "We" and "They", and, even in this war in which all were involved together, by the feeling of a cleft between the "two nations"'. Typical assertions quoted were: 'there'll never be much improvement so long as the country is run by people with money', 'the working class should be given a fairer do than they have had', and 'MPs have no worries, they've all got money in the bank.' The war itself had done little or nothing to broaden horizons. Nearly all the male conscripts, Slater and Woodside found, 'were bored and "fed up", took little interest in wider and impersonal issues, and were only concerned to get the war over and get home again'. As for their wives, 'the war was a background to daily life, irritating, endless, without significance other than its effects on their personal lives.' And for 'men and women alike patriotism was a remote conception, not altogether without meaning, but associated with feelings which were entirely inarticulate'.

For the husbands in particular, Slater and Woodside emphasised, one concern dominated above all:

> The spectre of unemployment is never very far away. Some have experienced it themselves; others remember its effect on their own childhood; and for still others it exists as a malignant bogy that must dog the steps of every working man. Again and again a preference is expressed for the 'steady job' as opposed to high wages, more especially by the older men. It is not likely that the lesson that England learned from the years of the trade depression will ever be forgotten . . . There was a strong feeling that the fate of the individual under the capitalist system had little to do with merit, and depended on nebulous and unpredictable social forces. If only these could be controlled, a rich reward for personal ambitions was of secondary importance.

None of which guaranteed any more than a minimal interest in politics: 'Politics, it was felt, had nothing to do with their ordinary lives, in which other interests, sport and home, predominated. Politics was a special subject, beyond the understanding of the uneducated, or too vast and impersonal for any individual effort to influence.' A mere 21 out of the 200 men took 'an active interest in politics', but the attitude of the overwhelming majority was summed up by assertions like 'I'm not interested in politics, it isn't my job', 'politics are a pain in the neck, I've not the education to understand them', and 'me being an ordinary working-class man, politics is nothing to do with me; we're too busy with our families and jobs'. Politicians themselves, moreover, were generally seen in a dim light – 'all politicians are rogues', 'I'm against political parties, they're only out for their own gain,' 'no government is any good'.

The wives, meanwhile, were not sufficiently engaged with politics even to be cynical, with 'a serious and intelligent interest' being taken by only seven out of 200. 'The remainder showed an extreme apathy and lack of interest. Politics are felt to be remote from real everyday life, as incomprehensible as mathematics, the business of men. Preoccupation with personal concerns, the affairs of the home, children, leave little room.' Slater and Woodside quoted some of them: 'I married young, and had no time, with the children', 'I don't read papers much about the Government', 'After being on your feet all day, you just want to sit down and have somebody bring you a nice cup of tea.' With a note of palpable disappointment, the authors concluded about the wives that 'their effect as a whole is negative, conservative, a brake on any change from the established order'.[38]

It hardly took a Nostradamus to see that the outriders for a New Jerusalem – a vision predicated on an active, informed, classless, progressively minded citizenship – were going to have their work cut out.

———

Britain in 1945. A land of orderly queues, hat-doffing men walking on the outside, seats given up to the elderly, no swearing in front of women and children, censored books, censored films, censored plays, infinite repression of desires. Divorce for most an unthinkable social disgrace, marriage too often a lifetime sentence. ('I didn't want it,' my own grandmother would say to me in the 1970s when, making small talk soon after my grandfather's death, I said that at least he had lived long enough for them to have their Golden Wedding party. 'All I could think about was the misery.') Even the happier marriages seldom companionable, with husbands and wives living in separate, self-contained spheres, the husband often not telling the wife how much he had earned. And despite women working in wartime jobs, few quarrelling with the assumption that the two sexes were fundamentally different from each other. Children in the street ticked off by strangers, children in the street kept an eye on by strangers, children at home rarely consulted, children stopping being children when they left school at 14 and got a job. A land of hierarchical social assumptions, of accent and dress as giveaways to class, of Irish jokes and casually derogatory references to Jews and niggers. Expectations low and limited but anyone in or on the fringes of the middle class hoping for 'a job for life' and comforted by the myth that the working class kept their coal in the bath. A pride in Britain, which had stood alone, a pride even in 'Made in Britain'. A deep satisfaction with our own idiosyncratic, non-metric units of distance, weight, temperature, money: the bob, the tanner, the threepenny Joey. A sense of history, however nugatory the knowledge of that history. A land in which authority was respected? Or rather, accepted? Yes, perhaps the latter, co-existing with the necessary safety valve of copious everyday grumbling. A land of domestic hobbies and domestic pets. The story of Churchill in the Blitz driving through a London slum on a Friday evening – seeing a long queue outside a shop – stopping the car – sending his detective to find out what this shortage was – the answer: birdseed. Turning the cuffs, elbow patches on jackets, sheets sides to middle. A deeply conservative land.

3

Oh Wonderful People of Britain!

'Seventeen days since V.E. Day, and never have I seen a nation change so quickly from a war mentality to a peace mentality,' observed the diplomat-turned-writer Sir Robert Bruce Lockhart near the end of May 1945. 'The war [ie that was continuing in the Far East and was expected to last well into 1946] has disappeared from the news ... Sport and the election now fill the front pages.' Sport included what was still the national game, and on 22 May the First 'Victory' Test ended at Lord's with Australia pummelling an ageing England attack to win by six wickets. For Gladys Langford there was a rare treat that day, in the company of Mr Burchell, a fellow-resident at her hotel: 'He took me first to the Saviours' Arms at Westminster where we had a substantial lunch – then we tried to get into a cinema but there were queues everywhere. We finally went to the Polytechnic after which, queues being in evidence, everywhere, we had fish & chips in a Soho "dive" where coloured men [probably American servicemen] were much in evidence. To be taken out at 55 is quite a triumph.' Anyone who had imagined that life would suddenly become easier in that first summer of peace was swiftly disabused. Judy Haines, however, took it all in her stride:

> *16 May*. Mother and Dad H. came to tea. Abbé [her husband, whose real name was Alfred] made the jelly and blancmange. Mother played and I sang – for 2 hours. The husbands seemed very happy about it. Then we became engrossed in KANUGO [a card game], till nearly 11 o'clock. Very satisfactory evening.
>
> *19 May*. As usual at holiday time [the Whit weekend], queues

everywhere in Chingford . . . The bread queue was the longest I have ever seen, and think many were disappointed. We had just about sufficient, and I have always Ryvita to help out.

26 May. Cleared out tallboy. Listened to *Pride & Prejudice*. The ration this week, of chops, contained some suet. Good! Chopped it and wrapped it in flour for future suet pudding.

For Henry St John, working a few days later in Midsomer Norton, there was as ever only frustration – 'I tried in vain to buy some Ovaltine, this being the 11th successive shop at which I failed to get it, although it continues to be widely advertised' – but there was some compensation when, on the train back to Bristol, an American soldier gave him a Camel cigarette. The American influence, and indeed anything that smacked of the modern, did not play well with Ernest Loftus in Essex. 'Mrs Williams [the French mistress] and I are taking joint action to stop our scholars attending Youth Clubs or, as I call them, Child Night Clubs,' noted Barking Abbey School's head in early June. 'So far as our type of school is concerned they are a menace. The world is sex-mad & they are the outcome of the sex-urge + the war + the cinema + evil books + a debased art & music + an uneducated parentage.'[1]

For one American, the writer Edmund Wilson, the experience of arriving in London later in June and putting up at the Green Park Hotel in Half Moon Street proved a salutary revelation of the Old World's post-bellum bleakness:

I was given a little room with yellow walls rubbed by greasy heads above the bed – little daybed with horrible brown cover that seemed to be impregnated with dirt – wooden washstand with no towel – brown carpet with rhomboidal pattern, stained and full of dust – piles of dirt in plain sight in corners – small shit-colored coal grate with dismal gas logs in corner. The dining room, with slovenly wretched waitresses – stains of soup, eggs, and jam on the table that seemed never to have been wiped off.

None of this, though, pierced Wilson's heart. But for Surrey's scholar-naturalist Eric Parker, driving through 'the Fold Country' (between Blackdown and Godalming) on the last day of May to see what had happened to his county's favourite corner since he had last been there in 1940, it was very different. 'The Fold Country was an aerodrome,' he found. 'Oak woods had been uprooted, engines of steel had torn out by the roots cottages and fields of corn.' Getting out of his car and wandering down a favourite lane, he suddenly found himself on a plain he had never seen before: 'The woods had gone. The lane had come to an end. Instead, in front of me stretched a vast flat space, a mile-wide level with a mile-deep highway broadening out to where I stood ... There in the mid-distance were the huge noses of steel machines lifting into the sky, monstrous waiting insects.' Consolation came only when he reached Dunsfold and 'its green with the old black-smith's shop, and the Bricklayers' Arms, and a cottage on the green covered with white roses, and another cottage with scarlet geraniums climbing to the windows – all as it used to be, years ago, in the Fold Country'.

Even in May 1945 there appeared two books that in time would fuel a nostalgia industry: Evelyn Waugh's *Brideshead Revisited* (early reviews dominated by perceptions of the novel's snobbishness) and the Rev. W. Awdry's *The Three Railway Engines*. The latter was published by Edmund Ward, a fine-art printer in Leicester who was, as Awdry later put it, 'appalled at the lack of good quality literature for children available in the shops'. The irresistible size and format were almost certainly chosen with the aim of saving paper, and in 'The Sad Story of Henry' there featured the Fat Director ('My doctor has forbidden me to pull'). The first performance of Benjamin Britten's *Peter Grimes*, at Sadler's Wells on 7 June, struck an altogether more pioneering note, as the National Opera Company returned home from a war spent touring. 'After each curtain call,' a member of the audience recalled, 'people turned to one another excitedly while continuing to applaud; it was as if they wanted not simply to express their enthusiasm but to share it with their neighbours.' Grimes himself, a rough-hewn fisherman, was a rounded, ultimately tragic figure, far removed from the usual dramatic depiction of the lower classes as little more than buffoons. 'It looks as if the old spell on British opera may be broken at last!' Britten wrote soon afterwards in response to an appreciative letter.[2]

But some things never changed, or closed, and less than a week later

Henry St John, briefly up in town, was in the fourth row at the Windmill: 'The first scene included a sideways view of a nude, and a front view of a woman whose breasts were bare. I delayed masturbation until another para-nude appeared seen frontways, with drapery depending between the exposed breasts. Actually the most erotic scene was one featuring Jane Rock with a diaphanous scarf across her bosom, because during her dancing this flimsy covering jerked away to expose the white globes of her breasts and the nipples.' The Lord Chamberlain's rules insisted on statuesque poses, but for the diarist it was still enough to make him entitle the top of his page 'A GLIMPSE OF BEAUTY'. Shortly afterwards, a young would-be writer, working for the Leeds firm J. T. Buckton & Sons, had the thrill of seeing his first article ('Music Hath Charms') appear in print, in the July issue of *London Opinion*, but sadly for its author, Keith Waterhouse, 'my fellow-clerks were more interested in the tasteful nudes'.

Another young provincial had a rather more shattering experience. Dennis Potter, the ten-year-old son of a Forest of Dean miner, spent most of the summer lodging (with his mother and sister) in his grandfather's small terraced house in Hammersmith, while they waited for a council house in the Forest. He went to a local school, where he was mercilessly teased because of his accent, and spent many hours in the Hammersmith Gaumont, a huge Art Deco cinema complete with a gleaming white Hammond organ, transparent curtains and a projector that shed 'blue tobacco smoke' light. But what affected him most intimately were the attentions of his just-demobilised Uncle Ernie, also lodging at 56 Rednall Terrace and deputed to share a bed with his nephew. Years later, Potter was asked if he had told anyone about the drink-induced abuse that he had suffered during those weeks. 'I couldn't talk about it,' he replied. 'You don't know the circumstances, the house, and the sense that I had, that it would be like throwing a bomb into the middle of everything that made me feel secure. So . . .'[3]

It was also an election summer. Churchill's strong preference – shared by Clement Attlee, leader of the Labour Party, and his most important colleague, Ernest Bevin – was for the wartime coalition to continue until Japan was defeated. But at its party conference in Blackpool on 21 May, Labour's rank and file almost unanimously endorsed its National Executive's unwillingness to extend the coalition's life beyond

October, whether or not Japan was defeated by then. Churchill responded by dissolving the coalition, forming a caretaker administration and calling a general election for 5 July. The Blackpool mood was almost rapturously optimistic, with loud and prolonged ovations being given to speakers old and new. 'It is in no pure Party spirit that we are going into this election,' the Tredegar firebrand Aneurin ('Nye') Bevan told them. 'We know that in us, and in us alone, lies the economic salvation of this country and the opportunity of providing a great example to the world.' He went on, with his matchless, inspiriting, immoderate oratory:

> We have been the dreamers, we have been the sufferers, now we are the builders. We enter this campaign not merely to get rid of the Tory majority – that will not be enough for our task. It will not be sufficient to get a parliamentary majority. We want the complete political extinction of the Tory Party, and twenty-five years of Labour Government. We cannot do in five years what requires to be done. It needs a new industrial revolution. We require that modern industrial science be applied to our heavy industry. It can only be done by men with modern minds, by men of a new age. It can only be done by the fine young men and women that we have seen in this Conference this week.

Few finer than Major Denis Healey and Captain Roy Jenkins – both prospective candidates, both in uniform, though Healey in battledress, Jenkins in service dress. Cuffs turned back and all eyes on him, Healey won applause by invoking his own experience of Europe in the past three years, claiming that 'the upper classes in every country are selfish, depraved, dissolute and decadent', and boldly insisting that 'the crucial principle of our own foreign policy should be to protect, assist, encourage and aid in every way the Socialist revolution wherever it appears'. It was, his friend and rival Jenkins would recall with wryness as much as affection, a 'macho' and 'striking' performance.[4]

Churchill could hardly have made a more counterproductive start to his campaign. 'No Socialist Government conducting the entire life and industry of the country could afford to allow free, sharp, or violently-worded expressions of public discontent,' he rashly declared in his opening radio broadcast on 4 June. 'They would have to fall back on some form of Gestapo, no doubt very humanely directed in the first instance. And this would nip opinion in the bud; it would stop criticism as it reared its head, and it would gather all the power to the supreme party and the party leaders.' The immediate reaction of Judy Haines was almost certainly typical of middle opinion: 'I thought it was awful. He condemned the socialists and used the word "Gestapo" on their policy of continuing to direct people into jobs until the world is a bit more put-to-rights.' Twenty-four hours later her reaction to the latest broadcast was very different: 'Attlee spoke, and after Churchill's outburst of last evening, I found it pleasant listening. He dealt with Churchill's accusation, but didn't counter-accuse.' Nevertheless, there remained a widespread assumption that Churchill's indisputably fine record as a war leader would be enough to see the Tories home. 'I think this election is going to be alright,' their licensed maverick, Bob Boothby, wrote to the press magnate Lord Beaverbrook on the 8th, 'and that the P.M. will pull it off. Without him I would not give the Tories two hundred seats.'

Churchill's three subsequent election broadcasts did improve some-what – though even so, Vita Sackville-West thought them 'confused, woolly, unconstructed and so wordy that it is impossible to pick out any concrete impression from them' – and towards the end of June he undertook a three-day tour of the north and Scotland in which, amid high levels of enthusiasm, he addressed no fewer than 27 meetings. In London, however, his appearances met with a less positive response. In Chelsea, as he drove down Royal Avenue making the inevitable but now anachronistic 'V' sign, 'nobody cheered, and the silence was dire'; in Islington it was the same, reducing the great man to taking off his hat to a passing bus, bowing to it and saying, 'Good night, bus!'; in Camberwell he was booed, and in Southwark he even had to be rescued by police from a crowd turning ugly. He continued to trust to the tunes he knew best. 'A glib and specious policy may have unpleasant booby traps attached to it,' he wrote in the *News of the World* the Sunday before polling. 'That is my view of nationalisation and socialism. History has shown – and this war has confirmed it – that the genius and greatness of our race lie in the encouragement and development of free enterprise and the spirit of adventure and self reliance which go with it.' But deep down he perhaps knew that this time around those tunes would not be enough. 'I've tried them with pep and I've tried them with pap,' he confided at one point (reputedly to Attlee of all people), 'and I still don't know what they want.'[5]

As in any general election, there was a patchwork of local colour. In Preston the young Tory candidate Julian Amery disconcertingly discovered in his canvassing that it was 'quite common to find eleven or twelve people sleeping in a single room'. In Dundee one of the Labour Party's leading left-wing theorists, John Strachey, made much of the fact that he was 'Wing Commander Strachey' and ensured that in his election address he was photographed in uniform. For another photo opportunity, Labour's candidate in Oxford, Frank Pakenham (later Lord Longford), hired a pony and cart, installed his many children in the back and set out holding aloft the placard 'A NON-STOP DRIVE FOR HOUSING'; unfortunately, the pony soon came to a halt and refused to be budged. In Grantham an Oxford chemistry undergraduate, Margaret Roberts (later Thatcher), spent the early weeks of her summer vacation supporting the Tory candidate, Squadron Leader Worth; she declared, in her capacity as a warm-up speaker at his meetings, that 'it is the people of my generation who will bear the brunt of the change from the trials of the past into calmer channels' and insisted that 'just punishment must be meted out' to the defeated German enemy. In Kettering the writer Naomi Mitchison, whose husband Dick was standing for Labour, noted of the Tory candidate John Profumo that 'when asked questions he runs away into the car', but that 'he has got the small shop-keepers frightened'. In Blackburn the young Barbara Castle, one of only 87 women candidates in the whole election (out of almost 1,700), told a packed, smoke-filled, almost entirely male hall to forget that she was a woman – 'I'm no feminist. Just judge me as a socialist.' In Plymouth the Labour candidate Michael Foot (still in his early 30s but, improbably enough, already a former editor of the *Evening Standard*) met his future wife Jill Craigie, who was making a documentary for Rank about the Abercrombie Plan. With complete confidence he told the electors, 'We really can have the most beautiful city in the world.' In feudal Northumberland, where Sir William Beveridge was standing for the Liberals at Berwick, the young Durham miner, Methodist preacher and tyro writer Sid Chaplin, on holiday in Alnwick, told a friend that 'the shadow of Percy Hotspur still hovers over the town – the Politics of the Duke are the Politics of the Town – Transport House is a rash dream, the *Daily Herald* a red rag! and Communism a nasty nightmare.' Accordingly, he added, 'when the Duke spoke for the Tory nincompoop that settled the interloper Beveridge!' And in Edmonton the Labour candidate, Evan Durbin, told the electors in his best LSE manner that 'we shall only win the battles of peace against unemployment, poverty and ill-health if we bring to the service of our common purpose the latest inventions of economic and political thought', while nevertheless emphasising at another meeting (held on Edmonton Green) that he 'was not asking for the votes of the people because he, or his Party, could produce a new heaven and a new earth in one day or in the lifetime of one Parliament'.[6]

As emblematic as anywhere of the bigger picture was Luton, home of the Vauxhall car plant. 'Electors Losing Apathy: Political Warming Up Beginning in Luton: First Assembly Hall Meeting Draws 2,000 Audience' ran the local headlines after the legendary journalist Hannen Swaffer had come to the town on 19 June to support the Labour candidate, William Warbey. 'There is tremendous enthusiasm within the ranks of our Party, an enthusiasm such as we have never seen before,' Warbey told those gathered. 'I firmly believe that for the first time in history we are going to win Luton for Labour on July 5.' As for Swaffer, he directly targeted Churchill: 'You haven't got a house? The reason is because there is no plan. He doesn't understand plans – a magnificent man of war, but he doesn't understand planning.' A week later, Warbey's star speaker was none other than Harold Laski, the Labour Party Chairman and LSE professor, who had been the object of sustained attack from Churchill and the Beaverbrook press following various indiscreet remarks. To a packed hall, requiring loudspeakers to be fitted outside for the overspill, Laski insisted, reasonably enough, that the election was not about him. Meanwhile, Warbey (in normal life a press officer living in Barnes) and his Tory opponent Dr Graham Brown were busy addressing an array of meetings, including lunchtime congregations of workers in canteens. Warbey visited the Vauxhall works, but it was in the heavy-machine shop of Hayward-Taylor & Co. that he got his most enthusiastic reception, as workers 'banged out a welcome with hammers and other tools'.

On the campaign's final day, 4 July, both candidates held meetings at the Assembly Hall. Brown went first, telling a women's meeting that 'the Socialists were making a determined attack to win Luton but, if elected, their programme would mean the end of a democratically-elected Parliament', while to a later, more male gathering, Warbey summed up the Labour case:

> The people wanted to make sure that the war in the Far East would be speedily and successfully concluded and that the men and women in the Services would return to a country in which we had a Government which knew how to plan for jobs for all; for the four million houses required; for all-round social security and for world peace. They were determined not to return to the bad old days of poverty and unemployment which was all they could get if Labour's opponents were returned to power.[7]

It was the case – plausible, direct, appealing – that in a pre-television age Labour candidates were making all over the country on that culminating, momentous, pregnant Wednesday evening.

Was it an enthused electorate? Certainly the legend of 'the spirit of '45' would be a powerful one. 'The packed eve-of-poll meeting in Canning Town Public Hall, scene of many famous trade union meetings, was tremendous,' a Labour Lord Chancellor, Lord Elwyn-Jones, recalled about his fight for Plaistow in London's East End. 'None of us who took part will ever forget it – the rows of intent, uplifted faces – dockers in their caps and white mufflers, the wives and children and old men and women who had been through so much.' So, too, Castle, who remembered the 3,000 people at her eve-of-poll meeting in St George's Hall, Blackburn, and 'a sort of unbelievable buoyancy in the atmosphere, as though people who had had all the textile depression years, the men and women who had suffered in the forces and the women who had been working double shifts, making munitions and the rest of it, suddenly thought, "My heavens, we can win the peace for people like us."' Or take a non-politico memoirist, the writer Nina Bawden, who as a member of the Oxford University Labour Club went with others to campaign for Ian Mikardo in Reading; there they found themselves 'caught up in an extraordinary atmosphere of political excitement that everyone seemed to share – soldiers on home leave, old men in pubs, tired women in bus queues'.[8]

Clearly, then, there were pockets of high excitement, perhaps especially on the Labour side. But the contemporary evidence suggests an electorate that was essentially jaded and sceptical. 'The war's got us down, what with the bombing and the blackout, and the worrying about coupons and queues, women like me haven't the mind to take to politics,' a Fulham resident told Mass-Observation early in the campaign. 'We want to be left alone for a bit – not worrying about speeches.' A woman from Bayswater agreed: 'I don't take any interest in it. Not a scrap. To me it's an awful lot of tommy rot, what with each party running the other down, and when they get in, they'll be bosom pals.' A Chelsea man was the most succinct: 'Dunno who I'll vote for. I don't like politicians anyway – they're all crooks.' In mid-June an M-O survey of Londoners as a whole found that only one in seven was 'happy or elated', that a third 'felt no different from during the war', that a quarter 'felt worried', that 15 per cent 'felt depressed', and that several 'simply said that there ought not to be an election yet'.

There is no doubt that the general interest did increase somewhat as the campaign went on – so that by the end only 24 per cent (as opposed to 57 per cent at the outset) admitted to taking no interest in the local outcome – but when George Orwell went looking in London in the closing weeks for signs of popular interest, he failed either to overhear 'a spontaneous remark' in the street or to see 'a single person stopping to look at an election poster'. Edmund Wilson, meanwhile, escaped from his squalid hotel on the penultimate Sunday before polling and went to watch Laski do his stuff at Southbury Road School, Enfield, on behalf of the local Labour candidate. Wilson's notebook jottings evoke a quintessentially English scene, in a quintessentially English suburb: 'Enfield – little bay windows and brick doorways – gray sandy-looking sides of houses (called rough cast or sprinkled ash) – meeting out of doors in noon sun – yellow bricks, dim or neutral red tiles: pale faces, quiet people – blue and gray, occasionally khaki clothes – all in Sunday clothes, the men wearing coats.' Even in Coventry, symbolic focus of post-war reconstruction hopes, there were few signs of election fever. Indeed, the only time the crowds there really came out, including no doubt many Labour voters, was to see Churchill – and thereby to be able to tell their grandchildren that they had done so.[9]

'This is not the election that is going to shake Tory England,' declared the *Manchester Guardian* the day before polling. Few pundits disagreed, even though that same day the *News Chronicle* published a Gallup poll giving Labour a six-point lead – a poll which the paper found so hard to credit that it ran the story as a low-key, single-column one full of caveats. Next day, polling began at 7.00 a.m. (except in 24 northern and Scottish constituencies where 'Wakes week' fell on the 5th, necessitating a week's, in one or two places a fortnight's, delay), and a quarter of an hour later the Home Service's *The Daily Dozen* gave all but the earliest voters a chance to exercise while they pondered their collective mind. We have a few glimpses from what turned out a pretty warm day. At Gladys Langford's Highbury hotel, another resident, Mr White, was 'furious' at breakfast when he read that a youth had flung a lighted squib in Churchill's face. '"*Very* reprehensible but NOT criminal," said I while *he* was advocating lynching.' In contrasting stages of life, H. G. Wells voted for the last time (unable to leave his car, he had to have the ballot paper brought to him for marking) while the five-year-old Patrick Stewart (many years later Captain Jean-Luc Picard in *Star Trek*) was briskly moved along by a policeman for marching with a placard and singing loudly outside a polling booth near his home in working-class Mirfield, West Yorkshire – a moment that turned him into a lifelong Labour supporter. For Durbin in Edmonton, standing in a truck all day touring the streets, these were tedious hours of what his wife remembered him calling 'just cheering and wasting time'. Ernest Loftus, down in Tilbury, exercised his democratic right after tea: 'I voted for the National Conservatives – that is Churchill. The least one could do for the man who has saved the country. His opponent here is a wretched Jew – the limit. Why can't we find English Gentiles to represent us?' Another diarist, St John, made no reference to voting but that afternoon travelled by train from Bristol to London, reaching Paddington by 6.20. 'I had to wait until after 6.35 for a train to Shepherds Bush, which came in packed. It stopped at White City, where many passengers alighted, presumably to attend a dog-racing meeting.'

The polling stations closed at 9.00 p.m., just as *Northern Music-Hall* was finishing on the Home Service and a quarter of an hour before Alistair Cooke's *American Commentary*. For those interested in the outcome, that left three weeks to wait before counting began, while the votes came in from the Forces abroad. 'If I may put down my forecast of the result,' the Tory-supporting Glasgow pattern-maker Colin Ferguson surmised, 'it is this: – For the Govt. 360; Labour 220; the rest 60.' Three days later, the *News of the World*'s jumping-the-gun headline was similarly sanguine: 'Mr Churchill Has Secured His Working Majority'. But whatever the eventual result, there was satisfaction in a general election successfully conducted, the first for almost ten years. Or, as the Pathé News commentator sententiously boomed out the following week to the cinema-going millions, over anodyne shots of the backs of people in polling booths, 'A good many European countries might learn a thing or two from the way a free people choose their government.'[10]

————

As ever, life's daily rhythms continued during those three suspenseful weeks before 26 July and the declarations in the constituencies. Royal Ascot may have resumed on Saturday the 7th for the first time since 1939 – 'It was something of a shock,' one report noted, 'to discover cloth caps, Panamas, and grey slacks in the Royal Enclosure, where peace-time etiquette demanded more formal clothes' – but for Nella Last in Barrow a week later it was an altogether more humdrum motif: 'Queues were everywhere, for wedge-heeled shoes, pork-pies, fish, bread & cakes, tomatoes – & emergency ration-cards at the food office.' Indeed, by this time such was the fed-upness with ever-lengthening queues that two determined London housewives (Irene Lovelock, married to a South London vicar, and Alfreda Landau, married to a Neasden rabbi) came together, following local campaigns, to form a British Housewives' League. Still, later on in the day during which Last gazed glumly at the queues, there was a major boost for all. 'The clocks are being put back tonight [marking the end of wartime double-summer time], and the lights are up!' Judy Haines recorded. 'I was very thrilled indeed to see Chingford lit up.' No longer the groping along with a torch looking for steps and obstacles, no longer either the windows of buses and Tube trains mainly covered by gauze netting, with only a little diamond slit to see where one was.

An impressed visitor was André Gide's translator, Dorothy Bussy. 'Everyone,' she wrote to him from London on 16 July, 'is extraordinarily kind and attentive and unselfish – bus conductors, the travellers in buses and trains and tubes, policemen of course, but food officials too.' She was also struck by 'London's ruins', which were 'now a garden of grass and wild flowers, green & pink and yellow, springing of their own accord in the wastes'. The following evening, some 27,000 kind and attentive Londoners packed into the Spurs ground at White Hart Lane to see Doncaster's Bruce Woodcock win the British and Empire heavyweight titles with a sixth-round knockout. 'For Jack Solomons, the promoter, the fight was a triumph,' the local Tottenham paper noted. 'The crowd paid from 5/- to 10 guineas to see it. About 5,000 came by cars which lined each side of 30 side streets around the ground.'[11] On the radio, clashing with a transmission of *Peter Grimes*, Raymond Glendenning's plummy, excitable commentary was complemented by the magisterial inter-round summaries of W. Barrington Dalby.

Nothing mattered more, though, than a roof over the head. 'In the country something stirs,' the Independent MP W. J. Brown observed in his diary on 12 July. 'A bunch of people at Brighton, calling themselves the Vigilantes, have set about solving the housing problem in their own way, by commandeering any house that is empty and installing in it a family in need of accommodation.' It was not a well-documented campaign, but later that month Frederic Osborn noted how in the past few weeks there had been 'organised squatting in empty mansions, with enough public approval to force the Government and the authorities into more active requisitioning'.

For those with a home or aspiring to one, there was the *Daily Herald* Post-war Homes Exhibition at Dorland Hall in London's Regent Street. 'They could just give me *any* of it, and I should think it wonderful,' a young middle-class married woman told Mass-Observation. 'Honestly I liked it *all*. I'm so desperate for a house I'd like anything. I can't criticise or judge it at all – four walls and a roof is the height of my ambition.' M-O found pessimism on the part of some of the working-class wives at the exhibition. 'I feel it's pretty hopeless,' one said. 'I'll never be able to afford to buy the fitments to modernise our kitchen. It would cost an awful lot to convert.' Asked what they liked best, more than three-quarters of those interviewed nominated the demonstration kitchens. 'The lovely kitchens, so fresh and clean,' said one woman. 'The kitchens, everything tucked away and all flush and it saves so much stooping,' replied another, and a third was yet more expansive: 'It was the kitchenette. I think that's what interests most women, all the cupboard room. It's a lovely idea, covered in under the sink. I've wanted that for years and we've never had it.'[12]

The members of the London Stock Exchange probably had no strong views either way about kitchenettes. What really mattered to those stockbrokers and jobbers, atavistically Tory almost to a man, was the outcome of the election. Their unofficial spokesman and bell-wether was a cheery, birdlike, veteran member called Walter Landells. Under the name 'Autolycus' – a snapper-up of unconsidered trifles – he had for years contributed a daily column to the City's pink bible, the *Financial Times*. 'That Mr Churchill and his party will be returned is practically taken for granted,' Autolycus declared on Thursday, 19 July; 'the point of uncertainty is the sum of the majority.' He was just as confident by the following Tuesday ('No sign exists in the Stock Exchange of apprehension'), while the paper's front-page headlines were similarly optimistic: 'Cheerful Market Tone Maintained' that same day, 'Market Steadiness Well Maintained' on the Wednesday, and 'Firm and Confident Tone of Markets' on the Thursday itself, the 26th. That, though, was merely the public face of the Stock Exchange. Were its habitués – widely if fallaciously assumed to have an unparalleled insight into the future – truly so certain there would not be a dreadful upset? Perhaps they were, but it is worth recording the remark to Mass-Observation by the manager of a London bookshop: 'Well, what's going to be the result on Thursday? I was told last week that the betting on the London Stock Exchange was 6 to 4 on Labour getting in.'[13] It is unlikely that Landells was part of the clever money and giving a deliberately misleading steer, but one never knows.

The Foreign Office, and Sir Robert Bruce Lockhart's pen, provide as good a vantage point as any for the crucial hours of a day of destiny: 'The election results began to come in as soon as I reached the office at about 10 a.m. The first returns showed Labour gains, but as they came from the industrial north no one was very excited. But as the morning approached midday, it was already clear that the tide was running strongly in favour of the Left. Early on, there were casualties among the ministers, Harold Macmillan being one of the first to fall.' All over the country, that morning and into the afternoon as the weather in many places turned wet, individual fates were determined. Durbin won comfortably in Edmonton; Castle was returned in Blackburn, Foot in Plymouth Devonport; Healey lost in Pudsey and Otley, Jenkins in Solihull; a promising young Tory, Flight-Lieutenant Reginald Maudling, went down in Heston and Isleworth. In Cardiff South exuberant Labour supporters carried the winning candidate, Lieutenant James Callaghan, shoulder high from the city hall; in Coventry there was only a sparse gathering to applaud the two winning Labour candidates, one of them the gifted intellectual Richard Crossman. In Abertillery (Labour majority over 24,000) a vengeful Labour agent insisted on a recount in an ultimately unsuccessful attempt to make the Tory lose his deposit; in Kettering, as it became clear that Naomi Mitchison's husband had won, 'Profumo himself was being very decent,' though later he 'made the gesture which was not really very tactful of giving Dick a sheet of House of Commons note paper'.

Bruce Lockhart, meanwhile, lunched at the Dorchester with the flour miller and film magnate J. Arthur Rank: 'There was a huge board (with results) in the hall. Many people were watching it, mostly with glum faces. Already Labour had gained over a hundred seats. When I came down from Rank's room, the faces round the board were even glummer. Labour had now over 300 seats with over 150 more results to come. A complete majority over *all* other parties was therefore certain.' The atmosphere was still gloomier at an election luncheon given by the press magnate's wife Lady Rothermere. 'Although the champagne was exiguous and the vodka watery, the spectacle of consternation as details of the massacre spread was a strong intoxicant,' Evelyn Waugh wrote home about a party 'full of chums dressed up to the nines and down in the dumps'. For Graham Greene, then literary editor of the *Spectator*, there was a purely private emotion involved. The writer Walter Allen met him for lunch at Rules, where as they sat down Greene's eye was caught by the dramatic *Evening Standard* headline 'SOCIALISTS IN'. 'Damn!' exclaimed Greene. 'Don't you approve, Graham?' asked Allen. Greene replied that he didn't care one way or the other, indeed hadn't even bothered to vote, but that on the assumption the Tories would win had been planning to make a telephone call at 3.00. 'There won't,' he added, 'be any point in doing so now.' It transpired that Greene had been intending to ring the Reform Club, where his magazine's editor Wilson Harris – a Churchill-supporting MP and detested by Greene – lunched every day. The message to be left was that Harris was to call at 10 Downing Street at 3.30.[14] Labour's first overall majority in its history had inconsiderately thwarted the practical joke.

Towards the end of the afternoon, after a family tea at the Great Western Hotel, the imperturbable Attlee arrived at Transport House in Smith Square. Among an excited crowd of Labour activists and others waiting to greet him was the 20-year-old Anthony Wedgwood Benn. A BBC man pressed a microphone in front of his face and asked, 'Will you shout, "Three cheers for the Prime Minister"?' but he was too shy and the honour passed elsewhere. At about 7.15p.m., having with Bevin's help thwarted an ignoble, last-ditch attempt by Herbert Morrison to wrest the party leadership, Attlee set out for Buckingham Palace, where Churchill was in the process of resigning. He travelled, as he had done throughout the election campaign, in a Hillman Minx family saloon, with his wife Vi driving. 'I've won the election,' he told the King, in a rather strained conversation between two decidedly non-loquacious men. 'I know,' was the reply. 'I heard it on the six o'clock news.' Vi then drove the new Prime Minister to Central Hall, Westminster. There were many other Labour celebrations that evening – including one at the Assembly Hall in Luton, where Warbey and his supporters celebrated a spanking majority of more than 7,000 – but this victory rally was the epicentre. The big words flowed freely. 'This great victory for socialism will bring a message of hope to every democracy all over the world,' Laski (mockingly calling himself 'the temporary head of the socialist Gestapo') told the faithful. Bevin promised that the new government would 'speak as a common man to the common man in other lands'. And Attlee himself announced, 'This is the first time in the history of the country that a labour movement with a socialist policy has received the approval of the electorate.' He then went on to the balcony to address briefly the crowd of cheering and chanting supporters outside. The rally ended with a rendition of 'The Red Flag', and as Attlee and his wife fought their way out, he told reporters, 'We are on the eve of a great advance in the human race.'[15]

If so, it was not an advance that many in the West End that evening
looked forward to with much relish. Beaverbrook, whose *Daily Express*
had led the demonisation of Laski and his colleagues, was in the
unhappy position of having arranged to host a large party at Claridge's.
'This occasion was intended as a victory feast,' he stood up and
announced to the assembled company. 'In the circumstances it now
becomes a last supper.' At another of Churchill's favourite hotels, the
Savoy, one lady diner was heard to say, 'But this is terrible – *they've*
elected a Labour government, and *the country* will never stand for
that.' The food turned even more to ashes in the mouth for the theatre
critic James Agate, despite his best efforts after hearing the appalling
news:

> I rang up the head waiter at one of my favourite restaurants and said,
> 'Listen to me carefully, Paul. I am quite willing that in future you address
> me as "comrade" or "fellow-worker", and chuck the food at me in the
> manner of Socialists to their kind. But that doesn't start until tomorrow
> morning. Tonight I am bringing two friends with the intention that we
> may together eat our last meal as gentlemen. There will be a magnum
> of champagne, and the best food your restaurant can provide. You, Paul,
> will behave with your wonted obsequiousness. The *sommelier*, the table
> waiter, and the *commis* waiter will smirk and cringe in the usual way.
> From tomorrow you will get no more tips. Tonight you will be tipped
> royally.' The head waiter said, 'Bien, m'sieu.' That was at a quarter-past
> six. At a quarter-past nine I arrived and was escorted by bowing menials
> to my table, where I found the magnum standing in its bucket and three
> plates each containing two small slices of spam!

Perhaps the most revealing detail, though, was Agate's rhetorical
question: 'Who would have thought a head waiter to have so much
wit in him?'[16]

That day and over the next few days, there were plenty of other
reactions to Labour's stunning overall majority of 146. 'It's an amazing
piece of ingratitude to Churchill,' asserted Loftus predictably enough,
while once she had got over the 'severe shock' Mary King in Erdington
declared that such ingratitude 'fills me with horror'. The diarist

Anthony Heap was yet more dismayed, anticipating 'the indefinite continuance of war-time controls, the incessant fostering of class-hatred, the stamping out of individual enterprise and initiative, the subjugation of everything and everybody to a totalitarian system of state control manipulated by a gigantic army of smug little bureaucrats'. Among Nella Last's fellow-sewers at the Women's Voluntary Service centre in Barrow, there was intense consternation as the news of the landslide percolated through: 'flushed and upset', Mrs Lord said that she *personally* feared riots and uprising' before Last calmed her down with 'two aspirins and a glass of muddy-looking liquid', purportedly sherry; and Mrs Higham said to Last, 'Don't you realise we may be on the brink of revolution?' Judy Haines's reaction was quite different – 'Labour in with a great majority, and I am thrilled!' – but significantly she added, 'People generally quiet – though it is the people who have done it.' One public schoolboy in Sussex, Bernard Levin, was positively ecstatic, hanging a red flag out of his window and braving the consequences. Two Oxford philosophers concurred: Isaiah Berlin danced a jig at hearing the news, while Iris Murdoch wrote with Wordsworthian fervour to a friend abroad, 'Oh wonderful people of Britain! After all the ballyhoo and eyewash, they've had the guts to vote against Winston! . . . I can't help feeling that to be young is very heaven!' Dylan Thomas was rather more understated. 'The rain has stopped, thank Jesus,' he wrote a few days later from a Carmarthenshire valley in his only apparent reference to the election result. 'Have the Socialists-in-power-now stopped it?' And soon afterwards, the poet W. S. Graham, Scottish but living near Marazion in Cornwall, was studiously indifferent: 'Yes I notice we have changed the government. It doesn't mean much though it's called Labour. Labour is now quite respectable.'[17]

Perhaps the most interesting response, however, came from the popular, ultra-patriotic historian Arthur Bryant. One might have expected indignation or anxiety to be the dominant note, but a letter that he wrote during August was very different in tone:

We can't return, even if we wanted to, to the social and economic frame-work of 1939, for it no longer exists, and the task of our rulers now is to create a new framework without causing social chaos in the meantime or saddling us with a totalitarian system. Without holding any exaggerated belief in the wisdom of Socialists, I believe the latter are more capable at the moment of doing this than the Conservatives, who are under the domination not only of vested interests but of something a great deal worse – vested ideas! And unlike the Conservatives, the Socialists do understand the discomfort and inhuman conditions under which so many people today are living and working.

It was a flexible, pragmatic reaction echoed by that of an underwriter at Lloyd's in the City of London. 'To my astonishment,' the future journalist John Gale would recall about returning to England after the election, 'I found that my father welcomed the Labour victory. "There might have been trouble if they hadn't got in," he said. I never asked how he voted.' But arguably, in terms of prophecy, the palm went to an old trouper. 'It may not be a bad idea for the Labour boys to hold the baby,' Noël Coward, no friend to the people's party, reflected. 'I always felt that England would be bloody uncomfortable during the immediate post-war period, and it is now almost a certainty that it will be so.'[18]

Why had it happened? Only two days after becoming Prime Minister, Attlee found himself at Potsdam being verbally strong-armed by Stalin, that electoral innocent, to account for Churchill's inexplicable defeat. 'One should distinguish between Mr Churchill the leader of the nation in the war and Mr Churchill the Conservative Party leader,' he answered. 'Many people looked upon the Conservatives as a reactionary party which would not carry out a policy answering to peace requirements.' For Beaverbrook, as for many contemporary analysts of the election, the current leader was not to blame. 'The unpopularity of the party,' he wrote soon afterwards, 'proved too strong for the greatness of Churchill and the affection in which he is held by the people.' Fortunately there were some, including one young reform-minded Tory, Cub Alport, who were able in their post-mortems to transcend the Churchill question. 'I think the election is a vote for the people who are least likely to involve us in foreign adventures, or bring us up against Russia,' he told Rab Butler. 'It is a vote for domestic security.' For a few intellectuals, that sort of interpretation was altogether too tame. 'It was not a vote about queues or housing,' declared Cyril Connolly in the September issue of

Horizon, 'but a vote of censure on Munich and Spain and Abyssinia . . . The Election result is a blow struck against the religion of money.' As usual, the views of his friend from prep school and Eton were more pertinent. 'No one, I think, expects the next few years to be easy ones,' Orwell wrote at about the same time, 'but on the whole people did vote Labour because of the belief that a Left government means family allowances, higher old age pensions, houses with bathrooms, etc., rather than from any internationalist consideration. They look to a Labour government to make them more secure and, after a few years, more comfortable.'[19]

Of course, there were plenty of other causal factors adduced then and subsequently.[20] The widespread belief that a Labour government would ensure a speedier demobilisation; the unusually even balance of political allegiance on the part of the press; the absence during the war of the familiar drip, drip of anti-Labour propaganda on the part of the fourth estate; the way in which that war had turned leading Labour politicians into familiar and trusted figures as senior ministers; the party's high degree of unity; above all, the general feeling that the number one immediate issue of housing could best be met by Labour's energetic message of can-do fairness: all these things contributed to the outcome. A significant minority of the usually Conservative-voting middle class switched to Labour and probably just as many abstained, often to decisive effect; for once, Disraeli's 'angels in marble', the working-class Conservatives, failed their betters; and across the classes, the young voted Labour in large numbers.

What about Churchill? In the eyes of a nation still hugely grateful for what he had done to help win the war, he was almost certainly still an electoral asset. But at the same time there can be no evading his prime culpability, as Tory leader from 1940, in the party's failure to develop and start to propagate realistic policies in response to people's understandable domestic concerns, above all in relation to housing and unemployment. 'Before the Election,' one Tory MP would recall, 'the Post-War Problems Committee's numerous reports, the "Signpost" booklets, the various pamphlets of the Tory Reform Committee, were all good, but they were not authoritative. They did not bear the *imprimatur* of the Prime Minister. There was no evidence that he had read them.'[21] Yet it is arguable that so powerful and pervasive was the mythology that had developed about the bleakness and inhumanity of the inter-war years – years dominated by Tory politicians and Tory policies – that no amount of domestic engagement by Churchill would have made much difference. Labour, after all, did not manage a decisive victory *during* those years, and indeed suffered three crushing defeats, culminating in 1935. Ten years and one arduous conflict later, a conflict which for an insular people had required an insular purpose, there was a strong desire not to return to the 'bad old days' – even though that desire paradoxically co-existed with a near-universal longing in other respects (above all the rhythms of everyday life) to get back to how it had been 'before the war'.

It would be both perverse and an error to exaggerate the revisionism. To take '1945' out of 1945 leaves a barren historical landscape indeed. The electorate may well have been voting more negatively against the Tories than positively for Labour, there may well have been relatively little popular enthusiasm for 'socialism' as such (as opposed to immediate material improvements), Orwell may well have been right when he asserted soon after the results that 'the mood of the country seems to me less revolutionary, less Utopian, even less hopeful, than it was in 1940 or 1942' – yet at some level most people realised that a rather amazing thing had happened, in effect marking off 'pre-1945' politically from 'post-1945'. 'My man,' called out a blazered, straw-hatted 14-year-old public schoolboy, John Rae, as he stood on Bishop's Stortford station with his trunk that late July. 'No,' came the porter's quiet but firm reply, 'that sort of thing is all over now.'

Even so, if there was such awareness, however inchoate or subterranean it may have been in many cases, it still had to fight for its place in the daily consciousness of the daily human round. Take a wonderfully revealing diary entry for Sunday, 29 July:

Weather has been lovely – such a difference from this time last year when we ran so often to shelter. The streets look so bright at night now, with all the lamps lit. We went to Kilburn & it was so nice to sit & chat & not have to listen for the warning. The election result is still creating talk – I wonder where this Labour Government will lead us to. I heard that Ladies shoes are going to 9 coupons on the new books. I expect it is true. I still don't believe Hitler is dead – & how much longer before the German war criminals are brought to trial. About time they were all shot else they will get off & start another war.[22]

Rose Uttin – mid-40s, married, living in Wembley, husband Bill in charge of stationery at the Royal Exchange Assurance, daughter Dora a clerical assistant at Harrow Education Office, elderly mother living upstairs in the back bedroom – had, like virtually everyone else, much else on her mind besides electoral earthquakes.

———

The pleasures of peace returned with a vengeance that weekend, as on the Saturday the trains of the London, Midland and Scottish Railway carried a record 102,889 holiday-makers to Blackpool's stations. On Sunday the new 'Light' Programme superseded the wartime 'Forces' Programme, and though Anthony Heap's immediate reaction was that 'there is precious little difference in the type of fare provided', there did take place on Monday afternoon the first episode of *The Robinson Family*, featuring 'the day-to-day adventures of a London family and their friends'. It is unlikely that there were any listeners among those present that evening at the dinner party given by Hugh Dalton (the new Chancellor) in a private room at the St Ermin's Hotel. The line-up was more or less the cream of Labour's up-and-coming talent, including Christopher Mayhew, Woodrow Wyatt and John Freeman, as well as Durbin, Crossman and Hugh Gaitskell. Also present were Harold Wilson, an archetypal grammar-school product who had made his name as an academic high-flyer helping Beveridge and who was already viewed by Harold Nicolson as 'brilliant', and the only non-university man, George Brown. Predictably, Wilson 'made me simply gape as he talked' (Mayhew wrote home afterwards), while Brown (according to Gaitskell) 'kept rather quiet'.[23]

Two days later, the new House of Commons met for the first time to elect its Speaker. 'When Churchill came in for the show he was greeted by the singing of "For he's a jolly good fellow" by the Tories,' recorded W. J. Brown (who had got back as an Independent). 'The Labour masses retorted by singing "The Red Flag" – which I thought was very bad tactics, doing no good and calculated to frighten all the retired Colonels in Cheltenham and Leamington Spa.' It was reputedly George Griffiths, a miner MP from South Yorkshire and member of the Salvation Army, who had started singing the socialist anthem; that evening Bob Boothby boasted at a London party that he was the sole Tory to have joined in. Strikingly, only 38 per cent of the Labour MPs came from a working-class background – compared with 72 per cent after the 1935 election.[24] Griffiths may have got them singing, but it was the lawyers, teachers, journalists, doctors, managers and technicians who would principally be calling the tune.

Monday the 6th – the day after the Giles cartoon 'Family' first appeared in the *Sunday Express*, on their way to the seaside – was the August Bank Holiday. There were large crowds at most seaside resorts (as many as 35 relief trains leaving Liverpool Street station) and the usual cultural preferences expressed at the main attractions (31,440 people at London Zoo, 4,553 at the V&A). At Lord's, where 10,000 were locked out ten minutes after the start of the Fourth Victory Test, play was interrupted at 1.00 by a terrific storm of hail and thunder – unluckily for listeners who, in an era before ball-by-ball, had been waiting patiently for Rex Alston's description of 'the closing overs before lunch'. Over at the White City stadium, some 100,000 tried, but only 52,000 managed, to watch a memorable athletics meeting. The stars were the two great Swedish middle-distance runners Gunder Hägg and Arne Andersson, the latter taking on Britain's pre-war record-holder Sydney Wooderson in the one mile and just winning. Wooderson, in the RASC, had reputedly travelled down from Glasgow by train and, not wanting to make a fuss about the fact that he was due to represent his country the next afternoon, had stood in the corridor all night. After the thunderstorm, the weather was cool and unsettled. 'Obviously no day for Hampstead [ie Heath] or anywhere like that,' noted Heap. 'So after an afternoon stroll round Bloomsbury and an early tea hied us round to the Regent to see "National Velvet".' He enjoyed it on the whole but despite Elizabeth Taylor's presence regretted that 'the essential English atmosphere is missing'.[25]

Meanwhile, some 25 per cent of the adult population had, as usual, been listening to the Home Service at 6.00:

Here is the News.

   President Truman has announced a tremendous achievement by Allied scientists. They have produced the atomic bomb. One has already been dropped on a Japanese army base. It alone contained as much explosive power as 2,000 of our great ten-tonners. The President has also foreshadowed the enormous peace-time value of this harnessing of atomic energy.

Hiroshima ('it's been an army base for many years') was identified as the target; but even on the nine o'clock bulletin, which included an official account of Britain's role in the development of the bomb, there was still 'no news yet of what devastation was caused – reconnaissance aircraft couldn't see anything hours later because of the tremendous pall of smoke and dust that was still obscuring the city of once over 300,000 inhabitants'.

The impact, nevertheless, was immediate. 'My husband looked at me across the lounge of the London flat, and I looked at him,' the writer Ursula Bloom remembered. 'Horror filled us both, and to such a degree that for a moment neither of us could speak.' Elizabeth Longford was sitting alone in her Oxford home when she turned on the wireless. 'For the first time in my life I had a strong presentiment about the future: that a brilliant scientific discovery would bring a balance of evil to the human race.' Later that evening, Joan Wyndham, standing around with WAAF colleagues at their Nottinghamshire air base waiting for transport to take them to the late watch, noticed Flight Sergeant Kelly hurrying towards them:

> First she walked a bit, then she broke into a run and walked again. It seemed odd because she wasn't late for the transport.
> When she came up to us she said, 'There's a terrible bomb been dropped on Japan – the worst ever! It's to do with re-directing the energy from the sun, or something. Everybody thinks the Japs will surrender any minute!'
> She probably expected a barrage of questions – or even cries of 'Good show!' – but there was nothing, only a shocked silence . . .
> I think I was stunned, not so much because of the bomb as at the thought of the war ending. Later, when the meaning finally sank in, I felt the strangest mixture of elation and terror.

For the Rev. John Collins, Dean of Oriel College, Oxford, the news marked the moment when 'I finally decided against the whole concept

of the Just War.' Within minutes of the bulletin ending, he was rung
by the left-wing publisher Victor Gollancz, who persuaded Collins to
call at once his friend Sir Stafford Cripps, the ascetic, high-minded
Christian who had just become President of the Board of Trade. Collins,
as he later recalled, got through without difficulty, to be told by Cripps
that 'the Cabinet had not been informed about what was to happen',
though he 'went on to assure me that no more atomic bombs would
be used against the Japanese'. Still that same evening, Collins rang
Lambeth Palace in the hope of speaking to the Archbishop of Canterbury, Geoffrey Fisher. However, he got only a chaplain, who told him
'that His Grace had "gone into hiding" – a favourite posture of the
Church in moments of moral crisis'.[26]

Over the next week or so – which included, notwithstanding Cripps's
assurance, an atom bomb being dropped on Nagasaki – most people
reacted in characteristic ways. Randolph Churchill, son of Winston,
was reported by Evelyn Waugh as 'greatly over-excited'; Joyce Grenfell
declared herself 'all for the Atomic Bomb, but not to drop it much';
Noël Coward reckoned that a bomb that was going to 'blow us all to
buggery' was 'not a bad idea'; and Vanessa Bell, writing to her daughter,
spoke for the Bloomsbury Group: 'What a to-do about the atomic
bomb . . . I wish they'd get to the stage of labour-saving devices instead
of destroying whole cities.' J.R.R. Tolkien was even prompted to make
a rare pronouncement, albeit private, on a public matter. 'The utter
folly of these lunatic physicists to consent to do such work for war-
purposes: calmly plotting the destruction of the world,' he wrote to
his son. 'Such explosives in man's hands, while their moral and
intellectual status is declining, is about as useful as giving out firearms
to all inmates of a gaol and then saying that you hope "this will ensure
peace".' He concluded, 'Well we're in God's hands. But He does not
look kindly on Babel-builders.' The pattern-maker Colin Ferguson,
writing his diary in Glasgow on the 8th, concurred: 'The papers are
still full of the Atomic bomb and what it may mean for the future.
They hope it will have beneficial effects & not a diabolic outcome. I
say, before they place any "hopes" on the future they'll have to get
men changed – not "political systems" . . . And in that they're hoping
against hope: there is *no hope* in *man*, and he is credulous who believes
there is. The end is near – maybe some years only.' As the news of

the appalling human and material destruction filtered through, perhaps most people felt like that at some level, even if less starkly. Yet the observation of Gladys Langford was telling. 'Everybody very proud of the Atomic bomb *we've* dropped on Japan,' she noted on the 7th, 'and yet those same people cursed the Germans for *their* cruelty when *they* bombed *us*.'[27]

The day after Hiroshima found Henry St John, briefly on second-ment in the north-east, working in Spennymoor: 'I tried in vain to buy cigarettes. The public lavatory had some fixtures missing, and an unusual wealth of scribblings on the door of the water closet. "I know a little girl of 11 who can take a man's prick. I broke her down in the woods, and did she enjoy it. I fuck my sister – she's 14," were specimens. A drawing showed a nude woman beside a bed, with a caption, "I'm ready, dean".' Two days later, the urban anthropologist returned to the scene 'to see if I could masturbate over the mural inscriptions', but vexingly, 'there was no lock on the door'. There was no such anti-climax for Nella Last and her husband on Saturday the 11th, when, having got 'the extra petrol', they set out from Barrow for the day, taking with them their next-door neighbours the Atkinsons:

> The thought that peace would soon be here, that mothers and wives could cease their constant worry, and anxiety, that people could begin to live their own lives again, seemed all mixed up with the warm sunshine and the fields of cut golden corn and the sea sparkling over the golden sands – a feeling of 'rightness'. We walked round Morecambe, *marvelling* at the tons of good food – things in Marks & Spencer's like brawn and sausage, thousands of sausage-rolls and pies, including big raised pork-pies.
>
> We went on to Heysham Head – surely the best shilling's worth in the whole world! Lovely surroundings, a show in the Rose Gardens, a circus, concert party, marionette show, little menagerie, dance board with relayed music, seats for everyone, either in the sun or the shade – all included! ... We sat on the slope of the Head to watch the circus, and I saw a group sitting near in very earnest conversation, with their heads together. I'd have loved to go and butt in. I love being in an argument, and thought, 'Perhaps they are talking about the atomic bomb – or the result of the Election.' I've very good hearing, and when I'd got used to the different sounds around, I could hear what they *were*

discussing – the new 'cold perm'! Every woman I know is interested in it – another revolution, when curly hair can be assured by a method so simple that it can be done at home.

'We felt in a real holiday mood' as, coatless, they drove home. And Last thought: 'It will be a good month for getting in the crops, for the moon rose fair when it came in.'[28]

Negotiations had dragged on for several days after the Japanese surrender on the 10th, but by Tuesday the 14th there was a general expectation that the end of the war could be only hours away. 'Crowds of small boys keep going by with packing cases for burning,' Gladys Langford tut-tutted that day. 'I think it is a great pity in view of necessary economy in fuel this coming winter.' The suspense mounted. 'We listened eagerly to the six o'clock news – still nothing tangible,' noted Last. 'I thought of a remark I'd heard: "Perhaps Japan, too, has a mystery bomb and is playing for time."' Later, 'when there was nothing on the nine o'clock news, I said that I was going to bed, as my back ached badly.' But finally, as Ernest Loftus near Tilbury succinctly recorded, it came:

At 11 p.m. – summary of news – we were told to stand by at 12 for an important announcement.

At midnight, therefore, I switched on and Attlee the new Prime Minister announced PEACE. The Japs had accepted our terms. Even while Attlee was speaking the sirens began to sound on the ships in the river & some of them are still at it at 12.55 as I write this.

The *Merthyr Express* described the memorable scenes and noises that ensued in South Wales – as in many parts of Britain – almost straight after the typically clipped announcement:

The streets in all the towns and villages in the Merthyr Valley, the Rhymney Valley and the West Monmouthshire area were thronged with singing and cheering people. Dancing and singing took place from soon after midnight until the small hours.

Those who did not hear the Premier's broadcast were awakened by their neighbours, and many left their beds, donned dressing gowns or overcoats and joined the ever-increasing crowds.

'The war is over' was a cry frequently heard, and for many the news was almost unbelievable at first. Many women were in tears at the thought of again seeing a husband or son soon to be released from prisoner-of-war camps.

Large buildings in many districts were floodlit – red, white and blue 'V' signs being very prominent. All our South Wales colliery hooters, train whistles, detonators, fireworks and rattles were used to swell the great chorus of celebration. Many bonfires were lit in the streets and on the mountain-sides, and shone out as symbols of Peace and Freedom.

Nella Last in Barrow was woken from her half-sleep by shouting and the noise of ships' sirens and church bells. For the next hour, as she looked through her bedroom window but could not quite bring herself to get dressed and go out, there were 'cars rushing down Abbey Road into the town', an excitable neighbour 'half-screaming "God Save the King"', from all directions 'the sound of opening doors and people telling each other they had been in bed and asleep', dogs 'barking crazily', ships' hooters 'turned on and forgotten', and 'the sound of fireworks coming out of little back gardens'. By 1.00 she had had enough. 'I feel no wild whoopee, just a quiet thankfulness and a feeling of "flatness",' she scribbled before returning to bed. 'I think I'll take two aspirins and try and read myself to sleep.'[29]

Attlee had announced in his broadcast that the next two days were to be public holidays, and as it happened Wednesday the 15th – VJ Day – had long been booked for the state opening of Parliament and the King's Speech. 'It was like old times even though there was no gold coach,' reflected one of the Tory survivors, Sir Cuthbert Headlam. 'The new Labour M.P.s are a strange looking lot – one regrets the departure of the sound old Trade Unionists and the advent of this rabble of youthful, ignorant young men.' Not everyone, to judge by Judy Haines's report, had been aware of the midnight revels:

We got up as usual and were breakfasting and listening to the 7 o'clock news, when we realised a V.J. day was on. People had started out for work and hardly knew which way to turn when it was conveyed to them today and tomorrow are holidays. Some had evidently been given instructions to join the bread queue in the event of VJ, for that is what they did. I have never seen so many people in Chingford. The queues were more like those of a football match. The queue for bread from List's stretched round to the Prince Albert. I was very glad Dyson's opened as it is my shopping morning and I needed my rations.

It was no better in Wembley. 'Women grumbling & arguing in the queues,' noted Rose Uttin, '& then it started to rain – everybody with heavy bags of shopping got soaked.' Elsewhere, once the shopping was in and with the weather brightening up, there were the familiar street tea parties for children, followed by victory dances and bonfires in the evening. 'All day long,' observed Langford in less disapproving mode, 'children have been passing with doors, window frames and other wood-work torn from buildings.' Anthony Heap and his wife, on holiday in Somerset when they heard the news, decided to 'dash up to London for the celebrations', catching the 10.35 from Frome. For a time, as they made 'a preliminary tour of the West End', he half-regretted their decision: 'Not quite so thrilling as we expected. The inevitable crowds gathered en masse in Trafalgar Square, Piccadilly Circus & Buckingham Palace listening to tinned music emanating from loud speakers. But otherwise the rejoicing seemed to be rather subdued. Just thousands of weary-looking people wandering round the streets or sprawling on the grass in the parks.' Sticking to their VE ritual, they went home for some tea before 'embarking on the evening excursion':

Had to walk there and back this time, but as it turned out to be so much more lively and jubilant a jaunt than the afternoon one, we didn't mind that so much. We waited among the multitude outside Buckingham Palace to hear the King's Broadcast speech at 9.0 and see the Royal Family appear on the balcony afterwards. We stood among the crowds in Whitehall and saw Attlee, Morrison and Bevin on the balcony of the Ministry of Health building, though we couldn't hear what the former was saying for his speech was continually drowned by shouts of 'We want Churchill' . . . We saw the floodlighting, we saw the fireworks, we saw the town literally and figuratively lit up – despite the deplorable dearth of drink – as it's rarely been lit up before . . . So far as revelry by night was concerned, VE Day had nothing on VJ Day. It was London with the lid off!

So no doubt it was, but for many people one day of celebrations was quite enough, even more than enough. 'Another V.J. day spent quietly at home,' wrote Haines on the 16th. 'So glad of the rest.'[30]

The election, the atom bomb, the end of the world war: all within a matter of weeks. It was a moment, inevitably, for taking stock. Frederic Osborn, starting on the 14th a long letter to the great American urban prophet Lewis Mumford, pondered the political upheaval:

> What has happened is a very big step in the British revolution – a shift of power to meet new conditions and new ideas. Britain will not willingly go far towards Communism; it will remain at heart a free-enterprise nation ... It does not accept the state-monopoly solution, despite Laski and Aneurin Bevan; and sooner or later it will revolt against the facile solution of state ownership and be driven to expedients of entirely new kinds, which Labour philosophy at present scornfully scouts.

Next day, amid the happy junketings, he turned to his obsession:

> I don't think philanthropic housing people anywhere realise the irresistible strength of the impulse towards the family house and garden as prosperity increases; they think the suburban trend can be reversed by large-scale multi-storey buildings in the down-town districts, which is not merely a pernicious belief from the human point of view, but a delusion. Many of our 'practical' people, including our Mr Silkin [Lewis Silkin, the new Minister of Town and Country Planning], share the delusion ... I am inclined to think the multi-storey technique will have to have its run ... It is a pity we can't go straight for the right policy. But it takes a long time for an idea, accepted theoretically, to soak through the whole of an administration; and the conflicting idea of good multi-storey development has enough enthusiasts to claim a trial in some cities on a fairly large scale. Damage will be done to society by the trial; but probably all I can do is hasten the date of disillusion. If I have underestimated the complacency of the urban masses, the damage may amount to a disaster.

Few of any persuasion imagined that the end of the war meant the end of Britain's problems. 'We have a lot in front of us in reconstruction,'

Grantham's Mayor-elect, Alderman Alfred Roberts, explained on VJ +1 to the local paper. 'When you have won the war you have to heal the wounds of war, and that is our next job.'[31]

PART TWO

4

We're So Short of Everything

The sporting highlight of the first autumn of peace was a far from peaceful British tour by the Russian football champions Moscow Dynamo. Amid much mutual suspicion and misunderstanding, four matches were played – draws against Chelsea and Glasgow Rangers, a narrow win over Arsenal and a 10–1 demolition of Cardiff City. The ill feeling that characterised at least two of the matches provoked George Orwell, writing just before Christmas in the left-wing magazine *Tribune*, to launch a full-frontal attack on professional football and its followers: 'People want to see one side on top and the other humiliated, and they forget that victory gained through cheating or through the intervention of the crowd is meaningless.' In short, 'serious sport . . . is war minus the shooting'. This was too much for E. S. Fayers of Harrow, Middlesex. 'George Orwell is always interesting,' began his riposte. 'But he does write some bilge.' And after defending football as a game to play, he went on:

> As to the spectators, with the greatest possible diffidence, I suggest that George is in danger of falling into the error of intellectual contempt for the 'mob'. These football crowds, if only he got among them, he would find are not great ignorant mobs of sadistic morons. They are a pretty good mixture of just ordinary men. A little puzzled, a little anxious, steady, sceptical, humorous, knowledgeable, having a little fun, hoping for a bit of excitement, and definitely getting quite a lot of enjoyment out of that glorious king of games – football.

The good-natured rebuke finished unanswerably: 'I'm sorry for George. He's missed a lot of fun in life.'[1]

There was no resumption of the Football League proper until the 1946–7 season, but happily for 'ordinary men' the FA Cup did take place in 1945–6, on a two-leg basis. Less than glamorous Accrington Stanley found themselves pitted in the third round against Manchester United, with the first leg at Peel Park. Two down at half-time, Stanley then, 'in as plucky a come-back as I have ever seen' (in the words of the local reporter 'Jason'), 'drew level with two minutes to go to the accompaniment of an almost hysterical roar of triumph from the crowd'. Predictably, United won the return 5–1 – but 'the game might have taken on a different aspect if two cruel pieces of ill-fortune had not come Stanley's way.' Three rounds later, at the Bolton Wanderers versus Stoke City match, there was disaster when 33 of the Burnden Park crowd were crushed to death. It could have been worse. 'I think I had a pretty narrow escape and it was because of the kindness of the men,' Audrey Nicholls recalled years later. 'That was typical of the spirit of the times that they were concerned for me, a girl, and they just lifted me up and off I went down. They were marvellous.' On 27 April 1946 the first post-war Cup Final, featuring Charlton Athletic versus Derby County, took place in front of almost 100,000 at Wembley's Empire Stadium. As an occasion it had everything: an intensely emotional singing of 'Abide with Me'; the appearance of King George VI in a grey overcoat ('Blimey, he's been demobbed too,' shouted a spectator through the cheering); Bert Turner managing within a minute to score for both sides; a burst ball (reflecting the prevailing leather shortage); three goals for Derby in extra time as they ran out 4–1 winners; and, in the absence of champagne, ginger beer celebrations in the victorious dressing room.

Almost everyone, it seemed, was hungry for escapism. 'The biggest entertainments boom ever known is now in full swing,' Anthony Heap noted in October 1945 against a background in the shops of an almost completely inadequate supply of goods for people's disposable incomes. 'Anything goes – good, bad or indifferent. Every theatre in the West End is packed out every night and to get reserved seats, one has to book weeks ahead.' A patriotic hit that autumn was *Merrie England*, enjoyed by a thoroughly sensible, suburban, church-going young woman, Erica Ford:

I put on scarlet & black jacket, black skirt, shoes & hat & bag. Went to N. Ealing Station & met Dumbo [an older man, called Harry Bywaters] 5.35. Went to Piccadilly & walked right up Shaftesbury Ave to Prince's Theatre ... Had two stalls. Very bright show & lovely music. Heddle Nash as Raleigh sang 'The English Rose' superbly ...

Went to Princes Restaurant 10.0 & had 4/6 dinner. Soup, plaice & chips & pears. Very nice. Bussed to Piccadilly & train to N. Ealing. Walked up Hanger Lane. Lovely night.

Elsewhere during these immediate post-war months, the dance halls were heaving (cementing the star status of band leaders like Ted Heath and Joe Loss); the country's 4,709 cinemas were almost invariably packed out (attracting in 1946 an all-time peak of 1,635 million admissions); and favourite programmes on the radio continued to draw huge listening figures, above all *ITMA*, the surreal yet warm Tommy Handley comedy vehicle which successfully relocated in peacetime to Tomtopia, a Utopia with Tommy as Governor. Colonel Chinstrap ('I don't mind if I do!') was still going strong, while new characters included Nurse Riff-Rafferty, Big Chief Bigga Banga and his daughter Banjoleo, according to Tommy a 'smashing portion of passion fruit, well worth a second helping'.

Not everyone appreciated these radio days. Mary King, impeccably middle-class but servantless in her Birmingham suburb, grappled one Monday in April 1946 with a particularly big wash load: 'Miss Newton, a young woman about 30 years of age living apart from her husband, had her wireless on in her bedroom with windows wide open (next door) from 9.30 to 2 p.m. All the jazz & what nots – a continual stream. It did not go in rhythm with my mangle, or aching arms ... I heard her mother ask her to shut it off – and her answer made me feel I should like to throw several of my buckets of suds right over her wireless. What a day!!!!' The disapproval, though, could go the other way. The middle-class cinema-going public may have lapped up *Brief Encounter*, but shortly before its official premiere in November 1945 its director, David Lean, had tried it out on a distinctly working-class audience in Rochester, where he was filming *Great Expectations*. The cinema, as Lean soon discovered, was full of sailors from the nearby Chatham dockyards. 'At the first love scene one woman down in the front started to laugh. I'll never forget it. And the second love scene it got worse. And then the audience caught on and waited for her to laugh and they all joined in and it ended in an absolute shambles. They were rolling in the aisles.'[2]

The high cultural mood, accurately reflecting the prevailing sense of fatigue even amid the pleasure-seeking, was one of isolation and retrenchment. A symptomatic episode was the enforced departure in October 1945 of William Glock as music critic of the *Observer* on account of his excessive enthusiasm for the difficult moderns, culminating in an obituary of Bartók which declared that 'no great composer has ever cared how "pleasant" his music sounded'. Two months later an exhibition at the V&A of Picasso and Matisse achieved notoriety. An outraged visitor threatening the paintings with his umbrella had to be forcibly removed; the elderly daughter of William Holman Hunt clapped her hands for silence and announced that the pictures were rubbish; Evelyn Waugh informed *The Times* that Picasso had as little artistic merit as an American crooner; and a columnist on the art magazine *Apollo* not only confessed that 'for me this stuff means precisely nothing' but compared Picasso and Matisse as artistic leaders to 'the more enterprising of the Gadarene Swine'.

Relatively few would have demurred, least of all the upper class, uneasily finding its feet after the war and the trauma of the Labour landslide, and now also unwittingly finding its Boswell – albeit a Boswell with a deeply imbued sense of what could be tastefully printed and what could not. On 7 November the *Tatler* introduced a new column, 'Jennifer Writes Her Social Journal'. 'Jennifer' was the redoubtable Betty Kenward, recently divorced by her Hussars husband and left financially high and dry. In her first entry she gave a detailed account of the wedding at St George's Chapel, Windsor, of Lord Kimberley to Miss Diana Legh, daughter of the Master of the Royal Household. 'The King of the Hellenes was among those present, and Lady Patricia Ramsay was there, as tall and good-looking as ever. Lady Grenfell, who is the bride's step-sister, was wearing a small cap of green cock's feathers, and it was amusing to note how popular feathers have become, ostrich being first in the running . . .' At times it was as if nothing had changed. 'At the fashionable, carefree Carcano–Ednam wedding reception,' the Tory MP, assiduous party-goer and cracking diarist Sir Henry 'Chips' Channon noted in early 1946, 'I remarked to Emerald [Cunard] how quickly London had recovered from the war and how quickly normal life had been resumed. "After all," I said, pointing to the crowded room, "this is what we have been fighting for."'[3]

Life was rather tougher for the men who had done most of the actual fighting. More than four million British servicemen were demobilised (too slowly, according to many) between June 1945 and January 1947, and probably for most the transition from war to peace was far from easy. Advice or support was not always available (partly because of the war in the Far East having ended so precipitately), previous jobs were often no longer open, the returnees were seldom treated as heroes by a deeply war-weary society, and the prosaic realities of peace frequently came to seem less attractive than the relative glamour (and male bonding) of war. 'Thoughts and plans begin to turn inwards in an unhealthy manner,' warned the *British Legion Journal*. 'This can lead to all sorts of pitfalls, not the least of which is self-pity, and should be shunned like early-morning PT.' The strains on marriages were severe. A couple might not have seen each other for several years; he expected to return to his familiar position as the undisputed head; she had become more independent (often working in a factory as well as running the home) – the possibilities for tension and strife, even when both were emotionally committed to each other, were endless. Inevitably, the number of divorces (in England and Wales) rose sharply: from 12,314 in 1944 (itself almost a doubling of the 1939 figure) to 60,190 by 1947.

Even if a marriage held together, as the great majority did, the experience for the children of a stranger's return home could be deeply bewildering and even damaging. 'I did not like this tall, weird, cold man,' Wendy Reeves remembered about the return of her POW father: 'After such a close relationship with my lovely warm, kindly grandad and uncle Colin, whom I worshipped, as they adored me. Of course, I did not understand at the time – but it became clearer as I became older – that Dad had become quite mentally unbalanced by his incarceration. He used to sleep in a separate room from Mum, was unkind to me – I received the first smack I had ever known, from him – and I became frightened of him.' It was little better in the case of

Brenda Bajak's father, a regimental sergeant major during the war:

> He was a total stranger to me and I didn't like him! He was moody
> and very demanding. He ordered us about as though he was still in the
> Army. He and my mother argued a lot and I wasn't used to grown-ups
> arguing. He had *no* idea how to behave with daughters. He shouted a
> lot and insisted things were done immediately. He told us little of his
> war. His moods were dreadful – he was great when out at work or with
> other people, but dreadful at home. He never participated in a 'family'
> life. He just worked and slept. My mother did everything for him and
> was the 'peacemaker'.[4]

Many such discordant stories were played out in these immediate post-
war years – the malign, destabilising legacy of a just conflict.

———

Was the woman's place still, as it had been before the contingencies of
war, in the home? A sharp if short-lived anxiety about Britain's apparently
declining population proved a key 'pro-natalist' weapon for the home-
and-hearthists, even persuading two well-known progressives, Margaret
Bondfield and Eva Hubback, to argue publicly in November 1945 that
'domestic work in a modern home will be a career for educated women'.
Coming from a different standpoint, the psychiatrist John Bowlby
published in 1946 his first major work, *Forty-four Juvenile Thieves*,
which found that the one common denominator in a group of adolescent
London criminals was prolonged separation from their mothers. Also
in 1946, the eminent paediatrician James Spence gave a well-publicised
lecture entitled 'The Purpose of the Family' in which he emphasised the
welfare of children, argued that the benign family unit had come under
unprecedented pressure during the war, and insisted that only through
preserving the art of motherhood could the family be saved.

Unsurprisingly, women's magazines seldom deviated from
upholding the domestic status quo ante. 'If men and women fail to
take their traditional positions in the dance of life,' declared the *Lady*
in January 1946, 'only a greater dullness is achieved.' Soon afterwards,
a fictional heroine in *My Weekly* put it succinctly: 'I've spent a week
discovering I'd rather be Mrs Peter Grant, housewife, than Rosamund

Fuller, dress designer.' On the flickering screen, the message of *Brief Encounter* (set in the winter of 1938–9) was similar. 'It all started on an ordinary day in the most ordinary place in the world – the refreshment room at Milford Junction,' begins Laura's voiceover. 'I was having a cup of tea and reading a book that I got that morning from Boots. My train wasn't due for 10 minutes. I looked up and saw a man come in from the platform. He had on an ordinary mac, his hat was turned down . . .' But in the end she does not have an affair and returns to her dull husband: a vindication of restraint, domesticity and pre-war values.

By September 1946 the number of married women at work (including part-time) was, from a wartime peak of more than 7.2 million, down to 5.8 million – a total that no longer included Judy Haines in Chingford. Some seven months after gratefully leaving her London office job, she spent a peaceful but potentially disturbing evening with her husband on the first Sunday in March 1946:

> Had Welsh Rarebit for tea. I must go to the Gas Company about the grill, the irons of which are missing, making it unusable. Welsh Rarebit isn't the same untoasted. Abbé washed up and I dried; we each read some chapters of 'The Outnumbered' and then listened to our serial, 'Jane Eyre'. I prepared our supper (cocoa and cakes) and put hot water bottles in bed while the news was on, to be in time for the speech by the Prime Minister, Mr Attlee. He was calling us all, especially women and the older people, to do a job of work [as] well. He added that he wasn't asking anyone to overwork. Oh dear! I don't want to go out working again. At the end of the speech Abbé said I had a job of work at home, and I was very happy. And I do do my own washing and make do and mend, which is all a help. I think Abbé deserves to be well looked after and a woman can't do this and go to work as well. If she does get through both jobs she cannot be much of a companion.

The nation's husbands agreed with Abbé. 'Am just beginning to appreciate some of the advantages that help to off-set the financial loss entailed by M's [ie his wife Marjorie's] change over from office work to house-wifery,' reflected Anthony Heap barely a fortnight later. These advantages included 'being able to have *all* my meals at home instead of going up to Mother's for breakfast and round to the British

Restaurant for lunch', as well as 'no longer having to do any housework, such as washing, wiping-up, sweeping, dusting, firelighting etc, etc'. In short, 'one certainly has a more comfortable time of it with a bustling wife around the house'. Or, as 'a solid trade unionist leader' in the north-east put it to the writer James Lansdale Hodson later in the year, 'Men hate their girls going out to work and impairing their own dignity as head o' the house.'[5]

Three women had contrasting destinies. Alison Readman (born 1922), daughter of a colonel of the Scots Greys, read PPE at Oxford before proving so efficient as R. B. McCallum's research assistant in his study of the 1945 general election that she finished up as co-author. Although their work was published in 1947 and immediately hailed as Britain's first book of psephology, that same year she married a White-hall civil servant and turned down an Oxford fellowship, believing that it would be incompatible with her future role of wife and mother. The first of five children was born in 1949, and in later years, in the words of her 2003 obituary, 'she worked on a book that was to combine a study of moral philosophy and contemporary ethics, but prolonged bouts of ill-health meant that it never came to fruition'. Margery Hurst (born 1913) chose another route. In 1946, with a £50 loan, a small room in Brook Street and a battered portable typewriter, she founded Brook Street Bureau of Mayfair Ltd, which soon became the Brook Street Bureau – by the 1960s a chain across three continents that was almost synonymous with the supply of secretaries and 'temps'. Marriage in 1948 and two daughters were successfully taken in her stride; a generally admiring obituarist in 1989, only a year after she stepped down as chairman of the plc, conceded that she could be 'infuriating, domineering, self-willed and insensitive to the effect that she had on others'; while as for her disinclination to stand up vocally for women's rights, at a time when the business world was almost wholly dominated by men, she would simply say, 'I can do more just by being me and letting it be seen what women can do.' For Judy Fryd (born 1909), the personal *was* the political. She married in 1936 and had four children, the first of whom had serious learning difficulties. Fryd encountered such problems and prejudice that in 1946 she was instrumental in founding the Association of Parents of Backward Children, from 1950 called the National Society for Mentally Handicapped Children, and now the Royal Society for Mentally Handicapped Children and Adults (MENCAP). 'My career was always going to be in politics,' she once remarked. 'I just didn't realise it was the mentally handicapped corner I would be fighting.' An obituarist in 2000 reflected that 'she taught us to help and learn from each other,' adding that 'Judy always reminded me of a cheeky little sparrow.'[6]

Still, even sparrows need nests. 'How I wish we'd a house to go to but still having my "main" piece of furniture will be "the best thing",' Muriel Bowmer, living with relatives in Sheffield, wrote to her soon-to-be-demobbed husband Fred in early October 1945. And a fortnight later, just before the great day, 'according to tonight's news they are going to "start at the bottom", & build houses to rent first – so it looks to me as though that dream of ours regarding "buying" is going to do a fade out. Perhaps it's as well we've got our name down at the Town Hall therefore.' Barbara Pym would have sympathised. 'Hilary [her sister] and I have taken a flat – in Pimlico, not a very good district, but perhaps we shall raise the tone,' the as yet unpublished novelist told a friend in November. 'It is on the corner of Warwick Square and really quite nice. Anyway we are so lucky to get anywhere at all, as it is practically impossible to get flats and you really can't choose at all.' Soon afterwards, Mollie Panter-Downes, another novelist but also the sender of a regular 'Letter from London' to the *The New Yorker*, noted that 'the personal columns of *The Times* are full of pathetic house-hunting advertisements inserted by ex-service men – the new displaced persons, who fought for the homes they are now desperately seeking, mostly, alas, without success'.

In March 1946 the housing shortage was just as bad, even in parts of leafy suburbia, as one rehousing officer, George Beardmore, privately recorded:

> Two wretched families have moved into one of our requisitioned mansions in Marsh Lane [in Stanmore, Middlesex] and are shortly to receive an injunction to leave. Have twice visited them officially and once unofficially, under pledge of secrecy, to give them some clothes and blankets Jean [his wife] has found for them. A scene of squalor and misery rare even in these days. A bus conductor, two women, and three schoolchildren, driven desperate for somewhere to live, camp out in a

large dilapidated room without light, water and (yesterday at least) without fuel for a fire. Sullen and dirty faces swollen with colds, an orange-box scraped dry of all but coal-dust, two saucepans on an unmade bed, a spirit-stove on which bacon was frying, and a green teapot shaped like a racing-car on a strip of newspaper many times ringed.

At about the same time, Glasgow Corporation commissioned a film, to be shown in Glasgow cinemas and called *Progress Report, No 1*, about what its housing department was doing. 'People everywhere are clamouring for houses,' the commentary declared. '94,000 names comprise the waiting list in Glasgow alone. Of these 40,600 are the names of people who are actually houseless. To provide more and more new homes in the shortest possible time is the aim of the Municipal Representative at George Square.'[7] Put another way, the numbers game was – for the best of reasons – now under way.

For a time, an important part of that game involved the construction of temporary homes using prefabricated materials – 'prefabs'. Churchill in 1944 had promised a programme of half a million new such homes, but in the event only 156,623 of these temporary bungalows – each with a similar two-bedroom layout and mainly occupied by young couples – were built between 1945 and 1949. 'You know we were offered the choice of a prefab?' a youngish working-class woman was overheard remarking to her female friend at the Modern Homes Exhibition at Dorland Hall in London in March 1946. 'Well, I wouldn't have it. They're nice inside but they look dreadful from the road. You don't like to feel ashamed every time you get near your own home.' The friend agreed: 'Those prefabs are awful – when you see a lot together they look like pigsties or hen-houses, I always think.'

Architects and other commentators were similarly dismissive – 'fungus-like outcroppings of those tin huts called "pre-fabs"' was how one saw them – but all the evidence is that those who lived in them were highly appreciative of having a fitted bath, constant hot water and a built-in refrigerator. 'I think everyone really felt they liked being in the prefabs,' one 1946 investigator, Peter Hunot, found after talking to almost thirty of the families in Clarence Crescent, a London County Council (LCC) run estate of prefabs in Wandsworth. No one wanted to live in a flat, 'many expressing a dislike of them', while 'hours and days had been spent on many of the gardens', with each prefab (as with prefabs generally) having one. Perhaps inevitably, Hunot's overall worry was that 'this contentment seemed to be individualist', though on hearing one man say that he had been among other people in the army for five years and was now glad to be on his own for a bit, the Hampstead-dwelling investigator 'felt sympathetic and not so certain that the lack of community was a fatal deficiency'.[8]

But of course, one word above all characterised life in immediate post-war Britain: austerity. Less than a fortnight after VJ Day, Panter-Downes outlined the grim implications of 'the sudden termination by the United States of Lend-Lease', the financial support that had got Britain through the war:

> The factories, which people hoped would soon be changing over to the production of goods for the shabby, short-of-everything home consumers are instead to produce goods for export. The Government will have to face up to the job of convincing the country that controls and hardships are as necessarily a part of a bankrupt peace as they were of a desperate war. Every inch of useable English soil will still have to be made to grow food. People are suddenly realising that in the enormous economic blitz that has just begun, their problems may be as serious as the blitz they so recently scraped through.

Writing to her absent Fred at about the same time, Muriel Bowmer in Sheffield was already sounding a somewhat pessimistic note:

> Everybody here aren't very thrilled by the news of the latest rationing hit, & also by the prospects of still more tightened belts. We did think that once Japan was beaten we should do away with queues, but it doesn't seem like it. Yesterday I queued 1/2 hour in Woolworths for some biscuits – & I was under cover. The fish problem seems to be a bit better here – it isn't quite so rotten although the queues are there still. As for me, I'm O.K. for coupons, as it happens, & well stocked for clothes also – so I shan't bother with much new this winter. I shall perhaps get a frock, & a new hat – I don't know yet. However once the new fashions start coming in there will be a new style of things I think . . .

Over the next few months there began to grow a pervasive sense of disenchantment that the fruits of peace were proving so unbountiful. 'No sooner did we awake from the six years nightmare of war and feel free to enjoy life once more, than the means to do so immediately became even scantier than they had been during the war,' Anthony Heap reflected in his end-of-1945 review. 'Housing, food, clothing, fuel, beer, tobacco – all the ordinary comforts of life that we'd taken for granted before the war and naturally expected to become more plentiful again when it ended, became instead more and more scarce and difficult to come by.' He concluded, 'I can remember few years I've been happier to see the end of.'[9]

In terms of everyday shortages, the greatest concern – and source of potential flashpoints – was undoubtedly food. This was clear as early as October 1945, when an unofficial dock strike, lasting several weeks, proved signally unpopular. 'Dock Strike Threatens Rations' warned the front-page headline of the strongly anti-Labour *Daily Express* (the most widely read daily paper) just as the Ministry of Food was about to announce that if the strike continued it might become impossible to distribute the full bacon ration. 'Meat And Eggs May Be Off Next Week' warned Beaverbrook's crusader a few days later, by which time Mass-Observation was conducting a series of interviews in Chelsea (then rather more downmarket) and Battersea. Both men and women were predominantly critical of the dockers, but whereas men tended to look at the political aspect, including the damage being done to the Labour government, women concentrated firmly on the food situation:

> The rations are bare enough as it is, without having to do without the bacon ... They should be satisfied with the wages and appreciate the fact that they're able to work without the Fly-bombs around.
>
> It's very selfish, I should say, making everybody suffer, instead of waiting a bit longer ... It's the food is going to be the worry; it's disgusting when we're so short of everything.
>
> I think it's very unfair – all the food going to waste. It's not right at all.

All those three (aged between 35 and 50) were working-class; but a more middle-class woman of 30 did not disagree: 'I think it's simply disgusting, stabbing the whole community in the back, just at this moment too when everything is so difficult; food's so short. The one way to stop it would be to take away their ration books!'

The strike was eventually called off in early November, but the grumbling about food was unabated. 'I had to hunt for bread,' Gladys Langford in her north London hotel noted on Saturday the 3rd. 'After mid day it seems well nigh impossible to get a loaf. Wandered around Seven Dials, also thro' Chapel St. market where I saw two raddled old hags telling fortunes and a queue of working-class women waiting to consult each one of them.' Five days later, another hotel resident, Henry St John in Bristol, went by train to Minehead and found that 'a small sandwich which had a smear of sardine inside it cost me 3d at Taunton station.' And the next day, in Birmingham, Mary King managed to get near to the car of the visiting King and Queen: 'She looked a little too matronly for her age. Considering the rationing of the people she certainly looked well fed.' In the House of Commons, meanwhile, the only meat on the menu was whale or seal steak – 'both disgusting', according to one new Labour MP, Aidan Crawley – while even a 'white tie and tails' banquet could disappoint. 'Of course the meal was terrible,' noted Raymond Streat in the New Year, down from Manchester for the *News Chronicle*'s big centenary beano at Dorchester House. 'A speck of hot lobster: an impossibly tough and exceedingly small leg of chicken: a tiny bit of not very sweet, sweet and a cup of coffee.'[10]

It is unlikely, though, that Streat or any of the other 424 guests often did the household shopping. Judy Haines did, and the third Tuesday of 1946 was probably no worse than most days:

> Got ahead with ironing and then felt I must go in quest of meat as that little chop left over from our Sunday joint will not make a very nourishing Shepherd's Pie. Dyson's very empty. I enquired tenderly if the van had called and they informed me 'no' and there should be some rabbits. I have had my hopes raised like this before, falsely. But I went home out of the cold, made myself a cup of cocoa and when half way through it saw the van. Hastily finished my drink and set off again. Yes, there were some rabbits but they weren't ready just yet. O.K. I'll come back again. Met Mother H. [her mother-in-law] who told me List's had some nice

Mince Tarts. I hardly liked leaving Dyson's, but she said she would wait there, which seemed a help though Dyson's would only let their registered customers have rabbits. Wondered if all the tarts would be gone, but I was lucky, and this will make a nice sweet with some custard. No sign of rabbits, so I went into the Post Office to draw my allowance, cash money order and buy National Savings Stamps. Crowds in there but I thought Dyson's couldn't sell out of rabbits very quickly. When I returned to the shop there was a queue and only about three rabbits visible. However, I waited and more came up. I was lucky.

'This shopping!' she added. 'All housewives are fed up to the eyebrows with it.'

Austerity took a new twist on 5 February when the Minister of Food, Sir Ben Smith, announced cuts in the bacon, poultry and egg rations – the last cut made much worse by the simultaneous decision to end the importing of dried eggs. The next few weeks saw a housewives' revolt, fuelled but not initiated by the anti-government press and at its liveliest in the middle-class parts of Liverpool. Smith eventually agreed to reintroduce dried eggs into the shops, but by then the episode had given a major fresh impetus to the British Housewives' League. In mid-March the appreciably more serious food shortage on much of the Continent prompted Mass-Observation to ask a cluster of working-class people, again in Chelsea and Battersea, 'How do you feel about giving up some of your food for Europe?' The replies of four men, followed by five women, were fairly typical:

No. I don't think we could do it at present, we're about down to rock bottom.

I'd be against it, myself. It's Germany's turn to go without.

If it came to it, I suppose I'd do it as willingly as the next. But not to help Germany – only the countries that's been overrun. I wouldn't care what happened to the Germans – they've asked for it.

No, I definitely wouldn't – I think it's up to America – when you read in the papers about what they eat – and it was just the same when they were over here – they're the biggest gluttons in the world now.

I wouldn't go short on half a loaf to benefit Germany.

Yes. Provided we still get something for every meal.

No, definitely not – if they were in our position they wouldn't help us, so why should we help them?

I think the Germans *ought* to go short, after all they've done.

I suppose we'd do it if we had to. I hope it won't come to that.

There was the occasional silver lining. The day after those interviews, on the 13th, Marian Raynham – middle-aged, living in Surbiton, mother of two – recorded a long-awaited moment: '*Bananas*. Yes, bananas!! The first for 6 yrs. They are Robin's [her son's] really, as they are only allowed for under 18's . . . Robin says the boys are bringing the peel to school & putting it down for others to slip on. The monkeys.' Two days later, 'Robin came in to room with banana & wanted to know which end to start peeling it from!! . . . We told him from stem end, & later I wondered if that was right.' In early April things got even better: 'The milkman brought mustard, semolina, & sultanas *asking* if I wanted them!! "Do you want" not "you can't have"! War *is* over.'[11]

But overall, the food situation was becoming a source of considerable and understandable discontent. An authoritative British Medical Association report in the late 1940s, based on studies between 1941 and 1948 about the availability of food for a family comprising a husband, wife and three children suggests a significant deterioration:

Throughout the war the 'housewife' of the 'standard' family would have had little difficulty in obtaining the 'human needs' diet . . . The picture changed somewhat in Spring 1946, for although the diet could still be obtained without much difficulty, the shortage of fats made it difficult for adults to obtain a sufficient calorie intake without considerable strain on the digestion, this being the cause of the 'recurrent complaints' that 'people have not enough to eat' . . .

After the end of the war the difficulties facing housewives in obtaining a sufficient and appetising diet for their families were increased, owing not so much to an actual shortage of food as to an insufficiency of the more palatable foods. Those especially affected were families who could not afford to spend much on food.

There was also an increasing concern about bread – in terms not only of quality (Panter-Downes referred in early March to the recent 'reversion to the darker, more nutritious, but obstinately disliked loaf') but also of quantity, given that bread had never been rationed at any point during the war. The war itself was still sufficiently recent for the principle of food rationing in general to be widely accepted – fair shares, etc – but a Gallup poll found that half of the public disapproved of the prospect of bread rationing; accordingly, bread and its waste now became something of a national obsession.

It was an obsession fully shared by Florence Speed. Aged 50 and unmarried, she had at various times worked as a commercial artist and also for her family textile business in the City before it was destroyed in the Blitz, as well as having had two novels published. By 1946 she was living with a sister and brother in a solidly middle-class part of Brixton (59 Vassal Road) and struggling with the twin problems of ill health and genteel poverty. A real writer, albeit in a sometimes indecipherable hand, her diary has a particular vividness:

> *7 April.* Took a book into the walled garden at Kennington Park but had only read a couple of pages when a chatty lady came and sat down beside me. 'Disgusting that children are allowed in here. They're so noisy & destroy everything.'
>
> *10 April.* A pleasanter day than usual as we [her sister Ethel and herself] spoke to one or two strangers. First as we passed a hotel at Victoria, a girl on the bus. Outside was a van loaded with buns, piled high with crusts cut from sandwich loaves. Ethel exclaimed at the waste & the girl joined in. 'Good crusts, fresh crusts. It's wicked, they should be eaten.'
>
> *11 April.* Going thro Kennington Park this morning, I saw three parts of a loaf thrown down under a tree. What sort of mentality have these food wasters?
>
> *26 April.* Owing to wheat shortage the 2lb loaf is to be cut to 1¾lbs, but price is to be 4½d just the same![12]

The Ministry of Food seems to have hoped, in a flash of Baldrickian cunning, that people would continue to consume the same number of loaves, even though those loaves were now significantly smaller.

It is not fanciful to argue that within a year of VE Day there had set in not only a widespread sense of disenchantment – with peace, perhaps even with the Labour government – but also a certain sense of malaise, a feeling that society, which broadly speaking had held together during the war, was no longer working so well, was even starting to come apart. To an extent it was an inevitable reaction. 'No one feels well or happy just now,' the novelist Sylvia Townsend Warner, living in Dorset, wrote to a friend in January 1946. 'No one in wartime can quite escape the illusion that when the war ends things will snap back to where they were and that one will be the same age one was when it began, and able to go on from where one left off.' Hauntingly, she added, 'But the temple of Janus has two doors, and the door for war and door for peace are equally marked in plain lettering, No Way Back.' A few weeks earlier, more prosaically, the *Barry Dock News* had identified a mood of 'anti-climax' in the South Wales town and described how Barry, like elsewhere, 'struggles on, a little bit war-weary and depressed, but accepting the situation with stoicism'. Few felt the anti-climax more keenly than Quentin Crisp. 'The horrors of peace were many,' the defiantly open homosexual recalled in *The Naked Civil Servant*. 'Death-made-easy vanished overnight and soon love-made-easy, personified by the American soldiers, also disappeared . . . Even mere friendship grew scarce. Londoners started to regret their indiscriminate expansiveness. People do when some moment of shared danger is past. Emotions that had been displayed had now to be lived down.'[13]

How much of an oppressive cloud, post-Hiroshima, did the atom bomb cast? 'There is no sense of stability,' Dr David Mace of the Marriage Guidance Council observed in a September 1945 analysis of why the war was a key factor in accelerating family disruption and marriage breakdown. 'We are forced to live in the "here and now" because we just do not know about tomorrow. That mood still prevails. The atomic bomb "question mark" means that it is no good planning.' Two months later, after the government had announced that the Civil Defence Services would be merely suspended and should 'keep together', Panter-Downes overheard on a bus 'a seedy cockney matron' talking to a friend: 'It 'asn't 'arf put the wind up people. They can't seem to settle to things, and no wonder. Funny thing, even though I've taken every stitch off me back every night since VE Day, I can't seem to feel easy, either. It's peace, I tell meself, but some'ow it don't feel like peace ought to feel.' Panter-Downes reckoned that this woman 'spoke for most disturbed Londoners', but it is at least equally possible that most Londoners and their fellow-countrymen fairly soon learnt to put to the backs of their minds such cataclysmic thoughts – as people usually do about the great unpalatables.

Almost certainly a bigger source of oppression, on a day-to-day basis, was the unattractive mixture, certainly in peacetime, of not only a ceaseless preoccupation with ration books, vouchers and 'points' but also enforced exposure to frequent displays of petty authority. The writer Rupert Croft-Cooke, demobilised in the spring of 1946 and returning to what was still bombed-out London, was struck by how often he saw 'the feelings of gentle people, of naturally timorous people being trampled on by loud-mouthed bullies, frequently in uniform', such as policemen or public-transport officials or cinema commission-aires. Such behaviour was hardly the result of the new political dispen-sation but in difficult times could not but stimulate anti-government feelings. Happening in April 1946 to catch *Workers' Playtime* (the radio variety programme that began during the war to boost production in the factories and continued long into peace), Vere Hodgson, a welfare worker in west London and, like many Londoners, much disgusted by the peacetime determination of bus conductors not to allow standing passengers, was 'amazed' by the programme's criticism:

> I do not listen very often, so it was all fresh to me. Much at the expense of Aneurin Bevan [the minister responsible for housing as well as health]. One comedian was going to Wales because a house had been built there last year! Then the song that struck me as being very remarkable was one called 'I'd Like To Be A Refugee From Britain'. All in rhyme it was . . . we were under fed and over taxed, and spent our lives in queues, etc, docketed and ticketed. But the most remarkable lines were the end . . . about they say they can do without Churchill, so they can do without me, I *want* to be a refugee from Britain.

'The factory girls,' she added, 'cheered to the echo.'

Crucial to the sense of malaise were the corrosive effects, in peacetime if not in war, of the overriding context of rationing, price controls and production controls. 'It's very easy to spot people who buy things without coupons in Barrow,' reflected Nella Last as early as September 1945. 'They have the Jewish stamp, over decorated & doll eyed bits & pieces of fur & tucks.' Ina Zweiniger-Bargielowska, historian of austerity, makes it abundantly clear that the black market and all its devices – including off-ration and under-the-counter sales as well as tipping and favouritism – were at least as extensive after the war as during it. Food orders, the Minister of Food noted in May 1946, were 'generally being ignored and evaded more flagrantly now than at any time during the war', while soon afterwards his ministry found that a 'substantial section of the agricultural community habitually disregard the Food Orders, adopting the attitude that they are just more regulations to be "got round" – at a profit – and not that such avoidance is fundamentally dishonest and unfair to the whole community', with farmers and dealers in Wales identified as the worst offenders. No doubt some of them had been partly responsible for the scandal that had done much to spoil the first peacetime Christmas (at least in London), with Panter-Downes reporting that 'most butchers refused to pay more than the legal prices for fowl and consequently had nothing but a nice row of empty hooks to show their customers'.[14]

It was about this time, moreover, that the black-market spiv really started to emerge as a well-known type: coat with wide lapels and padded-out shoulders, tight collar on shirt, big knot in tie, hair parted in middle with wave on either side, pencil moustache, he was grudgingly admired, essentially disliked. Yet the fact was that a significant part – perhaps even the majority – of the respectable middle class, and indeed of the respectable working class, simultaneously condemned *and* used the black market, without which they would have been hard pressed to maintain an even barely recognisable quality of life. Some even found themselves succumbing to the temptation of coupon fraud. 'I suspect there's more dishonesty in this country today than for many years,' Hodson reflected in May 1946. 'Rationing, controls of material, very high income tax [9 shillings in the pound], a feeling of despair at the state of the world – all these contribute to it.' Returning servicemen could, in this as other ways, find it particularly difficult. Thomas Hanley, 28 and just married, decided to try his luck in Devon. Half a century later, his memories were still sharp and painful:

I found business, even in a small seaside resort [probably Paignton], was run on chicanery and spivvery. I found that men, some not much older than myself, who had managed either by reason of age or health to miss a call-up, controlled all aspects of public life. In an atmosphere of rationing and shortages, interlopers like myself had a hard time. Helping hands were weighted by self-interest. Even persons of the utmost integrity, after six years of war, were motivated by self-preservation. It wasn't so much of 'dog eat dog', rather to make sure that no opportunity of easing one's existence was missed. I doubt if a single Englishman did not avail himself of the help of the 'black market'. Expedience was the name of the game.

In such a situation, Hanley reflected in retrospect, a returned serviceman's 'main attribute was the stoic acceptance of the inevitable, so much a part of his service life'. His formative years may have been taken from him, but 'at least he was alive'.[15]

There were plenty of other signs, big and small, of a society apparently out of joint. 'The trains are lighted now,' the headmaster Ernest Loftus conceded in October 1945, 'but the lighting is not always good & it is not easy to read unless one is lucky & manages to get a compartment with single lights behind the seats. People are awful vandals & some compartments are in darkness through the bulbs being pilfered – the window straps are also cut off – war disease – little sense of honesty.' That month was the busiest that Scotland Yard had ever known, and shortly before Christmas the Independent MP W. J. Brown considered in his diary the 'vast crime-wave in Britain today':

A most disturbing feature of it is the number of crimes with violence. In an effort to keep the thing within bounds the police have taken to large-scale raids on the public. Without warning they cordon-off a large area and make everyone produce his identity card [introduced during the war]. They take anyone who cannot satisfactorily account for himself to the police station for further enquiries. The first of these raids took place in the West End this last week. Many deserters were picked up and many clues found to gangs of robbers responsible for recent crimes. But it adds a new terror to pleasure-seeking in the West End . . .

It was also reported that one butcher in the pre-Christmas period, having managed by hook or by crook to obtain some turkeys, slept in his shop with a loaded revolver.

The crime wave, especially in the form of burglaries, did not abate in 1946; Panter-Downes that spring spoke for upper-middle if not middle England when she lamented the fact that 'practically nobody has a servant to leave on guard in the kitchen'. She then related the story of how a Chelsea householder had recently come home from the cinema one evening only to find that burglars had visited for the third time and taken his last overcoat, some tinned sardines, a pound of tea and two pots of marmalade. 'These are things,' she hardly needed to add, 'which are painful and grievous to lose nowadays.' The figures are patchy, but it seems that an appreciably higher proportion than usual of these burglaries were committed by juveniles – a fact that subsequent police reports not implausibly attributed to the way in which 'during the war years children have lacked fatherly control and restraint and in a large number of families mothers have obviously tended to allow too much freedom'.[16] What was indisputable was that a moral panic was brewing up nicely.

Reassuringly, during the spring and disappointingly poor summer, the old sporting rituals reappeared, apparently unscathed: not only the Cup Final but the Boat Race ('the Prime Minister was there, the swans were out, young men back from the services wore beards, folk picnicked on roofs, ate ice-cream, let off crackers,' noted Hodson), the Grand National (Captain Petre, on leave from the Scots Guards, winning on Lovely Cottage, very much the housewives' choice) and Wimbledon (the British players routed by the French, American and Australian ones). Then there was that traditional highlight of the social calendar, the Eton versus Harrow match at Lord's. 'There were only five tents in the usually close-packed stretch of turf,' reported Panter-Downes, 'and . . . the men looked an extremely shabby bunch. As a parade of the upper crust, valiantly pretending that everything was still the same, the occasion was a little saddening.'

Still, the cricket authorities made a fair show in this first peacetime season of pretending that nothing had changed. Although professionals were at last given their initials on the scorecards at Lord's, they were carefully put after the surname, with the initials for amateurs continuing to precede the surname; while the two classes of cricketer continued for the most part, though no longer invariably, to change in separate dressing rooms. Moreover, of the 17 first-class counties, only one was captained by a professional, Les Berry of Leicestershire. 'There has probably never been a better collection than those who have been appointed for this year,' the *Daily Telegraph*'s new cricket correspondent, E. W. Swanton, declared reassuringly on the season's eve. 'Better in the sense,' he explained, 'of having a truer notion of the essentials of a cricket match, of whatever kind.' Perhaps so, but the year's crop included not only at least three non-bowling amateurs who by no charitable stretch of the imagination were worth their places as batsmen but also Surrey's Nigel Bennett, an undistinguished club cricketer who got the job only through a case of mistaken identity. 'Want of knowledge of county cricket on the field presented an unconquerable hindrance to the satisfactory accomplishment of arduous duties' was the mild but telling verdict on him of *Wisden Cricketers' Almanack*, no friend of the open society.

Large crowds watched the run-stealers flicker to and fro. As usual, the final test (against India) was at The Oval, and on the first day 'rain that fell until one o'clock so affected the ground that it was doubtful if play would have been attempted even at five o'clock but for the crowds of people who waited around the walls from early in the morning'. Elsewhere, the wet summer did not hinder the pursuit of the poor man's opera – March 1947 would prove to be the peak of the post-war Bulge – and indeed 1946 set a new record for venereal infections. There was also the dream of the first proper summer holiday for at least seven years, but for many it remained a dream. In Coventry, when the factories closed in late July, the local paper described 'thousands of people, walking aimlessly through the streets or standing in queues for buses to take them a few miles away for a change from the every-day'. A 60-year-old working-class man, outlining his holiday plans to Mass-Observation at the start of August, was more enterprising or perhaps fortunate: 'We tried everywhere but we couldn't get in – they're so packed. People have booked up months ago, they're all full up. So in the end I told the wife to write to a place we stayed in Margate . . . We're very fond of Margate, it's lively and the air's good and we're going to make day trips to Ramsgate and elsewhere. It'll be a change.' For a 30-year-old more middle-class woman, waiting for her husband to be demobbed, common sense vied with natural yearnings:

> Well, we're going up North to Glasgow. We've gone up there every year for the simple reason it's cheapest and Mum and Dad are always glad to see us, and what with this rationing business and now the bread, well, it's too much bother going anywhere else. Besides think of the money it would cost to have a seaside holiday . . . Oh, but I'd give anything to give Johnny a real holiday – one where he could make sand-pies on the beach. He's never been to the seaside . . .

The Friday before the August Bank Holiday weekend (still then at the start of the month) saw huge queues for trains out of London, and at Paddington the railway officials for once relented and put up a notice: 'All platform tickets suspended'.[17]

The generally downbeat summer mood was epitomised by the lack of popular enthusiasm ahead of the full-scale Victory Parade in London on Saturday, 8 June. 'Are you going to put out your decorations?' Florence Speed asked a Brixton neighbour on the Thursday. 'No, things are worse,' was the gloomy reply. The same day a couple of Nottingham working-class women gave their reactions. 'I don't know what they want to have another V Day Parade so long after the war [for],' one said. 'People have had enough of it.' The other was even more negative: 'I don't agree with it at all. We haven't got much to celebrate about. The food is bad, the young fellows are still in the Forces – what will those women who have lost their sons in the war think?' On Friday afternoon, joining a queue of about 30 outside a baker's shop in London, a Mass-Observation investigator found the grumbling positively savage. '"I've been queuing ever since eight o'clock this morning, what with one thing and another," says F40D. "I'm about done for. I'd like to take that Attlee and all the rest of them and put them on top of a bonfire in Hyde Park and BURN them." "And I'd 'elp yer," says F65D. "Same 'ere," say several other angry women.'

On the day itself, marred by rain, some six million (by one estimate) assembled to watch the parade. 'The crowds were huge, Joyce, but really *huge*,' the well-bred journalist Virginia Graham assured her friend Joyce Grenfell soon afterwards. 'Most of the people had slept in the streets all night, & been rained upon, but there they were, paper caps & all, fainting like flies, cheering every horse or dog or policeman, as merry as grigs.' Certainly there was pride among the spectators and the many other millions who listened to it on the radio – the latter including Marian Raynham in Surbiton, who wondered 'what other country can make up such a varied performance' and marvelled at 'what organisation to do it' – but for the most part grig-like they were not. A note the following Tuesday by Mass-Observation's invaluable Chelsea-based investigator makes this clear:

> Almost everybody Inv met on the 10th and 11th, whether friends or tradespeople or strangers in shops, were saying loudly how utterly exhausted and washed-out they felt, not only those who had gone to see the procession but those who had stayed at home and merely heard it over the wireless. The remark incessantly repeated, both on Victory Day and afterwards, was: 'Well, it's the last of its kind – I don't suppose we shall ever see another'. Sometimes this was followed by 'The next war'll be short and sweet,' or 'We just won't be there at the finish, next time'.

One or two women did remark that there was still Princess Elizabeth's wedding to look forward to – but that 'it wouldn't be the same because there wouldn't be the troops'.[18]

The Victory Parade had – for relatively few, relatively well-off people – a side benefit. 'Remember me?' asked the announcer Jasmine Bligh on Friday the 7th, as BBC television began post-war broadcasting by showing the same Mickey Mouse cartoon that had been on the small screen when television had ceased in September 1939. That same day, the opening Variety Party featured Peter Waring, star of radio's *Variety Bandbox*. 'I must say, I feel a trifle self-conscious going into the lens of this thing,' ran his rather arch patter. 'But since I'm here I might just as well tell you a little about myself and my hobbies. I have one or two hobbies you know that Sir Stafford [Cripps, the famously austere Labour minister] can't control. No, I thought that now I'm being televised, you might see the jokes quicker.' Next day,

Freddie Grisewood was the main television commentator on the parade, with Richard Dimbleby (who had made his name describing the liberation of Belsen) as second string. 'You will forgive a man for saying that it is only a hat with feathers on it' was his surprisingly flip comment on Princess Elizabeth's elaborate headgear.[19] At this stage there existed only some 20,000 television sets (all pre-war), mainly within 30 miles of Alexandra Palace (from where programmes were transmitted), and as yet not many were inclined to take the new medium seriously as a force for the future.

The muted response to the Victory Parade was the first of three key symbolic events during the summer of 1946. The second was the imposition of bread rationing, announced four weeks in advance on 27 June by the new Minister of Food, the highly cerebral John Strachey. The generally negative reaction, especially on the part of women, was epitomised by a letter to her local paper immediately afterwards by E. Harris of 97 Cedars Avenue, Coventry:

> I am a housewife, and I wish to protest against this last burden which is to be put upon us. We have stood everything else, but this is the last straw. I have two menfolk. I cut up one large loaf every morning for packing, and my son can eat the best part of another for breakfast. How do they think we can live on the ration they are going to give us? Are we housewives to starve ourselves still more to give to those who go to earn our living for us? We give up most of our food to them now, and many of us are at breaking-point.

Over the next few weeks, much of the public protest was channelled through the Housewives' League, a largely middle-class organisation, which by mid-July had presented two petitions (one to the House of Commons, the other to the Ministry of Food), each with some 300,000 signatories. Judy Haines was probably not one of them. With the scheme due to start on Monday the 22nd, her approach was typically robust:

> *19 July.* How bakers are quibbling over bread rationing. I think Strachey is very patient with 'em. First they think it unnecessary (who should know?!), then they want it postponed! As if the Govt. are doing it

for fun! I welcome it. Probably see more cakes, and the ration is generous anyway. People will just be more bread conscious.

20 July. Housewives go 'bread crazy'. Shortages or queues everywhere. As if it will keep! Unfortunately I had my hair to rinse and set. Then tried Chingford, Walthamstow and Leyton for bread. Mum was able to buy rolls at Mrs Negus's and let me have half a loaf, which will do beautifully.

She was right. The amount of bread available on the Monday proved more than adequate; while as Grace Golden, a London-based commercial artist, perceptively put it in her diary, 'significant to see the patient tired faces of people queuing at Food Office, most of us too tired & apathetic to resist any stricture'.

Nevertheless, over the next few days not only did bread supplies often run out with dismaying speed, but there was the harrowing, widely publicised story of a girl of 19 who, fearful of a fine if she put six slices of bread in a bin, tried to burn them by pouring petrol over them and in the process burned herself to death. 'How do you feel about bread rationing?' Mass-Observation asked some working-class women in Kilburn and Finsbury Park in mid-August. One of the main reasons for the government's action had been to bring pressure on the Americans to do more to feed Germany, but the replies were unremittingly narrow in focus:

It's been good for us, we've got more points as a result.
    Disgusting. If anything it's making people more discontented.
    I'm well pleased with it. I haven't used all my bread units and so I get extra points.
    Well, I think it's stopped a lot of waste.
    It's a damned nuisance more than anything.[20]

Even if the bread ration was adequate, as most acknowledged it was, the very fact of peacetime bread rationing would remain a symbolic sore as long as it remained in force. This was especially so on the part of the middle class, and it was a straw in the wind when in a clutch of by-elections in July, two working-class Labour seats were held with only a small swing to the Tories, but in suburban, middle-class Bexley, captured by Labour in 1945, an 11 per cent swing to the Tories almost cost Labour the seat.

Of course, *everyone* apart from spivs and their suppliers became to a greater or lesser degree fed up with the inescapable reality of continuing rationing, shortages and all the rest of it. But broadly speaking, it does seem that the middle class lost patience more quickly and more conclusively than the rest. Clues lie in Florence Speed's Brixton diary entry about the baker's the day before the Victory Parade:

Mrs Randall when Mabel [probably a friend or neighbour of Speed] went in for the bread about 10.30 said 'Sold out, & no more today'.

Mabel replied 'Well I do think you might save a loaf for regular customers'.

Mrs R. flared up & retorted, 'Don't you talk to me like that' . . .

Mrs R. looked sick when Ethel [Speed's sister] went & paid the bill & said she wanted no more.

'I think you've treated me badly!' she told us. Treated *her*!!

We've dealt at no other shop for 35 years despite change of ownership, & as Ethel said, 'It's like begging for your bread. We've never had to do that.'

A week later, forsaking Brixton, the two sisters observed the black market in something like close-up:

While queuing in Regent Street, we watched a hawker with a barrow amply laden with peaches at 1/6d. In about 20 minutes he sold 25/6d worth. A boy with a whip, from a van, not more than 14 or 15, bought two & promptly ate them crossing the road back to his van. It is the most unlikely people who have the money! . . .

Peaches imported from France are very plentiful, but much too costly for most people.

Gladys Langford was similarly struggling to hold her own in what felt like an increasingly alien, unfriendly world. On a Monday in August, mercifully on holiday from her miserable schoolteaching, she spent a day in the West End:

In D.H. Evans hordes of highly perfumed and under-washed women
thronged the departments. Assistants ignored my presence – the only
one I questioned announced she was not a saleswoman – so I walked
out . . . No queues for ice-wafers and cornets since typhoid has been
traced to ice-cream. By Piccadilly Tube Station – outside the Pavilion
– a woman about my age was playing a piano-accordion. She was
plastered with rouge and powder, wore a smart black costume and
black peaked cap and a scarlet scarf was knotted about her neck.
Another woman, also a beggar, one-legged and grimy, sat slicing a
large peach!

Then came the poignant pay-off: '*I* cannot afford anything more tooth-
some than plums at 4½d lb.'[21]

Two contrasting novels explored the middle-class predicament
during these attritional times. *One Fine Day* (1947) by Mollie Panter-
Downes was written during the spring and early summer of 1946 and
set contemporaneously in a quiet part of the Surrey countryside. Laura
and Stephen are learning to make do without domestic servants, a
sympathetically depicted struggle in difficult circumstances, and
contemplate selling up and moving somewhere smaller and more
manageable. Revelation comes to the husband, the inevitable 'something
in the City', in the penultimate chapter:

No, damnit, he thought, let's hold on a little longer and see if things
improve. And it suddenly struck him as preposterous how dependent
he and his class had been on the anonymous caps and aprons who
lived out of sight and worked the strings. All his life he had expected
to find doors opened if he rang, to wake up to the soft rattle of
curtain rings being drawn back, to find the fires bright and the coffee
smoking hot every morning as though household spirits had been
working while he slept. And now the strings had been dropped, they
all lay helpless as abandoned marionettes with nobody to twitch
them.

There was no such mellowness in Angela Thirkell's *Private Enterprise*
(1947), explicitly set in 1946, in this case among the minor gentry of
'Barsetshire'. Dissatisfaction with the present state of affairs ran

through the whole novel, but it was bread rationing that really got Thirkell going:

> In addition to pages in the ration book called 'Do Not Fill In Anything In This Space', and 'Points' and 'Personal Points', and 'Do Not Write On This Counterfoil Unless Instructed', and large capital T's and K's and little things called Panels whose use nobody knew, and a thing called Grid General which meant absolutely nothing at all, the harrassed and overworked housewife was now faced with large capital L's and M's and small capital G's, each of which, so she gathered from the bleating of the wireless if she had time to listen, or the Sunday paper which she hadn't time to read, meant so many B.U.s. And what B.U.s were, nobody knew or cared, except that B seemed an eminently suitable adjective for whatever they were ...

All in all, Thirkell shrilled on, there was after a year of so-called peace 'a great increase of boredom and crossness, which made people wonder what use it had been to stand alone against the Powers of Darkness if the reward was to be increasing discomfort and a vast army of half-baked bureaucrats stifling all freedom and ease, while some of the higher clergy preached on Mr Noël Coward's text of 'Don't let's be beastly to the Germans'', only they meant it and he didn't'. Tellingly, Thirkell's hatred of what she saw as the destruction of old England struck a deep chord, and in the immediate post-war years her Barsetshire sequence of novels (begun in the 1930s) sold prodigiously. 'A clever though reliably conventional school friend rebuked me for never having heard of Angela Thirkell,' the future novelist David Pryce-Jones would recall of this time. '"At home we think she's the best living author. Everyone reads her." Home was in Camberley.'[22]

Yet even a Labour-supporting, mass-circulation paper like the *Sunday Pictorial*, in effect the Sunday version of the *Daily Mirror*, conceded that things were pretty grim when in July 1946 it launched its panel of '100 Families to speak for Britain' and give free rein to their many problems. 'I can't get shoes for my kiddies,' complained Eileen Lewis, a printer's wife of 246 Watford Road, Croxley Green. 'A couple of weeks ago I spent all day trying to buy two pairs of shoes. I must have called at twenty shops.' Generally the women volunteers on the panel complained about food rations, while the men (more than a third of whom smoked 100 or more cigarettes a week) were especially put out by being unable to buy a new suit. The paper, though, had no doubt about the headline story: '43 Families Out Of 100 Are Wanting A New Home'. And it was the continuing housing shortage that precipitated the third key episode that summer: the squatting movement.

It began with the mass occupation of disused service camps – eventually involving as many as 40,000 people in more than a thousand camps – but really attracted attention when families, either homeless or living in appalling lodgings, started occupying empty hotels and mansion blocks in central London, most notably the seven-storey Duchess of Bedford House just off Kensington High Street. Eventually, by late September, eviction and a certain amount of rehousing had taken place. Although they had been helped by the organisational skills of members of the Communist Party, there is no evidence that the bulk of the squatters in Kensington, and probably elsewhere, had any political motives other than wanting somewhere decent to live. An observer, Diana Murray Hill, asked one squatter what sort of house she would prefer if given the choice. 'A prefab,' she replied. 'They look so neat and you can keep them nice. With a garden in front and your own bath. Then you could have the key to your own door and come in and go out as you liked.'

Arguably, though, the real significance of the episode was not the additional spotlight it put on the housing question, with its accompanying embarrassment to the government, but rather the distinctly mixed response of the public at large – partly in the context of most of the press vigorously insisting that, whatever the human predicament of the squatters, such flagrant breaking of the law was liable to open 'the floodgates of anarchy' (as W. J. Brown put it in the *Evening Standard*). On the day the Duchess of Bedford squatters departed, Murray Hill listened to a young woman, apparently employed as a domestic at a neighbouring block of luxury flats, chatting with a middle-aged friend:

Well, really, how anyone has the face to behave in such a silly way beats me!
     Ridiculous, isn't it!

I wouldn't do a thing like that; not unless the Government told me to!

Well, I mean, just look at the Types!

Yes, it's only types like that'd do a thing like that. Some lovely kiddies though.

Poor little souls, fancy bringing your kids along to a place where there's no food! No electricity or anything! Poor little souls must be starving!

It's ridiculous! Why, these flats aren't fit to live in – they're in an awful state! They've got to have a lot done to them before they're fit to live in.

It's not as though doing a thing like this helps them at all, it only makes things worse in the end . . .

That's right. They should learn to be *patient* and *wait*.[23]

Being patient, waiting your turn, behaving with restraint, respecting the law: even in the difficult, disturbed conditions immediately following six years of war, these remained formidable codes to break. The squatters were still in situ when on 16 September the Wilfred Pickles quiz show *Have a Go!* was broadcast nationally for the first time, radio's first real vehicle for ordinary working-class voices to be heard. Ten days later, the new series of *ITMA* began, soon introducing an all too expressive character, Mona Lott ('it's being so cheerful as keeps me going'), while on 7 October there was the debut of *Woman's Hour*, scheduled for 2.00 on the grounds that that was when women were doing the washing-up and thus had plenty of time to listen. For almost its first three months it was presented by a man, the journalist Alan Ivimey, and the opening of the edition on 7 November gives a flavour of its tone and contents:

Ivimey: Good afternoon. I have three ladies round the table to keep me in order today – Edith Saunders, who has been to a fascinating exhibition of Second Empire Styles at a big West End store –
Saunders: Good afternoon.
Ivimey: Marion Cutler, who's been looking into the working of that splendid service to housewives and mothers begun during the war, the Home Help scheme –

Cutler: Good afternoon.

Ivimey: And Marguerite Patten, who wants to save some of those tea-time tragedies when the lovely cake you've baked comes out of the oven with a hole in the middle instead of a nice brown bulge . . .

Four days later, the *Daily Mirror* condemned the programme as 'uninteresting, waste of time, full of old ideas', but the very next day Judy Haines was more charitable: 'Washing already damp and ironing quickly done. "Woman's Hour" does improve.' Soon afterwards, 61 members of the BBC's London Listening Panel attended meetings at the Aeolian Hall and were asked to evaluate extracts by different football commentators. Among them was one Wolstenholme, presumably Kenneth, but he fared poorly, with negative ratings for 'skill in giving a picture of play' and 'knowledgeability of soccer'.[24]

A new arrival this autumn was Franklin Birkinshaw (the future Fay Weldon), whose voyage from New Zealand ended as both dawn and her 15th birthday broke. 'Was this my mother's promised land?' she asked herself:

> Where were the green fields, rippling brooks and church towers? Could this be the land of Strawberry Fair and sweet nightingales? Here was a grey harbour and a grey hillside, shrouded in a kind of murky, badly woven cloth, which as the day grew lighter proved to be a mass of tiny, dirty houses pressed up against one another, with holes gaping where bombs had fallen, as ragged as holes in the heels of lisle stockings. I could not believe that people actually chose to live like this.
>
> 'It's just Tilbury,' my mother said. 'It's always like this.'
>
> Just Tilbury? The greyness was so vast, as far as the eye could reach.

About this time, Mass-Observation's Tom Harrisson returned from a lengthy spell in Borneo and was struck by 'the lack of dynamic enthusiasms, the apathetic mood of the moment, the decline in laughter'. There were moments of uplift – the Britain Can Make It (cruelly dubbed 'Britain Can't Have It') exhibition of industrial design at the V&A attracted one and a half million visitors, the 300,000 waiting list for private telephones started to come down ('I only want a footman and a large income to complete the picture,' observed a delighted Vere

Hodgson after getting hers), and the first British-made, American-style nylon stockings went on sale, albeit in tantalisingly small quantities. But overall Florence Speed's experience, lunching one Thursday with her sister at Fleming's in Oxford Street, was about par for the course. The fish, supposed to be plaice, was 'a horrible piece of fin' and the price of 2s 6d was exorbitant; altogether, she reflected, 'old Mr Fleming who took pride in quality & service must turn in his grave at the deterioration.'

It was also by December 1946 getting ominously chilly. 'Mr Thomson in particular is "blue" – says he is too cold to sleep altho' he has four blankets, an eiderdown, a travelling-rug and a great-coat on his bed,' Gladys Langford in her north London hotel was writing by the 8th of a fellow-resident. 'He has been buying socks at 3/6 per pair at WOOLWORTH'S!! Not the kind of place you expect the director of a big firm to use as a shopping centre.' It was not a great time to be having one's first baby. 'Sick,' scribbled an understandably frazzled Judy Haines in St Margaret's Hospital, Epping, on the 19th, two days before the birth. 'Had a bad night with Sister Hilton nagging me the whole time. I had pains every few minutes and she said I was all right till *she* came on. She told me to forget myself and think of babe and termed me neurotic. Said I was disturbing the patients who had *had* their babies.'[25]

***

Another rather cheerless Christmas was approaching. 'Prefab houses in Lottman Road have already hung up their Christmas decorations (paper chains, etc),' sniffed Speed in Brixton as early as 5 December. 'Anything less gala in appearance than the houses themselves couldn't be imagined.' Three days later, Henry St John in Bristol went to Sunday evensong, not a habitual occurrence, and found he was one of only 16 people in the congregation, that church's lowest figure in its 90 years of existence. 'Are we a pagan country?' asked James Lansdale Hodson on the 13th. 'Few of my friends go to church. I read in the report of an Archbishop's Committee on the Use of Modern Agencies for Evangelistic Propaganda that 90 per cent of our people seldom or never attend church. The church each week has five million attendances; the cinemas have 40 million.'

About this time, Mass-Observation conducted a survey of 500 residents of a semi-suburban London borough, 'Metrop', most probably Fulham; three-fifths of the sample did not belong to any sort of organisation, and predictably their favourite unorganised activities were the cinema and pub. The investigation, published as *Puzzled People*, found that two-thirds of men and four-fifths of women believed, 'or believed more or less', in the existence of a God. 'Yes, I think there is a God,' said a 20-year-old girl, 'but He seems a bit preoccupied at the moment.' Only 61 per cent of those believing in God also believed in the divinity of Christ; paradoxically, 25 per cent of those *not* believing in God *did* believe in the divinity of Christ. Only one person in 10 in Metrop went to church 'fairly regularly', and congregations had roughly three women to one man, with the women being mainly old and mainly educated. The survey threw up 'frequent' criticism of institutional religion and those who practised it, with double standards a favourite target:

> A lot of bloody hypocrisy, if you ask me. Go to church and then tear your neighbour's character to tatters, that's all it is. There's worse people goes to church than stays at home, I can tell you that.
>
> Going off to church on Sundays and bowing and scraping to others that does the same.
>
> Oh, the parsons and the churchgoing and all the setting yourself up to be better than ordinary folk.

But when asked their attitude towards religion as such, most people were tolerant enough, if hardly enthusiastic. As two women and a man replied:

> I dunno, I've not got any attitude, because I've not got any interest.
>
> It's all right for them as has time and inclination.
>
> Doesn't touch me much – it's all right for women, especially when they're getting on a bit – but I don't think I need it just yet, thanks.

A 40-year-old man captured the prevailing view – low-level tolerance of what was essentially an irrelevance – exactly: 'I think it's all right in a way, provided it's not overdone.'[26]

Ferdynand Zweig may or may not have visited Metrop, but between August 1946 and February 1947 he immersed himself in London's working-class districts and interviewed some 350 working men – interviews that this Polish-born economist (before the war a professor at Cracow University) conducted in pubs, cafés, parks, dog-racing stadiums or wherever he could get his subjects to talk freely. The inquiry began as a study of spending habits and poverty but rapidly broadened into a portrait of the English working class, that flesh-and-blood fodder for so many ambitious post-war plans. 'A working man is a great realist,' Zweig found in his eventual book:

> He sees life as it is – as a constant struggle, with its ups and downs. He has no illusions about life. He is little influenced by books or literature, and is more genuine and natural than people coming from other classes.
>
> If you ask working men about their views on life, in a large majority of cases you will get the invariable answer: 'Life is what you make it.' This English proverb is ingrained in every working man's brain. It is astonishing how many times they express this as their philosophy of life.
>
> The same meaning is conveyed by answers like this: 'I take life as it comes,' or 'I try to make the best of it' . . .
>
> The other view which is most common is to regard life as flux, and reality as a system of change. What is today is not decisive, and might change tomorrow. Tomorrow the lucky hour might strike or the conditions might improve.
>
> But the worker does not think about the future in the way of making provisions for it or worrying about what will happen next.

Zweig also found 'no class hatred or envy or jealousy'; an attitude to money defined in terms of 'beer, smokes and food'; and a far greater interest in sport than politics. 'What the working man dislikes most is preaching, moralising and edification,' he discovered. 'He has "no time for that", as he would say.'

The book includes a rich array of case histories. There is the blacksmith in a transport-maintenance shop whose wife is still suffering mentally from the Blitz and who knows, despite working incredibly long hours, that 'he has a bad time in front of him and needs all his will-power to get through'; the small-time decorator, divorced and living alone in a furnished suburban room, who goes each evening to the pub ('drinking six or seven pints') for want of anywhere else, chain-smokes and 'has no set purpose in life – he just drifts along'; the Irish building labourer who 'dislikes responsibility' and has stayed unmarried, 'goes in for football pools and lays out 5s or 7s 6d a week but has never won anything', and is happiest playing darts in the pub; the paper-picker-up in one of London's public parks who is paid so little that he tells Zweig frankly, 'I wish I were dead, because I have nothing to live for – I have no recreation, and can't even afford a glass of beer – you have no friends if you have no money'; the 'under-nourished' sandwich-board man who makes 'half an ounce of tobacco for cigarettes last him about four days'; the road-sweeper who has only been on holiday once in his life and insists, 'If a working man can't have a smoke and a drink, he might as well be dead'; the Red Line bus conductor who rolls his own cigarettes, who is fond of gardening and whose main complaint is that since the war 'the speed of the buses is greater, with greater stress on the body, so that you require more rest'; and so on.

Altogether, the seven months of intensive fieldwork proved (as he explained in his introduction) a transforming, deeply educative experience for Zweig. It was a lesson that he for one would try not to forget:

> I approached the inquiry in the spirit of the traditional economist who knows everything about everything, who has neatly classified all things and put them into separate pigeon-holes. But I came to realise how little is really known about life itself. We can only catch a glimpse from time to time of real life with its constant changes, unexpected turns, enormous variety and richness, but how often do we content ourselves with outworn models, textbook patterns and artifice clumsily put together for certain analytical purposes which are taken as real. The renovation of economics and sociology can come only from the source of all being – i.e. from minute, conscientious and truthful observation of real life.[27]

Constructively Revolutionary

'Are you still a socialist?' the historian Raymond Carr asked his friend Iris Murdoch the first time they dined together after the war. She turned on him savagely: 'Yes. Aren't you?' That brusque Oxford exchange probably postdated the Fabian Society's away-weekend in September 1945 in the city of dreaming spires. A notable line-up assembled to discuss 'The Psychological and Sociological Problems of Modern Socialism', and presciently the most prestigious think-tank of the newly elected Labour Party was at least as much concerned with exploring how society at large might become 'socialist' as it was with analysing 'socialism' itself. Unlike their party leaders, most of the speakers did not assume that party and people were automatically in harmony.

The psychiatrist John Bowlby set the tone. 'In our enthusiasm for achieving long-sought social aims,' he argued, 'we should not overlook the private concerns of the masses, their predilections in sport or entertainments, their desire to have a home or garden of their own in which they can do what they like and which they do not frequently have to move, their preference in seaside resorts or Sunday newspapers.' Given the undeniable fact of these 'private goals', each of which had not only 'the attraction of being immediately and simply achieved' but also 'the sanction of tradition behind them', Bowlby asked how it would be possible to ensure 'the understanding and acceptance of the need for the inevitable controls required for the attainment of group goals such as, for instance, full employment, a maximising of production by reorganisation and increase of machinery, or a maximising of personal efficiency through longer and more arduous education and other social measures'. His solution was a mixture of democracy and psychology: 'The hope for the future lies in a far more profound understanding of the nature of the emotional forces involved and the development of scientific social techniques for modifying them.' In response, Britain's most venerated ethical socialist, R. H. Tawney, was relatively sanguine about the possibility of subsuming the private and pursuing group goals – 'the common people had enormous resources of initiative and ability that were hardly used at all' – but Bowlby's friend Evan Durbin, leading Labour thinker and now an MP, was deeply sceptical. 'People were far more wicked, i.e. mentally ill, than was commonly supposed,' he insisted, adding that 'as a whole we were all very sick and very stupid'. As for a solution, 'selective breeding was probably the answer'.

This was all too much for Frank Pakenham, the future Lord Longford: 'He failed to understand how virtue was to be promoted by psychologists, who, great as their therapeutic services had been, had as yet given little help in political matters. The conception of wickedness was very important and must be retained; our goal should be a race of *good* people.' Another rising star, Michael Young, principal author of Labour's victorious manifesto, agreed that he had not 'obtained much direct guidance from the psychologists'. Instead, 'his mental picture of the future was one of more planning at the top and more democracy at the bottom', and he explained what he meant by the latter:

As the result of the election, the idea of a ten-year plan had been accepted, but was not really understood by the bulk of people; the work of carrying it out must be publicised and dramatised, and progress must be clearly shown – even symbolic progress. It was dangerous to wait and hope for the best. Herein individual members of the Party must themselves get going and assist the process. He envisaged a whole host of local Advisory Committees in all subjects connected with the social programme of the new Government, for running health centres, for example; and, if the result of setting them up was to raise the minority of the population which actually took part in the work of government by 100% – from 5% to 10% of the total – it would be a great democratic step forward.

In the conference's final session, a characteristic contribution came from one of Labour's acknowledged intellectual giants, G.D.H. Cole. He 'did not agree with Mr Durbin that most people were either wicked or stupid'. Furthermore, he 'disliked the sharp separation which had been made by some speakers between leaders and led'. And as for what the aim should be, he posited a society in which 'a large proportion would participate in leadership in some field' – a fine aspiration which clearly not everyone present thought plausible.[1]

Different people, different visions. For a couple of particularly articulate workers, both of them miners, contrasting political futures were soon unfolding. 'What strange patient enduring brutes men are!' Sid Chaplin wrote in February 1946 to his friend John Bate. 'You can shepherd them to your will, but in their secret way they know and wait. And they are really brilliant at times, astonishingly awkward, but mostly devilishly stupid.' Chaplin, born in 1916 the son of a Durham pitman, had himself been in the mines since the age of 15, first as a blacksmith and then as an underground mechanic; he was now reflecting on his recent work ('taking in contributions, negotiating about ½ pensions and hunting out details of compensation') for the Durham Colliery Mechanics' Association. 'You get rid of all fancy illusions and ideals,' he went on. 'No, Jean Jacques R., man is not everywhere born free, he is born in harness, and you get so close in this work that you can see his nose twitch, the saliva dribble as he strains for the carrot that is always just beyond reach of his champing jaws.' Chaplin was also (though not for much longer) a Methodist lay preacher, and four months later he wrote again to Bate: 'I believe in God and I believe in human beings. I believe that human beings can make socialism work, eventually, as they have made other forms of society. But socialism as a panacea I take with a pinch of salt.' *The Leaping Lad*, Chaplin's first collection of stories, appeared in December 1946 and won warm reviews in the national press for its sympathetic, realistic, unforced depiction of life on the South-West Durham coalfield. 'Ferryhill Miner as Story Teller' was the local paper's front-page headline, and it quoted appreciatively from one of the stories, 'Big Little Hab': 'He lived close to all living and growing things. He was the most fascinating of companions although he was the most inarticulate of men.'[2] For Chaplin himself, who would never dream of voting anything other than Labour but no longer believed in a paradise on earth, the book's success stimulated him to try to become a full-time writer.

The other miner, Lawrence Daly, did believe in a heaven on earth – Soviet-style. He was born in 1924, the eldest of seven children of a miner who was an early member of the Communist Party of Great Britain. With his father being blacklisted by the coal owners and finding work hard to get, he had a tough Scottish upbringing before leaving school at 14 and going down the pit at Glencraig in Fife. Soon afterwards, abandoning his Roman Catholic faith, he joined the Young Communist League, and after two years the CP itself. 'The Communists were to the forefront in seeking to improve the low wages and terrible working conditions in the coal mine,' he recalled, 'and also in seeking to overcome the appalling social conditions in which we lived.' Daly was also through his teens a vigorous autodidact, taking correspondence courses (through the National Council of Labour Colleges) in economics, trade unionism, English and social history. Determined to expand his horizons, in November 1945 he attended the World Youth Conference in London, representing Young Miners of Great Britain; two months later, he was one of a British party (comprising parliamentary and non-parliamentary delegates) that visited Russia for several weeks. From Leningrad he wrote home describing the ballet at the Kirov Hall and its appreciative audience: 'It is only one of the many incidents I have seen which make an absolute mockery of the phrase "menace to Western civilisation". Here culture flourishes in its highest & finest form because it is used to elevate the whole people to the highest possible physical and moral plane.' Back at Glencraig, Daly became a National Union of Mineworkers (NUM) part-time lodge official and an increasingly active, committed member of the CP. Early in 1947, an episode involving a fellow-miner led to Daly being strongly criticised by some party members. Typically, in a long letter to the local area committee, he came out fighting: 'I have been taught by the C.P. to study *all* the factors in a situation taken together & in their movement. I knew *all* the local & personal circumstances – far better than Comrade McArthur did – & I believe that when the comrades consider these circumstances, as I have stated them, they will agree that my action was consistently Marxist.' Daly's mother may have once used her husband's copy of *Das Kapital* to kindle the fire, but the old man, who in letters to young Lawrence signed himself 'Comrade Pop', surely approved.[3]

In the country at large, there was still a considerable amount of understandable pro-Russia sentiment by the end of the war, and although in the 1945 election only two Communist MPs were elected (one of them in Fife), the British Communist Party's membership had tripled during the war to about 50,000 (including Iris Murdoch and Kingsley Amis). As for attitudes to Britain's other main wartime ally, the picture was distinctly mixed. There was an element of gratitude, certainly, and many personal entanglements, together with a largely frustrated longing for American material goods, but at the same time resentment of a newly risen superpower that seemed unpleasantly inclined to throw its weight around. 'Personally I'm sick of the sight of Yanks over here and will be mighty glad to see the back of them' was how Anthony Heap put it in September 1945.

Among the political class, on both right and left, these feelings were intensified by first the abrupt end of Lend-Lease and then the harsh terms, almost certainly reflecting distaste for the Labour government's nationalisation programme, of the proposed $3.75 billion American Loan. 'What is your alternative?' asked the Chancellor, Hugh Dalton, in the critical Commons debate in December 1945; he invoked the unappetising prospect of a dollarless Britain in which 'all those hopes of better times, to follow in the wake of victory, would be dissipated in despair and disillusion'. In effect there was no alternative but to accept the loan. 'It was extraordinarily unreal, even absurd, and shabby,' reflected Malcolm Muggeridge after two long days in the press gallery. 'Speakers took up their position, but the only reality was the fear which none of them dared to express – the fear of the consequences if cigarettes and films and spam were not available from America.'

Nevertheless, the 23 Labour MPs who voted against included not only predictable left-wing figures like Barbara Castle and Michael Foot (soon afterwards warning that American capitalism was 'arrogant, self-confident, merciless and convinced of its capacity to dictate the destinies of the world') but that future epitome of pragmatism and moderation, James Callaghan, who condemned 'economic aggression by the United States'. Callaghan and the others may have had good grounds for complaint – the American insistence on immediate multilateral trade was to prove as economically damaging to Britain as the other stipulation, that Britain by 15 July 1947 must allow convertibility, ie of sterling into dollars – but the bottom line, fairly or unfairly, was that beggars could not be choosers. A strong sense of grievance would persist on the part of the British left. 'It is clear,' complained the *New Statesman* in November 1946, 'that on the matters that most affect Britain today, the United States is nearly as hostile to the aspirations of Socialist Britain as to the Soviet Union.'[4]

None of which cut much ice with Ernest Bevin – creator between the wars of the Transport and General Workers' Union (TGWU), a crucial figure during the war as Minister of Labour, and now Foreign Secretary. 'His heavy, bullish frame, his rough and uncouth English, his blunt style of speech all combined to make a very powerful performance' – was how W. J. Brown admiringly described him in February 1946; more recently, one historian has made the bold, counter-Churchillian claim that 'this bullying, capricious, sasquatch of a politician, was also the most effective democratic statesman that this country produced in the twentieth century'. For Bevin, who had distrusted both Communists and the Soviet Union for more than 20 years, the fundamental premise of British policy towards Moscow had to be one of suspicion, or at best watchfulness. As for the alternative idea, broadly favoured by the Labour left, that Britain might pursue an even-handed path between the Russian and American power blocs, neither Bevin nor Clement Attlee saw it as a realistic possibility. It has been argued that the real instigators of a post-1945 anti-Russian policy, even before the Russians had unambiguously shown aggressive intent, were the mandarins in the Foreign Office. But that is surely to underestimate Bevin's considerable capacity for independent thought as well as his unrivalled force of character.

He also was well aware that his combative attitude would strike a chord among working-class patriots – so much so that George Orwell noted in the spring of 1946 that 'the public opinion polls taken by the *News Chronicle* showed that Bevin's popularity went sensationally *up* after his battle with Vishinsky [head of the Soviet delegation at the first meeting of the United Nations General Assembly, held in London], and went up most of all among Labour Party supporters'. Moreover, Bevin's strongly anti-Russian stance, typified by his statement to the UN that 'the danger to the peace of the world has been the incessant propaganda from Moscow against the British Commonwealth as a means to attack the British', also played extraordinarily well with his natural political opponents, possibly to his consternation but possibly not. Within a week of VJ Day, making his first major parliamentary speech as Foreign Secretary, he was, according to 'Chips' Channon, 'cheered and applauded by our side' for 'almost a Tory speech, full of sense'. Mollie Panter-Downes observed in October 1945 that 'people who three months ago were horror-stricken at the thought of Ernest Bevin negotiating England's foreign policy are now admitting, handsomely and unexpectedly, that they admire him'. Even high society welcomed the rough-tongued West Countryman, with 'Jennifer' recording how at a West End function a few weeks later Lord and Lady Rothermere had been spotted 'chatting to Mr Ernest Bevin, who was in great form with a fund of amusing stories'.[5]

Where Bevin and the rest of the Attlee government were less realistic was in their deep reluctance to accept that post-war Britain could no longer afford to enjoy great-power status. Admittedly there were retreats in these years from Greece, India and Palestine – with the granting of Indian independence a genuinely major if flawed achievement – but the illusion stubbornly persisted that Britain's rightful and permanent place was at the top table. Perhaps if Bevin had been at No. 11 (as Attlee had originally intended before being dissuaded by the King), fighting the financial battle for overseas retrenchment in a more tough-minded way than Dalton managed, it might have been different – but probably not. After all, assumptions of British superiority, and the rightness of large swathes of the globe being coloured red, were deeply rooted in the national psyche – and continued to be inculcated. 'The Empire Day celebration at school was absurd,' Gladys Langford noted disapprovingly in May 1946: 'Watts [presumably the headmaster at the north London school where she taught] had had posters made bearing names of Dominions and children held these aloft reciting doggerel rhymes – presumably of his composing – relating to their flora, fauna, and products. A few hymns were sung – quite out of tune – and we were exhorted to tell tub-thumpers to pack their bags and go away – that Russians were unpleasant people and Arabs wicked slave-dealers.' In such a climate it seemed only proper that Britain should have its own independent nuclear deterrent – in short, a British bomb – an objective agreed by the government in January 1947. This very secret decision was 'not a response to an immediate military threat', Margaret Gowing would write in her definitive study, 'but rather something fundamentalist and almost instinctive – a feeling that Britain must possess so climacteric a weapon in order to deter an atomically armed enemy, a feeling that Britain as a great power must acquire all major new weapons . . .' Or as Bevin had put it a few months earlier at a meeting of the relevant Cabinet committee, 'We've got to have the bloody Union Jack on top of it.'[6]

What, in the generally difficult circumstances, was the economic way ahead? 'I find myself,' John Maynard Keynes privately reflected in April 1946, 'more and more relying for a solution of our problems on the invisible hand [ie of the market] which I tried to eject from economic thinking twenty years ago.' He died a few days later, but Keynesianism – seeing that invisible hand as at best a regrettable, to-be-circumscribed necessity – was poised to enter into its inheritance. First, though, there was the playing out of the new government's commitment, explicit in its election manifesto, to socialist planning.

For at least two years, the rhetoric that planning from the centre was the key to a prosperous economy rarely faltered. 'Planning as it is taking shape in this country under our eyes,' declared Herbert Morrison, the minister responsible for co-ordinating the planning machinery, in October 1946, 'is something new and constructively revolutionary which will be regarded in times to come as a contribution to civilization as vital and distinctly British as parliamentary democracy under the rule of law.' Not long afterwards, there appeared a new edition of Douglas Jay's *The Socialist Case*, first published in 1937. Jay himself was now an economic minister, and he not only reaffirmed the immortal maxim that 'the gentleman in Whitehall really does know better what is good for people than the people know themselves' but argued that, within the context of a properly planned, centrally run economy, 'economic freedom – the freedom to buy or sell, to employ or refrain from employing other people, to manufacture or not manufacture – is a secondary freedom, often approaching a luxury, which can and should be limited in a good cause'.[7]

Yet the reality was very different. 'Nebulous but exalted' was how one of the government's economic advisers, Alec Cairncross, would in retrospect caustically describe central economic planning during these immediate post-war years, while according to Kenneth Morgan, probably the most authoritative historian of the Attlee government, the 'attempt to plan private industry through the Treasury and the Board of Trade was half-hearted, indirect, and in many ways unsuccessful'. Indeed, he contended, 'so far as Labour had a strategy of planning it was largely to renew and continue the physical and financial controls of wartime, to help exports, to direct industry towards development areas, and to direct the use of vital raw materials' – in short, 'nothing that resembled the *dirigiste* economic strategy of de Gaulle's "popular front" government in France in 1945–6'. No output targets (even for industries identified as key), no way of fitting together manpower and cash forecasts, above all no powerful, autonomous institutional mechanism to give muscle to vague nostrums: the planning deficit was insurmountable.[8]

There were several main reasons for this anticlimactic outcome. The Treasury, not for the first or last time, gave a masterclass in institutional scepticism; there was much intellectual confusion as to what economic planning in peacetime actually meant and entailed, as epitomised by the muddle-headedness of Morrison, theoretically in charge of planning; and for more than two years there was the unwillingness of either the Ministry of Labour or the trade union leaders (for all their considerable goodwill towards the government) to countenance a wages policy, seen as a direct threat to the long, jealously guarded tradition of free collective bargaining – an unwillingness that more or less scuppered the chance of any meaningful manpower planning.

But ultimately, what really killed central economic planning was the lack of willpower on the part of government. In particular, the Labour Party's commitment to *democratic* socialism meant in practice an aversion to either new, unaccountable administrative mechanisms or any form of tripartism (ie government, management and labour) that seemed to threaten the sovereignty of the familiar parliamentary system. As for either the compulsory allocation of manpower or the planning of wages, neither was consistent with the traditional 'voluntarism' of the labour movement, with its deep distaste for outside interference, certainly in peacetime. 'If the maximum of persuasion and inducement fails to attract enough men and women into particular occupations to fulfil the plans laid down at the centre,' Durbin insisted as early as September 1945, 'then the plans must be changed.' Just over a year later, Sir Stafford Cripps at the Board of Trade was publicly accepting that no comprehensive plan could be carried out completely 'without compulsions of the most extreme kind, compulsions which democracy rightly refuses to accept' – which was why, he hardly needed to add, 'democratic planning is so very much more difficult than totalitarian planning'.[9]

Not that planning would have been easy, even if the iron political willpower had existed. Quite apart from institutional and labour difficulties, there would have been intense resistance on the part of privately owned industry, which was hostile enough anyway towards such government schemes as Development Councils, intended to stimulate co-operation between firms in specific sectors. Given, in the words of the economic historian Jim Tomlinson, 'the absence of a large cadre of potential industrial managers sympathetic to any form of socialism', it was hardly surprising that the charge was sounded so faintly. The 1940s may have been the least unpropitious decade in the twentieth century for peacetime economic planning, but that did not make it propitious.

Yet another reason why such planning failed to get off the ground after 1945 was the continuing existence of important physical controls exercised by the government, including controls on labour machinery, building and materials allocations. Such controls helped explain the almost complete absence of anything significant by way of investment planning, seen at this stage as superfluous. '"The City" in the middle of a socialist state is as anomalous as would be the Pope in Moscow,' Attlee had observed in 1931, just after (in instantly created Labour mythology anyway) a 'bankers' ramp' had destroyed Ramsay MacDonald's minority Labour government, but in practice, Attlee's own government did remarkably little to undermine the functions of the Square Mile and its inhabitants. In particular, the proposed National Investment Board, billed in the 1945 manifesto as the way to 'determine social priorities and promote better timing in private investment', was never established. Instead, in its place there was an almost wholly lame-duck, purely advisory National Investment Council, of nugatory achievement.

There was also, looked at from a socialist or planning point of view, the feeble, half-cock nationalisation of the Bank of England in 1946. The minister largely responsible was Dalton, who despite his acknowledged expertise on public finance had a sketchy grasp of the City and by the time he became Chancellor still did not understand the functions of the government broker, let alone the difference on the Stock Exchange between brokers and jobbers.[10] Certainly he did not strike a great deal: the Bank kept its essential institutional autonomy, quite unlike that of a government department; governors were to be appointed for a fixed term of years and could not be dismissed; and the Treasury failed to secure the power to issue directives to the clearing banks, effectively putting it at the mercy of the Bank's mediation. It is hard to resist the conclusion that the purpose of this particular piece of nationalisation was essentially symbolic – a way, in short, of appeasing the party's demons after the 1931 fiasco.

Of course, the taking into public ownership of a sizable chunk of the British economy was integral to the planning dream. The Bank of England was followed in fairly quick succession by Cable and Wireless, civil aviation, electricity, the coal mines, transport (including the railways and road haulage) and gas. Between them these newly nationalised industries employed some two million workers, with the majority either on the railways or in the mines. And, together with the postal and telephone services that were already in state ownership, these industries would for the next three decades form the core of the public part of the 'mixed economy'.

The principal architect-cum-draftsman of the 1946–9 wave of nationalisations was Herbert Morrison – usually depicted as the ultimate machine politician (especially in his capacity as leader of the London County Council through much of the 1930s) but also in fact a sincere believer in socialism's ethical dimension. 'Part of our work in politics and in industry must be to improve human nature,' he would tell Labour's conference in 1949, adding that 'we should set ourselves more than materialistic aims'. He believed, as did the party as a whole, that the nationalisation of several key industries would generate a wide range of economic, social and political gains. These included helping to co-ordinate production, distribution, investment and pricing policies within and across industries; encouraging economies of scale that in turn would provide opportunities for modernisation of plant and equipment; creating a virtuous circle of a more contented workforce, improved labour relations and rising productivity; and making it harder for the despised *rentier* class to prosper through unearned income (memories perhaps of Aunt Juley in E. M. Forster's *Howards End* and her tidy, predictable dividends from shares in Home Rails).

In May 1946, shortly after James Lansdale Hodson had noted, almost certainly accurately, that 'the nation isn't behind grandiose nationalisation to anything like the degree the Front Bench pretends', Morrison explained to the Commons, in the context of the Civil Aviation Bill, how it was to be done: 'Competent business people will be appointed to manage the undertaking, with a considerable degree of business freedom; on the other hand, it will be a public concern, appointed by public authority, and therefore, the spirit of the public interest must run right through the undertaking.'[11] Based to a large extent on the inter-war public corporation, this model for the post-war years was accepted with remarkably little debate – and with remarkably few realistic alternatives being put forward.

Over the years, though, there would be many criticisms of the way in which nationalisation took place. The financial and business guidelines were unduly restrictive, resulting in an unrealistic pricing policy and an inability to diversify into such areas as manufacturing; too many 'non-believers' were appointed to the nationalised boards, including not just businessmen but a motley crew of peers and retired generals; it was too easy for ministers to interfere or, according to some, too difficult; there was little coherent planning that related the newly nationalised industries to the economy as a whole; and so on. The criticism, though, that would resonate most through the years, at least from the left, was that a golden opportunity had been missed to institute a meaningful form of workers' control.

Yet at the time there were few who saw this as a runner. 'From my experience,' Cripps discouragingly told a Bristol audience in October 1946, 'there is not as yet a very large number of workers in Britain capable of taking over large enterprises.' He added that 'until there has been more experience by the workers of the managerial side of industry, I think it would be almost impossible to have worker-controlled industry in Britain, even if it were on the whole desirable.' Morrison did not disagree, and, more significantly, neither did the left-wing Aneurin Bevan. There is no evidence, moreover, that the workforces themselves, certainly in the form of their union leaders, wanted control or even a measure of control. When Emanuel (Manny) Shinwell, responsible for the nationalisation of the coal mines in his capacity as Minister of Fuel and Power, on two separate occasions in 1946 offered two seats on the National Coal Board (NCB) to the miners' leaders, he got nowhere. 'They refused, saying that administration was not their affair' was how he recalled the outcome. But it went down in the folklore of industrial relations that (in the subsequent words of the veteran industrial correspondent Geoffrey Goodman) 'the NUM President, Sir William Lowther, awkward and gruff as they used to chisel them in the Durham coalfield, told Shinwell to go to hell'.

Indeed, it is far from certain that the majority of workers in the relevant industries were especially keen on the prospect of nationalisation as such. Hodson, visiting South Yorkshire in May 1946, was told by a colliery managing director that his workers were about equally divided on the subject: 'Of those for it, 25 per cent are Socialists who accept it as they accept all the Government does, and the other 25 per cent believe it means more pay for less work. Of those against it, 25 per cent think these particular pits are well run and will be less efficient under the government and that they'll suffer; the other 25 per cent hate change of any sort.' It was a lack of enthusiasm that contrasted sharply – and ominously – with the scenes in Westminster a few months earlier, as old miners, now Labour MPs, shed tears as they passed through the 'aye' division-lobby to vote for the takeover of the coal mines and even burst into song. 'The strains of "The Red Flag" and "Cwm Rhondda" were heard clearly in the Chamber,' recalled one very socialist, already rather bored newish Labour MP, Tom Driberg, pre-war founder (as William Hickey in the *Daily Express*) of the modern gossip column.

Still, these were early days. Clause Four may have become the cornerstone of Labour's constitution back in 1918, but in his book-length tract *Labour's Plan for Plenty*, published in early 1947, Michael Young saw public ownership as only at the start of its journey:

No one in the Labour Party would claim that the last word has been said about nationalisation, or that the Party's views on the subject need not undergo further development... There is scope for variety in structure and for continuous experiment in methods of public administration. That is the way in which the organisation of nationalised industries can be steadily improved and the ground cleared for a rapid extension of public enterprise.[12]

6

Farewell Squalor

What really enthused the Labour Party and its supporters was welfare and the Attlee government's creation of the modern welfare state. Even *The Times*, daily organ of the British establishment, was strongly in favour of a national health service, seeing it as a desirable trade-off between state and citizen. 'The new social services will come to claim too large a share of the national income,' it warned in friendly rather than threatening fashion in May 1946, 'if the citizen, in pursuit of security, leisure, and comfort, fails to understand that what he expects of society can only be secured by the enterprise, diligence, and self-discipline with which he makes his personal contribution to the enlargement of the national product.'

The optimistic assumption that welfare and productivity would go hand in hand was not shared by the *Financial Times* and (presumably) its readers, still mainly in the City. 'Britain is piling up a large burden of social services in outlays on health, education, national insurance, family allowances and subsidies for housing and for food,' it had declared balefully a few weeks earlier:

> We are a nation of producers with an ever-increasing overhead of social charges ... With these extensive commitments, we shall have to meet the competition of the United States for the markets of the world, once the immediate famine for goods of all kinds has abated. When we have topped our potential wave of prosperity, how shall we deal with the challenge of reviving German and Japanese exporting industries, now temporarily out of commission?

Forty years later, the historian Correlli Barnett took up the charge, arguing forcibly in *The Audit of War* (1986) and then *The Lost Victory* (1995) that Britain during and after the war had made a profoundly mistaken choice by not giving economic reconstruction clear, unambiguous, unsentimental priority over social reconstruction. Instead, according to his pungent reading, the country fell victim to a hugely damaging and economically illiterate virus of elite-driven 'New Jerusalemism' – in his caustic words, 'the creation of that better, more equal Britain to be built when there were blue birds over / the white cliffs of Dover'.

Barnett's assessment of the existence of that mood, at least among the 'activators', is surely correct. Yet as others have pointed out, the notion that a long, arduous, ultimately victorious 'people's war' did not have to result in welfare improvements for that people, at least in the short term, is essentially ahistorical – flying in the face of the inescapable political realities of that time. If the Tories had been returned to office in 1945, they almost certainly would have created a welfare state not unrecognisably different from the one that Labour actually did create. Moreover, even within the strictly economic parameters of the debate, it is possible that Barnett has significantly overstated the cost of that welfare state. 'An austerity product of an age of austerity' is how one of his main adversaries, Jim Tomlinson, has crisply characterised it, showing in detail how, whatever may have happened later, the Attlee government could not be justly accused of extravagance in its welfare provisions. By 1950 the 10 per cent of British GDP that comprised public spending on social welfare may have been above the comparable proportions in Scandinavia, Italy and the Netherlands but was significantly below those of Belgium, Austria and West Germany. 'The welfare state was created,' Tomlinson gladly concedes, 'but in a context where it consumed a quite limited level of resources, and where it was continuously vulnerable to a resource allocation system which gave priority to exports and industry, and restrained both private and collective consumption.'[1]

Unsurprisingly, at a time when relatively few activators quarrelled with the assumption that a collectivised economy was not only more benign than a free-market economy but also more efficient, there was little debate about whether the *public* provision of health, education, housing and so on was the right road to be going down. Anyway, it seemed glaringly obvious to almost everyone that only if the state were actively involved as provider was there a chance of reasonable equality of outcome in the receipt of welfare services. Might the welfare state lead to a dependency culture? Barnett has written, in a notorious passage, of how the New Jerusalem 'dream' turned into 'a dank reality of a segregated, subliterate, unskilled, unhealthy and institutionalised proletariat hanging on the nipple of state maternalism'. To which one can retort that there were indeed many free lunches between 1945 and 1979 – but that it was not society's losers who ate most of them, let alone the best of them.

Instead, if there was a flaw at the heart of the classic social-democratic welfare state, it was the assumption that those operating it were by definition altruistic and trustworthy, together with the accompanying assumption that those receiving its benefits should be passive, patient and grateful. Or, as Julian Le Grand has put it, echoing the Scottish philosopher David Hume, it was a system designed to be 'operated by knights for the benefit of pawns', certainly not by 'knaves' on behalf of 'queens'.[2] That paternalist model may have seemed psychologically convincing in the 1940s – though even then it was questionable, given a realistic analysis of popular attitudes – but over the ensuing decades it would become ever less so.

'He is a big, heavy man, not very tall but thick set, with very powerful arms and shoulders, dark, round-headed, and beetle-browed with eyes, nose and chin all rather prominent and large, speaks with a lisp and a Welsh intonation' was how in August 1945 a Ministry of Health official, Enid Russell-Smith, described her new chief, Aneurin ('Nye') Bevan. Some months later, on a visit to Doncaster with him, she noted that 'here and there among the audience one sees that beatific expression on a worn old face which means that some pioneer in the Labour movement is seeing all Heaven in a Labour Minister in a Labour Government expounding a Socialist policy'.[3]

But if no one denied that Bevan was a fine, inspiring orator, capable also of considerable personal charm, what surprised many – friends as well as enemies – was the remarkably effective way in which he pushed through the creation of the National Health Service. Inevitably the scheme had many complexities, but at root there were seven key elements. Access to health care was to be free and universal; costs would be met from central taxation, not insurance; all hospitals – whether local authority or voluntary, cottage or teaching – were to be nationalised; the great majority of these hospitals would be run by regional hospital boards; the other two legs of a tripartite overall structure would be executive councils (overseeing GPs, dentists and opticians) and local authorities (still responsible for such miscellaneous activities as vaccinations, ambulances, community nursing, home help and immunisation programmes); NHS 'pay beds' would enable consultants to combine private practice with working for the NHS; and GPs would no longer be allowed to buy and sell practices but would not be put on a full-time salary basis, with the capitation (ie per patient head) element in their income making it easier for patients to move between doctors. There were plenty of dramas to come, but the NHS Bill that Bevan put forward in March 1946 more or less became actuality just over two years later.

Producing and implementing a broadly coherent, working scheme out of the medley of conflicting vested interests that he inherited was indisputably a virtuoso performance. There were, nevertheless, significant sacrifices involved. When Herbert Morrison, in a fierce Cabinet tussle, unsuccessfully fought for the continuing, even expanded, control of hospitals by local authorities, he was invoking not only his own faith and roots in municipal socialism but also, in the recent words of Rudolf Klein, 'a view of the world anchored in the values of localism: a view which stressed responsiveness rather than efficiency, differentiation rather than uniformity'. 'If we wish local government to thrive – as a school of political and democratic education as well as a method of administration – we must consider the general effect on local government of each particular proposal' was how Morrison himself put it. The regional boards, moreover, were appointed rather than elected and distinctly lacking in accountability. Apart from the almost statutory tame trade unionist, their social composition over the years would tend strongly to the upper-middle class; as for the NHS's foot soldiers, Bevan at the outset ruled out specific representation on either the regional boards or hospital management committees. 'If the nurses were to be consulted, why not also the hospital domestics? the radiotherapists? the physiotherapists? and so on,' he rather querulously asked the General Secretary of the Trades Union Congress (TUC), Sir Walter Citrine. Perhaps the most telling criticism of Bevan is that he succumbed to the consultants, not wanting to fight against them as well as the deeply suspicious GPs. Accordingly, the consultants had their fears of having to work for local authorities allayed; financially, had their mouths (as Bevan himself would later concede, or perhaps boast) 'stuffed with gold'; and generally saw their role exalted way above that of the GPs. 'The consultants ruled the new health service' would be the verdict 40 years later of David Widgery (East End GP and socialist intellectual), 'and they were bound to shape the health service, above all the new generations of doctors, in their own image.'

However, the biggest disappointment at the time, at least on the left, concerned Section 21 of Bevan's Act. 'It shall be the duty of every local health authority to provide, equip, and maintain to the satisfaction of the Ministry, premises which shall be called "Health Centres" . . .' – that was the promise. Long a socialist aspiration, these centres would not only house GPs, dentists, chemists and the local authority clinics but also receive visits from hospital consultants. Preventive and curative medicine would be equally emphasised, and in time all general practice would take place within them. Such aims inspired a young London doctor, Hugh Faulkner, demobilised in 1947. 'When I came into general practice and began to look at it,' he recalled, 'I found myself in conflict with the basic development of the general practice as basically a cottage industry, as very much a series of small businesses, which were quite openly in conflict with one another; the GPs that used to talk about the opposition, meaning the GP in the next road, and none of the GPs round here spoke to one another . . . It seemed to me that the isolation of doctors was perpetuating a very low level of medical care.' Faulkner, based in Kentish Town, responded by building up his own group practice, which focused on the social context of health and developed a team that included a health visitor, a midwife and a social worker.

But for a long time the larger trend ran the other way, with the British Medical Association (representing GPs) in particular dead set against health centres – so much so that after ten years of the NHS only ten had been built. For Rodney Lowe, a leading historian of the welfare state, the fate of health centres exemplified 'the balance of power enshrined in the new organisational structure', in that 'patients were expected to seek out professional care – doctors were not expected to make themselves readily available to patients'. Strikingly, there is no evidence of Bevan exercising any political will and trying to bring the apparently cherished concept to fruition; indeed, the probability is that, aware of the medical profession's widespread opposition, he deliberately sat on it. Virtually no health centres, municipal control eroded, the consultant as king – it is apposite to quote the bittersweet words of Sir Frederick Messer, a Labour MP and one of the minister's better-informed critics. 'I think his outstanding success,' Messer reflected after watching Bevan perform in the Commons, 'was the way he applied the anaesthetic to supporters on his own side, making them believe in things they had opposed almost all their lives.'[4]

The natural complement to health was social security, and it largely fell to another Welsh ex-miner, James Griffiths, to implement Sir William Beveridge's celebrated wartime proposals, though building on the existing Family Allowances Act that took practical effect from the August Bank Holiday in 1946. There were two key measures.

The 1946 National Insurance Act, fully operational from July 1948 (as was the NHS), sought to protect the population, on a basis of universality, from the financial perils of sickness, unemployment and old age. Everyone from 16 to 65 (60 in the case of women), 'from the barrow boy to the field marshal' as Griffiths later put it, would be required to make flat-rate contributions to the state in return for flat-rate benefits. Whereas Beveridge had recommended old-age pensions to be phased in over a 20-year period, Griffiths was adamant they should be paid in full from the start. 'The men and women who had already retired had experienced a tough life,' he later explained. 'In their youth they had been caught by the 1914 war, in middle age they had experienced the indignities of the depression, and in 1940 had stood firm as a rock in the nation's hour of trial. They deserved well of the nation and should not wait for twenty years.'

The purpose of the 1948 National Assistance Act, the work of Bevan as well as Griffiths, was essentially to provide a safety net for the poor – non-contributory and paid out of central taxation. It was a measure formed by the long shadow of the 1930s. 'Let us remember the queues outside the Poor Relief offices, the destitute people, badly clothed, badly shod, lining up with their prams,' the robust Liverpool MP Bessie Braddock reminded the Commons in November 1947. 'They used to make soup every day and take it down to the central area of the city in a van and distribute it, and a piece of bread, to those who were hungry and waiting for it at a cost of a farthing a bowl. I have always remembered since then the terrible tragedy and horror on the faces of those in the queue when the soup was finished and there was no more to be sold.' Assistance was to be means-tested, but the fact that the much loathed whole-household means test had been abolished during the war, with the focus instead being on the means-testing of individuals and couples, meant that much of the old stigma had gone. 'I have spent many years of my life in fighting the means test,' Bevan declared. 'Now we have practically ended it.'[5]

But again, as with health, there were serious flaws amid the undeniable huge positives. For one thing, the flat-rate contributory basis to the National Insurance Act, as originally enshrined by Beveridge, was deeply regressive, though mitigated by the taxpayer's contribution through the Exchequer. For another, the accompanying benefits proved in real terms to be almost a third below what even the parsimonious Beveridge had calculated as necessary for subsistence. Analysis differs as to why this was so, but Tomlinson has convincingly demonstrated that a characteristic Treasury mixture of meanness and pessimism played a key role. There was a significant knock-on effect of these inadequate benefits. Griffiths and his senior civil servants had confidently assumed that a properly functioning national insurance scheme must irresistibly lead to the need for national assistance more or less disappearing. But the reverse proved the case, and over the years the numbers applying for national assistance (or supplementary benefit, as it was later renamed) would grow like Topsy.

There was also, once again, the whole question of the local and the national. The historian David Vincent has convincingly argued that 'Beveridge's greatest achievement may have been not to convert the Tories to the welfare state, but Labour to state welfare', given that historically Labour had tended to look to local authorities rather than the state for the relief of poverty. The practical consequence, following the wholesale shift of attitudes to the state as a result of the war, was an 'extensive indifference to the dangers of a system in which every official from whom claimants received money was controlled from Whitehall' – a system involving 'the creation of a huge new bureaucracy answerable to its clients only through the cumbersome mechanism of ministerial responsibility'.[6] A sometimes Kafkaesque trial – endured mainly by those least able to complain – was only just beginning.

Education, however, was where the left would really scent betrayal, in retrospect if not always at the time. Red-haired, diminutive Ellen Wilkinson, Minister of Education until her death in February 1947, may have been its feisty Jarrow heroine in the 1930s, but now she saw her prime task as the implementation of the essentially centrist 1944 Butler Act. Against a difficult background of very tight Treasury purse strings, not helped by the rising birth rate since 1942, she presided over the introduction of free school milk; managed against serious Cabinet opposition to push through the raising of the school-leaving age to 15, taking effect from April 1947; and was also able to get a modest school-building programme under way, exemplified by the prefabricated work in Hertfordshire of the modernist, socially concerned architect Stirrat Johnson-Marshall – a classic activator figure, 'Socratic in manner of discussion and intolerant of formality in any guise'. Structurally, Wilkinson followed the explicit line of the wartime Norwood Report, and the tacit line of Butler, by not only accepting but positively encouraging tripartism in secondary schools – that is, an overall mix of grammar schools, secondary moderns and secondary technical schools, each in theory enjoying parity of esteem.

The new secondary moderns, to which the majority of children went, 'were to be modern in aim as well as name and in no sense dumping grounds', Wilkinson assured her party conference in June 1946. But less than a fortnight later, the headmaster of a secondary modern in Middlesex publicly conceded that, given that his school's intake largely comprised pupils of 'under-average intelligence' who as adults would 'fill the more lowly positions in life', his object was 'not to get his children through the examinations but to make their school life happy and, at the same time, provide a background of interests and a balanced view that will serve them after they leave school'. Michael Young, charting *Labour's Plan for Plenty* soon afterwards, did not in essence dispute this analysis: 'The majority of children will go to the modern secondary schools . . . Many of those will unfortunately have to work in routine or semi-routine occupations which do not give them full scope for the expression of their personalities. Consequently, the curriculum will be designed primarily to equip the children to make full and creative use of their leisure time and to look after their own homes with skill and imagination.' By the time Wilkinson died, to be replaced by the stolid, commonsensical George Tomlinson, it was becoming crystal clear that the grammar schools enjoyed vastly more prestige, significantly greater financial resources and a far more middle-class intake than the secondary moderns. Moreover, few of the most able out of the 75 per cent or so of children allocated at the age of 11 to secondary moderns were subsequently given the chance to transfer to grammars.

As for the third leg of tripartism, the secondary technical schools, they proved almost a complete non-starter, never educating more than a small minority of pupils. Although launched with high hopes – 'work, and training for work, must be given an enhanced social significance, and general and vocational education fused into a purposeful whole', an advocate trumpeted in the *Times Educational Supplement* in February 1946 – they seem to have fallen foul of a mixture of parsimony (it being appreciably more expensive to equip a school training up engineers or technologists than one concentrating on arts subjects and pure science) and Wilkinson's instinctive opposition to narrow vocationalism, believing that it limited expectations and thus life chances. These technical schools would eventually take their place in the Correlli Barnett cosmology as the great white hope that 'might have fostered a technological national culture in place of a literary one' but were 'simply never to be built'.[7] Put in these terms, it is not absurdly Hampstead to feel only modified grief.

There was an alternative to tripartism – and, in particular, the division at 11 into sheep and goats. The movement for 'multilateral' (ie comprehensive) schools went back to the 1920s and had gathered momentum during the war, especially through the National Association of Labour Teachers, which had persuaded successive Labour Party conferences to accept pro-comprehensive resolutions. They found no echo at the Ministry of Education, whose pamphlet 'The Nation's Schools', published on VE Day, not only upheld a sharp distinction between the traditional grammar and the new secondary moderns (the latter being for working-class children 'whose future employment will not demand any measure of technical skill or knowledge') but made a four-fold case against multilateral schools: they would necessarily be very large, in order to have a viable sixth form, and that was intrinsically a bad thing; in practice, selection would continue within them; it was generally best if a school had one specific aim or function; and anyway, alternative plans for the future had already been formed. 'It would be a mistake,' in short, 'to plunge too hastily on a large scale into a revolutionary change.' Seven months later, in December 1945, the ministry's Circular 73 insisted that '*it is inevitable* for the immediate purposes of planning and in the light of the existing layout of schools, for local education authorities at the outset to think in terms of the three types'.

At this point, Wilkinson was the minister, and although not without sympathy for the egalitarianism of multilaterals – which, she told the Commons in July 1946, would 'mix all the children together in the corporate life of one community' and 'avoid snobbish distinctions between schools of different grades' – what truly stirred her was the prospect, in the wake of the 1944 Butler Act, of a new generation of bright, self-motivated, self-improving working-class children going to the traditionally elite, middle-class grammar schools and using that experience as a platform for future advance and fulfilment. 'The top few pupils were intelligent and could mop up facts like blotting paper,' she once recalled of her own non-grammar education in Manchester, 'but we were made to wait for the rest of the huge classes . . . We wanted to stretch our minds but were merely a nuisance.' Or as she told her party conference in 1946, 'I was born into a working-class home and I had to fight my own way through to university.' Put another way, socialism to her – and indeed to most of her Cabinet colleagues – was at least as much about equality of opportunity, for those with the brains and ambition to grasp it, as it was about equality of outcome.

Significantly, there had been no commitment to multilaterals in the 1945 manifesto. Anyway, the prevailing educational mood, not only in the ministry, was that immediate, on-the-ground reconstruction – finding enough teachers, finding enough decent buildings – mattered at this stage far more than the pursuit of alternative structures. Some local authorities (including by the spring of 1947 Coventry, Swansea and London) did submit plans with a greater or lesser multilateral component, but the majority, including Labour-controlled ones, were content to stick to tripartism. After all, it bore a reassuring similarity to the pre-war pattern of grammar schools, senior elementary schools and junior technical schools; neither educationalists nor laymen doubted the accuracy of intelligence testing; and the understandable bogey of hugeness had been instilled ever since the London County Council (LCC) in 1944 had first put forward 'a system of Comprehensive High Schools', each to have at least 2,000 children.[8] Nevertheless, a corrosive, long-running national (England and Wales) saga was under way.

There was another great educational might-have-been in these years. Labour was in with a thumping majority, a bewildered upper class had not yet had time to regroup, and there would never be a more plausible moment for seeking to abolish what was arguably the single most important source of political, social and economic privilege – the public schools. 'Attlee asked me what I thought of Geoffrey de Freitas who was there to be vetted as a candidate for Parliamentary Private Secretary,' Jock Colville (the Prime Minister's private secretary) recalled of a visit to Chequers the weekend after VJ Day. 'Charming, I said, and highly intelligent. "Yes," replied Attlee, "and what is more he was at Haileybury, my old school."' The following June, the PM returned to Haileybury to offer personal reassurance. 'He saw no reason for thinking that the public schools would disappear,' ran the report of his speech. 'He thought the great traditions would carry on, and they might even be extended.' A fortnight earlier, Wilkinson had sought to persuade her party's delegates that the right approach to the public-school question was 'to make the schools provided by the State so good and so varied that it will seem quite absurd to send children to these schools'. A noble aspiration, and undoubtedly there also existed in the Labour Party a widespread feeling that not allowing schools to exist outside the state system would be incompatible with prevailing notions of liberty; but it *might* have been a different story if there had been another figure at No. 10 than the deeply middle-class (son of a City solicitor), deeply respectable Attlee.

Nearly as much of a non-starter, moreover, was the Fleming Report's 1944 recommendation that public schools should voluntarily make available a quarter of their places to children from the state system. In practice there was a total lack of enthusiasm all round, whether on the part of the public schools themselves (once their fee-paying places started to fill up, as they quickly did), the Ministry of Education (which resisted the idea of state bursaries), the local education authorities (which had no wish to see their brightest pupils being creamed off) and working-class parents (naturally reluctant to have their children taken away to such an alien milieu). A 1946 play, *The Guinea Pig*, was soon afterwards turned into a successful film by Roy and John Boulting, starring the young Richard Attenborough as a 14-year-old cockney, Jack Read, sent to an ancient foundation. After early, heartrending scenes of bullying and unhappiness, the boy gradually adjusts and loses his accent, eventually winning a scholarship to Cambridge. 'Gosh sir, jolly good show' is his grateful response to the news.[9] The film portrays a triumph of social mobility, but in reality the Fleming scheme never got off the ground, and private and state education continued to co-exist as two utterly separate systems inhabiting utterly separate worlds.

The belief in 1945 that the public could match the private ran deep. Co-compiling that autumn a *Report on Luton* for the local council, Richard Titmuss ended the section on housing with a clarion call:

> There is evidence that the country is moving towards a wide acceptance of the principle that services provided by the people for themselves through the medium of central and local government, shall compare in standard with those provided by private enterprise. As it is with hospitals and clinics, so it should be with schools and houses. The council house should in the future provide the amenities, space and surroundings which hitherto have often been the monopoly of private building.

This was a vision fully shared by Bevan, perversely enough responsible for housing as well as health, two immensely challenging tasks. His unambiguous policy was severely to restrict private house-building and instead to pour as many resources as he could muster into new local-authority housing. Although there had been a significant growth of such housing between the wars, this policy marked the beginning of a fundamental and long-term step-change, so that by the end of the 1970s as much as a third of the national housing stock was in the hands of local authorities.

The most powerful historical critique of this strategy has come from Alison Ravetz. Noting that 'the weight placed on local councils as housing authorities – as developers, owners and managers – turned them, for several decades, into virtually unchallengeable landlords,' she particularly regrets Labour's lack of enthusiasm for such alternative housing agencies as housing associations, housing co-operatives and self-build societies. As a result, and aggravated by the lack of subsidy for private rented housing, the post-war British housing system had 'a distinctive, monolithic quality that set it apart from virtually all other European housing systems' – a system that 'befitted a centralised, collectivist, expertly advised and caring, but ultimately paternalistic, State'. To all of which one might add that there was also what now seems the glaring and obstinate refusal to admit that most people actually wanted to own their own homes. Yet was that true at the time? Tellingly, out of the *Sunday Pictorial*'s '100 Families' in July 1946, only 14 were reported as either owning or buying (ie from private landlords) 'the houses in which they lived'.[10] For most of the others, almost certainly, home ownership – in the middle of a serious national housing shortage – was simply not on the agenda.

At the heart of the new vision of public housing was quality as much as quantity. Typically, Bevan had no time for prefabs, not recognising their popularity and contemptuously dismissing them as 'rabbit hutches'. Instead, he wanted permanence and the highest standards possible, including lavatories upstairs and down as well as overall minimum room space increased from 750 to 900 square feet. 'We shall be judged for a year or two by the *number* of houses we build,' he declared. 'We shall be judged in ten years' time by the *type* of houses we build.'

Was Bevan's hope, as with Wilkinson in education, that if the quality was good enough in public housing, then there would be no demand for private? It is impossible to know, but certainly he placed much faith in mixing the classes together. 'You have colonies of low-income people, living in houses provided by the local authorities, and you have the higher income groups living in their own colonies,' he complained in October 1945. 'This is a wholly evil thing, from a civilised point of view . . . It is a monstrous infliction upon the essential psychological and biological one-ness of the community.' Subsequently, he invoked the ideal community as one where 'all the various income groups of the population are mixed' – an ideal that had once existed in some English villages, 'where the small cottages of the labourers were cheek by jowl with the butcher's shop, and where the doctor could reside benignly with his patients in the same street'.[11] What this might mean in practice, though, was another matter. Building council houses in districts dominated by homeowners? Persuading the doctor to live in a council house? The contrast with health, Bevan's other responsibility, was painfully stark. In that area there was every chance of persuading the middle classes to embrace a nationalised health system, knowing that the medical-cum-financial benefits more than outweighed the temporary discomfort of a socially mixed doctor's waiting room or even, if the worst came to the worst, hospital ward. A socially mixed 24/7 was, for all concerned, a very different prospect.

In the short, quantitative term, faced by a daunting set of circumstances (including severe economic constraints, fiercely competing priorities for building materials which were in short supply anyway, and the immediate need for at least a million homes), Bevan made a patchy start, leading directly to the squatters' movement in the summer of 1946. But he recovered sufficiently well to be able to announce by September 1948 that 750,000 new homes had been provided since the end of the war – a mixture of new permanent houses (almost half the total), temporary housing (including the despised prefabs), repaired housing and house conversions. However, a huge problem of unmet demand still remained. It was estimated that several million new homes would be required by the mid-1950s and that was even before the slum-clearance programmes, halted at the onset of war, were restarted.

A survey of Willesden, conducted in late 1946 and early 1947, found 61 per cent expressing dissatisfaction with their present housing (dominated in that inner London suburb by decaying terraced houses), with 'overcrowding' and 'lack of privacy' as the most frequent complaints, followed by 'inadequate amenities'. Moreover, 62 per cent (especially younger people) said that they would like to move from their present home in the next two or three years; of these, 72 per cent did not want to stay in Willesden, with a majority expressing a preference to live either in an outer suburb or outside London altogether. The makings, in other words, were already apparent of a great, essentially voluntary exodus – one already begun before the war – from the streets upon streets of substandard, nineteenth-century inner-city and inner-suburb speculative housing, most of it privately rented, that Bevan understandably viewed as the spur to a golden age of public housing.

The Willesdenites were also asked what form their ideal new housing would take; as usual, only a small minority (15 per cent) opted for the self-contained flat. But by this time the government had already introduced new subsidy scales for local authorities that in effect gave them a significant financial incentive to build blocks of flats of four storeys or more, as long as they had lifts. 'People would not consent to live in the clouds if land was available,' complained one Labour MP in March 1946, describing the measure as 'so much flat-doodle'; but it still went ahead. Woodberry Down estate in Stoke Newington and Churchill Gardens estate in Pimlico, each including blocks of at least eight storeys, were early responses: high enough in comparison with the standard four-storey LCC blocks of the 1930s but not yet skyscrapers. Elsewhere in London, at East Ham, the attitude in 1946 of the local council mirrored that of several other Labour authorities in bombed-out districts, with a simultaneous reluctance to accept either blocks of flats or a significantly reduced population. In the end, firmly told by its experts (the Chief Housing Officer and the Borough Engineer) that these two policies were mutually exclusive, the council did agree in principle to allow flats, though only for single people or childless couples.[12] Overall, the majority of new council housing in the 1940s was along well-established 'cottage' lines, with (outside London anyway) few blocks of flats being built.

For most architects, eager to get involved in rebuilding Britain, the economic circumstances were such that they had no alternative but to bide their time. Ernö Goldfinger, ultra-modernist and left-wing, was lucky, receiving a commission just after the war to convert a bomb-damaged Victorian warehouse in Farringdon into new premises for the Communist Party's newspaper, the *Daily Worker*. A fractious process ensued – the builders objecting strongly to taking orders from someone palpably not English born and bred – during which Goldfinger stuck to his modernist guns by removing most of the Victorian mouldings.

The end result won many architectural plaudits, but the journalists who had to work there every day soon identified two major flaws: the unpleasantly noisy main newsroom, built in a pioneering open-plan style, and the very low toilets, unrepentantly justified by Goldfinger on the grounds that the nearer one got to squatting Continental-fashion over elephant's feet, the more complete the bowel evacuation. 'The journalists,' according to his biographer, 'were not convinced.'

'"Everybody" is talking Dispersal, Satellite Towns, Green Belts, Location of Industry, etc,' Goldfinger's old sparring partner, Frederic Osborn, noted with satisfaction in September 1945. That indeed was the spirit of the age – a planning zeitgeist that looked with dismay not just on the rundown inner cities but also on all the proliferating Acacia Avenues and Chestnut Groves. 'The suburbs have generally developed as an unplanned growth,' complained Coventry's mayor, Councillor J. C. Lee Gordon, in August 1946. 'In order to develop a social sense it is very necessary to divide the suburbs into definite zones, each with its own identity, and each with a social centre, or focal point, at which group activities may be carried on which are wider than the activities of a small family group.' What Gordon envisaged, he explained to a local paper, was 'a neighbourhood unit' – the increasingly popular town-planning concept, imported from America, which ignored Dennis Chapman's inconvenient Middlesbrough findings and argued that community spirit would be fostered through the creation of zoned, residential-only neighbourhoods that each had its own school, church, community centre and so on.

Later that year, J. M. Richards, editor of the *Architectural Review*, was broad-minded enough to put in a word for the much-maligned existing suburbs, pointing out that for all 'the alleged deficiencies of suburban taste', there was no denying 'the appeal it holds for ninety out of a hundred Englishmen, an appeal which cannot be explained away as some strange instance of mass aberration'. But Richards's short book, *The Castles on the Ground* (1946), was, he would recall, 'scorned by my contemporaries as either an irrelevant eccentricity or a betrayal of the forward-looking ideals of the Modern Movement'. The notable exception was John Betjeman, who found in John Piper's accompanying illustrations of 'the fake half-timber, the leaded lights and bow windows of the Englishman's castle' what he called 'a new beauty – the beauty of the despised, patronised suburb, the open heart of the nation'.[13]

The time, though, was far from ripe for Metroland nostalgia. Another book, also published in December 1946, caught much better the prevailing mood: 'Let us close our eyes on the nineteenth-century degradation and squalor, and let us only look with unseeing eyes on the sordid excrescences of the first decade of this century, let us blind ourselves to the septic and ugly building wens and ribbons perpetrated and planted on us between the wars, but let us open our eyes and look brightly forward and onward to the new town, the new living . . . Peterlee.' *Farewell Squalor* was the work of C. W. Clarke, Easington Rural District Council's Surveyor. Clarke called for a large development of new, better housing for Durham's miners, to be named after their legendary former leader, Peter Lee. They certainly needed it, to judge by James Lansdale Hodson's account shortly before of visiting a pit village near Bishop Auckland:

> Three long streets on a slight rise stood at right angles. We drove up one and down another, going very slowly, for the streets are unpaved, with small knolls of hard earth and cinders and runnels caused by rain. Patches of grass grew boldly. The streets were almost an unbroken line of miserable brick hovels, each street about 400 yards in length, most horrible and dreary. Our coming brought a few unkempt women and ill-clad children to the doors. Two hefty young men eyed us sullenly. It was nearer to hell, I thought, than anything I had seen since Belsen.

'Yet it exists in 1946,' reflected Hodson, 'and hardly more than an hour's journey from Newcastle-on-Tyne.'[14]

Peterlee was one of 14 New Towns designated between 1946 and 1950. In line with the wartime *County of London Plan*, more than half were for Greater London – in order of designation, Stevenage, Crawley, Hemel Hempstead, Harlow, Hatfield, Welwyn, Basildon and Bracknell. The other six were Corby in Northamptonshire, Newton Aycliffe and Peterlee in the north-east, East Kilbride and Glenrothes in Scotland, and Cwmbran in Wales. Developed partly to relieve the housing shortage but also with explicit brave new world ambitions, they would become emblematic of the whole 1945 settlement.

The essential guiding spirit of these new towns followed on from Ebenezer Howard's garden-city movement: they were to be economically self-contained and socially balanced communities that in national terms would stimulate decentralisation from the overcrowded big cities. Reporting in 1946 to the new Minister of Town and Country Planning, Lewis Silkin, the Reith Committee (with Osborn a prominent member) placed particular stress on the need for a strong sense of community and highlighted the potential benefits of the neighbourhood unit – which indeed was the model explicitly used in 11 out of the first 14 new towns. As with his inter-war stewardship of the BBC, Lord Reith did not really embrace popular culture. He hoped that each new town would have 'a civic cinema', thereby counteracting the commercial cinemas with their 'limited cultural range and American productions'; he did not mention commercial dance halls; and he specifically repudiated greyhound racing: 'While there may be a demand, it would bring in its train consequences likely to be specially objectionable in a new town because displeasing to a large proportion of the residents.'

How were these fun factories to be run? The Reith Committee canvassed various possibilities, but the New Towns Act 1946 which quickly followed its report came down decisively for government-funded, government-appointed public corporations, in the event called development corporations, with no directly elected element. It was a fundamental breach of the Howardian vision, which had involved the bottom-up creation of what have been called 'self-governing local welfare states'. Not that this worried Silkin, whose much greater anxiety, he told the Commons in May 1946 in the course of moving his bill's second reading, was that 'the planning should be such that the different income groups living in the new towns will not be segregated':

No doubt they may enjoy common recreational facilities, and take part in amateur theatricals, or each play their part in a health centre or community centre. But when they leave to go home I do not want the better off people to go to the right, and the less well off to go to the left. I want them to ask each other, 'Are you going my way?' ... Our aim must be to combine in the new town the friendly spirit of the former slum with the vastly improved health conditions of the new estate, but it must be a broadened spirit, embracing all classes of society.

A final burst of eloquence, perhaps helping to produce the notably bipartisan spirit that characterised the passage of his bill, reached for the sunlit uplands: 'We may well produce in the new towns a new type of citizen, a healthy, self-respecting dignified person with a sense of beauty, culture and civic pride.'[15]

By this time Stevenage had already been publicly identified as the first new town, with its population of some 6,000 expected to increase tenfold. 'How do you feel about it?' a Mass-Observation investigator asked some of the indigenous residents. 'It's time this town was woken up,' replied a 45-year-old signwriter. A 30-year-old coachbuilder agreed: 'It's progress, and it's what we badly need here.' So, too, a 50-year-old housewife: 'I think it will be a benefit myself. If you've got a family, well, it's a good thing to know there'll be work for them.' Those expressing definite opposition included a 60-year-old car-park attendant. 'My great grandfather was here, and his father before him,' he explained. 'We belong here, and I shouldn't like to see the beauty taken away ... Have you seen the beauty of the place? That avenue of chestnuts up by the school and parish church? You should see it.'

A few weeks later, on 6 May, Silkin himself was in Stevenage, to address a packed, tumultuous meeting in the small town hall, with up to 3,000 locked outside listening to loudspeakers. 'I want to carry out in Stevenage a daring exercise in town planning,' he declared at one point. 'It is no good your jeering: it is going to be done.' Silkin argued that Stevenage was ideally placed to attract both people and light industry from overcrowded London; called on the existing residents to 'make some sacrifice' in order to 'provide for the happiness and welfare of some 50,000 men, women and children'; drew a picture of the new Stevenage recreating a village-like 'spirit of friendliness and neighbourliness, the sense of belonging to a large family, a community'; and once more insisted that there was no choice in the matter: 'The project will go forward, because it must go forward. It will do so more surely and more smoothly, and more successfully, with your help and co-operation. Stevenage will in a short time become world-famous. *(Laughter)* People from all over the world will come to Stevenage to see how we here in this country are building for the new way of life.' Amid cries of 'Gestapo!' and 'Dictator!', Silkin left the meeting and walked to his ministerial car, a 25 h.p.

Wolseley, only to find that some boys had deflated the tyres and put sand in the petrol tank.

Less than a fortnight later, a referendum was held: some 2,500 residents took part, with 52 per cent voting that they were 'entirely against the siting of a satellite town at Stevenage'. But it availed them little. Although considerable national publicity was garnered when Stevenage signs at the local railway station were temporarily replaced by Silkingrad ones, and although the High Court in February 1947 agreed with the Residents' Protection Association (mainly comprising the well-to-do) that Silkin had not properly considered the objections raised at the public inquiry the previous October, the government was not to be thwarted, with Silkin later in 1947 winning first at the Court of Appeal and then at the House of Lords. The juggernaut was rolling. Old Stevenage had been the setting for the house in *Howards End*; new Stevenage would, as an unsympathetic, non-connecting E. M. Forster now put it, 'fall out of a blue sky like a meteorite upon the ancient and delicate scenery of Hertfordshire'.[16]

Not surprisingly, given this sort of local opposition (apparent also in Crawley and elsewhere), it took several years to get the new towns up and running. Faced by an acute housing shortage, the LCC responded by expanding the programme of 'out-county' estates that it had started between the wars, notably in Becontree, St Helier and Downham, which by the end of the 1930s were three of the largest housing estates in the world. The LCC also between 1946 and 1949 built more than 31,000 dwellings (a mixture of unprepossessing but functional houses and low-rise flats) on new estates at Harold Hill, Aveley, South Oxhey, Borehamwood, Debden, St Paul's Cray and Hainault – all of them beyond the LCC's boundary and in several cases, as was often pointed out, in the green belt that it was wanting to protect. Harold Hill in Essex was the largest of the estates, but its near neighbour Debden, together with South Oxhey in Hertfordshire, would attract the most sociological attention. From the start, these out-county estates suffered, like their inter-war predecessors, from an image problem. Suddenly the new dwelling places for many thousands of working-class Londoners, entirely bereft of architectural distinction and often communal facilities such as churches and pubs, the estates were in effect, to quote the architectural historian Andrew Saint, 'lower-grade new towns without new town privileges'.[17] They were also the cause of considerable tension at the LCC. While the Valuer's Department under Cyril Walker got on with its job of achieving 'maximum output' in new housing, the Architect's Department (under Robert Matthew from 1947) was full of frustrated young graduate architects unable to implement their strongly modernist ideas about public housing. Not that this mattered much to the new residents of Harold Hill, Debden et al, happy enough to get on with their own lives with a roof over their head, an indoor lavatory, and hot and cold running water.

The new towns and out-county estates both reflected the widespread faith put in the 1940s on dispersal as the best way to relieve the familiar problems (overcrowding, congestion, poor health etc) of the modern industrial city. No city in Britain had worse problems – or a worse reputation – than Glasgow. 'It is a disgustingly ugly town, a huddle of dirty buildings trying to outdo one another and not succeeding,' Naomi Mitchison wrote in 1947. 'The population is as ugly as the buildings. Walk down the Gallowgate; notice how many children you see with obvious rickets, impetigo or heads close clipped for lice, see the wild, slippered sluts, not caring any more to look decent!'

Two competing visions were now set out for Glasgow's future. The first, the work of the City Engineer Robert Bruce, was essentially an urban one. The Bruce Plan advocated a radically new, high-speed road system, a geometrically planned city centre, the demolition of more than half the city's housing stock, and the decanting of the urban poor to developments on the city's periphery but within its boundaries. Ultimately, it was the vision of a Glasgow that would retain not only all its population but also its nineteenth-century heavy industrial base. By contrast, the Clyde Valley Regional Plan, appearing in interim form in 1946 and predominantly the work of the ubiquitous Sir Patrick Abercrombie, envisaged a depopulated, de-industrialised Glasgow, surrounded by a green belt and sending many of its ill-housed inhabitants to healthier, 'overspill' new towns beyond the city's boundaries. 'Whole districts are obsolescent and past the possibility of reconstruction to modern standards, alike for industry, commerce and housing,' Abercrombie would declare in his final report, published in 1949; all told, he expected that nearly half of Glasgow's 1.1 million population would move to outside the city.

This latter approach, seeing Glasgow as part of the region's problem rather than as part of its solution, naturally appalled Glasgow Corporation – above all its Housing Committee, which stood to lose many thousands of tenants as well as (through the green-belt provisions) much potential building land. It was as if Abercrombie was preparing to blow up one of the great municipal power bases. The gloom deepened when the government, attracted by the prospect of (in Miles Glendinning's words) 'a constellation of planned, Whitehall-controlled garden cities set within a Green Belt', plumped for Abercrombie, not Bruce.[18] The designation in 1947 of East Kilbride as Scotland's new town was an unmistakable signal of intent. Yet for the Corporation, and for all those who still believed in Glasgow as 'the Second City of the Empire', the game was far from over.

Overall, looking at town planning in the 1940s, it is easy to exaggerate the radicalism and modernism. For instance, in Portsmouth, where a redevelopment plan was accepted by the city council in February 1946, not only was the gutted Guildhall to remain the city's focal point, but the existing road pattern was to be kept, supplemented by a few new cross-routes. In Manchester, where a plan was formally unveiled in the first winter of peace, the City Surveyor and Engineer R. Nicholas accepted that some 100,000 of the city's slum dwellings needed to be pulled down but specifically repudiated the high-rise solution. 'It would,' he insisted, 'be a profound sociological mistake to force upon the British public, in defiance of its own widely expressed preference for separate houses with private gardens, a way of life that is fundamentally out of keeping with its traditions, instincts and opportunities.' Adding that 'the advocates of large-scale flat-building greatly overestimate the proportion of people now living in the congested areas who might thereby be decently housed on the site', he concluded bluntly, 'It is impossible to get rid of the effects of congested development by turning it on edge.'

Even in Coventry, epitome of the modern with its central area delineated by an inner ring road and containing zoned clusters of building types (shopping, entertainment, civic), Donald Gibson and his planning colleagues were far from slavish in the way they followed Le Corbusier's *City of Tomorrow*. 'We did not think that very high buildings were necessary for the centre of a smallish city which was unlikely ever to have more than 400,000 people,' Percy Johnson-Marshall (brother of Stirrat) recalled. 'We would have liked to have incorporated his dream of multi-level communications, but we were worried about expense, and felt that, anyway, our precinct form of development went a long way to bringing safety and convenience to the pedestrian.' As with some other badly bombed cities, including Bristol, Exeter and Plymouth, the outcome was indeed modern, in the sense of not following the familiar pattern, but it was – quite deliberately on Gibson's part – a generally restrained, unthreatening sort of modernism.

Nor were these immediate post-war planners as brutally unforgiving of the past as has sometimes been assumed. Thomas Sharp's declaration in 1946 that 'the watchword for the future should be – not restoration, but renewal' ran directly counter to the *Advisory Handbook for the Redevelopment of Central Areas* issued by Silkin's ministry the following year. This emphasised the importance of new buildings not swamping the old and pushed for retention of the 'existing main street pattern'. Moreover, as Peter Larkham has shown in a detailed study of urban-reconstruction plans up to the early 1950s, conservation played a surprisingly prominent role in them. Sharp himself, in his plans for Exeter, Oxford and Salisbury, was not entirely insensitive to their special architectural qualities, while plans for Edinburgh, Norwich, Warwick and Worcester all had a reasonably conservationist element, though in places only implicitly.[19]

Where there was virtually no call for conservationism was in the plans made for industrial cities and towns: there, the notion that the nineteenth-century industrial heritage might be worth preserving for aesthetic reasons did not feature. 'The city's buildings, with few exceptions, are undistinguished,' stated the plan for Manchester. 'Moreover, our few noteworthy buildings [identified as non-industrial] are obscured by the dense development surrounding them.' It was different, though, in the other great Victorian economic powerhouse. 'It would not be wise to adopt a new aesthetic and a new scale for building for the City of London until the old one has been definitely lost or outmoded,' asserted the architect Charles Holden and the town planner William Holford, the City Corporation's consultants for its rebuilding programme. 'The seventeenth-century scale should be preserved and

St Paul's Cathedral – the noblest in the City – should remain architecturally, as in other ways, its chief building.'

Yet despite all their relative moderation, the planners in these years found it desperately slow going when it came to trying to put their plans into practice. Most obviously, they and their local sponsors faced a series of trying economic constraints, including patchy financial support from central government and the severe rationing of building materials – constraints which invariably led to delay and sometimes to abandonment. Nor could they assume, however much they may have tried to, that the popular will was always behind them. In Bristol, for example, a poll organised in early 1947 by the local Retail Traders' Federation found that only 400 people wanted the proposed new Broadmead shopping centre, as against some 13,000 wishing to see the old shopping centre reinstated. The planners, for their part, simply ignored this unfortunate result.[20]

Regrettably, no comparable poll was taken in Coventry, where it would have been fascinating to test empirically the generally prevailing assumption that Gibson's plan was welcomed by the majority of Coventrians. Admittedly an impressive 57,000 people attended the Coventry of the Future exhibition held for a fortnight at the city's Drill Hall in October 1945, but the *Coventry Evening Telegraph*'s assertion on the third day that 'the public reaction appears to be that the schemes outlined are on the lines along which they would like to see the city developed' was somewhat belied by a letter it printed from Herbert E. Edwards, who had visited the exhibition 'along with a party of others':

We were unanimous in our strong criticism of the central area lay-out as shown in the large model.

The general feeling was that the hard, rigid lines of those monstrous buildings would utterly spoil Coventry's unique city centre, with its fine old churches, etc. The treatment seemed to us entirely foreign and out of touch with the traditional setting – which demands real harmony in its surroundings.

The City Fathers must be blind indeed if they suppose this massed barracks-like ensemble could possibly appeal to citizens with a grain of artistic feeling.

Over the next week, other critical letters appeared. 'The general concept of the scheme is not in keeping with the characteristics of the Coventry people, who would not feel at home in it,' wrote C.S.P. 'They all say, "Give us Coventry back as we knew it". What is wanted is the old Coventry, restored with a new Sunday dress, but old Coventry nevertheless.' Other letters dissented ('We have,' affirmed one, 'a wonderful opportunity to rebuild a city in accordance with the spirit of our age'), but certainly the overall balance of the correspondence was not in favour of the plan.

Subsequent oral testimony similarly suggests mixed feelings. 'It showed the raised ring road, all where the Cathedral was and all the rest of it,' recalled one visitor, Basil Whitham, more than half a century later. 'And we thought that this was fascinating ... we were all into spaceships, you know ... Buck Rogers and so forth.' That, though, was a young person's perspective; among older people the rather jaundiced recollection of Celia Grew was probably more representative. 'Whatever they proposed to do in the rebuilding, you sort of went along with it in a sort of zombie-like fashion, at least I did,' she explained. ''Cause you see I had got things happening in my own life with my husband getting wounded and being brought to Bromsgrove Hospital and me going over there to see him and all that kind of stuff.' While as for those who *did* take an interest, the experience of Dorrie Glass, a council employee who one day saw in Gibson's department a model of the new Coventry, was illuminating: 'It was a proper model really. You were sort of looking down, you know, like an aerial view. But they were all buildings, it wasn't a picture it was models, you know. We went and had a look at that. You couldn't sort of visualise it really.'[21]

The relative lack of interest on the part of architects, planners and others in popular taste was neatly encapsulated by a snatch from a 1946 round table (convened by *Building* magazine) of some leading architects. 'The public generally have no knowledge of what they want,' declared one. 'The public generally are only concerned with their own house,' responded another. 'It is questionable if they have any views at all.' Unsurprisingly, the next year's Town and Country Planning Act had no mechanism for getting the public involved in the planning process, apart from the right to object to the development plan after publication. In practice, according to Alison Ravetz, 'probably most people were quite unaware of this right, and ... the Minister was not obliged to hold a public enquiry.'

The aspect of Silkin's measure that caused most controversy was the 100 per cent development levy on appreciating land values. It was a provision never destined to have a long-term life, being (again in Ravetz's words) 'universally blamed for putting a stop to development'. But the Act as a whole was a stayer. Above all, it enshrined the principle that all development was to be subject to planning controls – or, as a delighted Frederic Osborn put it, 'it gives effect to the supremacy of public control of land use, without abolishing private ownership'. A further plus in his and many other well-meaning, progressive, middle-class eyes was that the act did much to protect the countryside from the threat of creeping, unplanned suburbia, the dreaded 'bungaloid growth'. Agricultural land, it insisted, was to be for agricultural use, but there was silence about the high-rise implication of high urban densities as the population grew. This was an implication that would have particular resonance given that the act also sanctified the idea of 'comprehensive' redevelopment of the inner city, which would follow compulsory purchase of (again in the words of the act) 'any areas which in the opinion of the planning authority suffered from extensive war damage, conditions of bad layout, obsolete development, or were in need of the relocation of population or industry'. Thus were born Comprehensive Development Areas (CDAs), though an economic upturn would be required for them to take major effect. Quite what that effect might be, no one at this stage could realistically envisage.

For one Tory backbencher, Sir Cuthbert Headlam, it was a case of seeing through a dark glass very darkly. 'I don't profess to have read one word of this most important measure,' he reflected on the evening in May 1947 when the bill was guillotined in the Commons, 'but can only hope that it may not be as devastating in its effects as some people say that it will be. I have an instinctive distrust of planners and always feel that "planning" merely makes confusion worse confounded – but then I am out of date and prefer things to grow up in their own way.' *The Times*, however, was sanguine, reflecting much of middle opinion. 'The British people,' it declared on the day in 1948 that the act came into force, 'almost without knowing it, are embarking upon one of the greatest experiments in the social control of their environment ever attempted by a free society. In the process they are also putting old individual liberties in trust for the common good.'[22]

The Town and Country Planning Act was in many ways complemented by the Agriculture Act, also 1947. While the former was designed to protect agricultural land and the rural character of the countryside, the latter specifically addressed what was to done on that land, with the threefold aim – entirely understandable in the immediate context – of feeding the population, keeping down food imports and maximising production. The solution adopted by Tom Williams, a former Yorkshire miner who now found himself Minister of Agriculture, was to give the farmers guaranteed prices and assured markets for most of their produce, as well as grants for modernisation and ready access to a government-run scientific advisory service. Back in 1937, Attlee had declared that 'the Labour Party stands for the national ownership of the land', but that was now off the agenda. Instead, for many farmers it was jackpot time. The National Farmers' Union would play a pivotal role each February in the annual price review; Williams himself became known as 'the Farmer's Friend'; and on eventually leaving office, he was given a small dinner party at Claridges, organised by the Duke of Norfolk.

The farm labourers fared less well. Although the act gave them improved security of tenure and a wages board, the system of tied cottages remained widespread and the farm worker was still very poorly paid (roughly two-thirds of average earnings in manufacturing industries) for often punishingly long hours. For the consumer, there was a new, longlasting era of cheap food; for the government, the heavy subsidies to be paid were amply justified by the spectacular success story to be told as farm productivity increased by leaps and bounds, with output as early as 1950 reaching 146 per cent of the pre-war level. And for the environment? The remorseless goal, shared equally by farmers and the Ministry of Agriculture, of maximising production had serious consequences for wildlife and landscape; but in the immediate post-war climate, with the food-producing farmer still almost a hero after his efforts during the war, organisations like the Soil Association, set up at its end and pushing for what would later be called organic farming, were completely marginalised. A golden future for industrialised farming lay, in every sense, wide open.

The illusion at the heart of the 1947 acts, taken together, was that agricultural Britain could be modernised without this fundamentally affecting the character of rural Britain. Even as the acts were coming into force, John Moore was completing his 'Brensham' trilogy of novels, lovingly detailing a Cotswolds way of life (intimate, domestic, with a benign, semi-feudal social hierarchy) that he believed to be under threat from a mixture of bureaucracy and technology.[23] Yet from another, arguably less sentimental point of view, it was the very insistence of government planners that agriculture be the only activity allowed on agricultural land that, together with the attempted prevention of suburban encroachment, had serious employment implications once agricultural modernisation had begun to reduce sharply the number of farm labourers required. Simultaneously romanticising and destroying the existing way of life, the urban activators did to the countryside what they would soon do to the – real or imagined – communities in their midst.

Glad to Sit at Home

All new governments enjoy something of a honeymoon, in this case prompting Raymond Streat to reflect in December 1945 that there had been 'extraordinarily little fuss or resistance' to 'the first moves in a comprehensive revolution within the economic and political life of Britain'. But as early as the spring of 1946, against a background of painful austerity, whatever honeymoon there had been with the middle class was more or less over.

'We are the masters at the moment – and not only for the moment, but for a very long time to come,' the Attorney-General Sir Hartley Shawcross unwisely pronounced on 2 April – words soon truncated to the notorious catchphrase 'We are the masters now.' On 16 April, inspecting Kenwood House for National Trust purposes, James Lees-Milne was 'surprised a little' by the secretary there 'saying that she considered any infringement of a law passed by this Government was justifiable'; two days later, the novelist Elizabeth Bowen told the diarist that 'we must all fight against being state-ridden'; and in early May the architect Professor Albert Richardson insisted to Lees-Milne that 'without aristocracy of the higher and lower grades there could be no beauty' and that 'consequently it was our duty to oppose this Government at every turn'. About this time, the young J. G. Ballard arrived in Southampton, having spent most of the war in a Japanese civilian camp, and travelled via London to relatives in Birmingham.

'Everyone looked small and tired and white-faced and badly nourished,' he recalled many years later. But what most struck him was the prevailing mindset:

All these middle-class people, my parents, friends and relations and the like, were seething with a sort of repressed rage at the world around them. And what they were raging against was the post-war Labour government. It was impossible to have any kind of dialogue about the rights and wrongs of the National Health Service, which was about to come in, they talked as if this Labour government was an occupying power, that the Bolsheviks had arrived and were to strip them of everything they owned.

That kind of atavistic loathing, vividly caught in Angela Thirkell's 'Barsetshire' novels, was perhaps at its most intense in the City of London. When the young Colin Knock, straight from school, attended an interview at the jobbers Prior & Williams, he made the mistake of wearing a red tie. 'Does that have any political implications?' he was asked by a partner. None at all, he replied, and thereby got the position of office boy. At another Stock Exchange firm, the brokers Panmure Gordon, the senior partner Richard Hart-Davis insisted that the Prime Minister was Chinese and invariably referred to him as A. T. Lee. At Midland Bank, the newly knighted and unashamedly pro-Labour chief executive Sir Clarence Sadd came under severe internal pressure and was eventually forced out in 1948. Nor was a virulent animosity absent from the Palace of Westminster, once the Tories had regrouped and begun to recover their nerve. 'I have not forgotten,' a junior minister, John Freeman, recalled in the late 1950s, 'the tension of rising to answer questions or conduct a debate under the cold, implacable eyes of that row of well-tailored tycoons, who hated the Labour Government with a passion and fear which made them dedicated men in their determination to get it out of office and to limit the damage it could do to the world which they saw as theirs by right.'[1] All in all, though we cannot recover those lost conversations in saloon bars or at 19th holes or local Rotaries, it is pretty clear that a strong, almost tribal middle-class backlash was well under way within a year of Labour taking power.

Certainly the well-to-do believed they had been soaked (James Lansdale Hodson wondered in January 1947 whether the Cabinet was 'aware of the bitterness and cynicism expressed in clubs and the mood that it's no use making money because you won't be allowed to keep it'), but what was the reality? Under Hugh Dalton's fiscal stewardship (until

November 1947), both surtax and death duties were increased quite sharply, but the temptation to introduce either a capital-gains tax or a one-off capital levy was resisted, and in general the City of London, for all its grumbling, survived quite comfortably. Nevertheless, it does seem that the cumulative effect of war and the Labour government was for the middle class to lose out quite significantly relative to the working class: at the end of the 1940s, the Inland Revenue estimated that whereas salaries (after tax) had declined in real terms by 16 per cent between 1938 and 1949, wages had risen by 21 per cent. Yet the angst of the middle class might have been alleviated if there had been greater awareness of the extent to which it stood to gain from the Labour government's proudest achievement – the welfare state. Not only was there its underlying (though not total) universalism – including such attractive benefits in kind as free secondary education and a free health service – but, in Kenneth Morgan's words, summarising a mountain of research, 'the very extent and cost of the welfare state after 1945 meant that many of the new social reforms were financed by transfers of income within lower-income groups themselves, rather than by transfers from the rich to the poor'.[2] It was not, amid the clink of G&Ts, a point much made.

What about the much-vaunted, much-predicted, much-feared social revolution? 'The Stock Exchange will be pulled down, the horse plough will give way to the tractor, the country houses will be turned into children's holiday camps, the Eton and Harrow match will be forgotten' was how George Orwell, in his celebrated 1941 essay *The Lion and the Unicorn*, had keenly looked ahead to the post-war socialist future. If by the end of the war he was significantly less optimistic, he hoped at least for an assault on that symbol of social privilege seen everywhere on the railways – 'the First Class nonsense should be scrapped once and for all,' he thundered in October 1944. But by the spring of 1946, some eight months into the Labour government, he was frankly conceding that there would be no social revolution:

In the social set-up there is no symptom by which one could infer that we are not living under a Conservative government. No move has been made against the House of Lords, for example, there has been no talk of disestablishing the Church, there has been very little replacement of

Tory ambassadors, service chiefs or other high officials, and if any effort is really being made to democratize education, it has borne no fruit as yet. Allowing for the general impoverishment, the upper classes are still living their accustomed life.

Orwell was surely right. The House of Lords did eventually have its power to delay legislation halved from two years to one, but any prospect of more fundamental reform, let alone abolition, was explicitly squashed by Herbert Morrison, who in 1947 told the Liberal leader Clement Davies that 'we should not set up something new and different from the past'. The public schools, of course, remained out of radical bounds, as did the privileges of Oxbridge. Other key areas where there was no government appetite for real change included company-law reform and gender equality. In the former, where the real possibility existed of deep-seated reform along German lines, tepid political willpower proved no match for City and Whitehall opposition allied to trade union leaders who saw workers' representation as jeopardising free collective bargaining; in the latter, the Labour leadership simply ignored an overwhelming card vote at its 1947 party conference in favour of equal pay.

Irrespective of government policy, moreover, society at large remained riddled by petty snobbery and infinite gradations of class. 'Among both the upper and middle classes,' Frederic Osborn reflected in October 1945, 'the word "garden city" stands for a working-class housing estate, with perhaps just a touch of philanthropy. It has therefore been something to approve but on no account to live in.' The following year, faced by rising costs, the traditionally select North Hants Golf Club elected 30 new members. Unfortunately, three of them were, as various letters of complaint to the committee put it, 'engaged in trade in Fleet'. The storm died down only when the committee pointed out that all three had played on the course regularly during the war and that no permanent 'change of policy' was envisaged.[3]

There was also, as ever, the uncanny ability of 'The Thing' (as William Cobbett called the British establishment) to reinvent itself. Perhaps the prime example in these years was the National Trust, almost entirely run by Old Etonians. Historically, the Trust's prime purpose had been to preserve actually or potentially threatened tracts of countryside, but that now changed to the acquisition and upkeep of country houses which would otherwise probably have been demolished. Public access to the nation's new treasures was in some instances fixed at no more than 50 days in the year and at hours which were, as the Trust freely admitted in 1947, 'settled as far as possible to suit the donor's convenience'. In October 1946 the Trust's relevant committee, including Sir Robert ('Bertie') Abdy, met at Montacute House in Somerset to discuss arrangements there. 'Meeting quite a success,' noted Lees-Milne, 'in spite of Bertie's sole comment which electrified the others. He remarked that the public could not of course be admitted to the house because they smelt. There was two minutes dead silence . . .' Still, perhaps the point of the story *was* the stunned silence; maybe things were changing after all.

Either way, what mattered to much of the progressive intelligentsia was not so much redistribution of wealth or social egalitarianism, planning or welfare as cultural renewal – the spreading to the mass of the population of what Matthew Arnold had famously termed 'sweetness and light'. The enemy was easy enough to identify. 'Refuse with scorn the great dope-dreams of the economic emperors and their sorcerers and Hollywood sirens,' J. B. Priestley implored in his *Letter to a Returning Serviceman*, published in late 1945. 'Don't allow them to inject you with Glamour, Sport, Sensational News, and all the Deluxe nonsense, as if they were filling you with an anaesthetic.' There was so much to deplore. Labour Party memos in 1946/7 on the need for a 'Socialist policy for leisure' lamented the 'failure of the majority of Britain's citizens to enjoy a full life through their leisure pursuits'; labelled the cinema and gambling as two prime examples of regrettably 'passive' and superficial leisure pursuits; and drew the rather defeatist conclusion that 'all forms of escapist entertainment or recreation are encouraged by the drabness, insecurity and hopelessness of daily life'.[4] All the more cause, then, to attempt to inject a large and improving dose of cultural uplift. But unfortunately for the uplifters, as three examples all too graphically showed, the mass of the population was simply not interested.

The first example was the Arts Council, direct successor to the wartime state-sponsored organisation CEMA, which had brought high culture (especially in the form of drama and music) to thousands of captive audiences, whether in army camps or air-raid shelters or factory canteens. The new body's first chairman was John Maynard Keynes, who in July 1945 declared his intention of making 'the theatre and the concert hall and the art gallery ... a living element in everyone's upbringing'. The initial strategy was to continue to take culture to the people, but in practice at least 80 per cent of the former wartime audience, now no longer captive, voted negatively with their feet. Activists, reported one regional office in 1947, were 'desperately worried' by 'their failure to establish contact with the ordinary folk in their towns'. Likewise, in a confidential report the same year, the Council concluded that its activities 'do not ... touch the mass of the working-class, even to the extent they did during the war'. By the late 1940s a full-scale retreat was under way from regional outreach, and soon afterwards the Council's ambitious motto, 'The Best for the Most', was replaced by the more circumspect 'Few But Roses'. A similar lack of broad appeal proved the Achilles heel of the adult-education movement. The vaunted if overestimated wartime impact of the Army Bureau of Current Affairs prompted in peace a big increase in government funding, especially for the Workers' Education Association, but in the immediate post-war period the WEA was only able to attract fewer then 20,000 manual workers to its classes across England and Wales each year, barely a fifth of its students as a whole.[5]

Finally, almost notoriously, there was the Third Programme, the BBC's high-culture radio channel that began broadcasting on Sunday, 29 September 1946. 'Its whole content will be directed to an audience that is not of one class but that is perceptive and intelligent,' promised the director-general Sir William Haley – whose private goal was that in time so many listeners would migrate to it from the Light Programme and the Home Service that the two older channels would no longer be required. A glance, though, at the *Radio Times* for the first evening suggested that it would be a long route-march from *ITMA*, *Variety Bandbox* and *Grand Hotel* on the Light to such offerings as 'Reflections on World Affairs' by Field-Marshal Smuts, the BBC Symphony Orchestra conducted by Sir Adrian Boult and gramophone records of madrigals by Monteverdi. Quarterly figures soon revealed the average programme on the Third to be securing only a meagre share of the BBC's overall listening audience: 2.2 per cent in October–December 1946, and down to 0.9 per cent by July–September 1947, with one listener in three not even having made an attempt to tune in. Another 1947 audience-research report found that whereas 30 per cent of the upper-middle class had given a 'warm welcome' to the Third, only 4 per cent of the working class had.

'I would prefer the Third Programme to be a little more familiar ground,' complained one member of the BBC's Listening Panel, an unemployed miner, fairly soon afterwards. 'After all, we are not all University Students or even past students.' A housewife agreed: 'It bangs us right into the middle of things we really cannot understand.' And an accounts clerk frankly admitted that 'the great majority of items' did not attract him because they were 'too remote, too heavy, requiring mental powers which I simply have not got at the end of an ordinary weekday'. Such lack of engagement was consistent with Tom Harrisson's early warning, in January 1947, that there was 'a real danger in the Third Programme becoming somewhat "cliquey", a bit of a mutual admiration society'; among recent examples he cited 'the amazingly unreal, donnish utterances of A.J.P. Taylor on foreign affairs', 'the lack of topical controversy', 'the total neglect of sociology' and 'the exaggerated use of Dylan Thomas's vocal qualities'. Among those even willing to be engaged, perhaps the best advice came from the novelist Rose Macaulay: 'One should have a long but not debilitating illness and really get down to it.'[6]

Significantly, Priestley's returning serviceman had to do more than just raise his cultural game. 'I think we make too much of our separateness in this country,' the great man warned, and, after a dark reference to how the pre-war suburbs had been like 'tree-lined concentration camps', he went on: 'Beware the charmed cosy circle. Don't stay too long in that armchair . . . but get out and about, compel yourself to come to terms with strangers (who will not be strangers long), make one of a team or a group, be both worker and audience, and put a hand to the great tasks.'

Was Priestley knocking at an open door? The testimony of Raphael Samuel – that most eclectic of historians, here recalling the years of his childhood – might easily make one think so:

Organization was regarded as a good in itself; it was fetishized in the conduct of personal life quite as much as in the office or the factory; it extended to 'dancing in step' in the ballroom, to organized fun in the holiday camps, to the orderly queues at the football grounds and the orderly crowds on the terraces. The 1940s constituted, in Britain, a kind of zenith of mass society . . . In London there were no fringe theatres, except for 'Unity', our Communist theatre in St Pancras, no alternative food shops, except for some delicatessens in Swiss Cottage and a vegetarian grocer in Tottenham Court Road. Clothes were worn as an affirmation of social position rather than as a display of personal self, and they were regimented to a degree. Skirt lengths rose or fell uniformly, above or below the knee, according to the dictates of the season; a man who wore suede shoes was morally suspect.

Those of us too young to remember the 1940s indeed look at the photographs of the massed ranks of cloth caps on the terraces, or the respectable-looking men wearing hats, jackets and ties as they watch the cricket or even sit by the sea, and assume that a uniform, collective appearance signified a uniform, collective spirit. Perhaps sometimes it did, but it was not a spirit inclined to forsake what Priestley, in his stridently communal '1945' mood, lamented as 'that famous English privacy' responsible for 'the apathetic herd we were in the Baldwin and Chamberlain era, when we messed about in our back gardens, ran about in our little cars, listened to the crooners and the comics, while the terrible shadows crept nearer'. Those shadows, after all, had now been banished, and for most people their *reward* was to return to their gardens and cars – cars that in time might even be a different colour than black.

This was a truth that Frederic Osborn recognised. 'In Welwyn, where everyone has a house and a garden, we find a moderate desire for social and communal life,' he wrote to Lewis Mumford in August 1946 from his garden city. 'The demand has definite limits; I am more communal in my habits than most people are. I find many women dislike the idea of nursery school and crêches; they want to look after their own children. And young men and women prefer lodgings to hostels.' How, then, was a more communally minded society to be encouraged? With great difficulty. In their pioneering account of the

Labour Party and popular politics in the 1940s, Steven Fielding, Peter Thompson and Nick Tiratsoo chart the post-war development of such largely *de haut en bas* initiatives as neighbourhood units, socially mixed housing, municipal eating facilities, popular participation in urban planning and joint production committees in the workplace, with in each instance only chequered progress being made at best. In terms of voluntary organisations like Co-operative societies, friendly societies and community associations, all their evidence points towards an essentially 'divi-minded', instrumental use of them (whether for benefits or facilities) on the part of members, as opposed to a more socialist or ideological motivation.[7]

Contemporary surveys flesh out the picture. In Willesden in the winter of 1946/7, more than twice as many preferred to live in a single-class street than in a mixed street; most drew a very careful distinction between 'friends', 'acquaintances' and 'neighbours'; and 75 per cent of housewives were not on visiting terms with their neighbours, let alone going out together. Soon afterwards, a survey of Watling, an inter-war LCC estate near Edgware, found that only 30 per cent of adults answered 'Yes' to the question 'Do you belong to any clubs, sports associations, guilds, etc., for leisure time activities, including those connected with politics and the social life of churches?' – a figure apparently *above* the national trend. And in August 1947 an investigator in Bethnal Green heard explanations from working-class people about why they preferred to give a wide berth to clubs, societies and suchlike:

I don't like mixing, I like keeping myself to myself.

I'm a married woman and I prefer staying in my home. I don't want to go and mix with other people, I've too much to do in the house.

I've got too much to do in the house, I'm glad to sit at home in the evening.

No, I don't want anything to do with that kind of thing. I just don't like it that's all.

I'm just not interested I suppose, there's plenty to do without joining one of those.

Well I like going out with the hubby, and I don't bother to mix much with others.

I've got these three kiddies, they take up all my time.

By now even Priestley was reluctantly coming to accept the sovereignty of the individual. 'There seems to be far less kind and neighbourly co-operation than there was a few years ago, during the worst of the war years,' he told his Light Programme listeners (presumably waiting impatiently for the next crooner) two months later. 'People are harder, more selfish, more intent upon looking after Number One. They are more likely to snatch, grab, lose their temper.' And, like a thousand intellectuals before and (especially) after him, he added, 'Now why is this? What has gone wrong?'[8]

———

Over the years, the '"we wuz robbed!" tendency within British Labour historiography', as the historian Dilwyn Porter has termed it, would exercise huge influence. If only there had been more systematic economic planning, if only there had been more extensive and full-blooded nationalisation, if only private education had been abolished – in fact, if only the Attlee government had been more *socialist*, and thereby engendered an irresistible moral and political force of popular enthusiasm for its policies – then the story of post-war Britain would have been fundamentally different and fundamentally happier. That was not how the *New Statesman*'s resident versifier, 'Sagittarius' (a pseudonym for Olga Katzin), saw things. In 'Let Cowards Flinch,' a brilliant long poem imitating Byron's ottava rima and published in October 1947, she surveyed Labour's first two years in power. Two verses had a special piquancy:

> But while they speed the pace of legislation
> > With sleepless ardour and unmatched devotion,
> The lower strata of the population
> > Appear to have imbibed a soothing potion;
> Faced with the mighty tasks of restoration
> > The teeming millions seem devoid of motion,
> Indifferent to the bracing opportunity
> > Of selfless service to the whole community.
>
> It is as if the Government were making
> > Their maiden journey in the train of State,
> The streamlined engine built for record-breaking,

> Steaming regardless at a breakneck rate,
> Supposing all the while that they were taking
>> Full complement of passengers and freight,
> But puffing on in solitary splendour,
>> Uncoupled from the carriages and tender.

Yet one can exaggerate the degree of uncoupling and indeed the breakneck steaming ahead. Precisely because the Attlee government was essentially practical and moderate in its approach, faithfully reflecting Attlee himself, it managed to create a settlement that in operational practice had – above all on the welfare side – considerable direct appeal. Crucially, it was an appeal not only to the working class, thankful (more or less) to consolidate its wartime gains, but also to significant elements of the middle class, who for all their lack of political gratitude were understandably reluctant to look an apparent gift horse, albeit a rather threadbare one, in the mouth. People may not have been as communally minded as Priestley and Labour's other cheerleaders might have wished, but they were for the most part perfectly willing, at this stage anyway, to look to collective provision in order to satisfy individual needs and wants. Put another way, the fact that BUPA started in 1947 did not mean that the majority of people were not welcoming the prospect of a national health service free at the point of delivery.

Moreover, for many of those who had lived through the worst of the inter-war years – the bleak 'Jarrow' version of those years rather than Margaret Thatcher's more upbeat 'Grantham' version – there was a deep satisfaction in the very fact of a government no longer run by the old gang. There might be serious economic problems, there might be miserable austerity, but at last the awful spectre of mass unemployment had seemingly been banished. One afternoon in April 1946, Florence Speed, an inveterate Conservative voter, was gazing at a shop window in Brixton:

There were lovely fabrics on display & streamlined wooden carvings & furniture which doesn't appeal to me.

As I looked a friendly little man in a cap, but neat & respectable, said to me, 'Beautiful stuff there'.

'Yes,' I agreed slightly sardonically.

'But it *is* good.'

'Yes it is, but I like curves, not all these straight lines.'

'I like Victorian mahogany,' he said then. 'More homely. But this stuff is good.'

'British craftsmen are the best in the world – if they'd work.'

'Digging that old one up' the man retorted contemptuously, & in a few seconds the friendliness had changed to fanaticism as bottled up hate, poured out in a spate of sing song Welsh.

He had been a miner . . . 'Won't work? I'd have walked from Land's End to John o'Groats to get work. Every man's entitled to a job. I've had nothing in a day but a cup of tea . . .'

He had no teeth & spoke so vehemently, & rapidly, that he sprayed my face with spit.

He told me of a friend who had fought in World War I . . . On his return he could find no work, & died from malnutrition. When he was dying he called his sons, & told them, 'If there's another war, don't fight. I did & I've starved.' Two of his sons were conscientious objectors in the last war.

The Conservatives in a 100 years had done nothing but keep down 70% of the population & let them starve. There had been starvation in every town in the country. They would never be in office again. In fifty years time there would be no bloody dukes & no parasites. Everyone would have to work.

A mild pleasant sociable old man, no one would have guessed at the deep-down burning hatred. The Labour Government are doing fine of course! – at least they haven't had time yet . . .

He had so obviously suffered that I couldn't help sympathising with him.[9]

PART THREE

Christ It's Bleeding Cold

New Year's Day 1947 was a red-letter day. 'The MINES HAVE BEEN NATIONALISED TODAY,' noted a somewhat sceptical Vere Hodgson in west London. 'All is fun and games at the pits . . . The worst of it is these remedies for the troubles of life never turn out so well as you expect!' Certainly that Wednesday and over the next few days there were some stirring scenes at Britain's 970 pits, employing some 692,000 miners. The National Coal Board (NCB) flag was hoisted (often by the oldest employee at the colliery), speeches were made, songs were sung, banners were unfurled, brass bands played. They were all now 'one family', declared the NCB's chairman Lord Hyndley at celebrations at Murton Colliery on the Durham coalfield, adding that 'if they all worked hard and worked together they would make nationalisation a great success'. At nearby Thornley Colliery the main address was given by Hubert Tunney, former chairman of Thornley Miners' Lodge and now assistant labour director of the coal board at Newcastle:

Thirty years ago a lot of us saw in a far distance a dream of the public ownership of the mines. Now we have realised that ownership we have the important duty of making that venture a success. You are now privileged to work for a model employer. You have had holidays recently with pay and without conditions attached to them, the Board taking the view that there is a value in stressing and expressing the human side of the industry. The responsibility is now upon the management and the men to recognise that they must also play their part as far as production is concerned. Absenteeism must be reduced, lightning strikes must be cut out. There is no necessity for these things.

Fine words, and at one Durham colliery they duly celebrated Vesting Day by burying a symbolic hatchet. But for Sid Chaplin, at the Dean and Chapter Colliery that dominated Ferryhill, it was a case of sitting in the canteen and hearing the sound of music in the distance, as lodge and colliery officials marched behind band and banner. 'We had been working all night to install a new conveyer,' he recalled. 'It had been a long shift and we were tired. But the conveyer was ready for coal-work, and we were satisfied.'[1]

For a glimpse of the distinctive mentality and culture of the miners in the immediate post-war years, our best guide is the indefatigable Ferdynand Zweig, who travelled around the main English and Welsh coalfields between July and October 1947. 'While talking to the miners,' he found, 'one is continually struck by the fact that the past is deeply ingrained in their minds' – above all the 1926 coal strike. 'Twenty years in the miner's life,' he added, 'is probably like a year for others.' Events between the wars had also led to a widely shared, deeply ingrained pessimism, which full employment and better wages since the early 1940s had done little to remove. 'The great majority of miners are not politically minded,' Zweig reckoned, 'but all of them have an enormous – I would say an overwhelming – class consciousness.' Outside working hours, miners' favourite pastimes included watching games (especially football), going to the cinema, going dancing and gambling (dog and horse racing, football pools, sweepstakes). 'In a village in West York-shire the people could name me nine bookies with their offices, and on racing days those places are simply besieged by the patrons, who want to know the latest results coming in on a teleprinter.' As for reading habits, Zweig noted how 'lately a great wave of cheap, rubbishy stories has invaded the mining villages, and at the stalls in any market you can see these booklets in exciting paper covers with glaring titles, changing hands like hot cakes . . . mostly second-hand, and very dirty.' *Dangerous Dames, Moonlight Desire, White Traffic, The Penalty is Death, Corpses Don't Care, The League of the Living Dead*: 'glaring' indeed.

Inevitably, to Zweig's silent but still palpable regret, 'some welfare institutes and clubs have closed their reading and library rooms because they were not used and turned them into games rooms', while 'even in South Wales, where the traditions of cultural interests cultivated by the institution of "Eisteddfod" were very high, I was told that the choirs, dramatic societies, poetry and musical clubs are not as popular as they used to be.' Zweig enquired why. "The buses have done that," someone told him. "You can move freely for a few pence and get any amusement you want outside the village." Zweig also went into miners' homes, finding 'a great contrast between the unpleasant appearance of the houses from outside and the nice appearance inside':

> The rooms are kept very tidy and clean, and the housewives take immense pride in keeping their houses spotless. Most miners go to considerable pains to have a yearly re-decorating of their living-room, which is always larger than any of the others. The living-room is often furnished with a leather suite, including an armchair and a couch. In general, miners prefer brass fire-irons to wooden or other modern ones, and they still have very large fire-places of the metal type, with large set-pots. Another noticeable sight are the gaily decorated mantel-pieces, with brass and other ornaments. Hand-made rugs and carpets are the feature in nearly all mining houses . . .[2]

For all the gambling and lurid paperbacks, for all the enhanced physical mobility, the pit villages were still deeply respectable, ultimately home-centred worlds of their own.

What at the start of 1947 did their inhabitants really expect from nationalisation? Clearly it was a moment not without high hopes. 'Nationalisation appears as the final and the only all-embracing security,' a Mass-Observation investigator had concluded in 1942 after lengthy stays in Blaina and Nantyglo on the South Wales coalfield; on Vesting Day itself that coalfield saw many scenes of excitement and enthusiasm, including more than a thousand miners gathering at Park Colliery to sing 'Cwm Rhondda'. Yet did the rank and file, as opposed to some union leaders and activists, truly see nationalisation as ushering in, either actually or potentially, fundamental changes in working conditions and employer/employee relationships? Unfortunately, we have no contemporary surveys, ie at the point of nationalisation. But Ina Zweiniger-Bargielowska's 1980s interviews with a range of retired miners from four collieries (Oakdale, Park and Dare, Penrhiwceibr, Seven Sisters) in South Wales – significantly, a more radical coalfield than most – broadly confirm the low-key assessment that a South

Yorkshire colliery manager had offered to James Lansdale Hodson some seven months before the event. The recollections she heard were of a solid but essentially narrow, pay-oriented trade unionism in these early post-war years. Bob Crockett 'never took it into [his] head' to go to union meetings, and 'once I came out of that pit I came home and I never thought about the pit . . . until I had to go back there'; Cliff Price frankly conceded that he was 'only interested in things appertaining to myself, my own work'; and according to Eddie Bevan, the men were solely interested in union affairs 'when it hit their pockets, when something within the pit happens'. Few recalled the work itself with any fondness. 'The worst occupation in God's earth,' declared Stanley Warnes; 'as long as I was getting a wage at the end,' was Bevan's view; or, as Glan Powell put it, 'wages, that's what everybody is going down the pit for, to earn money'. Perhaps inevitably, such men tended to see the prospect of nationalisation as something which in itself did not particularly concern them. A 'pie-in-the-sky sort of thing,' remembered one, another that he 'didn't much think about it, to be honest', a third that '[I]wasn't really bothered myself.' If it brought tangible, bread-and-butter benefits, well and good; if it did not, too bad; but either way, there were no ideological hopes invested.

Other oral evidence, from Midlands coalfields where there had been a long, pre-1947 history of harmonious industrial relations, predictably presents an even less politicised picture. Coventry Colliery, for example, was held up by one miner as having had 'great sports grounds, great pavilions, they spent money on providing silver bands, a very good cricket team, parks, leisure, it's all part of village life as I was brought up'. At the time of the changeover, his main hope was that benign paternalism under private ownership would continue under public ownership.[3] Overall, a range of expectations and non-expectations obtained at the start of 1947, but few miners seemed to equate nationalisation with workers' control, whatever that might mean.

It was anyway a propitious moment for pragmatism rather than ideology, given that by the time of Vesting Day the government was in serious difficulties over the production of coal – responsible for more than 90 per cent of Britain's energy requirements – and in no great position to resist the implementation of union demands for improved pay and conditions. The previous spring the National Union of Mineworkers had drawn up the 'Miners' Charter', a broad-based wish list (including the modernisation of existing pits, the sinking of new ones, proper training for young miners, and improved social and welfare provision) that had at its core several key demands: average wages not to fall 'below those of any other British industry'; a five-day week without loss of pay; and miners to receive two consecutive weeks' paid holiday. Over the rest of 1946, the response of Manny Shinwell, Minister of Fuel and Power, was essentially to give way – over holidays, the principle of a guaranteed weekly wage and, above all, the five-day week, to come into operation by May 1947. In so doing he overrode the wishes of the fledgling NCB, though such was the parlous state of the industry that arguably he had little choice: not only was there a shortage of manpower (14,000 down on August 1945), but absenteeism rates were still high (running at about 15 per cent) and much-exhorted productivity improvements were barely coming through. Strikingly, the prospect of nationalisation – forced through by the government with what one historian has called 'almost indecent haste' – did as little to improve the situation in the closing months of 1946 as did Shinwell's concessions to the Miners' Charter, so that by the end of the year many factories in the Midlands and north-west were on short-time working because of the lack of coal.

Shinwell himself, for all his bluff and bluster, was a disastrous minister at this difficult time. Hugh Gaitskell, who had drawn the short straw as his Parliamentary Secretary, would observe that 'he walks alone one feels because he has never been able fully to trust anyone', that his usual traits were 'suspicion and aggression', and that 'as an administrator' he was 'hardly a starter' – all fair charges. Working-class and left-wing, Shinwell felt an intense allegiance to the miners, who for so many years had enjoyed a unique position in the labour movement, and he obstinately believed that somehow they would see things through. 'Prime Minister,' he blithely remarked at one point to a sceptical Attlee, 'you should not allow yourself to be led up the garden path by statistics. You should look at the imponderables.'[4]

———

On Thursday, 23 January 1947 – the day after Anthony Heap noted that 'more and more shops and offices seem to be going in for the new pale blue "fluorescent" system of electric lighting' – snow began to fall in the south-east. It was the start of Britain's most severe and protracted spell of bad weather during the twentieth century. Florence Speed was one of millions who shivered:

24 *January*. I was frozen today, gas is on at such low pressure. Worked with scarf over my head, mittens on my hands, & a rug round my legs.

25 *January*. Open spaces look as if sugar has been dredged over them.

28 *January*. Freeze up continues . . . Thermometer been at freezing point all day. Waste pipe in the bathroom & the geyser frozen.

29 *January*. *Even colder* the forecast for tonight, so I've borrowed a balaclava helmet from Fred [her brother] to wear in bed!

30 *January*. The cuts last night put lights out in the streets. Hyde Park was closed because there were no lights there.

On Sunday the 26th, as the big freeze started to tighten its grip, the annual meeting was held of Oakdale Navigation Lodge, the miners' lodge for Oakdale Colliery in South Wales. 'It was regrettable to hear over the Wireless that Factories were closing down for lack of coal,' remarked the chairman, Sam Garland. 'This was not the fault of the Miners.' Was the importation of Polish miners the answer? Not according to Garland: 'We are in dire need of coal and previously it had been Miners' sons that had filled the pits, changes had come and Miners' sons were looking for a larger life, there were other people's sons who could well do their share before the introduction of foreign labour.' Three days later, the coldest day for more than 50 years, the lights went out not only in London but all over the country; the electricity was off for long spells; gas in most big cities was at about a quarter of its normal pressure; and amid huge snow-drifts transport virtually ground to a halt. 'Wearing my snow boots and fur-lined coat I was not once warm,' grumbled James Lees-Milne. 'All my pipes, including w.c. pipes, are frozen, so a bath or a wash is out of the question. W.c. at the office frozen likewise . . . And we live in the twentieth century. Even the basic elements of civilization are denied us.'[5]

A visitor to London at this miserable time was Christopher Isherwood, over from America for the first time since before the war. Londoners themselves 'didn't seem depressed or sullen' – though 'their faces were still wartime faces, lined and tired', while 'many of them stared longingly at my new overcoat' – and his only criticism of the prevailing stoicism was that 'perhaps the English had become a little too docile in their attitude toward official regulation'. By contrast, he found London's physical shabbiness 'powerfully and continuously depressing':

> Plaster was peeling from even the most fashionable squares and crescents; hardly a building was freshly painted. In the Reform Club, the wallpaper was hanging down in tatters. The walls of the National Gallery showed big unfaded rectangles, where pictures had been removed and not yet rehung. Many once stylish restaurants were now reduced to drabness and even squalor . . . London remembered the past and was ashamed of its present appearance. Several Londoners I talked to at that time believed it would never recover. 'This is a dying city,' one of them told me.

As for the snow, 'it soon assumed the aspect of an invading enemy':

> Soldiers turned out to fight it with flame-throwers. The newspapers spoke of it in quasi-military language: 'Scotland Isolated', 'England Cut in Half'. Even portions of London were captured; there was a night when no taxi driver would take you north of Regent's Park. With coal strictly rationed, gas reduced to a blue ghost and electricity often cut off altogether, everybody in England was shivering. I remember how the actors played to nearly empty houses, heroically stripped down to their indoor clothes, while we their audience huddled together in a tight clump, muffled to the chins in overcoats, sweaters and scarves. I remember a chic lunch party composed of the intellectual *beau monde*, at which an animated discussion of existentialism was interrupted by one of the guests exclaiming piteously: 'Oh, I'm so *cold*!' Two or three of my friends said to me then: 'Believe us, this is worse than the war!' By which I understood them to mean that the situation couldn't by any stretch of the imagination be viewed as a challenge to self-sacrifice or an inspiration to patriotism; it was merely hell.

Such were Isherwood's recollections, published some nine years later, with only a passing reference to English supineness in the face of officialdom. Yet at the time, his visit made a considerable impact upon his friends and acquaintances. 'We realised we had become shabby and rather careless of appearances in our battered surroundings,' recalled his host, the writer and editor John Lehmann. 'That we had become crushed as civilians to accept the ordering about of officialdom. That we had become obsessively queue-forming, and were priggishly proud of it.' Such feelings, induced by Isherwood's 'sharp observation of the altered London', were heightened by the ghastly winter:

> The adrenaline [ie of war] was no longer being pumped into our veins. We endured with misery and loathing the continual fuel cuts, the rooms private and public in which we shivered in our exhausted overcoats, while the snow blizzards swept through the country again and yet again. Were there to be no fruits of victory? The rationing cards and coupons that still had to be presented for almost everything from eggs to minute pieces of scraggy Argentine meat, from petrol to bed-linen and 'economy' suits, seemed far more squalid and unjust than during the war . . .
>
> Worse, still, to my increasingly disillusioned eye, was the kind of mean puritanism that the newly triumphant Labour MPs and their officials appeared to have decided was the proper wear of the day. Too many of them seemed to think there was a virtue in austerity and shabbiness, in controls and restrictions . . .

It was a significant alienation. The metropolitan intelligentsia had mainly welcomed the 1945 election result, but the socialism of daily privation and daily restrictions was not their kind of socialism. Moreover, it was symptomatic, not least in their eyes, that a magazine like *Penguin New Writing* (edited by Lehmann himself) was by this time on a sharply downward spiral in its circulation, having hit a peak of 100,000 in the spring of 1946. This dispiriting trend, Lehmann explained, meant the end of the fond hope, shared by the publisher Allen Lane (founder of Penguin paperbacks), that 'given the right formula an enormous public was now ready to devour what would have been considered almost entirely highbrow fare before the war'.[6]

There was nothing highbrow about the Levenshulme Palais, where Frank Lewis – still working in Manchester, having failed most of his economics exams the previous summer at the University College of South Wales in Cardiff – went on the evening of Monday, 3 February:

2 dances with 'Port Madoc'; she's nice; I'd like to go out with her. ('Wouldn't I with any of them,' repeats a dark hidden voice.) She told me her nickname was 'Smiler'. She showed me running steps during the last quickstep at 10 to 11.

I dance with 'Blondex'. Boy, what legs?

I dance with 'Belle Vue', who also taught me running steps.

There was heavy snow that day in the north and Midlands, but Lewis seems to have been too preoccupied to notice. Not so an anxious Mary King in her Birmingham suburb. 'Tonight 17,000 employees will be idle at the Longbridge Austin Motor Works through lack of fuel,' she recorded that evening. 'Many other firms are in the same plight. It is a dreadful thing to face.' Two days later, in the context of a weather forecast of 'more snow, & wintry conditions to continue', her anxiety deepened: 'One thinks of the shortage of fuel, and home comforts, such as blankets & sheets, & carpets – the scarcity of food – the difficulty of transport, and the unemployment of thousands of workers in factories due to lack of coal & materials. Never in my lifetime have I known such a period of history ...'

Finally, on Friday the 7th – the day after Ellen Wilkinson's death (possibly suicide), barely a week since she had told an audience at the Old Vic that she wanted Britain to be a Third Programme nation – Shinwell and his colleagues acted. With sufficient supplies of coal failing to reach power stations in London, the Midlands and the north-west, he announced that from the following Monday not only would electricity supplies to industry in these regions be suspended, but householders there would have to make do without electricity daily for three hours from 9 a.m. and two hours from 2 p.m.

'Somebody has been short sighted somewhere, sometime,' was Mary King's immediate reaction, and over the weekend much wrath, public and private, was directed at the hapless Shinwell. Repudiating his attempt to blame the weather ('Let the Minister look to himself'), and reckoning that 'never since the Industrial Revolution have we seen a crisis come in this way', the *Financial Times* declared that the situation was 'as serious a threat to prosperity, in peace time, as the events which brought down Mr Neville Chamberlain's Government were to victory in war time'. The staunchly pro-Tory Glasgow pattern-maker Colin

Ferguson castigated Shinwell's 'crass ignorance' and saw the crisis as conclusive evidence that the government was 'the silliest set of sneering gas-bags we've ever been cursed with in this country'; the reasonably objective James Lansdale Hodson, after noting 'drifts fifteen feet deep in Northumberland, railways in parts impassable, and queues of professional women in St John's Wood with buckets at a water-tap in the road', called Shinwell 'a modern phenomenon – muddling, insouciant, and a yoke round our suffering necks'. Even Vere Hodgson, not unsympathetic to the aspirations of the Labour government, accepted that 'we are in an awful MESS', could not understand why Shinwell had not resigned and asserted that 'there is not a leader amongst them'. On Sunday afternoon it did start to thaw in London. But on Monday, to mark the new restrictions, 'it froze again very hard, so that,' in Lees-Milne's words, 'the slush is like slippery brick'.[7]

The next 12 days or so, through to about 22 February, were the height of the crisis, with the weather unremittingly grim and unemployment rising to more than 1.75 million (compared to just over 400,000 in mid-January). Government-imposed restrictions were intensified: no electricity for five hours a day across the nation's households; television, the Third Programme and many magazines suspended; major cuts in transmission times for the Home and the Light programmes; newspapers even more severely cut down in size than before because of newsprint rationing; most forms of external lighting forbidden; and no electricity to be used in relation to superfluous activities like greyhound racing. There was also an intense propaganda campaign urging the public to use, when it could use, as little electricity and gas as possible. Inevitably, the miners in these weeks came under acute pressure to raise their levels of production. By and large they seem to have responded, with output per man-shift being as high during February as at any point over the previous 12 months, though such weather-induced problems as inaccessible mines, frozen-solid pithead stockpiles and transportation difficulties once the coal was ready to leave the colliery could not but affect overall production. On Sunday the 16th, 'Coal Sunday', many miners in the South Wales coalfield voluntarily worked a full shift, winning widespread praise for the 'Dunkirk spirit'.

Could more be done? Sydney T. Jones of Pengam Road, Penpedairheol, Hengoed, Glamorgan, was probably motivated by public interest as well as self-interest when the previous week he took his case direct to 'Mr Shinwell':

I hope you will forgive me for writing to you at this critical time, but it is a matter of the utmost importance in as much as it concerns the very problem with which you are grappling now – the Fuel Shortage.

I am a South Wales miner, and I write to ask – not only for myself – but for several of my butties, that you use your good influence with the Ministry of Transport to get him to restore to us miners the Travel Priority on our local Bus Services, especially those of us who work on the afternoon shifts. I myself, having been home two weeks with flu and bronchitis through having to walk half a mile to the nearest bus stop from the colliery, and waiting about at the end of the queue for the last bus to our village, a mile and a half away, we find at 10.30 p.m. the queue is made up of half-drunks, picturegoers, dance hall riff-raff, and we who have been sweating our guts out at the coal face are left to shiver in the bitter cold wind and hear the bus conductor say – 'Sorry, only three or four' as the case may be. Those types of pub crawlers can get home, but we miners have to walk through the torrents of rain or snow storms across the fields over the mountains to get home about 11.30 p.m., or near mid-night, and then perhaps we have to return in the morning to perform some special job. That means getting up at 4 a.m. to catch the Workers Factory Bus at 5.15 a.m. from the village. So you will see Sir how important it is. Tons and tons of coal is being lost to the nation through miners going to work at (1 p.m.) lunchtime for the afternoon shift and unable to get on the crowded buses through the Priority Ruling having been removed. As you are no doubt aware there are no Collieries, at least, very few are in big towns, and in the Rhymney valley especially miners have to travel miles on buses. So please do your very best to get us to work, and get us home at the end of the afternoon shift. For the day shift it matters not so much; because there are plenty of buses if they miss one. But at 10.30 p.m. at night the last bus from town means everything to us who work on this shift.

Contemporary observers made much of the miners' deep sense of social inferiority, arising out of their bitter, humiliating experiences between the wars; Zweig in his study asserted that this 'inferiority complex' was 'especially strong in South Wales'.[8] If anything, this plea to Shinwell would suggest that things were changing. But in any case, it is undeniably the authentic miner's voice – one obscure, now-forgotten Jones among many obscure, now-forgotten Joneses – and one is grateful it survives.

Few people enjoyed these mid-February days and nights. At Oxford, where the editor of *Cherwell* had just been sacked for publishing a questionnaire that asked female undergraduates if they were still virgins, 'CHRIST ITS BLEEDING COLD' was how the very male (and army-coarsened?) undergraduate Kingsley Amis put it to his friend Philip Larkin. 'Life here is quite impossible,' Evelyn Baring of the merchant bank Barings, probably the most august house in the City of London, reported to a fellow-banker, 'and really no-one would have believed it if they had read it in a novel. From 9 to 12 and 2 to 4 we work in the dim glow of candlelight or nightlight.' The diarists, meanwhile, shivered like the rest:

10 *February (Monday).* We walked down Baker St & Oxford St. The sky was heavy, the day grey & dark but the stores inside were gloomier still ... Assistants were straining their eyes trying to write out bills, the darkness was depressing. Coming out onto the streets again the dull light was almost dazzling. (*Florence Speed*)

11 *February.* Go out shopping – much windier & colder – astonishing to see Woolworths, like every other shop, lit by odd gas lamps & candles by cash registers. At 2 pm – sudden plunging into gloom. (*Grace Golden*)

12 *February.* Tonight it is announced that the cuts are to be extended throughout the whole country, Scotland & Wales ... Also that we are to return to a 'black-out' on the streets. Traffic lights will remain ... Yet for all the seriousness of the Country's situation, Ethel & I saw *crowds* – women chiefly! – mob Laurel & Hardy outside The Monseigneur [cinema] at Trafalgar Square this afternoon, to get their autographs ... Hardy – the fat one – is revolting. Huge & grotesque ... Both were hugely delighted at their reception; only moved on when the Policeman said 'Enough'. (*Florence Speed*)

13 *February.* No soap to be bought anywhere, & I feel ready to drop with fatigue by 2 pm. Lily sent me 2 lbs potatoes through the post & I am saving them for Sunday's dinner ... Last night I went to the

Red House to play cards in my fur coat & turban it was so cold there. (*Rose Uttin*)

Penalty now for using current during restricted times, the situation being 'dangerously critical', is a fine of £100 or three months jail . . . Yet despite this a woman in a queue in Brixton declared defiantly, 'Well anyway, I'm going to switch on the iron & do my ironing as soon as I get home'. It's because so many haven't played fair – the worst offenders are shopkeepers it is reported – that the penalties have been imposed. (*Florence Speed*)

Gas fire very low, but Ione [her baby daughter] and I managed. Shortage of pennies and shillings announced! . . . Down to last nappy but managed to get more dry between 12 and 2 and after 4. We froze up again. (*Judy Haines*)

14 February. Long queues for potatoes . . . Reduced clothing coupon allowances. No wonder people steal coupons and clothes . . . Blackout so batteries for torches are scarce. (*Gladys Langford*)

16 February. Restrictions and arctic conditions persist . . . Several people here ignore lighting regulations and use lamps & radios at forbidden hours. (*Gladys Langford*)

18 February. Yesterday Selfridge's was packed as though there was a bargain sale there. 'Nothing else to do, nowhere to go,' we heard a man say, obviously one of the nearly 3½ millions stood off through the fuel crisis. Today we saw men carrying their wives' shopping baskets. (*Florence Speed*)

19 February. In addition to my usual winter apparel, am now wearing four woollen pullovers (three sleeveless ones under my waistcoat, one with sleeves over it). And yet I still get chilled to the bone sitting in that bleak, unheated office all day. (*Anthony Heap*)

22 February. The weather is atrocious and now gas supplies are threatened. The streets are seas of slush and to cross a wide road means flirting with death. (*Gladys Langford*)

But for Frank Lewis, at the Great Universal Stores warehouse in Manchester, the weather still failed to impinge. 'Getting bloody boring at work, on the bloody shoot [ie chute],' he noted on the 14th. 'If only, too, the British working man didn't do so much bloody grumbling.' And the following Wednesday he went to a 'rag dance' at the

Plaza: 'Bloody awful! Too hot. Terrible women . . . I'll have to take "stronger love measures" to get a girl. I can't go on like this. This sex business is positively getting me down.'[9]

What were other reactions at the height of the fuel crisis and accompanying cuts? Mass-Observation sounded out, between the 10th and 14th, various working-class Londoners:

> I think it's ridiculous for the Royal family to go on such an expensive tour [they had left for South Africa on the 1st] – it should have been put off – the country can't afford it.
>
> Shocking – the position is absolutely shocking. The country is deteriorating rapidly. Thank Goodness I had nothing to do with voting Labour in. They're not the right kind to be at the head of affairs. What with one thing and another life's very trying. And the food – there isn't enough fats to keep oneself fit in this sort of weather. The diet is much too starchy. Oh, I could go on by the hour but what's the good.
>
> Rotten isn't it? Can't be helped though, wouldn't be done unless there was any real need for it. I'm sure everybody is doing their best.
>
> Shinwell? Ha! ha! ha! Don't know much about him, suppose he's doing his best.
>
> They should have warned us that the position was bad. Same as old Churchill did even in the blackest days. Came on the wireless and let us know how we stood, and even if the news wasn't good he somehow gave us confidence. But old Attlee doesn't do that.
>
> It's very bad in our line – the tailoring trade. When we're working on black we're practically working in the dark.

A coalman in Croydon spoke with particular personal experience. 'It's like everything else, the people with a lot of money get all they want,' he explained. 'I delivered half a ton this morning to a house in Purley, their fair ration mind you, but they've already got a stock of about a ton and a half and a couple of tons of coke besides. Now you can't get any coke, but those fellers can, they've got the money see.'

In general, in terms of obeying the restrictions on the use of power – restrictions to some extent based on voluntary compliance – it is clear enough that, as Florence Speed among others complained, not everyone played the game. Nevertheless, in the weeks beginning on 10 and 17 February there were rates of saving of respectively 29 and 28 per cent, ie by comparison with the level of coal consumption immediately before the cuts. Such figures, according to the authoritative history of the fuel crisis, 'attested to the public's willing co-operation with official attempts at enforcement'.[10] This did not necessarily mean, though, that they co-operated with a song in their hearts.

For one child this winter the big freeze was a mixed blessing, for another it was an unmitigated disaster. Roy Hattersley, growing up in a Sheffield suburb, went sledging after school every day – 'tearing downhill on home-made toboggans as we used the public highways as our Cresta Run', for at that time 'there were few motor-cars in Wadsley'. But at night he would leap into bed, still with the socks on that had protected him from 'the freezing linoleum', and huddle under an 'immense weight of sheet, thread-bare blankets, home-made eiderdown and coats carried up from the wardrobe at the bottom of the stairs'. For Bill Wyman (then Bill Perks), growing up in Penge, the atrocious weather meant that his bricklayer father was laid off work and no money came in. 'There wasn't enough food to go round, so he'd hit a couple of us, send us to bed without any dinner,' one of Bill's brothers recalled. '"Get to bed, don't argue!" Then you'd get hit, kicked up the stairs – vroom, that was it . . . And in the house we lived in, you didn't *want* to go to bed. It was freezing cold, really nasty, with ice on the inside of the windows and bedbugs that drove us crazy.'

But for two adults these uncongenial weeks proved the great turning point in their lives. Dirk Bogarde was among the cast (along with other unknowns Kenneth More and Dandy Nicholls) in a new play, *Power Without Glory*, about a working-class London family that opened in late February at a theatre club in Notting Hill Gate. Bogarde, only recently demobbed, played the male lead, Cliff, a neurotic who kills a girl in a *crime passionnel*. The play got rave reviews, with particular praise for Bogarde ('an excellent casual murderer, all egotism and nerves'), and within weeks he had signed a seven-year film contract with Rank. Meanwhile, Elizabeth David found herself stuck in a hotel in Ross-on-Wye, a far cry from Athens, Alexandria and Cairo, where she had spent most of the 1940s. 'Conditions *were* awful, shortages *did* make catering a nightmare,' she recalled years later with only moderate equanimity. 'And *still* there was no excuse, none, for such unspeakably dismal meals as in that dining room were put in front of me. To my agonized homesickness for the sun and southern food was added an embattled rage that we should be asked – and should accept – the endurance of such cooking.' So she began 'writing down descriptions of Mediterranean and Middle Eastern cooking. Even to write words like apricot, olives and butter, rice and lemons, oil and almonds, produced assuagement.' Subsequently, she added, 'I came to realize that in the England of 1947, those were dirty words that I was putting down.'[11]

The weather remained bitterly cold until well into March, but industry gradually got its power back and almost all the temporarily unemployed returned to work. The February restrictions on domestic use of electricity, however, remained in force until the end of April, and significantly, the clear evidence was of a rising trend from late February of covert consumption, suggestive of a general unwillingness to make peacetime sacrifices beyond a certain period. Although there were virtually no prosecutions for breaches of the domestic restrictions, the fact was that those restrictions were backed by legal sanctions; Vere Hodgson was one of the law-abiding millions getting increasingly browned-off. 'We have struggled on all the week with no light and restricted hours of electricity,' she noted on 3 March. 'This is to go on. They have domestic consumers well under their thumb now. We are helpless and we just have to do as we are told.' There were still two atrocious snowstorms to endure – in the south and Midlands on the 4th and 5th, when a train from Wolverhampton to London took 26 hours to complete its journey, and just over a week later in Scotland and the north – but eventually the weather did turn. 'The thaw is here!' exalted Gladys Langford on the 10th, and within a week it had spread from the south of England to elsewhere.[12]

For Erica Ford, the young woman living in the queen of suburbs, Tuesday the 18th was a day of almost sublime, unquestioned normality:

After doing my housework & putting on black suit, Daddy dropped me at Ealing Common [ie station] & I went to Knightsbridge & had look round Harrods. No good. Went up to Leicester Sq. for look at shoes – no good. Had snack lunch at Lyons. Met Gwen 1.30 at Swan & Edgars. Walked up Regent St. She got nice navy costume at Peter Robinson. Had tea Dickins & Jones. I got two-way stretch & sports belt at Lewis's & some Goya perfume.

Got home tired out 6.30. Bussed from town.

But even as she wrote, widespread floods, caused by heavy rain accompanying the thaw, were affecting as many as 31 counties south of the River Ouse, destroying 70,000 acres of wheat and 80,000 tons of potatoes. It was the final supply-shortening, queue-lengthening twist to an unforgettable winter.

To a government already much exercised by absenteeism, the temptation to make permanent the temporary ban on midweek sports meetings was irresistible. Although in the event toned down to a statutory ban only on midweek greyhound racing (the sport that was the particular bête noir of high-minded progressives), with more informal midweek restrictions applying to other sports (including football for the rest of the season), it could hardly have been a less popular initiative. 'Austerity for the sake of it' was the inevitable reaction of the *Daily Express*, while on 18 March a *Daily Herald* reader protested strongly, 'The Government must give us some light in these days of austerity. Football and the dogs have been some of that light.' That evening, as Erica Ford flopped down in Ealing, the limits to people's willingness to continue to prioritise the largely cheerless concerns of the public weal were eloquently shown when a radio broadcast by Attlee on the current situation clashed with a rival attraction. Next day, Mass-Observation asked working-class Londoners between the ages of 30 and 55 whether they had listened to the Prime Minister. Four women are followed by five men:

Yes I heard it. I didn't pay much attention to it, it didn't seem important and certainly wasn't interesting.

Yes I did, oh it wasn't bad – nothing startling was there? – I don't like the way he speaks, as if he is reading from a book.

No, I haven't read the paper today either.

No – I had to go out most of last night – my daughter had a baby you know – a boy, 7 pounds it is.

No, no I didn't – I was listening to the boxing.

No mate I didn't, I heard somebody talking about it a little while ago, don't know what they said – they just mentioned it.

No I didn't, it wasn't advertised much was it? As a matter of fact there was something else on which I wanted to listen to very much – the boxing match.

No, sorry chum I didn't.

I listened to half of it, that's all. I got fed up with it and switched over to the fight . . . I was very disgusted with the result of the fight, the referee must have been 'colour blind'. Ha! ha! ha! It wasn't at all fair – & everyone else seems to think the same thing as well.

The fight in question was the British Empire featherweight championship, at the Royal Albert Hall. Al Phillips of Aldgate won on points against Cliff Anderson from British Guyana – 'an extremely unconvincing decision', reported *The Times*, producing 'a very mixed reception'.[13]

It is debatable, though, how much the government's standing was fundamentally affected by the big freeze. Polling figures by Gallup indicated a sharp short-term rise in dissatisfaction with Attlee and his ministers that was almost wiped out by May. Rather, the events of early 1947 should surely be seen as part of a longer-term continuum, in which *existing* weariness with life in post-war Britain merely deepened – a weariness that in itself did not automatically assume a concrete political form. By the end of March, one of the top hit tunes around, in the dance halls and elsewhere, was 'Open the Door, Richard', a recent number one in the US. 'Wanting a thrill?' asked one of *Melody Maker*'s columnists. 'Get a load of Jack White . . . and see the jam-packed floor crowds lapping up the Astoria maestro's sock version of "Richard", with Sonny Rose at the burlesque end.' Over the next few months, 'Open the Door, Richard' became a great catch-phrase, applicable to almost any kind of restriction in everyday life; Attlee was even advised to 'Open the door, Richard' and replace some of his less thrilling elderly ministers.[14] The political prize was there, in other words, for whoever could find the door's key, real or rhetorical.

'But the same owners and managers are still in charge of collieries, and they are doing the same things' was the answer frequently given to Zweig that summer and autumn as he toured the coalfields and asked what difference the new dispensation had made. 'We see hardly any difference in their behaviour.' Those miners who were members of the new, much-trumpeted Colliery Consultative Committees tended to be particularly disenchanted: 'We have no access to the books; the co-operation on the part of the managers is not genuine . . . Our suggestions are completely disregarded and little encouraged . . . We have as little to say about the colliery as before.' A further problem was the excessive centralisation. 'Before, we knew where we stood,' a Derbyshire miner explained. 'When we had a grievance the manager could settle it in five minutes, if not on his own responsibility, after a short conversation on the telephone with the Agent. Now we cannot settle anything with the manager. When we come to the manager, he always shifts everything on to the back of the NCB. "I can't do anything without the NCB," he says. But we don't know the NCB . . .' Inasmuch as miners did know the NCB, Zweig found, 'irritation and indignation are expressed against the high salaries of officials who have no special qualification'. Furthermore, 'One often hears a certain irritation expressed when the miner is told he is now a partner. "Since the Government took over the mines," a miner said to me, "the popular saying of the managers is, 'It's your pit now,' but it is a mockery, because to most of us it does not matter, or benefit us, whether the mine pays or not." If you mention to the miner that he is a partner, he can be very bitter about it.' All in all, Zweig concluded, 'there can be no denial that at present the miners are disillusioned about the outcome of nationalisation'.

The fact that there were more strikes in the year after nationalisation than in the year before – including a long, high-profile dispute at Grimethorpe that spread across the Yorkshire coalfield – lends credence to the Zweig 'disillusioned' thesis. Yet ultimately it is a thesis predicated on the shaky assumption that most miners had 'illusions' in the first place about a fundamental reordering of social and industrial relations. Moreover, if in reality their aspirations for nationalisation were mainly more modest – focusing in the best 'labourist' tradition on solid, unglamorous, incremental improvements – then it is at least arguable that in the course of 1947/8 these pragmatic hopes started to be realised. 'Working conditions improved markedly almost from the beginning,' Roy Mason, a Yorkshire miner who later became a Labour minister, recalled. 'Training was introduced for newcomers before ever they went down to the coalface. A ban was introduced on young boys going underground before they were sixteen. We had a national safety scheme, with proper standards at every colliery. And for the first time, pithead baths became a standard facility.'[15] There were also improved wages and, despite ministerial and NCB misgivings, the introduction of the five-day week.

So much depends on how one sees the miners – specifically, whether one buys into the somewhat romantic view, prevalent in the 1970s, that they were natural militants who wanted workers' control and had been cruelly betrayed by the stodgy, bureaucratic form that public ownership took. But a rather different narrative starts to emerge if one accepts that the miners, for all their class solidarity and physical courage, were real – and therefore flawed – people: conservative (including about such matters as Polish labour and new forms of mechanisation), usually money-minded, sometimes bloody-minded, always deeply mistrustful.[16] In about June 1948 Mass-Observation surveyed 50 miners and 50 miners' wives in the Doncaster area about their attitudes to nationalisation. Just over three in five expressed 'unqualified approval', mainly on the grounds of the improved wages; just over one in ten expressed 'disapproval', predominantly because 'the old owners of the mines still wielded considerable power'; and among the others, approval was qualified by 'much vocal criticism' about 'the organisation of specific jobs, the alleged increase of officials, and the growth of impersonality in organisation generally'. There were the familiar complaints, echoing Zweig's findings, about remote, overpaid, high-handed 'top hats', but there was no sense of the strong wish to see more consultation of the 'man on the spot' being translated into a desire for the miners to assume strategic control of the industry.

Three pieces of testimony were especially suggestive. The first was by a packer maddened by the impractical *specifics* of nationalisation:

Oh, I don't know what goes on at the Coal Board. I expect it's even worse than down here at the pit. But down here there's far too many non-producers. I can't see the necessity for an 'over-man', a 'deputy', and a 'shot firer' for each district. That's what we've got now in the pit. Before nationalisation we only had one deputy for the same district and we got on all right. They seem to have plenty of money to throw about. They could produce cheaper coal if they got rid of the wasters.

A scientist at one of the pits, himself the son of a miner who had been killed at that pit during the war, presented an unflattering but convincing snapshot: 'The other day I was underground taking samples, and I happened to come to a face where the men didn't know me and they definitely treated me as a spiv – they said so ... A lot of the miners think if you are not producing coal then you are a spiv ... The be all and end all is the wage packet and anything likely to affect that is taboo. I am sure they think that my wages are coming out of their pay packet.' The third slice of testimony was by a rank-and-file miner, reflecting what the report found to be a widespread suspicion of the union leaders: 'They're all piss and wind ... Talk, talk, but when it comes down to doing anything, that's another matter ... The trouble is especially with the Welsh bastards, they all think in the past and not the present.'[17] With coal in high demand, and with apparently no significant rival source of energy on the horizon, it was a present and immediate future that was looking surprisingly good.

9

Our Prestige at Stake

'How do you feel about unmarried people living together?' was the question that Mass-Observation put to various Londoners in March 1947. 'I think it's perfectly terrible,' replied one middle-class woman in her 50s, 'because the woman always gets the worst of it and it's the beginning of heartbreak.' By contrast, the working-class response was notably non-judgemental:

I wouldn't do it myself, but I've an open mind on it, and circumstances may have a lot to do with it.

I suppose it's up to those people themselves – it's up to them entirely.

I mind my business and I don't care what others do – that's theirs.

I don't feel nothing.

Don't know, never thought about it.

If you love one another, it's all right I suppose.

I'm not a prude by nature, it's their affair.

Significantly, this unenthusiastic but ultimately pragmatic reaction to sex before marriage was partly repeated – but only partly – when it came to the accompanying question, 'How do you feel about divorce?'

It depends on the people. If either is to blame they should have a divorce.

Well, I mean to say, it's a good thing if the couple are unhappy.

No. A man takes a wife for better or worse, doesn't he?

I wouldn't grant divorce, they should get on with it.

I feel very sorry for the kiddies. It's very hard on them but if Mother and Father can't agree it only makes the children suffer worse – they suffer inwardly.

I think it's an awful thing to happen to anyone – everybody turns away from a divorced woman.

Better to divorce than live unhappily.

I don't like the idea of a divorce – all the publicity and scandal.

In some cases, yes. Marriage is a gamble anyway.

The divorce rate may have been rising – inevitable in the immediate aftermath of war – but across society the stigma remained. Sir Francis Meynell, creator and editor of the long-running, best-selling annual anthology *The Week-End Book*, was from 1946 no longer welcome at royal garden parties on account of his divorce that year, nor from 1947 were two judges who had been discovered by the Lord Chamberlain to have neglected to mention their divorces in their *Who's Who* entries. Divorce law itself had been liberalised in 1937, to the extent that cruelty and desertion had joined adultery as legitimate grounds, but this was still a long way from divorce by mutual consent. 'Would you approve or disapprove if it were made possible to get a divorce simply by agreement between the two parties?' asked Gallup in April 1948. Tellingly, only 27 per cent replied positively, with a bias towards the young and the middle class.[1]

For those visiting the first post-war *Daily Mail* Ideal Home Exhibition at Olympia in March 1947 ('Queues in all directions,' noted a hungry Vere Hodgson. 'We never got a bite.'), the publicity brochure of the furniture-makers James Broderick & Co. left little doubt about woman's place in the overall scheme of things. 'What every newly-wed should know' included a 'Day-to-Day Plan' for new brides:

Monday. Is not essentially a day for laundry. Scour the kitchen after week-end catering activities, check up on rations and shop for vegetables, canned foods and breakfast cereals for a few days ahead.

Tuesday. Manage the light personal laundry, leaving the sheets and bath towels. Get all items dried and ironed during the day whenever possible.

Wednesday. Clean thoroughly bedrooms and bathrooms and use early afternoon for silver cleaning.

Thursday. Change bedlinen, launder 'heavies'. While they dry, clean the
lounge. Iron early afternoon.

Friday. Plan meals for week-end, making provision for Monday 'left-overs'.
Shop. Give dining room or dining alcove a thorough clean and polish.

Saturday. Keep this free for the family as far as possible. Prepare vegetables for Sunday and manage some cooking in the morning. Then
relax.

Sunday. Belongs to you and those who share the home with you. Confine
all essential cooking to early part of morning.

'What you wear in the house for the working hours is important,'
added a section on appearance. 'Crisp, easily removed gay overalls,
smocks, nylon or spongeable plastic aprons look attractive. Wear your
hair as you would do for the man-of-the-house's homecoming.'

At this point only about a quarter of married women were in the
labour force, and during much of 1947 and 1948, as in 1946, there
was considerable pressure from the Ministry of Labour on young
married women to return to work. If there was a representative
woman's voice in the face of nothing less than a propaganda bombardment, it was surely that of Mary Grieve, editor of the top-selling
women's magazine, *Woman*. '"But surely you don't think they will
call up women!" said my friend in tones of horror in the middle of
our discussion on Britain's dire shortage of manpower,' she reported
in February 1947. 'Looking at her shocked face I hardly knew what
to say.' Over the ensuing months, Grieve and her columnist Joan
Lambert stressed how exhausted the housewife at home already was
and called on husbands, industry and government to offer practical
help to make it more realistic for married women, particularly if they
were mothers, to return to the workplace. In short, 'appeals to women's
patriotism are not enough.' And, daringly, 'perhaps what we need is
a Mothers' Union affiliated to the TUC!'[2] The suggestion was half
tongue-in-cheek, but only half.

It remained clear what most men thought. A snatch of saloon-bar
conversation at the Travellers Rest in Aston was overheard in June
1947. Said one man: 'It's all very well asking women to come back
into industry but there are plenty of men out of work. It beats me.'
His fellow-drinker of mild agreed: 'A woman's got a day's work in

the house anyway . . .' As for women themselves, a survey of almost 3,000 of them soon afterwards found that 'apart from small percentages who were either positively in favour of women working or positively against it, the majority thought that women should go out to work only if they can carry out their duties to their homes and families' – that, in other words, 'a woman's first duty is to her home'. Strikingly, less than a third of 'the occupied women' in the survey 'thought that in general women should go out to work'; among 'unoccupied' women, the proportion was less than a fifth.

Yet if there existed – as clearly there did, especially among many women who had worked during the war – a profound desire to get back to (and then stay put in) homemaking normality in familiar surroundings, that was not the exclusive sentiment. 'It's ridiculous to be forced to live like a schoolgirl at the age of twenty-four,' Phyllis Noble wrote in her diary in May 1947. 'The war pulled me out of Lee [a mixed Victorian suburb in south-east London], and now I must make my own road. There is no doubt in my mind that I must get "a room of my own".' She had recently been demobbed from the WAAF, and like many young women – and young men – she had every intention after the war of continuing to broaden her horizons. Later that summer, waiting to start a course to train as a hospital social worker, she went one day to Westminster Abbey in the hope of seeing the Battle of Britain Memorial. 'A long, unpleasant queue put me off,' she noted. 'Odd to see many women (including self) hatless. Such a revolution in so short a time!' Did this sudden hatless-ness presage a new sense of female independence? The emergence by 1947 of Christine Norden (daughter of a Sunderland bus driver and reputedly spotted in an Edgware Road cinema queue) as Britain's first post-war blonde, busty film star only arguably supports the thesis. Either way, the harsh home and/or work dilemma remained, as implacably expounded in the brilliant 1948 Michael Powell and Emeric Pressburger film *The Red Shoes*. Moira Shearer, playing a talented young dancer, is compelled by her lover to choose between giving up her career and giving up her would-be husband. It is a choice she is unable to make, and, in the absence of a third way, she dies.[3]

How did the nation's home-dwellers, whether homemakers or not, spend their free time? Not on the whole in reading, let alone self-improving reading. A Mass-Observation survey in the summer of 1947, carried out among almost a thousand Tottenham residents, revealed that '"reading" was given as the favourite hobby by three in ten of the middle class, by two in ten of the skilled working class, and by one in ten of the unskilled'. Almost half the sample said they never read books at all, but only one in ten went without reading a daily paper (the *Daily Mirror*, the *News Chronicle*, the *Daily Herald* and the *Daily Express* being the most popular), and a mere one in 20 did not read a Sunday paper (with three out of five favouring the *News of the World*). As for magazines, they were preponderantly read by the middle class. Non-readers of books, a group far more working-class than middle-class in composition, were asked to explain their lack of interest:

> None of them subjects is interesting to me. All I like is gangster stories, though there's precious much chance of reading here. Three rooms we got and three kids knocking around. No convenience, no nothing except water. I'm glad to get out of the house I can tell you.
>
>   Cos I ain't got no interest in them – they all apparently lead up to the same thing.
>
>   I'm not very good at reading, I never was. I've never liked it some'ow.
>
>   Too long. I like to get straight into a story. I have started books and I have to read through the first pages two or three times. I like to get stuck straight into a story – there's too much preliminary if you see what I mean.

Less than a quarter of the sample belonged to Tottenham Public Library. 'I don't want to bother' was one explanation; 'I ain't never even thought on it, never mind a reason' another.

Among readers, five preferred fiction to every one favouring non-fiction (in which the two most favoured topics were sport and health). 'I like something I can relax in,' reflected an elderly man. 'Don't like anything that gets me worried and wondering.' Crime and mystery stories were almost twice as popular as any other subject. 'There's nothing to beat a good detective story,' declared a young manual worker. 'Keeps you interested all the way through. When I get into a good murder story I don't hear any of the noise what's going on in the house or anything.' Working-class female readers had, predictably, a penchant for romance:

> My friend is very keen on love stories and when she gets a real good one she brings it in. Some of them are very good and I enjoy a real good cry when I read them . . .
>   My friend lives two doors away and I get books for her too. She likes the same kind of stories as well. It's nice to read about that sort of love and better class people, for you don't notice things as much then. It's a real pleasure to read Ruby M. Ayres' books and I often cry over them.

Ayres was one of Tottenham's six most popular authors – behind Edgar Wallace, Charles Dickens and Ethel M. Dell (a rival purveyor of the old-fashioned love story), ahead of Naomi Jacob (who wrote family rather than love stories) and Agatha Christie.[4] A list of only patchy quality admittedly, but not out-and-out rubbish either, its inclusion of Dickens reminding one that this was a world nearer to the Victorian era than to the early twenty-first century.

Reading (whether of books, papers or magazines) played second fiddle to the wireless in most homes. A survey of domestic evening activities in almost 2,000 households over a wide range of urban dwellings across the country, completed in the spring of 1947, found that whereas the percentage of people reading for half an hour or more was never more than 15 per cent in any two-hour period, there were for equivalent half-hour periods never less than 20 per cent of households with the radio switched on and often more than 30 per cent. The radio was on in no less than 40 per cent of households where school homework was in progress, while the other three most frequent pairs of conflicting activities taking place in the same physical space were radio and reading, radio and conversation, and 'radio and resting'. Given all these and other conflicting activities (including 'between children playing and other people resting' and 'between visitors and meals'), it might be expected that bedrooms were utilised for activities other than sleeping and dressing, but in practice, no doubt partly because of lack of heating, less than 10 per cent were.

Besides, to go upstairs might mean missing *Dick Barton – Special Agent* (15 million listeners a night, a cliffhanger at the end of every episode), or *Twenty Questions* (featuring Richard Dimbleby), or *Down Your Way* (Dimbleby again), or *Variety Bandbox* (making an instant star of Frankie Howerd) or even Benny Hill, who made his radio debut later in 1947. Startlingly, a survey done in June that year of more than 3,000 of the adult listening public found that 77 per cent usually listened while eating each of the three main meals of the day – including eight out of ten for the evening meal, which for two-thirds had taken place by 6.30. Not that these habitual listeners heard much in the way of vigorous airing of the issues of the day, with the BBC in 1947 formally issuing a self-denying ordinance which forbade discussion of any matters either currently being debated in parliament or due in the next fortnight to be debated there. Known as the 'fourteen day rule' or 'fourteen day gag', it was all too typical of an organisation (starting to be known as 'Auntie') that, in the acerbic but just words of one historian, 'shunned controversy and censored itself'.[5]

Similarly symptomatic of the BBC's lack of a hard journalistic edge was the continuing unwillingness to provide regular news bulletins on television. A first generation of television personalities was emerging, including Richard Hearne (aka Mr Pastry) and the bearded cook Philip Harben, famous for using his actual family rations on screen, though programmes could be received only within an expanding but limited radius of about 50 miles from Alexandra Palace, sets were still expensive and difficult to get, and by 1948 a mere 4.3 per cent of the adult population had one in their homes. Even within the BBC, there was little faith in the new medium. In June 1947 R.J.E. Silvey, in charge of audience research and a professed Home Service rather than Light Programme listener, gave three reasons, in addition to 'the extremely high standard of sound broadcasting', why he would not buy a set on his own account if he did not already have a staff set:

The picture itself still seems very primitive. Once the miraculous aspect of television has faded, as it inevitably does, the picture tends to be compared with that of the cinema. The comparison is least odious in respect of television studio productions, but in respect of O.B.s [outside broadcasts] the deficiencies of television are very obtrusive . . . Watching television for as much as an hour is, in our experience, liable to give one the same kind of headache as going to the early cinema did.

For 'people like us' the programmes themselves contain much which is of very little appeal. For example, we just aren't Variety-minded. An occasional little revue is the most in this field which we should ask for from television. In practice, once a fortnight would be the upper limit of our demands for this kind of thing ... Magazine programmes such as *Kaleidoscope* and *Picture Page* seem to us amusing enough if one wishes to demonstrate television to a friend but never of sufficient appeal to warrant switching the set on specially ...

Finally, by no means the least potent factor militating against television in my kind of home is the sheer palaver involved in having to watch it. It means putting the light out, moving the furniture around and settling down to give the programme undivided attention.

But for the less favoured, including Judy Haines in Chingford a few weeks later, the acquisition of a set was exciting enough:

26 July (Saturday). Escott's could get Pye television by Monday!

9 August. Abbé off and put his name down for television. Missed recent good opportunity to buy.

11 September. Had Pye Television Set delivered.

13 September. Abbé had televised cricket while I took Ione to park.

16 September. Television aerial fixed. It took from lunch until nearly 7 o'c.

4 October. Mum and Dad H. came for television variety.

Over in even leafier Ealing, Erica Ford's family got their set early in 1948:

9 February (Monday). It is a Murphy. In the evening we saw television music hall & winter sports. Very good.

10 February. In afternoon looked at television film about Mounties – quite good.

12 February. We saw play 'Gaslight' which was very interesting & so of course knitting remained undone.

29 February. Saw 'Muffin the Mule', a marionette – very good.

1 March. Spent evening looking in & then went off to bed in bit better time [ie than after the previous evening's viewing].

15 March. More knitting & saw television *Dancing Club*. I listened to
play in kitchen, while rest of family saw more television.

That summer, some 900 viewers, predominantly 'suburban, middle
class and middle aged', returned a BBC questionnaire asking about
their television-watching habits. It transpired that an evening rarely
passed in which the owner of a set did not switch on, with no fewer
than 91 per cent saying that it was their habit to watch from 8.30 p.m.
(or earlier) to close-down. Some 16 per cent said they had to make
'frequent' adjustments to the set, and 58 per cent 'occasional' adjustments, in order to get a better picture. As for programme content, the
tone of the replies reflected, according to the BBC's analysis, 'plenty
of enthusiasm for plays – but not "morbid" plays – plenty of prejudice
against dance music, and so on'.[6] All in all, television was hardly yet
the people's medium, but it was clearly starting to be somewhat
addictive for those who had it.

An older addiction was well served on both mediums. Fred Streeter
(former head gardener at Petworth House and almost instantly celebrated for his Sussex burr) emerged as the first regular television
gardener in 1947, the same year that *Country Questions* began (in
April) on the radio at Sunday lunchtime. A direct forerunner of
Gardeners' Question Time, it fielded listeners' queries 'about the countryside', with the celebrated farmer-journalist A. G. Street in the chair
and a panel that featured the West Country's quasi-professional – and
deeply reactionary – countryman Ralph Wightman, the voice from
Piddletrenthide on VE night. The programme's regular listeners may
have included the 400 members of the Bethnal Green Allotments and
Gardens Association. 'Curiously enough they won't go in for competitions,' the group's middle-class-sounding secretary observed in
August 1947 to an investigator into voluntary activities and groups.
'They won't believe they're good enough.' The investigator observed
that the members did not seem to have much contact among themselves:

Yes, that's true. We have no meeting place and it is largely an individual
affair and the Association helps with tools and advice ... There was a
scheme: we got some waste ground on the Wellington Estate: there were

40 gardening members there who thought it was a grand idea to start a sort of cultural centre and they're doing very well I think: there's a Mr H. who lives there and is very keen on it ... I tried to start the same scheme in three other estates but it did not work. I've come to the conclusion that you must have the leadership from among the people themselves, it's no good otherwise.

Elsewhere, the gardening signals were mixed. Contemporary illustrations of suburban back gardens suggest a new premium being put on order, often taking the form of a rectangular lawn, a single tree positioned in the middle, regularly placed square paving stones, and each plant surrounded by a large amount of soil. But for the many thousands of married women now staying at home, willingly or otherwise, there was the inspiriting Constance Spry, who started her flower-arranging school in 1946, wrote prolifically in magazines and, in Jenny Uglow's words, 'liked boldness, old roses, unexpected wild flowers, flashes of lime-green – just what was needed after wartime gloom'.[7] Although the future ultimately belonged to colourful display and dense planting-cum-foliage, there remained a stubborn puritanical streak in the British gardening psyche.

The nation's supreme demotic moment in 1947 came soon after the debut of Street, Wightman et al. On Saturday, 10 May, at the huge terraced bowl that was Hampden Park in Glasgow, 134,000 (out of the 500,000 who had applied for tickets) watched Great Britain versus The Rest of Europe. 'Britain Must Beat Europe: Our Prestige At Stake' was that morning's *Daily Express* headline about what had, the paper's Frank Butler declared, 'become known as the Match of the Century'. Butler was adamant that even a draw 'would be regarded as a moral victory by the Continentals and leave us the laughing stock of Europe'; among the opposition, he singled out the 'sinister figure' of Parola, 'the sallow-skinned and dark curly-haired Italian centre half, who is said to be a master stopper'. Moreover, he warned about The Rest of Europe team as a whole: 'They cleverly avoided revealing any of their talents to the British reporters who watched them yesterday. All they showed was some mighty fine acrobatics and high kicking.'

He need not have worried. Stanley Matthews of Stoke City enjoyed on the right wing an afternoon of mazy dribbles, Chelsea's Tommy

Lawton and Middlesbrough's Wilf Mannion each scored twice, and despite the best efforts of Parola (wearing 'the briefest of briefs') the home team ran out comfortable 6–1 winners. 'Europe is now convinced that the British are bosses of Soccer,' Butler duly wrote, and that evening, in a Glasgow hotel, Matthews signed for Blackpool for £11,500 and a deceptively hedonistic bottle of champagne. By this time the football season was going into overtime because of the many post-ponements caused by the big freeze, and the first post-war Division 1 championship was not settled until mid-June. In a tight finish it went to Liverpool, whose decisive goal in the last match at Wolves was scored by their red-haired centre forward Albert Stubbins. Established that day as a Liverpool icon, he would feature (with a broad grin) almost exactly 20 years later on the cover of *Sgt. Pepper's Lonely Hearts Club Band*.

In the 1940s there were still several professional sportsmen who combined soccer with cricket – among them the gifted, charismatic Denis Compton, who in 1947 experienced a true annus mirabilis. It was not just that he broke all batting records for England and Middlesex, scoring an astonishing 18 hundreds in the course of the season, but the spontaneous, life-affirming way in which he played at such a drab and depressing time. Neville Cardus, finest of English cricket writers, was among those cheering:

> Never have I been so deeply touched on a cricket ground as I was in this heavenly summer, when I went to Lord's to see a pale-faced crowd, existing on rations, the rocket bomb still in the ears of most folk – see this worn, dowdy crowd watching Compton. The strain of long years of anxiety and affliction passed from all hearts and shoulders at the sight of Compton in full sail, sending the ball here, there and everywhere, each stroke a flick of delight, a propulsion of happy sane healthy life. There were no rations in an innings by Compton . . .

Quite early in the season, on 11 June, in the first Test against South Africa at Nottingham, Compton made a match-saving 163. That same day, from the hills above Florence, Dylan Thomas wrote to one of the BBC commentators, 'I hear your voice every day from Trent Bridge . . . You're not only the best cricket commentator – far and away that; but the best sports commentator I've heard, ever; exact, enthusiastic, prejudiced, amazingly visual, authoritative, and friendly.' The recipient was John Arlott, who, in two remarkable years since the war, had stopped being a Southampton policeman and become first a poetry producer at the BBC (working closely with Thomas) and then a cricket commentator and writer. During the 1947 season, he emerged as a nationally known voice and name, his Hampshire burr (what the Head of Outside Broadcasts called 'a vulgar voice') in striking contrast to the conventional, upper-middle-class tones of E. W. Swanton and Rex Alston. For Arlott, at best a mediocre cricketer himself, these immediate post-war years were like a dream; he fell more than half in love with professional cricket as a way of life and with those who played it. 'On a sane and economic level no argument can be adduced for a man becoming a county cricketer,' he wrote soon after the season ended, in a sober assessment of the professional cricketer's many uncertainties and lack of material rewards. 'He is valuable to the student of social history only as an example of the incurable romantic – but it is difficult indeed to deny him sympathy, perhaps even envy.'[8]

During the hot summer of 1947, benefiting from the pre-war Holidays with Pay Act that gave most of the workforce a mandatory and paid one-week annual break, about half the population took a holiday away from home, the overwhelming majority staying within Britain. 'Blackpool: The Holiday Playground of the World' was the title of that premier resort's 1947 brochure, advertising a huge array of hotels, 'boarding establishments' and so on, each invoking a key phrase designed to allure: 'good English cooking', 'separate tables', 'very homely apartments', 'personal supervision', 'central for amusements', 'Vi-spring beds'. Sid Chaplin confined himself to a day trip in June. 'What impressed me most was the number of fish & chip shops, and the high quality of their service,' he told a friend. 'I'm afraid the air isn't very bracing, especially round about ten p.m., when it's full of the stench of stale beer . . . I enjoyed myself in the Pleasure Park, won five woodbines at the rifle stalls and a tin cigarette ash tray . . . Blackpool is a paradise for pleasure.'[9]

Seaside resorts attuned to the urban millions had been flourishing since the late nineteenth century, but the holiday-camp phenomenon was much newer. Although there were other chains – most notably Pontin's and Warner's – the concept became over the years almost synonymous with Butlin's. Billy Butlin's first camp started at Skegness in 1936, to be followed by Clacton two years later; by 1947 he had added Filey, Ayr and Pwllheli. He was certainly on to a winner. In May 1947 W. J. Brown (the Independent MP) went to Butlin's house-warming party at his new home – Dane Court, Bishop's Road, Hampstead – and found 'a magnificent house standing in spacious grounds' and 'furnished most sumptuously', with appreciative guests tucking into 'mountains of lovely food – cold chicken, tongue, crab, salad, asparagus, vegetable salads, and heaven knows what'. Butlin, a driven man, had a flair for publicity; and that summer saw the release of *Holiday Camp*, a sentimental drama introducing the lovable cockney family the Huggetts to the British screen and starring Jack Warner and Kathleen Harrison, with Petula Clark as their 12-year-old daughter. It proved a major box-office success, and Gladys Langford, after going to the Marble Arch Pavilion, thought it 'one of the funniest films I ever saw', though she did add that 'if this be a real picture of a holiday camp, God forbid I should visit one . . . I'd rather live out my life in a basement flat in quietude.'

The idea for the film came from the immensely popular writer (especially in women's magazines) Godfrey Winn, who had been enthused by a brief visit to Butlin's at Filey. Significantly, he depicted the holiday camp as a social melting-pot, where the different classes could come together – on the face of it a fanciful notion, yet it seems that for several years after the war the clientele were as much middle-class as working-class. That did not stop the camps acquiring, in some eyes, a reputation as little better than concentration camps for the proletariat. At a cocktail party in September 1947, a Mass-Observation investigator heard a young middle-class actor from the film being asked if he had gone on location (Butlin's in Skegness) for it. 'My God no, thank heaven,' he replied. 'But a lot of them did – they were there seven weeks – ghastly – it's miles from everywhere and they were stuck.' And as he eloquently added – 'Can you believe it – it's all so hearty and childish they even have "Lads and Lassies" on the Cloakroom doors – Christ!'

Soon afterwards, another Mass-Observation investigator travelled up to Filey in Yorkshire to see a Butlin's Holiday Camp for herself – unfortunately rather late in the season, but the half-empty site still had about 5,000 campers. Her first meal proved a bit of a culture shock – no choice of dishes and being designated to sit with strangers at the same table all week – and then on Saturday evening came the first entertainment, *Butlin Follies of 1947*, a variety show: 'The theatre was packed out, and the audience most appreciative, applauding each turn vociferously.' Next morning, after the daily reveille sung over the tannoy ('There's a new day a tumblin' in') and breakfast, she joined the queue for Sunday papers. 'Standing about outside the shop,' she noticed, 'were small groups of people feverishly looking at the football results and checking on their coupons to see if they had won anything on their Pools that week. Everywhere you walked people were doing the same.' Each day's programme had at least one contest, and on Sunday afternoon it was 'Holiday Lovelies', with the winner getting a loud round of applause at dinner that evening 'when she was asked to stand up so we could all have a look at her'.

Over the next few days, the investigator settled in, on Tuesday evening even enjoying the dancing:

At 10.30 two of the Red-coats disappeared from the Ballroom with a big drum ready for the 'Penny-on-the-Drum' parade. This is a nightly occurrence which everyone appears to thoroughly enjoy. The main idea is that the Red-coats bang the drum as they walk along and gradually collect a long string of campers behind them by singing

> 'Come and join us
> Come and join us
> Come and join our merry throng.'

The procession begins in the Regency Bar, works its way all through the camp, through the Viennese Bar and ends up with everybody in the Viennese Ballroom. Everybody is laughing and singing at the top of their voices and the procession winds round and round in the Ballroom and finally breaks up when the orchestra strikes up for the final dance of the evening.

Thursday evening featured the Campers' Concert – 14 items, each 'greeted with vigorous applause' – and on Friday afternoon there was 'Fun and Games' at the giant Bathing Pool: 'Everybody seemed in particularly good spirits . . . and felt a special kind of mateyness and comradeship with all their fellow campers.' The camp as a whole was divided into four houses (Gloucester, Kent, Windsor, York); in her concluding remarks on her week's experience, the investigator reckoned that the many inter-house competitions worked as well as they did because there was 'a suspension of disbelief sufficient to give them a sense of communal effort and general mateyness'. The campers, in other words, did not suddenly abandon their critical faculties once they entered this cocooned world of communal pleasures on tap. 'The picture sometimes painted of a set of solemn, suspicious, inhibited people arriving, and a set of slap-happy, healthy, gloriously carefree, 100% Butlinites leaving is distinctly wide of the mark; the vital thing is that some progress is made with everybody, giving a social atmosphere more healthy than the norm.'[10]

The summer of 1947 was dramatic and expectant for Glenda Jackson. A labourer's daughter, growing up in Hoylake, she took her 11 plus – only to find that on the day of the results there was a mix-up, involving a long, dreadful period at her girls' primary school being given pitying looks by everyone while those who had passed received multiple congratulations. Eventually, on returning home, she found and read the letter announcing that she had passed. 'I saw adults whom I had known all my life change their attitude to me twice in the space of a very small time,' she recalled. 'Contemptible.'

That autumn, Jackson started at West Kirby Grammar School for Girls, where the expensive, distinctly middle-class uniform require-ments included one's own gym outfit, hockey stick and tennis racquet. Albert Finney, a bookmaker's son from Salford and born on the same day as Jackson, also started at grammar school then, as did Bill Wyman, in his case at Beckenham and Penge Grammar School. 'Ninety per cent came from upper- or middle-class homes in the expensive parts of suburban Kent,' Wyman remembered. 'Penge, my home, was definitely the wrong side of the tracks. I was inhibited by what other kids called my "working-class" accent, and a sense of inferiority prevented me from inviting them to my small and spartan home.' Meanwhile, 'local kids in Penge threw bricks at me, knocking my grammar-school blazer and cap (which my father could ill afford to buy).' Altogether, it was 'a no-win situation', not least because 'if I tried "talking posh" as they called it when I got home, I was mocked by everyone around me'.

There were, however, significant straws in the wind pointing to a different, potentially less divisive future. At that year's Labour Party conference a resolution from Bristol calling on the minister George Tomlinson to consider 'the rapid development' of common secondary schools, 'in order to give real equality of opportunity to all the nation's children', received unanimous support, while over the next year a handful of local authorities were pushing hard for at least a quorum of comprehensives to be established. The new (but as yet far from universal) egalitarianism was epitomised by the 1948 report entitled *The Comprehensive School* by the National Association of Labour Teachers: 'So long as this stratification of children at the age of eleven remains it is in practice useless to talk of parity in education or of equal opportunity in later life.' After dismissing intelligence tests as 'pseudo-scientific' and intended 'to create an intellectual aristocracy', the report declared, 'It is high time that we forgot the unverified assumption that only a small percentage of our children have sufficient native ability to move on to advanced work of a high standard.'

Three Schools or One? was the title of Lady Simon of Wythenshawe's discussion of the subject that same year. A leading, progressive-minded figure for many years on Manchester's education committee, she here willingly accentuated the drawbacks of tripartism (grammar, modern, technical) and the positives of the comprehensive secondary school. Simultaneously, however, she felt bound to point out that 'middle-class parents will not readily send their children to a school in which they feel that the tone of speech and behaviour will be set by children coming from the poorest homes.' And she made an equally pertinent further point: such parents in this situation would, if they could afford it, look instead to the private sector.[11]

The Whole World Is Full of Permits

There was much on the Labour Party's mind by 1947/8 as – following the great burst of legislation since 1945 – it sought to orientate itself for the 1950s. Would it, for instance, tamely line up behind Ernest Bevin's strong pro-American, anti-Communist line? Over Easter 1947, shortly after President Harry Truman had proclaimed his fiercely anti-Soviet Doctrine, denouncing Communism for its inherent expansionism and promising on the part of the free world an 'enduring struggle' against it, three youngish Labour MPs (Richard Crossman, Michael Foot and Ian Mikardo) wrote an almost instantly published pamphlet, *Keep Left*. Critical of Bevin's 'dangerous dependence' on the US, it demanded that British and French Socialists form an alliance sufficiently strong 'to hold the balance of world power, to halt the division into a Western and Eastern bloc and so to make the United Nations a reality'. Within weeks there appeared a counter-pamphlet, *Cards on the Table*, written by Denis Healey on Bevin's behalf and pouring the coldest of cold water on the notion that Britain had anywhere else but the US to turn to if it was serious about wanting to moderate Russia's 'aggressive anti-British policy'.

Over the following nine months, two crucial developments persuaded Crossman et al to turn right. The first was the American initiative (first flagged in June 1947) that in due course became Marshall Aid: large-scale economic assistance to enable Europe's (including Britain's) post-war reconstruction, welcomed almost as much on the Labour left as on its right. The other, in February 1948, was the Communist coup in Czechoslovakia, which was extraordinarily hard to reconcile with a benign reading of Soviet foreign policy. The dramatic events in Berlin during the spring and summer – Russian blockade followed by Western airlift – merely confirmed the point. Benn Levy, briefly a Labour MP after becoming a well-known playwright, spoke in 1948 for many bruised and disillusioned Keep Lefters: 'There is no longer a third choice. We must travel the Russian road or the American road . . . Are we to choose the American alignment which it is widely feared may jeopardise our Socialism, or the Russian alignment which, with the object lesson of Czechoslovakia in mind, we may reasonably believe would end in the loss of our democracy? For better or worse, the choice is made.'[1] Levy did not need to add that that painful, deeply unenthusiastic choice was for the almighty (and more or less democratic) dollar – a choice that from the start precluded neither a continuing visceral anti-Americanism nor a lingering sentimental attachment to the Soviet Union and its stout-hearted people.

As the Cold War set in during 1947/8, so the British Communist Party inexorably hardened its line and narrowed its options. The Labour government was now attacked by it at every opportunity, above all for its subservience to America, while Stalin and the Soviet Union received unstinting, unwavering support, whatever the circumstances and tergiversations. Inevitably, there were defectors. 'I gradually became uncomfortable in the Party and hostile to it,' the playwright Robert Bolt, then a student at Manchester University, recalled of this time. 'I could get no sense out of the people I revered in the Party and no honest answers to the questions I was asking. So I left.' Nor was there much evidence that the shift of approach was striking any great popular chords. Quite the reverse, as the writer (and youthful CP member) Mervyn Jones discovered when he went to Wigan in February 1948 to help the Communist candidate in a by-election:

A few days before the poll, the Communists took power in Czecho-slovakia. It was true that the crisis was provoked by the right-wing parties, who miscalculated their strength; but it was also obvious that the CP would establish a monopoly of power. Up in Wigan, Party leaders, including Harry Pollitt, hastily conferred and produced a leaflet which began: 'Rejoice! Democracy has triumphed in Czechoslovakia!' In the gloom of a snowy morning, I helped to hand it out at the gate of a cotton-mill. The workers littered the ground with it. We polled about 1,300 votes. A Communist candidate today [1987] would be more than satisfied with that figure, but in 1948 it was seen as disastrous.

Overall, the onset of the Cold War could not but affect the temper of British public life. As early as May 1947, Attlee began to chair a Special Cabinet Committee on Subversive Activities; in early 1948 the government established the Information and Research Department (IRD), essentially an anti-Communist propaganda unit; and on 15 March, soon after the Prague coup, Attlee announced that members of the CP and those 'associated with it' would henceforth be forbidden from undertaking work deemed 'vital to the security of the State'. The immediate consequences were dramatic. There began the process of systematically investigating individual civil servants; new academic appointments were more or less closed for Communists or Communist sympathisers; and the BBC summarily dismissed Alex McCrindle, a Communist actor known to millions as 'Jock' in *Dick Barton*. Altogether it was hardly an edifying spectacle; yet whether the Attlee government's quite aggressively illiberal anti-Communism necessarily occupied the moral low ground is arguably another matter. Context, the historian Alan Bullock would remind younger readers almost 40 years later, was all:

> There was a real danger of the Soviet Union and other communists taking advantage of the weakness of Western Europe to extend their power. We know now that this did not follow, but nobody knew it at the time. This was a generation for whom war and occupation were not remote hypotheses but recent and terrible experiences. The fear of another war, the fear of a Russian occupation, haunted Europe in those years and were constantly revived – by the communist coup in Czechoslovakia, by the Berlin blockade.

It was unhistorical, in short, 'to dismiss those fears as groundless because the war and occupation did not occur'.[2]

There were similar heart-searchings over nationalisation. By the summer of 1947, all the public-ownership commitments in the election manifesto had been implemented or were in train – with the exception of the iron and steel industry, always the most controversial of the

1945 promises. Utilities and transport, after all, were publicly owned in many other capitalist countries, while the coal industry in private hands had been generally acknowledged to be in the knackers' yard. But the steel industry, although widely recognised to need a shake-up, was something else. Aneurin Bevan, whose constituency included the Ebbw Vale steelworks, pushed the hardest for early and full nation-alisation, positing it not only as an economic and social good in itself but also as symbolically crucial in demonstrating that Britain's first socialist government with an overall majority had not run out of steam. His opponents included the steelmasters, Lincoln Evans (leader of the steel workers' union) and Herbert Morrison. Eventually, after some heated discussions, including at what was described as a 'very hysterical and steamed up' meeting of the parliamentary party, the Cabinet decided in favour of full nationalisation but not until the 1948/9 parlia-mentary session.

For Morrison, it was a battle lost; henceforth, despite being the principal architect of the way in which nationalisation worked in practice, he was determined to impose an 'enough is enough' line, conscious no doubt that public ownership had never been a great vote-winner in the first place. 'We definitely do not want to nationalise the small man – the shop round the corner,' he told his party's NEC Policy Committee in November 1947. 'We must take care not to muck about with private enterprise, merely for the purpose of being spiteful.' The following May, at the party conference in Scarborough, he similarly insisted that the government should now go slow on nationalisation and instead concentrate on consolidating its existing achievements.

The whole question by this time seems to have touched a raw nerve, whatever the indifference of most workers in the nationalised industries themselves. 'Nationalisation without democracy is not Socialism,' Manny Shinwell told the same conference, 'and we cannot claim that an industry or service is socialised unless and until the principles of social and economic democracy are implicit in its day-to-day conduct.' That was also the view of Michael Young in Labour's research department, but when in 1948 he wrote a party pamphlet on 'industrial democracy', privileging the rank-and-file worker above the union leadership and even flirting with the idea of workers' control, the first edition had to be withdrawn after objections from both Bevan and Morrison. It was a revealing if heavy-handed intervention, for in the end the problem of how to make nationalisation work better would turn not on social liberation from below but on political and economic decision-making from above. Hugh Gaitskell, Shinwell's successor as Minister of Fuel and Power, did not doubt where the sharp end lay, and a diary entry from June 1948 suggests that he was not the only one:

> An argument last night with Nye Bevan at our group dinner about nationalisation. Being, of course, a glutton for power he does not like the present policy of setting up the semi-autonomous Boards. He wants to control and answer for them; in fact to have them under him like departments. There is of course a good deal in what he says. Certainly it is no easy job to try and establish just the necessary degree of control without going too far. Also it is irritating not to be able to keep them on the right lines all the time. On the other hand there would, I think, be even greater dangers if, for instance, the Coal industries were run entirely by the Department. In any case we are now committed in the case of my industries to the principle of the semi-independent Board, and that being so one must give this particular form and relationship a fair trial.[3]

Gaitskell from the right and Bevan from the left were tacitly agreed, in other words, that control of the commanding heights was not for those toiling in the foothills.

Even as the decision to defer steel nationalisation was being taken in August 1947, the Labour government was wrestling with what became known as the convertibility crisis. The implacable, inescapable problem was that from 15 July, in accordance with the terms of the American Loan over a year and a half earlier, sterling was fully convertible into dollars. Almost immediately there ensued an appalling drain of dollars from the country, accompanied by a run on the pound. A new round of belt-tightening – and all the attendant criticism – soon became inevitable. 'At dinner we guessed what awful impositions Attlee would announce tomorrow,' noted James Lees-Milne on Tuesday, 5 August, while staying at the Chequers Hotel in Newbury with Harold Nicolson and Vita Sackville-West. 'Harold admits that he foresees no solution to the predicament we are in, and his reason for becoming a socialist is that socialism is inevitable. By joining he feels he may help by tempering it; by remaining outside he can do nothing. He says the sad thing is that no one dislikes the lower orders more than he does.' Next day in the Commons, Attlee duly announced a range of cuts, involving food, petrol and films among other things.

Over the next few days, the political temperature rose with the actual temperature, and Mass-Observation's investigators managed a couple of good 'overheards'. The first was two middle-aged, working-class men on a bus in the City:

> Gor blimey Charlie – wot a bloody outlook etc. When are they going to stop cutting things I'd like to know. Still the people wanted em in, didn't they? Now they've got em they've found out a thing or two.
>
> Worse than the war mate ain't it?
>
> At least you knew wot was appening then but yer don't know wot to expect now do yer.

The other was a middle-class man travelling on a Southern Region train to Raynes Park: 'They have got to do these things – after all you must admit they are luxuries. I don't go to the films much so it won't affect me, the cutting down of films. Rounding up the spivs is a good thing – they are a burden on the national effort. They will be doing more drastic things in the winter, you mark my words.'

On the evening of Sunday the 10th, the day after Denis Compton and Middlesex had run riot at The Oval in front of 30,000, Attlee spoke to the nation – 'surely the most colourless politician who ever broadcast', according to Nella Last in Barrow. 'Listen with me to the end,' he asked before seeking to justify his measures, 'and think and talk over what I have said afterwards.' They half-obeyed that injunction at the Royal Clarence Hotel in Exeter, where Lees-Milne heard the speech. 'In the crowded lounge it was received in grim silence,' he observed. 'When over not a soul spoke or made a single comment. Instead, he and she went on with their reading, so typically English. A sign of native phlegm or stupid indifference, who can tell?' In any case, the measures failed to stem the crisis, as over the following week Britain's dollar reserves continued to drain away with alarming rapidity. 'The Government are in these matters, as in all others, worried, nervy, and incapable of reaching decisions,' privately declared one of the Bank of England's executive directors, 'Ruby' Holland-Martin, towards the end of the week.[4]

Finally, on Sunday the 17th, the Cabinet decided there was no alternative but to suspend convertibility. There were three more days of the Fifth Test at The Oval – Compton taking another century off South Africa, while according to *Wisden* 'the terraces presented a dazzling scene with the sun blazing down on the compact mass of people in the lightest permissible summer attire' – before Hugh Dalton on the 20th announced suspension on the radio. 'It is in fact a default,' was the implacable verdict of the *Financial Times*. 'Such a misjudgement of the situation and such precipitate abandonment of the position taken up so recently cannot fail to bring the gravest discredit upon this Government of self-styled planners.' For most people, however, national humiliation probably mattered rather less than the further cuts announced exactly a week later. '"LESS–LESS–LESS" shrieks the "Daily Express" headline this morning,' noted Florence Speed on the 28th – with the weekly meat ration, for example, being cut from 1s 2d to 1s – while Lees-Milne reported himself that day as 'terribly upset by the announcement that the basic petrol ration is to be cut off and all foreign travel to cease'. Yet in Henry St John's office in Bristol, this announcement of the latest cuts 'was freely commented on, but there was no sign of revolt, or any constructive criticism'.[5] Phlegm? Or indifference? A good question, to which perhaps the most plausible answer is that it was a bit of both.

In the short term, the response of the 'self-styled planners' was seemingly to turn to more planning, with Stafford Cripps in September assuming the newly created position of Minister of Economic Affairs, effectively replacing Morrison as planning supremo and enjoying, at least on paper, more clout than the somewhat beleaguered Dalton at the Treasury. On the face of it representing a renewed commitment to centrally directed economic planning, in reality it was the deftest of ploys by Attlee, who in the face of a possible putsch against his leadership thereby neatly detached Cripps from the fellow-plotters Dalton and Morrison. Only weeks later, Dalton was forced to walk the plank after carelessly revealing part of the contents of his Budget speech shortly before delivering it; Cripps replaced him, with his new ministry effectively being subsumed into the Treasury. Over the following year, Cripps proved to be a remarkably effective and dominant Chancellor – arguably the outstanding occupant of No. 11 since Gladstone, certainly since Lloyd George before the First World War. One consequence was a huge boost to the institutional authority of the Treasury, where by this time the out-and-out planners, advocating physical controls (especially over manpower) to achieve a planned economy, were heavily outgunned by the supporters of Keynesian demand management. Indeed, Dalton's ill-fated November 1947 Budget, seeking through fiscal policy to reduce the level of demand, had already made it clear where the Treasury stood; and Cripps, though nominally a committed planner, in practice became increasingly aware of planning's defects and limitations.[6]

Nevertheless, not only did many controls remain in place, but the intellectual shift itself took time to take effect. The influential Evan Durbin, for instance, was hardly a left-winger, yet he was deeply reluctant to abandon socialist planning. Typically, he did not duck the problems, arguing in a 1948 essay that if it was inefficient allocation of manpower that had been mainly responsible for weakening the economy by the time of convertibility, then the only way in which that difficulty could be addressed in a democratically planned manner was through a differential wages policy – given that it was unacceptable to increase significantly the degree of compulsory direction of labour that already existed. Durbin, like everyone else, knew that the stumbling block to his strategy was the trade unions and their deep attachment to free collective bargaining.

Moreover, although the TUC did, through gritted teeth, agree in the spring of 1948 to an informal policy of wage restraint, essentially as a quid pro quo for government efforts to restrain inflation, this agreement neither contained a differential element (such as might stimulate labour mobility) nor implied any endorsement of a wages policy as part of the permanent landscape of a planned economy. 'We shall go forward building up our wage claims in conformity with our understanding of the people we are representing' was how the most powerful union leader, Arthur Deakin of the Transport and General

Workers' Union (TGWU), had put it in 1946, adding that 'any attempt to interfere with that position would have disastrous results'. Nothing had changed fundamentally since then or was likely to change. For all those temperamentally and philosophically wedded to pulling levers from the centre, Keynesian demand management offered a more or less acceptable way out of the planning impasse.

The convertibility crisis also undermined planning in the sense of reconstruction, inevitably leading as it did to a number of major capital-investment cuts. Work on the first wave of New Towns almost ground to a halt, prompting some tellingly patronising, Goldsmithian lines from 'Sagittarius':

> O thou, the city planner's lawful pride,
> With industry and housing side by side,
> Abandon'd ere thy ground-plan was unroll'd,
> Farewell, sweet Stevenage! thou art pigeon-hol'd.
> Here winsome rented dwellings would have been,
> With sun-trap fronts towards th' unlitter'd green,
> Thy Civic Centre, seat of sober pomp,
> Thy glitt'ring Dance-Hall for the modest romp,
> Thy communal canteen and cultural hub,
> Thy decent shop and semi-rural pub.

It was almost as slow-going in the blitzed cities, where large swathes of bomb sites seemed to be settling in for a new duration, while in one, Hull, council elections in November 1947 showed clearly that local people were far more concerned with getting housing as soon as possible than, as they saw it, with watching the local authority engage in expensive, high-falutin' town planning for some distant point in the 1950s – or beyond.[7]

There were even continuing misgivings in Coventry. 'We all wish to see a beautiful and well-planned city rise from the ruins of the old,' one Coventry resident protested earlier that year, 'but you cannot expect people who are living in overcrowded conditions, with meagre supplies of food and clothing, properly to appreciate the present scheme of transformation in Broadgate. When they see the tons of cement and brickwork, together with the labour personnel involved upon the project, it only seems to widen the gap between their present conditions and the

VE Day celebrations in Lambert Square, Coxlodge, Newcastle upon Tyne

The Tory candidate addresses an election meeting in Bethnal Green, June 1945

Aneurin Bevan in Ebbw Vale during the 1945 election

Above: The Haymarket, Sheffield, 1946

Right: Museum steps, Liverpool, 1946

Mrs Francis, Christmas Street, off the Old Kent Road, 1946

The Gorbals, Glasgow, 1948

'Mr Browning's Winning Team': West Sussex, 1947

England versus South Africa at Lord's, June 1947

Margate, June 1948

hopes of something better in the near future.' The scheme, though, went ahead, and in May 1948, on a Saturday of blazing sunshine and huge crowds, Princess Elizabeth visited Coventry to declare the redeveloped Broadgate open and lay the foundation stone for its new shopping precinct. 'With your blessing we shall create not only a city of fine buildings, but a happy and prosperous community,' declared Alderman George Hodgkinson, the prime moving force behind Coventry's rebuilding, in his speech of thanks. That day the main local paper was similarly bullish: 'As we look around us we have reason for satisfaction. The old, homely Broadgate we knew was obliterated by bombing. That could never be restored, but in recent months new roads have been constructed, and a garden island has appeared where not so long ago was desolation. Truly Broadgate is a fitting centre-piece for a well-planned city. The foundation stone of the shopping precinct marks the beginning of bigger things.' In sum, Elizabeth's visit 'has given Royal recognition to Coventry's post-war achievements and aspirations'.[8]

Certainly immediate economic difficulties did not stop the activators looking ahead. In 1947 the Labour-run Birmingham City Council, very much under the sway of its dynamic City Engineer Herbert Manzoni, managed to raise a huge loan for the compulsory purchase of five of the city's most run-down areas, more than half of whose 30,000 dwellings were back-to-backs. The move confirmed that in Birmingham, as in other big British cities, there would one day be the juggernaut of large-scale slum clearance. A meeting in April 1948 of the Society of Women Housing Managers tackled the question of how it might work:

> Miss Thompson said the breaking up of an old community was a serious thing, as there was often a strong social bond in these areas. The key, she thought, was to get to know the people first, find out the forces making the social cohesion, and try to work in harmony with them.
>
> This point was taken up by Mrs Barclay, president, who said that even when a community was only being moved a short way it seemed almost impossible to re-create the same social bond. The very fact of living in new houses seemed to produce a kind of exclusiveness.

The Danish architectural writer Steen Eiler Rasmussen would almost certainly have agreed with this patient, listening, female approach.

Author of *London: The Unique City*, an instant classic on publication in 1934, he included a solemn warning in his new edition in 1948:

> The evil comes in when architecture is treated as free art, like music and ballet, with the aim of expressing the special mind of its originator. Some so-called modern architects prefer to pose as romantic figures like Beethoven whose countenance seems to reveal the vast profundity obscure. It is good for picture papers and promotes respect for the profession. But as we see today that even music has suffered from over-emphasis of the emotional side it is obvious also that the art of domestic architecture cannot stand a too romantic interpretation.

Instead, as a less hubristic but indispensable goal, 'it must find its justification simply in forming a satisfactory setting to modern life'.

Yet what exactly was 'modern life'? And what in urban terms might be 'a satisfactory setting' for it? 'I have never seen any scientific calculation as to what is the right density either for a town or a part of it,' the minister Lewis Silkin brusquely told a gathering of town planners in July 1948. And he specifically queried those planners' most sacred cow, the concept of the neighbourhood unit: 'The assumption is that by dividing up your population into groups of 10,000 to 20,000 and surrounding them by open spaces, railways and main roads you will get nice little communities living happily and sociably together. On what evidence is that based?' The door was swinging open for a whole new world of applied social research. Or as James Lansdale Hodson had reflected shortly before, 'We remain very ignorant of the state of the nation. Not half enough social scientists are examining what's going on.'[9]

———

Altogether, the mood by 1947/8 on the non-Communist left was undeniably mixed but still at some fundamental level united. Not everyone might have agreed with Michael Young's nomination of 1960 as a realistic target date for the building of a socialist society, but most would have empathised with the defence of post-war changes made by the central character in J. B. Priestley's *The Linden Tree*, opening in London in August 1947:

Call us drab and dismal, if you like, and tell us we don't know how to cook our food or wear our clothes – but for Heaven's sake, recognise that we're trying to do something that is as extraordinary and wonderful as it's difficult – to have a revolution for once without the Terror, without looting mobs and secret police, sudden arrests, mass suicides and executions, without setting in motion that vast pendulum of violence which can decimate three generations before it comes to a standstill. We're fighting in the last ditch of our civilisation. If we win through, everybody wins through.

Shortly afterwards, in early September, one of Young's colleagues in Labour's research department, the young writer Vincent Brome, had a lengthy, revealing conversation with Bevan. 'Inevitably we spoke of democratic Socialism. We analysed what the Labour Government was trying to do, we examined the difficulties surrounding it, and then, suddenly, he defined Socialism in terms very different from the normal':

Democratic Socialism he said was an instrument for implementing the social conscience, and his case seemed to develop along these lines: – The social conscience expressed itself in thousands of families where children were taught the virtues of compassion and kindness and consideration for others. These beliefs were reinforced by Christian teaching which established fresh links in a long tradition of service as well as self, but when the child left the circle of the family, it found the outer material world largely uninterested in such attitudes. 'Economic necessity quickly frustrated the moral impulse. The very structure of society insisted on disillusionment which led to moral neuroticism . . .

'If you look at some of the points in the Labour Party programme you will see that they are, in a sense, tantamount to an attempt to let society "resolve its guilt anxieties" – or, putting it another way – to do the bidding of conscience . . .'

Many people sympathized with the sick person, everyone wanted the poverty-stricken mother to find a house for her children, but it was assumed by too many that the resolution of these difficulties was entirely the responsibility of the individual concerned. Under Capitalism poor people were thrust back upon their own limited resources and some encountered inordinate hardship. 'But if we do what the Labour Government is doing – transform all these thousands of personal and private headaches into public headaches – we can get something done . . . To preach and not to practise, to be obliged by the structure of society to act inadequately or not at all, is to become a moral cripple . . . It is to thwart instead of implement the social conscience . . .'

There was much more in a similar vein

Brome was impressed. 'Forty minutes and still the phrases came pouring in like Atlantic rollers, full, rich, measured. For a whole hour it went on with hardly a pause, hardly a word from me, and then abruptly he stood up, pleaded pressure of many things and escorted me to the door.'[10]

Anthony Wedgwood Benn – son of a Liberal-turned-Labour peer, in his early 20s, about to come down from Oxford after being a fighter pilot in the war – did not yet have executive responsibilities but in early 1948 he composed his private 'Thoughts on Socialism'. Arguing that pre-war 'poverty and squalor and undernourishment' had made 'a mockery of the price mechanism as a means of translating needs into economic demand', he nevertheless accepted that 'economic efficiency demands a degree of inequality because of the need for incentives'. Even so: 'A certain standard of health, nourishment and housing must be maintained for all. No one else can do it but the state and in Britain a new paternalism is state paternalism: looking after those who cannot look after themselves. This involves interference, but if this interference is democratically controlled we need not fear that an unwieldy bureaucracy will clasp us in its grip.' In short, the answer was democratic socialism, with the emphasis at least as much on the first word as the second: 'We in the English-speaking world have created a wonderful machinery for peaceful change in parliamentary democracy. It has taken 1,000 years . . . Socialism is important, I feel certain, but socialism achieved by force is no good.'

Others sounded a wearier, more sceptical note. 'The honeymoon between literature and action, once so promising, is over,' bleakly declared Cyril Connolly, ultimate literary mandarin, bleakly in his magazine in July 1947, some six months after John Lehmann's Isherwood-induced disenchantment:

We can see, looking through old *Horizons*, a left-wing and sometimes revolutionary political attitude among writers, heritage of Guernica and Munich, boiling up to a certain aggressive optimism in the war years, gradually declining after D-day and soon after the victorious general election despondently fizzling out ... A Socialist Government, besides doing practically nothing to help artists and writers, has also quite failed to stir up either intellect or imagination; the English renaissance, whose false dawn we have so enthusiastically greeted, is further away than ever ... Somehow, during the last two years, the left-wing literary movement has petered out.

Nor was a society seemingly pervaded by pernickety, pettifogging bureaucracy any more attractive even for a veteran Fabian. 'The whole world is full of permits and control of people,' Lord Passfield (better known as Sidney Webb) lamented two months later in his final letter. 'I am afraid the old ones such as I fall to have to put up with much.' Everything, of course, would be all right so long as the people's party and the people were on the same wavelength. A perceptive observer as well as participant, Gaitskell privately reflected at about this time how often Labour MPs for marginal seats were 'most unrealistic about the Left Wing character of the electorate', and he argued that they made the mistake of 'identifying their own keen supporters – politically conscious and class-conscious Labour men – with the mass of the people, who are very much against austerity, utterly uninterested in nationalisation of steel, heartily sick of excuses and being told to work harder, but probably more tolerant of the Government and appreciative of its difficulties than many suppose'.[11]

Gaitskell's reading of a misalignment between party and people was endorsed in December 1947 by a poll which found that 42 per cent thought the Labour government had so far been 'too socialistic', 30 per cent 'about right', and a mere 15 per cent 'not socialist enough'. For Gaitskell's close friend and contemporary Durbin, such a poll served to confirm that (as he tersely put it in some notes written around 1947/8) 'British people not socialists' and 'the political future is not hopeful'. He had already, in earlier notes, called for 'co-operation between Public Opinion experts and sociological minded politicians' in some 'consumer's research – to find out what our people really want from the State'. Socialists, he now contended,

> must realise that the British people soon tire of any one set of changes
> – and will soon need a *new emphasis upon the values of personal life* –
> in a more complex and powerfully unified society.
>   improved communication with them
>   services that deal with personal problems
>   more provision for fun

The fragmentary, unpunctuated nature of Durbin's notes fails to mask the fact that, by this third year of the Labour government, he was working towards a new, potentially very fruitful, more consultative politics that would be predicated on a realistic assessment of the electorate's values and priorities.

None of which meant that Durbin himself made much political headway. 'You will see that God continues to strike heavily,' he had complained to a friend in October 1946. 'Trouble at Edmonton, chest trouble and no job in the Government.' Five months later he was at last given a position, but only as Parliamentary Secretary at the Ministry of Works – one of the less inspiring posts. Nor did the autumn 1947 reshuffle bring any joy. 'I feel a little separated from the consideration of economic policy,' he wrote with understandable disappointment to Attlee. 'I know that I have something to contribute to the Government in this direction.'[12]

The contrast was stark with another economist-turned-politician, Harold Wilson, who in the reshuffle became President of the Board of Trade – at 31 the youngest Cabinet minister of the twentieth century, though in appearance and manner (moustache, incipient paunch, invariable waistcoat, little small talk or sense of humour) middle-aged before his time. It was not quite Pitt the Younger, but it was in its way an equally remarkable advance. The son of an industrial chemist, Wilson in background was solidly northern (mainly Huddersfield), Nonconformist (Congregationalist) and more middle- than working-class. From grammar school it was a sure-footed ascent: scholarship to Oxford, a top First, fellowship at an Oxford college, research assistant to Sir William Beveridge, wartime work at the Ministry of Fuel and Power that won him an OBE, a seat (Ormskirk) in 1945, a government position from the start, the call to the Cabinet. The appointment received much publicity – almost all of it favourable – and within days the Cotton Board's Sir Raymond Streat was watching Wilson open a textiles exhibition and participate in a conference on the export task ahead. 'I think Wilson made a good impression on my cotton friends and on me personally,' Streat noted. 'He is quick on the uptake – too well versed in economics and civil service work to rant or rave like a soap-box socialist.' A second encounter with the new man followed soon after:

> Harold Wilson reacts too quickly, too smoothly and readily for any impression of particular purpose to emerge. Maybe he hardly gives himself time to identify purpose and if his romantically early start in politics is to lead to the acquisition of the qualities of statesmanship he would possibly be well advised to take himself in hand and leave part of the garden in which such plants could grow . . .
>
> He is nice enough as an open-hearted sort of young man and a fond father of a young family to be all right if he does not entirely forget big things by allowing himself to be pre-occupied with a million small ones.

One of Wilson's biographers, Ben Pimlott, has argued that this was somewhat unfair, given that 'a million small things' were at this time the very business of the Board of Trade. But Streat's was still an acute assessment.

What was Wilson's 'particular purpose'? Much has been made of his attachment to Liberalism until the late 1930s and his subsequent lack of a moment of socialist epiphany. Yet what is most striking about his personal-cum-political formation is the cumulatively conclusive evidence that at no stage was he interested in ideas – as opposed to economic statistics, the names and numbers of steam engines, and football and cricket scores. Formidably clever and industrious, he was not (for better or worse) an intellectual. 'Harold Wilson was a rule-governed convergent thinker,' reflected one historian, David Howell, after reading Pimlott. 'He performed according to the rules.'[13] And, unlike the young Gladstone when sent to the Board of Trade, he never complained that he had been 'set to govern packages'.

For the Conservative Party, so crushingly vanquished in 1945, it could be only a long night's journey into day.[14] At its first post-war conference, at Blackpool in October 1946, the mood on the platform was still pessimistic. 'These great, intelligent thoroughbreds, trained from their earliest years to prudent administration and courteous debate, were in their hearts not far from accepting as definitive their electoral defeat,' one observer, the French political scientist Bertrand de Jouvenel, wrote soon afterwards. But on the conference floor there was a much greater sense of defiance – not least (if one accepts her retrospective account) on the part of Margaret Roberts, newly elected President of the Oxford University Conservative Association. The right-wing newspaper proprietor (and wartime Minister of Information) Brendan Bracken reported to Beaverbrook that the delegates 'would have nothing to do with the proposal to change the Party's name' and that 'they demanded a real Conservative policy instead of a synthetic Socialist one.' Although Churchill was initially disinclined to undertake a fundamental review of policy at this stage, in due course a committee chaired by Rab Butler (architect of the 1944 Education Act) was set up.

The outcome was *The Industrial Charter*, published in May 1947 and recognised from the outset as a major policy statement. Less than two years after Churchill's ill-considered 'Gestapo' jibe, the document apparently marked a broad acceptance of the emerging post-war settlement. There would be no denationalisation of the Bank of England or the coal mines or the railways; the new orthodoxy of Keynesian deficit finance – government increasing its spending in order to boost demand and thus employment – was accepted; workers' rights were to be protected; and producers' monopolies and cartels were denounced as vigorously as trade union restrictive practices. One passage particularly caught the prevailing pragmatic tone: 'We Conservatives want to release industry and those who work in industry from unnecessary controls so that energy and fresh ideas may be given their head. But we know that, as things are, there must be some central planning of the nation's work. The world is topsy-turvy. Raw materials are scarce. Stormy weather must be foreseen. There must be a hand on the helm . . .' Altogether, commented the *Spectator*, the document removed any 'excuse for labelling the Conservative Party as at present constituted as reactionary', adding that 'in most cases the difference with Labour is more of degree than of fundamental principle.'

That October, at the party conference in Brighton, the progressive-minded, thoroughly non-grandee (son of an actuary) Reggie Maudling, prospective candidate for Barnet and one of the bright young things on the research side, moved an amendment that the *Charter* be accepted by the party as a whole. Sir Waldron Smithers, the entirely unreconstructed MP for Orpington, protested that 'the party must not allow itself to become infected with the Socialist bug, and it must stick to its principles or perish'. But amid soothing words from Butler (including the phrase 'private initiative in the public interest') and a certain amount of well-rehearsed procedural legerdemain, the Maudling amendment was carried with only three dissenters. It was, the *Spectator* reflected with overall satisfaction, 'a responsible act' that demonstrated 'a positive will to govern on the part of the rank and file'.[15]

In reality, the Tories were not in quite such ideological retreat. Not only did *The Industrial Charter* consistently identify private enterprise as the rightful mainspring of economic activity, but the language almost throughout emphasised the individual at the expense of the collective. 'The ultimate restoration of freedom of choice' for the consumer, 'status as an individual personality' for the worker, and 'a personal incentive to reap a greater reward for greater responsibility' for the manager: all were contrasted, in 'a free and resourceful nation', with Labour's belief that 'the men and women who fought and worked together in the war can now be exalted, controlled and regimented into producing goods, building houses and rendering services in time of peace'. Variety as against uniformity, 'humanising' as against nationalising, giving people 'opportunity' as against orders – this was to be the new, distinctive rhetoric of post-war Conservatism, a rhetoric far removed in the late 1940s from Labour rhetoric, even right-wing Labour rhetoric.

Moreover, although no one in the Tory leadership imagined that there could be a return to the minimalist, 'nightwatchman' state of the nineteenth century, it was far from clear that old-fashioned economic liberalism had been totally banished. 'I do not agree with a word of this,' Churchill memorably told Maudling after being given a five-line digest of the newly endorsed *Charter*; the next most senior Tory, Sir Anthony Eden, was already pushing hard for 'a property-owning democracy' despite the fact that public housing was poised to expand as never before; and a possible Tory Chancellor, Oliver Lyttelton, a hard-money man from the City, was privately contemplating the radical free-market solution of floating the pound. In short, the 'pinks' like Butler (who himself plugged 'co-partnership' essentially as a tactical antidote to nationalisation) and Harold Macmillan (author of *The Middle Way* in the 1930s) were far from having captured the party. A few weeks after the Brighton conference, the somewhat puzzled thoughts of Sir Cuthbert Headlam, a backbencher instinctively sceptical of Keynes et al, were probably representative of much of party opinion:

> I find that this pinkish portion of our party are more prominent but less popular with the rank and file than they used to be. People instinctively dislike their economic planning and plotting and yet can see no alternative to some policy of the kind in present conditions. In this I fancy they are right – the great thing, however, is not to emphasize the necessity for controls so much – if and when we come back into power, it will be time enough to decide how much Govt. intervention in the conduct of industry is required.[16]

There was still, in sum, much to play for – both within the party and, notwithstanding Labour's partial retreat from planning, between the parties.

Not that most people were fussed either way. 'A very large number of people know little about party politics and care little,' declared a Mass-Observation report in the summer of 1947 about public reaction to the *Charter*. 'Any effort at all to obtain interest in a particular political party or policy is immediately confronted with a solid wall of disinterest and disbelief in at least a third of the people of this country' – a state of mind co-existing with 'extreme confusion on any subject even remotely concerned with party politics'. Asked about the differences between the two main parties, most of the survey's respondents were unable to identify any; as for those who did, the analysis rarely went beyond the personal or the non-political. 'The Labour are out for themselves and don't care about the people, but the Conservatives are wonderful, Mr Churchill should be sitting on the throne of Heaven' was a not untypical reply, in this case given by a 55-year-old charwoman. Less than a fifth of the sample, shown copies of the

Charter and other recent political pamphlets, confessed to having ever seen or even heard of any of them. Among those willing to engage with its policies, a worker's charter was generally seen as irrelevant and profit-sharing as impractical. 'It's all right on the outside but it's the inside that counts' was how a Labour-voting baker summed up his response to the pamphlet. 'I just don't trust them, that's all.'

Still, whatever its limitations in terms of popular appeal, there is no doubt that the *Charter* played an important part – if probably more by language than content – in making the Tories once again electoral contenders. For one septuagenarian, obstinately unwilling to stand down even as his finest hour passed into the history books (at this stage mainly being written by himself), this was a gratifying development. 'She told me that her father was very elated by the municipal election results, and was now confident that his party had a following in the country,' Lees-Milne noted in November 1947 after dining with Sarah Churchill. 'Already people in the streets were more respectful to him.'[17]

Ain't She Lovely?

The forces of conservatism were not to be underestimated. In March 1947 Bishop Barnes of Birmingham set out in *The Rise of Christianity* a theology that rejected the evidence of the Virgin Birth, the Miracles and the Resurrection. Over the next year his book sold more than 15,000 copies and generated a huge, wildly varied postbag. 'It is such a brave book,' the actress Sybil Thorndike wrote to him, 'and coming from a priest of the Church it is more than brave. It has been a releasing for me, and I am sure it must have been for many people.' The controversy came to a head in October 1947 when, at a meeting of Convocation, Geoffrey Fisher – Archbishop of Canterbury and uncomfortably aware that a majority of bishops were itching to pass a vote of censure for heresy – explicitly disavowed Barnes. 'If his views were mine,' he added, 'I should not feel that I could still hold episcopal office in the Church.'

Soon afterwards, the *Sunday Pictorial*, noting that 'at the very least the fundamental beliefs of millions are called into question', asked its readers to send in their views. The upshot was a torrent of words (more than three-quarters of a million in one week), with 52 per cent of letters supporting Barnes, 32 per cent against and the rest neutral. Tellingly, his opponents highlighted hypocrisy at least as much as doctrinal impurity. 'Dr Barnes should be expelled from the Church of England for denying the very truths he is paid a large salary to defend,' declared P. G. Thurston of Waterworks Road, Hastings. Ruth B. Hall from Ashford, Middlesex, agreed: 'Resign, man! And at least be honest. At the moment you are taking money under false pretences, in my opinion.' There was, as Mass-Observation's *Puzzled People* survey had shown, a widespread dislike for the established church, seen by many – in a way that had little or nothing to do with theology – as smug and excessively privileged. Barnes himself did not step down. But it was clear that within the church leadership the liberals were in a distinct minority, a minority that did not include Archbishop Fisher, a man of 'benign authoritarianism' (in the phrase of his *Times* obituary) who had earlier been a public-school headmaster and intended to run the Church of England along similar lines.[1]

A few weeks later, Fisher was solemnising the first post-war royal marriage. It had been a contentious choice of husband on Princess Elizabeth's part. In January 1947, before the engagement was announced, a *Sunday Pictorial* poll found that although 55 per cent were in favour of a marriage between her and Prince Philip of Greece (with the stipulation 'if the Princess and Prince are in love'), 40 per cent were against. Many readers felt that she ought to marry a commoner, one declaring that 'the days of intermarriage of royalty have passed'; others saw the marriage as frankly 'a political move'; and plenty echoed the xenophobic view of one household in the Euston Road: 'We, the Russell family – a father and two sons who have served in both wars – say, "Definitely no!" to a marriage with a foreign prince.' Lord Mountbatten, Philip's uncle, was already sufficiently rattled that he had asked the editors of the hostile Beaverbrook press whether they thought opinion would soften if his nephew were naturalised. They had agreed it might help, and Prince Philip of Greece in February duly became Lieutenant Philip Mountbatten, RN.

In July the engagement was at last announced. 'Any banqueting and display of wealth at your daughter's wedding will be an insult to the British people at the present time,' the Camden Town branch of the Amalgamated Society of Woodworkers immediately warned the King, 'and we would consider that you would be well advised to order a very quiet wedding in keeping with the times.' Amid a generally warm press response, the reaction of Florence Speed was probably representative. 'Princess Elizabeth is engaged (official),' she noted, '& judging from the laughing photographs of her taken after a dance at Apsley House last night it is the "love match" it is claimed to be & we are all glad about it.' As for Philip, she added that he was 'the type "easy on the eye", which any young girl would fall in love with'. Although a poll taken soon afterwards revealed that 40 per cent professed indifference to the prospect of the royal wedding in November – typical remarks including 'Feel? What should I feel?', 'I don't care, it doesn't affect me' and 'It's not my business, it's up to them' – by October those actively approving of the marriage were up from 40 to 60 per cent. Even so, James Lees-Milne recorded some disturbing news on 18 November, after dining with Simon Mosley of the Coldstream Guards: 'Says that 50 per cent of the guardsmen in his company refused to contribute towards a present for Princess Elizabeth. The dissentients came to him in a body and, quite pleasantly, gave him their reasons. *One*, they said the Royal Family did nothing for anybody, and *two*, the Royal Family would not contribute towards a present for their weddings.' Moreover, 'when Simon Mosley said that without the Royal Family the Brigade of Guards, with its privileges and traditions, would cease to exist, they replied, "Good! Let them both cease to exist."'

Thursday the 20th was not a public holiday – deemed inappropriate, in the economic context – but there was still enormous interest in the wedding (flower arrangements by Constance Spry). 'How we love the Crown and a wedding!' wrote James Lansdale Hodson next day:

> Our work in the office was put quite out of gear by all the staff listening-in. A newspaper records that Trafalgar Square was so crowded that not a pigeon could find foothold, and I'm told you could shop comfortably in the remoter streets, rows of tempting iced cakes lying untouched. Overnight Londoners brought out their blitz mattresses and blankets and lay on the kerbstone route; hard lying for pleasure now instead of for Jerry, and in the morning women washed in warm water from vacuum flasks before putting on their new make-up.

Not everyone was *quite* bowled over. Finding himself close-up to the happy couple on their way to Waterloo and their honeymoon (at Broadlands), the journalist John Clarke privately thought that 'she looked to have a great deal too much make-up on', while 'he' (that morning created the Duke of Edinburgh) was 'rather grey-faced and already long-suffering'. The following Monday, dining at the Beefsteak, Sir Cuthbert Headlam was told by the King's Private Secretary, Sir Alan ('Tommy') Lascelles, 'that Philip Mountbatten is a "nice boy", but not much educated – should do all right he thinks for his job'. Later that week, the commercial artist Grace Golden went to a news cinema to see the film of the wedding and observed that 'Princess Elizabeth's charm must lie in her expressions.' But by the New Year there was still undimmed, mainly female enthusiasm to see the wedding dress and presents that had been on display since November. 'Mrs C. and I dragged ourselves out of bed at 7 a.m.,' Vere Hodgson, a staunch royalist, recorded in mid-January, 'and on a cold, wet and windy morning found ourselves in a long queue outside St James' Palace at 9.15 a.m. It was none too soon. At 10 o'clock we were let in with the first thousand.'²

There is the odd quasi-intimate diary glimpse of Elizabeth herself. 'She had a very pretty voice and quite an easy manner but is not, I think, very interested in politics or affairs generally,' reckoned Hugh Gaitskell in April 1948 after a quarter of an hour's conversation with her. Soon afterwards, Violet Bonham Carter went to a ball at Buckingham Palace for the King and Queen's silver wedding. 'I have *never* seen Pss E. look better,' she told her son Mark. 'She looked really *pretty* . . . She strikes me as being rather "delié" by marriage – with fewer "stops".' The report went on: 'Pss Margaret on the other hand has *none* – as you have always said. Talking to her is not like talking to a "royalty".'

Not long afterwards, on 2 June, the princesses' mother paid a visit to the Lancashire cotton industry. It turned out to be 'a wet day, thoroughly wet, with a raw cold wind', in the words of Raymond Streat, one of the party that met the Queen at Blackburn station and then followed her in the second car of the procession. Early on she visited a mill and talked to the weavers, with Streat struck by 'the positive rapture indicated on the faces of those to whom she spoke'. Lunch at Rochdale Town Hall followed, and afterwards she appeared on the balcony 'and the vast crowd in the Town Hall Square cheered her mightily'. The procession then made its way to Oldham and from there, with the rain still pelting down, to Manchester. During those 7 miles there were 'people all the way on both sides of the road', and 'they surged off the pavement to get a close view of the Queen'. For Streat, it was the culmination of a rich anthropological experience:

Through the windows of our car we heard the voices of the crowd as they looked with fond affection on the receding car of the Queen and expressed their reaction to their immediate neighbours. Many hundreds of times that day I heard the phrase 'Ain't she lovely?' . . . That was the comment of more than three-quarters of the onlookers – just that and nothing more. They had come in curiosity to see a Queen, some no doubt for the first time and wondering what majesty did to a woman: they had seen a sweet and kindly face and shining friendly eyes, a wave of the hand and a little bow in their direction: that was all and their outstanding thought was that 'she' was lovely.

The Firm did not rely on just waves and smiles. Less than a week later, Harold Nicolson went to Buckingham Palace to be sounded out by Lascelles about writing an official life of George V. 'He said that I should not be expected to write one word that was not true,' Nicolson recorded. 'I should not be expected to praise or exaggerate. But I must omit things and incidents which were discreditable.' Nicolson agonised but in the end agreed. And privately he conceded, shortly before getting down to work on the commission, 'I quite see that the Royal Family feel their myth is a piece of gossamer and must not be blown upon.'[3]

For royalty and subjects alike, at least in theory, there was no getting away from continuing austerity. When Gallup in 1947 asked people what would be their ideal, no-expense-spared meal for a special occasion, their lovingly detailed answer – sherry; tomato soup; sole; roast chicken with roast potatoes, peas and sprouts; trifle and cream; cheese and biscuits; coffee – belonged in large part to the realms of fantasy, certainly in terms of assembling it all on any one domestic table at any one time. By the autumn of that year, following the convertibility crisis, not only had the butter and meat rations been cut again, including the bacon ration halved, but potatoes were on the ration for the first time. In early December, from the vantage point of a Wembley housewife, Rose Uttin summed up a year that had been 'depressing in all ways except the weather':

Our rations now are 1 oz bacon per week – 3 lbs potatoes – 2 ozs butter – 3 ozs marge – 1 oz cooking fat – 2 ozs cheese & 1/- meat – 1 lb jam or marmalade per month – ½ lb bread per day. We could be worse – but we should be a lot better considering we won the war. Cigarettes are 1/8 for 10 our only luxury except for 1 drink on Bridge evenings. Dora [her daughter] became engaged to Mac in October – we did manage a party, but I am wondering how long it will be before they can afford to marry with prices high as they are. One bag coal last week cost 4/10. America & the Labour government say we are producing more – what a joke. They forget to count the lumps of slate & stone in it. Used all the points up by last Wed on oats & mashed potato powder. Hard frost last two nights. Fog yesterday. My dinner today 2 sausages which tasted like wet bread with sage added – mashed potato – ½ tomato – 1 cube cheese & 1 slice bread & butter. The only consolation no air raids to worry us.

Nor was eating out, assuming one could afford it, necessarily a panacea. 'It used to be a treat to have a meal there,' commented Florence Speed in September after a dismal experience at Peter Jones. 'Our lunch costing 3/- was a waste of money,' with the lowlight being 'half-cold at least just tepid fish au gratin'. Or as Lees-Milne, speaking for everyman, put it two months later, 'The food in England is worse than during the war, dry and tasteless, even at Brooks's.'

One food above all became a byword for these straitened, unappetising times. 'A new South African fish on the market – snoek!' noted Speed in October 1947. 'Fred expressed a desire to taste it, so I got a tin when I saw it in Collins. Not cheap – 2/9 a tin.' Fred's reaction went unrecorded, but from the first there seems to have been little enthusiasm for this vaguely mackerel-type fish, seen by the government as the ideal replacement (largely because it came from within the sterling area) for Portuguese sardines. Ten million tins were due to reach Britain, and when in May 1948 there arrived the first large consignment the Ministry of Food celebrated by putting up snoek posters and publicising eight snoek recipes, including a concoction to go with salad immortally called *snoek piquante*. By this time a tin cost only 1s 4½d and took only one point (five less than household salmon) – necessary inducements with so many half-pound tins to get rid of. 'If you have not yet tried the new allocation of snoek, you may be wondering what it is like,' Marjorie Huxley wrote encouragingly soon afterwards in her 'Recipes for the Housewife' in the *Listener*. 'It is rather like tunny fish in texture, but with snoek, it is best not to try serving it as it is, but to break it into flakes and moisten it with some kind of sauce, dressing or mayonnaise.'⁴

Not everything fell victim to the government's – above all Sir Stafford Cripps's – determination to achieve a relentless drive for exports and reductions in unnecessary personal consumption. Cigarettes, for example, stayed off the ration: although their price had gone up sharply (from 2s 4d to 3s 4d for a packet of 20) in Hugh Dalton's penultimate Budget, no minister dared tamper with the working man's inalienable right to smoke, a right barely yet connected with lung cancer. 'All we need to do,' Dalton had reassuringly boomed, 'is to smoke a little slower, make our cigarettes last a little longer, throw away our stubs a little shorter, knock out our pipes a little later; and all this might be good for our health.' Nevertheless, in a thousand and one ways, everyday life remained difficult, perhaps typified by the qualitative as well as quantitative problems involved in that indispensable necessity for almost every household – coal supplies. 'There seems to be more coal dust in the delivery nowadays,' one housewife, Mrs Mary Whittaker, complained in October 1947 on *Woman's Hour*. 'I know we're asked to make briquettes of it, but can you tell me why we get so much of it?'

Housing remained a continuing, high-profile worry, though at least the much-disparaged prefabs (described by Mary King in her diary as 'a blot on the lovely English scenery') were for the time being still going up. Neil Kinnock's family moved in November 1947 to a new two-bedroom prefab on a council estate at Nant-y Bwch. 'It was like moving to Beverly Hills,' he recalled. 'It had a fridge, a bath, central heating and a smokeless grate . . . and people used to come just to look at it.' As for clothing restrictions, Anthony Heap's experience a few weeks earlier was probably typical:

Hopefully hied up to Burton's branch at The Angel, to order one of the fifteen 'made to measure' suits that comprise their present weekly 'quota'. Wanted a grey tweed, but as luck would have it, they hadn't any in this week's 'allocation' of patterns – only blue worsteds. They would, however, try and get me a length next week. In which case, the suit would be ready in about nine months' time! And with that dubious prospect I had to be content.

It was probably even more frustrating for women. 'Proceed early to Marshall & Snelgrove,' Grace Golden noted in January 1948, 'only to learn that they do not change utility garments – I almost burst into tears.'[5]

Gallup revealed that spring that as many as 42 per cent of people wanted to emigrate, compared with 19 per cent immediately after the end of the war. But soon afterwards there were merciful signs that Cripps's strong medicine was starting to work, with a modest petrol ration for pleasure purposes being reinstated from 1 June, together with 12 extra clothing coupons. And in her *The New Yorker* letter a week later, Mollie Panter-Downes optimistically reckoned that such concessions would be 'uplifting in their effect on the public, who are apt to accept controls as a sort of evil forest that has grown up around them and become a tedious but quite natural part of their lives'. Still, Tennessee Williams probably had the right of it. 'I guess England is about the most unpleasant, uncomfortable and expensive place in the world you could be right now,' he wrote not long afterwards to his agent in New York. It was a Sunday, he was staying at the Cumberland Hotel, and on going hopefully to the bar at 2.10 in the afternoon he had discovered that 'there wasn't a drink to be had in all of London until seven'.

Whatever the problems, whatever the sense of monotony and restricted choice, most people *coped*. Take Marian Raynham in Surbiton on a Wednesday in July 1947: 'Had a good & very varied day. Went to grocers after breakfast, then on way home in next door, then made macaroni cheese & did peas & had & cleared lunch, then rest, then made 5 lbs raspberry jam, got tea & did some housework, listened to radio & darned, wrote to Jessie Gould. In bed about midnight.' A key coping mechanism for many women, especially working-class women, was the bush telegraph. 'Round about us we have got a good shopping centre, so we are very fortunate,' explained a miner's widow when asked that year about the effect of rationing on her family budget, 'and I find in getting about you pick up windfalls and swop ideas and hints (for I am not too old to learn).' There was also the indispensable safety valve of humorous grumbling. *Punch* as usual had its finger on the pulse of Middle England, typified by these more or less amusing snippets between October and December 1947:

'Excellent meals *can* be obtained if you know where to go,' says a correspondent. He claims to have found a restaurant where food is fully up to war-time standard.

The Government policy of encouraging large families is emphasized by a recent statement that only in households of six or over is it worth while collecting the new bacon ration weekly.

'What could be better than a comfortable old arm-chair, a cosy little fire, and a good book?' enthuses a reader. We don't know; but no doubt some Ministry or other will soon be telling us.

Since caterers' supplies were cut we hear many people have taken to rations to eke out their eating out.

'Fry your whalemeat with an onion to absorb the oil,' advises a chef, 'and throw away the onion.' As well?

Anyway, there was remarkably little hard, objective evidence to back up the Tory claim that the unappetising austerity diet was actually leading to malnutrition. When the Hunterian Society debated the question in November 1947 at the Apothecaries Hall, nutritionists demonstrated that it was extremely difficult to detect even limited malnutrition. 'The biological system of man was infinitely adaptable to circumstances,' insisted one of them, Magnus Pyke. They did not perhaps go quite as far as Michael Foot had in a recent parliamentary debate – claiming that the children of 1947 were 'healthier, tougher, stronger than any breed of children we have ever bred in this country before' – but their central point was not disproved.[6]

Things looked pretty good to one outsider. Enid Palmer was in her late 20s when in April 1948 – after military nursing service in India and Burma followed by a lengthy stay with her parents in Kenya – she disembarked at Liverpool and caught the train to London. 'The sun shone most of the way – & England looked very pleasant,' she wrote home soon afterwards. 'Little green fields full of apple trees in blossom – sheep and white lambs gambolling about. Children every-where – dogs all over the place – particularly wire haired terriers like Whiskey. We passed farms – with great English Carthorses pulling loads – and of course the rows and rows of tiny houses with their front and back gardens, washing hanging out.' That Friday evening she reached Addlestone in Surrey, where she was staying with her uncle George, aunt Beattie, cousin Joan and her baby Graham, and 'The Granny'. Uncle George took her on Saturday afternoon to the shops in Woking. 'They are full of nice things,' she reported. 'I eventually bought a pair of blue leather shoes at Dolcis – they cost only 51/- and are beautifully made with a crepe sole. I had to give 7 coupons for them. We walked round Woolworths, it was packed with people.' That evening a trip to the Weybridge Odeon ('comfortable plush seats') was followed by supper back home of 'sardines, tomato & lettuce, bread & margarine & coffee'. All in all, she told her parents, she was impressed:

> I have decided that England is not such a bad place after all. As for the stories one hears about it – they are quite untrue! Everybody looks very well – the children with beautiful rosy cheeks – and what numbers of children – there are crowds of them everywhere. The People are cheerful & happy – everybody is kind & polite & they smile – all the bus drivers & conductors, the railways officials, taxi drivers, porters etc, are polite & pleasant & helpful.
>
> The shops are full of flowers & fruit, sweets, cigarettes, clothes, shoes, everything one could possibly want. The only snag about clothes & shoes is the lack of coupons – one cannot buy them without. Fruit one can buy. There are fine apples, Jaffa oranges, South African grapes. The apples & oranges are 9d a lb. Daffodils are 24 for a shilling. Sweets are rationed – each person is allowed ¼ lb per month. Cigarettes are expensive, and not always easy to get. Other things are plentiful & everything is so much cheaper than in Kenya.

Nor was that all. 'Everybody is well dressed – far better than you or I even are – they may be old clothes but they are smart and well cut . . . Few people wear hats or stockings. The commonest working man looks smart in his utility clothing.'

Over the next few weeks, while Palmer waited to go to a maternity home in Colchester to continue her training as a nurse, the honeymoon did not quite last. 'England's countryside is beautiful,' she wrote, 'but there are too many restrictions – everything is crowded & there are queues everywhere.' And: 'Life is narrow and bound by documents.' And again: 'There is one standard topic of conversation in England –

"coupons", "food", "clothes".' She was also rather dismayed by the lack of hygiene, and one day in London, finding herself near Victoria station, she did the enterprising thing:

> I found a public Baths building – after queuing for an hour got a good hot bath for 6d. It was most enjoyable as it was 6 days since I had had one. They are short of coalite here. Today Uncle George said, 'You may have a bath today'. I am afraid he runs this house. I was rather amused at being told when I may have a bath. Nobody else seems to have a bath except Uncle George who has one on Sunday night. Other nights I have a kettle of hot water, heated on the gas.

She also in her letters stopped extolling the abundance of food.

But whatever the objective truth about that, or indeed about the malnutrition question, the crucial, all-pervasive *subjective* reality for most people was that morale generally, and food morale in particular, was low. In the same month that Palmer arrived in England, an official survey asked a representative sample of the population whether they felt they were getting sufficient food to stay in good health. Fifty-five per cent answered 'no', with another 7 per cent doubtful; when a similar survey was conducted two months later, the respective figures were 53 and 9 per cent. '"Something tasty" is the key-phrase in feeding,' Richard Hoggart would memorably write about the working-class Hunslet of the 1950s – but in reality of the 1930s when he was growing up there. 'Something solid, preferably meaty, and with a well-defined flavour.'[7] Given the shortages of anything tasty, especially with the low ration of fats, it was little wonder that almost half of a weary, put-upon population wanted to try pastures new.

Meanwhile, the sense of social malaise if anything deepened. Thirteen million pounds' worth of property was stolen during 1947, more than five times as much as in 1938. 'Newspapers are sprinkled with stories of rascals at work,' noted Hodson in December 1947 – stories that included the *Barnsley Chronicle*'s report of how the town's market had been invaded by 'strapping young men dressed in gaily ribboned slouch hats; the loudest and latest Yankee ties (nude figures painted with luminous paint); fancy overcoats with padded shoulders;

highly-polished pointed shoes'. And all rounded off with 'David Niven 'tashes, cultivated with the aid of a black pencil'. These spivs, 'driven from their holes and corners in London by the manpower hunt, the closer attentions of the police, and income tax officials', attempted to sell toy balloons at 2s 6d, paper flowers at 5s a bunch, and 'worthless glass trinkets at 10s' – '"All very speshull" they whined in their best Cockney accent.' But they got little joy from the Barnsley housewives. 'Why should such fit young men be allowed to carry on like that,' demanded one, 'while my husband is at the coal face risking his life to get coal to keep the likes of those comfortable?'

Soon afterwards, in early 1948, the black market was the subject given by Mass-Observation to its regular panel. 'Do you know of any such dealings in your area? If so, please describe them. (No identification, please.)' More answers than not emphasised their prevalence:

Yes, I do know of such dealings locally. Eggs are sold at from 6d to 1/- each; dead birds at much above the controlled price; milk at 1/- per pint and moreover if one leaves a little extra each week in the empty bottles more milk is forthcoming. Conversely if one stops the tribute the milk stops immediately. No words are used in this little comedy . . . Black market dealings pervade every sphere of life and every commodity. (*Grocer*)

If the Black Market exists as it seems to in the minds of Fleet St then I've not come into contact with it. There's a hell of a lot of a sort of barter going on. Which is very different. (*Commercial traveller*)

My aunt (otherwise a scrupulously honest woman) gets extra supplies of eggs, butter, cheese and fruit from her regular grocer – at fabulously high prices. (*Designer*)

From my experience the focal points in my neighbourhood centre in the local Conservative Clubs. The people who, day in and day out, pour rancorous abuse upon the Government's restrictions are, I find, the very folk who dabble dirtily in this sort of anti-social business. (*Local government officer*)

In common with everyone else in this country I know of such dealings and I would require strong proof to convince myself that we do not, all of us, take part in them. (*Advertising*)

The other day I was in a baker's shop. A woman whispered to the assistant who glanced at me, hesitated, then brought a bag from under the counter (literally) and handed it over. No money passed. I knew at once that about half a dozen eggs had changed hands. (*Pianist and housewife*)

My experience is I don't know anyone who is not in the B.M. (*Steel worker*)

My friends tell me that any number of clothing coupons can be bought at 2/- each; that bus conductors offer nylons to passengers on their buses; I know people who can get all they want in the way of 'points' goods without surrending a point – these they sell. Nearer home, I know a Methodist parson who collects eggs from one of his former 'cures' and who retails them at 6/7 per doz – quite cheap, when one considers that the regular B.M. rate is 10/- per doz. He also can produce silk stockings or marmalade – whichever you want! (*Housewife*)

About the same time, Kenneth Preston was told that the Bishop of Bradford and an ecclesiastical colleague had been overheard 'discussing a 40 pound ham they had secured and which they were going to share between them'. To Preston, a middle-aged English teacher at Keighley Grammar School and the most conscientious of diarists, it was yet one more sign that there was something fundamentally amiss with the post-war world: 'They were paying 10/- per pound for the ham. It is rather shocking to think of one's bishop engaged in black market transactions.'

Most people – respectable and law-abiding – probably shared Preston's dislike of the very fact of the black market, instinctively seeing it as unfair. A Gallup poll in April 1947 found that only 14 per cent thought the authorities were doing enough to stop it. Did that, though, translate into widespread reluctance and/or shame about using it? The Mass-Observation replies in early 1948 suggested, perhaps inevitably, a range of attitudes:

My husband insists that anything one gets over and above the ration is morally a black market transaction. I prefer to call it grey – though I admit he is really right. (*Housewife*)

Generally speaking I feel that the ordinary Englishman leaves such dealings to the selfish who will have this or that no matter who else goes without, and to the shady character who makes his living in the business and has no qualms at all. (*Civil servant*)

A number of my neighbours buy sacks of potatoes ['controlled' rather than rationed between November 1947 and April 1948], onions, oranges when no one else can get them – 'well my dear we pay a bit over the odds but one must have the stuff'. (*Housewife and voluntary social worker*)

I would say that the Black Market is treated as a semi-joke, although a serious one. People feel they are very clever if they can say they have obtained something or other outside the rations or without coupons. (*Sales manager*)

Unfortunately almost everybody I know does these things to a greater or lesser degree . . . I myself must admit that I am not quite without blame myself, where getting things for my family is concerned, although I honestly hope I do less wrong than most. (*Export and production manager*)

I guess we are all human, who wouldn't like some ham, petrol, nylons, all those things that make life worth living (or do they?). No, I think my only dislike in this line is the slimy types who seem to deal in the 'market'. I've no scruples about where the thing comes from really, but some of the slick boys who seem to live by this business get me down. Put it this way. If a Service man came to me and said, 'this rum or whatever it was "knocked off" what's it worth to you?' I'd deal. But when it comes to some flash looking 'won't work' type of Spiv, a guy living on his wits, no fixed abode, no guts, no papers etc, cut me out. If he is a fat cigar-smoking Jew – well I'd rather starve. (*Electrician*)

In fact there is some evidence that by this time – almost three years after VE Day, virtually everyone fed up with continuing rationing – the spiv was becoming a less demonised figure. March 1948 saw the first issue of the *Spivs' Gazette*, a humorous magazine which among other things gave details of the Spivs' Union ('Only genuine spivs, drones, wide boys, eels, butterflies and black marketeers to be eligible for membership . . . All members must wear the official spiv uniform – shoulders to be not less than 46 inches wide . . . Members are not expected to "do" each other – only the public').[8] Put another way, the morality of shared sacrifice no longer seemed quite so compelling as – perhaps – it once had been.

Two developments in 1947/8 pointed the way to a more expansive, acquisitive future. The first took its cue directly from the United States, where self-service shopping had been pioneered in the early 1930s, to the extent that by 1946 almost a third of retail food stores were entirely or partially self-service. The first British experiment along these lines probably took place in a section of the Romford Co-op in 1942, in the context of a staff shortage. The Romford example was soon followed by other London Co-operative Society shops, but it was not until some time after the war that the requisite fixtures and fittings became available for authentic, full-scale self-service conversion. One enthusiast, after a revelatory eye-opening visit to the States, was Tesco's Jack Cohen, the self-made founder of a chain of grocery shops (by this time about a hundred strong) that faithfully obeyed his dictum 'pile it high and sell it cheap'. In 1947 he put his St Albans store on a self-service basis, an experiment that began well but ended after 12 months – partly because the equipment was not yet quite right. Elsewhere, in January 1948 Marks & Spencer introduced at its store in Wood Green, north London, what Kathryn Morrison, the historian of English shopping, has called 'the first full-fledged version of self-service in the UK'. It was only the food department, but in style and layout it was unmistakably on the American model. 'It would appear so far, at least, that shoppers are well pleased with the innovation, several writing to express their satisfaction to the store manager,' reported *Store* magazine in February, though early users were sufficiently cautious that in the first few weeks their number of purchases per visit rarely rose above two or three. About the same time as the M&S initiative, several London Co-ops (including at Upton Park, Barkingside and West Hounslow) were putting entire grocery counters on a systematic self-service footing, while in March one of the more dynamic figures in the co-operative movement, the Portsmouth-based John Jacques, opted for self-service across his domain. Was it the start of an inexorable transatlantic revolution? 'This England of ours is not America,' R. Hardstaff ('Royal Arsenal Grocery Shop Assistant') warned in the *Co-operative News*. 'We live as English, not in the cosmopolitan manner of Americans. The English housewife wants personal service, she likes to shop with salesmen who know and understand her wants and likes.'[9]

The other development was heralded by *Vogue* in the autumn of 1947:

> Fashion has moved decisively in Paris. One has seen changes coming for many months but now they are here, inescapably. Our Fashion Editor sums it up: 'Take last season's round hipline, small shoulder, pulled-in waist, longer skirt, and emphasize each; stress the bosom, stress the *derrière*; add a side-moving hat; and you will have a composite view of the Paris form for the new season.' The skirt may be full – petal-shaped or spreading with unpressed pleats. It may be straight. But either way it descends to anything from fourteen to eight inches from the floor.

From the first, there were opponents of this new, feminine style (largely the work of Christian Dior). 'The ridiculous whim of idle people' was the trenchant view of the Labour MP Bessie Braddock. 'The problem today as it affects British women is to get hold of clothes. They have not agitated for the longer skirt. Their strong feeling is that things should be left as they are. Most women today are glad to get any clothes they can get hold of.' The British Guild of Creative Designers agreed: 'We just have not got the materials. We cannot give way to Paris's irresponsible introduction of the longer skirt.'

For British women, there was a six-month wait before clothes in the new style started to come through to the shops, though in January 1948 there was an early sighting of the soon-to-be-ubiquitous port-manteau term when Panter-Downes noted that 'women's winter coats are being offered at knock-down prices to tempt customers who are gambling on a mild winter and saving their coupons for a spring New Look – Cripps or no Cripps.' The Chancellor was another of the New Look's non-admirers, soon abetted by another Labour MP, Mabel Ridealgh, who in February denounced it as an 'utterly ridiculous, stupidly exaggerated waste of material and manpower, foisted on the average woman to the detriment of other, more normal clothing'. For her as for some other Labour critics, it was not just that the New Look was a needless extravagance at a time of dire shortage of materials, but that it was also a seriously retrogressive step. 'Women today are taking a larger part in the happenings of the world,' she wrote in *Reynolds*

News, 'and the New Look is too reminiscent of a caged bird's attitude. I hope our fashion dictators will realise the new *outlook* of women and will give the death blow to any attempt at curtailing women's freedom.'

Alas for Ridealgh and others, the New Look began in March and April to sweep almost all before it. 'We are selling nothing but New Look clothes, with nipped-in waists and rounded shoulder lines,' reported Marshall & Snelgrove. 'The longer skirt is here, let's face it,' Norah Alexander wrote in her fashion column in the *Daily Mail*. 'You'd think that after all these austere years no one would grudge us this small token of pleasanter things to come . . . Don't let anyone persuade you that it's wanton to covet the sort of clothes they're wearing in the other cities of the world.' A spokesman for the London Model House group, which had tried to persuade the Board of Trade to regulate hemlines, conceded defeat: 'It's impossible to stop the New Look. It's like a tidal wave.' By late April it was popping up in diaries. 'Saw several examples of the New Look, none of which was interesting to me,' sniffed Gladys Langford after a trip to Richmond, where the 'long queues outside all tea-shops' had reduced her to 'orangeade and jam sponge roll at Woolworth's'. But for Grace Golden, standing in a bus queue in Piccadilly was an opportunity to view 'a number of charming "new look" women – the full long skirts quite delightful'. The final, clinching breakthrough came on the 26th, with the outfit worn by Princess Margaret (who a few months earlier had been given a private showing by Dior) to the celebration in St Paul's of her parents' silver wedding anniversary. 'She had fully adopted the tightly waisted, bouffant-skirted, ankle-length New Look,' in the words of a biographer, 'with which she wore – and would always thereafter wear – very high heels and platform soles.' By the end of the year, soon after Mass-Observation had found that 'opposition comes mainly from men over thirty-five', it was estimated that as many as ten million women either had or desired the New Look.[10]

Was the widespread adoption of this new style really such a defeat for female emancipation? 'There was nothing intrinsically submissive about the New Look,' one cultural historian, Angela Partington, has forcefully contended, 'even though it restricted movement and emphasised the curves of the body.'

Its strong colours, severe shapes, and theatrical styling could equally well be read as 'stroppy' and defiant compared to the twee floral prints and sensible cuts of utility styles. The way it was adapted and worn by working-class women transformed it into a hybrid style, 'unfaithful' to the designer's vision, and they appropriated it for working and for relaxing in, as well as for 'dressing up' occasions . . . By refusing to keep the functional and the decorative separate, consumers were not only breaking the rules of good design and taste, but using goods to satisfy desires other than those assumed by the marketing industries.

Such assertions may demand fuller empirical testing than is possible, but any argument that gets away from the consumer as a passive, undifferentiated dummy deserves respect.

For at least two women – and their children – the New Look was not unmomentous. In 2002 an interviewer asked David Bailey (brought up 'in a little terraced job in East Ham' with an outside toilet) about his first strong visual memory: '"Going to Selfridges in 1948, where my mother tried on a New Look dress. She couldn't afford it, but tried it on anyway. I remember her twirling around and thinking how beautiful she was, and that was my first fashion picture, I suppose." Taken in your head? "Yeah."' For Carolyn Steedman, born in March 1947 and living in Hammersmith until she was four, an even more graphic early memory was dreaming about her mother. 'She wore the New Look, a coat of beige gaberdine which fell in two swaying, graceful pleats from her waist at the back' – and for Steedman much of the retrospective point of the dream was the fierceness of her mother's desire for the New Look, which in real, impoverished life was too expensive to be attainable. In her memoir, *Landscape for a Good Woman*, she draws a picture of her mother (the daughter of a Burnley weaver) who in two particular respects contradicted the conventional, salt-of-the-earth wisdom about the working class: not only was she politically a Tory, but she had almost overwhelming – and guiltless – material urges, together with powerful resentments if they were not fulfilled. Steedman's remarkable book is, among other things, a plea against the overdeterministic reduction of working-class individuals to flattened figures in a Lowry-type setting, 'washed over with a patina of stolid emotional sameness'. The New Look was, not only for Steedman's mother, a very real as well as symbolic goal.[11]

———

Even so, there seems little doubt that it was the middle class that *felt* a relatively greater sense of deprivation during these austerity years. In Ina Zweiniger-Bargielowska's words, 'the staples of the middle-class lifestyle – domestic service, ample food and clothes, consumer durables, motor cars, and luxuries such as travel, entertainment and subscriptions – were squeezed by labour shortage and rationing as well as high taxation and rising prices.' Papers like the *Evening Standard* were full of malcontent correspondents. 'Before the war,' complained one in April 1947, 'we could afford to go abroad for holidays. Last year we imposed ourselves upon relatives. We used to play golf, tennis and badminton. How can we afford them now?' Another, a grammar-school master, was only marginally less down-beat: 'We could give up the car; but we cling to it as a last link with comfort and luxury, having surrendered so many other things, including annual holidays, library subscriptions and golf.' By 1948 at the latest, it had become almost axiomatic that it was the middle class that had taken the biggest hit since the war. In a radio talk given in May, four months after the *Economist*'s finding that 'at least ten per cent of the national consuming power has been forcefully transferred from the middle classes and the rich to the wage earners', the economic journalist (and prolific broadcaster) Graham Hutton similarly argued that 'the well-to-do and better-off, the middle classes, have taken the biggest material cuts and sacrifices, as persons or households', whereas 'the less well-to-do have had their material standards raised'.[12]

The obvious temptation – to emigrate – was manfully resisted in Evelyn Waugh's case. At around the time of the cuts following the convertibility crisis, he explained in his diary why he had decided not to decamp to Ireland: 'The Socialists are piling up repressive measures now. It would seem I was flying from them.' But for the veteran travel writer H. V. Morton, the lure of South Africa was irresistible. Not only, he told a friend during the winter of 1947/8, had the Attlee government 'put over more unpleasant measures than any other in history', but England had become a society where 'things moved steadily towards Communism' and 'everything that can be done is being done to pamper the masses and to plunder anyone with capital or initiative'. Soon afterwards, a City banker, Ernest Muriel, was similarly contemplating his sunset years in South Africa: 'A country,' he informed a no-doubt sympathetic correspondent in Cape Town, 'which has many attractions as against Britain, where we are hedged around with so many restrictions and frustrations and where the retired rentier has to pay penal taxation, and, in the Socialist mentality, is looked upon as a cross between a drone and criminal.'

Most stuck it out, including the indomitable 'ladies' for whom Derry & Toms was almost a second home. 'Quite a number of the original upper middle class Kensingtonians survive,' noted the writer John Brophy (father of Brigid) in April 1948:

> All over sixty, now, some over eighty. Most of the men are bewildered and defeated. The old ladies are invincible. Neither rationing, queues, the disappearance of servants, nor heavy taxation and the lowered purchasing power of money gets them down: the unforeseen bad times give them something to talk clichés about. They wear long, rustling skirts, flowered hats, and carry reticules and, in summer, silk sunshades with long handles. The 'New Look' has for the first time in forty years brought them almost within range of contemporary fashion.

These old dears mainly ate their meals in restaurants, where 'they talk[ed] to each other across the small tables as though from mountain top to mountain top. And all banality . . .' They were also, Brophy observed with grudging admiration, 'quite unscrupulous': 'They were born to privilege, and in the days of their decline they fight for it. Given half a chance, any one of them will sail in ahead of the longest bus queue.'[13]

In general it is clear which political party stood to benefit from an increasingly aggrieved middle class. 'Two villages in the Home Counties have each subscribed about £500 for Lord Woolton's Tory fund to fight the next General Election,' Hodson had already noted in January 1948, adding that 'the middle class are rising up.' And that summer, a memo from the Conservative Party's research department set out what it hoped would be the next election's battleground: 'The floating vote is mainly middle class (incomes £700–£1,200 per annum). These people are now finding it impossible to live. The chief fear of the middle-class voter is being submerged by a more prosperous working class. Our whole appeal must be in this direction.' How would Labour respond? Manny Shinwell may have infamously declared in May 1947 that his party did not care 'a tinker's cuss' for any class other than 'the organised workers of the country'; Cripps in his April 1948 Budget may have indulged in a one-off capital levy; but for one of Labour's more thoughtful MPs, Maurice Edelman (sitting, like Richard Crossman, for a Coventry seat), there was a key distinction to make. 'Morrison has spoken of Labour's concern for the "useful" people,' he wrote in the *New Statesman* in June 1948:

> Among the middle class the description 'useful' applies from the white-collar clerk to the working director; it includes Civil Servants, teachers, working shopkeepers, technicians, managers, doctors, journalists and farmers . . .The useful middle classes are an integral part of the Movement.
>
> But there are others among the middle classes whose prosperity and advancement is tied up with a *laissez-faire* economy. Every measure of a planned economy is to them a poisoned draught. Often they owe their careers, started in the working class or the lower middle class, to the competitive nature of business, which has given their commercial aptitude opportunity, and their aggressiveness scope. They include company secretaries, commercial travellers, sales managers and small business men. These, then, are the irreconcilables among the middle classes. Labour's victory is, by definition, their defeat.

In the latter category, Edelman did not even bother to mention the rentiers of Kensington and Cheltenham, of Bournemouth and Budleigh Salterton, the ultimate irreconcilables.

The increasing middle-class sense of being somehow muscled out of the picture by the working class was nicely caught by Gladys

Langford. 'It is very noticeable that nowadays the well-fed, well-clad, sweetly smiling bourgeoisie male & female have disappeared from poster and advertisement,' she reflected in May 1947. 'It is the broadly grinning and obviously unwashed "worker" who appears in more than life size on our hoardings and Tube stations.' The chances are that hostility flowed mainly in one direction, at least to judge by the experience of a friend of Hodson who spent that summer in a hospital ward. 'I hadn't been so close to the working class before,' he told the diarist. 'I didn't find a trace of class antagonism. The chap in the next bed was a Cockney who had three tricks, imitating pheasants, imitating the nurse when she asked "Have a cup of tea?" and creating a rude noise.'[14]

That cheerful chappie was lucky not to be waiting to catch a train from Hungerford station on Tuesday, 6 January 1948. 'A number of prosperous, well-dressed families were collected, who talked loudly about their personal affairs, ignoring the rest of the world and making me ponder the phenomenon of Class, and ask myself how the war had affected it.' Frances Partridge (translator, diarist and member of the Bloomsbury Group) went on:

> When the pressure was on us all, it had seemed as though the relation between master and man, for instance, was suffering a sea-change, and it was a common sight to see a Colonel in a good but worn suit almost cringing to a waitress as he pleadingly enquired 'Do you think I might have a little water?' Today I felt we were in the presence of 'conspicuous padding' – that is to say I was aware that the gentry had reassumed their right to the privileges and support that money gives. Two elderly ladies got into our carriage in the train and drew back their lips from their yellowing teeth with identical snarls of concentration as they pecked about in their handbags. 'Thought for a moment I'd forgotten my handkerchief,' said one. '*Very* nosy day, isn't it?'

The previous day had featured the start, at 4.00 on the Light Programme, of *Mrs Dale's Diary*. Directly replacing the more down-market *The Robinson Family*, each day it told the story of the Dales, a family living in a comfortable house in an outer suburb, Kenton in

Middlesex, though soon moving to a fictitious London locality (Virginia Lodge, Parkwood Hill). Dr Jim Dale had been a GP for 25 years; their son Bob had recently been demobilised from the army; their 19-year-old daughter Gwen worked in an office in town; and there was a cat, called Captain. As for Mrs Mary Dale herself, she enjoyed the services of a domestic help (Mrs Morgan, who seldom stopped talking) and before long came up with a catchphrase – 'I'm a little worried about Jim' – that over the years seeped into the middle-class collective consciousness.

Certainly the two cultures – middle-class and working-class – seldom mixed happily. In the autumn of 1947 the Bristol Empire, situated in the city's east, decided as an experiment to put on eight plays. Those chosen were hardly highbrow, including *Arsenic and Old Lace* and Ivor Novello's *I Lived with You*, but the experiment proved a resounding flop. 'Simply,' explains that theatre's chronicler, 'the Empire audiences did not expect or want to see this type of production, while keen playgoers from other areas of Bristol were not willing to visit the Empire, seen as a working-class home for variety and revue.' Going legit was not a mistake that the London Palladium ever made, though as everywhere the quality could be mixed. 'It was a rotten variety bill, with far too many acrobatic affairs – some of which were positively obscene,' a just-demobbed Kenneth Williams noted in January 1948. 'Sid Field was marvellous, and received terrific and well-merited applause – what camping! I simply roared!'

Field, particularly celebrated for his 'Slasher Green' spiv sketch, was probably *the* variety performer of the late 1940s, but younger ones still had it all to do. A glance at the line-up at the Aldershot Hippodrome a month later reveals Dave and Joe O'Gorman ('celebrated comedians') as top of the bill, with other attractions including Arthur Dowler ('The Wizard of Cod'), Peter Sellers ('Bang On'), Wimpey ('Acrobatic Novelty'), and Cynthia and Gladys ('A Juggling Delight'). Sellers, at this stage an impressionist, was paid £12 10s for his week of twice-nightly appearances, which his friend Graham Stark remembered as a disaster. But on 5 April a star *was* born. 'Wisdom's the name,' the *Daily Express* proclaimed. 'He Woke to Find he had Joined the Star Comics.' Such was the enthusiastic reception for Norman Wisdom's first-night performance at the London Casino. The paper described his act: 'His face is mobile, can be twisted into any shape. He tumbles on the stage, shadow-boxes, tries to play the piano, pulls out a clarinet, tires of it and turns his attention to . . . a vast sandwich. Then he pleads with his audience to follow him in an Eastern song – in gibberish. His props? A stringy tie, an old shirt, and a baggy evening suit, several sizes too large.'[15] Wisdom was 33 (though billed at the time as 27), a former shop assistant, and, like so many of his contemporaries, had begun entertaining while in the army.

At the big football grounds, huge, almost entirely male working-class crowds continued to pour through the turnstiles – in January 1948 the highest League attendance ever, 83,360, saw Manchester United play Arsenal at Maine Road (Old Trafford being still out of commission following bomb damage). Sadly, few Lancastrians ever thought of going to watch Accrington Stanley in the Third Division North and thereby boost the seldom large crowd at Peel Park. Even so, the club by this time had just managed to pay off the mortgage on the ground, and on 10 February a ceremony took place at the Mechanics' Institution. 'The gathering was a happy one to celebrate a happy event,' reported the *Accrington Observer*, 'and the red and white motif was in evidence, from an iced cake bearing the words "On, Stanley, On" to the red and white table flowers.' The main speech was given by Councillor S. T. Pilkington, JP, associated with the club as player, official, director and chairman (for the past 12 years) since 1906. 'He referred to football finance at the present time as being "daft". To pay £20,000 for one player [as Notts County, of all clubs, had recently done for Chelsea's Tommy Lawton], he said was "absolutely silly, crazy finance".' The first match after the ceremony was at home to Wrexham, with a predictable outcome: 'Bad Luck and Bad Shooting beat Stanley.'

Two months later it was the Cup Final, Manchester United versus Blackpool, billed as probably the last chance for the 33-year-old Stanley Matthews to get a winner's medal. But United won 4–2, and years later their winger, Charlie Mitten, recalled a conversation with his opponent that did not exactly focus on the glory aspect (or lack of it): 'I walked off the field with Stan Matthews. He said, "Look at that, Charlie? A silver medal and we get no money." But we never gave much thought to the money side. I said, "Yes, I believe the band get more than us, Stan." "Yeah," he said. "Bloody disgrace, isn't it?" I said, "They must have played better than us, that's why."' 'Anyway,' concluded Mitten with the mellowness of time, 'it was all a bit of a joke and a laugh.'[16]

There was little inclination yet to abandon cultural hierarchies. 'A certain Professor Zweig has been doing a little mass-observation in England all by himself, has had 400 conversations with men earning between £4 10s 0d and £6 a week,' noted Hodson in April 1948, before summarising some of Zweig's findings. Up to half of a wage could go on tobacco; 3s a week was the usual outlay on football pools; one in five betted on the dogs; 'real recreational spending' was 'small'; and 'time after time men said, "I have no interests."' Hodson went on:

> As a picture of Britain I find this decidedly inglorious. Every evening I see folk queued up for the cinema. Whatever picture is on, whatever drivel it is, the queues are there. Dogs, pictures, tobacco, drink, football pools, crooners – what an indifferent lot of pastimes for our people. To do a monotonous repetition job you loathe, and to use these anodynes to help you forget tomorrow's work! If this is Western civilisation, there is a R.A.F. phrase that can be used – we've had it!

A few days earlier Kenneth Preston, on holiday from school, cycled with his wife and son from Keighley to Nelson. There, after inspecting the open market ('We always think there is far more food in the Lancashire shops than here'), they went to a second-hand bookshop:

> Whilst we were having a look round we heard the voices of two women in a really incredible conversation. One yelled out to another, who was evidently looking at some books, 'Nah! then, don't buy all e' booiks'. The other said 'Nay, we don't read much at our 'ouse'. The other replied 'No! we don't. I've nivver read a book i'my life'. The other said 'No! I often wish I'd read a bit more. You learn stuff from books, don't you?' It seems incredible that there could be anyone who had never read a book. The woman who said she hadn't, Kath said, would be over fifty. These are the folk who vote!!

Attitudes were perhaps not so different in the people's party. Some weeks later, the Labour conference at Scarborough included an eye-opening diversion. 'Paid our first visit to a Butlin Camp [ie at Filey] where the N.U.M. were entertaining us on our last night,' noted Hugh Gaitskell (Winchester and Oxford). 'Very efficient, organised, pleasure holiday making. Everybody agreed they would not go there!'[17]

Over the years, the profound cultural mismatch between progressive activators and the millions acted upon would inevitably be played out in some of the most emotive policy areas. In retrospect, two stand out from the late 1940s: crime and race. The first was already becoming the cause of major fractures – not only within elite opinion but also between elite liberal opinion and non-elite illiberal opinion – while the other, even more resonant, was poised to be similarly destructive of any forward-looking, modern-minded consensus.

'More brutal crimes,' recorded an unhappy, almost bewildered Gladys Langford in June 1947. 'Have I been all wrong? Is it that these vicious criminals need flogging and harsh treatment or are they cases for a psychologist?' There were many causes of the increased crime, brutal and otherwise, in immediate post-war Britain – most obviously the pressures and inducements deriving from the rationing of the majority of key everyday requirements – but what was undeniable was that it was happening. During the summer of 1947, the most headline-grabbing case was that of poor Alec de Antiquis, a respectable motor mechanic in his 30s who, as he rode his motorcycle down a London street, was shot dead by fleeing jewellery thieves. The culprits were quickly found (a vital clue being the clothing coupons for a discarded RAF raincoat), and two men were hanged at Pentonville, with the lugubrious Albert Pierrepoint doing the honours. When Cyril Connolly later that year weighed into the government in another disenchanted *Horizon* editorial, one of his main charges was that a regime that did not 'even dare to propose the abolition of the death penalty' bore 'no relation to the kind of Socialism which many of us envisaged'. Yet the fact was that twice already in 1947 the question 'Do you think the death penalty should be abolished?' had been put by Gallup; and each time only 25 per cent had answered 'yes'. Developments in 1948 were unlikely to sway this hardline majority. 'A vast crime-wave is sweeping Britain,' W. J. Brown noted in February. 'And last week a policeman was killed in London.' Indeed, over the year as a whole the number of indictable offences recorded in Britain turned out to be 522,684, almost double the total in 1937.[18]

Unpromising mood music, then, for the abolitionist amendment by Sydney Silverman (Labour MP for Nelson and Colne) to the Criminal Justice Bill being brought forward by Chuter Ede, the Home Secretary. On the day of the debate and vote, 14 April, Cuthbert Headlam on the Opposition backbenches was a sardonic, unsentimental observer of a deep split in the ruling party:

> The H of C (free vote) decided tonight to put the death penalty for murder into cold storage for 5 years which presumably will mean the abolition of capital punishment in English law. The Home Secretary and the Cabinet advised the House that in their opinion this was not the moment to make the experiment – the police and the judges are said to be against the change – but the Comrades as a body were not convinced. Human life is sacred, hanging is no deterrent to murder, other countries have abolished it without any increase of murder – why should not we? All very plausible – all very noble-minded – but what does all the fuss amount to? Chuter Ede gave us figures to show that about 11 or 12 people are hanged every year – that a majority of murder cases are reprieved – that the chance of a miscarriage of justice is very slight ... We are asked therefore to do away with capital punishment against the advice of responsible authority at a time when criminal violence is on the increase ... The speeches today were good, bad and indifferent – and each speaker in turn congratulated the one who spoke before him on his high morality and sincerity. There was a deal of sob stuff which depressed me as it always does.

The majority of 23 in favour of an experimental suspension of the death penalty would have been greater if it had been a genuinely 'free vote'. In fact, Attlee on the morning of the debate curtly told his junior ministers that, given the Cabinet's position, they were not to vote for Silverman's amendment. Among those who protested – and in due course abstained – was the rather incongruous pair of Evan Durbin and James Callaghan.

It proved a short-lived triumph for the mainly middle-class Labour backbenchers. Four days later, the *Sunday Pictorial*'s headline was '"Hanging" Vote Worries Public', with the paper's reporters having conducted an intensive two-day inquiry 'all over Britain' which found that 'the majority of the public, while welcoming an end to hanging as the sole penalty for murder, feel it should be kept as protection from the worst criminal types'. Accordingly, 'nine out of ten people favoured degrees of murder, with death for killers in the first degree'. The paper also quoted some representative vox pop:

Criminals will stick at nothing now they know they cannot be hanged. (*Capt. A. E. Tarran, Shadwell, Leeds*)

With this last deterrent gone, no woman will feel safe in London after dark. (*Miss A. Bennett, Martin Way, Merton*)

It is a mistake to remove the only punishment of which armed thugs are afraid. (*Mr T. Ashton, Holloway Road, N7*)

I think Members of Parliament should have their heads examined for coming to such a decision. (*Mr H. Ronson, Deane Road, Bolton*)

How dare the Commons abolish the death penalty without hearing the views of the people they represent! (*Mr T. O'Neil, Wadham Road, Liverpool*)

Now it was up to the Lords. But meanwhile, Gladys Langford noted in early May, '. . . another policeman shot – Forest Gate this time', and later that month another Gallup poll revealed that 66 per cent were opposed to suspending capital punishment for five years and only 26 per cent in favour. The Lord Chief Justice, the uncompromising Lord Goddard, had already made clear his view that criminal law would be respected only if it remained in line with public opinion, and on 2 June (the day the Queen toured the Lancashire cotton mills) the Lords rejected suspension by a crushing 181 votes to 28. At a Cabinet meeting soon afterwards, Attlee – well aware of where public feeling lay – successfully insisted that, for the time being at least, the abolitionist game was up; Hartley Shawcross, no longer the master, left the room in tears.[19]

The summer of 1948 was even more of a defining moment in the centuries-old story of immigration to Britain. For many years the most widely stigmatised 'others' in British society had been the Jews and the Irish, by the end of the war numbering respectively some 400,000 and 600,000 (ie on the mainland). Although it is possible to exaggerate the extent of the prejudice, Jews in particular were demonised, even after the film cameras had entered Belsen and Auschwitz; shockingly, British fascism revived quickly after the war, little impeded by the men in blue. 'I suppose it is perfectly in order for a lousy swine like Jeffrey Hamm [Oswald Mosley's main sidekick] to get up on a street corner in the East End of London and shout, "Down with the Jews. Burn the synagogues. Kill the Aliens," and he gets away with it, but if a person tries to pull him up, what happens?' a concerned local person asked the Home Secretary rhetorically in October 1946. 'The so-called keepers of law and order, the police, go up to this person and tell him he'd better move away before he gets hurt . . . These guardians of the law and order from Commercial Street Police Station openly boast about being members of Jeffrey Hamm's fascist party.' The following year saw anti-Semitic riots in several British cities. These were triggered by lurid headlines about the hanging in Palestine of two captured British sergeants but also involved a widespread belief that it was Jews who were responsible for running the black market – and making a killing from doing so.

There was likewise some persistent anti-Semitism in the higher echelons of society. Frederic Raphael's schooldays at Charterhouse were famously made a misery because of it, while in the City of London the malign legacy survived of Montagu Norman, the notoriously anti-Semitic Governor of the Bank of England between the wars. 'Mr Randell of Bank of England says he is a very pushing individual – German Jew – who established himself here in 1938,' stated (early in 1948) an internal note of the Issuing Houses Association, to which Walter Salomon had applied for his firm to join. 'They don't know a lot about him, but think it would do no harm to let him cool his heels a bit more.' And, damningly: 'His office is full of foreigners.' When the IHA took other soundings, no one denied that Salomon was a man of ability and energy, but – the face not fitting – he did indeed have to cool his heels.[20]

However, the Jew was about to be replaced by the black immigrant as the prime 'other'. At the end of the war, some 20,000 to 30,000 non-whites were living in Britain, and studies were starting to be made of the attitude of whites towards them. Kenneth Little's *Negroes in Britain* – published in 1948 but mainly based on fieldwork done in the late 1930s and early 1940s in Cardiff's Tiger Bay (where Shirley Bassey, seventh child of a Nigerian seaman, was growing up) – concluded hopefully that 'a great deal of latent friendliness underlies the surface appearance of apathy and even of displayed prejudice in a large number of cases,' though he did concede that it was difficult to generalise, given that as yet 'relatively few English people have made close contact with coloured individuals.' The other port with a sizeable number of black immigrants was Liverpool, where Anthony Richmond in the early 1950s examined what became of several hundred West Indians who went there during the war (under an officially sponsored scheme to boost production) and subsequently stayed on. Richmond found that by 1946 at the latest they were encountering considerable prejudice in the workplace from skilled tradesmen who, having served their apprenticeships, 'resented being associated in the minds of English people with the unskilled negro labourer': 'Outside the field of employment there can be little doubt that the area of most intense prejudice against the West Indian Negroes is that of sexual relations,' in that 'men who are accepted in the ordinary course of acquaintance are subjected to serious insults if seen in the company of a white girl', and 'the girl herself is often stigmatised among all "respectable" people'.

A Guyanan at the sharp end of prejudice in 1947/8 was Eustace Braithwaite, who after demobilisation from the RAF struggled, for over a year and despite having a Cambridge physics degree, to get a job: 'I tried everything – labour exchanges, employment agencies, newspaper ads – all with the same result. I even advertised myself mentioning my qualifications and the colour of my skin, but there were no takers. Then I tried applying for jobs without mentioning my colour, but when they saw me the reasons given for turning me down were all variations of the same theme: too black . . .' Eventually, sitting one day beside the lake in St James's Park and watching the ducks, he fell into conversation with 'a thin, bespectacled old

gentleman' and related his plight. The stranger told him there were
many vacancies for teachers in the East End, and soon afterwards
Braithwaite secured a job at an LCC school in Cable Street, scene of
the pitched battle between fascists and Communists in 1936. He was
the only black teacher in London, and the eventual literary (and
cinematic) upshot was *To Sir, With Love*.

Ignorance about black immigrants and where they came from no
doubt played its part in shaping indigenous attitudes. A survey of
almost 2,000 adult civilians, conducted mainly in May 1948, revealed
the following:

What people know	*% of persons*
That native peoples in the Colonies have a lower standard of living than ourselves	67
That Colonial inhabitants are mostly coloured, not white	62
People who can name at least one Colony	49
People who can name at least one food or raw material from the Colonies	37
That the new ground nut scheme is in East Africa	16

'Housewives, unskilled operatives, and people over the age of sixty,
are the least well-informed sections of the population,' observed the
report, adding that among even the most knowledgeable occupational
group, comprising professional, managerial and higher clerical
workers, less than two-thirds could explain the difference between a
colony and a dominion. The report went on: 'Public opinion is
inclined to be complacent about the work that Britain has done in
the Colonies. Only 19% think that we have "tended to be selfish in
the past" – though this feeling is stronger among the better informed
sections of the population than among the more ignorant. In any
case, the great majority of people believe that we are doing "a better
job now".'[21] These were significant findings. Whatever people's
instinctive attitude towards black immigrants, not many believed that
Britain morally owed them a favour. The guilt factor, in other words,
was still the preserve of a privileged minority.

At the Ministry of Labour (MOL), faced by a serious labour shortage, the need to attract migrants was obvious. But whereas it went out of its way in these years to bring into the British labour market many thousands of white European workers, a high proportion of them Poles, its attitude to Caribbean labour was essentially negative, albeit sometimes covertly expressed. 'Whatever may be the policy about British citizenship,' Sir Harold Wiles, Deputy Permanent Under-Secretary, told a colleague in March 1948, 'I do not think that any scheme for the importation of coloured colonials for permanent settlement here should be embarked upon without full understanding that this means that coloured element will be brought in for permanent absorption into our own population.' The colleague, M. A. Bevan, agreed: 'As regards the possible importation of West Indian labour, I suggest that we must dismiss the idea from the start.' And in May, submitting a report on the question of employing 'surplus male West Indians', the MOL came up with an avalanche of reasons (or what it called 'overwhelming difficulties') why this was a bad idea. There was the major problem of accommodation; Caribbean workers would be 'unsuitable for outdoor work in winter owing to their susceptibility to colds and the more serious chest and lung ailments'; those working underground in coal mines would find conditions 'too hot'; and anyway, 'many of the coloured men are unreliable and lazy, quarrels among them are not infrequent'.[22] That, it seemed, was that.

How did such attitudes chime with questions of British citizenship? The issue had been raised by Wiles in his March 1948 memo, in the knowledge that legislation was in the pipeline for what, following its second reading in May, became by the end of the summer the British Nationality Act 1948. This legislation, distinguishing between citizens of the United Kingdom and Colonies on the one hand and citizens of independent Commonwealth countries on the other, was essentially a response to Canada's recent introduction of its own citizenship and sought to affirm, in the authoritative words of the historian Randall Hansen, 'Britain's place as head of a Commonwealth structure founded on the relationship between the UK and the Old Dominions'. It was not in any sense a measure centrally concerned with matters of immigration; and nor was it really about the colonies. Although in practice it sanctioned what over the next 14 years would be a very liberal immigration regime, it was (again to quote Hansen), 'never intended to sanction a mass

migration of new Commonwealth citizens to the United Kingdom' –
and, crucially, 'nowhere in parliamentary debate, the Press, or private
papers was the possibility that substantial numbers could exercise their
right to reside permanently in the UK discussed'.

Significantly, with cross-party support and little public interest, the
bill's passage was smooth and quick. Inasmuch as politicians considered
the immigration aspect, no one expected the legislation to have more
than a marginal impact. The subsequent recollection of one Tory,
Quintin Hogg – 'We thought that there would be free trade in citizens,
that people would come and go, and that there would not be much of
an overall balance in one direction or the other' – would have applied
equally to Labour.[23] After all, the general expectation was that any
future labour shortage could continue to be met by European labour;
no one anticipated the increasing availability of cheap transportation
from the Caribbean. The act was thus a fine example of liberalism at
its most nominal. Yet by a delicious irony, even as the legislators legislated,
that liberalism was starting to be tested.

On 24 May the *Empire Windrush*, a former German troop-carrier, set
sail from Kingston, Jamaica, with 492 black males and one stowaway
woman. Their destination was Tilbury, and as early as the 26th the London
office of the Ministry of Labour reacted to the news with 'considerable
dismay', predicting that if the men tried to get jobs in areas of worsening
unemployment like Stepney and Camden Town (in both of which there
were quite a few black workers already), 'there will probably be trouble
eventually'. By 8 June the minister, George Isaacs, was emphasising to
MPs that the job-seekers had not been officially invited. 'The arrival of
these substantial numbers of men under no organised arrangement is
bound to result in considerable difficulty and disappointment,' he declared,
adding, 'I hope no encouragement will be given to others to follow their
example.' Over the next fortnight the MOL tried in vain to delay the
Empire Windrush's arrival but did arrange jobs for many of its passengers
– mainly out of London and mainly well apart from each other.

Within the Cabinet the flak for this untoward turn of events was
directed at the Colonial Secretary, Arthur Creech Jones. He was blamed
on the 15th for not 'having kept the lid on things' and was requested,
amid considerable press interest (curious rather than hostile) in the
ship's imminent arrival, to 'ensure that further similar movements either

from Jamaica or elsewhere in the colonial empire are detected and checked before they can reach such an embarrassing stage'. Replying to his critics three days later, Creech Jones did not deny that the men were fully entitled to come to Britain but sought to offer reassurance for the future: 'I do not think that a similar mass movement will take place again because the transport is unlikely to be available, though we shall be faced with a steady trickle, which, however, can be dealt with without undue difficulty.' Fewer than 500 constituting a 'mass movement'? Given that over the previous 12 months as many as 51,000 white European voluntary workers had been placed in one sector alone of the British economy (agriculture), the subtext was almost palpable. Soon afterwards, in a letter sent to Attlee by 11 anxious Labour MPs, there was no beating about the bush:

> This country may become an open reception centre for immigrants not selected in respect to health, education, training, character, customs and above all, whether assimilation is possible or not.
> The British people fortunately enjoy a profound unity without uniformity in their way of life, and are blest by the absence of a colour racial problem. An influx of coloured people domiciled here is likely to impair the harmony, strength and cohesion of our public and social life and to cause discord and unhappiness among all concerned.

Accordingly, the MPs suggested that the government should, 'by legislation if necessary, control immigration in the political, social, economic and fiscal interests of our people'. They added that 'in our opinion such legislation or administration action would be almost universally approved by our people'.[24]

This petition to Attlee was sent on Tuesday, 22 June – the very day that the *Empire Windrush*'s passengers disembarked at Tilbury. The *Star*'s report that evening concentrated on '25-year-old seamstress Averill Wanchove':

> She stowed away on the ship and was befriended by Nancy Cunard, heiress of the Cunard fortunes.
> Tall and attractive Averill was discovered when the ship was seven days out from Kingston.

Mr Mortimer Martin made a whip round and raised £50, enough to pay Averill's fare and to leave her £4 for pocket money.

Nancy Cunard, who was on her way back from Trinidad, took a fancy to Averill and intends looking after her.

Pathé newsreel film of the new arrivals featured the calypso singer Lord Kitchener (real name Aldwyn Roberts) performing his latest composition, 'London Is the Place for Me', a buoyantly optimistic number which he had started composing about four days before the boat landed. 'The feeling I had to know that I'm going to touch the soil of the mother country, that was the feeling I had,' he recalled almost half a century later. 'How can I describe? It's just a wonderful feeling. You know how it is when a child, you hear about your mother country, and you know that you're going to touch the soil of the mother country, you know what feeling is that? And I can't describe it. That's why I compose the song.'

About half the men, presumably those without jobs already assigned to them, stayed temporarily at Clapham South's wartime deep shelter, run by the LCC. On the first Saturday afternoon, the vicar of the Church of the Ascension, Balham, invited them to a service the next day, to be followed in the evening by tea in the hall. About 80 took up the offer. 'The Jamaicans were charming people,' the *Clapham Observer* quoted W. H. Garland, a representative of the church, as saying afterwards. 'They were churchmen and keen.' The following Saturday – five days after some 40,000 mainly rain-soaked spectators at Villa Park had watched the middleweight Dick Turpin become Britain's first black boxing champion – five of the shelter's residents 'introduced the "Calypso" to Clapham, when they played at the baths at a social held by the Clapham Communist Party'. Under the headline 'Jamaicans Thrill Communists', the local paper went on: 'The chief exponent [Lord Kitchener?] of the calypso was called again and again to the microphone. Some of the verses he sang to the intriguing West Indian rhythm had been given before: others he made up as he went along, poking sly fun at members of the audience.'

Two days later, on 5 July, Attlee replied to his 11 worried backbenchers. 'I think it would be a great mistake to take the emigration of this Jamaican party to the United Kingdom too seriously,' he told them.

'If our policy were to result in a great influx of undesirables, we might, however unwillingly, have to consider modifying it. But I would not be willing to consider that except on really compelling evidence, which I do not think exists at the present time.'[25]

A Change in the Terms of Struggle

Tuesday, 22 June may have been Windrush Day, but *Woman's Hour* that afternoon had cricket on its agenda. 'Yes, I'm one of the awful men you keep switching off,' the cheery commentator Rex Alston told the listeners. 'But please give me a chance this time. I won't keep you more than five minutes – so don't dash off into the kitchen and see if your cakes are burning. I promise you I won't talk about silly mid-on and gully and maiden overs and all the other jargon that must perplex you. All the same, don't tell me that, some time during the week, you won't be bowled over, completely stumped, or even badly caught out!' The occasion for this patronising guff was radio's forthcoming coverage of the England versus Australia Test starting at Lord's two days later. The outcome of the match itself was predictable. England as usual were captained by a well-meaning amateur (Yorkshire's Norman Yardley), and Don Bradman's 'Invincibles' won by the crushing margin of 409 runs.

On Tuesday the 29th, about an hour after the match had finished, the regular 'What's Your Worry?' slot on *Woman's Hour* featured the reassuring voice of Marion Cutler:

> It's hard to believe that next Monday will be the much talked about 5th July when both the Health Service and National Insurance Scheme come into force. So today I'll try to clear up some of the points from your questions which have been worrying you – and sure I'm not surprised they worry you . . .
>
> Lately many of you have written to say, 'I'm over age – that's over 60, and too old to join the National Insurance. Does that mean I won't

be able to get the free medical treatment and advice under the Health Service?'

No, indeed it doesn't. Let me say once again, joining the National Insurance has nothing to do with what is offered by the Health Service. It doesn't matter what your age is, whether you're married or single, whether you're rich or poor . . .

But I *was* told the other day of one thing that is causing a lot of delay and extra work in getting the Service going.

You know the form E.C.I. which many of you have filled up already and sent in to join the Health Service. In some districts nearly 80 out of every 100 have been returned with the answers to some of the questions left blank. Two spaces in particular – and two important ones – have been left just empty. One is you can't remember, or haven't been told to produce, your Identity Card number, and the other one is you've completely forgotten the day, month and year of your birth.

Well, we've often heard that *not* telling her age has been a woman's weakness, and most of us hope it will be hidden in a birth certificate, or our marriage lines. But alas it has to go down on paper sometimes, and putting it on this Health Service Form is one of the times.

'By next Monday,' Cutler confidently declared, 'it's expected there will be over 14,500 doctors working in the Service, and if you want to you ought to be able to get on the list of one in your district before then – be able to enrol and be accepted as a patient.'[1]

It had been a far from smooth ride to get to this point, with Aneurin Bevan engaged for two years in a fierce war with the British Medical Association (BMA). 'The Act is part of the nationalization programme which is being steadily pursued by the Government,' that body's chairman, Dr Guy Dain, declared in November 1946, the day after the National Health Service Bill had received the Royal Assent. 'What the Minister appears to have done is to have taken the Bill which we had partly fashioned and to have inserted into it the Socialist principles of State ownership of hospitals, direction of doctors, basic salary for doctors, and abolition of buying and selling of practices.' In the event it required some concessions at the margins by Bevan, and no less than three plebiscites of GPs, before an adequate number of doctors were willing to enter the scheme.

Feelings undoubtedly ran high – 'We have not fought and won a war against dictatorship only to submit to it disguised as democracy of the Soviet pattern,' protested J. S. Laurie, a GP in Fitzwilliam, Yorkshire – but there were many doctors, often practising in poorer areas and not always well represented on the BMA, who positively looked forward to a national health service free at the point of delivery. One was probably Gladys Langford's GP in Islington. 'Despite all his trouble on my behalf he utterly refused to accept a fee,' she gratefully noted in May 1948. Another was Mike Leigh's father Abe, practising in Salford. 'He always cursed his private patients and couldn't wait to get rid of them,' the film director recalled. 'When the day came when he had no more private patients, that day was one of celebration as far as he was concerned. He also worked as a visiting factory doctor, mostly around Oldham.' Even so, the more typical GP at this stage was possibly Dr R. P. Liston of Tunbridge Wells. At a BMA representative meeting barely a week before the NHS came into effect, a Scottish doctor argued that it might be necessary to form a trade union to protect the interests of doctors, given that 'clearly we must protect ourselves against the forces of tyranny so latent in a state service'. Liston did not deny the point but insisted that a 'Guild' would be much preferable. For as he added, pressing every middle-class button in the room, 'This word trade union sticks in our gullets.'[2]

During the months leading up to 5 July 1948, there was a torrent of government propaganda – cartoon films, lectures, leaflets and pamphlets, travelling exhibitions, advertisements, broadcasts – explaining and justifying the new welfare arrangements. Press opposition came from predictable quarters, above all Beaverbrook's *Daily Express*, which loudly and insistently banged on that the whole exercise was a waste of taxpayer's money. As for the new dispensation itself (involving a weekly deduction of 4s 11d from the wage-earner, of which only 8½d went to the new health service), there was also a negative note struck by parts of the local press, though more about the insurance than the health aspect. 'The appointed day!' declared the *Falkirk Herald* in its last issue before the 5th:

Not the day appointed for the annual exodus to coast or country, but the day on which the new National Insurance scheme comes into operation.

It will give Falkirk folk on holiday at the seaside something to think about, and the whelks and mussels may remind them that they will be called upon to 'shell' out some more of their hard-earned cash to purchase the much-vaunted cradle-to-the-grave security.

Among the weeklies, the *New Statesman*'s support was hardly surprising – 'That we are doing this undismayed by debt and deficit, dubious international relations and an ageing population is a great tribute to the courage and resilience of our people' – but more telling was the attitude of the tough-minded humorist (and Independent MP for Oxford University, in the last years of that seat), A. P. Herbert. 'July 5th, 1948! Boys, this is going to be a big day,' he began his weekly column in *Punch* at the end of June:

> This column has, at last, obtained a 'Family Guide', with all those delightful Government owls [anthropomorphic drawings, presumably denoting wisdom]: and, being a comparatively elderly column [Herbert was 57], it has suddenly sprung into quite unexpected enthusiasm for the Whole Affair. It had been pretty lukewarm. Indeed, it had been wandering round trying to find out what were the penalties for non-cooperation (there is nothing about *them* in the Family Guide). 'What,' it had muttered darkly, 'would happen if one *declined* to contribute – simply did not stick on the stamps?' But, now that it has read the Family Guide, all that nonsense is ended. Listen, uncountable readers.

There followed from Herbert a broadly sympathetic examination of the new National Insurance arrangements.

But the real plus for the government, in terms of truly uncountable readers, was the sympathetic treatment given by the women's magazines, owing something to personal cajolery by Bevan and other ministers. 'They're a happy family – 8½d a week isn't much to pay to keep them healthy' was *Woman*'s caption on 12 June to a photograph of a smiling quartet (the obligatory father, mother and two small children). And in the accompanying article, Norah Kingswood emphasised that readily available medical treatment under the NHS, free at the point of access, would soon put paid to the grumble she had recently overheard while waiting in the fish queue for her weekend kippers, that

'We'll be paying large sums of money each week and getting precious little back.' At the top end of the market, even *Vogue* was onside. 'The social conscience of the country has been growing steadily,' noted its July issue. 'Progress has been made under Liberal, Conservative and Labour governments. Now we are due to take another stride.' The magazine's editor, the Labour-sympathising Audrey Withers, then had words specifically for her well-heeled readers: 'It has taken a long time to scotch the Class fallacy: to admit that rich and poor are "subject to the same diseases, healed by the same means" – and to ensure that lack of money shall not stand in the way of that healing.'[3]

One element in society hostile – or at best ambivalent – to the July revolution was the Catholic Church. 'It will be a sad day for England when charity becomes the affair of the State' was the underlying view of Cardinal Bernard Griffin, Archbishop of Westminster; seemingly indifferent to larger questions of national welfare, he managed to nego- tiate the opting-out of Catholic hospitals from the new NHS. Public opinion as a whole was broadly if not overwhelmingly supportive: according to Gallup in March 1948, 61 per cent saw the NHS as a 'good' idea and only 13 per cent as 'bad'. Nevertheless, the apparently mixed feelings of Marian Raynham in Surbiton were probably not unrepresentative. 'Receive leaflet about National Health Service,' she recorded in late April: 'It seems medicine, teeth, glasses, hearing appa- ratus will all be free when July 5th comes, & after paying the insurance of 4 or 5 shillings. Robin is too young & Daddy too old & I am a housewife, so only Ray pays. What with old age pensions, 7/6 for Robin, free school milk & free hearing for Dad & free teeth for me & any new glasses free it seems a crazy world.' Vere Hodgson was, perhaps befitting a voluntary welfare worker, still more sceptical. 'It seems to be all right if we could afford it,' she reflected on the eve of the NHS's start. 'It seems to me just Bankrupt Hospitals being taken over by a Bankrupt Country. You pass on the baby.' Was there fear at this stage about welfare 'scroungers'? It does not come through in the mainly middle-class diaries, but at the start of July the *Liverpool Daily Post* made a front-page attack on 'coloured' stowaways on ships from South Africa who were coming to the city to 'obtain employment, receive dole, a ration book and even free clothing'. And, in a pre-echo of much that lay ahead, the paper demanded that the law be changed, to enable deportation of British subjects and thereby 'curtail the daily increasing numbers' of the uninvited.[4]

There was, by any objective assessment, a huge amount to be done. Earlier in the year, as part of her social-work course, Phyllis Noble spent some time in a Family Welfare Association office in Deptford. She recorded a visit to a poor Irish family living in one of the nearby slums:

To think such squalor can still exist! Surely I can never forget that smoke-filled room, the mouldy cabbage in the corner, the bowl with the dirty water on the bare boards, the toddler wandering about in threadbare shirt and no shoes. Nor the horror I felt when Mr Doyle said in his heavy Irish accent, but so *casually*, 'There's another behind you' – and I turned and saw a pile of rags on the bare springs of the bed, and hidden in the rags a dirty, tiny baby.

Soon afterwards, a national survey was undertaken of more than 5,000 children, across the social classes, who had been born in the first week of March 1946. The findings were unsensational but important. Maternal efficiency was poorest on the part of the wives of unskilled manual workers, not least because they were often in poor health themselves; a two-year-old from such a family was already virtually an inch shorter than his or her counterpart from a professional and salaried family; there was almost double the relative probability of having had frequent colds over the previous winter; and it was only children of the self-employed who were taken less often by their mothers to child welfare centres.

In practice so much would depend upon ease of access – psychological as well as physical – to the new services. In May, following her Deptford experience, Phyllis Noble went as a student almoner to St Thomas' Hospital. There, at the end of each interview with a patient, she was supposed to ask if the patient could make a donation to hospital funds and, as encouragement, to shake the small tin box that stood on her desk. But at last the much-awaited 5 July beckoned. 'On the final days before the "Appointed Day" in Casualty we joyfully abandoned the little tin boxes,' she recalled. 'It was the symbolic new beginning of a health service that was intended to be free to all.'[5]

On Sunday the 4th there were two starkly contrasting speeches. A radio broadcast by Attlee, after the nine o'clock evening news, summarised and put into historical context the main changes taking place next day; emphasised that 'all our social services have to be paid for, in one way or another', so that only 'higher output can give us more of the things we all need'; expressed the hope that all those who had 'served in the past' on a more voluntary basis would 'still find a field for your generous impulses and public spirit'; and finished with a typically understated peroration: 'Here then is our new scheme of social security for all. I believe that it will increase the health and happiness of our peoples and I ask you all to join in working wholeheartedly for it so that it may bring new strength and well-being to our country.' There was nothing bipartisan about the other speech, given at a Labour rally at Belle Vue and reported thus in *The Times*:

> Mr Bevan, Minister of Health, recalled what he described as the bitter experiences of his early life when he spoke in Manchester yesterday. For a time he had to live on the earnings of an elder sister and was told to emigrate. 'That is why,' he said, 'no amount of cajolery, and no attempts at ethical or social seduction, can eradicate from my heart a deep burning hatred for the Tory Party that inflicted those bitter experiences on me. So far as I am concerned they are lower than vermin' ...
>
> Mr Bevan referred to the launching of the new health service and said that during the next few months there would be complaint after complaint about what they were not able to do. In the past the distress was there, but the complaints were not heard.
>
> 'After tomorrow,' Mr Bevan said, 'the weak will be entitled to clamour ...'

That striking v-word made an immediate impact. 'Had a heated political discussion in the Staff-room, arising out of Bevan's latest exhibition of himself,' Kenneth Preston at Keighley Grammar School noted on the 5th. 'He has been calling Conservatives scum and vermin.'[6] In a prevailing culture that still prized self-restraint above all on the part of its politicians, the gifted and passionate miner's son from South Wales had lapsed – and would never be allowed by his opponents to forget that lapse. The fact that it occurred at the very moment of an unquestionably great achievement only accentuated the piquancy.

The Appointed Day itself was littered with claims and warnings. 'We are leading the whole world in Social Security,' boasted the *Daily Mirror*, adding: 'Our State belongs to the people – unlike so many countries where the people belong to the State – and Social Security converts our democratic ideal into human reality.' *The Times* wondered whether the next generation would be able to 'reap the benefits of a social service State while avoiding the perils of a Santa Claus State' but insisted that 'it would be a grave mistake to overlook the deep feelings and sense of purpose and common humanity which all the new social services are trying, however imperfectly, to express.' A surprisingly sour note came from the *Manchester Guardian*, which – true to its nineteenth-century laissez-faire roots – feared that the state provision of welfare would 'eliminate selective elimination' and thus lead to an increase of congenitally deformed and feckless people. Among the diarists there was grudging acceptance from Anthony Heap ('sounds all right on paper, but how will it work in practice?'), but Cyril Leach, who lived in Harrow and was a senior figure in the insurance world, reckoned that 'it looks like being a fine old muddle'.[7]

Bevan himself, by now in thoroughly benign mood, spent the day in Lancashire. The symbolic keys of a hospital in Manchester were handed over to him; he said that patients in hospitals were 'just human beings wanting help', not members of political parties; and in an afternoon speech in Preston he argued that progress was less 'the elimination of struggle' than 'a change in the terms of struggle'. For some, this momentous day was the day of their birth. They included Lynn Creedy; half a century later, on the NHS's 50th anniversary, she told her story:

> I was a home birth. I was born in 41A Victoria Road, Deal, Kent. I was due to be born the day before, but I was born about midday on the fifth, so my father didn't have to pay anything. The midwife was then a lady to be feared; she had a lot of authority. She instructed my father not to let the fire go out in the flat so that she could burn the placenta. Things went on for a while and my father got so engrossed in his cowboy books, which were popular at the time, that he let the fire go out.

'The midwife was not very happy,' she added. 'My mother often reminded him of that . . .'

For Nella Last in Barrow, it was a typically busy, purposeful day – preparing for the WVS garden party, taking her order to the grocers, getting her hair done, sending a box of new potatoes and some onions to her Aunt Sarah, turning away a hawker selling 'patent' brushes – until soon after tea:

I must have shown the effects of my rush & bustle of the day. My husband said kindly 'would you like to go to a show – have you anything yet to do?' I said 'yes, I've jam to make & fruit to bottle, but all is ready, the fruit would sterilize by itself, & the jam being raspberry only needs 4 minutes quick boil!' . . . I said 'I'd love to go for a little run' & he finished 'round Coniston Lake'. It was such a sweet fair night, the top was off the car & I felt akin to my little Shan We [her cat] who lay relaxed on my lap, stretching & flexing his paws at intervals . . . I felt the creases all fading out of my tired soul as the peace & beauty of hills & moors came into view. We paused to look at the Lake. My mind was as blank as it's possible for a busy mind to be. I felt I was trying to be one with the rhythm & utter peace. My husband said 'you *shall* lie here if it is in my power – I'd like the same'. I felt startled. I felt it so 'revolutionary'. My queer ideas have so often irked & annoyed that poor dear, try as I would. We smiled at each other. Odd how a shared 'wish' can be so friendly. We were home by 8.30. My bottles had sterilized & my jam soon made – the fruit was 'mashed' with the sugar, & ready for putting on the stove.[8]

SMOKE IN THE VALLEY

This book is dedicated to Michael

PART ONE

PART ONE

What Do You Say?

The world came to London on Thursday, 29 July 1948. On a sweltering hot afternoon, a crowd of 85,000 – shirt-sleeved, lemonade-swigging, knotted handkerchiefs covering heads – gathered in Wembley Stadium to watch the opening ceremony of the first post-war Olympics. There was a special cheer for Princess Margaret as the royal party took their seats; the loudest applause during the march past of competitors was for the small countries ('a very typical British touch', thought *The Times*, silent like the rest of the press about the banning from the parade of the unsightly Jack Dearlove, the cox of the British VIII who had lost a leg as a boy); King George in naval uniform declared the Games open in 16 mercifully stammer-free words; and the massed bands of the Brigade of Guards, conducted by Sir Malcolm Sargent, played Kipling's hymn 'Non Nobis Domine' before the dedication address from the Archbishop of York. The most dramatic moment was the arrival in the stadium of the Olympic Torch. The identity of its bearer had been kept secret – some even speculated that it might be the Duke of Edinburgh – and it turned out to be a little-known 22-year-old from Surbiton, John Mark. Fair-haired, 6 feet 3 inches and a recent Cambridge Blue in the quarter-mile, he cut a figure very different from Britain's just-retired champion runner, the slight, bespectacled Sydney Wooderson. But barely three weeks after the start of the National Health Service, the fact that he was also a young doctor, at St Mary's in Paddington, was perhaps credential enough.

Two days later, with British athletes struggling in vain for a gold medal, the Bank Holiday weekend began. Huge queues snaked back from the main London railway stations as extra trains took day-trippers and holiday-makers to the seaside: from Victoria, 25,700 people to the Kent coast and 63,287 to Eastbourne and Bognor; from Waterloo, 21,200 to Portsmouth and the Isle of Wight, 27,200 to Bournemouth, Weymouth and the west of England; from Liverpool Street, 150,000 to points east; and from King's Cross, 60,000 to the Lincolnshire coast (bracing Skegness et al). Late that afternoon, a severe thunderstorm blew up over the north-west, leading to the abandonment of the last race at Aintree amid scenes of largely cheerful chaos. But there was less goodwill in Liverpool itself that Saturday evening, as just after ten o'clock a white mob attacked the Anglo-Indian Restaurant in St James's Street, as usual full of 'coloured' customers. Fighting ensued and, by the time the police arrived, the café had been wrecked. Only one person was arrested – a black seaman.

There were more Liverpool 'race riots' over the rest of the weekend. On Sunday evening the attack by another white mob on a black seamen's hostel was the cue for a spate of attacks on cafés and lodging houses favoured by Liverpool's black population, with the inevitable fighting and six arrests made (five of them black); on Monday evening there were further attacks and further arrests (32, all of them black). A series of court cases took place during the rest of August in which claims about police brutality and the planting of weapons in police cells were brushed aside; there was no questioning of the veracity of police evidence, and most of the defendants were found guilty of disorderly behaviour and assaulting and wounding police officers. Neither in court nor in the accompanying press coverage was there any serious attempt to get to the bottom of the disturbances. 'What the trouble was about I don't think I need go into,' remarked the police prosecutor, while headlines included 'Police Stoned', 'Whites Stoned', 'Had Loaded Pistol' and 'Screaming White Girls'. Less than two months after the *Empire Windrush*'s historic docking at Tilbury, the police claim that 'there isn't any colour question in Liverpool at this moment' rang hollow at best.

But at least the brotherhood of man prevailed at the Olympics. There, the 30-year-old mother-of-two Fanny Blankers-Koen, 'the Flying Dutchwoman', stole the show with four gold medals, narrowly defeating Dorothy Manley, a 21-year-old shorthand typist from Woodford Green, in the women's 100 metres final. At one point it seemed the British had finally struck gold, in the men's 400 metres relay – but the decision disqualifying the Americans was reversed. The Games drew to an end on Saturday, 14 August, just as England crashed at The Oval to 52 all out and the legendary Australian batsman, Don Bradman, played his last Test innings. 'Two slips, a silly mid-off, and a forward short-leg close to him,' John Arlott burred, 'as Hollies pitches the ball up slowly and – he's bowled! Bradman, bowled Hollies nought. Bowled Hollies nought. And – what do you say under those circumstances?'[1]

At any one time that day, only about 9 per cent of the adult civilian population of some 36 million was listening to the cricket commentary. Most people, battling with the obstinate twin blights of rationing and shortages, had other priorities. Nella Last, a middle-class, middle-aged housewife living in Barrow-in-Furness, spent the afternoon in Kendal:

> I'd 21 points left in our four books. I felt I *must* spend them, with rumours of less points – hoped to buy marmalade. Beyond piles of pressed veal, & lots of Canadian chopped ham, not to be compared to any made in America & sold as 'Spam' etc & of course high pointed, there was very little in the shops, in fact the grocer where I spent my points agreed that he had never had so few points goods, or such a poor choice. We felt puzzled – & skeptical – that the rumour of so many things going off points, would prove to be true. I got dried eggs – begrudging the 2/6 & the 10 points.

The day's work done, listening figures really picked up in the evening. Whereas the most popular programme during the day had been *House-wives' Choice* (12 per cent), the top three on the Home Service between 8.15 and 10.45 were *Henry Hall's Guest Night* (25 per cent, ie some nine million listeners), the news (28 per cent) and *Saturday Night Theatre* (26 per cent), with *Saraband for Dead Lovers*.

Over the next week, the sporting round continued. The Don departed the Test arena shortly before noon on Wednesday the 18th, with Australia winning by an innings and plenty. Less than two and a half hours later, the first race at Haydock Park was won by The Chase, a 10–1 shot 'styl-ishly handled', according to *Sporting Life*, 'by the trainer's son, L. Piggott, who is only 12 years of age'. It was the first winner for a prodigy soon to be described as having 'the face of a well-kept grave'. Saturday the 21st saw the start of the football season. Darlington and Gateshead won 3–0 in the Third Division North against Accrington Stanley and New Brighton respectively, while in the First Division Derby County beat Manchester United, Arsenal drew at Huddersfield, and 57,885 packed into Stamford Bridge to watch Chelsea beat Middlesbrough 1–0. There the visitors were without their England star forward Wilf Mannion, fit and well but in a bitter, protracted dispute with his club over its unwillingness to supplement his maximum wage (£12 per week). None of which vitally affected Princess Margaret, still often known as Margaret Rose: eighteen that day and already a head-turner, her picture was in almost every paper, amid rumours that she was about to announce her engagement to the young Marquess of Blandford, heir to the Duke of Malborough and, befitting a Guards officer, currently staying at Balmoral.

Henry St John, a pernickety civil servant who in his diary made grumbling an art form, was staying with relatives in Shackleton Road, Southall. Having left the Westbourne Hotel in Bristol on the 9th and started work a week later at the Ministry of Food (room 93A on the fifth floor at 15 Portman Square), he was now looking for somewhere to live in west London. On Saturday the 28th – a pleasantly warm afternoon that across the country attracted a record aggregate crowd at League matches of 1,160,000, including 64,000 at Newcastle to see Preston North End run out 5–2 winners – St John first 'proceeded to Ealing Common':

I walked to an address in Creffield Rd, where I was told a single room had been let.

I walked to a hotel in North Common Rd, where no single room was immediately available and where, if it had been, the cost would have been at least 4 guineas a week.

I walked to South Ealing, proceeded to Boston Manor, and set out to walk to a certain road where an official address had been notified. I had not the courage to walk so far in such a district, so proceeded to South Ealing, and walked to 41 Woodville Gardens.

Here I was shown a large bedroom with a gas fire, but breakfast was timed for 7.50 am, there were 6 guests and no facilities for washing in one's room, although there were said to be 2 bathrooms.

A hard man to please, St John 'walked to Ealing Common, and proceeded to Southall'.[2]

It was still the holiday period, and five days later one of the Labour government's junior ministers, Evan Durbin, was with his family at Strangles Beach, south of Bude. There was a heavy sea, one of his daughters got in difficulties, and he drowned while managing to save her. To a more senior minister, Hugh Gaitskell, he had been mentor as well as close friend; in his heartfelt tribute in *The Times*, Gaitskell identified Durbin's 'clarity of purpose', his 'very well defined set of moral values and social ideals', and his 'rocklike quality when dealing with either personal or social problems'. Gaitskell added that Durbin 'insisted in applying the process of reasoning unflinchingly and with complete intellectual integrity to all human problems' – typified by his adamant hostility (even when it was fashionable to profess otherwise) to the Soviet dictatorship, for 'he would not sentimentalize about tyranny, which seemed to him equally odious everywhere'. Altogether, it was not an excessive tribute, for in his writings as well as his person Durbin had pointed the way to a realistic social-democratic future for the Labour Party, a future that might plausibly run *with* the grain of human nature and desires. A 'lost' leader? Probably not. But he was, as Gaitskell sadly and privately reflected, an irreplaceable guide 'on the most fundamental issues'.

St John, after more trudging, at last found adequate lodgings (at 18 Acacia Road, Acton) on Wednesday, 8 September, the day that Gaitskell's tribute appeared. Summer was almost over, and on Saturday the 18th there was the final performance at the Spa Theatre, Scarborough, of *Out of the Blue*, a variety show that, in the staid local press, enjoyed the more dignified term of a 'concert party'. It had been playing since June and its stand-out turn was the young comedian Norman Wisdom. In the course of the run he had developed, with the help of the conjuror David Nixon, a distinctive character that would enjoy huge appeal and resonance over the years. This was the seeming simpleton, invariably wearing a scruffy, undersized check suit with a check peaked cap to match – in other words The Gump, that most unwittingly subversive of post-war figures, ensuring without apparently meaning to that the best-laid plans of his social superiors never came to fruition.[3] The rigid hierarchies might remain in place, but every now and then the underdog would have his day: a consoling if illusory thought in what was still a deeply stratified society.

Oh, for a Little Extra Butter!

'What do you consider to be the six main inconveniences of present-day living conditions?' Mass-Observation asked its regular, largely middle-class panel in autumn 1948. The male replies tended to terseness – 'Lack of Homes, Food Rationing, High Cost of Living, Insufficiency of Commodities causing Queuing, Crowded Travelling Conditions, Expenses of Family Holidays' was an engineer's top six – but the female responses were more expansive. '1. High cost of living,' declared a housewife. 'This means a constant struggle to keep the household going and there is very little left over for the "extras" that make life. 2. Cutting-off of electric power in the morning (usually just before 8 o'clock). 3. Shortage of some foods, particularly butter, meat and sugar.' For a doctor, 'queues at food shops instead of ordering by phone and having things sent' vied with 'lack of gardener' and the laundry problem: 'Reduced times of collecting (fortnightly only) means doing a lot of it at home.' Another housewife, aged 52, let herself go:

1. Not being able to plan (and purchase) dinners ahead. The housewife wastes an immense amount of time in small-scale shopping, and money also when rabbit and offal appear at the weekend when she has the week's meat ration.

2. Absence of delivery service. Having to carry home the food, cleaning materials etc means an incredible amount of labour. She must go out every day in order to cope with it and is literally a beast of burden.

3. Absence of counter-space for her shopping basket. She has to grovel on the floor among fellow-shoppers' feet in order to re-arrange wet or fragile foods. Allied to this is the absence of chairs which means

that women have to stand and stand. We are the voiceless, submerged half of the population, unable to organise or to strike.

4. Clothing coupons, because of one's liability to forget to carry them when off duty. Hence when unexpectedly seeing some article (while perhaps going to a theatre, visit a friend, or jaunt of some kind) one cannot buy it. The greatest disaster is the inability to buy a handkerchief if one has sallied forth without one.

5. Paper shortage. While flowers are wrapped in large white sheets of it, and even boot repairs are put into a large paper bag, food is put into newspaper which has been goodness knows where. The small print used in order to cram in the maximum amount of news is a great eye strain.

6. Fuel shortage, because it entails poor lighting on railways, in waiting rooms etc, with consequent eye strain and depression.

M-O also asked if attitudes to clothes had changed since the end of the war. 'Yes,' replied one jaundiced housewife. 'I used to look upon "making do" and renovating as a national duty and make a game of it. Now it is just tiresome necessity.'

In fact, though it would remain 'austerity Britain' for the rest of the decade and into the 1950s, there was some significant easing by 1948/9. 'Clothes rationing gradually becoming less stringent,' the minor civil servant Anthony Heap noted the day after the Olympics began. '36 coupons "on tap" for next six-month period beginning Sept 1. All footwear off ration from tomorrow. Men's suits down from 26 to 20 coupons. Women's from 18 to 12. And so on.' Even so, 'prices continue to rise to such an extent that all clothes now cost at least three times what they did before the war.' In early September, in her regular, shrewdly observed 'Letter from London' to the *The New Yorker*, Mollie Panter-Downes accepted that despite the current shortage of Virginian cigarettes (an issue that was being 'debated seriously at Cabinet level and furiously in the queues, often hundreds strong, that form up daily outside the tobacconists'), rationing and shortages were generally less prevalent. 'It is again possible to go into a shop and buy a loaf of bread [off the ration since July] or a pair of shoes or a package of corn flakes without tendering a coupon.' The supply of nylon stockings was severely curtailed by an October fiat but, between November 1948 and March 1949 a series of so-called 'bonfires' of controls led to abolitions and relaxations in relation to many goods and commodities, culminating in the end of clothes rationing. 'On Sat I bought 2 shirts – 17/3 each (utility) – & 2 semmits [ie undershirts] – 16/2 each; 2 white handkerchiefs – ½ each – & a rain coat – £5.6.2,' exalted Colin Ferguson, a pattern-maker in Glasgow, after an instant 'clothes spending spree'. He also called in at Burtons to see if his new suit was ready. 'They have the 2 extra pairs of trousers, but not the suit. I'll be post-carded.'[1]

The man responsible for these gratifying conflagrations was the President of the Board of Trade, Harold Wilson, still in his early 30s. It is clear that there was an element of opportunism on his part – like the Chancellor, Sir Stafford Cripps, all his deep-rooted administrative instincts lay in the direction of planning and controls rather than the market and the price mechanism – but he was well aware of the favourable personal publicity that his 'bonfires' would attract. He could also talk a good game. 'A Housewife Argues with Harold Wilson' was an encounter set up by *Picture Post* at the start of 1949, as Mrs Lilian Chandler of Bexley Heath, Kent, complained on behalf of women generally about shortages, high prices and the lack of quality in essential goods such as shoes, clothes, sheets, towels, saucepans and furniture. 'I'd like to point out that I'm a father myself' was how Wilson began his able, detailed defence. 'I've got two small boys – one five years old and the other only seven months – and I assure you that my wife wouldn't let me go for long without learning about the difficulties the mother and housewife has today.' In March, not long before he was photographed tearing up a clothes-ration book, he sat next to the Liberal grandee Violet Bonham Carter at a dinner at the American Embassy, with the Foreign Secretary, Ernest Bevin, on her other side. 'I started off with Harold Wilson, who didn't attract me at all,' she noted. 'He is short, fat, podgy & rather pushing & seemed anxious to be "in" on every conversation that was going – & to tell his own stories instead of listening to Bevin's when Bevin turned to me.' By contrast, she found Bevin 'absolutely natural, solid, 3-dimensional'.

It was still a drab, drab world. 'Dreariness is everywhere,' lamented Gladys Langford, a schoolteacher in north London, on a Sunday towards the end of 1948. 'Streets are deserted, lighting is dim, people's clothes are shabby and their tables bare.' The drabness pervaded small things as well as big – 'We miss very much the coloured and decorated crockery we used to get before the war,' Mrs Chandler told Wilson – but it was rumbling stomachs and unsatisfied tastebuds that really lowered spirits. 'Oh, for a little extra butter!' wailed Vere Hodgson, a welfare worker in west London, in March 1949, just after it had been announced that the meat ration was to go down again. 'Then I should not mind the meat. I want half a pound of butter a week for myself alone . . . For ten years we have been on this miserable butter ration, and I am fed up. I NEVER enjoy my lunch . . .' The immediate result of the further cut in the ordinary meat ration was lengthening queues at horse-meat shops, while soon afterwards disgruntled butchers were reported as saying that they needed not scales but a tape measure to do their job.

At least the lights in shop windows and electric signs were by now going on, while also in April there was another bright moment when sweets at last came off the ration after seven long years. 'It's wonderful to see all children munching sweets,' declared mother-of-two Judy Haines in Chingford, but in the event the demand proved so great that in August they returned to the ration. Accompanying the deep, wide-spread, natural desire to get back to pre-war abundance (relatively speaking) was an instinctive reluctance to try newfangled ways of countering the shortages. That summer, one of the Ministry of Food's regular consumer surveys discovered that more than 73 per cent of households were finding the present ration of soap insufficient – and that well over two-thirds of working-class households were unwilling to experiment with soapless detergents. 'Ten years ago the war started,' Rose Uttin, a Wembley housewife, noted bluntly on 3 September 1949, '& we are still on the rations.'[2] With every peacetime day that passed, the 'fair shares' rationale seemed that much less compelling.

Inevitably, the black market remained in robust existence, if not quite so ubiquitous as in the immediate post-war years. In January 1949 a much-publicised judicial inquiry (the Lynskey Tribunal) found that John Belcher, a junior minister, and George Gibson, a former chairman of the Trades Union Congress (TUC) who was now chairman of the North-Western Electricity Board, had granted favours in return for what Panter-Downes summarised as 'the pathetically minor rewards of a few good dinners, a few bottles of Scotch, and a few free suits of clothes' – their road to ruin in what she called 'a fantastic fairy story of human frailty lost in a jungle of spivs'. The spiv himself remained a far from universally loved figure, not least the super-spiv of this particular scandal, a high-living, smooth-talking Polish immigrant calling himself Sydney Stanley who was condemned by the judge for his 'reckless disregard of the truth'. 'He looks the SPIV type,' Gladys Langford in her Highbury hotel sniffed at the end of 1948 about the new occupant of the next-door room, 'small, dark, sallow in silver grey rather shoddy suit – like a recent bridegroom'. And when in September 1949 Joyce Grenfell's husband was assaulted by a young man in Piccadilly in a dispute about a taxi, her lengthy account to a friend referred to him throughout as 'the spiv', though in fact he was a bookmaker's assistant. 'The bland smoothness of the little man *was* maddening,' she added in justification of her husband pressing charges after 'the spiv denied the whole thing with the innocence of a new born baby'.

Nevertheless, as had already started to become apparent during 1948, attitudes to the black market were softening significantly as the passive acceptance of the patriotic-cum-socialist necessity of rationing and shortages steadily dwindled. The emblematic figure was Arthur English, a house painter from Aldershot who made his debut at the Windmill Theatre in March 1949 and by the end of the year was a radio star on *Variety Bandbox*. Wearing a white suit with huge shoulder pads ('I 'ad to come in the swing-door sideways!') and a flowery kipper tie down to his knees ('Keeps me knees warm in winter!'), he would invariably start his routine with a conspiratorial opening line, ''Ere, Tosh', before launching into a mixture of catchphrases ('Sharpen up there – the quick stuff's coming') and high-speed patter. Almost instantly he became the archetypal – and loveable – cockney spiv, 'The Prince of the Wide Boys'. The verse with which he rounded off his first broadcast unerringly presaged the end of austerity as a source of social unity:

> Shove on the coal, blow the expense,
> Just keep the 'ome fires burning.
> Perhaps I've made you larf a lot,
> I 'ope I've brought yer joy,
> So 'ere's mud in yer eye from the end of me tie,
> Good night – and Watch the boy![3]

'Fancy coming home from the Motor Show and kicking our poor old car,' said the wife to her husband in a Giles cartoon in October 1948,' as he clutched his foot in agony. The frustration was understandable. At what the *Daily Express* called 'the biggest "Please-do-not-touch" exhibition of all time', 32 British car manufacturers were showing more than 50 models at a time when, because most of the motor industry's production was compulsorily reserved for export, the delivery dates for the home market ranged from 12 months to two and a half years. Such was the hunger for almost anything on four wheels that that painful circumstance did not stop huge crowds coming to the first post-war Motor Show at Earls Court, over the ten days a total of 562,954, almost double the previous record.

The Vauxhall Velox and the Jowett Javelin both drew many admirers, but without doubt the star attraction was Alec Issigonis's Morris Minor, an attempt to create a British counterpart to the Volkswagen Beetle. Having been dismissed at the drawing-board stage as 'a poached egg' by Lord Nuffield, founder-owner of Morris Motors, it was in fact a brilliant design: no chassis but an all-in-one body shell; independent front suspension; and rank-and-pinion steering that made the car easy to drive. 'Women loved the Morris Minor,' recalled one car salesman, John Macartney. 'It was very light, it was very responsive – there was a saying that if you drove over a penny in a Morris Minor you knew whether you'd gone over heads' or tails' side up.' Not every alpha male approved of women drivers, but for Barbara Hardy, a married woman who acquired her Morris Minor in the 1950s, it was as if the distinctive, jelly-mould shape became an emblem of emancipation. 'I could fit five in the back and put two on the seat beside me,' she remembered about her time as leader of a cub pack. 'There were no seat belts in those days, and there weren't the cars on the road. I did my own thing in those days.'[4]

The appetite for motor cars was matched by that for news and gossip about the Royal Family. 'It looks as if Princess Margaret will one day be Duchess of Malborough,' reckoned Vere Hodgson in December 1948. The so-called 'Margaret Set' was at this point aristocratic rather than bohemian in composition – with 'Sunny' Blandford himself and the Earl of Dalkeith (Johnny Dalkeith) as the two leading members, though there was also the very rich Billy Wallace. Margaret's recent

18th birthday had been the cue for endless profiles, in the provincial
as well as the national press. After calling her 'a leader of youthful
fashions', typified by her beaver-trimmed coats, the *Middlesbrough
Evening Gazette* went on: 'This Princess who loves to rumba, to wear
high heels and to use lipstick, brighter and thicker than her mother
really approves, is still a child in many ways. She has great poise, but
sometimes a youthful nervousness breaks through.' The following
spring, 'Princess Margaret Leaves By 'Plane for Italy' was a front-page
story for the *Coventry Evening Telegraph*, with the obligatory reference
by the reporter at London Airport to how she 'waved from the window
to the crowd as the 'plane rose into the air'. A world to conquer lay
before her. 'High-spirited to the verge of indiscretion,' a mutual friend
informed the diarist James Lees-Milne soon after Margaret's return
from her four-week holiday in Italy. 'She mimics lord mayors
welcoming her on platforms and crooners on the wireless, in fact anyone
you care to mention ... She has a good singing voice. In size she is a
midget but perfectly made. She inadvertently attracts all the young
eligibles to her feet, which doesn't endear her to the girls.'

Not everyone was quite as staunchly royalist as Lees-Milne, as he
found one stormy afternoon in Hyde Park not long after Margaret's
birthday celebrations in August 1948:

> A violent cloudburst of rain descended so I sheltered in a temple alcove.
> In it were two working-class men talking disrespectfully of the Royal
> Family. Some women driven in by the rain joined in the conversation,
> and agreed that the Royal Family were an unnecessary expense. All
> spoke without vitriol and quite dispassionately. I was surprised, and
> merely said that I totally disagreed. Wished them good-day and osten-
> tatiously walked off. Got soaked.

There was no room for cynics among the patiently waiting crowd outside
Buckingham Palace on the evening of Sunday, 14 November. 'It's a boy,'
a policeman eventually announced through cupped hands. 'Both well.'
The word 'boy' quickly went round, and the crowd (mainly men) stayed
on 'to cheer, to sing and to call for the father, until asked to go home
in the early hours', while in Trafalgar Square the illuminated fountains
were lit with blue lights, the pink ones being redundant. The next day

saw more crowds milling round the Palace and shouting 'Good old Philip', the ringing of bells at Westminster Abbey and St Paul's, and the royal salute of 41 guns from Hyde Park and the Tower. But Anthony Heap was cross that the bells and guns had not been heard straight after the birth the previous evening. 'Have the officials responsible for these things *no* sense of drama?' he asked himself. It was not until the eve of the christening on 15 December that the public was let in on the name of the new Prince, but this time Heap gave a nod, approving of Charles for its 'right royal ring'. A big crowd standing outside the Palace watched people arrive for the event. 'It is,' reflected Harold Nicolson (himself about to start work on the official life of George V), 'the identification of natural human experience with this strange royal world that causes these emotions; one's own life enlarged into a fairy story.'[5]

Another happy family were the Huggetts. After appearing in the 1947 comedy *Holiday Camp*, they got the first film of their own in *Here Come the Huggetts*, released in November 1948. 'The lively, laughing, loveable Huggetts are Britain's very own family,' declared the poster, with Jack Warner as the father in this middle-class suburban family and Petula Clark as one of his daughters. The fairly feeble plot turned on the visit being paid by a flashy blonde cousin (Diana Dors as a 15-year-old jitterbug queen) and the mistaken belief that the father was having a fling with her. 'It's an unpretentious affair and none the worse for that,' thought *Picturegoer*, which praised the 'requisite touch of sentimentality', but for Anthony Heap, who saw it at the King's Cross cinema, it was at best 'pleasant entertainment', handicapped by a 'persistently pedestrian' script. Two more films followed in quick succession – *Vote for Huggett* (revolving round a promise to construct a war memorial) and *The Huggetts Abroad* (not their kind of place, with Mrs Huggett lamenting the absence of queues) – before the series came to a more or less unlamented end. In retrospect, the films' main interest lies in the role of the father, Joe Huggett. Often he seems to be marginalised ('Nobody does anything I ask them round here,' he complains) as events and misunderstandings go on around him, but in the end it is he who sorts things out and has his position of authority validated and reinforced. But if the contrast with his affectionate but scatterbrained wife Kathleen and their three daughters was stark, it raised few eyebrows at the time.

Here Come the Huggetts was never likely to get a Royal Command performance, unlike the epic, slow-moving, intensely patriotic *Scott of the Antarctic*, released at about the same time and starring John Mills as Captain Scott, with a suitably grandiloquent score by Vaughan Williams. 'Such a film as *Scott* is welcome at a time when other races speak disparagingly of our "crumbling empire" and our "lack of spirit"' was the unashamed response of the *Sunday Dispatch*. 'It should make those who have listened too closely to such talk believe afresh that ours is the finest breed of men on this earth. And so it is.' Above all, there was the film's emotional continence, the very quintessence of still-prized stiff-upper-lippedness. 'What iron discipline and self-control!' reflected Vere Hodgson after seeing it. 'They joked to the last, and never said one word to each other of what they really thought . . . I am sure no men but those of English race could have kept up that courtesy and nonchalance to the last, in the face of such terrible physical suffering.' Soon afterwards, a Mass-Observation study of weeping in cinemas found that whereas men tended to weep at moments of reserve in a film, women wept at moments of parting and loss – here, when Scott says goodbye to his wife on the quay and when the ponies are shot. One adolescent male could have wept with frustration. Having taken the 15-year-old Joan Rowlands (the future Joan Bakewell) to their local picture house in Stockport and found her discouragingly unresponsive to his advances, he turned to her and declared that she was as cold as the film.[6]

Cinema's nemesis was still at the fledgling stage. In February 1949 the *Sunday Pictorial* (in effect the Sunday version of the *Daily Mirror*) revealed 'The Truth About British Television':

Are the programmes bad?

Yes. Transmission most days is only an hour in the afternoon and about two hours in the evening . . . Afternoon programmes are mainly old American films. They are terrible . . . Major sports promoters are bitterly opposed to television because they know attendances will suffer. Consequently most sportscasts are of amateur events . . . Variety programmes are poor because the big combines put a television ban on their stars.

Nevertheless, between June 1948 and March 1949 the number of television licences doubled from 50,000 to 100,000. Moreover, by 1949 there were, a BBC inquiry found, 'unmistakeable signs of TV becoming less and less a "rich man's toy"' – indeed, by the start of the year, 'although TV was still *relatively* more common in wealthy than in less comfortable homes . . . more than half the TV sets in use were in Lower Middle Class and Working Class homes'.

Mass-Observation at about this time asked its national panel ('generally above average in intelligence and education') for its views on television. Only 2 per cent of the 684 respondents owned a set, which had cost almost £100, but about half wanted one ('Can stay at home for entertainment' and 'Educational, widens and stimulates interest' were the two main reasons), and many tended to see it as inevitable anyway. 'No, I won't have television – until all my neighbours have it' was how a 33-year-old publicity assistant put it. One-third were definitely opposed, while even those wanting one, especially the female panellists, emphasised Television's prospective disadvantages. 'I would very much like to have a television set in my own home,' noted a young housewife, 'but I'm afraid that my needlework and mending and all the jobs which normally get done in the evening, would be sadly neglected.'

For those who actually had a set, the biggest problem was often where to put the thing. 'Make Room for Television' was the title of a spring 1949 *House and Garden* article, reckoning that 'for winter viewing, a good place for television is near the fire where chairs are usually gathered'. It seemed the obvious solution in an era before central heating became ubiquitous; yet, given the huge emotional baggage attached to the domestic hearth, the very essence of homeliness, there existed an understandable anxiety about the newcomer supplanting the time-honoured fireplace. 'Most of the day your set will sit lifeless in the room, so its looks are important,' warned the magazine. 'As the cabinet is bulky and creates special problems of accommodation, its position shouldn't be obtrusive. Your room must be re-arranged for its new function.' In addition, curtains or Venetian blinds were recommended in order to divide up a living room in which 'the viewers need less light (especially round the set), while the others may be distracted by the performance'.[7] The domestic ecology, in short, was starting to change.

In virtually every household the wireless was still the principal source of home entertainment and, arguably, imaginative life: between 1948 and 1950 the total of radio licences climbed from just over 11 million to a record 11,819,190. For Marian Raynham, living in Surbiton, there were some trying times in September 1948:

> *17 September.* Settling down this evening to the return of Eric Barker [star of the comedy show *Waterlogged Spa*, with its catchphrase 'Ullo, cock, 'ow's yerself?'] on radio when radio went off & fused lights. Robin fixed lights but the radio smelt awful. It has had nothing done to it since we had it about 9 years. Been wonderful . . . It is going to be terrible without it, no news, no fun, no In Town Tonight.
>
> *20 September.* Electrician came. New transformer needed in radio. They will try & get one & let me know . . .
>
> It is awful without wireless. I go in to hear Mrs Dale at 4pm next door. Without there seems no time & no news & it is miserable. Must try & hire one . . . My world has gone to pieces without it.
>
> *23 September.* Missing first of Tommy Handley tonight.
>
> *30 September.* No sign of wireless being fixed.

Eventually, Raynham got a temporary radio, by which time the latest series of Tommy Handley's catchphrase-rich comedy vehicle, the renowned and still hugely popular *ITMA*, was well into its stride. At the end of October there was the 300th show since the first series shortly before the war, with Princess Margaret and a party of friends in the audience. *ITMA* number 310 was broadcast on Thursday, 6 January 1949, as usual at 8.30 p.m. Tommy had become manager of a tea and coffee stall ('Uncle Tom's Cabin'), and among those paying him a visit were Basil Backwards ('Sir – morning good! Coffee of cup. Strong too not. Milk have rather I'd.') and Sophie Tuckshop (played by Hattie Jacques), while Mona Lott declined to cheer up after her election as Miss Waterworks of 1949. 'In fact,' recalled the show's scriptwriter Ted Kavanagh, 'it was just an ordinary *ITMA* saga of craziness.'

Three days later, at noon on Sunday the 9th, Handley had a stroke while stooping down to pick up a dropped collar stud and died in hospital at 3.45. He was 56. The news reached the BBC just as the 5.30 repeat of Thursday evening's transmission was going out on the

Light Programme. 'I'd washed up & was clearing away, when the 6 o'clock news began,' Nella Last in Barrow wrote in her diary that evening. 'I was putting some spoons in the drawer of the side board, & heard Tommy Handley's death announced. My husband heard me say sharply "oh No" & hurried in. I felt I could hardly say "Tommy Handley is *dead*" & saw his face whiten, & we sat down silently to hear the scanty details.' 'I heard it on the wireless, & I didn't believe it,' one man told Mass-Observation a day or two later. 'I sat for a while, & then went in & told my daughter. She just looked at me & burst into a flood of tears.'[8]

For two young scriptwriters, Frank Muir and Denis Norden, the news came at a particularly ticklish moment. From 4.00 to 8.00 that day, their recently launched comedy programme, *Take It From Here*, was in rehearsal at the BBC's Paris studio in Lower Regent Street, with recording due to take place from 8.30 to 9.00 for transmission on the Tuesday evening. The original typed script survives, together with the frantic pencilled amendments:

Joy Nichols: I'm worried about Jimmy [Edwards]. He should be here. Dick – do you think he's met with an accident?

Dick Bentley: There you go – day-dreaming again.

Joy: Dick, how can you talk like that? Poor Jimmy, he may be stretched out somewhere, stark and cold. [Last six words deleted, and instead, 'locked up in prison, broken a leg or something'.] Think of it, Dick.

Dick: Yeah. (LAUGH) Yeah! What a terrible thing! (LAUGH)

Joy: It'll mean that only you and I will be left to carry on the TIFH tradition.

Dick: There, there, little woman, we can do it. The two of us, pulling together. It just means changing the title. We'll call it the Teen-age Show. I'll take care of *all* the funny lines now. After all, Tommy Handley [crossed out, and 'Charlie Chester' inserted] does, and I'm as good as he is.

Joy: Are you, Dick?

Dick: Well, *half* as good.

Joy: Half?

Dick: Well, a quarter as good. ['as T.H.' inserted]. Well, an eighth . . . well, a sixteenth . . .

Not everyone mourned Handley's passing. Anthony Heap noted that he had 'hardly ever listened' to *ITMA*, 'because like all the other ostensibly comic features the BBC doggedly inflicts on us week after week, its humour was of a stereotyped, repetitive, machine-made variety that didn't appeal to me in the least'. Kenneth Preston (an English teacher at Keighley Grammar School) and his wife had been similarly indifferent to the programme's charms, with Preston reflecting that 'apparently Handley earned £10,000 a year – a sad commentary on the times'. But these were far from the sentiments of Marian Raynham ('How can we do without him? It's almost a personal loss . . .') or Nella Last ('The very way he said "Hallo folks" seemed the warm greeting of an old puckish friend') or Vere Hodgson ('It has haunted me that we shall never hear his "Hullo, folks" again'). Or, as a young housewife on Mass-Observation's panel put it, 'other people I've met feel exactly the same – the sense of losing part of their life almost'.[9]

Then came the funeral (as described by Kavanagh in his 'instant', evocative biography of Handley):

> Six deep they lined the streets; they were of all ages and of all classes, many were in tears. Slowly our car nosed its way through the thousands who milled round the Private Chapel in Westbourne Grove and, at the other end of the route [ie Golders Green Crematorium] ten thousand and more awaited the arrival of the hearse. Through slum streets, through squares that had seen better days, on through more fashionable districts, past blocks of expensive flats, everywhere it was the same – the crowds had come to pay a last tribute to one whose voice had cheered them through the years, to one who had indeed been part of their very lives.

Later in January there was a memorial service at St Paul's. The doors had to be closed before the start, many thousands waited outside to hear the service relayed to them, the broadcaster John Snagge read 'Let Us Now Praise Famous Men', the Bishop of London praised Handley as one whose 'raillery was without cynicism and his satire without malice', and naturally many millions listened on the radio.

The sheer depth of the popular grief suggests that it was not only about a much-loved comedian but also about something else – perhaps about Handley's death as symbol of the inevitable fading into the past of the wartime spirit, or anyway what was remembered as the wartime spirit. 'He shares with Mr Churchill the honour of keeping us going during the War,' reflected Vere Hodgson, a notably level-headed diarist. Yet only a year later, in January 1950, a survey of Londoners found that although everyone knew who Handley was, and 31 per cent thought that *ITMA* remained unique, as many as 35 per cent declared that *Take It From Here* was better than *ITMA* had ever been.[10]

Muir, Norden and the others were by this time labouring under considerable constraints. 'Programmes must at all cost be kept free of crudities, coarseness and innuendo,' insisted the *BBC Variety Programmes Policy Guide For Writers & Producers* (generally known as 'The Green Book'), a long-lived document assembled and taking force during the second half of 1948. 'Humour must be clean and untainted directly or by association with vulgarity and suggestiveness. Music hall, stage, and to a lesser degree, screen standards, are not suitable to broadcasting . . . There can be no compromise with doubtful material. It must be cut.' The following were the subject of 'an absolute ban':

Jokes about –
   Lavatories
   Effeminacy in men
   Immorality of any kind

Suggestive references to –
   Honeymoon couples
   Chambermaids
   Fig leaves
   Prostitution
   Ladies' underwear, e.g. winter draws on
   Animal habits, e.g. rabbits
   Lodgers
   Commercial travellers

Extreme care should be taken in dealing with references to or jokes about –
   Pre-natal influences (e.g. 'His mother was frightened by a donkey')
   Marital infidelity

Good taste and decency are the obvious governing considerations.
The vulgar use of such words as 'basket' must also be avoided.

Religion, politics and physical infirmities were all heavily restricted
areas, though 'references to and jokes about drink are allowed in strict
moderation so long as they can really be justified on entertainment
grounds'. As for expletives, 'they have no place at all in light entertainment and all such words as God, Good God, My God, Blast, Hell,
Damn, Bloody, Gorblimey, Ruddy, etc, etc, should be deleted from
scripts and innocuous expressions substituted'. Any jokes that might
be taken to encourage strikes or industrial disputes were to be avoided,
while 'the Corporation's policy is against broadcasting impersonations
of elder Statesmen, e.g. Winston Churchill'. Altogether, it was Auntie
at her most auntie-like. For a 'blue' comedian like the great Max Miller,
with his roots in the old music hall, it made radio appearances almost
an impossibility, but for others like Frankie Howerd, with a career
still to forge, the answer (in his biographer's words) 'was to make the
audience – via the use of a remarkably wide range of verbal idiosyn-
crasies in his delivery – hear the sort of meanings in certain innocent
words that no English dictionary would ever confirm'. Or, as Howerd
himself later put it, 'To say "I'm going to do you" was considered
very naughty, yet I got away with the catchphrase: "There are those
among us tonight whom I shall do-o-o-o."'[11]

The inhibitions of popular radio were complemented, at the other
end of the cultural spectrum, by the constipation – or, put more kindly,
narrow parameters – of the prevailing literary culture. If there was a
quintessential mandarin of the late 1940s, it was perhaps the distinguished literary critic and Oxford don renowned for his aristocratic
manner, distinctive voice ('like a crate of hens being carried across a
field', according to Isaiah Berlin) and marriage into the Bloomsbury
circle. A *Vogue* profile in July 1948, accompanied by a soulful Cecil
Beaton portrait, practically said it all:

Lord David Cecil possesses a mind as elegant, in the best sense of the
word, as his long fingers. In an age when style in everything is fast
becoming as extinct as the dinosaur, his fastidious prose touches the
mind and heart with its grace and beautiful precision. He is Tutor of

English at New College, Oxford, and his weekly lectures are as remarkable for their perfect delivery as for their content. He is famous for his life of Cowper, and has just published 'Two Quiet Lives', a study of Dorothy Osborne and Thomas Gray . . . The values which shine through his work are prized by those who look for brilliance without false glitter, balance without dusty academicism.

For the young, lower-middle-class Kingsley Amis, briefly assigned Cecil as his BLitt supervisor, he was 'that POSTURING QUACK Cess-hole', as he informed Philip Larkin two months after the *Vogue* piece. Later that autumn, when Amis actually tried to make contact with Cecil in order to discuss his thesis, he found it impossible ('Oh no, sir,' chuckled the porter. 'Lord David? Oh, you'd have to get up very early in the morning to get hold of him. Oh dear, oh dear. Lord David in college, well I never did') and decided to switch to another don, F. W. Bateson ('A bit leftie in a sort of Bevanish way, which was all right with me at that stage,' he recalled some 40 years later). The defection did not dismay Cecil, who two years later enjoyed failing the thesis. And when in 1953 the veteran American actress Ruth Draper visited Oxford, she took special delight in seeing him. 'Of course,' she told her sister, 'David is one of the most rare and quaint and distinguished young men [in his early 50s by this time] to be found anywhere – *such* brains – *such* race – such sensitivity, but a darling person.'

It is hard to avoid the e-word. A trio of 1948/9 snippets from Lees-Milne's diary accurately reflect a prevailing elitism, reinforced rather than subdued by Labour's 1945 landslide and the ensuing legislative programme of the Attlee government. Walking in Hyde Park one summer evening, the diarist 'had an uneasy feeling that the proletariat, sunning themselves so happily, truly believe that all is well with the world and themselves just because they are richer than ever before and work less than ever before'. At the annual meeting of the National Trust, the Bishop of London (in his capacity as chief speaker, not admirer of Tommy Handley) 'said that the social revolution we were going through would prove disastrous if this country did not preserve for the masses the culture which had been lost to France during the French Revolution'. And at dinner one evening, the novelist Ivy Compton-Burnett, talking 'of the uneducated English masses', said that 'hitherto England had come out on top because she had been pushed along by the educated few,' but 'now that there was open competition between nations England must go down owing to her standard of education being lower than that of every other European country' – with which Lees-Milne agreed, adding that 'the situation seemed to me even more serious in that the educated few were being pushed around by the uneducated many'.[12]

Near the end of 1948 there appeared, within a few weeks of each other, two important, influential books, both of them predicated upon strictly hierarchical cultural assumptions: *The Great Tradition* by F. R. Leavis and *Notes Towards the Definition of Culture* by T. S. Eliot.

It is absurd, on the face of it, to call Leavis an elitist. Born in 1895, he was the son of a piano dealer in Cambridge, spent most of his adult life there as an English don fiercely at odds with the university establishment, and never lost his visceral hatred of what he saw as a malign metropolitan literary clique, above all the Bloomsbury Group. By the late 1940s he was in the process of becoming the most influential English literary critic of the century – an influence that owed at least something to his striking appearance and take-no-prisoners personality. 'Leavis was a familiar figure in the Cambridge streets,' Peter Hall recalled:

> He rode an absurdly old-fashioned tall black bicycle. His shirt collar was always wide open, even in the worst weather, and he was the original corduroys-and-open-sandals man. He wore socks with his sandals. His delivery at lectures was dry and witty, with an in-built sneer in virtually every phrase. We attended in order to be shocked and outraged by his judgements, though actually we were delighted to hear all the great reputations overturned.

In schools, in adult-education colleges, in other universities, even in the wider world, successive generations of Leavisites would spread the stirring, unambiguous word: only five novelists (Austen, Eliot, James, Conrad and Lawrence) belonged to 'The Great Tradition'; these writers mattered supremely not only for their art's sake but also for how they promoted 'awareness of the possibilities of life'; only through nurturing the right relationship between life and literature might it be possible to return to the organic society destroyed by modern industrial civilisation.

It was in many ways a profoundly illiberal vision. The creation of a so-called 'great tradition' was in effect a grandiose, self-serving collective mask to justify Leavis's choice of five favourite novelists; the puritanical moralising barely concealed his disdain for everyman's desire for material progress; as for popular culture, he saw himself in absolute black-and-white terms fighting on behalf of taste and sensibility 'against the multitudinous counter-influences – films, newspapers, advertising – indeed, the whole world outside the class-room'. Nevertheless, its very dogmatism was a strong part of the Leavis appeal, especially by the late 1940s. With the Cold War intensifying and Communism losing much of its appeal to those in search of intellectual direction, Leavis offered to his followers what John Gross has acutely described as 'a doctrine which sees the established order as hopelessly corrupt but in no way pledges them to try and replace it'. Put another way, the sage of Downing College filled a vacuum while the old left of the 1930s died and the new left was as yet unborn.

Unlike Leavis, T. S. Eliot was interested – at least notionally – in real people doing real things in the modern world. 'Derby Day, Henley Regatta, Cowes, the twelfth of August, a cup final, the dog races, the pin table, the dart board, Wensleydale cheese, boiled cabbage cut into sections, beetroot in vinegar, nineteenth-century Gothic churches and the music of Elgar' ran his celebrated list in *Notes* of 'the characteristic activities and interests of a people', demonstrating 'how much is embraced by the term *culture*'. That did not mean, however, that Manchester United versus Blackpool at Wembley was equal in value to a Pugin church. 'What is important,' declared Eliot in a treatise imbued almost throughout with a pessimistic strain, 'is a structure of society in which there will be, from "top" to "bottom", a continuous gradation of cultural levels', adding that 'we should not consider the upper levels as possessing *more* culture than the lower, but as representing a more conscious culture and a greater specialisation of culture'. Indeed, 'to aim to make everyone share in the appreciation of the fruits of the more conscious part of culture is to adulterate and cheapen what you give', for 'it is an essential condition of the preservation of the quality of the culture of the minority, that it should continue to be a minority culture'.

Eliot did not mention by name the Butler Act, which four years previously had significantly expanded access to secondary education, but he did express his unhappiness about the way in which education had recently been 'taken up as an instrument for the realisation of social ideals'. In particular, he dubbed as 'Jacobinism in Education' the notion that education should be the means of achieving equality of opportunity in society – a notion he dismissed as 'unobtainable in practice' and which, 'if we made it our chief aim, would disorganise society and debase education'. After a swipe at how the purveyors of 'the Equality of Opportunity dogma' had derived spurious 'emotional reinforcement' through citing the unproven example of 'the mute inglorious Milton', Eliot finished by solemnly warning that 'in our headlong rush to educate everybody, we are lowering our standards' and, in sum, 'destroying our ancient edifices to make ready the ground upon which the barbarian nomads of the future will encamp in their mechanised caravans'.

To at least one ambitious educationalist, Eric James, head of the prestigious Manchester Grammar School since 1945, Eliot's strictures against the dilution of elite culture came as valuable ammunition. In 'The Challenge to the Grammar School', a *Times Educational Supplement* piece subtitled 'Attack upon Standards and Values', James had already condemned the idea of the common (or comprehensive) school on the grounds that it would inevitably lead to 'grave social, educational and cultural evils' – in contrast to the grammar school, whose fundamental purpose was to provide 'an education of the fullest kind for the academically most gifted section of the population'. There followed in 1949 James's more detailed, and very influential, *An Essay on the Content of Education*, which argued along similar lines. Admittedly, James and other advocates of a strict hierarchy in secondary education conveniently ignored Eliot's caveat that 'the prospect of a society ruled and directed only by those who have passed certain examinations or satisfied tests devised by psychologists is not reassuring', but Eliot's staunch defence of the culture of the governing elite, even if in his own mind it was not a grammar-school elite, was clearly grist to their mill.[13]

It was not only the culture wars that left one visitor cold during the winter of 1948/9. For almost four months the American film star Ronald Reagan spent his working days at Elstree Studios, making an instantly forgettable movie, *The Hasty Heart*, set in a hospital compound in Burma. 'You won't mind our winter outdoors – it's indoors that's really miserable,' an Englishman had helpfully warned him, and – wearing either pyjamas or shorts for the entire picture – Reagan froze most of the time. His otherwise determinedly cheerful memoirs recall a series of gloomy images and episodes: an appalling London fog that 'was almost combustible, so thick was it with soft-coal smoke', lingering for almost a week 'until a kind of claustrophobia threatened to drive everyone stir-crazy'; the only outdoor illumination coming from 'dim and inadequate street lamps'; the 'severe limitation on food'; and a hotel in Cardiff where Reagan in the small hours ran out of shillings for the gas fire and 'finished the night wrapped in my overcoat'. At Elstree itself he was also unimpressed by the contrast between the 'tremendously talented, creative people' he was working with and the 'incredible inefficiency that makes everything take longer than it should', not helped by union restrictions on the hours available for filming.

A jocose Christmas letter to Jack Warner in Hollywood suggested disenchantment with Britain ('what they do to the food we did to the American Indian', while 'cheerio' was 'a native word meaning good bye – it is spoken without moving the upper lip – while looking down the nose'), but it was in the New Year that he had a serious conversation with the film's director, Vincent Sherman. 'They had,' according to Reagan's most intimate biographer, 'some long arguments over the Labour government's so-called Welfare State. As far as Reagan could see, nobody was well, and everybody fared badly. If this was socialism – stoppages, six-hour hospital queues, mile after mile of slate-roofed council houses – what price the New Deal?' Reagan himself wrote in the 1970s that this trip to Britain had marked a defining stage in his political journey. He had seen the consequences of the natural economic order being turned upside-down, with civil servants becoming civil masters; accordingly, 'I shed the last ideas I'd ever had about government ownership of anything'.

In the Dorset parish of Loders and Dottery, the focus on the second Thursday of 1949 was very much on the parish party held at 7.30 in the Ex-Service Men's Hut. There were prizes for fancy dress, plenty of refreshments and an overall profit of almost £11. 'Believe it or not, some people are troubled lest the ham they ate at the party might have been eaten illegally!' recorded the recently installed vicar, Oliver Willmott, in his wonderfully readable parish notes. 'It is unlike Loders to be sensitive to the nice points of the Law, but so like Loders not to have doubts before the ham was digested. Tender consciences should be relieved to know, on the authority of the Bridport Food Office, that the giving away of one's own ham, killed under permit, does not offend the Law.' Soon afterwards, Willmott reflected on how vicars like himself were enjoying a newfound social popularity. 'What,' he asked, 'is the cause of this wondrous transformation that the clerical collar should be sought after?':

> A revival of religion? Alas, no. The answer is 'Forms'. It is they that have made the clerical collar popular, because its wearer is privileged to testify that the form filler is what he makes himself out to be. Forms are much sworn at, but it may prove their passport to heaven that they gave many a dejected parson an agreeable sense that his people needed his services, and that he was able to do a thing for which they were grateful. But, you form-fillers, be not zealous overmuch! The cleric who was called out of the Bridport sausage queue to sign a form, never retrieved his place in the queue.[14]

In August 1948, living on the Isle of Jura and struggling against mortal illness to complete a novel to be called either *The Last Man in Europe* or *Nineteen Eighty-Four*, George Orwell assessed for an American magazine where the Labour government stood after three years in power. There did not exist, he insisted at the outset, 'any positive desire to return to capitalism', despite the 'disproportionately vocal' noise being made by 'the big capitalists and the middling entrepreneur class', eager to convey the impression of a country 'groaning beneath bureau-cratic misrule'. Rather, 'the great majority of people take it for granted that they will live on wages or salaries rather than profits, welcome the idea of birth-to-death social insurance, and do not feel strongly one way or the other about the nationalisation of industry'. As in July 1945, allegiance to Attlee and his colleagues was far from ideologically rooted: 'The change-over to national ownership is not in itself an inspiring process, and in the popular regard the Labour party is the party that stands for shorter working hours, a free health service, day nurseries, free milk for school children, and the like, rather than the party that stands for Socialism.' Not that Orwell ignored the physical downside of life in Attlee's Britain: 'The housing situation is extremely bad; food, though not actually insufficient, is unbearably dull. The prices of cigarettes, beer, and unrationed food such as vegetables are fantastic. And clothes rationing is an increasing hardship since its effects are cumulative.' Would the government be more popular if its publicity was more effective? Orwell did not deny that 'the housing shortage, the fuel shortage, bread rationing, and Polish immigration have all caused more resentment than they need have done if the underlying facts had been properly explained', but the fact remained that, with the exception of the *Daily Herald*, 'all that matters of the British press is controlled either by Tories or, in a very few cases, by left-wing factions not reliably sympathetic to a Labour government'. In spite of everything, he still expected Labour to win the next election, given that 'the mass of the manual workers are not likely ever again to vote for the Conservative party, which is identified in their minds with class privilege and, above all, with unemployment'.

It was in many ways a typically persuasive piece – but one question that Orwell did not confront was whether Labour, having completed its welfare reforms and most of its promised nationalisation programme, would decide to undertake a major new wave of public ownership. On that vexed front, there was one important piece of unfinished business: the iron and steel industry. The bill to nationalise it was put forward in October 1948, and it proved a significantly more divisive issue across the political spectrum than previous nationalisation measures. 'It is not a plan to help our patient struggling people,' the Conservative leader Winston Churchill declared during a notably heated Commons debate, 'but a burglar's jemmy to crack the capitalist crib.' There was never any doubt that the measure would get through parliament, but it took a long time, and in the end it was agreed that the first properties would not be transferred to the Iron and Steel Corporation before 1951.

Nevertheless, by the start of 1949 the question was being insistently asked: what would Labour's nationalisation programme be if it retained power? One Tory backbencher, the veteran Sir Cuthbert Headlam, probably called it right when he reflected in his diary in January that 'the Government side are out of breath – have over-strained themselves – don't quite know what to do for the remainder of the Parliament – whether to go on nationalizing or to try and consolidate what they have already nationalized – what course is calculated to gain votes . . .'[15] In the light of opinion polls, by this time consistently showing a majority against further nationalisation, the answer might have seemed obvious.

After a fierce right/left tussle within the party's National Executive, Labour in April 1949 published its policy statement *Labour Believes in Britain*, in effect a draft manifesto. The relatively few parts of the economy that were put forward for second-term nationalisation included sugar-refining and industrial and life assurance, and there was a clear commitment to the mixed economy, ie a mixture of public and private industry. The hand of Herbert Morrison, the Cabinet's chief 'consolidator', was almost visibly on the document. Then in June, against a background of recent poor local election results, the party assembled in Blackpool for its annual conference. All eyes were on Nye Bevan.

It was, in oratorical terms, one of his great speeches. 'We have to exercise our imaginations as to what we can do further,' he declared. 'Indeed, we have to restate the relationship between the public and the private sector.' But as to precisely *how* that relationship was to be recast, Bevan was silent, beyond placing his faith in 'all the essential instruments of planning' being 'in the hands of the state'. Indeed, he even conceded that 'we shall have for a very long time the light cavalry of private, competitive industry'. The verdict of John Campbell, Bevan's most insightful biographer, is harsh but compelling: 'The truth was that Labour was approaching a crossroads. While fiercely contemptuous of those like Morrison who wanted merely to "consolidate" what had already been achieved, Bevan could see the way ahead, after steel, only in generalities.' His speech then took refuge in socialism's spiritual uplands. 'The language of priorities,' he famously insisted, 'is the religion of Socialism. We have accepted over the last four years that the first claims upon the national product shall be decided nationally and they have been those of the women, the children and the old people. What is that except using economic planning in order to serve a moral purpose?' He finished with a peroration in which he called on 'this great movement' to 'raise its head high and look at the stars':

> We have become so preoccupied with documents and papers that we sometimes fail to realise where we are going. These are merely the prosaic instruments of a masterly design. These are merely the bits and pieces

we are fitting into the great structure, and I am convinced that, given another period of office, we shall not only materially improve the well-being of Great Britain but we shall have established a British society of which Britons everywhere can be proud and which will be an example to the rest of mankind.

Campbell's reading of the passage is again devastating. 'Bevan was happy,' he argues, 'so long as he thought the *direction* was right and was satisfied that socialist *principles* were still intact.' The upshot, he adds, was that 'the debate within the party over the next two years – of which he was increasingly the storm centre – revolved less around issues in their own right than around issues as symbols: symbols of priorities.'[16]

For all the applause ringing in Bevan's ears, Blackpool confirmed that the consolidators had won – a victory further strengthened when Morrison in tandem with other senior ministers subsequently managed to dilute the commitment to nationalise industrial and life assurance, so that it instead became a 'mutualisation' proposal, in effect a mechanism by which a proportion of insurance funds could be compulsorily put into government securities. By the time that compromise had been accepted by the party's executive, the insurance industry, led by the Prudential, had launched a fierce campaign against any state involvement, and it is unlikely that the watering down did much to allay stoked-up fears.

The most memorable anti-nationalisation campaign, however, was that waged by the sugar monopoly Tate & Lyle. An animated cartoon character, 'Mr Cube', was created in July 1949; for the rest of the year and into 1950 the little man seemed to be everywhere. Daily he was to be seen on sugar packages, on ration-book holders (given away free to housewives) and on Tate & Lyle delivery trucks, while intensive advertising in the press was supplemented by shopkeepers handing out millions of leaflets to customers. 'Take the S out of State,' was one of Mr Cube's easy-to-grasp slogans, 'Tate not State!' another. The campaign even enlisted the services of Richard Dimbleby, the broadcaster who was well on his way to becoming a national institution. Visiting the company's refinery at Plaistow 'with an open mind and an open mike', he found a strong 'family spirit' among the workforce and an 'astonishingly unanimous' desire to 'stay as we are'. The interviews he conducted were made available on no fewer than four million 12-inch records. Altogether, it was an astonishingly effective, American-style campaign, which the government was quite unable to counter.

But arguably, the whole question of nationalisation stood proxy for something larger: a creeping sense that organisations were getting too big, too remote and too bureaucratic. Writing in a mass-circulation Sunday paper in January 1949, the best-known Labour-supporting public intellectual, J. B. Priestley, asserted that irrespective of which party was in power, 'the area of our lives under our own control is shrinking rapidly' and that 'politicians and senior civil servants are beginning to decide how the rest of us shall live'. There was a rapid rebuttal from Michael Foot, who in the Labour left's house magazine, *Tribune*, accused Priestley of being the 'High Priest of the new defeatist cult'. Foot did not deny that 'bigness is an enemy', nor that 'once the advantages of some centralised planning have been secured or once a private monopoly has been transferred to public ownership, the next step must be to establish a wider and more democratic diffusion of responsibility', but he was insistent that post-1945 British socialism was imparting a 'new meaning' to democracy itself:

All over Britain the housing programme is being directed and organised by local councillors elected by their fellow citizens. Most of these, together with the chairmen of finance committees and the rest are ordinary men and women, probably most of them working-class. Never in municipal history were local councils charged with such a tremendous responsibility. Never were the trade unions called upon to play a bigger role in the nation's economy.

In essence, Priestley was suffering from 'the nihilism of the intellectual who will not deign to join the strivings of the common people'.[17]

On Michael Young, head of research at the Labour Party and principal author of the 1945 manifesto, it was starting to dawn that it was the very task of public-minded intellectuals to understand the lives and aspirations of 'the common people'. *Small Man, Big World* was the haunting title of his pamphlet published in the winter of 1948/9. After a homely opening paragraph describing a family working together as they put up and decorate their Christmas tree, he set out his guiding preoccupations:

> There is no doubt that democracy can most easily flourish in the family and in other small groups built to the scale of the individual. All the members there meet face to face; if a decision has to be made, all can have a direct and personal part in making it, and all can perceive the results of their decisions.
>
> Democracy therefore seems to require smallness. But efficiency, promoted by the growth of science, often requires bigness. This is the great dilemma of modern society . . .
>
> There is no salvation in going back to some misty past in which the small man lived in a small world, no salvation in putting multi-coloured maypoles in every city square or even substituting William Morris for the Morris car. Destroying bigness would not only reduce the standard of living; it would also destroy democracy . . .
>
> But higher efficiency has not been gained without social cost . . . In the small group – in the family, amongst friends at work or in the pub, in the little ships of the Navy – the person has a feeling of comradeship and a sense of belonging: the individual matters and his self-respect is supported by the respect of his fellows. But in the large group the individual is only too likely to be and to feel powerless and insignificant.
>
> How can the individual be made to matter more?

The bulk of the pamphlet then offered some rather mechanistic ways – befitting a party publication, albeit for discussion purposes – in which the right kind of democratic leadership could be secured, closer two-way communication between those at the bottom and those at the top could be established, and the size of organisations could be reduced without harming efficiency.

Towards the end, after duly lauding industrial democracy, 'the small New Towns which the Labour Government has bravely launched', community associations, and parish and neighbourhood councils, Young extolled the way in which 'some of the social scientists, with the psychologists in the lead, are analysing from a new standpoint the complex motives of man' – and in the process revealing man's deep need, whatever his aggressive impulses, 'to love, or contribute to the good of others, and to be loved, or receive the affection and respect of others'. Fortunately, he reflected, 'the strength of democracy is that it can so fully satisfy these human needs'. Much more research was needed ('research based on field work in the social sciences is every bit as – in my personal view much more – important than research in the natural sciences'), but the incentive was that 'this new knowledge will enrich socialism as it will enrich the new society which socialists are making':

> British socialists have been broadly of two kinds – the Fabians with their emphasis on efficiency and social justice, and their devotion to facts; and the idealistic socialists, inspired by such men as Robert Owen and William Morris, with their emphasis on the dignity of man and of labour. The time is coming when the two strands can blend. If the Fabians are ready to follow the facts – the new knowledge about human relations which the social scientists are producing – they may find they are led to conclusions which differ little from those of the socialist idealists. If the latter are ready to restrain their more impractical ideas and compromise with efficiency, idealism need not lead to economic collapse and democratic disaster but to a society, built on the model of the family, which is not only more comradely but more efficient. In this new society human nature itself will increase its stature and the small man at last come into his own.

Fieldwork, the family, the small man: a life-change was beckoning.

'A pamphlet very much off the beaten track' was *Tribune*'s verdict, though the magazine conceded that 'the questions he raises and seeks to answer respond perhaps more directly to the worries of the rank-and-file of the Labour movement than the apparently more practical issues of day-to-day policy'. How had Young reached this point in his thinking? No doubt he had been much struck by the large gap that had seemingly opened up between rulers and ruled since the 1945 election, a gap symbolised in many eyes by the perceived failure of nationalisation to usher in a new set of social relations. But he was also perhaps influenced by his mentor, Leonard Elmhirst, co-founder (with his rich American wife Dorothy) of Dartington Hall, the progressive school near Totnes which Young himself had attended. 'Remember,' Elmhirst wrote to him in July 1948, 'that the social sciences is only another term for political dynamite, because psychology and economics must drive right at the heart of human affairs and will inevitably upset any realisation of the immediate needs of party politicians.' Young himself later that year described economics to Elmhirst as being 'to social psychology like hacksaw surgery to chemotherapy'.

He was also about to forge a new, fruitful alliance. 'Did you see a note about Michael Young in yesterday's *Observer*?' Peter Willmott, a mature student at Ruskin College, Oxford, wrote in early 1949 to his wife Phyllis in London. 'He seems a good chap, right on the line, and I have thought that I might write to him.' Willmott, whose personal background was far less easy than Young's, got hold of the pamphlet, liked it, and over a pub lunch in early summer the two men clicked so well that Willmott joined Young in Labour's research department that autumn. 'Tall and hollow-chested, bony-limbed and flaxen-haired, with clean-cut jaw, pale-blue eyes and a pale, damp face, he seemed as he stood there to be oblivious to his surroundings' is how Phyllis Willmott (née Noble) has vividly described her first encounter with Young, at a party where uncharacteristically he was 'roaring drunk'. It was not long before she came to realise that he was almost invariably 'diffident and reserved to the point of inhibition when talking about himself' – but, crucially, 'showed a keen interest in everything around him (including people) that was at once striking and flattering'.

If Young was on a journey moving inexorably away from party politics, one Oxford economist was poised to go the other way. Born in 1918, educated at Highgate School and Oxford, and a protégé of one of Attlee's senior ministers, Hugh Dalton, the notably handsome, intelligent and (when he wanted to be) charming Anthony Crosland was by 1949 actively looking for a parliamentary seat. That September, about the time he was adopted as Labour candidate for South Gloucestershire (which fortunately included Bristol's northern suburbs), he reflected in his diary on how for all the good that Sidney and Beatrice Webb and their fellow Fabians had once done, especially in terms of stimulating state action to counteract economic inequality, it was high time that the labour movement outgrew the puritanism and priggishness of their latter-day followers:

I want more, not less, 'spooning in the Parks of Recreation & Rest', more abortion, more freedom & hilarity in every way: abstinence is not a good foundation for Socialism, & the almost unnatural normality of the Webbs, & their indifference to emotional & physical pleasures, really would, if universally influential, make the Socialist State into the dull functional nightmare wh. many fear.

Crosland's liberalism contrasted sharply with the social conservatism of most Labour politicians, especially those from a trade-union background. Indeed, it was at about this time that Young (with whom Crosland was becoming friendly) commissioned a group of Labour-supporting lawyers to produce a report on law reform, with a view to including some of its proposals in the manifesto he was working on for the election due in 1950. 'The report when it arrived contained a large number of well-reasoned proposals for reform, such as abolishing the "crime" of homosexuality, modernising the divorce laws, removing censorship of plays and films, and abolishing capital punishment,' Young recalled a decade later. 'The members of the [Policy] Committee were acutely embarrassed. Far from considering the proposals on their merits, they showed concern only that no word should ever get out that such a dangerous report had been received.'[18]

Of the two intellectuals, Young at least would come in time to appreciate through first-hand experience the deeply entrenched world view of the party's core supporters. But perhaps not even he ever quite took on board the full force and significance of the findings, applicable to both sexes, of a gifted (and now almost completely forgotten) sociologist, Pearl Jephcott. After working incognito for several months in a light engineering factory on a London bypass, she reported in September 1948 on the virtually non-existent interest of her fellow-employees in current affairs:

The girls' talk hardly ranges beyond two themes, personal appearance and personal relations. The latter means fellows – mine, yours, hers. Even among the older women the only public event in the last three months which has fished folk out of the sea of personal and domestic affairs has been the Derby.

'What we need,' she concluded, 'is some mental stimulant connected with our working life.'[19]

3

Jolly Good as a Whole

Two of 1949's innovations were Longleat and launderettes. On 1 April the sixth Marquess of Bath, wearing a pair of baggy old corduroys, stood with his wife on the front steps of one of the great Elizabethan houses and welcomed the first coach of visitors, each paying half a crown. A guidebook written by the marchioness, picture postcards and tubs of ice cream were all on sale, while her young children acted as tour guides or car-park attendants. The visitors poured in, up to 135,000 in the first year. 'Of course,' Lord Bath explained some months after his pioneering move, 'the only way now is to run one's house as a business, then it's subject to the same taxation as other businesses. Like this it's possible to keep things going.' But for the landowning aristocracy as a whole, faced by unprecedentedly stiff peacetime taxation (including death duties of 75 per cent on estates of more than £1 million), the outlook seemed terminally grim. 'A house such as Rowcester Abbey in these days is not an asset, sir, it is a liability,' P. G. Wodehouse's Jeeves authoritatively explained a few years later to an American visitor. 'Socialistic legislation has sadly depleted the resources of England's hereditary aristocracy.' Ironically, it was the system of agricultural subsidies introduced by the Labour government that would, at least as much as charabancs, save many of the stately homes of England and their ungrateful inhabitants.

Britain's first self-service, coin-operated launderette opened, for a six-month trial, at 184 Queensway in Bayswater on 10 May. 'All that housewives have to do is bring the washing, put it in the machine and come back 30 minutes later (charge 2s 6d for 9lbs),' explained the local paper. After the film star Jean Kent had done the ceremonial honours, first through the doors was 14-year-old Ryan Hyde of Woodfield Road, Paddington, carrying a large white linen bag. 'Mum's doing the cooking,' he told the reporter. 'This is going to save my big sister a lot of work.' The experiment proved a success, and gradually other Bendix branches spread across London and elsewhere. When one opened in Fulham Broadway, the working-class mother of Janet Bull (later Street-Porter) 'decided to forgo the cheap bagwash (only a shilling a week, and our clothes went in a sack with those of our upstairs tenants) at the Sunlight Laundry around the corner'. For the four-year-old Janet it was a thrilling experience – 'as we didn't have a tele-vision, I found the hour or so spent watching our sheets and towels being washed in a machine every week totally mesmeric'.

About the same time as Bayswater's launderette opened, a national survey of housewives found that less than half used laundries, with most either doing their own washing or (for the better off) having a washerwoman come in to do it for them. To possess a washing machine was still rare; almost everyone had a scrubbing board or hand-turned mangle. But there had already been a significant moment in October 1948 when Hoover, hitherto best known for its vacuum cleaner, offi-cially opened a factory for the manufacture of its new electric washing machine near Merthyr Tydfil. Initially almost all the machines were for export only, though that did not stop Hoover's chairman and managing director, Charles Colston, from indulging in some pardonable rhetoric (probably written for him by a young Muriel Spark):

> The introduction of this machine, I believe, is going to be welcomed by countless housewives throughout the country. During the War they carried a tremendous responsibility, and since the end of the War condi-tions have been none too easy for them and to relieve the housewives of much of the laborious work which they have to do is, I believe, one of the most effective ways in which we can raise their general well-being. Our Electric Washing Machine should be most valuable to mothers of babies and young children.

'It is not an expensive model intended for the few,' he emphasised. 'It has been built with the intention that it shall be for the million.'[1]

The National Health Service, by this time turning into a robust if greedy infant, was undeniably for the million. Right from the Appointed Day there was huge demand for its services, far from confined to elderly ladies wanting their varicose veins done. 'I certainly found when the Health Service started on the 5th July '48,' Dr Alistair Clark, an ordinary GP, recalled half a century later, 'that for the next six months I had as many as twenty or thirty ladies come to me who had the most unbelievable gynaecological conditions – I mean, of that twenty or thirty, there would be at least ten who had complete prolapse of their womb, and they had to hold it up with a towel as if they had a large nappy on.'

Overall, though, the three great, almost feverish rushes were for drugs, spectacles and false teeth. As the drugs bill spiralled in two years from £13 million to £41 million, even Aneurin Bevan, the NHS's architect and still Minister of Health, was heard to complain about the 'cascades of medicine pouring down British throats – and they're not even bringing the bottles back'. As for the lure of free spectacles, some eight million pairs were provided in the first year, double the anticipated total. 'Officials in the Service,' reported Mollie Panter-Downes, 'say that this is partly because of the hundreds of thousands of citizens – mostly among the poor – who have been fumbling around all their lives in glasses bought at the five-and-ten [traditionally a lucky (or unlucky) dip counter at Woolworths], the only kind they could afford.' There were two NHS frames to choose from: the 422 Panto Round Oval (anticipating the glasses immortalised by John Lennon in the 1960s, though in the NHS case with unsightly, pinkish plastic) and, far more popular, the 524 Contour (as worn years later by Elvis Costello). In the case of teeth, it could be a question of finding a dentist. 'Colonel Whiter explained that dentists are under no legal obligation to treat anybody as a Health Service patient,' officials of the John Hilton Bureau (in effect a citizens' advisory organisation subsidised by the *News of the World*) found in December 1948 when they went to see the Ministry of Health's Deputy Senior Dental Officer. 'They can, if they wish, in urgent cases say "I will treat you as a private patient but not as a Health Service patient." He is aware that dentists are doing this all over the country. He agrees that it is against the whole spirit of the Health Service Scheme.' The same issue of the bureau's *Journal* that related this encounter also included a pithy anecdote in a reader's letter: 'The dentist froze my jaw and said "I will not take your tooth out under the Health Service. It will cost you 5/-." What could I do?' Altogether, there were many stories of abuse circulating during the NHS's first year, not a few involving dentists succumbing to the obvious financial temptation posed of being paid by the filling.

Nevertheless, Panter-Downes was surely right when in January 1949 she noted the existence of 'a feeling that the Service is not working out as chaotically as was expected by its critics' and that 'the bitter blood between the Minister of Health and the medical men has diminished'. If there were storm clouds, they had to do with costs, almost from day one revealing that Sir William Beveridge's confident expectation earlier in the decade – that a national health service would make the nation healthier and thus reduce health costs – was diametrically wrong. As early as December 1948, Bevan was warning his colleagues that the original estimate of £176 million for the NHS's first nine months was going to be overshot by almost £50 million, and when two months later he came to the Commons for that extra money, or what Sir Cuthbert Headlam privately termed 'Mr Bevan's monstrous Supplementary Estimates for the national health business', he had to see off attacks on his profligate stewardship. 'Pale and miserable lot,' Bevan called the Tories, 'instead of welcoming every increase in the health of the nation . . . they groan at it. They hate it because they think it spells electoral defeat.'[2]

One articulate doctor was disinclined to call a truce with the minister. 'I am firmly convinced that at the present rate of expenditure it will involve us in national ruin,' Ffrangcon Roberts (from Addenbrooke's Hospital, Cambridge) declared in the *British Medical Journal* about the cost of the NHS, before going on:

> Our duty as a profession is clear. We must teach our students and the lay public that the fight against disease is part of the struggle for existence; that medicine is not above economic law but strictly subject to it; that the claims of health, so far from being absolute, are relative to national well-being; that the country will get not the finest Health Service in the world but the Health Service which it deserves.

By May an unabashed Bevan was telling the Cabinet that there would have to be another 'supplementary', for the financial year 1949/50. But he was adamant that the introduction of prescription charges would 'greatly reduce the prestige of the Service'. Perhaps unsurprisingly, given that the first phase of the NHS coincided with a period of considerable economic stringency, a survey soon afterwards found that 'there exists among a substantial proportion of the population an exaggerated idea of the cost of the Health Service in relation to other items which tends to be associated with belief that the Government is spending more than it should be on the service'.

In April 1949 a Mass-Observation series of interviews across England asked people what they thought of 'the new scheme as a whole'. There was as ever a range of responses:

> As a whole it's been all right, but like everything else it's getting abused. People are using any excuse to go to the doctor when they never would have gone before. (*Married woman, 58, Kentish Town*)
>
> It's pretty good. It's what is needed. (*Carpenter and joiner, 49, Selsdon, Surrey*)
>
> It's not as good as it was. The doctor isn't so friendly as he was, now it's nationalised they're just like the rest of the civil servants and they don't want to have you more than they have to. When I took him the card he wasn't very pleased about it. I've always paid for what I had from him and now he's got to take everybody at so much a year. You can't expect to get the same service. (*Tobacconist, 58, Croydon*)
>
> A very good idea. Necessary to international interests. (*Village postmaster, 33, Danbury, Essex*)
>
> I think it's good because I used to have to pay 4/- every time he came when we were sick. (*Wife of crane driver, 34, Liverpool*)
>
> Jolly good as a whole – it may be the members themselves spoil it by abuse. (*Librarian, 36, Ferndown, Dorset*)
>
> I've had no advantages myself yet. (*Civil servant, 56, Kensington*)
>
> Well, myself, I think it's good. But I think there's a lot of extravagance on the part of the doctors. (*Housewife, 24, Kimberley, Notts*)
>
> It's a waste of money, and I'm sure the poor could be helped without it. I don't feel we have a family doctor any more. The surgeries are

crowded and there is too much waste of time while we wait. (*Housewife, 60, Birtley, Co. Durham*)

It could be a good idea if people didn't take advantage of it – as it is, no. My husband hurt his back playing rugger and he caught a cold and it went to his back. He had to go to the doctor and he waited goodness knows how long. He had to go again, and each time he went he more or less saw the same people, and the doctor more or less reckoned half of them had nothing wrong with them – just went for the sake of going. (*Policeman's wife, 32, Marylebone*)

The English may have been a people with a disposition to grumble, but overall, M-O reported on its survey, 'unqualified approval was nearly twice as common as approval hedged in with reservations'. The 'main thing' liked about the scheme was 'the obvious point of cheapness, and the fact that it put everyone on a basis of medical equality'. Against that, 'the commonest criticism concerned the time wasted in the doctor's waiting room, followed by less frequent charges of abuses and malingering amongst some patients, and a feeling of increased regimentation'. The report added that 'only a very few were able to venture any idea of the cost of the service.' Among the ingrates was an aspiring young actor. 'Went to Doctor about warts on my left hand,' Kenneth Williams confided to his diary in April, the same month as the M-O survey. 'They are becoming unsightly. Have to go to University College Hosp. to see Skin Doctor on May 5th! – ghastly business this National Health Scheme! – one might be dead by then!'[3]

It was Bevan's other responsibility, housing, which remained, in the continuing context of shortages of manpower and materials, the government's Achilles heel.[4] So much so that Gallup in early 1949 registered 61 per cent dissatisfaction with the progress being made. Those who did have somewhere to live did not dare jeopardise losing it. 'Have you ever wondered why so many old people can be seen roaming the streets of Malden?' asked a September 1949 charity appeal from the heart of Surrey suburbia. 'Does it shock you to hear that it is because many of them are only tolerated in their lodgings on condition that they keep "out of the way" during the hours of daylight?' Young Harry Webb, the future Cliff Richard, was seven when he, his parents and his three sisters left India for England in 1948. 'At first my grandmother found us a room next to her in Carshalton,' he recalled. 'That room was our living room, bedroom, kitchen – the lot.' After a year, 'my aunt gave us a room in her home at Waltham Cross in Essex – but it was no bigger and the five of us went on living in each other's pockets.' Eventually they got a council house in Cheshunt, but they were still reliant on packing cases to serve as chairs.

In the capital new housing at this stage usually meant flats (for which the Treasury was prepared to subsidise the purchase of expensive land by local authorities), though rarely high-rise flats. In inner London, in the six years after the war, the London County Council (LCC) built 13,072 flats but only 81 houses, while in the boroughs of outer London the respective figures were 13,374 and 2,630. In July 1948 Panter-Downes visited Lambeth, where four-fifths of the housing stock had been damaged or destroyed in the war. There she found 'excellent new permanent housing' which, along the lines envisaged by Sir Patrick Abercrombie's wartime plan for London, involved 'the population's expanding vertically rather than horizontally'. Admittedly, she added, 'the average Londoner wants a little house and a garden,' but 'according to the new plans, he'll have to settle, nine times out of ten, for a flat and a window box'. *Picture Post* was a less ambiguous cheerleader when, the following January, in an article stridently headed 'Housing: London Shows How', it featured the work under way in the heavily blitzed Stepney-Poplar reconstruction area, where two-thirds of the new dwellings were to be flats. Many of these flats contained 'four rooms, a utility room, a drying balcony, a sun balcony, and a boiler in the kitchen to provide domestic hot water, or else gas or electric water-heaters. All living rooms will have open fires.' In short: 'What a contrast to the rooms pictured by Charles Dickens!'[5]

The houses versus flats issue continued to be debated among activators, generally, but for Donald Gibson, City Architect of Coventry and mastermind of that city's much-lauded post-war redevelopment, the answer was obvious. In April 1949 the local paper reported his speech on the city's prospective new estates:

On the question of lay-out, Mr Gibson said: 'I do not see why there should be any front gardens, for most people do not seem prepared to devote enough time to them. The street is the concern of the whole city, and these gardens destroy its appearance.' He considered there should be no gates or fences and that central greens should be the responsibility of the Baths and Parks Committee.

The city should go in for flats in a big way and have really high ones, even up to 20 storeys in a block.

The paper's editorial in the same issue was essentially in agreement, especially on the horticultural aspect: 'Almost anywhere it can be seen that many people do not want, and do not deserve, their gardens.'

Inevitably, these were bad days for Frederic Osborn. 'Relatively to the knowledge and aspirations of the times, the wholesale building of multi-storey flats at 40 an acre today in Stepney or Bermondsey is less enlightened than the building there of terrace-houses at much the same density 100 years ago,' he declared in the spring issue of *Town and Country Planning*. And by July he was inveighing to Lewis Mumford about how 'in London just now the authorities are building eight and ten storey flats, intended for families', though with an average floor area of only 650 square feet, compared to the 1,000 or 1,050 square feet for 'the current two-storey house'. Yet 'Royal personages open these wonder-flats, admire the gadgets, the central heating and hot water, the automatic lifts, etc. Mayors wear halos, women's columns write as if the millennium of the housewife had arrived...' It was a passage that revealed the limitations of even as practical and humanitarian an idealist as Osborn. Most people might indeed prefer houses to flats, but if a flat was the only way to obtain central heating and hot water, let alone 'gadgets', that for very many (and not only housewives) was an irresistible lure.

The architects and architectural critics, increasingly cross that the LCC in 1945 had removed housing from the Architect's Department to the Valuer's, were also missing the point. Arguably the key figure was J. M. Richards, editor of the *Architectural Review* and for a time the *Architects' Journal* as well as architectural correspondent for *The Times*. In February 1949 the LCC held an immensely popular Homes for London exhibition in the entrance foyer of Charing Cross tube station, viewed by more than 120,000 commuters. But for Richards, this was the cue to launch a fierce attack on the iniquity of London's new public housing being in the hands of non-architects – 'whether,' as he told radio listeners at the end of February, 'you take the grim concrete barracks recently provided for the people of Bethnal Green and Deptford and Islington or the immense scheme now under construction at Woodberry Down, a fine site in North London now being covered with flats of an ineptness in design and crudity of detail that London shouldn't be expected to put up with in 1949'. In the *Architects' Journal* an anonymous writer (perhaps Richards himself) predictably agreed with that critique and cited the Valuer's most recent development, the Flower House Estate at Catford, comprising 15 blocks 'in monolithic concrete' of three or four storeys each, as ample justification for it. Yet to read the *Lewisham Journal*'s report of the opening by Herbert Morrison of the first five blocks on 11 March is to sense a proud local occasion and many happy new residents. At one point Morrison presented the key of flat number 4 of Morse House to George Jones, a salesman at Sainsbury's in Catford. He, his wife and their 18-month-old twin boys had been living in a small room in Eltham, with Mrs Jones in poor health; they were clearly relieved and delighted to be moving to a three-room flat, with kitchenette and bathroom.

That did not stop the *Architects' Journal* being filled for several weeks with letters from architects supporting the Richards attack, eventually prompting the LCC to put on another exhibition, at County Hall in May, of its housing work – in turn attracting yet more strident criticism from the architects. 'If one single building had been able to compare with the clarity of Gropius's block of flats in Siemensstadt Siedlung, Berlin, built, mind you, 20 years ago, one might have felt that there was some encouragement for the future' was a fairly typical specimen. Significantly, also on display at County Hall were the designs for what would become the Royal Festival Hall, principally the work of the LCC's Architect and Deputy Architect, Robert Matthew and Leslie Martin. 'It shows,' asserted Richards, 'every promise of performing that rare feat: combining a frankly modern expression with a monumental character and real refinement of detail.'[6] The architects were poised to regain control. But for the punters, who just wanted somewhere to live, it was a squabble that at this stage mattered not a whit.

Coinciding with the displays at County Hall was the Royal Academy's annual Summer Show, and for the first time since the war the traditional eve-of-show banquet was held, with the speeches going out live on radio. In the chair was the RA's doughtily reactionary septuagenarian President, Sir Alfred Munnings, whose speciality was very popular (and lucrative) paintings of horses. He was, as heard by a delighted Vere Hodgson, determined to give it to them straight:

> What a speech! He entirely forgot he was being broadcast. He could see no ladies present – forgot many of them were listening in – and simply crashed out at Modern Art. I hugged myself as I listened . . . He damned that and damned that . . . Said he has asked Mr Churchill if he saw Picasso walking down Piccadilly would he join him in a bodily assault . . . And Mr Churchill replied – WILLINGLY. So it went on . . .
>
> I could feel the BBC officials were fainting in the background – not knowing whether to switch him off or not. But they did not. Someone tried to tell him he was overstepping his time. He waved them on one side, and said it was the last time he was President and he intended to have his say . . .
>
> Apparently the BBC was bombarded with phone calls as, never before, has an Academy Banquet been so exciting. Artists interrupted the President during his speech. This is unheard of . . .

The provocation was undeniable. Attacking experts 'who think they know more about art than the men who paint the pictures', Munnings mentioned by name the Surveyor of the King's Pictures, Anthony Blunt, who had once said in his hearing that Joshua Reynolds was inferior to Picasso. 'What an extraordinary thing for a man to say!' declared Munnings. Then, after a swipe at Matisse for his 'aesthetic juggling' (leading to cries of 'beautiful' and 'lovely work'), he turned on a recent, well-publicised sculpture by Henry Moore. 'My horses may be all wrong,' he added, 'but I'm damned sure that isn't right.'

It was a diatribe that certainly made an impact. 'Much talk at dinner table of Sir Alfred Munnings' last night broadcast speech,' noted Gladys Langford in her Highbury hotel. And in her next entry: 'Very gay breakfast-table, Freddy White on Munnings & The Moderns was very

funny.' Not long afterwards, Munnings was booming away in the
Athenaeum when he spotted Britain's greatest living sculptor and his fellow-
modernist friend, J. M. Richards. 'There's that fellow Moore,' exploded
Sir Alfred. 'What's a bloody charlatan like him doing in this club?' Moore,
perhaps influenced by the worldly-wise Richards, ignored him.

At the Summer Show itself, Munnings's own paintings found particular
favour with the paying public. 'I think they're very good, outstanding,
somehow,' a working-class man told Mass-Observation's investigator.
'They're lifelike, not just paint and canvas. They stand out.' A 65-year-
old woman was especially struck by his *Coming Off the Heath at
Newmarket*: 'It's very nice, isn't it? I like the dust coming up from the
horses' feet.' Almost invariably, the highest value was given to pictorial
realism. 'Now that's beautiful,' said a young middle-class woman about
a painting called *Generation to Generation*. 'Every detail is there. The
oil lamp and even the spoon in the teacup. It's one of the best of the
views.' A slightly older middle-class woman liked a portrait of the Lord
Chief Justice, Lord Goddard: 'There's a lot of detail in that. It's just like
a photograph, but that's just what you want.' Not all the subjects,
however, met with approval. 'I think that's dreadful,' said another middle-
class woman about *Mother and Child*, in which the child was suckling.
'I see nothing beautiful in that. And when the baby grows up he won't
be so pleased either. It's all right from a medical point of view, but that's
about all.' A working-class man was similarly dismissive about *Spit and
Polish*, a still-life: 'There's far better stuff to paint than old boots like
those. I don't like that.' Overall, M-O's report rather reluctantly accepted,
'the general public are quite clear in their own minds about what they
like and what they dislike.'⁷

———

Amid architectural and artistic controversy, the annual sporting rhythm
did not miss a beat. Russian Hero was the 66–1 winner of the Grand
National – tipped, appropriately enough, by the *Daily Worker* – while
in the Boat Race the normally imperturbable commentary of John Snagge
(his throaty chant of 'in, out' timing the strokes) went somewhat awry:
'Oxford are ahead. No Cambridge are ahead. I don't know who's ahead
– it's either Oxford or Cambridge.' Two days after the Munnings broadside, Wolverhampton Wanderers (captained by Billy Wright) met

Leicester City (missing their 'schemer-in-chief' Don Revie) in the Cup
Final. Valerie Gisborn, growing up in Leicester (where television was
not yet available), listened to the match on the radio with her mother,
but her father travelled down to Isleworth, where he had an ex-naval
friend who had invited him to stay, specifically to watch the match on
their set. Although City lost, the womenfolk keenly anticipated the report
of his trip:

> He was so thrilled he could hardly wait to get indoors to tell us about
> it. What a weird and wonderful thing it was. He kept us in suspense as
> he related every step from arriving at their home to leaving. He told us
> that the house was full of men who had been invited to watch the match
> on the small television in the lounge. Dad described how the set was
> held in a large, dark brown cabinet, with the television set in the top
> half. The screen measured nine inches square and the picture was black
> and white. Constantly there were white flashes and a muzzy picture but
> the cameras followed every move the players made. He reckoned it was
> better than actually being at Wembley.

Just over a month later, 46,000 crammed into White City stadium to
watch Yorkshire's taciturn heavyweight, Bruce Woodcock, defeat
London's cheerful brawler, Freddie Mills, in 14 rounds. Interest in the
fight was so intense that thousands had packed Great Windmill Street
off Piccadilly just to see the boxers arrive for the weigh-in. For Woodcock, it was a last hurrah, but another Yorkshireman, the cricketer
Brian Close, was just starting out. At Old Trafford in July he played
against New Zealand at the age of 18 – more than half a century later,
still England's youngest-ever debutant. He was out third ball for a
duck, caught on the square-leg boundary, but was praised by *Wisden*
'for his effort to follow the correct policy of big hitting'. With greased-
down, combed-back hair, complete with Frank Sinatra quiff-wave, he
signed the young Frank Keating's scorecard at teatime behind the
pavilion while asking him to hold his smoking Woodbine.[8]
    In the cinema that summer, there were no fewer than three superb
comedies from Ealing Studios to enjoy. *Whisky Galore!* was a tale of
Scottish islanders determined to keep a shipwrecked cargo of whisky
out of the hands of killjoy Customs and Excise officers; *Kind Hearts*

and Coronets ('I enjoyed it very much and thought the script very amusing,' noted Gladys Langford) concerned an aristocratic outcast killing off his unlovable relatives; but the most resonant, and for most people closest to home, was *Passport to Pimlico*, starring Stanley Holloway and Margaret Rutherford. It was, on the surface, anti-state in its message (like *Whisky Galore!*) and indeed anti-Labour government. The plot hinges on Pimlico, very much a working-class district, declaring itself independent from the rest of Britain – an independence immediately resulting in freedom from restrictions, rationing, purchase tax, ID cards and so on, with a scene in a pub of ration books and ID cards being torn up that apparently provoked roars of applause from the cinema audiences. Or, in the words of a placard, 'Forget that Cripps Feeling'. Civil servants from Whitehall try to bring the natives back into the fold, but their leader brutally tells them, 'We're sick and tired of your voice in this country.' Soon things go wrong. Pimlico becomes a 'spivs' paradise' (as the Holloway character calls it), 'crowds of cup-tie proportions' (in the phrase of the mock radio report) flood in from outside, and law and order breaks down. In fact, complete freedom from rationing and controls is shown to be frightening, not something to be desired, and in the end, after the fracture is repaired between Pimlico and Whitehall, we see the warmly greeted return of the ID card and ration book. 'I never thought people'd welcome the sight of these things again,' remarks Pimlico's policeman. To which Holloway's wife replies, 'You never know when you're well off till you aren't.' The film ends in nostalgic wartime mood, with the state once again benign, community spirit strong, and an unnatural heat wave giving way to reassuring rain and cold. The left-of-centre '1945' verities had been reasserted.[9]

They were not verities to which by 1949 much of the middle class was any longer inclined to subscribe. An autumn 1948 survey of British standards of living – the work of Mark Abrams, starting to carve out a notable career as one of the closest observers of social and economic trends – revealed that whereas the standard of living of the average working-class family had increased by 10 per cent since 1938, that of the average salary earner had slumped by 20 per cent. Even though the fact remained (as Abrams also showed) that the average middle-class family was still 50 per cent better off than the average working-class family, the middle-class reaction to such a stark contrast in recent fortunes was understandably unenthusiastic.

Nevertheless, pending an opportunity at the ballot box, stoicism – and an almost iron will not to let hard-won personal standards and social position slip – tended to rule the day. 'The interesting thing is that they are contriving to send their children to the same sort of schools, are as determined as ever to take the same sort of holidays, and are in some way managing to fit their lives into a reduced but roughly recognizable pattern,' observed Panter-Downes in February 1949, after describing how the middle class were 'beginning to feel with fright the effects of prices that have crept up so quietly and steadily that they are now perched, like ghostly black dogs, on everyone's back'. Three months later, Mrs Lola Archer's new column ('Over the Tea Cups') for the local paper in Weston-super-Mare exuded similar values:

> Once upon a time, way back in the halcyon days of the nineteen-thirties, a woman's column meant clothes, holidays, and recipes that started: 'Take six eggs . . .' Today, though holidays may be nothing more than making the best of your free time at home, and recipes are expected to combine equal proportions of ingenuity and frugality, the latest fashion still holds place of honour. Owing to this fact it has been decided to run a pattern service for 'Mercury' readers. In future, every week an 'easy to make' pattern, featuring the style of the moment, will be reproduced in this column. So, put your work baskets in order . . .

Elsewhere in the column, she told the story of her nine-year-old son Jeffrey being refused a new pair of white flannels for the cricket season and saying scathingly, 'But mummy, you only need money now', as she wondered aloud to her readers how to teach children the value of money.

For *Picture Post*, running a major investigative feature in June, the question was simple: 'Is the Middle Class Doomed?' The writer, Ruth Bowley, itemised their plight:

> Those with less than £1,000 are really up against it. They are facing that hardest thing to face – a move down the scale through inescapable necessity. The average budget here gives no scope for substantial adjustments, like

doing without the family car and the maid. When the coalman calls, the family cuts down on housekeeping extras. When the dry-cleaning bill turns up on Thursday, there is no cinema on Friday night. Salaries cannot catch up with prices, and there are few savings to fall back on. Now the wife knows that she must do all the housework and look after the children.

Yet middle-class standards are still somehow kept up. Meals are eaten in the dining-room, though it would be less work to eat in the kitchen. The children still go out for a walk in the afternoon, but mother is now the nursemaid, and often has to finish the housework when the children are in bed.

'Today the middle class, as our parents know it, is indeed disappearing' was the bleak conclusion. 'A new standard of living is taking shape.' Among the many letters which the piece provoked, that from Mrs N. E. Walkey of resolutely lower-middle-class South Lane, New Malden, read in toto: 'Re your article "Is the Middle Class Doomed". Heaven forbid! They are the only people left who have good manners, brains and honesty. Lack of money will not destroy them. P.S. My first correspondence with a newspaper.' Although further up the middle-class pecking order, the residents of the Grand Hotel at Frinton-on-Sea would no doubt have agreed. 'Pre-war British customs may be dying (as they say abroad) but they are dying hard,' noted the veteran journalist Sydney Moseley after staying there in August. 'Almost everybody at this hotel "dressed" for dinner.'[10]

The *Picture Post* issue with Bowley's investigation was still on sale when, on 8 June, Secker & Warburg published George Orwell's *Nineteen Eighty-Four*, with a justifiably confident initial British print run of 25,500 copies. Six months earlier, reading the typescript, Fred Warburg himself had had no doubts about the novel's central message: 'Here is the Soviet Union to the nth degree, a Stalin who never dies, a secret police with every device of modern technology . . . A deliberate and sadistic attack on Socialism and socialist parties generally' – and to Orwell's chagrin that tended to be the immediate, reductive reaction of the critical world at large. Some even interpreted the book as an attack on the Labour government. 'My recent novel,' he publicly insisted barely a week after publication, 'is NOT intended as an attack on Socialism or on the British Labour Party (of which I am a supporter) but as a show-up of the perversions to which a centralized economy is liable and which have already been partly realized in Communism and Fascism.' In practice, the perceived anti-socialist thrust, accurate or otherwise, proved impossible to dispel.

Given the intensifying Cold War – especially once NATO had been formed, with the reluctant acquiescence of the Labour back benches, in April 1949 as an explicitly anti-Soviet alliance – this was surely inevitable. 'It is an open season for communists,' the young left-wing but not quite Communist literary critic and Workers' Educational Association (WEA) tutor Raymond Williams had already noted in 1948, and during 1949 this was abundantly true in small as well as large ways. 'It's a fine state of ecclesiastic affairs when the Dean of Canterbury [the infamous Dr Hewlett Johnson, the 'Red Dean'] believes everything he reads in *Pravda*,' declared one outraged elderly clergyman to another in March in an Osbert Lancaster cartoon in the *Daily Express*; soon afterwards, the news that the relatively radical schoolmaster Robert Birley, predictably dubbed 'Red Robert', was to be given the headmastership of Eton caused much needless parental apprehension. Rather more importantly, that summer saw a major industrial dispute in London and elsewhere. 'There has been a disgraceful Dock Strike all the week,' noted Vere Hodgson on 10 July. 'No one knows why . . .' The same day, in its main front-page story that faithfully echoed the government line, the *Sunday Pictorial* had no doubts about the cause:

> This is the time to speak bluntly. Thousands of honest, decent workers in Britain are being hoodwinked and perverted by a contemptible little gang of unscrupulous rogues. They are menacing the nation at the time of its acute economic crisis. That, indeed, is their evil plan.
>
> Who are these rogues? They are the Communists, who seek to impair our country's recovery by such wrecking tactics as the senseless, purposeless strike at the docks. To them honour is worthless and the welfare of their fellows is of no account if it obstructs their ruthless progress.

'These are the Men of Shame,' thundered the paper. 'Let Britain be warned now . . .'[11]

Certainly, in 1949, to be a Communist, or even merely a 'fellow-traveller', was not (in the short term at least) an astute career move.

Civil servants continued, as they had been since the spring of 1948, to be vetted; scare tactics resulted in the removal of most Communists from the National Union of Teachers (NUT) Executive; the historian George Rudé was dismissed from his teaching post at St Paul's public school and found it impossible to secure either an academic or a BBC position; the Transport and General Workers' Union's implacably right-wing leader, Arthur Deakin, banned Communists from holding office in his union; the educationalist Brian Simon thought he had got a job at Bristol University, but it proved a mirage after his CP membership was discovered; it was on pain of dismissal that any John Lewis employee did not sign an anti-Communist declaration; and so on.

Yet for all that, the witch-hunt could have been much more extreme. 'The Cold War mentality which developed in Britain did not reach the state of paranoia which sometimes afflicted the United States,' the cultural historian Robert Hewison persuasively writes. 'No House of Commons committee solemnly examined the works of art chosen for exhibition abroad by the British Council, in search of Communist tendencies . . . Britain had no Senator McCarthy.' And by way of explanation, he quotes from *A Summer to Decide* (1948) by the young novelist Pamela Hansford Johnson, in which the hero explains to an American why there is much less fearful preoccupation in Britain with the prospect of a war with Russia:

> One, the ordinary person is too busy. I mean he's too busy coping with the daily problems of his rationed life, and trying to see a clear road for his own future. Two, he sees the ruins of war all round him – along the railway lines as he goes to work, along the bus routes. He sees the place where the pub was, and the children's playground on the cleared site. He's still wondering how long it'll take to tidy them all up. He hasn't got round to contemplating new ruins. And despite sporadic hullaballoo in the newspapers, he simply doesn't see Russia as a threat to himself.

That did not mean there was any great popular love for the Communists in Britain, Russia or elsewhere. In April the shelling by Communist forces of British ships on the Yangtse, together with the heroic if bloody escape of HMS *Amethyst* into the open sea, seems to have struck a deeply patriotic chord in the working-class breast. But as so often, Labour's intellectuals did not get it. 'British warships,' Richard Crossman (Winchester→Oxford undergraduate→Oxford don→ people's tribune) declared in the *Sunday Pictorial*, 'are as out of place on the Yangtse as Chinese warships would be on the Thames.'[12]

Broadly speaking, it was from the intelligentsia and the trade unions that the bulk of the British Communist Party's fewer than 50,000 members came. Mervyn Jones, a young writer in the late 1940s, recalls how, despite spreading doubts about Soviet Russia, it was the very 'ferocity' of the Cold War that held the party together, with the 'incessant onslaughts' from the press and two main parties including 'some home truths' but also 'a torrent of distortions and slanders'. As for himself, he stayed a member because he could not yet find in the Labour Party an alternative 'focus of dissent'. For Lawrence Daly, a young Fife miner who was also a part-time National Union of Mineworkers (NUM) lodge official and, from 1949, chairman of the Scottish TUC Youth Advisory Council, there was not a sliver of inner doubt as he stood that spring as a Communist candidate in the Fife County Council elections. '"Vox" and "Anti-Humbug" may talk as much as they like about "Police States" and "Ruthless Dictatorships",' he wrote defiantly to *The Times for Lochgelly, Bowhill, Dundonald, Glencraig and Lochore*, 'but I prefer to accept the opinions of the founders of the Labour Party, Sidney and Beatrice Webb, who, in their monumental work, "Soviet Communism", described it as a new civilisation and as the greatest democracy on earth.' Gratifyingly, two days later, the *Daily Herald* called him Fife's 'chief Communist orator and theorist', but Daly still went down heavily to Labour.

Generally, what sort of culture prevailed in the British CP? The evidence, cumulatively, is not flattering. For all the seriousness and noble intentions of many of the members, there was an almost unwavering allegiance to the Stalin line (at times descending into Stalin worship), and from the leadership an aggressive unwillingness to allow any dissent or deviation. 'That time produced one of the sharpest mental frosts I can remember on the Left,' the historian E. P. Thompson would recall from personal knowledge of the CP in the late 1940s and early 1950s. 'Vitalities shrivelled up and books lost their leaves.' The stultifying, repressive flavour comes out well in a 1948 internal statement by the party's cultural commissar, Sam Aaronovitch. 'There are still too many of you,' he told the writers' group, 'who are not making a serious study of Marxism as a science. Because of that there are tendencies to compromise on basic principles, tendencies which light-heartedly reconcile, for instance, materialism and idealism . . . To engage more actively in the ideological struggle, our ideological workers must become Communists.' It was an atmosphere that could not but encourage intellectual dishonesty, notoriously so when in 1948/9 the CP's most famous scientist, J. D. Bernal, endorsed the wretchedly fraudulent 'proletarian science' of Trofim Lysenko, Stalin's pet scientist and proponent of the Marxist theory that genes have no independent existence or influence.

In February 1949 Penguin published *The Case for Communism* by one of the CP's two MPs, the veteran Scottish activist Willie Gallacher. Naturally it came with a heavy health warning: 'As publishers we have no politics . . . Whether we like it or not Communism is one of the major political forces in the modern world . . . Readers must judge for themselves how far his case is based upon objective analysis, and how far coloured by partisanship.' At one point, in his chapter 'Advancing Socialism – Declining Capitalism', Gallacher considered Russia's satellite states – countries like Poland, Czechoslovakia, Bulgaria and Hungary – and discussed whether they were democratic:

> The parties in the countries of east Europe, where the Communist parties are exerting a decisive influence, are all working together in the Govern-ments to reconstruct their countries. But what about the opposition? What opposition? The parties in the Government bloc represent the people, and carry forward a policy in the interests of, and for the welfare of, the people. Those who want to put the clock back are enemies of the people. There can be no toleration for such.

'In the democratic countries of east Europe they give no scope to the enemies of the people, and their nationalised industries have workers' participation at every stage, from top to bottom,' he added. 'That's the Communist idea of democracy, a new and far better type of democracy than the slow, dragging, Parliamentary sham of fighting that goes on in this country.'[13]

In the early summer of 1949, there arrived from Salisbury, Rhodesia, a Communist sympathiser (though not yet a party member). 'High on the side of the tall ship,' Doris Lessing recalled, 'I held up my little boy and said, "Look, there's London." Dockland: muddy creeks and channels, greyish rotting wooden walls and beams, cranes, tugs, big and little ships.' She came with her two-year-old son, little money and the manuscript of her first novel, *The Grass is Singing*. The London she found 'was unpainted, buildings were stained and cracked and dull and grey; it was war-damaged, some areas all ruins, and under them holes full of dirty water, once cellars, and it was subject to sudden dark fogs . . .' It got worse:

> No cafés. No good restaurants. Clothes were still 'austerity' from the war, dismal and ugly. Everyone was indoors by ten, and the streets were empty. The Dining Rooms, subsidised during the war, were often the only places to eat in a whole area of streets. They served good meat, terrible vegetables, nursery puddings. Lyons restaurants were the high point of eating for ordinary people – I remember fish and chips and poached eggs on toast . . . The war still lingered, not only in the bombed places but in people's minds and behaviour. Any conversation tended to drift towards the war, like an animal licking a sore place.

For Lessing, a redeeming feature (in addition to London's over-whelming lack of provincialism in comparison with her hometown) was the general lack of affluence. 'Nobody had any money, that's what people don't understand now,' she told Sue MacGregor in 2002. 'Nobody had anything. We didn't bother about it . . . It wasn't a question of suffering in any way. Nobody went hungry or anything like that, or went without clothes – it's just that we weren't suffering from this itch to possess more and more and more.'

Needing somewhere to live, Lessing spent six weeks 'tramping the streets with a guidebook, standing in queues outside telephone booths, examining advertisement boards'. These were weeks of 'interminable streets of tall, grey, narrow houses' with 'pale faces peering up from basements, innumerable dim flights of stairs, rooms crowded with cush-ioned and buttoned furniture, railings too grimy to touch, dirty flights of steps – above all, an atmosphere of stale weariness'. Eventually she met a jeweller's assistant called Rose, who found for Lessing and her small boy a garret in the working-class lodging-house in Denbigh Road, Notting Hill, where she herself lived. 'I don't care who gets in,

I'll get a smack in the eye either way' was Rose's view of politics. 'When they come in saying "Vote for Me", I just laugh.' But Lessing, soon if not already aware of how the pervasive Cold War climate had sent many intellectuals running to (as she later put it) 'The Ivory Tower', was determined to keep a political edge to her life and writing.[14]

Walking in the Shade, Lessing's compelling autobiography about her first 13 years in England, periodically includes brief sections on 'the Zeitgeist, or how we thought then'. Included in the one relating to her early impressions is this quartet:

> Britain was still best: that was so deeply part of how citizens thought, it was taken for granted. Education, food, health, anything at all – best. The British Empire, then on its last legs – the best.
>
> Charity was for ever abolished by the welfare state. Never again would poor people be demeaned by gifts from others. Now we would dismantle all the apparatus of charity, the trusts, the associations, the committees. No more handouts.
>
> In Oxford Street underground, I watched a little bully of an official hectoring and insulting a recently arrived West Indian who could not get the hang of the ticket mechanism. He was exactly like the whites I had watched all my life in Southern Rhodesia shouting at blacks. He was compensating for his own feelings of inferiority.
>
> Everyone from abroad, particularly America, said how gentle, polite – civilized – Britain was.

The evidence suggests that in the late 1940s there was not invariably hostility towards black people. Mass-Observation, for example, reported that among young white factory girls in the cavernous dance halls there was 'great competition to dance with the blacks' on account of 'their superb sense of rhythm'. But at least as often as not, there does seem to have been some degree of prejudice against the 25,000 or so (more than half living in either Cardiff's 'Tiger Bay' dock area or the rundown streets of Liverpool's South End) 'coloured' people in Britain, including Africans, Somalis and Sudanese Arabs as well as West Indians.

A Ministry of Labour survey in early 1949 found that in the Midlands black male workers were placed 'in firms like Lucas, BSA, and Singers on dirty and rough finishing work', but that 'as regards vacancies in building, Post Office, transport, coalmining, railways, clerical, and draughtsmen's work, coloured labour would not be accepted'. As for the employment, just starting, of West Indian women in NHS hospitals, a Home Office memo in March noted that 'it has been found that the susceptibilities of patients tended to set an upper limit on the proportion of coloured workers who could be employed either as nurses or domiciliaries'. Soon afterwards, Harold Nicolson was prevailed upon by his friend Jimmy Mallon, Warden of Toynbee Hall, to give a lecture to the Citizens Council in Whitechapel. 'I dined with him first at the Reform Club, and then we took a taxi to the East End,' Nicolson related to his wife Vita Sackville-West. 'My audience, I regret to say, consists very largely of West Indian negroes, who, it seems, have flooded into London in the hope of high wages. All they get are rude remarks, the denial of white women and a sense that they are shunned.' 'I do not think,' he added, 'that many of the Jamaicans, Haitians and Trinidadians who were present quite understood my elaborate explanation of tolerance and the democratic State.'[15]

By July it was just over a year since the *Empire Windrush* had docked at Tilbury, and during that time there had been only a trickle of further West Indian workers arriving in Britain, perhaps about 600. Even so, there existed sufficient tension for a Colonial Office working party on Britain's black Caribbeans to suggest that month that 'dispersal of these aggregations would lessen the special social problems which result from their presence', thereby enabling them to 'be trained in the British way of life'. At the same time, 'Is There a British Colour Bar?' was the question asked by *Picture Post*'s Robert Kee. He concluded, broadly speaking, that there was – 'invisible, but like Wells' invisible man it is hard and real to the touch . . . and it is when you get lower down the social scale that you find it hits the hardest'. It was, for instance, 'often extremely difficult' for a black man to find a furnished flat or room, and Kee quoted the classic landlady line: 'I wouldn't mind for myself. But there's no telling what the other lodgers might say.' As for getting a job, 'the coloured man meets prejudice in connection with his employment from all classes', including 'the white workers themselves'. Kee's article inspired some supportive letters, including one from the black British athlete McDonald Bailey, but D. R. Smith of Bramham Gardens, SW5, attacked his 'drivelling cant' and asked how he would feel about his daughter marrying a Negro: 'While I am quite prepared to admit that there are many good people in the coloured races, we cannot recognise them by inter-marrying with them or by introducing them into our social life.' G. Carter from Croxley Green, Herts, agreed: 'One can hardly imagine the British people becoming a mulatto nation . . . I believe the best solution is to prevent any large number of coloured people taking up permanent residence in this country. Why import a social problem where one did not previously exist?'

Soon afterwards, in early August, there was an unpleasant episode in the West Midlands when 65 Jamaicans were expelled from Causeway Green Hostel near Oldbury, following attacks on them by the more numerous Poles staying there. 'It is no good arguing about the matter' was the response of one of those expelled, Harold Wilmot, an ex-airman who had been six years in England. 'We are black men, and must bear the black man's burden.' Another, Horace Halliburton, a skilled metal turner who was still looking for work 15 months after arriving in England, wrote an eloquent article for the *Birmingham Gazette*. 'What really annoys my countrymen,' he emphasised, 'is the constant baiting and jeering which is directed at the coloured man. He is unrepresented and invariably victimised.' As evidence, he quoted what an Employment Exchange manager in Birmingham had said to him: 'I am sorry for you. It is talent wasted, but the factories will not employ coloured men. Do not blame us. Blame the management – and they in turn will blame their employees. British workmen do not like sharing their benches with a coloured man and that is an end to it.' 'Even the landladies at boarding-houses will not have us as lodgers,' Halliburton added in confirmation of Kee's finding, before ending on a wrenching, even pitiful note: 'I am heartbroken when I hear mothers point out a coloured man to their children and say: "I'll set the black bogy man on you if you are not well behaved."'[16]

'Very serious dollar situation,' noted Hugh Dalton, senior minister and former Chancellor, in his diary for 15 June 1949, less than two years after the convertibility crisis. 'Cripps says that the danger is that, within twelve months, all our [gold] reserves will be gone. This time there is nothing behind them, and there might well be "a complete collapse of sterling".' Over the next three months there was a curious disjunction: the balance-of-payments position remained dire; international (especially American) confidence in the British economy steadily deteriorated; the country's threadbare reserves continued to drain away; Sir Stafford Cripps authorised a new round of cuts in imports, ie trying to reduce dollar expenditure while formally denying that he intended to devalue sterling; the financial markets operated on the tacit understanding that the currency (long thought to be overvalued at $4.03 to the pound, the rate agreed at the outbreak of war) would be devalued sooner rather than later; and *The Times* published many letters that sought to diagnose the causes of Britain's economic problems. Yet, perhaps because it was summer, there was no great sense of crisis felt by the mass of the population. 'Any visitor hoping to discover what the ordinary Londoner is thinking about the dollar crisis could wear his ear off laying it to the ground, and get no result,' Panter-Downes rather plaintively remarked at the start of September. 'What he is currently talking about is his holiday or the drought or the new price cuts in utility clothing.' She went on:

> Short of the Prime Minister coming to the microphone and saying, 'Sorry, no rations next week,' it is hard to see how the worker can be made to realise that things are critical when, from his angle, they are looking nothing less than prosperous. Though Britain's vital dollar exports are down, their industry is still managing to show every sign of lively good health, to judge by the full employment and increased productivity. Some luxury lines, always the first to feel the pinch, are feeling it, but on the whole the industrial picture is so surprisingly, if deceptively, bright that there is every reason for workers to believe that if this is a crisis, it's the most comfortable crisis they ever took a ride in.[17]

It was enough, she might have added, to make a *Times* letter-writer despair, let alone a government exhorting ever-greater efforts.

The eventual decision to devalue was a slow, painful and at times muddled one, not helped by Cripps being in a Swiss sanatorium for part of July and most of August. The process included a perceived act of double-crossing, a heated discussion about bread, and a critical if predictable non-decision.

In Cripps's prolonged absence, the three ministers left in day-to-day charge of economic matters were Hugh Gaitskell, Harold Wilson and Douglas Jay. Gaitskell and Jay were pro-devaluation, viewing it as preferable to deflation and likely to enhance competitiveness, while Wilson was seemingly of a similar mind. But at a crucial meeting at Chequers, he appeared to be covering his back, leading on Gaitskell's part to a permanent attitude of mistrust towards him. 'What emerged during the summer of 1949,' Wilson's straight-as-a-die adviser Alec Cairncross recalled, 'was Harold's fondness for keeping his options open, his disinclination to say unpalatable things to his colleagues, his tendency to see economic issues in purely political terms (in this case, the date of the next election) and, most of all, his deviousness.'

On 12 September, just over a fortnight after the Cabinet had reluctantly concluded that there was no alternative to devaluation, Cripps and Ernest Bevin were both in the British Embassy at Washington, where together they decided what the new fixed value of sterling should be. Among those present was the Treasury's Sir Edwin Plowden:

> There were two rates put forward, $2.80 and $3.00, and I think the majority of us felt that $2.80 was the right rate. When we went upstairs to a meeting in Ernie Bevin's sitting room, he'd been ill and he was still in his dressing gown and pyjamas. Stafford was there and his view was that $3.00 was the right rate and we argued for the lower rate. Ernie then turned to me and said, 'What effect will this have on the price of the standard loaf of bread?' Fortunately, thinking he would ask this, I'd sent a cable to the Treasury asking what effect it will have. It was a penny. We put that forward and he said, 'Oh all right, but I hope we can have a whiter loaf. It makes me belch, this stuff.' So it wasn't the $2.80 argument that was decided, it was the price of bread that decided it.

So, $2.80 it was – but in the event, without (to Bevin's regret and Cripps's nutritional satisfaction) going back to the pre-war white loaf. 'When they looked into the cost,' Cairncross subsequently explained, 'it turned out that there would be more dollars involved because they would have to buy offal and throw it away and need more flour, so to speak, than otherwise and that caused the Treasury to oppose it.'

The non-decision was the failure to give serious consideration to the economic merits of floating the pound, so that it no longer had a fixed value that had to be defended at nearly all costs. But for the instinctively *dirigiste* Cripps and his fellow-ministers, such a market-oriented policy was almost beyond the bounds of rationality. 'If by a floating rate its sponsors mean to imply that all our exchange and import controls should be taken off and the pound allowed to find its own level,' he told the Commons soon after devaluation, 'we could not possibly think of such a course.'[18]

Cripps announced devaluation to the nation on the evening of Sunday, 18 September. After an explanation of what he was doing and why, together with a 'most earnest' appeal to manufacturers and exporters to 'redouble their efforts' and an insistence that 'this is a step that we cannot and shall not repeat', there was one passage in his broadcast that had a particular resonance:

> We have decided upon these steps because we are determined not to try and solve our problem at the cost of heavy unemployment, or by attacking the social services that have been expanded over the last few years. This drastic change is the only alternative and it offers us a chance of a great success, but only if we all play the game and do not try to take advantage of one another; if we take fair shares of our difficulties as well as of our benefits.

Different listeners reacted in different ways. 'Cripps very parsonical in an evangelical sort of way,' thought Malcolm Muggeridge, while for Vere Hodgson it was 'a lot of meaningless soft soap', though she added that 'he was upset to announce it'. The unforgiving Kenneth Preston in Keighley recorded grimly that 'Cripps has had to eat his words' and reflected that 'the dollar has come to assume such an importance in our lives at present that, as Vallance [his local vicar] said this morning [ie in church], the dollar bill, in the minds of some people, has come to take the place formerly occupied by God as the universal provider'. For one diarist, as no doubt for many other listeners, the global seamlessly merged into the local. 'It sounded like a schoolmaster explaining citizenship to young people,' noted Gladys Langford. 'I cannot believe people will respond to his plea for more and more effort. They have been offered nothing but disappointment for so long. I wonder how long before Mr Lee raises our rents?'

In her next letter to the *The New Yorker*, Panter-Downes described the wider impact:

The devaluation of the pound went off like a bomb that you can hear coming but that makes you jump just the same. The public is still rocking from the startling effects of the explosion, unsure as to whether things will be looking better or worse when, eventually, the smoke clears. Certainly a good deal of the shock proceeded from the fact that the Chancellor had become identified in most people's mind with the maintaining of the precious pound sterling. All his utterances on the subject had given the impression that he intended to stand or fall with it. Though making allowances for the necessary lack of frankness preceding the operation, even those Britons who expected devaluation seem somewhat astonished by the briskness with which he has bent the pound, not to mention its staggering new angle.

The morning after, Cripps himself held a large press conference, at which, according to Panter-Downes, he 'looked far more a spruce figure at a wedding, come to give away a cherished daughter, than a coroner sitting on the facts of a sensational demise'. Indeed, 'the assembled journalists hadn't a chance against a fascinating performance that crackled with good humor and vigor'. Nevertheless, whatever the economic arguments in its favour, the very fact of devaluation inevitably had powerful connotations of volte-face and humiliation. These were not connotations that any political party would want to be associated with twice in living memory.

The day that Panter-Downes wrote her letter, Thursday the 22nd, saw the staging at Wembley of the first World Speedway Championship since the war. No fewer than 500,000 cinder-track fans applied for the 85,000 tickets on sale in advance. It was a sport that had been invented only in the late 1920s, gates in the current season were already up by more than a million on the previous year, and 16 riders were due to compete for speedway's greatest honour, never previously won by a home rider. The *Daily Mirror* headline the next day celebrated a triumphant outcome: '93,000 Cheer The New Speed King – An Englishman!' Tommy Price had won all five races, and for 'a wildly cheering crowd' the question of a new exchange rate was, for a few hours anyway, neither here nor there.[19]

4

A Decent Way of Life

'I was sorry myself to miss Wilfred,' Nella Last in Barrow noted in her diary on 14 October 1949 (ten days after her sixtieth birthday) about missing that Friday evening's edition of *Have a Go*, starring the great Pickles – probably the most popular man in the country. 'It's not just that I like his handling of people, it's the "genuine" feeling I get – of homely every day people, with humour, courage & ideals as steadfast as ever, in spite of all the talk of "decadence", slacking, problem youth, etc, etc, which seems so insistently brought to sight nowadays, in press, books & cinema.' The next afternoon, 37,978 squeezed into Meadow Lane to watch Notts County trounce the visitors Bristol City 4–1. Tommy Lawton at centre forward was 'his usual brilliant self', according to the local reporter, A. E. Botting, and scored County's fourth after 'a typical solo burst'. One watchful presence in the exultant crowd was probably Alan Sillitoe, who transmuted the experience into a short story, 'The Match', with County going down to a bitter defeat. As the mist rolls in from the Trent and it becomes impossible to see the advertising boards above the stands 'telling of pork pies, ales, whisky, cigarettes and other delights of Saturday night', one of the characters bites his lip with anger. '"Bloody team. They'd even lose at blow football." A woman behind, swathed in a thick woollen scarf coloured white and black like the Notts players, who had been screaming herself hoarse in support of the home team all the afternoon, was almost in tears: "Foul! Foul! Get the dirty lot off the field. Send 'em back to Bristol where they came from. Foul! Foul I tell yer."' Still, whatever a weekend's ups and downs, there was always *Variety Bandbox* on Sunday evening, with some 20 million regularly tuning in. 'Now, ah, Ladies and Gentle-*men*,' began the star turn's 'lion tamer' monologue on the 16th. 'Harken. Now – harken. This is, no – harken! Now har-*ken*! *Har-ever-so-ken!* Now, that's the life: the circus! What? That's the life! If you live. I know! What? I'm telling you this. *Liss-en*! There's one phase in my life, there's one phase – and I never forget a phase! Ha ha ha ha! Every gag fresh from the quipperies!'¹ The script was by Eric Sykes, and for the intense, insecure man delivering his lines, Frankie Howerd, these were golden days.

It was a month since devaluation. 'Everybody is waiting to hear what cuts & changes the Gov. will make on Mon.,' noted Marian Raynham in Surbiton on Saturday the 22nd. 'Attlee will speak. It is supposed to be drastic & touch us all. People fearing clothes rationing have been buying a lot.' Two days later did Attlee indeed speak to the nation, outlining expenditure cuts amounting to some £250 million and emphasising that his government had 'sought to make them in such a way as not to impair seriously the great structure of social services which has been built up and which we intend to preserve'. The package included reductions in capital (including housing and education) and defence expenditure, but one listener, Judy Haines, naturally saw it from the point of view of a Chingford housewife trying like everyone else to make ends meet. 'More austerity to cope with devaluation of £,' she recorded. 'Drs prescriptions 1/ – or what they're worth if less; dried egg dearer; decontrol of fish prices.' The most controversial aspect was the new intention, barely 15 months into the life of the NHS, to charge for prescriptions. A swiftly taken Gallup poll revealed that although 44 per cent were opposed to this policy shift, as many as 51 per cent agreed with it. Overall, reckoned Anthony Heap in St Pancras, the expenditure cuts – 'anxiously awaited' for the previous two or three weeks – were 'in no way as alarming as we'd been led to expect'. Given that a general election was due within the next nine months, it would have been surprising if they had been.

Life, though, remained difficult enough in the last autumn of the 1940s. 'Wanted: A Housewives' Strike' was the provocative title of a *Picture Post* article in late October, detailing the high prices of everyday items compared with pre-war and producing a predictable flood of supportively indignant readers' letters. 'One of the biggest rackets at the present time is the high price of sanitary towels, surely an absolute necessity,' wrote Mrs Laurel Garrad from Weston-super-Mare. 'Is it possible to organise a real nation-wide housewives' strike?' Joan Comyns from Carshalton, for all her similar anger, thought not: 'Pans have to be bought to cook for one's family; darning wool must be paid for, or children go sockless to school; string is necessary to tie up parcels to send to loved ones. I have tried to strike about face towels, and have cut up every conceivable bit of garment which might do for them. Tell me, how can we strike, except by continually placing worried heads in gas ovens?' The middle class, as ever, was at the cutting edge of the masochism that accompanied austerity's trials and tribulations. 'Excellent women enjoying discomfort – one bar of a small electric fire, huddled in coats,' the soon-to-be-published Barbara Pym, still living in Pimlico, suggestively jotted in her notebook in November. For that questionably excellent man, Henry St John, it was not so much self-abnegation as grumbling that remained a way of life. 'I had a poor lunch in Lyons' cafeteria at Hammersmith,' he recorded about the same time, 'where a clearer-up told me trays were to be put in a "rack", by which she meant a trolley.' Not long afterwards, on 8 December, a young Czech woman arrived in England, staying in the capital for a few days before travelling north:

> There were still bombed-out ruins all over London, and the post-war drabness was far worse than that in Prague. The English women I saw walking about London seemed to me sloppily dressed, with scarves tied round their heads and cigarettes hanging from their lips. The shops, too, were a great disappointment to me. I had expected wonderful shops, but most of what I saw in London shop windows seemed to me to be shoddy stuff, with little attempt to display it elegantly.[2]

These recollections belonged to Olga Cannon, recently married to the determined, high-minded Les Cannon, Lancashire's representative on the executive of the Electrical Trades Union and still a fully committed Communist.

For some 6,000 people, most of them young, 1949 was the year of being struck down by polio – in 657 cases fatally. Ian Dury was seven when in August he contracted it in the open-air swimming pool at Southend: 'I then went to my granny's in Cornwall for a couple of weeks' holiday, an incubation period, and it developed. I spent six weeks in an isolation hospital in Truro, because I was infectious. I was encased in plaster, both arms and both legs. My mum came down on the milk train and they said I was going to die but I rallied round after six months in the Royal Cornish Infirmary. They took me back to Essex on a stretcher.' His left side remained paralysed for a time, and thereafter he walked with a pronounced limp. Another victim, Julian Critchley, was eighteen when one Saturday morning in early November he 'set out to walk to John Barnes, the department store next to Finchley Road tube station, but felt so ill I was compelled to turn back and make my way home'. By Tuesday, after three feverish days in bed and with his left leg much the weaker, it was clear that he had what his anxious parents had not brought themselves to say aloud. 'It is hard to exaggerate how frightened people were of polio,' he recalled many years later about a disease of which for a long time from 1947 there was a serious outbreak every summer:

In August, swimming-pools would be closed [but presumably not in Southend] as a precaution; the press would be full of speculation as to its cause; at one time it was believed that the virus was spread by excrement deposited on railway lines by passing trains. There was no cure; no way in which the paralysis, which occurred once the fever diminished, could be halted; it could lead to death by suffocation or, even worse, a life imprisoned in an iron lung. I was fortunate; the paralysis stopped at my right buttock, robbing me of the ability to run (I could not stand on tip-toe on my right leg) and withering the calf and thigh.

Critchley was back from hospital by Christmas, but for many there were long weeks (or more) in the dreaded iron lung – a huge, fearsome contraption that made the patient feel he or she was being buried alive – followed by almost punitive physiotherapy, with little or no allowance made for human frailty. 'I'm not having any bent cripples going out of this ward' was how one specialist put it to a young sufferer, Marjorie Crothers. 'You will go out vertical if it kills both of us.' Across in the United States, whose greatest President had been stricken by polio, the race was on to produce an effective vaccine, but no one knew when or if that might happen.

Mercifully, most children were polio-free. For Judy Haines's two little girls, late November brought the novelty of a double pushchair. 'Joy of joys!' their mother wrote (on the same Tuesday as St John's unsatisfactory meal at Lyons):

> My dear Mother-in-law came round & minded children, washed up, prepared vegetables & did ironing while I went to Percival's, High St & bought cream and fawn folding car for £7.15. 8d. It's just what I've dreamed of (except colour, which was all they had). I can tuck babes up in travelling rug & use the cushion-covers I embroidered & take them out in all weathers. Oh I'm so thrilled ! It's coming tomorrow. *Do* hope it does.

It did. 'Oh happy day! Lucky me!' she gleefully recorded. For small children everywhere that winter, there were two new delights that between them would go a long way to defining a whole era of childhood. Enid Blyton's latest creation, hard on the heels of the Secret Seven, included (in her explanatory words to her publisher) not only 'toys, pixies, goblins, Toyland, brick-houses, dolls houses, toadstool houses, market-places' but also 'Noddy (the little nodding man), Big Ears the Pixie, and Mr and Mrs Tubby (the teddy bears)'. First up in the series was *Little Noddy Goes to Toyland*, seductively illustrated by a Dutch artist, Harmsen Van Der Beek; it and its rapidly produced successors were soon selling by the million. Then on the third Monday of 1950, at 1.45 p.m. on the Light Programme, were heard these even more seductive words: 'Are you sitting comfortably? Then I'll begin.' There followed a quarter of an hour of stories and deliberately rather pedestrianly sung songs – a hit from the start. 'First reports indicate that *Listen with Mother*, the programme for "under fives", is being received with enthusiasm by little children,' noted BBC audience research in March. 'We know of one small boy who said to his mother at breakfast, "Aren't you e' sited when *Listen with Mother* comes on?" and of another who fairly pushes his mother out of the room at 1.44 each day on the grounds that the programme is not for her!'[3]

On 17 December, almost exactly a month before *Listen with Mother*'s debut, the great childminder of the future had taken another big step forward. 'Television Marches On' declared the *Listener* in an editorial to mark the opening at Sutton Coldfield of 'the world's biggest and most advanced television station' – the BBC's first high-power transmitter outside the London area, bringing television into the orbit of much of the Midlands. Advance local reaction was distinctly nervous. 'Change in our habits television will certainly bring,' reckoned one Birmingham paper. 'Let us hope, however, that the change will be less drastic than is feared.' Another expressed only quasi-confidence that 'if it is necessary in some households to exercise some form of disciplinary restraint, it should be possible to do this without overmuch wrangling' – in which regard 'the setting aside of a television room may be advisable'. Unsurprisingly, the press was out in force on the opening evening, a Saturday. 'No more snooker at the club for me if there's sport or opera being televised,' declared Mr H. A. Catton of 63 Silhill Hall Road, Solihull; over in Warwards Lane, Selly Oak, not only did Mrs M. Walker profess herself 'absolutely amazed' and predict that 'this will be the death knell of the cinemas,' but in the next-door house six-year-old Martin Woodhams resolutely refused to budge from his seat until ten o'clock. For the moment at least, Norman Collins spoke in vain as Controller of Television: 'Please don't let the children view too much. At least send the little beasts to bed when the time comes.'

The new transmitter marked a significant stage in the television audience becoming more representative of society as a whole, but the fact remained that by the end of March 1950 there were still only 343,882 sets in the country, in other words in fewer than one home in 20. Nevertheless, given that the total number of sets a year earlier had been a mere 126,567, there could be little doubt that television was the coming medium. Writing not long before the Sutton Coldfield opening in the *BBC Quarterly* (a revealingly self-important title), the director-general, Sir William Haley, fondly anticipated the time when television would result in something 'which, working with all the other beneficent influences within the community, will have the capacity to make for a broader vision and a fuller life'. The *Listener*, in its by now well-accustomed role as cultural watchdog, naturally agreed: 'That the extended service now opening will bring a fresh pleasure to thousands is hardly to be doubted. That television, as it spreads, may bring about a keener, more sensitive, and more intelligent appreciation on the part of all who see it of the world about us – this is a hope that cannot be too often

emphasised.' Early in the New Year, the BBC's newly established Television Panel (of about 2,500, from almost 25,000 applications) started
watching programmes in order to provide the Corporation with feed-
back. 'A very high proportion of sets,' reported the first bulletin on
its activities, 'are switched on for the main Light Entertainment show
on Saturday nights', notably *Vic Oliver Introduces* – not quite what
Haley had in mind. In one home in Chingford, all such concerns were
purely academic. 'The girls draw up their chairs for a Hopalong Cassidy
film,' noted Judy Haines on 9 January, 'but the Demonstration Film
(with a visit to the zoo) remains their favourite.'[4]

The people's will was about to be expressed. Florence Speed in
Brixton noted caustically on New Year's Day how 'for the forthcoming
election, several things have been taken off points [rationing] for the
period starting today' – including 'canned meat puddings, canned pork
hash or sausage meat, boneless chicken, turkey, rabbit, spaghetti &
sausages in tomato sauce, vegetable & macaroni casserole, canned tomatoes, snoek & mackerel'. Three days later, Michael Young in Labour's
research department wrote to his Dartington benefactors, the Elmhirsts.
'What on earth am I doing hurling myself into this election organisation,
thinking out ways of outwitting the Tories?' he asked. 'And yet I do
so much want this odd, pedestrian, earthy and loveable Party to win.
I am fearful of what would happen to our society if the Conservatives
succeed. And they may.' Eventually, on the 10th, Attlee formally
announced that the general election would be held on Thursday, 23
February. He and Herbert Morrison would have preferred to go in
May, by when it might have been possible to deration petrol, but his
Chancellor, the ailing Stafford Cripps, was adamant that it would be
immoral to deliver a budget just before an election – and threatened
to resign over the issue. Such was Cripps's standing in the country,
even after devaluation, that Attlee felt he had no alternative but to
yield to Cripps's wishes. But as he remarked privately and with some
asperity of his colleague, 'He's no judge of politics.'[5]

The election was not yet in full swing when on the 26th at the
Old Bailey a 29-year-old 'company director' called Donald Hume
– in reality a spiv who specialised in aerial smuggling, of goods or
people or currency – was found not guilty of murdering Stanley
Setty, a used-car dealer, but was given 12 years for being an accessory

after the fact. The verdict came some three months after the discovery of Setty's headless and legless body in a parcel floating in the marshes at Tillingham, Essex. Hume was a member of the United Services Flying Club at Elstree, and while denying the murder, he admitted that he had dropped the parcel from his plane. 'For no other reason than for money, the sum of £150,' declared the judge in sentencing him, 'you were prepared to take parts of a body and keep the torso in your flat [above a greengrocers' shop in the Finchley Road] overnight, and then take it away and put it in the Thames Estuary.' A manifestly sensational case, it received massive press coverage – and hardly suggested that the quality of the English murder was in decline. As it happened, George Orwell's funeral took place at Christ Church, Albany Street (lesson chosen by Anthony Powell, clergyman 'excessively parsonical', coffin poignantly long) on the same bitterly cold Thursday as the verdict on Hume.

The case almost entirely overshadowed another murder trial earlier in the month. On the 13th, also at the Old Bailey, a mentally backward 29-year-old lorry driver called Timothy Evans – originally from near Merthyr Tydfil but for the previous two years living at 10 Rillington Place, a tiny house in a cul-de-sac near Ladbroke Grove Tube station – was found guilty of murdering his pregnant wife and one-year-old daughter. In effect the police had had to identify as the murderer either Evans or the occupant of the ground-floor flat, John ('Reg') Christie, a 51-year-old Yorkshireman who during the war had served for four years as a special constable based at Harrow Road police station. Perhaps inevitably, they chose to believe in the innocence of the former copper. Some five weeks after the trial, Evans had his appeal dismissed by Lord Chief Justice Goddard and his colleagues, and on 9 March, at Pentonville Prison, he was hanged by Albert Pierrepoint. His last words to his mother and sister were the same: 'Christie done it.'[6]

The Blue Lamp premiered less than a week after Evans had been sent down. Starring Jack Warner as a kindly, imperturbable, home-loving, pipe-smoking, begonia-growing veteran police constable called George Dixon – attached to Paddington Green station, less than two miles from Rillington Place – it was dedicated to the British Police Service and unquestioningly endorsed its fight against crime. Early on, the maturely authoritative voice-over sets out the film's defining context. After referring to childhoods in homes 'broken and demoralised by war', the male voice goes on:

> These restless and ill-adjusted youngsters have produced a type of delinquent which is partly responsible for the post-war increase in crime. Some are content with pilfering and petty theft. Others, with more bravado, graduate to serious offences. Youths with brain enough to plan and organise criminal adventures and yet who lack the code, experience and self-discipline of the professional thief – which sets them as a class apart, all the more dangerous because of their immaturity. Young men such as these two present a new problem to the police.

The two in question are Tom Riley (played by Dirk Bogarde) and his sidekick. The film turns on the scene, roughly halfway through, in which, in the course of robbing a box office in a Harrow Road cinema, Riley fatally guns down Dixon. The rest of the film is about getting Riley, who is finally hunted down in a remarkable closing sequence, partly shot during an actual greyhound race meeting at the White City stadium. It is as if *everyone* – police, bookmakers, tic-tac men, the crowd itself – is united in the pursuit of not just a criminal but a transgressor. 'Riley's real crime has not been the killing of P.C. Dixon,' one cultural historian, Andy Medhurst, has acutely noted, 'but his refusal to accept his station, his youthful disregard for established hierarchies, his infatuation with American culture.' There was, Medhurst adds, no place in the British cinema of the early 1950s for 'charismatic, sexy, insolent, on-the-make individualists'. Instead, the film is a hymn to shared values – of decency, of honest hard work, of understated humour and emotion, indeed of the whole Orwellian 'English' package, minus of course the politics. Or as Dixon puts it when confronted with a difficult situation, 'I think we could all do with a nice cup of tea.'

The reviews were generally positive. Gavin Lambert, the young and already unforgiving editor of *Sight and Sound*, used the film as a vehicle in his campaign against mainstream British cinema, while *The Times* suggested that its depiction of policemen was unduly indulgent. But

Woman's Own spoke for the majority in praising an 'extraordinarily vivid, realistic and exciting story'. At least three London diarists saw it. Gladys Langford 'enjoyed it' but thought Jimmy Hanley 'badly cast for the young policeman'; Grace Golden called it an 'excellent film' and reckoned Bogarde 'very good as young crook who accidentally murders a policeman – the inevitable Jack Warner'; and Anthony Heap, an assiduous cineaste, found it 'at least as tense and thrilling as all but the very best American gangster films – and for an all-British effort, that's darned good going'. Some six months after the film's release, Mass-Observation's questioning of its panel demonstrated a similar gender pattern of reaction to that of *Scott of the Antarctic*: 'Men weeping (or at least gulping) at moments of reserve (the Hanley character painfully breaking the news to the initially stoical but soon distraught Mrs Dixon), women at moments of parting and loss (the murder itself)'. What is surprisingly difficult, though, is to find contemporary evidence backing the conventional wisdom that *The Blue Lamp* scandalised its audiences – whether in terms of the murdered policeman or language (including reputedly the first use of 'bastard' in a British film) or the Bogarde character as an American-style punk. Still, it was revealing that within weeks of release Bogarde was making a guest appearance on *Variety Bandbox* as a violent criminal. 'Now come along, Mr Bogarde,' twittered Howerd. 'You must take that mask off. Oh, *dear*! You have given me such a *shock*!'[7]

According to Ted Willis, who co-wrote the story on which *The Blue Lamp*'s script was based, the inspiration for George Dixon was one Inspector Mott, whom Willis watched in action for several weeks. 'A middle-aged officer who had risen through the ranks', he 'had spent years in his East End manor, seemed to know every crack in every pavement and was instantly recognised and greeted respectfully by half the population'. He was also kindly, understood human psychology and could be tough if need be. This emphasis on local knowledge – acquired only through pounding the beat – certainly came through strongly in a study made in the early 1950s by John Mays of a police division in a working-class part of Liverpool. Not only was it 'felt by many men that the sight of the uniformed constable constantly patrolling his beat had considerable preventive value', but it was 'agreed that nothing could replace the constable moving on foot in a limited area, knowing the alleys and backways where patrol cars could not penetrate, familiar with the people and knowing many of them by name and address'. Indeed, almost half the police officers interviewed by Mays revealed that they were 'fairly often consulted by inhabitants of the district on matters that were not purely police concerns':

> The man on the beat is often asked in to help settle some family dispute or to adjudicate in an argument. Matrimonial advice is often sought where husbands and wives are at loggerheads. One of the boys may be insolent and so the policeman is asked to speak to him. One constable said he was asked to thrash a boy for his mother but wisely declined. A woman will stop a policeman on his beat and ask him how to apply for assistance or how to bring a complaint against a landlord. Does he know a club where Charlie could go to at night? Is 14/6 a week a legal rent for their sort of house?

There were signs, though, that a new, less intimate style of policing was starting to evolve. The pioneer city was Aberdeen, where since April 1948 there had been a system of so-called 'team policing', whereby an area of traditionally ten beats was instead policed by a single team, comprising four constables and a sergeant, with a police car with two-way radio ready to be summoned to any trouble spot. Over the next few years, this was an experiment copied in several other cities (Mays in Liverpool referred to 'the increased use of motor patrols') but for the most part only if a force was suffering from recruitment difficulties. The evidence is that the great majority of chief constables much preferred, if at all possible, to rely on what Bolton's chief constable called in 1951 'the traditional system of beat working'. It was, in the words of a historian of the police, 'a conception of policing that placed overriding emphasis on prevention rather than the detection of crime' – and, crucially, it assumed close, continuous and broadly harmonious contact between the police and the policed.[8]

'What do you think of the police?' was one of the questions asked in a remarkable survey of English behaviour and attitudes undertaken by the anthropologist-cum-sociologist Geoffrey Gorer in the winter of 1950/51. His sample comprised some 11,000 readers of the *People*, a Sunday paper with an almost entirely working-class and lower-middle-class readership; his expectation in advance was that 'a very considerable number of the respondents would take advantage of the anonymous questionnaire to express feelings of hostility to the representatives of the state, of law and order, of the repressive aspects of society'.

He could hardly have been more wrong. Less than a fifth of the sample had any criticisms at all to make, prompting Gorer to conclude that (more or less equally across class, age, gender and region) 'there is extremely little hostility to the police as an institution'; from many, there was positive enthusiasm:

> I believe they stand for all we English are, maybe at first appearance slow perhaps, but reliable stout and kindly. I have the greatest admiration for our police force and I am proud they are renowned abroad. (*Married woman, 28, Formby*)
>
> The finest body of men of this kind in the world. Portraying and upholding the time tested constitution, traditions and democracy of the British Way of Life combining humble patience with high courage and devotion to duty. (*Married man, 38, New Malden*)
>
> Underpaid and overworked in dealing with masses of petty bureaucracy. Admire them for the results they get, and also for surprisingly little evidence of 'fiddling' among the Police force itself. (*Unmarried civil servant, 30, Surbiton*)
>
> Oh I like them. I wish I could marry one. (*Unmarried girl, 18, London*)

As for the dissenting minority, Gorer noted that their criticisms were 'mostly on points of character or behaviour, that the police as individuals are "no better than anybody else", and the human failings of persons in the police'. For instance:

> I think the police in big towns and cities do a grand job and their work is hard, but in villages such as this we become their friends and they ours, and they often turn a blind eye. (*Married woman, 21, village near Newark*)
>
> Majority of them show off when in uniform as if everyone should be afraid of them. Yet they seem kind and considerate to children. My children love to say Hello to Policemen and it isn't very often they are ignored. (*Mother, 24, Birmingham*)

Too much time is taken up with minor traffic offences on the roads.
Freemasonry should be barred in the Police Force. (*Man, 26, Sidcup*)

'Some 5 per cent of the population is really hostile to the police,' Gorer
reckoned, 'and with about 1 per cent of these the hostility reaches an
almost pathological level.' Tellingly, he added, little of this hostility
was political in nature but rather stemmed from 'the belief that they
misuse their power, are unscrupulous, avaricious or dishonest'. And
Gorer, who could speak with some authority, declared his belief that
such suspicions 'would be much more widely voiced in most other
societies'.[9] It was, all in all, a graphically consensual picture that this
aspect of his survey evoked.

The Blue Lamp was equally topical in terms of the prevailing moral
panic about youth into which it so deftly tapped. 'Rarely a day passes
now without some act of criminal violence being committed,' noted
Anthony Heap in March 1950: 'Gangs of young teen-age thugs,
emulating the American gangster "heroes" they see regularly on the
screen, go around "coshing", robbing, and beating-up people with
impunity. And on the few occasions when some are caught, what sort
of punishment do they get? The good flogging [made illegal in 1948,
along with birching] they so richly deserve? Oh dear no! That's too
"degrading". It might hurt their feelings.' 'Women are quite nervous
to go out alone after dark – a thing quite unknown before,' observed
Vere Hodgson in west London soon afterwards. 'You do not need to
have thousands of pounds of jewellery in your bag,' she added about
her particular fear of being 'yammed on the head with a Cosh' by
youths. 'They will yam you for 3½d and think it is all fun ... I agree
with the Birch.'

Was the immensely popular daily radio thriller, *Dick Barton*, an
unintentional stimulus to juvenile delinquency – unintentional because
Barton himself was a detective of impeccably upright language and
lifestyle? Ever conscious of its responsibilities, the BBC in early 1950
sent out a questionnaire to more than 70 child-guidance clinics about
the possible effects of the series. Several replies expressed concern:

Nightmares and undue mental tension are produced in some children ...
The educational value seems poor ... Many of them look on Barton as

a fool who gets away with too much, and miss the moral issues raised. (*Portman Clinic, W1*)

It fills a vacuum but it is not constructive. There is no indication that years of strenuous preparation precede heroic exploits. The characters are shadowy. The heroes are complementary to 'spivs', rather than their opposites. (*Department of Psychological Medicine, The Hospital for Sick Children, Great Ormond Street*)

The fact that the child listens to Dick Barton is frequently mentioned by mothers of over-anxious children. (*Child Guidance Clinic, Chatham*)

Generally, though, the experts took a reasonably robust line – 'It is a useful medium for the projection of phantasy,' asserted the Royal Hospital for Sick Children in Edinburgh – and by almost two to one they voted for the programme's continuation. Henceforth, though, each episode was lumbered with a gratuitous tailpiece, in which a voice-over solemnly mulled over the moral issues that had been raised – a device that perhaps hastened the programme's end in 1951.

Juvenile delinquency, although undoubtedly a real phenomenon, was almost certainly not as widespread as the moral panic imagined. One suggestive fact is that out of 1,315 working-class Glasgow boys who left school in January 1947, just over 12 per cent had been or would be convicted in the courts at least once between their eighth and eighteenth birthdays. Analysing the lives and outcomes of these boys over the three years after they left school, Thomas Ferguson (Professor of Public Health at Glasgow University) identified the main factors behind juvenile crime: low academic ability, employment problems, bad housing and criminal habits or tendencies in the family background. These were hardly unexpected findings, but the research was full and convincing.

However, where one gets closer to the subjects themselves is through John Mays, Warden of Liverpool University Settlement, who in 1950, before his work on the police, embarked on an in-depth study of 80 boys growing up in an impoverished, rundown area of central Liverpool. The majority of his sample admitted having committed 'delinquent acts' at some point during childhood and adolescence, with 30 having been convicted at least once and with 13 as the most common age for acts of delinquency. Mays's findings were significant – emphasising the malfunctioning family and the importance of group solidarity in temporarily overriding individual conscience – but the real value of his study was, rather like Ferdynand Zweig's, in the psychological depth of his case studies. Take one, with the interviewee probably in his mid- to late teens:

He has never appeared at a Juvenile Court but has committed offences which might very well have brought him there if he had been less lucky. All his delinquencies are typical of the pattern for the neighbourhood and were steadily but not excessively indulged in. He said 'we' used to steal fruit regularly from a shop on the way to school in the afternoon. When on holidays he shop-lifted in the company of other boys. Woolworths at— — was mentioned. He has also stolen from a large Liverpool store and described how parties of schoolboys used to set off for town on a Saturday morning with the intention of shop-lifting. They carried with them a supply of paper bags so that they could wrap up the stolen goods and pass them off as purchases. The stealing was worked by a team with the usual 'dowses' and attention-engagers posted. He added some points on the ethics of shop-lifting. He 'wouldn't think twice' about stealing things from a large store because 'they rob you' by 'their fantastic prices'. However, he gradually broke away from such activities because had he been caught his mother would have been very upset and this acted as a deterrent. He did a lot of lorry-skipping but never took anything off the back. This he attributed to the fact that he knew that the driver would be held responsible and he felt sorry for him and didn't want to cause him suffering. In the big stores he did not feel conscious of a similar personal relationship with the assistants behind the counter and did not think they would have to make good any losses.

Significantly, almost all of Mays's interviewees were members of a youth club; he conceded that 'the many young people who are at present inaccessible to research because they have never, and will never, submit themselves to the restraints of formal association are more deeply committed to delinquent habits than the youths who have co-operated in this project'.[10]

An array of different residential institutions sought to reform these delinquents. 'There can be no finer calling than that of moulding and fashioning the character of a wayward boy . . . and the ultimate realisation of the useful purpose of life,' declared Harold Hamer, President of the Association of Headmasters, Headmistresses and Matrons of Approved Schools, at its annual conference in 1950. Two years later, a member of staff at High Beech, a probation home in Nutfield, Surrey, for male juvenile delinquents, agreed: 'We are trying to turn out good citizens and good men . . . we are not just a place of detention.' Or, in the words of that home's mission statement (formulated in 1949), its purpose was to provide 'the means whereby young offenders from unsatisfactory homes, who do not require prolonged periods of re-education [ie in an Approved School], may learn to discipline their lives and to develop qualities of character'. On the basis of a close study of High Beech's records, as well as the revealing if sometimes sententious monthly issues of the *Approved Schools Gazette*, Abigail Wills has concluded that by the 1950s 'the project of reforming male delinquents centred around the notion of *mens sana in corpore sano* (a healthy mind in a healthy body), which involved ideals such as strength of character, emotional independence, restrained hetero-sexuality and disciplined work ethic' – a set of ideals ultimately 'conceived in terms of the reclamation of delinquents "for the nation"'.

In practice, a high premium continued to be placed on conformity, and in practice also, some of these residential institutions could be brutal in the extreme. In the rather patchy report on juvenile delinquency that he submitted for Mass-Observation in 1949, H. D. Willcock quoted the experience of a 14-year-old at an Approved School some distance from London: 'One Sunday morning we went for a walk in the country and one boy with us messed his trousers, and, when we got back, the officer took his trousers off and rubbed them all over his face. The stuff went into his eyes, his mouth, and his hair, so that you could not see his face from the brown mess.' Once, after trying to escape, the 14-year-old was summoned to the governor's office:

First he started by getting hold of me by the hair and giving me two black eyes. He then kicked me in the stomach and winded me. I ran to the fireplace and picked up a poker and threatened to hit him with it. Then two officers pounced on me and held me down whilst the Head beat me something terrible. When I got to my feet it was only to be knocked down by a terrific blow on the mouth. He then laid me across a chair and gave me fourteen strokes with the cane on the back and backside. After this he took off his coat and belted me all round the office. I must have lost consciousness because I remember coming round crying, 'Father, father, stop, stop.' I was completely out of my head. When he had finished beating me he led me down to the showers, kicking me all the way.

'Strange and improbable as such accounts may seem,' commented Willcock, 'this one is not unique in our files.' And after citing 'the case of the six boys in a northern Approved School who shot a master – and intended to murder the Head', he remarked, 'That school is probably an admirable one. But of others we hear fearful things.'[11]

It is clear that young people generally were increasingly being perceived as a social category – and social problem – of their own. 'Was talking to a Hoxton greengrocer this morning who was inveighing against the behaviour of children of today,' noted Gladys Langford in June 1949:

He said he heard a noise of cheering last winter after he had closed and opened his door to find some little girls of 8 or 9 lying on their backs with boys of 12 or 13 lying on top of them indulging in sex play – or even worse. He also said when he drove back thro' Epping Forest the other night, by the Rising Sun among the bushes several little girls about 13 with faces mock made up were lying with boys & men in very abandoned attitudes. He blames the lack of home-life due to married women's going to work. He says the Council provides houses but the homes no longer exist.

The nation's youth, and not just its delinquent portion, became the object of sociological scrutiny. Mark Abrams, investigating leisure habits as early as 1947, found in a national survey of boys aged 16 to 20 that no fewer than 23 per cent said they spent their spare time doing 'Nothing'. When Abrams specifically asked young people in a London borough how they had spent the previous evening, almost a third had been in either the cinema or the dance hall. In the spring of 1949, two researchers from the Social Medical Research Unit sought to investigate 'the physical, mental and social health' of 85 males living in a particular outer London borough and born between April and June 1931 – or, in the study's evocative title, 'Rising Eighteen in a London Suburb'. Their fieldwork did not contribute hugely to national uplift. Among only eight was 'an outstanding aptitude, or strong interest in a specific subject, the main influence in deciding their choice of job'; most of the labourers and machine-minders concentrated their future hopes on 'unrealistic dreams of becoming champion cyclists, football stars or dance-band leaders'; the 'lack of creative or constructive leisure pursuits of these lads' was 'striking', with 'very few signs of any awakening interest in wider civic or community activities'; in terms of sexual mores, 'the majority did not acknowledge the older sanctions of formal engagement and marriage'; and as for mental health, 'a good deal of emotional disturbance was found'. Overall, the picture of these 18-year-old boys was one of 'physically fit young men' in a state of 'passive acceptance of the world around them' – a state very different, the researchers astutely reflected, from 'the prevalent notion of restless youth eager to explore and experiment'.[12]

For almost all 18-year-old males, still three years shy of being entitled to vote, there was the awkward, almost unavoidable fact of conscription – formally known from 1949 as National Service and lasting for up to two years. Peacetime conscription was unique in modern British history, but the Labour government was insistent that it was the only way in which the country could meet its extensive military commitments across much of the world. Such was the general assumption – in all parts of society – that Britain must continue to be a main player on the international stage that there was at most only muted opposition to the policy. And equally tellingly, in the broad support given to that policy until at least the mid-1950s, the latter-day notion that the discipline of National Service would somehow act as a magical moral stiffener for errant, delinquent youth played little or no part. In other words, some 2.3 million men were called up between 1945 and 1960 for essentially geopolitical purposes.

Among those who got the summons (invariably in a buff envelope), some 16 per cent were rejected as physically unfit, compared with only 0.4 per cent who successfully claimed conscientious objections. Invariably, there were many urban myths in circulation about surefire ways of failing the medical – such as throwing a fit, eating cordite to induce sweating, and sticking a knitting needle into the ear in order to perforate an eardrum – as there were also about trying to fail the intelligence test. Kenneth Tynan gave a notably 'successful' performance, smothering himself in Yardley scent and cutting an outrageously camp figure, while his fellow-thespian Tony Richardson was so genuinely nervous and nauseous during his medical that he won a reprieve – to the eternal shame of his father, an earnest, moralising man who kept a pharmacy on the main road from Bradford to Bingley.

In general, the probability is that resentment about being called up was less common than a fairly passive acceptance of the inevitable. Such at least is the conclusion of Stephen Martin, on the basis of an oral-history survey conducted in Essex in the mid-1990s. One of his interviewees, Peter Hunt, put it as well as anyone:

> I mean it was purely, in my case anyway, something that everybody had to do. You know, you just waited for it to come, went for the medical and that was it. There was no questioning it at all, not as far as I was concerned. Having thought about it, I suppose because it was only five years after the war and we lived in a sort of very, I won't say repressed, but suppressed society, whereby you were used to taking orders without question such as the blackout and queues and rationing and things like that. So against that background it doesn't seem so unusual now to say, 'Oh well, we just went and did it!'

Indeed, several of Martin's sample recall positively looking forward to the call-up – the chance to 'cut the apron strings' and get away from home, to stop doing a boring job, to visit foreign countries at someone else's expense. 'Attitudes surrounding the question of National Service,' he concludes, 'owed more to the concerns and aims of growing teenagers rather than any ideas about the rights and wrongs of conscription.'[13]

Even so, it is possible to argue that the way in which National Service operated had a significantly destabilising – if not necessarily radicalising – effect on the assumptions and norms of British society. For one thing, it served as a melting-pot, especially during the early weeks of square bashing and basic training, for people from different classes and regions who were often living for the first time outside their familiar home environments. Confronting 'the revelation of another England', the future writer Edward Lucie-Smith, 'a middle-class product of a scholarship mill', was 'shattered to discover how poorly most [men] had been taught' at school. For the future cartoonist Mel Calman, the revelation was coming across people who 'spoke a language that said "cunt" instead of "woman" and "fuck" instead of "love"'. Another eye-opener could be watching the officer class in action, as the young doctor (and poet) Dannie Abse did in the officers' mess on dining-in nights after he had been posted in 1951 to the mass radiography unit at Cardington, near Bedford:

> Two teams lined up, in single file, each team member having been supplied with a snooker ball that was held high up between thighs and crutch and buttock. At the other end of the room two buckets had been placed and towards these, now, each player awkwardly progressed in a relay race. At the bucket, each in turn would stoop in the posture of defaecation in order to drop the billiard ball with a zinc clang into the receptacle. Or two men, blindfolded, would lie prone on the carpet as they tried to hit each other with a rolled-up *Picture Post* or *Life* magazine. These two blind antagonists lay on their stomachs, horizontal on the floor, swinging their arms and crashing down their weapons mainly on the carpet while other officers gathered round frenetically shouting, 'Smash him, Jocelyn. Attaboy, Robin'.

Eyes were also sometimes opened in the wider world. 'I felt increasingly distressed by what I was being asked to defend – it seemed to be a system based on political injustice,' one ex-National Serviceman recalled about his time in Malaya, a British colony beset (like Cyprus and Kenya) by a strong and growing independence movement. Moreover, many young conscripts were caught up in fighting; indeed, in the course of the 1950s several hundred died in action.

Far more common, though, was the need to endure long hours of boredom and mind-numbing tasks. It was in this context that there developed a culture where skiving – best defined as looking busy while doing nothing – was made into a fine art. The Boulting brothers (John and Roy) commemorated the culture, undeniably subversive if sturdily apolitical, in their 1956 satire *Private's Progress*, featuring Richard Attenborough as Private Cox, the arch-skiver. Whether two years of skiving in the army automatically led to 40 years of skiving on the factory floor is a hypothesis not yet empirically tested. More plausible is the view that these two years spent as involuntary conscripts with a bunch of other 18- and 19-year-olds provided a shared experience – living away from home, going out together to pubs, dance halls and so on without any parental restraint – that did much to accelerate the arrival of 'youth' as a category in its own right. Indeed, by happy chance National Service got properly under way just as the term 'teenager' was being imported from the United States and rapidly becoming a staple of social reportage.[14]

That said, it is equally if not more probable that National Service served at least as much to reinforce as to undermine existing social structures and attitudes. Take the question of who got a commission from among the conscripts. 'The potential National Service officer had to possess a good education, social confidence, some previous military training and a certain conceit,' Trevor Royle has noted in his survey of the National Service experience. 'Most of these qualities, the Army generally agreed, were to be found in the products of a public or grammar school education.' And he adds that 'there were many National Servicemen who would have applied for officer selection but for their fear (not altogether groundless) that they did not have the right accent or social background, or that they would be unable to afford the higher expenses of the Officers' Mess'. Moreover, the whole basis on which the army was run was consciously designed to encourage conformity and stamp out independent, critical thinking, especially of a left-wing variety. Instead, it offered a wonderfully self-contained world in which tradition, hierarchy, authority and discipline were privileged above all else.

Crucially, the evidence we have is that most conscripts – themselves predominantly working-class – did not in any fundamental sense challenge that value system. A survey of almost 500 young Glaswegians, who had left school in 1947 aged 14 and were called up and accepted in the early 1950s, found as follows on questioning them two years after return from National Service: 59 per cent had 'enjoyed Service life'; 27 per cent had 'actively disliked it'; and the remaining 14 per cent were 'more or less neutral, regarding it as "just a job that had to be done"'. The majority, in other words, would probably not have disagreed with the more or less contemporaneous view of a young factory worker quoted in the 1955 collection *Called Up*: 'When I was back in Civvy Street and looked back on all the good times I'd had with my friends, my National Service didn't seem so bad after all. But I do think that a lot of time is wasted in the Army just hanging around.' There could even be something else involved. The future writer Colin Wilson, conscripted into the RAF and immediately nicknamed 'Professor', wrote home in the autumn of 1949 about his passing-out parade:

> It was an odd experience. I'd come to feel such contempt for the R.A.F. and everything it stood for. I used to repeat to myself that comment of Einstein about strutting imbeciles in uniform. Well, on the last morning in Bridgnorth, we were all on the square, and all I wanted was to get the whole stupid farce finished with and get home. Then suddenly the sun came out. I stood there, with the band playing the R.A.F. march-past and the sun shining and all of us moving like a single great machine, and suddenly I felt a tremendous exhilaration and a love for it all.

'It was,' in fact, 'quite irrational.'[15]

If National Service was unconnected in most people's minds with the state of the nation's moral fibre, that was much less the case with matters of sexual attitude and behaviour. Mass-Observation in early 1949 asked 2,052 people, chosen randomly on the streets of a cross-section of British cities, towns and villages, whether they thought 'standards of sex morality today' were 'getting better or worse or remaining about the same'. Some 39 per cent were either 'undecided' or 'vague' or reckoned they were 'much the same as ever'; 44 per cent (with a bias towards the elderly) said they were 'declining'; and only 17 per cent (with a bias towards the young) thought they were 'improving'.

The question was part of a survey subsequently dubbed 'Little Kinsey' – in the event never published but having some limited affinity to the recent celebrated (or infamous) American sex survey. It did not get very far in terms of uncovering actual sexual behaviour – beyond revealing that 33 per cent thought 'sexless' happiness was possible and

32 per cent thought it impossible, with a judicious 9 per cent reckoning it 'depended on the individual' – but it was quite revealing in terms of broad attitudes. For instance, 76 per cent were in favour of sex education and only 15 per cent (including a high proportion of church-goers) positively against; 63 per cent approved of birth control and 15 per cent disapproved; 58 per cent were 'unreservedly in favour of marriage', with most of the rest in favour depending on circumstances, and only 8 per cent either having 'mixed feelings' or giving 'unfavourable opinions'; and 57 per cent 'more or less' approved of divorce, with the emphasis almost invariably, Mass-Observation noted, 'on divorce as a regrettable necessity, to be avoided wherever possible, but not at the expense of happiness'. Tellingly, when M-O put this last question to its largely middle-class (and somewhat leftish) National Panel, as many as 83 per cent expressed broad approval of divorce – 26 per cent higher than the mainly working-class street sample.

Inevitably, there was also a question about people's attitude to extra-marital relations. 'That's wrong', 'I don't agree with that', 'It's filthy', 'Well, I think that's awful', 'Oh no, that's not done, that's lust' – such were some of the brief, indignant replies. Others elaborated somewhat more on their views:

> I feel very strongly about this. I've seen a lot of the harm it causes. I may say my wife and I have dropped one or two people who weren't playing the game, we didn't think they were worth knowing. (*Taxi-cab proprietor*)
>
> I don't believe in it, it's not right, it's going like animals. (*Painter and decorator, 70*)
>
> You can't stop the feeling, I agree with it. It's to try people out – you never want to buy a pig in a poke. (*Steeplejack, 37*)
>
> It's hard to say. As far as I can see everybody does it. If I was single I wouldn't refuse, would I? (*Dock labourer*)
>
> After I had been going with her for two months, I tried to go all the way with her, but it wouldn't work. She wants a white wedding and marriage in a Church, and to be a virgin. I agree with her and I don't try any more. (*Londoner, 20*)
>
> That shouldn't be allowed. Just because I do it, I don't think it's right. (*Lorry driver*)

Overall, 63 per cent of the street sample disapproved of extra-marital relations, compared with only 24 per cent of Mass-Observation's National Panel. And within the street sample, there was above-average opposition from regular church-goers, people who had left school by the age of 15, those living in rural areas, women, and married people over 30. As for the 37 per cent of the street sample who did not express outright disapproval, the M-O report stressed that only a minority 'gave even lukewarm unqualified approval'. Accordingly, 'There is certainly no easy or widespread acceptance of sex relations outside marriage in the population as a whole.' Even so, the report's accompanying assertion (largely on the basis of illegitimacy statistics) that 'there is ample evidence for assuming that at least one person in three, probably more, has intercourse either before or outside marriage' suggested that what people did was not always the same as what they said when confronted on a street by an inquisitive stranger.[16]

It was a picture – of social conservatism in attitude and, to a somewhat lesser extent, in behaviour – broadly confirmed by Geoffrey Gorer's much more extensive 1950/51 *People* survey. 'Not counting marriage, have you ever had a real love affair?' he asked. Out of the 11,000 or so questionnaires returned, 43 per cent admitted to having had one (which Gorer understood to mean in the vast majority of cases a sexual relationship) and 47 per cent 'gave an uncompromising No'. It was the latter figure that struck Gorer most forcibly in terms of 'the sexual morality of the English':

> I should like to emphasise that half the married population of England, men and women alike, state that they have had no relationship, either before or after marriage, with any person other than their spouse, and that the numbers are even greater in the working classes. My personal impression is that this is a very close approximation to the truth; and although there are no extensive figures available comparable to these [with Gorer footnoting that the Kinsey sample was 'in no way comparable'] I very much doubt whether the study of any other urban population would produce comparable figures of chastity and fidelity.

He also asked the *People*'s readers whether in their view young men and women should have some sexual experience before getting married:

I can only answer this. It was a joy on my wedding night to know this was my first experience. (*Working-class Man, 42, Sutton-in-Ashfield*)

I had no sexual experience before my marriage and I'd never want to experience my wedding night again. (*Divorced working-class man, 31, Greenwich*)

Not knowing much about the facts of life before marriage, it came as rather a shock to my nervous system. (*Working-class married woman, 42, Bradford*)

A girl should not, because I did – with my husband and I've often wished we'd waited. Neither of us ever refers to it and we are very happy in our marriage even so. (*Working-class married woman, Yorkshire*)

I would rather have my husband know what he is doing, but for a girl I do not consider this necessary as she takes more risks. (*Unmarried working-class woman, 25, Southampton*)

Anyone who tackles a big job should be trained for it. Marriage and sex life is a big job, and for women my answer obviously has to be the same, but I suggest the woman does not obtain her training from too many teachers. (*Married working-class man, 33, Lincoln*)

In all, 52 per cent were opposed to pre-marital sexual experience for young men and 63 per cent for young women. Gorer made three main accompanying points: that 'whether pre-marital experience is advocated or reprobated, the effect on the future marriage is the preponderating consideration'; that 'the high valuation put on virginity for both sexes is remarkable and, I should suspect, specifically English'; and that the view, common in some other societies, connecting 'sexual activity with physical and mental health' had in England 'apparently achieved very little currency'.[17] It was still, a year after the publication of Nancy Mitford's novel, a case of love in a cold climate.

One type of sexual activity – little studied in either survey – dared not speak its name: homosexual intercourse. Unsurprisingly, the moral panic of the late 1940s and early 1950s generated a sustained campaign to stamp out such wicked congress, with indictable offences (mainly for sodomy and bestiality, indecent assault and 'gross indecency') rising sharply. The Director of Public Prosecutions, Sir Theobald Mathew, was a zealous homophobe; successive Home Secretaries were disinclined to restrain either him or the police; and the men in blue now started using agents provocateurs to catch homosexuals, as often as not 'cottaging' in public lavatories. Predictably, there is no evidence that this campaign was out of step with public opinion.

To take people's minds off such upsetting matters, there was the emergence by 1950 of a blessedly heterosexual film star. In the weeks and months after *The Blue Lamp*'s release, Dirk Bogarde ('all Brylcreem and liquid eyes') was assiduously groomed and publicised by Rank to become the great British male heart-throb of the new decade – a process typified by his open letter to *Woman's Own* about the qualities he demanded in 'The girl that I marry'. From a formidable list, they included:

Do not smoke in public.

Do not wear high heels with slacks.

Wear a little skilful make-up.

Never draw attention to yourself in public places by loud laughter, conversation, or clothing.

NEVER try to order a meal from a menu when I am with you.

Never laugh at me in front of my friends.

Never welcome me back in the evening with a smutty face, the smell of cooking in your hair, broken nails, and a whine about the day's trials and difficulties.

From one reader, Evelyn S. Kerr of Gidea Park, Essex, there came a memorable riposte: 'After reading Dirk Bogarde's article, I find that I am his ideal woman. The only snag is, I breathe. Do you think it matters?'[18]

———

The electorate's hour was at hand – an electorate that, Mark Abrams found in a July 1949 survey, was a distinctly polarised one. 'Among all electors, except Conservative supporters, substantial minorities were convinced that a Conservative victory in the next general election would mean mass unemployment, the dismantlement of the Welfare State, more industrial disputes, and an abrupt extension of private enterprise'; at the same time, 'all but Labour supporters feared that another Labour victory would lead to a much wider application of nationalisation, the neglect of national material prosperity, and excessive class-oriented legislation', with a third of all Conservatives asserting that 'in its four years of power the Labour government had done nothing that was worthy of approval'. Much would depend on whether Labour could hold on to the significant degree of non-working-class support that it had attracted in 1945. One of Mass-Observation's panel, a clearly well-off 37-year-old housewife, explained in August 1949 why she felt she could no longer vote Labour:

> Like many 'upper class' socialists, I thought with security of employment and adequate pay, as well as a Government of their own, workers would act as we should act in similar circumstances, i.e. work with a will, and enjoy doing so. In the event, it seems that we have been wrong and that removing the threats of unemployment, starvation, etc has only made the workers more discontented, which also seems to apply to nationalisation which certainly is a failure up till now. I think it will be possible to make it work in the case of railways, etc (it had better be) but I do not think that this is the time for more similar experiments ...
>
> The other reason is more intangible, it is a matter of atmosphere. Somehow, a Labour Government has managed to take a lot of the joy and the interest out of the atmosphere. I feel that it is not so much 'austerity' – I can eat like a king if I have the money, and now also dress well, so it wouldn't be that – but the general discontent, the lack of eagerness to serve among the people accompanied by a lack of eagerness to play, to have any social life, to do anything at all.

'The atmosphere is one of lassitude,' she concluded. 'Perhaps by taking so much of the fight out of life, it gets less interesting, less worth while.'[19]

Let Us Win Through Together was the unexceptionable title of Labour's deliberately low-key election manifesto. Apart from a rather shapeless-looking 'shopping list' of industries (including water supply, cement, meat distribution and sugar refining) for which some form of public ownership was proposed, the main thrust was on the horrors of the past – above all dole queues, means tests and inadequate social services – and how these had been banished by the post-war Labour government, often against Tory opposition. 'Clearly Herbert [Morrison] & Co are trusting to do nothing except to frighten the electors about what the wicked Tories will do if they are given a chance' was the realistic appraisal of the Conservative backbencher Cuthbert Headlam, 'and a reminder of the terrible times between the wars.' A rare exception to the almost palpable intellectual exhaustion was the inclusion of a commitment to introduce a consumer-advisory service – on the face of it, an important shift by the producers' party. The reality was rather different. 'Since I was writing the election programme,' Michael Young recalled years later, 'I slipped it in and no one on the National Executive Committee made anything of it.'

As for the main opposition's response, one supporter, Florence Speed in Brixton, summed it up on 25 January:

> The Conservative manifesto published this morning. A fighting one, with freedom the keynote.
>
>   Freedom of labour to choose its own job; freedom to build houses, freedom for private enterprise. No more state buying. Food off ration as quickly as possible. Freedom for doctors to practise where they like. Good strong stuff – and yet? The young of the world have had Socialism drilled into them from the cradle.

In reality, *This Is The Road* was a pretty skilful document. It gave plenty of reassuring emphasis as to how a Tory government would build on rather than undermine the foundations of the newly constructed welfare state, declaring outright that 'suggestions that we wish to cut the social services are a lie', but it also included three strongly worded sections ('Reduce Taxation', 'Limit Controls', 'Stop Nationalisation') that together made it unambiguously clear that the party stood for 'the encouragement of enterprise and initiative'. The manifesto got a generally good press. 'Even *The Times* appears to approve of it,' noted Headlam, 'and admits that it is a far better thing than the Socialist manifesto.' Typically, he added, 'Of course 20 years ago one would have taken it for a Socialist pamphlet – but times have changed.'[20]

A general election in the early 1950s was still a predominantly local affair, with more than half the electors personally canvassed by one or more of the parties – testimony to the armies of unpaid activists the two main ones could rely on (Reginald Maudling, standing for the Tories in Barnet, had no fewer than 12,000 members at his disposal). As for the playing out of the 1950 election at a national level, there was of course the press (overwhelmingly anti-Labour), but apart from allowing the main politicians to make party political broadcasts – which they decided to do only on radio, not yet trusting television – the BBC 'kept as aloof from the election as if it had been occurring on another planet', as a somewhat exasperated Herbert Nicholas put it in his authoritative Nuffield study of the election. 'Every programme was scrutinised in search of any item, jocular or serious, which might give aid or comfort to any of the contestants, and after February the 3rd virtually all mention of election politics disappeared from the British air.' Indeed it did, with R.J.F. Howgill (Controller, Entertainment) having explicitly warned 'all producers, announcers, commentators and other users of the microphone' against 'making political allusions, cracking political jokes, and using the microphone in any way that might influence the electors', with 'special care' needing to be taken 'over O.B.s [outside broadcasts] from music halls'. Even so, Nicholas's overall verdict was telling: 'Undoubtedly in view of the enormous power wielded by such a monopolistic instrument the decision to carry neutrality to the lengths of castration was the only right one.'

Perhaps for this reason among others, it was not an election that ever really caught fire. 'All along,' Mollie Panter-Downes reckoned just over a week before polling day, it 'has had a curious, fuzzy aura of unreality about it', with the 'subnormal' election temperature not helped by 'torrents of icy rain and gales of wind rampaging over the country'; while after it was all over, she called the campaign 'as thrilling as a church bazaar'.[21] Still, a quickfire tour of the constituencies suggests it had a bit more life to it.

One of the closest, most spirited contests was in Plymouth Devonport between Michael Foot and Winston Churchill's talented but bombastic son Randolph. 'The reason I haven't talked about Plymouth housing is that I don't know much about it,' the latter foolishly admitted with ten days to go; thereafter it was easy for Foot convincingly to depict his opponent as having 'as much knowledge of the real political and economic issues facing the British nation as the man in the moon'. The two men were already well-established public figures, but it was different for a clutch of young – and ambitious – Tory hopefuls, among whom there were four men fighting eminently winnable seats and one woman who was not. 'It's the future that matters' was the simple but effective (and also revealing) slogan of Maudling in Barnet; another moderniser, Iain Macleod in Enfield West, did not harm his cause by declaring that it was in the field of social services that 'my deepest political interests lie'; in Wolverhampton South-West Enoch Powell conducted a short, intensive, military-style campaign that made much of how 'we have watched our country's strength and reputation in the world going to pieces in these years immediately after victory'; there was a similar briskness and efficiency about Edward Heath's campaign in Bexley, despite an embarrassing moment when his claim that the housing situation would have improved if Aneurin Bevan and his wife Jennie Lee had had to live with their in-laws was met by a heckler's decisive intervention, 'They do!'; and in Dartford, a neighbouring seat, Margaret Roberts (the future Margaret Thatcher) insisted, in more or less blatant disregard of her party's accommodation with the post-war settlement, that Labour's policies for universal welfare were 'pernicious and nibble into our national character far further than one would be aware at first glance'. For Labour hopefuls, the high tide of opportunity had obviously been 1945, but Anthony Crosland was optimistic enough in South Gloucestershire. 'A really crowded meeting at Staple Hill – very enthusiastic – I'm really becoming quite a popular figure!' he noted in his campaign diary on 3 February, before adding: 'A letter from a woman with a dropped stomach, demanding that I should get her a truss. This is too much.' The following week he was in a village called Dyrham: 'Member of squirearchy asked interminable questions about dental fees, & why he had to wait 3 months for an appointment: they *do* ask silly questions.'[22]

Naturally all candidates had their awkward encounters with voters. Headlam, fighting his last election in Newcastle North, spoke in a school off Elswick Road and recorded with satisfaction the failure of a bunch of 'men hecklers' to break up his meeting. Another Tory, Dr Charles Hill (famous during the war as the 'Radio Doctor'), held three lunchtime meetings in the large canteen at Vauxhall Motors – on one occasion being disconcerted by 'four men ostentatiously seated in the front' who 'ignored me completely' and stayed 'deep in concentration in their game of solo'; on another, being photographed for the local press, revealing that, 'while I was in full flood, a serious-looking young man seated at the back was engrossed in *Forever Amber*'. And over in South Bucks, the freelance broadcaster Bruce Belfrage, standing for the Liberals, had a bad time of it among the atavistic 'hard core of the Tory supporters' living in Beaconsfield and Gerrards Cross. 'Grim and determined characters whose political knowledge was in most cases non-existent,' he wrote soon afterwards, 'they were inspired by an implacable loathing of the Socialist Government and all its works . . . They were not open to argument or persuasion, and my wife and I, together with all Liberals, were, in their eyes, traitors, renegades, fellow-travellers and foul splitters of the anti-Socialist vote.' Judy Haines in Chingford would have sympathised. 'As we have Conservative notices either side and all round us, got a trilly delight out of putting "Labour" notice in our window,' she noted just over a week before polling day. 'Will I be sent to Coventry tomorrow?'[23]

Was the overall rather tame campaign a sign of democratic progress? Harold Macmillan thought so, claiming subsequently that 'the high poll (at 84 per cent) showed that the lack of rowdyism and excitement was due not to the apathy of the electors but rather to a serious approach to their responsibilities.' Evidence on the ground suggested a less sanguine conclusion. In his Greenwich survey, involving interviews with 914 people in that constituency, Mark Benney found that ahead of the election barely half could name even the party of their local MP and only a quarter the MP's name; that during the campaign only 7 per cent went to an election meeting; that 'those who had not made up their minds how they were going to vote bothered least of all about reading the campaign hand-outs'; and that although the parties were 'reasonably successful' in their efforts 'to hammer home the names of their candidates', the overwhelming indications were that 'neither the candidates nor their electioneering activities aroused much enthusiasm.'

It was pretty much the same with Mass-Observations's survey shortly before polling day of 600 voters in six London constituencies. Not only had 86 per cent not been to any meeting, but 44 per cent had not even read an election leaflet (in an election where probably well over 30 million were distributed). Nor, among the 56 per cent who had picked one up, were there many signs of serious scrutiny. 'Looked at the man's face on it' was how an accountant's wife put it, while another woman replied, 'I have glanced through them but I think they are a waste of paper.' Touring East Ham on the Saturday before polling day, a Panel member noted: 'In the afternoon I could not discover a single remark with any bearing on the election – on the streets, outside shops, in cafés – the people were shopping and that's all.' Or take the vox pop culled three days later from potential voters in Islington East. One 40-year-old working-class woman, a baker's shophanger in Canonbury, based her voting intentions on the twin premises that 'you've got to have money before you can do anything' and that 'there isn't a single gentleman in the Labour Party – with the exception of Mr Attlee, and he's too much of a gentleman to manage that crowd'. Another working-class woman, the 27-year-old wife of an asphalter in Aberdeen Park, had not got quite that far in her analysis: 'To tell the truth I haven't thought about this voting business. I want a house. I live with a relative, and I think she wants it for her daughter so my main concern is to find a place.'[24]

Where the electorate were most engaged was through listening to election broadcasts. During the fortnight from 4 February, the proportion of the adult population tuning in ranged from 31 per cent to 51 per cent (for Churchill) and averaged 38.1 per cent – a bit of a drop on 1945 but still pretty impressive, albeit that in Greenwich (and presumably elsewhere) 'many of those who listened did so with half an ear, for no more than an average of 26 per cent claimed to have heard the whole broadcast'. Research immediately after the election found that the broadcasts by Attlee and Churchill had changed the minds of less than 1 per cent of the electorate – Churchill, after his 1945 radio fiasco, was perhaps grateful for that – and of course there were many households that did not tune in at all. These seem to have included Nella Last's in Barrow. 'We listened to Music Hall,' she reluctantly noted on the 4th. 'I wanted badly to listen to the political broadcast [by Morrison] but "controversy" of any kind upsets my husband.'

One broadcast did make a difference. 'It isn't as the Radio Doctor that I'm speaking tonight,' began Charles Hill on Tuesday the 14th. 'And it isn't about aches and pains or babies and backaches. It's politics. I shall say what I honestly think – speaking not for others, not for the doctors, but for myself – one of the many candidates.' Over the next

20 minutes he argued forcibly but not fanatically that the miseries of the past had been grossly exaggerated by Labour politicians (whom he like most Tories invariably referred to as 'the socialists'); that the welfare state had essentially bipartisan foundations; that the recent devaluation of the pound (announced by Cripps 'with that touch of unction all his own') had signalled an economy in serious trouble; and that the fundamental choice facing the electorate was whether 'we really want a world in which the state's the universal boss'. A particular passage entered electoral folklore:

> Why are the socialists trying to fill us up with ghost stories about the inter-war years? Well, not all of us, because many of us can remember what they were like. But there are many voters who can't. I am not surprised that the socialists gave up that 'Ask your Dad' campaign. I suppose Dad was beginning to give the answers! And did you hear that great writer of fiction, J.B. Priestley [who had given a party political broadcast for Labour a month earlier], super-tax payer and good luck to him – did you hear him tell us that last Christmas was the best ever? Oh, chuck it, Priestley. Anybody would think that we had no memories . . .

It was a formidable target – as Hill himself would recall, Priestley 'in his rich, Yorkshire homespun voice had given the impression of an honest-to-God chap who was having a fireside chat with blokes as puzzled and eager for the truth as he was' – but that one, seemingly spontaneous phrase, 'chuck it, Priestley', brilliantly did the job and would long be remembered.

Among the 42 per cent listening were Kenneth Preston in Keighley and Vere Hodgson in west London, both admittedly Tory supporters. 'He was very effective and must have done a great deal of damage to the Socialist cause' was Preston's instant verdict, while Hodgson reckoned that he 'wiped the floor with Mr Priestley' and added: 'The broadcast is to be on gramophone records by Monday . . . It would touch every home, as he has a homely manner.' Nicholas in his election study agreed about Hill's effectiveness. 'Here was expressed, in popular phraseology, in an occasional pungent phrase and in a continuously "folksy" delivery, the politics of the unpolitical, the plain man's grouse' – or, put another way, a 'narrative of the adventures of *l'homme moyen sensuel* in Queue-topia' (the term recently coined by Churchill) that was 'winged straight at the discontents and prejudices of the lower middle class, full of the changeless wisdom of common-sense and constructed according to the most sophisticated formulas of applied psychology'.[25]

Even so, the 1930s 'myth' remained a potent weapon in Labour's hands. One of its national posters featured marchers with a 'Jarrow Crusade' poster and the accompanying caption 'Unemployment – don't give the Tories another chance'. And although for the Tories there was, as Hill showed, some mileage in challenging the myth, the leadership and candidates broadly preferred to follow the *Spectator*'s advice to 'make it abundantly clear that as a party they have learned much from the years of travail, and that the Tories of 1950 are not the Tories of 1935'. Churchill in particular stayed more or less on-message, though naturally he could not resist the temptation to play the world statesman. In a speech in Edinburgh on the 14th – a speech reported by all the world's radio services except those of the UK and the USSR – he spoke of how, if restored to power, he would seek to convene 'a parley at the summit' with the Soviet leaders, so that 'the two worlds' could 'live their life, if not in friendship at least without the hatreds of the cold war'. Churchill's proposal coined the diplomatic term 'summit', but Ernest Bevin immediately labelled it a stunt, while Harold Nicolson agreed that it was 'unworthy of him': 'To suggest talks with Stalin on the highest level inevitably makes people think, "Winston could talk to Stalin on more or less the same level. But if Attlee goes, it would be like a mouse addressing a tiger. Therefore vote for Winston."' There was also soon after this speech a whispering campaign to the effect that Churchill was dead; a robust denial quickly put an end to it.

As for Attlee, driven around the country by his wife in a Humber (having traded up from a Hillman), he was happy enough to exude reassurance and for the most part stick to the largely domestic agenda that concerned the electorate. According to Mass-Observation's London survey, asking its sample to name the election issues they thought most important, housing came easily top, followed by shortages, wages and taxation, nationalisation and cost of living. To Attlee fell the final broadcast, on Saturday the 18th and listened to by 44 per cent:

The choice before you is clear. During these difficult years Britain
by its example has done a great service to democracy and freedom.
We have shown that orderly planning and freedom are not
incompatible. We have confirmed faith in democracy by the example
of a Government that has carried out its promises. It is utterly untrue
to say that our prestige has been diminished. On the contrary, it
stands higher than ever, for we have added to the triumphs of war
the victories of peace.

'I do not suggest that all our problems have been solved,' he conceded,
'but I do say that great progress has been made, that if we continue
with the same steadiness, cheerfulness and hard work that have been
displayed during these years I am convinced that we can solve them.'
Though as he added with an honesty that may only arguably have
been advisable, 'I am not going to make promises of quick solutions.
I am not going to offer you any easement unless I am certain that it
can be done.'[26]

As during any election, there was plenty else going on. On Friday
the 3rd, the day of the old parliament's dissolution, probably the
most popular British comedian, Sid Field, collapsed and died at the
age of 45, after a short life of heavy drinking. Evocatively described
by one historian of comedy, Graham McCann, as 'ranging freely
from coarse, back-throated cockney, through the nasal, drooping
rhythms of his native Brummie, to the tight-necked, tongue-tip
precision of a metropolitan toff', Field was the special hero of another
son of Birmingham, the aspiring comedian Tony Hancock, and on
hearing the news, Hancock wept – the only time his agent saw him
in tears. On the same day as Field's death, the German-born nuclear
scientist Klaus Fuchs, who had fled Germany in the 1930s and had
been working at the Atomic Energy Research Establishment at
Harwell, Oxfordshire, was charged with passing information to
Russian agents about how to construct a plutonium bomb.
Apparently disenchanted with Communism, the previous week he
had made a full confessional statement at the War Office that included
a remarkable passage:

Before I joined the [Harwell] project most of the English people with whom I made personal contacts were left-wing, and affected in some degree or other by the same kind of philosophy. Since coming to Harwell I have met English people of all kinds, and I have come to see in many of them a deep-rooted firmness which enables them to lead a decent way of life. I do not know where this springs from and I don't think they do, but it is there.

Fuchs in due course received a 14-year sentence; but on 8 February a Liverpudlian gangster called George Kelly was sentenced to death for murdering the manager of the Cameo cinema in the suburb of Wavertree during a bungled burglary. The Crown's case against Kelly was entirely circumstantial, lacking any scientific support – but his conviction was not quashed as unsafe until 53 years after he had been hanged.

Meanwhile, for one Surbiton housewife, as for millions, the quotidian dominated:

10 February. The greengrocer came very late, so we had to wait a long time for our second course of a fresh salad before the rice pudding.
13 February. I like to see boys [including her son Robin] carrying attaché cases instead of satchels as they did in the war, not being able to get the cases then.
14 February. Lay down to rest at about 2.30 exhausted, went to sleep in middle of Woman's Hour.
16 February. Ray [her daughter] went out this morning to get some stuff for a skirt. Was I glad to see the Pudeena she brought me, the first since 1939. Of course, I make steam pudding with ordinary flour, but these make such light ones, lighter than with our heavy flour.
19 February. Robin's cold is better & went quickly. Wonder if it was the Ribena, the pure blackcurrant juice the Health Act provided for mothers & children, & which anyone can now get. It is lovely, & 2/10 [for] a quite big bottle.

For all her keenness as a radio listener and generally serious attitude to life, Marian Raynham did not mention listening that month to Fred Hoyle's series of talks *The Nature of the Universe*, in which the term

'Big Bang' was coined. The astronomer's robust, down-to-earth approach was for some an acquired taste – the BBC's Listening Panel reported how his 'way of speaking was not particularly well liked', undoubtedly referring to the incongruity of a northern accent on the Third Programme – but the series established his reputation as the first popular scientist in the age of mass media (even though the listening figures, being for the Third, were unremarkable). 'It has been the most satisfying & enjoyable series I think I have ever heard,' declared one panel member, a gas inspector, after it was over, '& I am very sorry we shan't have this Saturday evening speaker to look forward to any more.'[27]

For politicians, the only focus that mattered in early 1950 was the electoral one. Before the campaign, seeking to relieve the tedium of a Cripps dinner party ('the meal was pretty foul and conversation, not surprisingly, drab and common place,' noted Hugh Gaitskell), a group of ministers and their wives had forecast the outcome. Everyone bar Douglas Jay assumed an overall Labour majority, with Gaitskell's the lowest estimate at 30. The Stock Exchange already agreed, by the end of 1949 having informally given odds of 11/8 against a Tory win, while the Tories themselves were split. 'Harold was somewhat cocksure I thought – I mean as to the result of the GE – the idea being that our manifesto is "a winner",' recorded Headlam after listening to Macmillan address northern candidates at the end of January. 'I wonder – my fear is that the working man won't change his attitude until he is in want – and that is not yet.' The only poll with any sort of credibility was Gallup's, which on 20 January revealed (in the *News Chronicle*) Labour having dramatically reduced a long-established Tory lead and then from the 30th moving narrowly ahead. Its final poll was published on Wednesday, 22 February, the day before voting, and showed Labour on 45 per cent, the Conservatives on 43.5 and the Liberals on 10.5. In truth it was too close to call, but the great thing for everyone involved was to stay as confident and motivated as possible. 'We've all worked like blacks – but I'm not worried – I tell you, I'm *not* worried,' the Tory agent for Islington North told a Mass-Observation investigator on the 18th. 'But I'd far sooner see a Liberal get in – if *they* [ie Labour] got back, this'll be the last election we shall see. There'll be no more voting and no more parties – it'll be straight totalitarianism.'[28]

Polling day was mainly fine, but by the evening there was plenty of rain about, making the eventual turnout all the more notable. From about eleven o'clock there was a large crowd in Trafalgar Square, where a big *Daily Mail* screen on the Canadian Pacific Railway building was showing the early results. 'There was no evidence of very deep personal feeling or concern except in a minority of cases,' reported Mass-Observation, while Panter-Downes that night was struck by the many young people, including students who 'swung along arm in arm, dressed, indistinguishably as to sex, in a uniform of old duffle coats or burberries, corduroy slacks, and huge party rosettes'. There were even thicker crowds in Piccadilly Circus, where the *Daily Telegraph* sponsored the scoreboards over the Criterion Theatre. There Panter-Downes overheard the exchange of views between 'a pretty little blonde' and a fat man next to her, after she had 'enthusiastically shrilled "Up Labour!"' after each government win:

He: Now, sweetheart, you don't bloody know what you're talking about. You was only a kid when there was a Conservative Government last, so what the hell do you know about it, sweetheart?

She: I know enough to know that they were rotten bad days for the workers. (*Applauded by several people standing nearby.*)

He (patiently): Look at me, dear. Don't I look like a worker? My dad was a foreman bricklayer, and we were seven boys, and always plenty to eat and us kids kept decent. No, sweetheart, this country won't be right till it gets some private bloody enterprise again, and don't you talk no more about bad old days to me, see, ducks?

For London's elite, there were election parties at the top hotels. At Claridge's part of the accompanying cabaret was provided by Tony Hancock – who became increasingly vexed as his *Hunchback of Notre Dame* impression was continually interrupted by the toastmaster raising his white glove to announce the latest result – but the bigger draw, attracting up to 2,000 guests (and almost as many gate-crashers), was the thrash at the Savoy hosted by Lord Camrose, the *Telegraph*'s proprietor. 'Practically everyone I've ever heard of there,' reported Malcolm Muggeridge, 'champagne flowing, ran into numbers of people, whole thing slightly macabre and eve of the Battle of Waterloo flavour about it – the bourgeoisie shivering before the deluge to come.' And indeed, once the results started coming in, 'it became clear very soon that there was no real swing against the Government'. Another diarist-guest, Cynthia Gladwyn, observed how 'faces became downcast and, in spite of the champagne, spirits low', so that 'finally, at about one o'clock the party was a feast at which there were only skeletons'.

Most people stayed at home that night. Some, like Judy Haines, were able to watch – 'we were continually reminded by Television Commentators (Conservatives, I'm sure) that the results so far were nothing to go by' – but far more listened into the small hours on the radio, including the 23-year-old John Fowles in his parents' house at Leigh-on-Sea. 'The constant interruption of the music and the numbers counted floating out of the loudspeaker,' he recorded somewhat loftily in his diary. 'Interest grows like a child's interest in a match boat-race in a gutter.' During the half-hour after midnight, some 36 per cent of the adult population were still listening to the results, and the only criticism of its coverage reported back to the BBC was that as the night wore on 'the fill-up gramophone records were much too loud'.[29] By dawn Labour were 61 seats ahead of the Tories, with ministers still confident of a comfortable overall majority, but only 266 constituencies had declared, and those that had not included many rural and suburban seats.

Friday the 24th proved a thriller. There was a steady flow of results from late morning to mid-evening, with many fluctuations in the relative state of the parties, but with the Tories having in general a far happier time than the previous night. At the Dorchester there was food and champagne provided by another newspaper dynasty, the Rother-meres. 'From time to time the loudspeaker calls, "Attention! Atten-tion!", and then gives the state of the parties,' noted a guest, Harold Nicolson. 'At about 1 pm the gap between Labour and Conservative begins suddenly to narrow. Excitement rises. People do not behave well. They boo a Labour victory and hoot with joy at a Conservative victory. They roar with laughter when a Liberal forfeits his deposit.'

By afternoon there was the unmistakable feel of a national nail-biter. 'Shopkeepers, bus-passengers, fellow-residents all full of election news and very excited about the neck-and-neck election results,' observed Gladys Langford in north London, while according to Panter-Downes it was as if the city generally had been 'hit in the face by a blizzard of newspapers': 'On every street, people walked along thumbing through the latest edition, or stood on corners intently reading, or dropped one paper and queued to buy two others.' Moreover, 'shops that had a radio turned on or had put some kind of arrangement for showing election returns in the front window were surrounded by absorbed crowds.' For a tired Judy Haines, who on Thursday night had stayed up watching the coverage until 3.00 a.m., the political and the personal understandably merged: '7 o'c came round so terribly soon. Had a dreadful day with babes & their colds. Kept grizzling. I tried putting Pamela to sleep but had to bring her down again when she was so weepy. To make matters worse I was straining hard to get Election Results. Made a game of it by booing Conservatives & cheering Labour, but it wore very thin long before nightfall.' Soon afterwards, no less than 43 per cent of the adult population listened to the six o'clock news to hear the latest position.[30]

By mid-evening, with 13 results still outstanding, it was pretty certain that Labour would still have an overall majority, but one that was far from comfortable. The eventual figures – Labour 315, Conservative 298, Liberal 9, Irish Nationalist 2, Communist 0 – set it at six. By then the Cabinet had decided, late on the Friday, to carry on in government, notwithstanding some excitable talk of a coalition. Among the victors were Foot, Maudling, Macleod, Powell, Heath, Hill and Crosland; losers included Margaret Roberts and Bruce Belfrage; and in Islington North the Tories went down by more than 9,000. Almost everyone expected another general election before very long.

'WHAT A SHAKING THEY HAVE HAD' was Vere Hodgson's immediate reaction to what had happened to the Labour government, while another diarist, the Liberal-voting Marian Raynham, agreed that 'they won't be able to have it all their own way'. Such was also the view of much of the press about the implications of Labour having, in the *Economist*'s words, 'suffered a Pyrrhic victory', or, as Nicolson privately put it, 'Labour cannot carry on with a Socialist policy when it is now clear that the country dislikes it.' But for one Tory supporter in Barrow (a rock-solid Labour seat), the defining moment was hearing her leader concede defeat. 'I listened to Mr Churchill's brave but broken voice with a pity so deep I began to cry bitterly,' Nella Last wrote on the Friday evening. 'I don't cry easily, or often, my husband said "now fancy you upsetting yourself over so small a thing", but somehow that brave gallant old voice got tangled up with my own worries & fears.' In Chelsea, meanwhile, Mass-Observation's investigators caught a couple of overheards more or less encompassing the socio-economic spectrum. 'If it's a stalemate it means they can't do just as they like any longer,' shouted a pleased-sounding coalman to someone on the pavement in Manor Street as he leaned down from his cart. A member of the Stock Exchange did not manage quite such a large view of the situation: 'My God it was funny all the time there was just the one Liberal member – the word went round that they were waiting for a second so that they could breed from them.'[31]

In an election in which the two main parties virtually squeezed out all other parties, why had Labour, landslide victors in 1945, lost so many MPs? Almost immediately afterwards, the political analyst Philip Williams persuasively attributed the collapse to two main causes. Firstly, there was the redistribution of seats that had been agreed during the previous parliament, with Attlee in this respect behaving with self-sacrificing integrity, in the knowledge that large numbers of Labour votes would be transferred from marginal to safe seats. So it transpired. In terms of the popular vote, Labour at 46.1 per cent were still well ahead of the Conservatives on 43.5 per cent. But it was seats that mattered. Secondly, there was what Williams termed 'the revolt of the suburbs'. As he explained, whereas the national swing from Labour to Conservative was 2.6 per cent, in London and the Home Counties it was 6, in Essex nearly 8 and in Middlesex 8.5 per cent. Put another way, Labour's working-class vote had stayed pretty solid (though there remained a significant obstinate minority of working-class Conservatives), but its unprecedentedly high middle-class vote in 1945 had shown itself flaky when put to the test after four and a half years of actual Labour government – years above all of rationing and high taxation, accompanied by a sustained press campaign against what was depicted as the doctrinaire and hypocritical socialism of ministers like Bevan, especially after his 'vermin' outburst in July 1948. The predominantly class-based character of the voting in 1950 was further borne out by Benney's Greenwich survey. There he found that 'for most voters, and in particular for working-class voters, party policy plays a smaller part in attracting or repelling support than the class character of the party's public image.'[32]

In all, it was an election that, from a Labour point of view, threw up three troubling questions as it prepared to govern again, albeit with a threadbare majority. Could the party win back its fickle middle-class supporters? Would its impressively loyal working-class base continue to be grateful for the full employment, welfare reforms and shift of wealth brought about in the immediate post-war years? And, with the working class in long-term secular decline (comprising 78 per cent of British society in 1931, 72 per cent by 1951), would that base be sufficient in elections to come?

PART TWO

A Negative of Snowflakes

Take a journey in 1948 from what one traveller soon afterwards reckoned 'the grimmest station in England':

Starting from Birmingham's New Street Station, the train runs between the old central factory quarter and streets of huddled dwellings, past a vista of Middle Ring industrial buildings, by Monument Lane and on to the edge of Birmingham. Here, without a break, begins the Smethwick industrial zone, with its jumble of roads, railways and canals. Running alongside the canal bank, the train enters the Black Country leaving the congested industry of Smethwick for the waste lands left derelict by earlier industries. Canal junction and old spoilbanks lie north of the line and to the south lies Oldbury, the first Black Country town. A steel plant shows the persistence of heavy industry in the middle of the Conurbation. The River Tame winds through a landscape of slagheaps and pitmounds. Open land stretches towards Rowley Regis. Houses advance across land evacuated by industry. Across the canal the carriage window still looks on to tracks of derelict land, with a brickworks marking the midway point. Close by, this desolation forms the setting of a new housing estate. The train halts at Dudley Port Station, a Black Country railway centre. Industrial buildings stand among heaps of ash, spoil and scrap. Roads, railway and canals overlap at Tipton and straighten to cut through terrace streets and new municipal housing as far as Tipton Station. Just beyond, new industry is using old derelict land across the line opposite the township of Tipton Green, and tips are filling the open space between three embankments. Through Coseley the train passes the backyards of houses and factories, and a stretch of loosely knit development, before reaching the extensive steel plant and rolling mills at Spring Vale, Bilston. Across the line is Rough Hills, a slum built on and among slag heaps. As the chimneys of Bilston recede, the train enters the fringe of Wolverhampton, from which the zone of increasingly older and denser industrial building reaches into the heart of the town, 14 miles from New Street.

This enticing travelogue was the work of the West Midland Group, authors of a resolutely optimistic planning study grappling with the legacy of two centuries in which 'the needs of man' had taken 'second place to the demands of manufacture', above all anything to do with metalworking (tubes and bolts, nuts and rivets, screws and nails) and engineering. Birmingham and the Black Country – together they were, this report did not exaggerate, 'the very hub of industrial England'.[1]

Hub, indeed, not only of a nation but of a universe, given that Britain remained – as it had been since beyond living memory – the most industrialised country in the world. The headline facts at the midpoint of the twentieth century spoke for themselves: responsible for a quarter of the world's trade in manufactured goods; the world's leading producer of ships; Europe's leading producer of coal, steel, cars and textiles. Yet the reality was more complex. Not only had the inter-war period strongly suggested that the two great staples – coal and cotton – of the nineteenth-century British economy were in long-term, perhaps irreversible decline, but it was also becoming clear that newer, science-based industries like electronics, chemicals and aviation were on an equally long-term rise. So strong, though, was the British self-image as pioneer of the Industrial Revolution, together with the accompanying dark satanic mills, that it would be a long time before 'manufacturing' stopped being almost exclusively equated with 'smokestacks'. It would take even longer for the economy as a whole not to be seen in almost purely manufacturing terms – even though the service sector in 1950 provided as much as half of Britain's gross domestic product and employed roughly as many people as the manufacturing sector. It is not fanciful to suggest that the overwhelming post-war emphasis on the virtues, importance and general superiority of manufacturing owed at least something to a male, virility-driven view of the world. Heavy industry was real men working in real jobs making real, tangible things; jobs in the 'parasitic' service sector, such as in offices and shops, were as often as not held by women. For planners and film-makers, economists and social-realist novelists, the cloth cap had the authenticity that the skirt, let alone the white collar, palpably lacked.[2]

Perhaps it could not have been otherwise, given the sheer physical impress of industrialisation. 'At Blaydon the murk sets in,' noted *Picture Post*'s A. L. ('Bert') Lloyd (the renowned folk singer) as he made his way 'Down the Tyne' in 1950. 'At Newcastle the smoke blows over the cliffs of brickwork that tower above the black river, and the soot falls like a negative of snowflakes on the washing strung across the ravines.' From there to the river mouth, 'the traveller walks along a Plutonian shore, among the rubbish heaps and the row-town rows whose little houses are overcast by the towering machinery of the shipyards', their cranes 'marked with such names as Swan Hunter and Vickers Armstrong'. Or take Sheffield – 'a mucky picture in a golden frame', as the local saying went. 'Our skyline was dominated by hundreds of smoking chimneys and the city lived to the constant accompaniment of steam hammers and the ring of metal meeting metal,' recalls Stewart Dalton about growing up on a council estate there. The steelworks' smell and smoke was everywhere pervasive. 'There's nothing wrong with him,' doctors would try to reassure anxious mothers, 'he's just got a Sheffield cough.'

Not very far away, the Pennines provided an even more striking industrial landscape than the Don Valley. Travelling by train in 1951 from Manchester to Leeds, via Oldham and Huddersfield, Laurence Thompson was not surprised to encounter ribbons of 'barrack-like' textile mills and 'drilled rows' of workers' cottages. But for the young Australian actor Michael Blakemore, who in two years in England had barely ventured north of Watford, the experience in 1952 of travelling to Huddersfield had the force of revelation:

Most of the journey had been grim, rattling through the bleak, mono-chromatic Midlands, or sitting stranded in a railway intersection so huge it was like a harbour clogged with a seaweed of dirty steel tracks. The last section, however, was spectacular in its awfulness. As the train wound through the devastated beauty of the hills, each valley was revealed as a sink of smoke from which, like neglected washing-up, bits of township projected – a chimney stack, a church spire, the long spines of terraced housing sloping upwards . . .

Down there entire lifetimes were ticking away as remorselessly as a chronic cough. I was appalled. Why had nobody spoken to me of this – not my godmother living in the orderly pastures of Sussex, not my teachers at RADA nor my fellow students?

The natives, of course, largely took for granted the industrial environment in which they, their parents, their grandparents and most likely their great-grandparents had lived, worked and died. An environment now almost gone, and visible only through the new industry of odour-free nostalgia, the sheer pervasive heaviness of its presence in much of mid-century Britain is one of the hardest things to recreate. For every Salford ('the ugly, scrawled, illiterate signature of the industrial revolution', as the novelist Walter Greenwood called it in 1951, with its River Irwell 'throwing up thick and oily chemical belches') or Oldham (with its forest of 220 tall mill chimneys pointing 'their cannon-like muzzles at the sky which they bombard day in and day out with a barrage of never-ending filth'), there were many lesser-known workshops of the world. Hunter Davies grew up in Carlisle after the war:

> An ordinary, smallish northern city, nothing as satanic as those in deepest Lancashire, but my whole memory is of dust and dirt, industrial noise and smoke. You couldn't see the castle, built in 1092, for the decaying slums. I was unaware that our little town hall was a 17th-century gem. It had become almost a bus terminus, surrounded by traffic. Walking down Botchergate was frightening, huge cranes and monster machinery lumbering towards you. Dixon's chimney and textile factory loomed over the whole town. Caldewgate was dominated by Carr's biscuit works. Going Up Street, as we called it, you listened for the factory horns and hooters, careful not to be swept over by the human tide vomited into the streets when a shift finished.

'That's my un-rose-tinted memory,' he adds defiantly. 'Hence my only ambition in life, when I lived in Carlisle, was not to live in Carlisle.'[3]

The pollution was endemic. 'Before Wigan at the approach of the dreadful industrial country, the sky darkened,' noted an apprehensive

James Lees-Milne during a motoring tour in 1947. 'I thought storm clouds portended much-needed rain, but not a bit of it, only the filthy smoke which gathers in the sky here every day of the year, fair or foul.' Five years later, Blakemore's Pennine experience was made all the more striking by the fact that it was a Sunday, in other words the 'stale haze was the residue of the previous working week'. London – itself with a still notably strong manufacturing base – could suffer, too. 'The streets were like those of Dickens' murky London by day and like Dante's Inferno by night' was how the writer Mollie Panter-Downes described the 114 continuous hours of late-November fog endured by poor Ronald Reagan in 1948.

Britain's rising consumption of coal, the cause of all this smoke pollution, had been inexorable for two centuries: some five million tons of it being burned in 1750; 50 million tons by 1850; and 184 million tons by 1946, with more than a quarter of that last total being consumed on the open domestic grate. 'In peace and war alike, King Coal is the paramount Lord of Industry,' declared the Minister of Fuel and Power in a 1951 radio talk, repeating the ringing words of Lloyd George some 30 years earlier. 'It is still more true today,' Philip Noel-Baker went on:

> When I go down a mine and watch the coal going out on the conveyor belt, I often wonder where it will at last be used: in some power station to drive our factories; in a gas works, to supply our cookers; [in] a blast furnace, smelting steel; in a grate at home; in a merchant vessel crossing the Atlantic to carry our exports overseas. On the output of these dark, mysterious galleries where our miners work, the greatness of Britain has been built and still depends.

Such seemed the abiding, bipartisan truth, barely challenged by an as yet ineffectual environmental movement (the Coal Smoke Abatement Society jostling with the British Ecological Society) that seldom penetrated the most industrialised parts of the country. But for one man, E. F. (Fritz) Schumacher, the 1950s would be years of intense agonising. An economist who had left Germany in 1937, Schumacher became in 1950 economic adviser to the National Coal Board – from which vantage point he was increasingly convinced that an ever-rising GNP and supply of material goods was no longer the route to a spiritually healthy society. Accordingly, he began to argue publicly not just that oil and nuclear power were unreliable alternatives to coal, but that coal itself, as a non-renewable fossil fuel, needed to be conserved. A prophet without honour, long before the seismic publication in 1973 of *Small is Beautiful* and an almost simultaneous energy crisis, Schumacher struggled to make an impact with either part of his message.[4]

The foot soldiers of the British economy, meanwhile, concentrated on getting to and from work each day. The average journey to work in the 1940s was some five miles – more than double what it had been in the 1890s, barely half of what it would be in the 1990s. The main mode of transport for that journey between the 1930s and the 1950s broke down (by percentage) as follows:

	1930–39	1940–49	1950–59
Walking	22.5	17.2	13.4
Bicycle	19.1	19.6	16.0
Tram/trolley-bus	9.7	6.7	2.5
Bus	13.8	23.0	23.3
Train (overground)	18.4	18.3	18.9
Underground	4.1	5.4	4.4
Motorcycle	2.3	2.2	3.0
Car/van	9.1	6.0	16.3

By the end of the 1940s, there were barely two million cars on the road, and for another decade it remained the prevailing assumption that the car was a middle-class luxury rather than a commuting necessity. Indeed, well into the 1950s a horse and cart (delivering milk or coal, or perhaps in the hands of a rag-and-bone man) was as likely to be seen as a car on a northern working-class street.[5]

By contrast, the pre-Beeching railway network lay thick across the country, creating sights, sounds and smells intimately known to every adult and child. The eventual, less vivid future was slowly dawning: 'The principal advantages are economy of coal; 90 per cent availability (the engine being ready for service at a moment's notice); no fuel consumption when at a standstill; simple fuel handling; greater cleanliness; smoother running; better conditions for driver and assistant,' bullishly declared the *Illustrated London News* in January 1948, in the context of Britain's 'first diesel-electric main line locomotive' having just done a trial run on the Derby–London line. But for the time being there were still plenty of steam locomotives for trainspotters and others to relish. Steam's relationship with coal was mutually profitable – coal in the tender, coal as freight – and in 1950 few eyebrows were raised when the newly nationalised British Railways formulated a plan for large-scale production of 12 standard designs of steam locomotives through the rest of the decade.

Even so, for most working-class people a railway journey was a fairly unusual occurrence, more often than not associated with going on holiday, and in general, railway commuting was a middle-class preserve. 'The train had its regulars, usually in the same place every day,' the broadcaster Paul Vaughan recalled about the start of his working life in 1950, when each morning he caught the 8.32 from Wimbledon to Holburn Viaduct. 'In one carriage there would be four men, always in exactly the same seats in their sober business suits, and they would spread a cloth over their knees for a daily game of whist, which I suppose they played all the way to the City.' Vaughan himself, working at a pharmaceutical firm near Loughborough Junction, some-times had to get out on their side, when 'they would frown and sigh and raise their eyes to heaven as they lifted their improvised card-table to let you pass . . .'[6]

It was for two other modes of transport that the first ten or so years after the war were the truly golden age. 'This was certainly a town of car-makers,' Peter Bailey wrote about growing up in Coventry, 'but bikes and buses provide the memorable images of town traffic in the early 1950s: dense surging columns of pedalling workers released from the factories at the end of the day; long snailing queues of workers, shoppers and schoolchildren waiting to board the bus home.' Men were twice as likely to use bicycles, with a 1948 survey finding that 'as the social scale is descended the proportion of men using bicycles increases and the proportion of women decreases'. As for the bus, it was by now decisively vanquishing the tram (killed off in London in 1952 but lingering in Glasgow for another decade), while the relatively newfangled trolley-bus, vulnerable to sudden power cuts, was never a truly serious competitor.

Arguably the most emblematic bus route was 'The Inner Circle'.

This was Birmingham's number 8 route, which from 1928 linked the city's inner suburbs and was invariably known as the 'Workmen's Special' because of the large number of factories and workshops it served. Beginning at Five Ways, the bus was soon (going anti-clockwise) passing through Sparkbrook and approaching Small Heath, where the B.S.A. (Birmingham Small Arms) factory in Armoury Road was by 1950 employing 3,500 workers making its world-renowned motor-cycles. Soon afterwards, going up the hill towards Bordesley Green and not far from Birmingham City's ground, there were the Meadway Spares scrapyard, several paint manufacturers and Mulliners, the vehicle bodybuilder that for many years made military buses for the British armed forces. The route then curved round to Saltley (with its West Midlands Gas Board yard always tantalisingly full of coke) and Nechells (with its towering gas-holders in Nechells Place). Then it was along Rocky Lane (with the H. P. Sauce factory, the Hercules Cycle and Motor Company and the nearby Windsor Street gasworks) before reaching Aston Cross, home to the impressive Ansells Brewery building. After Six Ways and Hockley, the swing south went through the justifiably famous Jewellery Quarter, a warren of small firms and passed-down skills, before a final turn took the workhorse bus, often at this time of a 'Utility' design with wooden-slatted seating, back to Five Ways.[7]

Most of the Inner Circle's passengers were short-distance; many of the workers who used it lived in houses cheek by jowl with the factories and workshops that lined the route; and – whatever the pronouncements of the planners – few conceived that its self-contained ecology would ever change.

6

Part of the Machinery

'Local men worked in local plants and factories,' the historian of Blackhill, a particularly tough part of Glasgow, has written of the 1950s: 'Braby's, the Maronite steel works, the St Rollox engine sheds, Alec Binnie's, the White Horse distillery, the Caledonian locomotive works, the Blochairn steel works, W. Lumloch and Cardowan pits, the Parkhead Forge, the Royston Road copper works, the Hogganfield creamery, the Robroyston brick works . . .' We will never know about the lives of the men – mainly, but not entirely, manual unskilled and semi-skilled – who filled those jobs, but one Scottish industrial life that has been memorialised by a son is that of Harry Jack (1902–1981), a fitter:

> Naturally as a boy, I regarded him as a genius. Certainly, he was conscientious. He took the problems of work home with him. Drawings of faulty steam valves would be spread on the kitchen table and he would sometimes speak bitterly of his workmates, scowling into his food and exclaiming:
>
> 'I told old Tom Ramsden where to stick his overtime!'
>
> 'That damned Macdonald! Calls himself a fitter! Took half the morning to take three washers off!'
>
> He did not prosper. He started work as a fourteen-year-old apprentice in a linen mill on five shillings a week and progressed variously through other textile factories in Scotland and Lancashire, into the engine-room of a cargo steamer, down a coal pit, through a lead works and a hosepipe factory . . . He ended his working life only a few miles from where he had begun it, and in much the same way; in overalls and over a lathe and waiting for the dispensation of the evening hooter, when he would stick his leg over his bike and cycle home.[1]

Jack in 1951 was one of an 'occupied' population in Britain of some 20.3 million people. Within that workforce, the proportion doing what were generally recognised as manual, working-class jobs had declined from 78.1 per cent in 1931 to 72.2 per cent twenty years later – a decline especially marked on the part of unskilled workers, with big drops in the coal and textile industries (especially in Scotland, Wales and the north) only partially compensated for by an increase in skilled workers (up from 1.56 million to 2.26 million) in the metal and engineering industries (especially in the Midlands – quintessentially Coventry – and around London). Within industry as a whole, the ratio of administrative, clerical and technical employees to operatives increased from 13.5 per cent in 1935 to 18.6 per cent in 1948. It was a workforce in which, as higher education slowly expanded and retirement provision became more extensive, the trend in terms of age profile was increasingly towards a middle-aged bulge: 43 per cent of the male workforce in 1951 was aged between 35 and 54, compared with 32 per cent half a century earlier. Gender was a different story, with the 30.8 per cent female component of the total workforce in 1951 barely a percentage point above the 1911 proportion. Nevertheless, women by this time were engaged in significant numbers in a far greater *range* of occupations even than in 1931.[2]

Any generalisation about work is easy to challenge. For one thing, so much depended – like almost everything else in mid-century Britain – on matters of class and accumulated expectations attached to class. In the late 1940s a leadpress cable-maker described to the ever-curious social anthropologist Ferdynand Zweig what he saw as the chief differences between a manual worker's situation in the workplace and that of an 'office man':

I start at 7.30 in the morning, an 'office-wallah' starts at 9. He works in a collar and tie and has clean hands, and I have to dirty my hands. What he does can be rubbed out with a rubber, while what I do stays. He keeps in with the boss class. He has a full sick-wage, while I have none. He has a salary, while I am an hourly rated man. His holidays are twice as long as mine. He has superannuation, while I have none. He eats in the staff dining-room and has a better-served meal, which he calls lunch, while we eat in the general dining-room and call it dinner.[3]

The world of work as experienced by working-class people – still by a considerable margin the numercially predominant group in British society – varied hugely, but the dismal ambience of a medium-sized bottle-making firm based in Hunslet, Leeds, may well have been typical of many family-owned, backward-looking manufacturing enterprises. 'One thing that the war did not change was the working conditions at Lax & Shaw's works,' observes that firm's notably unsentimental historian about conditions that remained largely the same until the late 1960s:

> The heat was terrific. The furnaces were much lower in those days, therefore they threw off considerably more heat. This was compounded by the hot, molten glass which dropped down behind the machines when they had to stop, and which had to be dragged out by hand and wheeled away in barrows by the 'flow boys', a back-breaking business. A machine operator would wear clogs on his bare feet, belted trousers, a waistcoat, and a towel around his neck. An operator's shirts would be white with the salt sweated out of his body.
>
> There wasn't even a tap from which to collect cold water to mop one's brow. There was nowhere to wash other than in the water which tumbled down behind the machines. The room set aside at the Albert Works for the men to eat their lunch in was filthy and never used. At Donisthorpe Works the canteen was a horrible, stinking, empty place. But such primitive facilities were on a par with the rest of the industry. The non-machine men usually brought sandwiches and ate them in the works. In the machine shops it was not unknown for men to cook a casserole or hang kippers in the lehr [a type of furnace].

An altogether larger-scale enterprise was Raleigh in Nottingham, kingpin of the British bicycle industry, where a very young Alan Sillitoe worked during the war. In *Saturday Night and Sunday Morning* (1958) he would evoke something of this formative experience: 'The factory smell of oil-suds, machinery, and shaved steel that surrounded you with an air in which pimples grew and prospered on your face and shoulders'; 'lanes of capstan lathes and millers, drills and polishers and hand-presses, worked by a multiplicity of belts and pulleys turning and twisting and slapping on heavy well-oiled wheels overhead, dependent for power on a motor stooping at the far end of the hall like the black shining bulk of a stranded whale'; 'the noise of motor-trolleys passing up and down the gangway and the excruciating din of flying and flapping belts'. Overall, it was not an enviable environment in which to spend most of one's waking hours.

Admittedly Sillitoe's hero, Arthur Seaton, found that he could think and daydream once he had got his lathe working properly, yet at the same time there was always the sense of someone – the rate-checker or the foreman or one of the tool-setters – being potentially on his back. It was that pervasive sense, in essence a loss of independence, that has prompted one historian of work, Arthur J. McIvor, to write of a 'degenerative transformation' as having taken place during the first half of the century:

> Almost all work was considerably more mechanised and capital-intensive by 1950 compared to 1880. Mechanisation and new structures of managerial control incorporating 'scientific' methods, the stopwatch and the rate-fixer meant that the all-round skills of the artisan in trades such as engineering, building, mining and printing were far less in evidence . . . The last vestiges of pre-industrial patterns of work – which had proven particularly persistent – disappeared and labour became regularised, intensified, monitored and codified within the context of a shorter work day and year. Work assumed its 'modern' form.

In the new order on the factory floor, power lay in the hands not of the old-fashioned foremen but of the specialised and highly functional supervisors and line managers.

It was a transformation perhaps most visible in that twentieth-century phenomenon, the motor-car plant. For Phyllis Willmott, visiting Ford's at Dagenham in October 1948, it was a Kurtz-like experience:

> Surely the wheel has completed its full circuit! Seeing those masses of men fixed to the assembly line, the furnace, the inhuman vastness of the power-transformer it is impossible to believe that the condition of man was worse when factory conditions were first in real swing. Hours are shorter, breaks are longer, materially environment is improved – but all, surely, sops to the enslavement, the dehumanisation, the degrading & humiliation of man as a whole person. The shuffle alongside of the moving belt, now this way, now that to fix one screw or add one further

bit of superstructure. The moving chair in all directions & at all levels.
The noise – The massiveness – The horror!

This procession of car bodies moving ceaselessly and relentlessly past
the assembly-line workers was what struck every observer of the
industry. One of those workers was Joe Dennis, working on the night
shift by the 1950s. 'My wife always insisted that I had my breakfast
before I went to bed,' he recalled. 'And I would get into such a state
that I would sit down to a bacon and egg and the table would appear
to be going away from me.' He himself stuck it out, he added, 'but
the elderly chaps couldn't stand the pace'.[4]

Nevertheless, there were (as Willmott conceded) some positives in
the workplace. In 1947, for example, soon after Hugh Dalton had
appealed to the women of the textile areas to 'come back to the mills
and speed the export drive', the *Illustrated London News* featured
photographs of 'Scenes in a Modernised Cotton-Mill' in Bolton,
showing how 'by the provision of fluorescent lighting and the painting
of the premises, together with welfare services for the employees, the
mills can be made attractive'. As for wages, the striking fact was that
by 1949 a manual worker's average earnings stood at 241 per cent of
their 1937 level, whereas the equivalent figure for a member of the
higher professions was 188 per cent. Even so, that professional man
was still earning as much as a skilled manual worker, a semi-skilled
manual worker and an unskilled manual worker put together. The hours
of work, meanwhile, were undeniably shortening by the immediate
post-war period. 'The five-day week is now almost universal,' declared
the Chief Inspector of Factories in 1949, by which point an average
manufacturing operative was working some 46 to 47 hours a week
(including paid overtime), compared with 54 on the eve of the Great
War. Moreover, the great majority of workers were by now entitled to
at least one week's paid holiday (in addition to six public holidays),
and in practice many manual workers received a fortnight's paid holiday.

Finally, on the improving side of things, it was irrefutable that the
British workplace had become by mid-century a significantly safer
environment: the annual average of persons killed in industrial accidents
declined from more than 4,000 in the 1900s and more than 3,000 in the
1920s to 2,425 in the 1940s and 1,564 in the 1950s. One of the most

compelling arguments for the nationalisation of the coal-mining industry had been the dreadful safety record under private ownership, but it still took until the second half of the 1950s for the annual level of fatalities regularly to get down to below 400. Moreover, in post-war British industry as a whole, workplace accidents remained an all too regular feature. Colin Ferguson, in the pattern shop at Babcock & Wilcox's Renfrew Works, was only a few feet away from one in October 1950:

> Last Thursday Willie Agnew was seriously injured while working at the Wadkin patternmaking machine just behind me. All the ribs on his left side were broken & he was caught by the cutter of the machine behind his left shoulder & badly lacerated. His shoulder blade is broken & the lung pierced. His clothing had to be cut to release him. He was unconscious but regained consciousness for a few moments. It was I who put off the power to stop the machine. Jas Edmond & C. Connell both ran for the D^r. He was carried in a stretcher to the ambulance room & injected with morphine . . .

Happily, the poor man regained full consciousness on the Saturday.[5]

Occupational safety, of course, was not quite the same as occupational health. If one of the traditional killers, lead poisoning, had been more or less eliminated by this time, there still remained the remorseless 'dust' diseases of silicosis (including coal miners' pneumoconiosis) and asbestosis. In 1950 there were more than 800 deaths directly from silicosis, rising to more than 2,000 by 1955. In the former year some 5,000 more men left the coal mines of South Wales – where the disease was mainly centred – than went into them, principally for fear of getting silicosis. The National Coal Board, to start with anyway, did not cope shiningly well with the problem: detailed scientific research did not begin until 1952 and made only slow progress, while a squabble with the NHS over the work and the cost meant that it was not until 1959 that there began, with a view to prevention and control, the systematic medical examination of all mine workers. Laurence Thompson's sentiments after visiting the South Wales pits at the start of the decade were understandably heartfelt. 'If I had to live or work with someone slowly choking of silicosis, I would leave too,' he declared, 'and I would never let a word pass my lips about lazy miners who won't get the coal.' Yet, as he added, 'someone must get the coal'.

The number of deaths caused by exposure to asbestos (specifically, the inhalation of asbestos fibres) was for a long time appreciably less, yet arguably it was the more shocking story, given that it was not until the 1960s that most of the workers engaged in asbestos-related industries became aware of the danger, which was at least 30 years after they could and should have been made aware. Asbestosis, lung cancer, mesothelioma – all were caused by the insidious dust, which (as victims from Clydeside shipyards and building sites would recall) came 'down like snow' on them, whether in the form of dust, asbestos cuttings or dried-out 'monkey dung', as asbestos paste was called. Britain's leading asbestos manufacturer was Turner & Newall, headquartered in Rochdale's Spodden Valley near Manchester. Its records have been comprehensively studied by Geoffrey Tweedale, who for the mid-decades of the century relates an appalling tale of management indifference to the dangers to which its workforce was exposed, allied to an almost systemic policy of trying to wriggle out of financial liability to the families of those who had died (usually in their mid-50s) as a direct result of those dangers. 'We have many cases of death obviously caused by the usual diseases to which man is heir,' privately grumbled the chairman, Sir Samuel Turner, in 1947, 'but if by any chance a few particles of asbestos happen to be found in the lung, then coroners invariably bring in a verdict which involves a claim.' Tweedale, however, shows in devastating detail that the odds were heavily weighted against a victim's family receiving an adequate (let alone an equitable) level of compensation; that Turner & Newall could very well have afforded in the post-war period to adopt a more generous policy; and that human sympathy was conspicuous by its absence. A hard-headed, unpreachy business historian, he is compelled to a class-based conclusion: 'The majority of sufferers were working-class people – usually manual workers – and their "masters" rarely developed asbestos disease. While hundreds of its workforce perished, Turner & Newall's higher echelons remained immune.'[6]

How typical was this cold-hearted exploitation? 'The neglect of the human side in industry was a frequent theme of my conversations with workers of all grades,' Zweig noted after some three years of intensive and extensive interviews, mainly in the late 1940s:

'My employer never looks at me,' a cotton spinner said to me, 'he just sees the £ s. d. I represent. For him I am manpower, not a man.'

'Men are treated here as part of the machinery and everybody knows that they are valuable pieces of machinery,' a factory engineer told me, 'but the funny part of it is that they are not studied as the machines are, and kept in good running order. No one is interested in finding out the needs and requirements of men. They are simply taken for granted.'

Zweig also talked to employers, among whom there were 'many good-natured men' determined to treat business and morality as separate spheres. 'You know business isn't charity or a club,' an employer in an engineering firm told him. 'It's fatal to be sentimental in your work.'[7]

Even so, for all the intensification of the work process since the late nineteenth century, the cumulative evidence is that there still prevailed in Britain circa 1950 a considerable amount of what over half a century later seems like very old-fashioned paternalism – a paternalism that, in the employer/employee relationship, transcended the cash nexus. The full-employment context of the post-war economy clearly made a difference, in the sense that labour became a far more precious commodity than it had been during much of the inter-war period, but that alone is not sufficient explanation for what were often historically very entrenched attitudes on the part of employers and management.

Take the big high-street clearing banks. The work was often tedious and repetitive, the pay nothing special (at least in middle-class terms), but the sense of security was overwhelmingly reassuring. 'You had a job for life, you got paid a little more each year, and the bank looked after you in all sorts of ways, through its concern for your well-being, your family, your finances and your social position,' notes the historian of that ritualised, self-enclosed world. 'Each employee was docked 2½ per cent of his salary for the widows and orphans fund. The only way you could be fired was by putting your hand in the till.' In many (though far from all) of the much smaller firms that made up the City of London, the spirit was somewhat similar, if more intimate. When a 16-year-old called Godfrey Chandler joined the stockbroking firm of Cazenove, Akroyds & Greenwood & Co during the war, he warmed from the start to the family atmosphere and could not help but think of the Cheeryble brothers in *Nicholas Nickleby*. At

Cazenove's as elsewhere, much depended on the office manager: it was a given that he was an autocrat, the question was whether or not he was a benevolent one.

In industry at large the classic paternalist firm was the soap and detergent manufacturer Lever Brothers, the nineteenth-century creation at Port Sunlight near Liverpool of William Lever, the first Lord Leverhulme. Housing, leisure, health, retirement – all were directly taken care of by the company, which unflaggingly stressed that employers and employees alike comprised one large family. In 1953 more than a third of its 8,389 workforce had served for 15 years or more, with almost a thousand having been there for 30 years or more. Three years earlier, when *Port Sunlight News* featured seven men who had completed more than 40 years' service, the accompanying article hailed them as exemplars and noted proudly that they had grown up in the 'Lever tradition' of 'enlightened industrial outlook'. By this time, indeed, the 10,000th gold watch had already been handed out. Yet there were limits to the family spirit: in the model village (where non-members of staff could not buy houses until the late 1970s) there operated strict residential segregation between workers and senior managers.

It was similarly not quite all roses at another arch-paternalist firm, the well-known machine-tool manufacturers Alfred Herbert Ltd. The founder and, right up to his death, dominant figure was Sir Alfred Herbert (1866–1957), whose approach is perhaps best described as an authoritarian and strictly hierarchical benevolence, offering moral as much as material guidance. Discipline was everything; workers knew that there would be no seasonal lay-offs; and the prevailing parsimony, for all the pioneering welfare provision (including sports and social facilities), was positively Gladstonian. That in essence was the 'deal' Sir Alfred offered – and during his lifetime many skilled workers in Coventry were glad enough to accept it. Or take the paternalism of the aggressively anti-nationalisation Tate & Lyle. For all those connected with its sugar refinery at Plaistow Wharf, the biggest in the world, there was a weekly treat at the social club. 'It was known as the Tate & Lyle Saturday night out,' recalled one worker, Ron Linford. 'It was really great. All the family would go including the kids. First thing we used to do was to make sure we had our seats right alongside the bar, so that we didn't have too far to carry the drinks. There was cabaret, fancy dress with prizes for the children, dancing to the band, spot waltzes and comedians doing turns.'[8]

In almost any manufacturing firm run along more or less paternalist lines, there was the annual ritual of the works outing – perhaps to one of the National Parks (such as in the Peak District) created by the government in 1949 but more often to the seaside. 'Rewarded for Their Labours' was how in July 1948 the *Merthyr Express* reported 310 employees of Hoover being 'treated to an outing to Weston-super-Mare' by the company the previous Sunday, including lunch and high tea at the Grand Pier Restaurant. 'The whole cost of the outing was borne by the company in recognition of the whole-hearted co-operation of all the workers within the organisation. Mr A. R. Northover, works manager, accompanied the party, which made the journey by coach and boat.' The imaginative importance of these factory outings, comparable to that of the Christmas office party in a later, more white-collar era, was nicely reflected in a Max Miller joke. The foreman asks four pregnant women at their sewing machines when their babies are expected. 'Mine's due in May,' replies the first, 'hers is also due in May, and so is hers.' 'What about the other girl?' asks the foreman. 'Oh, I don't know about her. She wasn't on the charabanc trip.'

The more prosaic reality is probably caught in Valerie Gisborn's account of her first factory outing, in 1950, as a 16-year-old working in a Leicester clothing factory. The coaches, each with a supervisor, left at 7.00 a.m. and just over four hours later pulled up along the seafront at the inevitable Skegness:

It was fine and windy but we made the best of it doing exactly what we pleased. We had many laughs and purchased silly 'Kiss me quick' hats. The fairground was a big attraction and we spent a couple of hours there trying to win something or other on the darts and shooting ranges. A couple of the young girls made themselves sick by having too many rides on a whiplash merry go round . . .

Everybody turned up for the coaches at 7 pm and, when the check-in was completed to ensure no one had been left behind, the coaches set off back to Leicester. Halfway home the coaches separated, each one taking a different route to a selected public house so that we could all have a drink. We stopped for one hour, and as I did not drink in pubs a girlfriend and I walked around the village, purchased some chips and a drink from the local fish and chip shop, and returned to wait for the others in the coach. Later as we drove towards Leicester the coaches caught up with each other and we all arrived back outside the factory about midnight.

'The day out was the talk of the firm for days,' she added, 'and the manager, Mr Pell, organised a letter on behalf of everyone to say thank you to the boss.'[9]

For women as a whole, the range of available jobs may have expanded during the first half of the century, but the work they actually did was still largely gender-determined. The figures are stark: 88 per cent of women working for wages in 1901 had been in occupations dominated by women; by 1951 the proportion was virtually unchanged at 86 per cent. Teachers, nurses, clerical workers, cleaners, waitresses, shop assistants, barmaids, textile-factory hands – these were typical female members of the workforce, with often not a man in sight, at least at a non-supervisory level. Most of that work, pending greater employer flexibility, was full-time: of the female workforce of just over 6 million in 1951, only 832,000 worked fewer than 30 hours per week.

Whether full-time or part-time, women seldom enjoyed other than lowly status in their jobs. In banks and building societies, for example, female clerical workers were largely confined to the 'back office', with many managers and customers unable to countenance lady cashiers before the 1960s. Moreover, although the 'marriage bar' (the policy of not employing married women) was gradually being lifted – from teaching in 1944, from the Civil Service in 1946, from the Bank of England in 1949 but still in place at Barclays Bank until 1961 – there was still the crucial question of pay. Here the gender differential was undeniably narrowing, with the hourly earnings of women increasing by 163 per cent between 1938 and 1950, compared with 122 per cent for men. But it was still huge. If one takes the last pay week of October 1950 in all manufacturing industries, the average earnings of women (over 18) compared with the earnings of men (over 21) amounted to about 53 per cent. In the 1950s as a whole, full-time female workers earned only 51 per cent of the average weekly pay of male workers. It was not so much a pay gap as a pay chasm.[10]

At a national policy level, the official desire by 1946/7 to see women back in the workforce (following their return home at the end of the war) was readily understandable in the context of the prevailing labour shortage, but, among other things, it ran up against an equally prevailing anxiety that the war and its immediate aftermath had done significant damage to the social fabric, which would be more readily repaired if women stayed in their traditional homemaking capacity. The outcome, predictably, was only modified encouragement – and certainly no dangling of the carrot of equal pay or anything like it. A particularly influential economist, Roy Harrod, emphasised to the Royal Commission on Equal Pay how important it was 'to secure that motherhood as a vocation is not too unattractive compared with work in the professions, industry or trade'. Even Bloomsbury's finest (and Harrod's hero), the liberal-minded John Maynard Keynes, was no crusader for equal opportunities. 'A world in which young married women spend eight or nine hours a day away from home doing office work when their husbands are doing alike, seems a gloomy one' was his view of the Bank of England's prospective removal of its marriage bar.

Amidst progressive opinion generally, there existed a distinct tendency to esteem hard, sweaty – and almost invariably male – labour above 'softer' forms of work, with inevitable implications for pay as well as status. The biography of Jennie Lee, Aneurin Bevan's equally left-wing wife, records a classic exchange (probably in the early 1950s) between her and another, rather younger, female Labour MP, Barbara Castle. 'Barbara,' said Lee, 'we cannot ask for equal pay when miners' wages are so low.' In that case, replied the red-haired one, 'we will wait for ever'. The weight of opinion – indeed of sentiment – remained with Lee. So, too, in the unprogressive middle-class world at large, where for a long time it remained a distinguishing mark of a man's assured position in his class if his wife was able to be at home – which obviously could be shown only by actually being at home. On the radio, in films, in women's magazines, femininity was almost exclusively identified with the home and the nurturing of children. For those women who sought to identify themselves through their careers, there was pity more than admiration. 'Business Girls', one of the most haunting poems in John Betjeman's *A Few Late Chrysanthemums* (1954), is an evocation of 'poor unbelov'd' businesswomen living in

Camden Town and having a precious if lonely bathroom soak before 'All too soon the tiny breakfast, / Trolley-bus and windy street!'[11]

Within the workplace the male attitude to upward female mobility was almost universally discouraging. 'Such women are the first to agree that they do not represent the general aspirations of their sex' was how *Midbank Chronicle*, Midland Bank's staff magazine, put it in 1949. 'They have not the least desire to impose conditions that would be suitable to themselves upon the great majority for whom the same conditions would be entirely unsuitable.' Barely half the pay, fewer perks (such as cheap mortgages), inferior pension rights – all were inherent, and duly played out, in the logic of that argument. Unsurprisingly, women working for the big high-street banks were seldom encouraged to take the exams of the Institute of Bankers and thereby achieve promotion. There was no doubt an element of fear involved – that if women advanced in numbers, they might start to threaten men's automatic position as chief breadwinners – but the male assumption of superiority in the workplace was also a deeply entrenched cultural norm. Listen to the voice of Frank Pound, who in the late 1940s worked in the toolroom at the Mullard Valve Company in south London. He was asked in the 1990s whether there had been women attached to the toolroom, traditionally the preserve of the skilled male elite:

> They had a little department, they called it the cow-shed, and the girls was in there doing turning, very simple engineering, which we hardly ever spoke to. You know, we occasionally saw them ...
>
> *And these women would not have had an apprenticeship?*
>
> Oh, no, no, no, they were, I believe they called them trainee workers, and they were trained during the war, I take it, to help people get things done in the war, you see.

The implications were clear. Women might have penetrated the toolroom during the exigencies of war, but their presence was no longer acceptable; there was no question of their receiving apprenticeships and thus becoming full toolmakers, and management and the male toolmakers between them would soon ensure that women were wholly excluded from the citadel. In short, it was back to the cow-shed.

Yet the fact is that in her oral history of Mullards, together with similar light-industry firms in south London, Sue Bruley has found 'no signs that women resisted the pressures to reinforce strict occupational segregation'. Furthermore, 'the only signs of unrest among the women in these years [1920–60] was over piece rates', though 'there is little evidence that dissatisfaction over pay rates spilled over into serious unrest'. Much turned, presumably, on the expectations of working women, as well as the extent to which they looked to their job as the central source of their identity. And certainly the Social Survey's study *Women and Industry*, based on 1947 fieldwork, made it abundantly clear that in the eyes of most women (working and otherwise) it was wrong to combine work and marriage, with work having to be second best unless that was financially impossible.[12]

This finding would not have amazed Pearl Jephcott. Through both her sociological fieldwork and her involvement in the girls' club movement in London, she had a thorough understanding of how young women entering the labour market saw work in the broad scheme of things. In *Rising Twenty*, her 1948 study of just over a hundred girls living in three parts of England ('a pit village in County Durham; a cluster of decaying and blitzed streets within a mile of Piccadilly Circus; and a northern industrial town [Barrow?] notable for its armaments and shipbuilding'), she set out her stall in a chapter called 'The Dominant Interest':

> Practically every girl says that she will want to give up her job when she gets married, and expects her career to continue for another five years at most . . . Those who consider that they might stay on at work give as their reason not a belief in the value of their job, nor even personal independence, but 'only if my husband's pay weren't enough' or 'if we need to get a good home together'. No one feels her job to be so important either for other people or in her own life that she ought to continue with it.

'Generations of tradition lie behind this outlook,' emphasised Jephcott. And she added that 'for the last 65 years, almost since the weddings of these girls' great-grandmothers, there has been no appreciable change (apart from the war periods) in the proportion of women of 15 to 45 who do go out to work'.

Jephcott's findings were particularly relevant given the youthful profile of the female workforce – an age analysis in July 1948 revealed that 57 per cent were 30 or under, compared with 37 per cent of the male workforce. But for a vivid picture of the female workforce as a whole, one turns to the tireless Zweig, whose *Women's Life and Labour* (1952) was based on well over 400 interviews, mainly in the late 1940s. He visited 'cotton and silk mills, engineering factories, potteries, woollen mills and finishing-up trades, shops, canteens, hospitals, glove and hat and shoe factories, printing offices and paper-sorting departments in Lancashire, Cheshire, Staffordshire, Yorkshire and London', comprising 46 workplaces in all.

There he found a predominantly unskilled workforce in which 'a strong preference for a concrete job of a specific nature' was voiced 'only infrequently'. A pronouncement like 'I was always interested in telephones, so I took a job as a telephonist' was 'rarely heard'. Instead, the 'one outstanding preference' was more often than not expressed in the assertion: 'This is a clean job.' And Zweig commented:

> The social prestige of jobs is primarily based on the cleanliness and tidiness of the jobs performed, as it has been tacitly assumed that like attracts like, the clean and tidy girls being on clean jobs. The low prestige of mill girls is basically caused by the fluff and dust of the cotton mill ... The cardroom tenters, who collect the highest share of fluff and dust, enjoy the lowest prestige, the spinners forming the middle and the weavers the upper class.

Many women also preferred what they called 'a light job' – interpreted by Zweig to mean light not only physically but also mentally. 'Maybe they have enough bother and worry of their own,' a supervisor explained to him about the general disinclination to stick at jobs requiring a significant degree of concentration or thought. 'When an easy job comes along I have to split it and let it go round.' There was, argued Zweig, an essentially different mindset involved:

> A woman has plenty of subjects which can occupy her mind and her mind is always busy with small bits of everyday life. Not only does she rarely complain of the monotony of her job, but in most cases she loves a repetitive job of such a kind which enables her to indulge in daydreaming or simply reviving pictures of the past. If she was in the pictures last night, she has something to remember the whole day afterwards if

the film was interesting. The other advantage of having a light repetitive job is the ability to have a chat: 'I must keep my eyes on the machines but I can talk'. If the noise is not too deafening the girls can talk freely about their experiences and last night's outings.

Predictably, *Music While You Work* (on the Home Service at 10.30 each weekday morning) was 'much more popular with women than with men'.

Were working women broadly content? Zweig had started his inquiry, he admitted, 'with a preconceived idea about the unhappy woman dragged from her home to work, the little slave doing a monotonous and uncongenial job, the victim of the industrial civilisation'. His eyes were opened:

> I can say definitely on the basis of my experience that industry has a great attraction for women workers, apart from a small minority of women whose health and energy are not sufficient to carry on two jobs and who are driven to industry by the whip of want. Women are not interested in industry as such but the industry stands in their mind for many things which they want and opens for them a new world. Here they come into contact with real 'life'; they feel that they are in a place where there is something worth while going on.

Friends and companionship, chatter and gossip, looking for a mate or just giving one an interest in life – there were many reasons, Zweig explained, why women enjoyed working, in addition to the obvious economic motivation. He went on:

> I do not like general theories, and least of all psychological theories, but the one thing which struck me in my inquiry was the sense of inferiority which many, if not most, women have. They accept man's superiority as a matter of fact and a man's job is as a rule superior to a woman's job. You can feel the regret that they were not born men, who have the best of everything and the first choice in practically all things. So they do as much as they can to prove equal to men, to prove that they are not drones or pleasure animals kept by men for their amusement, or sleeping partners to men's booty. Paid work, especially work in industry, relieves that sense of inferiority.

'I don't need to ask my husband for permission to spend a shilling as others do,' he was told. 'I spend my own money in my own way.'

This was far from Zweig's only inquiry in these years, but it seems to have been the one that meant the most to him. He described in his foreword how it had revealed to him 'a whole world of distinct female values', exemplified by 'the amazing endurance and struggle against the adversities of life on the part of many married women with large families'. It was not unusual, he explained, 'to find a mother of five small children going out to work full-time, getting up at 6 a.m. and going to bed at 12, doing her washing on Sundays, and accepting all this with a smile as a matter of course'. Such women, he asserted, 'were an inspiration to me – as they can be to anyone who looks deeply into the turbulent waters of life'.

But perhaps the most haunting of the individual case-studies he provided was of a childless married woman, aged 36, working in a factory:

> Her steady wage on a machine is £4 plus 15s bonus. She worked for three years during the war and has since been working two years. She likes her job; it's interesting and of course she likes the money. Her husband is a skilled fitter and turner in the same firm, but she doesn't know how much he earns. He gives her £4 a week. She saves for a nice house, because for the time being they live with in-laws.
>
> They have no children. Why? 'It is up to him. I would like to have children and I am not getting any younger.'
>
> Her greatest hope: 'To get a nice house.' Her greatest fear: 'To die.'
>
> The basis of happiness consists of a nice house and a good married life. ('I can say that because I haven't got it.')
>
> She doesn't go in for pools or other gambling, 'that I leave to my husband'.
>
> She enjoys life as far as she can. She goes three times a week to the pictures, at the weekends to the pub; she reads Western stories. No churchgoing.
>
> 'Life is what you make it.'

'She has never heard about the devaluation or cheapening of the pound or the economic crisis,' Zweig's pen picture added. 'What is meant by economic crisis to her is that there are no nylons in the shops.'[13]

In 1952 Zweig also published *The British Worker*, pulling together
the fruits of his hundreds of interviews in the late 1940s with male
manual workers. In the book he drew similarly positive conclusions
about the human effects of industrial work. A worker who complained
about a monotonous job was usually unhappy in his home life; most
male jobs were not monotonous; and even if up to a third of the
male working-class population did 'dull, repetitive, and uninteresting
jobs', that did not mean that they were all bored stiff with them,
given the twin observed facts of the sociability of the workplace and
that 'machines are often very interesting and many people like
handling them.'

Yet as Zweig fully conceded, the question of job satisfaction
depended on a range of variables, even within the same grade of the
same industry in the same region:

> Cleanliness, the right temperature, good air, light, private lockers, good
> washing facilities, good canteens, the good repute of a firm, a genial
> atmosphere, friendly relations on the floor, fairness in dealing with the
> worker, a good foreman, and a good boss, may turn even a distasteful
> job into an attractive one. No one of these factors can be singled out
> as more important than the others. Men react to the general conditions
> of the work, not to any individual factor in it.

There were two even more important variables – the size of the wage
packet and the extent of job security – with Zweig in both cases emphasising the social as much as the economic aspect. All in all, he concluded,
'there is an element of hate in the most valued jobs, and an element
of love in the most hated':

> The factor of habit clearly comes into men's feelings towards a job, and
> makes them like even a job they originally disliked. But the hateful
> thought that they are bound to a job for life is an unpleasant feature of
> even the most interesting jobs . . .
>   The vast majority of men if asked whether they like their job will
> answer thoughtfully 'I suppose I do'; but their further comments are
> often revealing.
>   Some men will tell you: 'I should think so. Think about the people

who have no job at all', or 'It gives me my bread and butter', or 'I am used to it now', or 'I mustn't grumble'.

Strong feelings for or against the job are less common than the combination of liking and disliking at the same time.

'I like the job but you get fed up with it at times.'

In short, 'the ambivalence of love and hate is nowhere more strongly expressed than it is in the attitude to work'.[14] Zweig's portrayal, here and in his other studies, of a fatalistic, suspicious, deeply conservative working class, finding a degree of satisfaction in its labours while overall stoically and unenthusiastically accepting its lot, is broadly convincing – not least because no other sociologist or commentator of the era came so intimately and extensively into contact with that class as he did.

Certainly there were some workers intensely proud of what they did. Take the Sheffield steel industry, where for so many years the crucible had nurtured what the industry's historian justifiably calls 'virtuoso skill in hand and eye'. That skill may have been under threat by the 1950s, but it still remained important. 'It was all rule of thumb,' recalled one operative. 'We did play around with devices such as thermocouples, but they were so unreliable, we tended not to use them.' Sheffield, remembers Stewart Dalton about growing up there, 'was a proud City, and its workers proud of their skills'. Not only the workers: 'Children on the housing estates could be heard arguing, "My dad works at ESC [English Steel Corporation]. It's better than Firth Browns." Pity the child whose father's occupation was so humble as to be ignored in the daily round of squabbles. The melter, the roller, the forgeman . . . these were the "worthy" occupations, not comparable in any way with the "wimpish" occupations found outside the factories.'

In general, such pride was unsurprising. Whatever the long-term trend towards deskilling that was undeniably taking place in British industry, the fact was that by mid-century less than 5 per cent of the overall workforce was engaged in mass-production processes, increasingly typified by the assembly line of the car plant. Nor does Zweig's emphasis on the positive social function of the workplace seem misplaced. As often as not there was humour and camaraderie, as well as a strict hierarchy within many of the workforces – a hierarchy which, by informally imposing its code of proper conduct, in turn contributed to the strength of civil society. 'If you didn't behave at the works,' the Labour politician Frank Field has recalled, 'you were taken behind the shed and dealt with, because you couldn't have people risking other people's limbs and lives.' That necessity, as well as the sense of solidarity in factory culture, comes through in Colin Ferguson's diary entry for the last Monday in August 1950:

> Worked only half a day in the Pattern Shop today. Just before dinner time a Shop Meeting was hurriedly called & within 2 minutes a vote was taken whether we would stop at the whistle & go home till tomorrow morning. This was agreed to on a show of hands without a count. The reason for this was a request, that our shop fall in line with the Dressing Shop & the Iron & Steel Foundries, which (as a mark of respect to a dresser who'd just been killed by a 3½ ton casting falling on him) had decided to stop work for the day. The man killed came from Paisley. His name was Patterson.

It was a discipline good at creating a sense of duty, even loyalty – primarily towards fellow-workers, but sometimes to employers. Field's father spent 48 years building carbon blocks for Morgan Crucible in Battersea. 'He got up every day, coughing his lungs out, hating his job, but he never went sick, never let them down.' His reward on retirement was £1 for every year of employment.[15]

In the end – whether or not the job was satisfying (and here Zweig may have been somewhat rose-tinted, ignoring for example the sheer numbing, alienating tedium of the vast majority of clerical work), whether or not there was solidarity within the workforce (at Lax & Shaw the sorters were the sworn enemies of the operators, the latter paid by the accepted bottle and often provoked to violence when 'idle sorters on a slow-moving lehr raked away perfectly good bottles simply to get away for their break more quickly'), and whether or not there was a good atmosphere in the workplace – every worker knew full well, like generations of workers before him, that he was not there for the fun of it.

'When a man receives his wages every seven days, and these on the whole not a great deal more than enough for comfortable survival, he is *bound* to his work,' noted the authors of a study of a Yorkshire mining community in the early to mid-1950s. 'By Sunday night the collier who starts work at 6 a.m. on Monday is not enjoying himself with the same abandon as he did the night before. By Wednesday, three hard days may have made him tired and dispirited and he consoles himself only with the remark that at least the back of the week has been broken.' While on the vexed question of the voluntary Saturday morning shift, that subject of much well-meaning exhortation and propaganda from above, the authors quoted a typical snatch of miners' dialogue:

Coming in on Saturday?
   No. Five days is enough for anybody.
   Oh, so you're not bothered about getting some extra coal out for the country?
   I suppose that's why you come in on Saturdays.
   Is it . . .! We come in for some extra brass and that's that.

It is a trend impossible to date precisely, but it seems plausible that it was during these relatively early post-war years that the shift began – at least on the part of a significant proportion of the working class – from 'living to work' (as the phrase went) to 'working to live'. Work, in other words, was starting to lose *some* of its traditional centrality in terms of defining a working man's life and purpose. 'If extra hours have to be worked at pressure periods, it is almost impossible to persuade workers to do them on Saturday mornings' was the 1949 finding of the Chief Inspector of Factories about the coming of the five-day week, not only in relation to coal miners. An important shift, it can only be understood against the background of full employment and rising real wages.

   Even so, for the workforce as a whole, it did not alter the dominant priorities identified by Zweig. Early in 1953, Research Services Ltd, the organisation run by Mark Abrams, interviewed 1,079 people who worked for a living across the country. They were shown a list of ten possible job satisfactions – nearness to your home; friendly people to work with; good wages or earnings; security of employment; opportunity to use your own ideas; good holidays; opportunities to get on; adequate pension; good training facilities; reasonably short hours – and asked to name which three they considered most important. Good earnings (placed in 58 per cent of people's top three) and security of employment (55 per cent) were easily the most popular, followed by friendly people to work with (39 per cent), while reasonably short hours and good training finished equal bottom at 8 per cent each. Predictably, middle-class workers attached greater importance to opportunities to get on and use one's own ideas; equally predictably, older people (who had lived through the inter-war slump) put job security above good earnings, while younger workers were the other way round. There was indeed a distinct generational gap emerging in attitudes to work. 'A middle-aged craftsman will say sometimes: "My work is my hobby", but a young man will very rarely say this' was Zweig's observation. 'He finds his hobbies somewhere else, and lacks the same firmly-established working habits.'[16]

Fortunately, it is possible to get a bit closer up. In 1946 a University of London psychologist, Norah M. Davis, conducted individual interviews across the country with 400 building workers, a mixture of skilled tradesmen (bricklayers, joiners, plasterers, etc) and labourers (mainly unskilled but including some semi-skilled like scaffolders). She found that 82.1 per cent of tradesmen expressed 'definite liking' for their jobs, compared with 69.6 per cent of labourers. 'Open-air life; healthy; sense of freedom' was the most popular explanation given (34.5 per cent) for liking the job, with – despite the acute national housing shortage – 'Job is of social importance' put forward by only 2.9 per cent. Whether liking or disliking the job, there were plenty of patently sincere views expressed:

Mine is a job on its own. Not everyone can get an eighth of an inch off 57 feet long of glass.

I feel that men's lives depend on my work [scaffolding]. The more ticklish a job the better I like it.

I dislike being a labourer and looked down on as an imbecile. It gives me an inferiority complex. Girls draw away from you in buses and say, 'He's only a labourer'.

I like being a labourer as we have less responsibility than trades-men.

The wages aren't enough to live on. I have slaved for fifty years and now have only one suit. Is that enough out of life?

It frightens me to think I'll do nothing but lay bricks all my life.

I like making a place look decent. I want a house of my own so I am interested.

I like the open air. I like laying bricks and the harmony among your mates.

Asked about their ambitions, more than 40 per cent of the tradesmen and over 52 per cent of the labourers replied – in what tone of voice is not recorded – that they had 'No ambition', with many men adding, 'It's no good having ambition.'

The interviews also revealed that a high degree of group solidarity, with overwhelmingly favourable attitudes being expressed about fellow-workers ('They're a good, sociable crowd of lads' was a typical assertion), co-existed with widespread grumbling about management:

There are too many walking about in hats. Why?

You can get no satisfaction out of the Head Office. They pass the buck and you get nowhere.

I wish they had a suggestion scheme. Of course I expect only one in a hundred suggestions would be any good and be accepted, but that wouldn't matter because it would be an encouragement to everyone.

I'm sure our squad is laying an average of about 800 bricks whatever the Corporation says. They never give us the facts or tell us how they get their figures.

It would be more interesting if they'd only tell us how the job is progressing.

'On most of the sites,' summarised Davis, 'the relationship of the operatives to the management was characterised by lack of contact and ignorance.' Significantly, private contractors were less the target of criticism than public contractors, in effect the local authorities – a discouraging finding in the light of Aneurin Bevan's systematic privileging of public above private house-building.

What really stirred the interviewees' emotions was being asked about their attitude towards their own sons entering the industry. Of those giving an opinion (the overwhelming majority), only 18 per cent expressed definite approval, as against the conditional approval of 33 per cent and definite disapproval of 49 per cent. Pervading many of the replies was a more or less resentful sense of the inferior status accorded in modern society to the building operative (whether tradesman or labourer) and indeed the manual worker more generally:

No. A collar and tie job for him.
  No. Any boy that dons overalls is a fool.
  The trade is too casual. He's got a horror of the tools because he knows what his Dad's life has been.
  I wouldn't like them messed around as I have been.
  I shall try to prevent them. It's too hard work.
  I wouldn't let him. Grandfather and me had too hard a time.

Tellingly, men with a family tradition in building were more than 9 per cent more likely to express that heartfelt disapproval.

Overall, the survey leaves an impression of a rugged, socially cohesive, probably fairly bloody-minded culture on the nation's building sites. It was not so different in another great nineteenth-century British industry: the railways. 'Job is utterly filthy,' noted a young middle-class Communist, Charlie Mayo, in October 1952 soon after getting a job at King's Cross:

Engines are covered in grease, dirt, soot, inches thick ... Prevailing picture one of utter drabness & dirt, oil, grease, black soot, oily water underfoot, the air dogged with steam ...
  A large part of the time is wasted. We hang about the canteen. I'm getting sick of bloody tea. It's like a drug, the drivers & firemen are permanently brewing tea. Even, I found, in the middle of shunting ...

The drivers were the elite group – the long-haul drivers anyway – but Mayo found them sadly limited in outlook: 'They say a lot of the old feeling of companionship has gone out of the industry. The older ones still talk in terms of "The Company". No one has a clue what nationalisation *should* mean. They all just know from their own experience that what they've got hasn't benefited them at all. Yet I'd say they were solid Labour voters.' Mayo's most poignant encounter, though, was with a driver on his 65th birthday. 'Small & worn away', with 'tired & dim' eyes, the man's compulsory retirement fell that day:

> 'They're mean, mate,' he said, 'mean as arseholes. This is my last day here, & they want me to work it. 48 years, & they can't give me half a day.' He shrugged. 'Well, fuck 'em, I'm taking it. They won't pay me for it, but I'm taking it. The missus won't be expecting me, but I'm clocking off at two.'
>
> 'I don't think I shall be staying here for life,' I said.
>
> 'Don't you, mate. Get yourself a job with a pension. When I was a lad, I didn't think about it, but from this end of the run it's a big thing.'
>
> I said, 'Still, by the time I'm due to retire, I expect we'll have won our pension. It's up to us to get the Union to fight for it.'
>
> 'Right, mate. Right enough,' he said. But there was no belief in his voice.
>
> 'You must have been in the general strike,' I said.
>
> 'Yes, I was in all of them. But the men haven't got the feeling for it. Even less now . . .'

Just before two o'clock, the man came to say goodbye. '"Goodbye, mate," I said, "& all the best." He walked off across the tracks, carrying in his hand his tea can.'

In the course of the winter during which Mayo kept his King's Cross journal – a winter that saw the young Communist having his idealistic assumptions about the working class challenged almost daily – one episode had a particularly brutal clarity:

> We were in the mess room when one of the shunters brought in a pigeon. It had got oil on its wings & was unable to fly. One of its eyes had been missing for a long time. Charlie took it and put it on the table, right between us. He held its wings out & examined it. Someone made a joke, & I was half smiling.
>
> 'It's a goner,' said Charlie. He hit it suddenly on the back of the neck, but it only struggled. So he took its neck in his fingers and pulled its head off, neck & all. It was so sudden & savage, right there among our cups of tea & sandwiches, that I'd hardly time to take it in before I witnessed the next nightmare. He just tossed the body onto the open fire. But the nervous reaction in the body made it jump out again, wings

on fire. Then it fluttered & scrambled about on the floor among our feet – a headless flapping horror.

'Oh fuck it,' said Charlie, getting up from his seat, 'look out, mate.'

He cleared a space & then he stamped on it with his big heavy boots; stamped & stamped until it was a flat, squashed still mess. Then he picked it up, slung it out the window, sat down again & took a large bite at a sandwich.

With a shock I found I was still half-smiling.[17]

Stiff and Rigid and Unadaptable

In November 1949, less than two months after the humiliating devaluation of sterling, *Picture Post* published a letter from Mrs C.M.J. Jackson of Preesall Avenue, Heald Green, Cheshire. 'Wanted: A New Britain' was the title of her *cri de coeur*:

> I am a housewife desperately trying to understand the present critical situation in this country. The Socialist Government seems to be unable to make the workers realise the seriousness of the present situation. Why wasn't a return to a 5½ (if not a 6) day week decided on at least two years ago? We should by now have started on the road to recovery. There is no remedy in increased wages, they only raise the cost of goods made (and sold) in England, and, worse still, they close the overseas markets to our exports. An immediate return to a 5½-day week at the same wage is imperative – with added incentives for those who *will* work a 6-day week. I can hear the cries of the Saturday afternoon sports fans, but isn't it time we put 'self' aside and worked for an ideal? After all, we *are* England and if she goes down we go down with her . . .

Undeniably, there was gloom in the air. 'What is Wrong with the British Economy?' was the title of the first of three radio talks given by Geoffrey Crowther (editor of the *Economist*) in the early weeks of 1950. 'Our system is stiff and rigid and unadaptable,' he declared. 'We all know what happened to the brontosaurus because he could not adapt himself to new circumstances. The fear that I have about the British economy is that it is getting a little into the state of the brontosaurus.' Or put another way, as he strove for the homely, topical touch: 'What we are suffering from is like a lack of vitamins. You can call it Vitamin C for cheapness, or Vitamin A for adaptability, or to sum up the whole thing you can say that we are short of Vitamin E for economic efficiency.'

Arguably, though, the British economy was not doing too badly. Mollie Panter-Downes, visiting a big textiles exhibition at Earl's Court in May 1949, may have heard foreign buyers 'frequently complain about the high prices and slow delivery dates', but the fact was that in 1950 Britain's volume of exports was running some 50 per cent higher than in 1937, with its share of world trade having increased from 21 to 25 per cent. Moreover, whatever the *immediate* post-war problems of dollar shortage, high taxation, reduced purchasing power and non-availability of goods, there did not exist any general sense that, *beyond* these problems, Britain was somehow locked into a perhaps irreversible cycle of long-term decline. Even Crowther, for all his warnings, was at pains to insist that there was 'plenty that is right' with the economy.[1] 'Declinism', in short, had still to set in.

Yet by any objective criteria there was no shortage of causes for concern about the underlying health of the British economy at the mid-century point – causes for concern all the more legitimate in that potentially serious competitors (including Germany, France and Italy as well as Japan), temporarily knocked out of contention, were by this time visibly starting to pick themselves up from the floor. The under-appreciated truth – at the time if not subsequently – was that circa 1950 there existed a unique but fleeting opportunity. The historian William D. Rubinstein (summarising and broadly endorsing the high-profile work of Correlli Barnett) has perhaps expressed it best: 'In 1945 Europe was in ruins; as it recovered and living standards rose, British export industries were in a position to become the powerhouse of Europe. Britain was also in a position to take an important slice of the markets of other countries around the world, including the United States. By the early 1950s, it ought to have begun a successful assault on the world's markets.'

Taking a realistic view of Britain's place in the geopolitical scheme of things would have been a good starting point. Barnett himself (in *The Lost Victory*, published in 1995) justifiably makes much of a baleful Treasury memorandum written just before VJ Day in August 1945 by none other than John Maynard Keynes. It was, contended Keynes, a serious 'over-playing of our hand' to 'undertake liabilities all over the world'; he referred specifically to how 'we have got into the habit of maintaining large and expensive establishments all over the Mediterranean, Africa and Asia to cover communications, to provide reserves for unnamed contingencies and to police vast areas eastwards from Tunis to Burma and northwards from East Africa to Germany'. Moreover, he added, 'none of these establishments will disappear unless and until they are ordered home; and many of them have pretexts for existence which have nothing to do with Japan'. Then came the policy crux:

> Very early and very drastic economies in this huge cash expenditure [some £725 million annually] overseas seem an absolute condition of maintaining our solvency. There is no possibility of our obtaining from others [ie the United States] for more than a brief period the means of maintaining any significant part of these establishments . . . These are burdens which there is no reasonable expectation of our being able to carry.

Put baldly, there was a clear need to make a peacetime strategic economic decision to, in Barnett's words, 'shrink Britain's war-bloated world and imperial role'.

It did not happen. The course of the war may have graphically demonstrated that there were now two superpowers, neither of which was Britain, and Britain's industrial base may have been palpably in need of modernisation, but neither the governing elite (including most Labour ministers) nor popular sentiment generally was yet ready to face up, coolly and unemotionally, to the idea of Britain no longer being able to afford the luxury of acting as one of the world's leading policemen. When Attlee in 1946 *did* call for such an appraisal, in particular questioning the necessity of the Mediterranean Fleet, he was quickly shot down by Ernest Bevin, who throughout his foreign secretaryship never deviated from his 'world role' assumptions – assumptions predicated in large part on the fear of Russia filling any 'vacuum' created by British retreat. Typically, when in June 1949 the Minister of Defence, A. V. Alexander, accepted that there was a 'problem' – which he defined as 'whether, after the economic exhaustion of the war years, we have the power and the resources to maintain the armed forces equipped to modern standards required to permit us to play the role of a Great Power' – he felt unable to avoid the conclusion that any 'wholesale abandonment of commitments' was 'unthinkable'. In the end, it is hard to evade the basic psychological point that long-term realism was unlikely from a nation that had just won its second world war in less than 30 years. It would not have been easy for Britain to shed at all quickly a major portion of her accumulated global commitments, but there was a dismal absence of grown-up public debate about the question.

It was much the same in the financial domain, where the continuing existence of the sterling area, accompanied by sterling's position as one of the world's leading reserve currencies, likewise resulted in over-stretch. The sterling area, operating in those parts of the world where the writ (whether formal or informal) of the British Empire still ran, had been a creation of the Bank of England during the 1930s, and although Keynes had bitterly observed in 1944 that 'all our reflex actions are those of a rich man', the conventional wisdom remained that it was desirable for sterling after the war to play a leading world role. 'The Sterling Area, and the countries which were linked with it, included about 1,000 million people and could therefore be associated with the United States and the dollar area on a basis of equality' was how Bevin saw it in July 1949 – notwithstanding that he was in the middle of a balance-of-payments crisis more or less directly caused by an overvalued pound. Devaluation was just round the corner, but it would not be long before there began a new cycle of quasi-fetishistic defence of the parity of sterling, on which it was widely believed that Britain's national prestige – and the prosperity of the City of London as an international financial centre – rested.[2]

Overall, most historians are agreed with Correlli Barnett that a more modest appraisal of Britain's place in the world, accompanied by lower levels of taxation, would have been beneficial to the productive economy – especially in terms of investment at a time when so much plant and machinery was rundown or even destroyed. Where his case becomes much more controversial is in his often polemical attack on what he sees as the unnecessary twin burdens of full employment and the welfare state.

'The Pervasive Harm of "Full Employment"' is one of the chapter titles in *The Lost Victory* – a doctrine embodied in the strongly Keynesian White Paper of 1944 and typically castigated by Barnett as 'not so much a *Schwerpunkt* as a shackle'. He argues vigorously that it was a doctrine that owed everything to faulty perceptions of the inter-war years, when in fact, 'except during the hurricane of the world's slump in 1930–3', unemployment had 'never constituted a *general* problem ... but a local and structural one'. Yet in reality, such was the folk memory of that time, involving an incredibly emotive set of images and associations (epitomised by the Jarrow marchers), that it would be many years before the fear of going 'back to the 1930s' lost its policy-making resonance. 'Full employment is practically dead as a political issue,' flatly stated a Treasury memorandum in November 1950. For the next two and a half decades, virtually no mainstream politician questioned the assumption that the automatic price of high unemployment was political suicide. It was much the same with the welfare state. It may or may not, in a strictly *economic* sense, have been a profligate waste of money – Barnett's figures to that effect have been sharply disputed – but what is surely incontestable was the prevailing *political* context. Whatever the precise detail about the scope, cost and funding of the welfare state, often a matter of intense debate, there was, put bluntly, no political mileage at all in advocating a wholesale return to the previous dispensation. Moreover, as state-provided welfare spread across a reconstructed Western Europe during the 1950s, it was soon clear that this was far from being a uniquely British constraint.[3]

In any case – irrespective of the economic consequences of the prevailing assumptions about Britain's world role and the creation of a New Jerusalem at home – the fact was that the British economy that emerged from the war was suffering from a far more important inherited burden: namely, a notably uncompetitive environment in which to operate.

A handful of main factors determined this non-Darwinian state of affairs. The first was the considerable if perhaps overestimated extent to which there existed for the British manufacturing industry an array of easy, undemanding, semi-captive export markets, usually linked with the Empire and/or sterling area. Such markets represented a comfort zone – a zone which, not unnaturally, few industrialists were inclined to leave voluntarily. The awareness that several other major manufacturing economies were temporarily *hors de combat*, not least in terms of exporting to Britain, merely added to the mental tranquillity. A further source of reassurance was the existence of exchange controls, meaning that the economy was not exposed to potentially unsettling movements of international capital. Introduced at the start of the war, exchange controls were made seemingly permanent by 1947 legislation which was, *The Times* reported, 'received with sober approval in the City' and more or less with indifference everywhere else. Similarly encouraging to a quiet life was the almost complete absence of a tradition of contested takeover bids, though here the 1948 Companies Act, insisting on more stringent financial disclosure, did at least in theory signal that things might change.

Above all, in terms of perpetuating a stagnant economic environment, there was the sheer extent of price-fixing (mainly in the form of resale-price maintenance), collusion and even cartelisation. The precise extent is the subject of debate, but one estimate is that by the end of the war there existed 'a proliferation of collusive agreements covering perhaps 60 per cent of manufacturing output and frequently sustaining inefficient producers'. It was an issue not without resonance. 'All parties in this Election are concerned about Monopolies,' noted the *Financial News* in July 1945, while Labour's manifesto condemned outright 'bureaucratically-run private monopolies' and promised that these would not be permitted to 'prejudice national interests by restrictive anti-social monopoly or cartel arrangements'.[4] In fact the government-encouraged merger movement of the inter-war years, followed by the intimate relationship between government and industry during the war, meant that there was a huge amount to be done before the economy could return to anything like its rawer, more competitive, pre-1914 character. It was a moot point, moreover, whether a Labour Party properly in power for the first time represented a plausible saviour of tooth-and-nail capitalism.

Was there also by this time a longstanding *cultural* bias against industry, indeed against money-making in general? Some historians have thought so – notably Martin J. Wiener in his influential if somewhat tunnel-vision 1981 overview, *English Culture and the Decline of the Industrial Spirit, 1850–1980*, a favourite text of Sir Keith Joseph and other ministers during the early years of Thatcherism.

A handful of snippets offer some anecdotal support. A 'nightmare uniformity of ugliness', for instance, was all that the popular, middle-brow travel writer S.P.B. Mais could find to say in 1948 about the drive from Stockport to Bolton – an ugliness all the more marked 'after the gracious meadows and lawns of the south country'. For Kenneth Preston, devoting his life to teaching English at Keighley Grammar School, the rewards for entrepreneurial activity were out of all proportion to their true worth. 'He was telling me about an insurance man who is making £2,000 a year and he is a man who cannot make his subject agree with his verb,' he noted somewhat resentfully in July 1949 after a conversation with a friend. 'He told me of a man who went round buying up derelict mills and sold one the other day for £7,000 for which he gave a few hundred a few years ago ... Of course, I know I could not do this sort of thing but why should people be able to make such easy money?' In May 1951 the Oxford undergraduate and budding writer V. S. Naipaul contributed an article, 'When Morris Came to Oxford', to *Isis*. The general thrust of the piece was that gown and town (in the form of the Morris plant at Cowley) had learnt to live with each other, but it was clear that there were still some lingering resentments and touchiness. 'If the University people had known that we were going to expand so much,' a car worker told Naipaul, 'they would have done their best to get rid of us.' And when at about this time a young industrialist called Quinton Hazell, managing director of a motor-components company that bore his name and in the process of rapidly becoming Colwyn Bay's biggest employer, applied to join an exclusive professional club there, he found himself being brusquely rejected – on the grounds that he was 'in trade'.[5]

High taxation; Victorian-style private enterprise stigmatised by its inter-war association with mass unemployment; large-scale concerns (public like the BBC or the Bank of England, private like ICI or Shell or the clearing banks) offering jobs for life and career paths predetermined to almost the smallest detail; the state fresh from its finest hour and now offering the opportunity to transform society – altogether, it is instinctively plausible that the '1945' moment represented a nadir of capitalism's animal spirits. Such a view holds almost irrespective of the extent to which one buys into Wiener's much-contested cultural critique. But in the end, an economy is only as good as its main functioning parts – and, in the post-war British economy, each suffered from crucial defects.

———

The most visible aspect of the financial sector was the high-street clearing banks, for half a century after the First World War dominated by the 'Big Five' of Barclays, Lloyds, Midland, National Provincial and Westminster. During most of this period, they operated more or less as a cartel, showing little appetite either for innovation or for new business – even though as late as the mid-1950s only about a third of the working population had their own bank accounts. Britain was a pre-plastic, cash society; deposit banking was a world run by the middle class for the middle class; and the lack of competition, including no obligation to publish profits, was hardly a stimulus to change. 'It was like driving a powerful car at twenty miles an hour' was how the gifted Oliver Franks (academic, civil servant and diplomat) recalled his chairmanship of Lloyds Bank that decade. 'The banks were anaesthetised – it was a kind of dream life.'

Most bankers, though, had no doubts about their linchpin role in what was probably the most stable financial system in the Western world. 'We should be proud of the universal respect our profession commands,' Franks's predecessor, Lord Balfour of Burleigh, told the Institute of Bankers in 1950. 'This is due not only to the faithfulness with which our members perform their responsible duties. It is also a tribute to the manner in which they are meeting the special difficulties of the times, and continuing to maintain a high standard of personal integrity amid the maze of regulations which complicate everyday affairs.' George Mainwaring, that pillar-of-the-community bank manager at Walmington-on-Sea by now approaching retirement, would no doubt have nodded sagely.

Balfour was speaking in the City of London, the very heart of the financial system. It was still by mid-century a club-like Square Mile – a village. Here thousands of small, often specialist firms did much the same work in much the same way that they had been doing 50 or 100 years earlier; connection (family/school/social/sporting) and a personable manner enjoyed a higher premium than more meritocratic qualities; trust ('My word is my bond') lubricated and made possible the whole undeniably impressive machine; and the village policeman (aka the Governor the Bank of England) had only to raise his eyebrows for his wishes to be obeyed. It was a village, in its higher echelons, of middle-aged or elderly men who unambiguously saw themselves as gentlemen performing gentlemanly tasks and adhering to a gentlemanly code. 'Shoes have laces', 'motor cars are black', 'jelly is not officer food': such were the timeless aphorisms of Cedric Barnett, the austere, digni-fied, top-hatted partner in charge of gilts (British government securities) at the leading stockbroking firm Cazenove's.

Deeply suspicious of any face that did not fit, it could be an intensely difficult village for an outsider – however able – to penetrate. Perhaps the most telling case involved Denis Weaver of the atypical, deliberately non-nepotistic stockbroking firm Phillips & Drew.[6] A trained actuary who by the late 1940s was expected to become the next senior partner, he hit an immovable roadblock when the Stock Exchange Council refused to countenance his membership. His crime was that he was a Quaker who during the war had registered as a conscientious objector. Nothing changed during the 1950s (with Weaver concentrating on becoming the British pioneer of investment analysis), and by the time the authorities eventually relented in 1960 his chance of becoming senior partner had gone. The fact that the Stock Exchange's chairman through the 1950s, the ultra-respectable, establishment-minded Sir John Braithwaite, himself came from a Quaker family background only added salt to the wound.

Between the wars, the City's traditionally rather remote relationship with British industry had become significantly closer: partly because much of its own international business had dried up, partly through its government-encouraged financial-midwifery role (especially on the part of the Bank of England) in response to the serious structural problems of steel and cotton. Indeed, by mid-century it almost seemed a consummated marriage. Industrials, as they were called, represented a key section of the stock market, giving it much of its daily tone (mainly through the FT 30-Share Index); the new issue market retained a strongly domestic orientation; and the newly established Industrial and Commercial Finance Corporation (subsequently known as 3i), with the clearing banks as its main shareholders, was the City's very deliberate riposte to criticism, especially from the left, that there was inadequate capital-raising provision for medium-sized companies.

Overall, the financial system seems to have played a positive if somewhat flawed role in this post-war phase of industrial finance. The commercial banks could be relied on to give rollover loans to well-established clients but tended to be less accommodating – and less willing to make a fact-finding effort – if the industrial supplicant was newer or more innovative; in the domestic capital market, there was often a similar lack of diligence on the part of the sponsoring merchant banks, though here the result was excessive liberality rather than restrictiveness; the ICFC was regarded by its shareholders as at best a regrettable necessity; and in general there was little sign of any change in the endemic condition, so eloquently lamented by Keynes, known as City short-termism. Yet the divide that persisted was less economic than social and cultural – and indeed political, given the not unjustified suspicion of leading industrialists that their City counterparts found it appreciably easier than they did to get close to the decision-makers in Westminster and Whitehall. Ultimately, the City–industry relationship was one of business rather than of the heart – a truth appreciated by Frank Perkins, a Peterborough-based manufacturer of diesel engines. Compelled in 1951 to decide between two of the City's historic merchant banks, Barings and Morgan Grenfell, as his issuing house, he chose Barings on the very sensible grounds that it had fewer peers as directors.[7]

Like Rothschilds, like Schroders, like Kleinworts, like other august City names, those houses had enjoyed their finest, most prosperous hour during the long nineteenth century, when London had been the world's undisputed leading international financial centre. The guns of August 1914 had changed all that, leading directly to New York's almost immediate ascendancy. Could London ever hope to restore its position and become once again an economic powerhouse in its own right? The prospects by the early 1950s were poor: exchange controls were firmly in place; sterling was prone to sudden collapses of international confidence; London's classic role as an exporter of capital barely functioned; and the City's international markets (such as the futures markets in commodities) were stagnant. Nevertheless, amid widespread sluggishness and deeply inbred conservatism, there were two outstanding figures who *did* have some sort of vision of how London might return to its past glories.

One was Siegmund Warburg, a cerebral, fiercely ambitious German Jew with *haute banque* in his blood, who had fled from Hitler in the 1930s and who in 1946 launched upon the City establishment his own merchant bank, S. G. Warburg & Co. He was no great admirer of the natives. 'One of the dominant attitudes in the City is tolerance towards mediocrity,' he noted in the mid-1950s, adding that 'most of the important people' were 'so anxious to avoid any unpleasantness that they will knowingly make blunders, with the sole aim of sparing themselves any conflict'. He was especially unimpressed by the English habit of meeting any prospective difficulties with the stock phrase 'Let's cross that bridge when we come to it' – and he would contemptuously call such people 'bridge-crossers'. Warburg did not know precisely how London was going to escape from being permanently condemned to an existence as a rather insular, largely domestic financial centre, but he did know that somehow it had to be done, preferably with his own merchant bank in the vanguard.

The other person with a visionary streak was George Bolton, a talented, restless banker who had come up on the Bank of England's international side but lacked the social poise and indeed breeding of his main rival Cameron ('Kim') Cobbold, the latter becoming Governor in 1949. 'A pleasant Etonian' was how Raymond Streat the next year described the City's new head. 'Able and adequate, but not tremendous.' Soon afterwards, Hugh Gaitskell was less polite: 'I must say that I have a very poor opinion of him – he is simply not a very intelligent man.'[8] In fact it was easy to underestimate Cobbold, who though certainly no intellectual was a pretty capable operator and had the great gubernatorial virtue of not getting flustered by events. But he was not (and would not have wanted to be) a man for the really big, demanding, risk-taking picture. As for Bolton, bitterly disappointed not to get the top job, he would bide his time and wait for London's circumstances to become more propitious.

Where Bolton, Cobbold and any number of practical City men would have instinctively agreed was about the general uselessness of politicians – of whichever party, though naturally with Labour politicians viewed as dangerous as well as hopeless. They might have relished Correlli Barnett's scathing verdict half a century later on the Labour Cabinet of 1945. Thirteen out of 20 were 'amateurs without direct experience in industry', with all but one of the other seven being trade unionists; of the seven members belonging to the 'upper-middle-class progressive Establishment', none had 'ever studied anything so rudely vocational as, say, engineering', with only one having 'ever stooped so low as to work in a factory'; Attlee himself 'lacked any direct experience of industry' and, with his 'deeply conventional and matter-of-fact mind' was 'happier in the efficient transaction of current business than in thinking strategically about Britain's long-term future, industrial or otherwise'. All in all, in Britain's unexpectedly harsh post-war circumstances, these 20 Labour politicians 'found themselves in a plight to which a lifetime's assumptions were quite inappropriate, for instead of redistributing wealth they were faced with the urgent and immensely more difficult task of creating it'.

The Barnett version carries a powerful charge, and certainly it is difficult to see the first Chancellor, Hugh Dalton, for all his being the author of an often reprinted textbook entitled *Principles of Public Finance*, as one of nature's wealth-creators. 'Stop talking details, Nicholas! Stick to principles!' he would boom whenever his friend Nicholas Davenport, City economist and writer, tried to explain the workings of capitalism's citadel. But his successor Stafford Cripps was a significantly different economic animal. The diary of Raymond Streat, who first got to know Cripps when he was still President of the Board of Trade, reveals an initial deep scepticism eventually giving way to outright admiration for his grasp of detail, superb brain and unmistakable sincerity of purpose. By November 1948, with the Chancellor's national reputation approaching its pre-devaluation zenith, Streat was telling Cripps to his face that he personally was 'in receipt of a remarkable degree of confidence and support from the business men, notwithstanding that so many were of another party colour'. Cripps, moreover, was at the forefront of the government's attempt to make British industry more efficient, more scientific, better managed, more rationally structured and more productive – in short, more modern.[9] Put another way, the goal of a flourishing economy (admittedly defined in terms of full employment rather than growth) was integral to the New Jerusalem and in no way extraneous to it. The point is sometimes forgotten.

As for the mandarins who serviced this aspiration, Barnett is predictably rude. 'The civil-service elite was in the method of its selection, in its concept of its role and in its way of working a Victorian survival overdue for root-and-branch modernization,' he argues. 'This elite being a stem of the liberal Establishment, its members were mostly the fairest blooms of an arts education at public school and Oxbridge.' Unsurprisingly, he adds, their knowledge of the outside world was 'largely restricted to the City, Oxbridge senior common rooms and what they read in *The Times*'. Here it is harder to quarrel. Take Sir Edward Bridges, Permanent Secretary to the Treasury. He was the son of a Poet Laureate; he did not pretend to know about economics; and in lectures and writings he celebrated what he liked to call 'the principle of the intelligent layman'. No one disputed his intelligence or administrative capacity, but his relationship with the real economy was at best tenuous.

The atmosphere more generally in post-war Whitehall is evoked in the vivid memoirs of Roy Denman, who, fresh from Cambridge, went in February 1948 to work in the Statistical Division at the Board of Trade. There he encountered a memorable assistant secretary (ie 'a fairly senior manager'):

> Mr Bacon had a square jaw, keen blue eyes and dressed, unusually for those days, with a certain elegance. These unfortunately were his main qualifications for senior office. Before anyone from the outside world came to see him he would get his secretary to stack his desk high with files garnered from obscure cupboards in order to show how busy he was. With a weary sigh, a wave of his hand indicated to his visitor the crushing burden of administration which he daily bore. 'These are difficult times,' he would say in a resonant voice. 'But if we all pull together the country will get through.'

After a year of frustrating inertia, Denman moved to the timber section of the Raw Materials Department, where to his relief he found that they 'actually did things'. The clear implication was that this was the exception rather than the rule. Admittedly the workings of government have always been an easy target, but to read William Cooper's novel *Scenes from Metropolitan Life* – a robust and intimate portrait of post-war

Whitehall, written in the early 1950s but for libel reasons unpublished for some 30 years – is on the whole to have prejudices confirmed. It depicts a world of (to quote the critic D. J. Taylor) 'highly intelligent men' absorbed in 'bureaucratic fixing and power-broking', between them 'conspiring to influence the world of "affairs" in the not quite conscious assumption that the whole business is an end in itself'.[10]

The newly nationalised industries involved much of Whitehall's time in the late 1940s and early 1950s. Inevitably, in operational practice, there was a series of turf wars, some of them acrimonious, between ministers and civil servants on the one hand and the boards appointed to run the industries on the other. Prices and wages, investment decisions, worker consultation, ministerial notions of 'standardisation officers' and an independent 'efficiency unit' – all were issues that created friction. 'The meeting with the Area Board Chairman was an uproar,' Gaitskell noted with Wykehamist tolerance in August 1948, four months after the nationalisation of the electricity industry. 'After I had spoken they got up and one after another opposed. I did not mind the opposition but the unbelievably stupid and muddled arguments they put forward! I was really horrified that so many men, earning so much money, should be so silly.' The problem, he added, was that 'they are all madly keen to sell electricity and just cannot get used to the idea that at the moment they should stop people from buying it.'

Undoubtedly, there existed by about 1950 a general sense of disappointment with the experience of nationalisation so far. Much of that disappointment was social – 'speaker after speaker reiterated the fact that no attempt was made on the part of the management to inform the employees of what they were doing and why' was the chorus in November 1950 at a conference of London employees of nationalised corporations – but it was also economic. Herbert Morrison, architect of nationalisation, had already told the emblematically named Socialisation of Industries Committee that it was necessary to put in place 'more effective checks upon the efficiency of their management', while over the next year or two research by the non-partisan Acton Society Trust revealed a degree of worker indifference-cum-hostility to the new dispensation that hardly stimulated higher productivity. Management structures, moreover, were unwieldy, overcentralised and rigidly hierarchical, all of which militated against encouraging talent, while that same management had no qualms about appointing ex-trade union officials as heads of personnel. Unsurprisingly, given that nationalisation in the first place was the result of social and political at least as much as economic considerations, there was also a deep and pervasive reluctance to use the price mechanism in resource allocation. Altogether, from the perspective of a twenty-first-century privatised world, it was far from cutting-edge.

Yet even in strictly economic terms, the story was perhaps not quite so black and white. The economist John Kay wrote almost movingly in 2001 about the recently deceased Central Electricity Generating Board (CEGB), hub for virtually half a century of the nationalised electricity industry:

> It represented the best of central planning. It was run by highly intelligent administrators and engineers who were dedicated to the public interest. It employed the most advanced techniques of risk management and economic analysis.
>
> Its pride and joy was the central control room of the National Grid. The engineers who worked there had details of the running costs and availability of every generating plant in England and Wales. They would constantly monitor and anticipate demand and instruct plant managers to produce electricity, or stop producing electricity, by reference to what they called the 'merit order'. The objective was to ensure that output was always achieved at the lowest possible cost.

Kay, though, does not regret the CEGB's passing. 'Centralisation, giganticism, secrecy and complacency – in retrospect, it displayed all of these.'[11] In the early 1950s, however, such perceptions were barely starting to take shape.

――――――

Anyway, the nationalised industries represented only about a fifth of the economy. Sir Topham Hatt on the Island of Sodor may have quietly changed from the Fat Director into the Fat Controller once the railways were nationalised, but the great majority of British managers spent their whole working lives in the private sector. There was no great premium placed on merit. 'It is true beyond any doubt that nepotism is still widespread in private industry, and so long as it persists on its present scale it frustrates all efforts to provide equality of opportunity in the business world,' Anthony Crosland complained in 1950. 'There are far too many firms which recruit, if not entirely from founder's kin, at least on a generally "old boy" basis, and there is nothing more exasperating than to observe, in the universities today, the appalling lack of correlation between ability and jobs obtained.' Soon afterwards, a survey of 1,243 directors from 445 large companies found that almost three-fifths had been to public school and a fifth to Oxbridge, predictably with arts graduates twice as numerous as science ones. Their average age was 55, and almost three-quarters had changed jobs either once or never at all. A subsequent survey of directors, in the mid-1950s, found that about a third were sons of directors, most of them directors of the same firms.

In a bravura passage, Correlli Barnett (who as a young man worked in industry in the 1950s) portrays the lifestyle of the British directorate:

At the summit of the industrial system stood an elite predominantly blessed with the accent of the officers' mess: men bowler-hatted or homburged, wearing suits of military cut either bespoke or at least bought from such approved outfitters as Aquascutum or Simpsons of Piccadilly; gentlemen indeed, confident of manner, instantly recognizable by stance and gesture. They lived in large detached houses on a couple of acres of garden in the suburbanized countryside that surrounded the great cities all within 'exclusive' private estates adjacent to the golf course. They drank gin and tonic; had lunch in a directors' dining room resembling as near as possible a club in St James's; dined in the evenings; drove a Humber, Rover, Alvis, Lagonda or perhaps a Rolls-Royce; and were married to ladies who played bridge.

It is a portrait that, notwithstanding an element of caricature, has the ring of authenticity about it. So, too, does Barnett's depiction of British middle management in the early to mid-1950s – a world in which the extent of promotion almost invariably corresponded with educational background and 'the snobbery of the socially unsure' permeated everything:

With the exception of the public-school men [probably about one in five], these managers were all denizens of that unchartable sea that lay between the two well-defined shores of the upper class and the working class. All spoke in regional or plebeian accents, with the original rough-ness sandpapered down to a greater or lesser degree; they ate dinner at midday (though this was changing); bought their ready-made suits from Meakers, Dunn's or Horne Brothers; wore at the weekends blazers with breast pockets adorned with the crests of such un-crack regiments as the Royal Army Service Corps; drove staidly respectable motor cars like Morris Oxfords or Austin Dorsets; and were blessed with 'lady wives' who were proud of their well-furnished 'lounges'.

As with the directors above them, this is an evocation of a profoundly conservative, risk-averse and mentally as well as materially unambitious culture – a culture in which managers were 'for the most part content to jog along decade after decade in the same cosy working and domestic routines'.[12]

Barnett's uncompromising reading of immediate post-war British history has provoked understandable dissent, even at times distaste, but it is surprising that his detractors, mainly from the left, have been unwilling to recognise the sheer weight and power of his onslaught on the complacent, insular British establishment of those years. It is possible, though, to make some sort of defence of the businessmen. Against an overarching twentieth-century background of family capitalism gradually giving way to managerial capitalism, there was among senior managers a slowly rising proportion of university graduates (some 30 per cent by 1954, only 1 per cent less than West Germany); a Labour government initiative led directly to the establishment of the British Institute of Management; and there were an increasing number of American companies (such as Ford) and management consultants eager to spread the gospel of modern management techniques. 'We're All Specialist Now' was one of the chapters in *Professional People*, written in 1952 by the renowned specialists on the middle class, Roy Lewis and Angus Maude, and it included a section on 'The Management Movement'.

Nor was the dominance of ex-public schoolboys in the upper echelons of British companies *necessarily* a formula for disdainful amateurism. Geoffrey Owen, in his authoritative survey of post-war industry, asserts that in the 1940s and 1950s 'it was common practice for public schoolboys, if they did not go on to university, to undergo some form of technical training after leaving school, perhaps as a premium apprentice in an industrial company'. Owen adds that 'if there was an anti-industrial bias in the education system, it was to be found at Oxford and Cambridge, where some professors regarded a career in business as intellectually and morally demeaning'. Owen also implicitly queries the conventional wisdom deploring the relative ease with which accountants – as opposed to engineers – were able to penetrate senior levels of management. 'Employers,' he writes, 'saw that the rigorous training which accountants had to undergo was a good preparation for management.' One such accountant, qualifying in the late 1920s, was the self-made, utterly capable but also visionary Leslie Lazell, who by the early 1950s was running the Beecham pharmaceutical group and beginning to turn it into a very successful – and international – science-based, marketing-oriented enterprise, all fuelled by a huge research effort which he ensured was properly funded.[13]

Moreover, whatever the overall sluggishness of the business world, some striking entrepreneurs were at work. Jules Thorn and Michael Sobell, for example, were both foreign-born outsiders who by the early 1950s were starting to shake up the still heavily cartelised electrical industry, with Sobell (father-in-law of Arnold Weinstock) about to make a fortune through the manufacture of television sets; Daniel McDonald, starting out with £300 capital and a shed in the West Midlands, was the inventor and manufacturer of Monarch gramophones, which from the early 1950s had a simplicity of design and lower unit costs that enabled him to take on the more upmarket Garrard model, eventually making him one of Britain's richest self-made men; the thrifty, driven and despotic Joseph Bamford, founder of J. C. Bamford, was the inventor and manufacturer of the hugely profitable JCB excavator; and Paul Hamlyn, a German Jewish refugee, began his innovative and highly rewarding publishing career in 1949 with an imprint characteristically called Books for Pleasure.

There was also, sui generis, the case of Alastair Pilkington. He was finishing his war-interrupted mechanical-sciences course at Cambridge when the turning point of his life occurred. It is an episode that has become shrouded in mythology; the historian Theo Barker tells the authorised version:

Alastair's father had become interested in his family tree and so had Sir Richard Pilkington, a shareholding member of the St Helens glassmaking family. When it became clear that there was no traceable link between their respective ancestors, the two men got round to discussing the rising generation. Would Pilkingtons be interested in employing an up and coming engineer when he had completed his degree? As it happened, the company was then very concerned about its shortage of well-qualified engineers. Harry Pilkington [a director] saw Alastair's father and subsequently had Alastair himself up to St Helens for close scrutiny over a three-day period. More remarkable, the board decided that 'a member of the Pilkington family, however remote, could be accepted only as a potential family director'. So it came about that Alastair, having passed the preliminary test, started work at Pilkington Bros Ltd in August 1947 as a family trainee.

This was also a turning point in the firm's fortunes. 'Four years after starting work at Pilkingtons, he conceived the idea that molten glass could be formed into a continuous ribbon by pouring it into a bath of tin and "floating" it while it cooled.'[14] Such was the revolutionary float-glass process, eventually to become world-famous. It had been a triumph of not-quite-nepotistic recruitment.

For every wealth-creator, unfortunately, there was at least one Lord Portal of Hungerford. An ace fighter pilot in one world war, Chief of the Air Staff in another, his first big peacetime job (1946–51) was as Controller of Atomic Energy. 'I cannot remember that he ever did anything that helped us,' the very able Christopher Hinton, responsible for the production of fissile material, unsentimentally recalled. By the late 1940s Portal was taking on directorships – of the Commercial Union, of Fords and of Barclays DCO, where after lunch he invariably picked up a copy of the *Field*, not the *Economist* – before in 1953 assuming the chairmanship of one of the country's most prestigious companies, British Aluminium. His principal qualities remained his distinguished war record and, of course, the famous 'Portal' nose.[15]

It was an emblematic career, in that British management in these years remained *essentially* unprofessional. In the 1950s it was still unusual for a top British company to be organised along divisional lines, while it was not until the 1960s that the first business schools began to appear.

Typical, moreover, of the often skewed priorities in British corporate culture was what seems to have been an almost systematic downgrading of the status of production managers, in accordance with the maxim 'Men who can manage men, manage men who can only manage things.' And what men who managed men needed was 'a balanced cultivated life', as one leading manager enjoyed telling an international conference in 1951. 'He should have long weekends,' the manager explained; 'he should play golf ... he should garden ... he should play bridge, he should read, he should do something different.'

Two witnesses of the industrial scene were unimpressed by what they saw. When Maurice Zinkin joined Unilever in 1947, he was 'shocked' to find how many of its British-based companies were 'old-fashioned and badly managed':

> One of the toiletry companies I went to see was still selling its perfectly good face cream on a silly advertising story about a dying sheikh and his secret desert well. Port Sunlight was still training for overseas service managers of a technical level not high enough to make them acceptable to the increasing nationalism of overseas governments. It was also, even to my inexpert eye, over-manned.

So, too, the economist Alec Cairncross, who after his stint in Whitehall returned to academic life, at Glasgow University, in 1951. There he tried to get the local shipbuilding industry interested in management studies but met a complete lack of interest. It was not, he recalled in the 1990s, as if that industry had nothing to learn:

> In a large yard, employing more than 5,000 workers, the organisation of the work below board level was in the hands of the yard super-intendent, who was distinguished from the other workmen by his bowler hat and not much else. But there was no planning staff of the kind customary in modern factories. That work was devolved to the foreman on the job, and he set about it like a foreman on any building site. Each ship was built as a one-off job.

In fact, 'management in the industry was almost non-existent.'

No single case study can claim to be representative, but there is something peculiarly compelling – and perhaps indicative – about Courtaulds, the large textile manufacturer based in Coventry. It is a story told with relish by the company's historian, Donald Coleman. In 1946 the ailing septuagenarian chairman, Samuel Courtauld, had to find a successor. In effect, the choice lay between P. J. Gratwick and John Hanbury-Williams. One had 'long textile experience, much shrewdness, and some enthusiasm for the bottle'; the other had 'presence, diplomatic skills, and splendid manners', not to mention a double-barrelled name. The position went to Hanbury-Williams – from a long-established landed family, son of a major-general, married to Princess Zenaida Cantacuzene, a director of the Bank of England and a gentleman usher to King George VI. Coleman's characterisation is savage:

> Hanbury-Williams knew little or nothing about production technology, despised technical men, remained ignorant of science, and wholly indifferent to industrial relations . . . He was contemptuous or patronizing to those he could refer to as 'technical persons' . . . His tactical ability to rule in a small and fairly homogeneous group, and to give suitably beneficent and urbane nods to the doings of the executive directors, allowed dignity to masquerade as leadership. But this activity, or inactivity, totally lacked strategy and ideas . . . There is no evidence that Hanbury-Williams had any innovative ideas whatever.

In 1952, six years into a reign that lasted into the 1960s, Hanbury-Williams reflected on the company's organisation: 'There has been a Gentlemen's Club atmosphere in the Board Room, and I believe it is in true to say that over the years this has spread to all the Departments of our business. It is in fact part of the goodwill of the Company which we must safeguard.' A rare iconoclast (and incisive administrative talent) on the board was Sir Wilfrid Freeman, who only the year before had flatly described Courtaulds as 'over-centralized, constipated, and stagnant' – a situation unlikely to change while the insufferably complacent Hanbury-Williams was still in harness.[16] But, bearing Portal in mind, the fact that the trenchant Freeman had in an earlier life been an Air Chief Marshal serves as a warning against facile typecasting.

Across the table from management sat the trade unions. During the war, the appointment of Ernest Bevin, the greatest living trade unionist, as Minister of Labour in Churchill's coalition had signalled their arrival at the national top table, along with the spread to many industries of national pay bargaining. After the war, their leaders continued to be consulted by government on a regular basis, and by 1951, against a background of full employment, their membership stood at an all-time high of 9.3 million. Some perspective is needed: the average *density* of trade union membership (ie in relation to the workforce as a whole) struggled in these years to rise above 45 per cent, while the sheer number of unions (735 in 1951) inevitably made it a somewhat incoherent patchwork quilt of a movement. Nevertheless, the contrast with the travails of the inter-war slump, when membership bottomed out at 4.35 million in 1933, was unmistakable.[17]

The inevitable concomitant to greater prominence was increased exposure to criticism. 'It takes some spirit,' complained the Cambridge economist Sir Dennis Robertson in his presidential address in 1949 to the Royal Economic Society, 'to state clearly and fairly the case for wage reduction as a cure for unemployment or an adverse balance of payments, or the case for the curtailment of subsidies and the over-hauling of the social services as a solvent for inflationary pressure, without being prematurely silenced by the argument that nowadays the trade unions would never stand for such things. Perhaps they wouldn't; but that is no reason for not following the argument whithersoever it leads.' For the most part, though, there existed by the end of the 1940s a broad-based, bipartisan acceptance that, whether a welcome development or not, organised labour had permanently arrived as a major and unignorable force to be reckoned with.

The high national standing of the unions by about 1950 – certainly compared with 20 or 30 years earlier or indeed later – owed much to their responsible behaviour during the difficult immediate post-war years. The key figure was the Transport and General Workers' Union (TGWU) right-wing leader Arthur Deakin, memorably characterised by Michael Foot as 'a fierce, breezy, irascible, stout-hearted bison of a man who genuinely believed that any proposition he could force through his union executive must be the will of the people and more especially the will of Ernest Bevin [the TGWU's founder] whose requirements he had normally taken the precaution of finding out in advance'. In effect Deakin saw the unions as an integral part of the labour movement, engaged in a social contract with the Labour government: in return for policies aimed at full employment, extended welfare provision and a measure of wealth redistribution, he would do his formidable best to ensure that the government's economic stability was not jeopardised by unrealistic wage demands.

Deakin's strong preference was for pay bargaining to be independent of any direct government involvement; eventually, faced by overwhelming evidence from Cripps about the extreme seriousness of the country's economic position, he had led the way to the TUC agreeing in March 1948 to accept the government's case for a more formal policy of wage restraint – a freeze that, albeit voluntary rather than statutory, lasted for two and a half often difficult years. The government was duly grateful. 'There can be no doubt that the trade union leaders have been wise and courageous since the end of the war,' a junior minister wrote in March 1950 to the TUC general secretary, the long-serving, self-effacing Vincent Tewson. 'It takes a great deal to explain to your members the intricacies of the economic situation and the General Council [of the TUC] has, in my view, done a splendid job.' Characteristically, the minister added that 'you have the satisfaction of knowing that you have been acting throughout in the best interests of the Trade Unionists and their families.'[18]

The minister was James Callaghan, his personal roots deep in white-collar trade unionism. Indeed, such were the historically intimate links between Labour and the unions – going back to the party's founding in 1900 – that even in the 1945 parliament, notwithstanding the rise of the professional classes as candidates, almost a third of Labour MPs were directly sponsored by unions (well over a quarter of them by the National Union of Mineworkers (NUM)). These trade union MPs had several defining qualities: almost invariably male; usually sitting for a safe seat; politically unambitious, or anyway seldom promoted from the back benches; obedient to the leadership; and hostile to middle-class socialist intellectuals. As for the unions themselves, they adopted a range of political positions on the left–right spectrum within an overarching loyalty to the Labour Party; the only important union with a Communist executive was the Electrical Trades Union, though the TGWU, NUM and several

others had Communists in leading posts. Predictably, it was Deakin who
fought a particularly sturdy and effective campaign against Communist
influence in the unions, including in 1949 persuading his own union to
bar Communists from holding office in it; by about 1953 it was generally
reckoned that Communist influence in the unions had dwindled significantly, though it was still far from extinct.[19] For the British Communist
Party, however, the workplace was a crucial location in the larger struggle,
given the party's almost complete lack of success in conventional electoral
politics, and it had in its ranks some very determined and motivated
people more than willing to play the long industrial game.

When agreeing in the late 1940s to go out on a limb for the Labour
government, Deakin was adamant that a temporary wage freeze should
in no way be taken as undermining the hallowed *principle* of free collective bargaining – a principle at the very heart of British trade unionism.
Allan Flanders, the leading academic analyst of industrial relations in
this period, explained in 1952 the all-important historical, largely
nineteenth-century, context:

> The significance of collective bargaining to the workers might be summed
> up in the word, self-protection. It enabled them to protect their interests
> in relation to their employment in three ways. First of all, in the presence
> of a reserve army of unemployed, it eliminated the competition which
> would otherwise exist among them to offer their services at a lower
> price than their fellow-workers for the sake of securing employment.
> Secondly, by the application of their collective strength they could in
> favourable conditions compel employers to concede wage advances and
> other improvements in their terms of employment. Thirdly, collective
> bargaining by introducing something of 'the rule of law' into industrial
> relations protected individual employees against arbitrary treatment by
> management in the form of favouritism or victimization.

Crucially, it was a *voluntary* system – which for the most part had
developed outside the auspices of government or the law courts. 'It is
a form of self-government and as such promotes the democratic virtues
of independence and responsibility,' asserted Flanders. 'Moreover it
has the great merit of flexibility. It would be impossible for industry
to operate with a sensitive regard for the varied human interests of all

Holidaymakers outside Waterloo station, July 1948

Elephant and Castle, December 1948

Mrs Lilian Chandler and the President of the Board of Trade (Harold Wilson)
discuss the housewife's plight, December 1948

Durham Miners' Gala, 23 July 1949

Reading the small ads, London, 1950

Blackpool, 1949

The *Ark Royal*, Birkenhead, 1950

The Pool of London, autumn 1949

The car dealers of Warren Street, autumn 1949

The victorious Newcastle team returns from the 1951 Cup Final the equally varied categories of workers by means of regulations imposed by an outside authority.' Such advantages, he was sure, had enabled 'the voluntary system' to achieve 'so decided and widespread an acceptance today'.

Flanders himself, who had fled from Nazi Germany in the 1930s, was a passionate social democrat and anti-Communist. In 1949 he began a class at Nuffield College, Oxford, on industrial relations, and the fruits appeared five years later in his authoritative *The System of Industrial Relations in Great Britain*, co-edited with another, younger Oxford academic, Hugh Clegg. The latter, many years later, recalled the very '1945' assumptions behind the 'Oxford group':

> We were pluralists, believing that a free society consists of a large number of overlapping groups, each with its own interests and objectives which its members are entitled to pursue so long as they do so with reasonable regard to the rights and interests of others. But we were also egalitarians, wishing to see a shift in the distribution of wealth towards those with lower incomes, and a shift of power over the conduct of their working lives and environment towards working men and women; and, for both these reasons, emphasising the importance of trade unions in industry, in the economy, and in society. We therefore attached special importance to collective bargaining as the means whereby trade unions pursue their objectives.

The book itself was imbued with the assumption that enhanced trade union power was, if exercised in the appropriate way, an almost unequivocal social and economic good. The appropriate way included moderation in recourse to the strike weapon; the use wherever possible of industry-wide collective bargaining; and such bargaining to be reliant upon long-nurtured codes rather than externally imposed legal contracts.[20] Altogether, it was in its way a noble vision.

Unfortunately for its long-term implementation, however, the fact was that British trade unionism, as it had evolved by the early 1950s, had three fateful Achilles heels. The first was the large and growing gap between the leadership and the rank and file. It was not, broadly speaking, an ideological gap. For all the socialist rhetoric over the years (applicable also to the Labour Party) about the led being well to the left of those leading them, there is little supporting empirical evidence – certainly not for the immediate post-war period. Indeed, in the case of the Electrical Trades Union it was the mass of members who for many years reluctantly put up with a Communist executive. In general, although the process of political consultation with members may have been far from perfect (exacerbated by the block-vote system at conferences), the determinants of the relationship lay elsewhere. 'The large unions have a great many advantages,' observed Ferdynand Zweig in his largely positive reading of the trade unions' role in the lives of the British male workforce, at a time when the 17 biggest unions accounted for some two-thirds of all members. 'They can give a more skilful and varied service to their members, and they have a greater power of bargaining for improved wages and working conditions, but their service is by their very nature more impersonal and the touch between the leaders and members less direct. From being local in scope they have become national, and so more remote from an individual centre of trouble.'

There was an inevitable consequence. '"The unions are just taken for granted by the younger generation," is an opinion one often hears,' Zweig also noted. 'There is no doubt that the active trade unionist who attends the meetings and takes an interest in the affairs of his branch is less frequent now than previously, and he is less frequent among the young men than he is among the older generation.' No union was bigger than Deakin's TGWU (some 1.3 million members by the mid-1950s, the biggest trade union in the Western world), whose governance was subjected in the late 1940s to a devastating scrutiny (not published until 1953) by a young American called Joseph Goldstein. Examining in particular its branch in Battersea, Goldstein found such overwhelming apathy on the part of rank-and-file members that the result was 'an oligarchy parading in democracy's trappings'. Deakin himself contributed a pained foreword ('He has, I feel, misunderstood what he has seen'), but the cumulative evidence was irrefutable. In practice, the growing gap between leaders and officials on the one hand, rank and file on the other, was creating a dangerous vacuum – dangerous anyway from the point of view of the rather Whiggish certainties of the Flanders vision, which trusted to an enlightened leadership being able in negotiations to 'deliver' its members.

Into this vacuum stepped the often unelected and only quasi-official figure of the shop steward, in these immediate post-war years an increasingly powerful presence in the workplace, especially in the engineering and allied industries. 'I'm not educated enough, it's like a puff of wind for me to say something,' one inactive member of the Battersea branch rather forlornly explained to Goldstein when asked if he thought that he as an individual could help to settle the union's policy. 'I leave it to the Steward,' he went on. 'He's doing a good job. I speak my mind to him.' Union leaders were for a long time reluctant even to admit the fact of the shop stewards movement, partly but not only because of its associations with the Communist Party. 'The opinion still prevails,' noted Flanders in 1952, 'that the strengthening of workshop organization might undermine agreements arrived at nationally or on a district basis or otherwise weaken the authority of the trade unions.' But, he astutely added, 'the risks involved in the growth of any kind of "factory patriotism" have to be weighed against the need for the unions to make their influence felt in the daily lives of the workers.'[21] It was not a challenge that most union leaderships – deeply bureaucratic, deeply conservative, deeply grounded in the verities of the past – were well equipped to meet at this point where British society stood on the cusp of major change, above all precisely in the sphere of 'daily lives'.

The second fundamental flaw in mid-century trade unionism concerned gender. 'I believe the majority opinion of women working in factories and mills, especially in large-scale factories and mills, is on the whole favourable to unions, but in a lukewarm way, as expressed in such phrases as: "Unions are useful", or "helpful", or "sometimes useful sometimes not",' noted Zweig in his survey *Women's Life and Labour*. Even so, the stark fact (of which he was well aware) remained that in these post-war years only about a quarter of the female workforce was unionised – a proportion that hardly shifted until well into the 1960s. Zweig emphasised two particularly formidable stumbling blocks to female unionisation. One was the attitude of employers, who 'more often object to women joining the unions than to men doing so', and indeed 'many non-unionist employers give preference to female labour for the very reason that they can more easily keep women out of the unions than men'. The other obstacle, even more important, was the covertly (sometimes overtly) hostile attitude of male trade unionists. Zweig explained how it was an attitude with deep roots:

> Women were historically the great competitors of men on the labour market, often in the past condemned as blacklegs who undermined wages and fair standards and trade union controls, so trade unions were always concerned with keeping women out of the labour market by various restrictions on female labour. When finally trade unions came to see that they have to organise women to get them under control, the organisation took place not for the interest of women but for that of men.

Accordingly, not only were women's own unions 'rarely strong', but mixed unions were 'dominated by the interests of the males'.

Would women fight back, or would they simply keep their distance from the whole alienating, very male world of trade unionism? In terms of both membership and active participation, Pearl Jephcott's mid-1940s sample of adolescent working girls strongly suggested the latter:

> Their general attitude to trade unions both in London and the North is disheartening. One girl who at 18 was in the Ladies' Garment Workers' Union and was prepared to argue with other boys and girls that a union was a good institution, by 20 had lost heart about her cause (when it did not get her what she wanted) and belongs to none now. Another, who was a union member as young as 14, has no use for any union at 18 because 'they promised they would get us a rise in six months and they never did'. Even the telephonist [aged 19, working at a government office] asks, 'Why pay your money to keep some man in a job?'[22]

In their smoke-filled rooms, few of the invariably male trade-union leaders concerned themselves overmuch if at all. But if these girls represented the future, it was a poor look-out for the vitality of the movement – especially once husbands and wives began to live less in separate designated spheres.

The third Achilles heel, and ultimately the most serious, was the economic dimension of trade unionism. Although Flanders himself in *The System of Industrial Relations* strongly attacked free-market economists who were demanding greater flexibility than that provided by industry-wide pay agreements – 'There is not the slightest possibility of the clock being turned back to individual or to works bargaining over wage rates . . . Only the breaking up of trade unions by a political dictatorship could conceivably accomplish this result.' – another of the book's contributors, the young historian Asa Briggs, looked to the future health of the British economy and argued that among employees as well as employers there still remained 'serious psychological obstacles' to 'a sizeable expansion of output in the future'. Briggs added that 'whether or not the challenge of difficult times is met depends upon a new attitude to productivity and a new willingness to experiment'.

Put another way, would organised labour be part of the economic problem or part of the economic solution? Written by someone as close to the industrial coalface as anyone, Zweig's words earlier in the 1950s had a special and ominous resonance:

Every union has its own character derived from the past; and has crystallized its past experience into rules and customs. The union is the greatest bulwark of industrial conservatism. 'That has been the practice of our union and it must continue.' 'That is our custom, and always has been.' 'That goes against our practice and we can't tolerate it.' These are the statements one hears time and again and reads in the union reports; and the first duty of the union officials is to defend the past against any changes put forward by employers or by their own members. These practices are looked upon as the wisdom entrusted to them by the founders, and they are ensuring that what was won with great difficulty and sacrifice in the past shall not be lost.[23]

8

Too High a Price

The term 'supply-side economics' was not coined until 1976, and it is often claimed that over the previous three decades the fatal flaw of economic policy – characterised as broadly Keynesian macro-economic demand management, in other words fine-tuning from the centre the levels of demand – had been its unwillingness to grapple with the micro-economic supply side. What follows is a brief look at how five key elements on that side of the economy were faring by the early 1950s: transport and telecommunications, training and education, incentives, competition, and restrictive practices.

In March 1951 the panel on radio's main current-affairs discussion programme, *Any Questions?*, was asked if the finances of British Railways would be improved if fares were reduced. 'Nobody's going to pay anything to go on the railways as they're getting now,' replied the novelist and farmer Robert Henriques bluntly:

> They're getting worse and worse and worse, and in fact, this country in communications and transport – that's to say, telephones and everything else as well as roads and railways – is rapidly becoming worse than almost any other in the whole of Europe. The roads are appalling; you get more accidents because the roads are so narrow. You get slower and slower times on the roads because they're so congested . . . You get your trains that are going at a slower time than they were half a century ago and that is absolutely true . . .

'We're absolutely hopelessly inefficient,' he concluded. 'The whole thing is muddling through.'

It was a justifiably damning charge-sheet. Admittedly nationalisation in 1948 had given the railway industry (like the coal industry) a near-impossible brief of combining public service with commercial efficiency, but the fundamental problem was crippling underinvestment, in freight as well as passenger services, reflecting the failure of politicians and mandarins to face up to the need for an extensive modernisation programme. The contrast with France was especially painful. There the gifted engineer Louis Armand was instructed by his government in 1946 to make the French railway system the best in Europe; he received the resources and political backing to do so, and by the early 1950s was delivering. It was a similar story on Britain's roads, where after the early abandonment of the ten-year national road plan announced in 1946 there was only nugatory investment in what was – long after the creation of Germany's Autobahns – a pitifully inadequate, slow-moving and bottlenecked network. Moreover, blighting the prospects of both road and rail, there was in these years no systematic appraisal by the Treasury of the long-term demand that the British transport system was likely to have to meet.

As for telecommunications (still run by the Post Office), the picture was if anything even more dismal than that painted by Henriques. By 1948 less than 10 per cent of the population had a telephone, while by 1950 demand was so far exceeding supply that the waiting time for installation was reckoned to be anything up to 18 months. Moreover, for those lucky enough to have one, there were for private users the joys of a party line and for businessmen (and others) the trying, export-order-threatening experience of, in Correlli Barnett's exasperated words, 'waiting and waiting for their turn to have urgent long-distance calls put through inadequate cabling' by telephone operators 'shoving jacks into the switchboards of ageing manual exchanges'.[1] It could hardly have been a more felicitous formula for telegrams and anger.

In the area of training and education, it had traditionally been the apprenticeship system that sought to ensure a well-trained workforce, but by the 1950s, even though that system was working reasonably if not brilliantly well on its own terms, the fact was that almost three-quarters of teenagers entering the world of work were doing so in jobs without any craft or career training available. Nor was the formal education system meeting the gap. At secondary level the technical schools, supposed to be one leg of a three-legged stool that also comprised grammars and secondary moderns, never began to get a proper head of steam behind them, not least because the requirements of industry were low down the priorities at the Ministry of Education. Meanwhile, wartime plans to develop a network of so-called county colleges, providing compulsory part-time vocational education for school leavers up to the age of 18, never got off the ground, with voluntary day-release – inevitably less focused and sustained – being substituted instead.

Higher education, in terms of providing the requisite scientists, engineers and others for a modern economy, was not much better. In 1945 the Percy Report advocated that local technical colleges (though only 'a limited number' of them) should be sufficiently upgraded, in status as well as educational content, that their courses would be comparable to university degree courses. They were in effect to be the forerunners of the latter-day polytechnics. It was a bold proposal that soon encountered significant opposition from the Advisory Council for Science Policy, comprising eminent scientists from university departments, the research councils and industry. 'We do not believe that the type of man we need can receive the right kind of education in a technical college,' that body insisted. 'For that, we are convinced we must rely on the universities.' Investment in these technical colleges proved spasmodic up to the mid-1950s, with the numbers increasing but still fewer than 40,000 attending them.

In the universities themselves, there was a certain amount of opening up, with numbers increasing from some 50,000 at the end of the war to some 80,000 by the early 1950s, along with greater financial provision for children from poor, working-class families. But as one historian has fairly put it, 'their traditional curricula remained largely unchallenged and unchanged', notwithstanding the establishment in 1950 of the more science-oriented Keele University (originally called North Staffordshire University College). Crucially, 'they adapted only slowly to the technological needs of the post-war economy'.[2]

In the area of incentives, Herbert Morrison's candid private assessment in July 1949 of the current high-taxation regime was that 'the incentive to effort for workers as well as professional and technical people and employers is seriously affected by this burden'. With the standard rate of income tax standing at 9s (45 per cent), and around 12 million people paying some form of income tax (compared with four million before the war), he was understandably concerned about the political as well as the economic implications.

Generally, among economists and economic-policy advisers, there existed a broad consensus that overly high taxation acted as a significant deterrent to efficiency and productivity. 'In these days most wage earners know enough about their income tax to realise how much of their overtime pay goes in income tax, and there is no doubt that this discourages extra effort,' noted Paul Chambers in 1948 – a view having particular authority because he was the architect of the recently introduced Pay As You Earn (PAYE) system. For Robert Hall, head of the Cabinet's economic section, the crucial thing was to get some hard information about how taxation and incentives actually played out in practice. Not that Hall did not have his own views. 'What I really want,' he reflected in 1950, 'is an authoritative and impartial statement, to which everyone in the country will have to pay attention, to the effect that there are features in the present system which in the long run are very likely to damage our industrial efficiency, and that the price of removing these features is fairly small, whereas the price of keeping them may in the long run be fairly heavy.'

The upshot was the Royal Commission on the Taxation of Incomes and Profits, which commissioned a report, *Incentives in Industry*, by Geoffrey Thomas of The Social Survey, involving 1,203 interviews in early 1952 with a range of male manual workers across the country. The findings confounded the conventional wisdom. Not only, in the summarising words of the Treasury, did 'few productive workers' have 'any detailed knowledge of the way they were affected by income tax', but there was 'no evidence of productive effort being inhibited by the income tax structure within its present limits'. Startlingly, Thomas reckoned that of the eight million or so manual workers about whom it was reasonable to generalise on the basis of his sample, only a sixteenth or so of them, if offered fiscal incentives, '*might* increase their speed of work to *improve* their standard of living' – and that 'the amount of the increase is undetermined'. Furthermore, when his interviewees were asked to name the main ways in which output could be increased, 'monetary incentives to production did not occur spontaneously to more than 6% of the men'.[3]

There was thus only very weak evidence that – whatever the public-bar mutterings about tax – the availability or otherwise of fiscal incentives significantly affected real-life behaviour in most workplaces. Whether it was a different matter for the more vociferous grumblers in the saloon bar remained uncertain.

The Labour government, with its inherently divided instincts on the subject, did not prove an effective champion of competition. Although it did (under American pressure) push through anti-monopoly legislation in 1948, this lacked an adequately coercive dimension, while over the next three years the newly established Monopolies Commission managed to produce a grand total of two reports on specific industries: dental goods and, bizarrely enough, cast-iron rainwater goods used in building. Indeed, if anything the business environment was over the long run becoming *less* competitive: it is plausibly estimated that whereas in the mid-1930s cartel agreements (usually managed by trade associations) were affecting some 25–30 per cent of gross manufacturing output, by the mid-1950s the equivalent level of collusion was at around 50–60 per cent.

Predictably, it was the businessmen themselves (largely through the Federation of British Industries) who were mainly responsible for emaciating the legislation. Indeed, such was their attachment to cosy price agreements that they also managed to deter ministers from introducing measures that would threaten resale-price maintenance. Collusion was seemingly everywhere – for example in the ice-cream industry, increasingly a carve-up between Lyons and Wall's, though the urban myth that kiosks on Brighton beach sold only Lyons ice cream because of a territorial 'fix' was untrue, at least in the sense that it was the local councillors and not the companies that did the fixing. Certainly it was a stitch-up in Steel City. 'Selling was a gentleman's existence, with Sheffield operating as a big cartel,' Gordon Polson of Firth Vickers recalled in the early 1990s about the steel industry 40 years earlier. 'Orders were reported first to the respective trade and association committee, and at the end of the day they would tell you what prices to quote. The price-fixing was incredible.'[4]

The preference for an easy life was understandable – there were still plenty of government controls in place; imperial and Commonwealth markets provided an apparently welcoming, uncritical home for British goods, and the import threat was no more than a cloud on the distant horizon – but such an approach was no sort of preparation should the weather change.

Finally, on the question of restrictive practices, one turns again to Ferdynand Zweig, who when he began his study of five sectors of industry in the late 1940s was under the impression that such practices 'were increasing, because of the strengthened bargaining power of the Unions'. (Typically, he conducted some 400 interviews in the course of his inquiry.) 'But fortunately the reverse is true,' Zweig went on. 'War economy, with its admitted need for more production and the national interest awakened and strengthened in all sections of the population, delivered a blow to many restrictive practices ... And many restrictive practices abolished or temporarily suspended during the war are still in abeyance.'

That seemed straightforward and optimistic enough. However, he explained, the reality was more complicated. Not only in this respect did the war deal 'not as severe a blow as might have been expected', but 'there is a group of restrictive practices which has been spreading since the war' – practices that included 'the embargo on overtime, "working to rule", withdrawal from Joint Committees deliberating on important and pressing issues, etc.' Unions found such restrictive practices to be an effective substitute for a strike, 'which is a costly affair, full of risks and too conspicuous, and up to now in most cases outlawed'. There was, Zweig emphasised, a similar lack of appetite for confrontation on the part of many employers, who were willing to acquiesce in piecework bans, overtime restrictions or closed-shop arrangements. '"Peace in industry is worthwhile paying for" they often say,' he noted, while not denying that it was a rational attitude. After all: 'Practically the whole field of industrial relations is covered by agreements, rules and practices accepted by both sides, and the industrial code is growing constantly. Many employers feel that these rules and regulations are restricting the field of free enterprise, but they cannot find any alternative to this, but industrial chaos.' In short, 'each industry has a system of industrial jurisprudence, and the boss's word is no longer law'.

Zweig's survey leaves the reasonably clear impression that although restrictive practices were not necessarily spreading or intensifying, nevertheless they remained, from the point of view of encouraging a productive economy, a serious problem. Indeed, at about the same time another inquiry (overseen by the distinguished economist Roy Harrod) discovered that more than 60 per cent of its business respondents reckoned that prevailing restrictive practices were responsible for reducing productivity.[5]

In few places were these practices more rife than the national newspaper industry – where the union chapels exercised an iron and highly profitable rule, to the dismay of successive generations of timorous management, for whom the overriding concern was to ensure that their papers never failed to get out, at whatever long-term cost. Take the *Financial Times*. In September 1946 the editor, Hargreaves Parkinson, sent an urgent memo to the managing director that in a sense foreshadowed all that lay ahead. 'Mathew [Francis Mathew, manager of the printing works] rung up after you had gone tonight,' he began, and – after explaining how advantageous they felt it would be 'for expediting the printing of the paper' if the men took their half-hour for supper from 6.30 to 7.00 instead of 7.00 to 7.30 – he set out the state of play:

> The men have now been consulted and have intimated their willingness to make the cut at 6.30. They will do it for an extra payment each night of 8d, which Mathew says would mean a total of £2 a night, i.e. £10 a week. They can do it starting Friday night, if it is authorised Thursday.
>
> I recommend it strongly. It would be well worth the money and it may be indispensable if we are to get our eight-page issue out tomorrow night.

The recipient of this message was Lord Moore (the future Lord Drogheda, chairman of the Royal Opera House and one of the classic great-and-good 'fixer' figures of the post-war era). Next day, he returned the memo with a laconic pencilled note: 'I have said OK to Mathew.'

The following July, a not yet upwardly mobile 16-year-old called Norman Tebbit went to the *FT* as a price-room hand. There, compelled to join the printing union NATSOPA, he was 'outraged at the blatant unfairness of the rules which provided for the "fining" or even expulsion (and thus loss of job) of those with the temerity to "bring the union into disrepute" by such conduct as criticism of its officials'. Accordingly, 'I swore then that I would break the power of the closed shop.'[6] But more immediately, the question was whether, given the Labour government's natural reluctance to jeopardise its social contract with organised labour, a future government of a different hue would have the resolve to attempt to put industrial relations on a more flexible and productive basis.

————

There was an alternative model to follow. Near the end of September 1949 – as Aneurin Bevan cheered up Labour spirits by launching a barnstorming attack on Churchill as well as the 'obscene plundering' of stockbrokers and jobbers in Throgmorton Street's unofficial market the Monday after devaluation – the *Daily Mirror* asserted that what really mattered in Britain's painful economic position was not 'the dreary political skirmishing' in the House of Commons but a just-published report which found that output in the American steel industry was 'anything from half as much again to nearly double the rate of ours'. Noting that 'America succeeds because U.S. workers *believe* in the benefits of high output', the paper concluded: 'Only when every industry and every trade union has been converted to this purposeful way of thinking will we be in the frame of mind to conquer our difficulties.'[7]

What is clear about these years, however, is that neither side of British industry was willing, when it came to it, to follow the American gospel of productivity, with its pervasive emphasis on new methods and new techniques of doing things.[8] Thus the largely fruitless endeavours of the Anglo-American Council for Productivity, which between 1948 and 1953 produced a considerable body of work detailing the stark contrast between the productivities of the two economies but made barely a dent in deeply entrenched attitudes. In particular, the American push for the '3 Ss' – standardisation, simplification, specialisation – met with much opposition on the part of managers, who were similarly unimpressed by American calls for greater professionalism and zeal, not to mention greater openness with the workforce. As for that workforce, as represented by their unions, there was little appetite for the American formula of attacking craft practices and putting enhanced mechanisation and productivity bargaining in their place.

Importantly, this joint resistance to Americanisation was very much in line with British attitudes generally to their cousins across the herring pond. 'What are your present feelings about the Americans?' Mass-Observation asked its panel in August 1950. The following replies (all from men) were broadly representative:

Cordial detestation. (*Schoolmaster*)

I like their generosity, but I dislike their wealthy condescension. (*Forester*)

I do not like their habit of preening themselves and their way of life before the world and of giving advice to the rest of us in a somewhat sermonising manner. (*Civil servant*)

I like them and consider them our absolute friends. They give me the feeling of being able to do anything if they put their mind to it. Nothing would be too big. (*Clerk*)

Something like horror though that is much too strong a word. Their strident vitality makes me want to shrink into myself. (*Vicar*)

As individuals charming. As a race 'We are it'. (*Sales organiser*)

I dislike their worship of Mammon and hugeness but one must admire their ability and success. (*Retired civil servant*)

I hate their 'high pressure salesman' society. (*Hearing aid technician*)

I feel that the Americans are rather too big for their boots. (*Civil servant*)

The Americans are obviously becoming the Master race, whether we like it or not, so let's all begin to hero-worship them. (*Designer*)

Strikingly, even a commentator like Geoffrey Crowther, far from happy about the state of the British economy, had serious misgivings. 'America is a country where to my mind they have too much competition,' he told his Home Service listeners earlier in 1950. 'It does indeed make them rich . . . But every time I go there I am struck again by how much personal instability and unhappiness comes with the heavy competition. It shows up, I think, in the greater incidence of things like suicides, of nervous breakdowns, of alcoholism; very few people there can feel economically secure.' Accordingly, 'I am not suggesting that we should go to the American extreme and imitate their degree of competition. They pay too high a price for their wealth.'

Ealing, its finger ever unfailingly on the national pulse, agreed. *The Titfield Thunderbolt*, premiered in March 1953, could not have made the case more explicitly against unsentimental, bottom-line materialism and modernisation. The film tells the humorous, heartwarming, defiantly emotive story of how the inhabitants of a village come together to save their branch line (the oldest in the world) from the attempt by both British Railways and the local bus company (Pearce & Crump) to have it closed down. 'Don't you realise you're condemning your village to death?' one of the campaigners, the local squire, asks passionately at a public meeting. 'Open it up to buses and lorries and what's it going to be like in five years' time? Our lanes will be concrete roads, our houses will have numbers instead of names, there'll be traffic lights and zebra crossings.' The story's ending is predictably happy – as it was in a remarkably similar film that Ealing Studios made later that year.[9] This time the object to be saved was a small cargo boat pottering about the Clyde, with an American tycoon cast in the role of the bad guy in its struggle for survival. The message by the end was the simple and uplifting one that loyalty and obligations are more important than mere money. The film and the boat shared the same name: *The Maggie*.

9

Proper Bloody Products

Within the British mid-century economy, three industries were peculiarly emblematic. Each was important in itself, but each was also a symbol of something larger. Up to the 1970s, and even beyond, each possessed a resonance that made it the object of much attention, not always either accurate or flattering.

———

'300,000 people were there,' noted Hugh Gaitskell in July 1949, after speaking at the Durham Miners' Gala in his capacity as Minister of Fuel and Power. 'There were only 200 police controlling this vast mass and so far as I know there were no incidents. I only saw two people drunk and they were harmless enough.' It was the red-letter day in the Durham miners' calendar – the day that they and their families took over the city, with spectators packing each side of Old Elvet 15-deep for several hours in order to watch them march with their banners and bands through the centre on their way to the racecourse, where each year a handful of luminaries in the labour movement addressed them. In July 1951 it was the turn of Attlee and Morrison as well as Michael Foot and the General Secretary of the NUM, Arthur Horner. 'The speeches were only incidental,' reckoned one observer, the Labour MP for Huddersfield, J.P.W. ('Curly') Mallalieu. 'They mixed with the sounds of the fair, of late-arriving bands, of sandwich papers and of popping corks.' That afternoon, long after the speeches, there occurred in the narrow bottleneck of Old Elvet, as the processions made their slow and crowded way back, the day's moment of epiphany:

Suddenly there was silence. The colours still danced, but everything else was still. For the banner we now saw was draped in black. It carried a flag sent by the miners of Yugoslavia. It carried also the name of Easington Colliery. In that colliery, 52 days earlier, 83 miners had lost their lives [as the result of an explosion]. Through the silence the Easington band began to play. It played 'Gresford', the tune which a miner himself had written in sorrow for the great Gresford disaster [of 1934 near Wrexham in North Wales, when an explosion had killed 266 miners]. When the tune came to an end there was again stillness and silence until Old Elvet gently relaxed his hold and there was space to move. With the first movement the great crowd set up a storm of cheering that could be heard in Paradise, dancers cavorted again and the sunshine wiped away all thought of tears.

'Miners rub shoulders with death,' concluded Mallalieu. 'They know how to face death. Last Saturday I saw, too, that they will not let death spoil life.'[1]

Gaitskell would have been moved, too, but his late 1940s diary gives overall a fairly unflattering account of an industry that was starting to settle down in the wake of its 1947 nationalisation. 'I met the Divisional Coal Board and was not impressed,' he noted after a visit to Lancashire in October 1948. 'The problem of finding good men to occupy high managerial positions in coal is appalling. The industry just does not breed them. All you have is engineers without any conception of leadership or administration.' The National Coal Board (NCB) itself was not much better. 'The awkward thing is that I agree with most of his criticisms of the organisation,' Gaitskell privately conceded earlier that year when one of its members, the distinguished if somewhat pig-headed mining engineer Sir Charles Reid, threatened to resign on the grounds that the NCB was over-centralised, too rigidly structured and did not allow its managers to manage. Gaitskell asked Sir Richard Burrows, the shrewd, common-sensical former chairman of Manchester Collieries, to investigate. Some seven months later, the minister recorded, 'Burrows gave me some rather hair-raising accounts of the way the Board does its business. It is astonishing that nine apparently intelligent men should behave in the way that, according to him, they do.'

Almost certainly the most culpable figure was the chief of those nine, the NCB's first chairman (until 1951), Lord Hyndley, who as John Hindley had entered the industry as an engineering apprentice back in 1901, having on leaving public school preferred the charms of Murton Colliery to those of Oxford University. 'His successive promotions within British coalmining in the 1940s owed more to his seniority, and his familiarity in official and political circles, than to inherent suitability' is his biographer's telling verdict; she quotes the view of his counterpart in the electricity industry, the tough-minded former trade unionist Lord Citrine, that Hyndley was 'a most likeable man, friendly, experienced and broadminded, but lacking in drive'. Although he was good with the miners' leaders (Hugh Dalton called him 'a human water softener', presumably a compliment), and although the NCB did manage by the early 1950s a degree of decentralisation, the coal-mining industry needed an altogether bigger figure at its head.[2]

Operating at a much lowlier level in the industry was Sid Chaplin, Durham's miner-writer. The publication in 1946 of his first collection of stories, *The Leaping Lad*, had won him praise and a Rockefeller Award, enabling him to leave the pits and devote 20 months to writing But by the end of 1948 he was back at his old colliery, before getting a London-based job writing, from May 1950, a monthly feature ('I Cover the Coalfields') for the NCB's magazine, *Coal*. In January 1949, while still a miner, he wrote a piece that looked ahead in highly positive terms:

There is a spirit of adventure and experimentation within the industry which will produce rich dividends. Every coalfield is searching for new untapped sources of coal. All wastage of manpower between coal-face and the shaft will have to be cut out, and we must think in terms of conveyor, diesel, skip-loading. The old cumbersome methods of screening will have to go, to be replaced by new techniques.

Above all there is a need for pit-level awareness of the problems and achievements of the industry. It is not enough that the Board itself, its administrators or technicians should be aware of them. Every rank-and-file miner should be conscious of the immensity of the task, and be prepared to play his part.

At the beginning of the third year of public ownership the foundations are well and truly laid. Our task is now to build well upon them.

Given his deep emotional commitment to the nationalisation of an industry that ran in his blood, there is no reason to question Chaplin's sincerity here or in subsequent articles, but if he could not yet become a full-time creative writer, it was surely a relief when he managed to escape from the pit.

In truth, the industry's performance in its first five or six years of public ownership was less than sparkling. Overall output did rise but not by enough to meet demand fully, despite continued rationing. As for productivity, the verdict of the American economist William Warren Haynes was probably accurate. 'When the expanding volume of investment under nationalisation is considered,' he concluded in his major 1953 survey *Nationalization in Practice*, 'the small rise in productivity is disappointing. Modernisation of the industry has barely kept pace with the deteriorating geological conditions and with the shorter work week. It is by no means clear that the miners are putting forth more effort.' Capital expenditure and mechanisation (especially power-loading) were indeed increasing. But apart from the 'effort' factor – by definition difficult to quantify – there were two main productivity problems: the need, for short-term output reasons, to keep poor, inefficient, high-cost collieries going; and, despite overall progress on the manpower front, some shortages of skilled labour, especially in the more productive areas like Yorkshire and the Midlands. Accordingly, operating costs by the early 1950s were starting to rise quite steeply.

Even so, the long-term outlook for the industry seemed broadly optimistic. *Plan for Coal* was published by the NCB on 14 November 1950, and that evening its director-general of production, E. H. Browne, explained its main points on the Home Service. The assumption was that demand would continue to rise over the next ten to fifteen years, with production being expanded by about a fifth, while over those years there would be a capital investment of some £635 million. Browne explained how some 250 of the existing 900 collieries currently in production would have to be reconstructed – 'many of them by major changes often amounting to complete remodelling' – in order to become technologically fit for the task of producing about two-thirds of all the coal required. 'There will also be a score of new large collieries,' he added, as well as the closure by the early 1960s of some 350 to 400 pits. 'It will not be possible to avoid a further decline in the central coalfield of Scotland, West Durham, Lancashire, the older parts of Cannock Chase, and the very small fields of the Forest of Dean and Somerset.' After stressing again that the purpose of the plan was to expand output and control costs, Browne finished on a sober note: 'Mere words on paper will not bring about the recovery of the industry. We have got to run fast in order to stand still.'[3]

How would the traditionally vexed aspect of labour relations fit in? Chaplin in his January 1949 overview conceded that, since nationalisation, significantly less progress had been made here than in mechanisation, that indeed 'as yet we have a great deal to learn about the human element in industry'. There was certainly no lack of commitment to making nationalisation a success on the part of what was a remarkably able and weighty generation of miners' leaders – some of them Communists, like Arthur Horner or the Scottish and Welsh leaders Abe Moffat and Will Paynter. There was always on the NUM's executive a solidly right-wing, pro-Labour government majority. Few areas were more politically moderate than the huge Yorkshire coalfield, with its 150,000 men in 130 mainly semi-rural pits. 'The problem we had was that the entire NUM leadership in the coalfield was right-wing,' recalled Bert Ramelson, a young and energetic Canadian lawyer appointed in 1950 as the CP's district secretary in Yorkshire. 'If I was going to do anything that was useful, of importance, it would be to change the character of the Yorkshire coalfield . . . The Yorkshire miners could change the character of the NUM, which in turn could change the composition of the labour movement as a whole.' It would clearly be a long haul – by 1953 there were still fewer than a hundred party members in the South Yorkshire pits – but that was the gleam in Ramelson's mind's eye.

Nevertheless, for all the prevailing political moderation, industrial relations in the coal industry were if anything deteriorating in the late 1940s and early 1950s. Not only did absenteeism rates (at around 12 per cent) fail to improve, but the frequency of strikes (almost all of them unofficial) was on an upward curve, quite sharply so after the already numerous 1,637 in 1951. Stanislas Wellisz, an industrial sociologist, examined the 640 stoppages between 1947 and 1950 in the North-Western Division, comprising some 65 pits in Lancashire and seven in North Wales. He was even-handed in his allocation of blame. 'In most of the conflicts over authority,' he reported, 'manage-ment uses stern or arbitrary orders, or fails to ascertain the miners' wishes, and the miners walk out in protest.' On the other hand, the 'clinging to inherent rights', not all of them rational, was 'at the root of the miners' refusal to abandon output restrictive practices', tending to push the managers into an unacceptably (from the miners' point of view) authoritarian response. This was an even-handedness absent from most press coverage, which in coal-mining disputes almost invariably sided with the NCB.

The worker's point of view was the subject of a report by the Acton Society Trust, based on a researcher's experience in 1951 of living for three months in a miner's home in a coalfield (given the fictitious name of Pollockfield). It was not an optimistic document. Miners were gener-ally cynical about nationalisation, believing that as soon as their industry had been restored to health it would be sold back to its previous owners at the earliest opportunity. As for the NCB, a quarter of miners could name neither the chairman nor their own area general manager, while 'the intensity of the hatred and scorn felt for the administration is perhaps conveyed by some of the nicknames freely given to them: Glamour Boys, Fantailed Peacocks, Little Caesars.' Typically, there existed a widely held belief – such was the NCB's congenital waste and inefficiency – that at head office in London there was at least one full-time car-cleaner who would clean any car parked anywhere near. Many wage disputes were 'expressions of a feeling that the men's services, and hence the men themselves, are undervalued', while the miners' resentment about the use of Poles and Italians in the pits stemmed from the implication that 'only unemployed foreigners can be conscripted to do miners' work'.

Above all, there was in the miners' world view a gaping dichotomy that no amount of exhortations or information campaigns seemed likely to bridge. 'Whatever falls within the miners' experience – the wages system as it affects his actual pay, conditions in the pit, local issues such as housing and transport – was known in great detail,' declared the report. But 'the wider issues and underlying causes – the economic reasons for importing American coal, the probable forthcoming shortage of manpower, the character of the National Plan, the functions of the administrative and technical machine – were largely unknown'.[4]

These were findings that made a cruel mockery of Chaplin's hopes about rank-and-file consciousness of – and positive response to – the stern challenges faced by this most high-profile of nationalised industries.

The relentless primacy of the local was hardly surprising. 'The life of the community is built around the pit,' observed Pollockfield's inquisitive guest, 'and events touching the pit form the subject of practically all conversation.' In *Coal Is Our Life* (1956), one of the classic community studies of the era, Norman Dennis, Fernando Henriques and Clifford Slaughter analysed a Yorkshire mining community called 'Ashton', in fact Featherstone. Based on extensive fieldwork there, mainly in 1952/3, the study provided an unsentimental close-up of what was still a world of its own.

'Ashton is predominantly a working-class town [population about 14,000] owing its development to the growth of its collieries,' the three authors wrote. 'The latter having drawn people and houses around them, the main pit is almost in the centre of the town. Most of the men in Ashton are miners.' Crucially, they found that though much had changed in the miner's life since the late 1930s – better conditions of work, rising wages, job security, nationalisation, enhanced status within the working class – his outlook was still in its fundamentals determined by the long preceding years of 'hard toil and social conflict'. They told the story of a 63-year-old pitman who on two successive night shifts found himself being given pony-driving duties. At the end of the second shift, he stormed into the deputy's cabin. 'What do you think you're doing?' he shouted. '*I'm not signed on as a driver; I'm signed on as a collier*, and that's the kind of bloody job I should be doing, not a lad's work.' All this, noted Dennis et al, 'was shouted loud enough for all the men near by, dressing to leave work, to hear' – and the pitman 'came away flushed and very pleased with himself, for he had, with this demonstration, removed, or so he thought, any reflection of inferiority cast upon him by his work of the last two shifts'.

In general, they found, the notion of co-operation with management, even after nationalisation, remained essentially suspect. 'It's a rotten scheme and you won't catch me having anything to do with it' was a 32-year-old collier's view of the industry's pension scheme. 'Anything the management wants the men to do is bound to be to our detriment. That's what I've always been taught.' Indeed, there was an increasing tendency on the part of miners to treat their union officials as management, such being by now their relative closeness; the clear implication was that this was why stoppages and go-slows were assuming an increasingly unofficial nature. Crucially, the difficult and sometimes dangerous work that coal mining still was (involving a close mutual reliance between miners), combined with the single-industry character of the town, meant that there was no sign of any significant weakening in solidarity as 'a very strongly developed characteristic of social relations in mining'. There was, as in other mining communities in West Yorkshire, a strong element of *contra mundum* in this solidarity:

> The mining villages, and Ashton is certainly a good example, are among the ugliest and most unattractive places to live; they are dirty, concentrated untidily around the colliery and its waste-heaps, and lack the social and cultural facilities of nearby towns. Passengers on buses going through Ashton will invariably comment on its drabness, and the place is often quoted as an example of the backwardness of the mining areas. In conversation with strangers, men and women of Ashton will defend their town almost before it comes under attack on such grounds . . .
>
> In addition, the backwardness of welfare developments in the Ashton Colliery – there are no baths and only inadequate canteen facilities – is part of the reason for a general belief that Ashton is neglected and something of a backwater.

One historical event still had, for the older miners, a particular resonance. This was the great strike of 1893, when the troops were sent in and two miners were shot dead and 16 others were injured. It was the moment in the history of 'Ashton' that, these older miners proudly believed, would never be forgotten.

Ferdynand Zweig (who visited most British coalfields in the late 1940s) probably had it right about those who worked in the nation's coal mines: 'They all live in closely-knit communities where there is a strong projection of the group on the individual. Their life is firmly circumscribed by pit conditions. The pit and the village control their

habits and rules of conduct . . .' And again: 'The miners, who often
hate their jobs, have at the same time a deeply-felt affection for them,
which is often expressed in the incessant talk about the pit.' He added,
tellingly, that 'younger men often interrupt this talk with "Pit, pit, and
pit again"'. Those younger miners included by 1953 the 15-year-old
Arthur Scargill. Years later, he recalled his initiation into the industry
at Woolley Colliery, just north of Barnsley:

> Melson [Alf Melson, the one-eyed foreman] used to stalk up and down
> a sort of raised gantry in the screening plant. He was just like Captain
> Bligh glaring at his crew. We were picking bits of stone and rock out
> of the coal as it passed us on conveyer belts. The place was so full of
> dust you could barely see your hands, and so noisy you had to use sign
> language. When it came to snap time, your lips were coated in black
> dust. You had to wash them before you could eat your snap [in his case
> a bottle of water and jam sandwiches] . . .
>
> There were two sorts of people in the section: us, and disabled rejects
> of society. I saw men with one arm and one leg, men crippled and
> mentally retarded. I saw people who should never have been working,
> having to work to live.

'It probably sounds corny,' this very atypical miner added, 'but on that
first day I promised myself I would try one day to get things changed.'⁵

Five years earlier, in February 1948, *Picture Post*'s focus was on a
different but not altogether dissimilar sector of the economy. Six individual dockers, each pictured with a confident, smiling face, were
selected as representative of 'The Men Who Can Do It':

> *Walter Eagle.* Forty-six, he lives at Forest Gate with his wife and three
> children. He has been a docker for over 25 years.
> *Patsy Hollis.* Nicknamed 'Flash-bomb', says he's about 45, from Poplar,
> and one of the 'pitch-hands', who load 'cargoes from ships' on to
> hand-barrows.
> *Wally May.* Thirty-four, he comes from Becontree. In his spare time is
> a chicken-fancier, but spends most of his time loading ships.

George Rutter. Thirty-five, married, with two sons, he comes from Manor Park. When he has time, he likes escaping to Epping Forest with the boys.

Arthur May. Thirty-nine, married, with two children, he comes from Manor Park. He works in the holds of the cargo ships.

George Moore. Sixty-two, worked in dockland for 37 years. Travels from Canning Town. He has two sons who follow his footsteps.

A mainly historical piece about the dockers and their leaders, by the middle-class socialist (and man of parts) Raymond Postgate, accompanied the pictures and captions. It ended with Ernest Bevin, who had won national fame in 1920 as 'the Dockers' K.C.' during a government inquiry. 'Now he has international fame,' wrote Postgate, 'but he is still a docker. Study that stocky, sturdy figure – its faults and its virtues – its courage, its solidity, its short temper, its readiness to fight, its imagination, its patriotism, its loyalty – all these are typical of dockland.'

The same issue also included a photo-essay and more critical piece on London's docks and dockers. 'Men Who Are Vital Links in the Nation's Import and Export Chain Work at the Port of London's King George V Dock' began one of the extended captions. 'After generations of industrial struggle, they now have a guaranteed daily wage of £1 0s 6d for a 5½-day week. Casual labour, which was the curse of dockland, ended last year. It is on men such as these that the quicker turn-round of ships, which can so help industrial recovery, depends.' The disturbing fact, however, was that turn-round time in British docks had, far from improving, 'fallen off badly'. 'Can we cut out this serious delay, which is costing us so much, and get back at least to pre-war turn-round figures?' asked *Picture Post*, identifying restrictive practices as the crux:

> The case can be quoted of six gangs on quay, all of which turned up one or two men short on a Saturday morning. These gangs would not manage to make five complete gangs, and they would not work short-handed. So no work was done on the quay that morning, and the gangs on the ship could not work either. The dockers' trade union leaders, responding to the Labour Government's appeal, are now doing their best to end these restrictive practices, and the powerful Transport and General Workers' Union has backed the Government's export drive.

'But the final answer,' the piece concluded with no wild optimism, 'is with the dockers.'[6]

Much would turn on how the National Dock Labour Scheme (NDLS), building on Bevin's wartime reforms of dock labour and coming into effect in July 1947, played out. In addition to decasualisation (aimed at ensuring a regular, well-organised supply of labour) and a guaranteed daily wage, it involved a disciplinary mechanism to be administered jointly by employers and unions. After so many years of chaotic, even vengeful industrial relations in the docks, there seemed a real chance that a new, more productive, more harmonious era might begin. Such hopes were quickly dashed. Not only were there major, high-profile strikes in 1948 and 1949 (in both cases centred on London and Liverpool), but between 1945 and 1951 as a whole, more than a fifth of the 14.3 million working days lost to strikes in all industries were attributable to industrial action in the docks – even though those docks employed only about 80,000 men out of a national workforce of some 20 million.[7]

'To some of us,' a bishop living in Eastbourne wrote to *The Times* during the 1949 strike (ended only by the government's resorting to no fewer than 15,000 servicemen to act as strike-breakers), 'it is all so desperately puzzling.' He went on:

> We are told that the majority of dockers are decent men, yet their reasoning powers seem paralysed. How can it be right to sacrifice England, to attempt to starve her, and to upset our already over-difficult national recovery by any sectional action? Is there some deep cause we do not know, or is it just rather sheer stupidity or selfish sectionalism? We are told to admire the 'solidarity' of a section (even though England is victimised), but when employers were accused of a similar 'common front' we were told that it was a conspiracy to victimise the public. What is the difference?

Nor did the NDLS seem to make much difference in terms of restrictive practices. 'They have the very finest machinery,' the President of the Glasgow Chamber of Commerce told the *Financial Times* about the new ships for handling ore cargoes on Clydeside, 'but meantime the dockers insist that the same number of men should be employed as in the old-fashioned ships, which means that in a gang of eight to twelve men only two do the actual work.' When a few weeks later a government-sponsored Working Party on Increased Mechanisation in British Ports published its report, it revealed that union representatives 'have told us that they are not prepared, except in certain circumstances, to depart from the present arrangements which call for certain numbers of men to be employed on stated tasks' – and that in those situations where dockers were paid for standing by watching the machine do the work, 'we have been informed that this is the only method in which machinery can be used without causing disputes and stoppages'. Or, as a report at about the same time by the British Institute of Management on the London docks flatly summed up the situation, 'The refusal of the workers to agree to alter long-established rules seems now so much to be taken for granted that many technical improvements are not even seriously considered by the employers.'

Probably the most militant dockers, certainly among London's 25,000 or so, were the roughly 10,000 who worked in the so-called Royal Group of Docks in the south of West Ham: the Victoria, the Royal Albert and the King George V (always called KGV). Where these docks led, London's other docks followed. 'Anybody with a cap and a choker, on a bicycle, could ride round the West India Docks shouting "they're out at the Royals",' one manager recalled in 1970. 'Men would come trooping off the ships with no questions asked and no regard to agreements or current work.' Defending piece rates and existing working practices – above all the size of gangs – lay somewhere near the heart of the prevailing militancy in the Royals, almost all of it channelled not through official unions like the TGWU but through the unofficial Port Workers' Committee, renamed the London Docks Liaison Committee in the mid-1950s.

'One of the protective practices was, if you loaded cargo in the centre of the hold and you got over 26 feet to walk your parcels in for stowing, once it went over 26 feet, you demanded pro rata, extra men because of the distance of walking,' recollected in retirement the rank-and-file movement's leading figure by the late 1950s – and, between then and the early 1970s, one of the most demonised figures in the country. This was Jack Dash. After an impoverished south London childhood, lengthy spells of unemployment, an early

conversion to Communism and a war spent with the Auxiliary Fire
Service, Dash was in his late 30s when he became a docker at the end
of the war. By 1949 his role in that year's major dispute led to him
being one of six dockers disciplined by the TGWU, and from that
point he did not look back. Nicknamed 'Nature Boy' on account of
his penchant for stripping to the waist, he had undeniable personal
charisma; a speaking style, at the countless unofficial meetings heralding
countless unofficial stoppages, that skilfully combined humour and
eloquence; and a political philosophy that may have been unsophisti-
cated but was undoubtedly sincere. Dash believed that (in the words
of his biographers) 'there were two classes, the exploiters and the
exploited, and that the downfall of capitalism would occur as Marx
had predicted'. By a pleasing irony, he had got a permanent job in the
docks – normally reserved for sons of dockers – only after an employer
had recommended him for full registration on the grounds that he was
'a good worker'.[8]

Why did the much-vaunted NDLS fail to transform industrial relations and instead lead to an explosion of unofficial militancy? Almost
certainly, despite some name-calling on the part of government, it was
not because the great majority of recalcitrant dockers were politically
motivated. Indeed, the blunt verdict of one well-qualified historian
about the 1945–51 period is that 'political subversion had nothing to
do with any of the main unofficial strikes'. Rather, the problem was
that for many dockers the new arrangements did not represent a sufficiently attractive deal to persuade them to moderate their traditional
occupational behaviour – indeed, the context of more or less full
employment served only to encourage them to exacerbate it.

The deal itself was well summed up in retrospect by a Liverpool
docker (Peter Kerrigan) who had entered the industry in 1935: 'The
Dock Labour Scheme was a two-edged thing. At the same time as it
gave the benefits of a guaranteed minimum sum if you didn't work,
you had to pay for it with a certain loss of liberty. The people who
ran it were the officials of the T&G and the employers. The people
who punished you were also the people who were supposed to be
your representatives.' In smaller ports, more dockers than not found
the improved security provided by the NDLS broadly acceptable, but
in larger ports, such as London, Glasgow and Liverpool, the reverse

tended to be the case. Peter Turnbull and two other sociologists have put it most lucidly:

> Quite simply, for better-organised groups such as Glasgow dockers and London stevedores, the NDLS held few attractions, imposing restrictions on what was previously regarded as the worker's 'freedom of choice' or established union procedures for the allocation of work. On the Thames, stevedores and the more skilled dockers, the so-called 'kings of the river', preferred irregular employment with the possibility of earning high wages when work was available, on the cargoes they liked best, rather than more regular but un-specialised work throughout the port. The NDLS was predicated on the latter, not the former.

The direct result in London and other major ports was an inordinate number of small but cumulatively disruptive and damaging disputes over such matters as allocation, transfers or demarcation – disputes in which the TGWU and other unions were increasingly marginalised.

The situation was not helped either by the nature of the work itself (the infinitely disputatious implications of variable payments depending on type of cargo, not to mention the frequent contrast between long working weeks and periods of short-time) or by the reluctance of the employers, customarily – and rightly – seen as reactionary, to invest in dock amenities. 'It is not surprising that the men avoid the lavatories whenever possible and have a real fear of infection,' noted a National Dock Labour Board report in 1950 on the latter aspect. Revealingly, in terms of their lack of knowledge, Board members were 'amazed and nauseated by what they saw and smelled'; the report added, somewhat condescendingly, that a 'general raising of standards' was occurring on the part of the dock workers, in that they were now demanding better toilet and washing facilities 'which but a few years ago would have seemed irrelevant in dock land'. And, of course, dock work in the 1950s remained as dirty and dangerous as it had ever been. A survey in 1950 found that although 41 per cent of accidents in the docks were, predictably enough, caused by handling, no fewer than 40 per cent were caused by being struck by a 'falling body', by 'striking an object', by falling or by what was rather sinisterly called 'hook injury'. Dash himself would become leader of the rank-and-file movement in

London after Wally Jones had been killed by a fall into a ship's hold.[9]

One source gives us an array of contemporary voices – not from London or Liverpool but from the much smaller docks at Manchester. During the winter of 1950/51, social scientists from Liverpool University interviewed 305 dock workers there, out of a total labour force of 2,426. Although most of the workers were more or less in favour of the NDLS, their tenor across a range of issues was generally negative:

Everyone round here ultimately drifts into the docks.

People wouldn't say that dockers were solid if they saw us in the 'pen' [ie the call-stand, resembling a cattle market, where jobs were allocated] squabbling like a lot of monkeys to do ourselves a bit of good.

People get sent to jobs they cannot do. Young men are put in the sheds, old men in the ships. This is very unfair.

Top management should get round a table with the men to discuss their problems.

The damned twisters would rob you of a halfpenny.

The branch meetings [ie of the union] are too dull and slow.

Everything's rigged in the meetings.

When there is a dispute, the officials should try the job themselves, not just look at it and keep their hands clean.

You have to have more skill and experience at this game than for any other job and yet road sweepers outside get more than us.

The bare lick is no good with the present cost of living; I dare not take £5 home to the wife. You can't be sure of overtime, although some men never seem to be on the bare lick.

You practically have to sleep here to get a good wage.

Blue eyes get the bonus jobs.

They twist us on bonus.

Treated like animals, we are.

I wouldn't wash my feet in their canteen tea.

We should be supplied with clothes in the same way that platelayers are. I have to depend on cast-offs.[10]

It was the same in the Port of London. When my mother arrived from Germany in the spring of 1950, her ship berthing at the West India, what most struck her was the sight of the dockers wearing not work uniform but instead their ordinary heavy overcoats.

––––––––––

The third emblematic sector was altogether more modern. 'The vitality of the British motor industry,' the Minister of Supply, George Strauss, told the annual dinner of the Society of Motor Manufacturers and Traders on the eve of the first post-war Motor Show in October 1948, 'has confounded the wiseacres who foretold that the industry would die a lingering death in the post-war world.' He added that 'the main reason for our export success is that British cars are exceptionally good'. Next day, the *FT* agreed: there could 'be no doubt that the industry has done very well, much better than its detractors can have thought possible'; if it had not managed to achieve 'the visionary target of "one car, one firm" which has sometimes been urged upon it', this was because 'this target is both impracticable and undesirable, not because the industry is not aware of the need for standardisation'; and in general the temporary lack of competition in the export market was far from meaning that there was no 'substantial underlying demand for British cars' – indeed, 'the quality displayed at the show should banish any doubt that they will be unequal to the opportunity' when circumstances changed. Or, as a talk soon afterwards on the Home Service put it with due caution, 'Britain, perhaps just for the time being, is the greatest motor-car exporting nation in the world.'

Nor had the situation changed by 1950, with the huge American motor industry still trying to satisfy its swelling domestic demand and Europe still recovering from the war. That year, the British motor industry enjoyed a staggering 52 per cent of world motor exports. In terms of overall production, whether for domestic or export purposes, the French, German and Italian combined total only just exceeded Britain's 476,000. Japan, meanwhile, produced only 2,000 cars in the entire year. A report on the British motor industry did concede that it would not be a seller's market for ever and identified Germany in particular as a potential future competitor of 'permanent importance', but that competition would not come from the Volkswagen, which the report reckoned 'by British standards' to be 'uncomfortable and noisy'. Despite increasingly persistent, disobliging complaints from abroad that British cars were becoming a byword for unreliability, it would take a lot to shake the industry's complacent assumption that British was still best.[11]

It was an industry clustered in five main places. Each had significantly different characteristics, but in all of them the conveyor-belt assembly line – 'the track' – was the relentless, remorseless, unforgiving nerve centre of operations.

Dagenham was the British home of Ford – a Detroit in miniature since the early 1930s. The works put a premium on continuous, integrated production and included a blast furnace, coke ovens, a powerhouse, iron and steel foundries, and fully mechanised jetties for loading and unloading that reached out into the Thames. 'Ford has always applied the principle that higher wages and higher standards of living for all depend on lower costs and lower selling prices through increasingly large-scale production' was how the British chairman, Lord Perry, summed up the Ford philosophy soon after the war. By 1948 Ford was the highest-volume as well as the most profitable car manufacturer in Britain, while by 1950 its production had trebled over the previous four years. There were also by the end of 1950 two new models about to come on stream – the Consul and the Zephyr, both very successful, heavily American-influenced family saloons – which for the time being most of the quarter of a million or more on Ford's home-market waiting list could only dream about. Meanwhile, the barely revamped pre-1945 models (the Anglia, Prefect and Popular) still enjoyed huge appeal at the less expensive end of the market.

In general, coming into the 1950s, Ford had the most professional management, the most systematic product planning and a powerhouse leader in Sir Patrick Hennessy. A self-made Irishman, with drive and strongly held free-market views, he was more frustrated than most by what he saw as the Labour government's congenital interference in the motor industry. 'They tell us what to do, what to make, when to make it and what to do with it when we have made it,' he complained to an American colleague in June 1948. Even so, when soon afterwards the Board of Trade tried to persuade him that the socially responsible way for Ford to continue to expand its production was by opening a new plant some 200 miles away in Kirkby (about to become an overspill area for Liverpool), he successfully stood his ground. 'It is neither good economic or business judgement for this Company, or the Country, to upset the balance of the only integrated factory in the motor industry by so distant a dispersal,' insisted a colleague on his behalf.[12] Ford, more than any other British motor company, was focused on the bottom line.

But there was a crucial flaw. 'Labour relations were perhaps the area in which Sir Patrick was least at home' is his biographer's verdict. 'So high were the standards of dedication and performance he set himself that he found it difficult to understand why every Ford worker could not be as disciplined and loyal.' That is one way of describing the implications of what was a wholly unsentimental deal on offer to the Ford workforce: in essence, reasonably high day wages (with no piece-work element) in return for accepting more or less all-encompassing management control. Typically, there had been no recognition of trade unions until almost the end of the war, and then only grudgingly. It was an overly inflexible, macho approach that had worked during the unemployment-scarred 1930s but it was much less suited to the rela-tively full-employment post-war era. In the three years from the spring of 1946 there were almost 40 strikes and go-slows at the Dagenham plant – or what management in March 1949 bitterly described to the TUC's Victor Feather as 'the lamentable, frequent, and serious breaches of the current Agreements'. A tough-minded approach on the part of management was probably inevitable, given the broadly sensible decision to pay largely by time rather than by piecework, with all the inevitable problems and disputes that the latter approach involved; at Ford, however, it seems as often as not to have been a tough-mindedness that, counterproductively, allowed an insufficient degree of dignity to the workforce.

A trio of recollections gives a flavour of Ford's methods since the 1930s and the ensuing atmosphere of resentment:

They were great disciplinarians. You'd go down to where the job was, and hang your clothes up, and there'd be a man standing by this rack arrangement that the clothing was put on to. And as soon as the hooter went you would all start work immediately and out of the corner of your eye you could see this rack start to sail up into the roof with all your clothing. And there it stayed until 4.30 in the afternoon . . .

Those of us who worked in the Dagenham plant recall the fear of talking out of turn and the suspensions and even worse if one spoke out. The Gestapo-like Service men, and the cat-walk high above the factory where the superintendent usually patrolled, for all the world like a prison warder ... Many former employees will remember the raids on the trim and upholstery departments to see whether a worker had committed the heinous crime of having his packet of sandwiches near his job. The company insisted that they be kept in a locker which was above the heat treatment, making the sandwiches uneatable at lunchtime ...

Working on the line was filthy, dirty and noisy. Basically, you had to have a bath every night. The metal dust that was flying around would turn all your underclothes rusty. No matter how much you washed the sheets they would go rusty and so would the pillows. But what really caused the trouble was the speed-up. We used to have a works standards man come round, and he'd time you with his watch. Then the foreman would come and say, 'Well, you've got to produce faster.' But it just didn't work out like that, because you felt you were working and sweating hard enough as it was ...

Over the years, observers of the industrial scene (such as Graham Turner) tended to find the factory and its environs a sullen, dispiriting sort of place. The work itself was so intensely narrow and repetitive that the concept of any intrinsic job satisfaction was unimaginable; a high proportion of the workforce, going back to the 1930s, were incomers to the area attracted solely by the material rewards of the work – men characterised by Turner as often 'at odds with their particular situation or with society in general, the misfits, the dissatisfied and the restless'. As for Dagenham itself:

The only relief amid the vistas of identical houses [almost entirely built by the London County Council between the wars] is the occasional mild rash of shops, garnishing the burial mounds thrown up to allow the District Line tube to pass beneath them. Wet or fine, the wind blows down the broad avenues and across the litter-laden open spaces. It carries the smoke and the smells from the factories by the river and deposits them among the houses.

Altogether, concluded Turner, there hung over this one-class, 'fossilized' community 'a towering sense of insecurity, an insecurity compounded of old and new fears, of past memories and current rumours'.[13] That was in the early 1960s; the collective psyche was unlikely to have been very different in the late 1940s. The human factor, in short, was where the Detroit model was found wanting.

Some 40 miles away, Luton was host to the other American-owned motor company among the British 'Big Six'. General Motors had acquired Vauxhall in 1925, and by 1949 it had an 11 per cent share of total British car production (compared with Ford's 18.7 per cent), as well as, through its Bedford trucks, a 17.7 per cent share of the British commercial-vehicle market. Vauxhall had also by this time streamlined its car production (making only the Velox and Wyvern models, both of them given Chevrolet-style makeovers in 1951) and started on a major expansion of the plant's infrastructure. But what made Vauxhall really distinctive were its harmonious labour relations, earning it the nickname of 'the turnip patch'. It was a harmony that may have owed something to Luton's location – well away from other major car plants or indeed any local engineering tradition – but undoubtedly there was a key individual involved. This was Sir Charles Bartlett, managing director from 1929 to 1953, a highly intelligent paternalist who liked his workforce to call him 'The Skipper'. Given considerable autonomy by his American masters, and inheriting a fairly brutal, hire-and-fire regime, he presided through the 1930s and 1940s over a gradual, quiet and almost entirely successful revolution – in which, crucially, workers were treated as human beings rather than Stakhanovite extras in a remake of *Metropolis*.

Bartlett's approach to industrial relations had several main features: avoiding lay-offs wherever possible, so that the workforce became more stable; paying good wages; using what was known as the Group Bonus System in order to enhance motivation and give the workforce at least a limited sense of control; introducing a profit-sharing scheme; developing an impressive range of social and welfare amenities; and, at the very core of Bartlett's strategy from 1941, promoting the Management Advisory Committee (to which each area of the factory sent a representative elected by secret ballot) as a forum for meaningful rather than fig-leaf consultation. Bartlett was no sentimentalist, not least in relation to the unions. They had been recognised at Vauxhall (as at Ford) only during the war, and thereafter he was determined to keep them relatively marginalised. Indeed, even during the 1950s less than half of Vauxhall's workforce was unionised, while it took a long time for a shop stewards' movement of any clout to emerge. As late as 1960, 'The Firm Without a Strike' was the straight-faced title of an *Economist* profile of Vauxhall. Of course, that was not *strictly* true. 'There wasn't a strike for twenty years,' an executive would wryly recall in the very different early 1970s. 'We called them "pauses for consultation". You can laugh, but that's really what they were. Nobody lost any money. We were paid while the work stopped and the MAC went into the trouble squarely.'[14]

There was by contrast no shortage of conflict at Cowley on the outskirts of Oxford, though in this case much of it was within the ranks of management. The ageing Lord Nuffield, formerly William Morris, was a classic example of a founding father – of Morris Motors – who, Lear-like, refused to let go. The upshot by the immediate post-war period was a disastrous managerial culture: lines of authority were at best ill-defined; Nuffield's own approach to man management largely consisted of telling people about the shortcomings of their colleagues; there prevailed what one historian has described as a 'distressing climate of suspicion and indecision'; and in general there was little in the way of clear-sighted or other than spasmodic strategic thinking. Market share (19.2 per cent in 1947) was declining, while a major management purge and reorganisation by a new chief executive, Reginald Hanks – who tactlessly told Nuffield that 'Rome is burning' – did not fundamentally change a divisive culture whose roots went back to the 1920s.

Would the Morris Minor, unveiled at the 1948 Motor Show, be the firm's saviour? In an obvious sense, yes, in that it soon became Britain's best-loved as well as best-selling small car. But Corelli Barnett is probably correct when he argues that Morris Motors, by failing to concentrate on the Minor and instead spreading its production resources over additional models (including the Oxford, the Cowley and the Morris 6), missed a golden opportunity to challenge Germany's equivalent small car, the Volkswagen, in the main export markets: 'Total output of the Minor over seven years [1948–55] only reached 387,000 – not much more than a third of the Volkswagen's total of one million cars in the same period achieved from a standing start in a bombed-out works.' Barnett also has a pop at the actual design of the Morris Minor by the 'supposedly brilliant' Alec Issigonis, claiming that it was not nearly so advanced as the motoring cognoscenti claimed at its launch. However, given its undeniable instant popularity, this is perhaps trying to have it both ways.

Management discord at Cowley was accompanied by a distinct abrasiveness in labour relations. Leading shop stewards were systematically weeded out, while union membership was sufficiently discouraged such that, as late as 1956, there was only 25 per cent unionisation at Morris Motors. A young shop steward in these difficult years was the remarkable Les Gurl. Born in 1921, the son of a labourer at a farm belonging to an Oxford college, Gurl started work at Cowley in 1935 and, after being demobbed from the navy, returned there in 1947. Soon afterwards, amid a sharp, pervasive divide between those who had left to fight and those who had stayed, he became a shop steward in the erecting-and-wiring shop:

Most if not all charge hands, foremen, superintendents, managers and company directors had worked in the factory throughout the whole war. Morris men through and through, whatever Lord Nuffield said or did it was OK by them. They were now dealing with mainly young ex-Servicemen [about 75 per cent of the workforce in Gurl's shop] who were looking for improvements in the factory way of life away from the hire and fire and the charge hands' pets, the men who came in regularly with the bag of garden products which they left by the charge hands' desks. Of course we had to be wide awake to the fact that if these old hands would bring in vegetables to get in with the bosses, then they would also run to them with any tales about the union or steward.

By the time he came to write his recollections in the mid-1980s, Gurl was convinced that a more understanding attitude on the part of the company in these early post-war years would have made a huge long-term difference:

Simple things were forced up into major problems because Mr Moore [the shop foreman] would seldom make the effort to solve our grievances.

There was the case of the coat rail where the line workers would hang their macs and coats. Under this rack travelled telpher trucks filled with greasy prop shafts, shackle plates, axles. The bottom of the clothes were soon blackened with grease. Most people in those days only owned one mac or overcoat, many worked in very old shoes wearing their good pair only to and from work. There was a simple solution to this complaint – raise the rack say two feet. Sadly it took weeks and was only solved when in frustration I told the line I represented, 'If you want action, then stop work'. It brought a quick solution. The maintenance men were soon down in the erecting shop and the rack was raised.

Gurl from 1949 led the campaign for a workable pension scheme for those workers at Cowley who were paid by the hour. 'We eventually won our case,' he recalled laconically, 'on the day British Leyland was taken over by the Government' – that is, in 1975.[15]

The fourth centre of production was Coventry: Motor City itself. Daimler, Humber, Maudslay, Singer, Standard, Rover, Riley, Hillman, Alvis, Triumph, Jaguar – between 1896 and 1928 all these firms had started producing cars there. By 1945 the city's two main players were Standard (who took over the Triumph name in 1945) at Canley and the Rootes Group (producing Humber, Hillman and Sunbeam Talbot models) at Stoke and Ryton. Jaguar was under the formidable William Lyons, Daimler concentrated mainly on commercial vehicles, while Alvis, Armstrong Siddeley and Riley (owned by Nuffield and leaving Coventry in 1949) were notable among the smaller-scale producers.

By 1951 the city's output of cars was more than 130,000, representing just under 28 per cent of total British output, and the place was manifestly booming. The population was increasing rapidly, from 232,000 in 1946 to 258,000 in 1951; hourly rates in the motor and other engineering industries were up to a third or even more above the national average; and among the city's 60,000 or so workers in the motor industry were many newcomers, of many nationalities, living in hostels or an improvised shanty town of derelict railway coaches while they waited for Coventry's housing to catch up with its explosive economic growth. 'A young city, virile, brimming over with skill and energy' was how the visiting Laurence Thompson found it in about 1950, adding that the place was 'the mother and father of British mass-production' and 'a town in which anything might happen'.[16] It was also one where, at least at Standard and Rootes, organised labour was far more powerful than anywhere else in the motor industry.

The key figure was the managing director of Standard Motors, Sir John Black, who during the war (when the firm built Bristol and, later, Mosquito aircraft) and in its immediate wake worked closely with the TGWU district secretary, Jack Jones, to implement a policy that combined high wages with high output. 'A dashing, debonair man with a touch of the dynamic,' Jones later wrote admiringly, 'he stood out in sharp contrast to many of his contemporaries in management. He enjoyed walking around the shop floor, chatting to the work-people and sensing the feeling which existed between line managers and the workers.' Black was convinced that in the post-war world an ever-expanding demand for cars would be matched by a serious shortage of labour, and by 1948 he had – entirely independently of the Engineering Employers Federation – negotiated with Jones a comprehensive agreement for Standard. Its three main elements were that it guaranteed high wages; effectively created a closed shop by giving the union the prime responsibility for hiring labour; and divided the workforce in the main plant at Canley into 15 large, inevitably powerful gangs, with whom piecework rates would be negotiated and to whom bonuses (dependent on output) would be paid. The upshot was that, for the next six years or so, the shop stewards more or less ran Standard.

None of the other employers in the motor industry quite followed Black's example, but at Rootes, run by the brothers William and Reginald Rootes, an initially aggressive approach after the war soon gave way to what one disgruntled manager there recalled as 'management by abdication', with their Coventry factories being 99 per cent unionised by 1950. Senior shop stewards met with management on most Friday nights to explain what they had been doing; the gangs by the early 1950s were able to elect their own leaders; strike action was relatively infrequent; and in a way that would have seemed inconceivable in the 1930s it was the workers who largely called the shots, albeit in a less institutionalised form than at Standard.

It is in the context of this broad shift of power – and in particular the emergence of the gang system – that the oral historian Paul

Thompson has penetratingly evoked the world of the post-war
Coventry car worker, in effect between the 1940s and the 1970s. He
portrays a world where the unions were in charge of recruitment,
which they tried to keep 'in the family' (ie of workmates and their
kin) as much as possible; where although in theory there was an elaborate system of apprenticeships, in practice almost all the training took
place on the job itself; and where the demands of 'the track' made a
potential mockery of the craft traditions so important in Coventry's
earlier industrial history. 'By the 1950s some of the major skilled crafts,
like hand tin-hammering and wooden joinery body building, had effectively vanished,' he writes. 'Even in the most conservative firms, moving
assembly lines were now the normal practice.' It was, in short, a
deskilled world of what one former car worker described as 'very
monotonous, terribly monotonous, repetitive work'. Or, in the words
of another, 'It was just pure drudgery. You became a wage slave,
nothing else – the only thing you could see at the end of the week
was your wages and that was it.'

Nevertheless, Thompson contends that this potentially dispiriting,
deskilled reality co-existed in Coventry – above all at Standard – with
a *culture* that owed much to earlier craft traditions. 'The essential aim,'
he argues, 'was to recapture traditional craft discretion in planning
work' – an objective made possible only through the post-war strength
of the gang system, whereby 'for more than twenty years' there was
're-created in the context of mass production something of the old
spirit of pride and mastery in skilled work, fused with a particular
group solidarity'. By swapping around on the assembly line, eventually
a worker could feel capable of carrying out all the multiple tiny
processes in making a whole car. The recollections of a trio of former
Standard workers give a flavour of this distinctive culture, a culture in
which (in Thompson's words) 'both control over the work pace and
also job shifts within the gang were determined, within the outer limits
set by management, collectively by the workforce':

> It was a rota for everything. There was a rota for overtime ... You'd
> be on primer in the morning, and you'd be on finish in the afternoon,
> and then the next day you'd go on preparation, preparing the work for
> the spray booth. (*Painter*)

> You could be finished by half-past two, three o'clock ... You got
> your day in, and that was acceptable in the company, because they were
> getting what they wanted, but of course at the same time they were also
> getting information about the job, they could find out the real times of
> the job. (*Polisher*)
>
> The discipline was built into the system by the men themselves, not
> by the authorities or the management. It was self-pride that made you
> get it right ... Nobody wanted to look like a silly arse by scrapping
> out a whole lot ... It was just a man's pride, it's his work and he should
> get it right. (*Grinder*)

Thompson does not deny either that the nature of the mass-production
work remained essentially unchanged by the gang system or that (as
recalled by a machinist) the shop stewards inevitably morphed into
'another layer of management' and 'sort of gloated over the fact that
they had this – certain amount of power over people'.[17] But undoubtedly
it was a system that made intrinsically attritional, unsatisfying work
somewhat more palatable.

Of course, from a strictly economic point of view there were some
serious flaws.[18] Empire-building by the gangs and their leaders, bitter
and protracted disputes over which gangs should do which jobs, endless
wrangling over the collective piecework rates, the overwhelming
inducement never to price a new job lower than its predecessor, often
well-founded accusations about favouritism in recruitment: all these
were inherent and pervasive. Even Thompson, for all the warmth of
his account of what he terms 'a type of egalitarian co-operation that
at least some workers believed to be the dawn of a new social world',
ultimately condemns the gang system as a case of collusive and Luddite
complacency on the part of management as well as organised labour.
'The key stage was in the immediate post-war years,' he claims, 'when
neither management nor the trade unions showed any significant
commitment to serious research and development programmes.'
Instead, 'they assumed a slow-growing world with an eternal taste for
British goods' while devising the gang system (providing an adequate
degree of flexibility and workforce motivation) to meet pressing short-
term production needs. He not only cites comparative studies with
North America and Japan to show that 'new technology need not

imply personal deskilling' but explicitly compares the Coventry experience – based essentially on negative workplace resistance – to that of Italy's equivalent motor city, Turin, where the metalworkers' unions made 'constant demands on management for more intensive investment and higher-level training for the workforce', as well as funding their own research centres on technological change. Altogether, it is a compelling analysis. Rather like Galsworthy's Forsytes at the height of their power, the Coventry car workers at the zenith of theirs exhibited an admirable tenacity matched only by a profound lack of imagination. 'Playing at being skilled men', to use Thompson's perhaps unkind but far from contemptuous phrase, was not enough.

It would have helped if the product ranges of the two big firms had been more satisfactory. The main white elephant at Rootes was the Humber Pullman – the civilian version of a wartime staff car – while at Standard there was the 1947 launch of the disastrous Vanguard, very much Black's flagship project. Freddie Troop, Standard's service manager in Scotland and the only person in the service department possessing a foreign passport, was soon summoned into the breach:

> My boss said to me, 'We've got a few problems with the Vanguard in Belgium. You know how these continentals panic. We'd like you to go over there.' When I got there I found they really had problems, particularly with the chassis and suspension. The fractures in the chassis had to be seen to be believed. The shock absorbers were weak after a few thousand miles. The Belgians put a stiffer oil in, and that just made the shock absorbers go solid when they hit a bump. It used to fracture the bolts to the chassis, and it used to come up and over and straight through the wing. We got over that by fitting a sort of fireman's helmet . . .

It was the same all over the world, with a disastrous trail of breakdowns and unavailable spare parts. Perhaps Black and his men should have listened more carefully to Sir Stafford Cripps before they let the Vanguard loose. Inspecting it at Canley, he declared it a failure because he was unable to sit in the back seat with his top hat on.[19]

Finally, just up the road, there was Birmingham, including Rover at Solihull (having left Coventry at the end of the war) and Austin at Longbridge. At Rover the cardinal mistake was not concentrating on the superb Land Rover, launched in 1948, but instead spreading resources across a range of solid but unexciting saloons, such as the P4 'Auntie' model that from its launch in 1949 became a favourite car of bank managers and doctors. At Austin, which had been making cars to the south of Birmingham since 1910, there was a similar lack of clear-sighted product focus. By the late 1940s the sensible thing would have been to concentrate mainly on the recently launched A40 and thereby attempt to challenge the Volkswagen head-on in the world's markets; in the event the emotional attachment to larger saloon models with reassuring names like the Hampshire, the Hereford and the Somerset was too great. Historically, the great rivalry of the British motor industry was between Austin and Morris, or between Longbridge and Cowley; between 1946 and 1950, however, their combined market share slipped four points to 39.4 per cent, with Ford emerging as an increasingly serious challenger. There was talk from the late 1940s of a merger between the two members of the old guard, but by the new decade nothing had been settled.

One man, originally a talented production engineer from Coventry and briefly in the mid-1930s Nuffield's right-hand man at Cowley (creating an undying mutual enmity), dominated management at Longbridge. He has been memorably characterised:

> Ruthless yet capable of touching generosity, frequently guilty of rudeness to the point of cruelty yet sometimes capable of admitting and apologising for his mistakes, Leonard Lord was both crude in speech and manner and the victim of an inferiority complex. He detested pomp and also distrusted anything approaching sophistication in the running of a business. He regarded both salesmen and accountants as overheads: if they were any good, cars sold themselves – 'make proper bloody products and you don't need to sell 'em'.

Told on one occasion that his cars did not stand up to Australian roads, Lord's typically brusque response was that the Australians should build roads to suit them. Certainly he did not lack drive – including embarking by 1948 on a major modernisation programme at the Longbridge plant

– but at this stage of its fortunes, the firm, and indeed the industry, could have done with a subtler operator.

Lord's credo was simple. 'Industry needs Freedom,' he declared in the *FT* in 1946. 'Freedom from control and inexperienced academic planning, freedom from interference arising from departmental indecision or jealousy; freedom to apply the principles and experience of production on which the foundations of British trade and prosperity were built.' Predictably, he saw the unions as at best a more or less evil necessity, and in the immediate post-war years his approach to them was almost unremittingly hostile. There were several waves of victimisation of shop stewards – at one point he made 600 of his workforce redundant with a week's notice – and his unwillingness to consult with the unions was encapsulated in the blunt public assertion that 'it is the directors and not the workers who run the factory'. Overall, the business verdict by Lord's biographer implies much: 'His priority was not the financial success of the enterprises he worked for, but extracting the maximum from the material and labour resources available to him.'

The other key figure, among the almost 20,000 who worked at 'The Austin' by the end of the 1940s, was on the other side of the industrial fence. Richard (Dick) Etheridge was the son of a Birmingham shopkeeper, joined the Communist Party in 1933 at the age of 23, and in 1940 went to Longbridge as a capstan operator. In 1945 he became convener of the shop stewards there – a position he would hold for 30 years. He is described by his biographer as 'over six feet tall, broadshouldered and robust of build'; as a 'teetotaller, non-smoker and non-gambler but a great trencherman'; and as a lover of Maxim Gorky, Jerome K. Jerome and Rudyard Kipling who 'for many years took his family holiday at Clarach Bay near Aberystwyth in a caravan that he built himself'.

As convener, Etheridge gained the well-justified reputation of being a painstaking organiser and adroit tactician who pursued an 'economistic' interpretation of Communism (ie the pursuit of improved immediate material conditions), as opposed to a more overtly political approach. Given that the CP branch at Longbridge had only a dozen members by the early 1950s, this was well judged. Predictably, his relationship with the take-no-prisoners Lord tended to be adversarial, a flavour of which comes through in a statement, in Etheridge's hand-writing, published in May 1949 by the Joint Shop Stewards Committee:

> We refute the statement of Mr Lord, when he says that the A.E.U. [Amalgamated Engineering Union] members will not operate new machinery at their disposal. Further we protest at his statement that A.E.U. members do not operate them fully. Every Austin worker knows that once the piecework price is fixed then they have to work to full capacity to get reasonable wages. The fact[s] are that operator[s] are expected to operate new machinery on price[s] which yield less wage than previously earned despite increased production.

By this time the Austin workforce was substantially unionised, and the scene was set for some titanic battles between two very determined men.

Meanwhile, for the car workers whom Etheridge represented, the daily reality was now – at Longbridge as elsewhere – immutable. Among his voluminous papers are some anonymous verses, undated but almost certainly written between 1947 and 1952:

> Crash; Bang; Wallop; and with a mighty roar,
> The great machine comes to life and shakes the ruddy floor.
>
> Tick, Tack, tick tack, the whole day long, till shadow of night do fall,
> The monotonous burden of its song, makes your stomach crawl . . .
>
> They bleed us white, they squeeze us dry, they treat us like a lemon,
> They little know what ire they rouse, what hatred and what venom.
>
> And when the day of judgement comes, and we all stand on the same level,
> Ratefixers will go to their proper place, and work beside the devil.[20]

PART THREE

Andy Is Waving Goodbye

On 16 March 1950, three weeks after 'the revolt of the suburbs' in the general election, there appeared for the first time in the *Daily Express* – Britain's best-selling daily paper – a cartoon for middle-class middle England: the Gambols. Within 15 months, as paper rationing eased, it was being published daily, and through the rest of the 1950s and then way beyond, it never failed to appear, after 1956 in the *Sunday Express* as well. The cartoonist was Barry Appleby, working closely with his wife Dobs, and together they created an ageless couple. George and Gaye Gambol have no children; they sleep in twin beds; he works as a salesman, she looks after the home; he is practical, she is zany. The Gambols inhabited a frozen-in-time world closely mirroring the Applebys' own in Kingston-upon-Thames, Surrey, in the early 1950s – a world that simultaneously repelled and fascinated Colin MacInnes, who evoked it in his brilliant 1960 essay 'The "Express" Families' (including those of Giles and Osbert Lancaster as well):

> They are, in fact, a couple of sexless sparrows in their suburban love-nest: where the major events are the annual 'spring clean', the summer tending of the garden and the domestic dramas in the kitchen – where Gaye 'cooks' largely out of tins and George 'does the dishes' . . . George talks in his sleep, and Gaye, who sobs easily, will emit, when afraid of a mouse (or the dark, or almost anything), a desperate cry of 'Eek!' . . .
>
> George and Gaye are, of course, very *nice* people: that is undeniable. But outside their tiny world of consecrated mediocrity, nothing exists whatever.[1]

Did anyone ever find the Gambols funny? Perhaps not. But clearly their companionable, unambitious, shuttered marriage struck a real – and abiding – chord with their readership.

A month later, on 14 April, a comic for the boys of middle England made its bow. 'EAGLE is here!' trumpeted the accompanying advertising campaign:

> On Friday you can get your first copy of EAGLE, the new national strip-cartoon paper for children – 20 big pages, 8 of them in *full-colour*. Start sharing the adventures of EAGLE heroes, in space ships, or in the red man's country – Read about your favourite hobbies, games and sporting stars – Laugh with EAGLE's comic characters – Learn how things work and explore the countryside. There will be competitions with prizes to win . . . and you can join the EAGLE Club.

The ad featured pictures of 'Dan Dare Pilot of the Future', 'Skippy the Kangaroo' and 'P.C. 49 of Radio Fame', as well as an irresistible come-on for the first issue: 'Pin-up for Boys: an Accurate Colour Drawing of the new British Railways Gas Turbine-Electric Locomotive'. *Eagle* came from the same stable (Hulton Press) as *Picture Post*; the latter, in an article consisting mainly of enthusiastic comments from children shown advance copies of the first issue, did include some grumbles. 'Some things I didn't care for much such as "Dan Dare" – I can't get interested in a hero who does things no one has really done yet,' said 13-year-old Giles Davison. 'I don't see why Bible stories should be there,' he added. 'They haven't anything to do with comics, really.' Another probably equally middle-class north London boy was similarly wary of the moral message. 'I shall enjoy being a member of the Eagle Club,' declared Stephen Aris, also 13. 'The Editor's article about its objects is all right but he ought to be careful not to make them sound too priggish.'[2]

Aris had a point. 'There are really only two kinds of people in the world,' declared the editor's letter in this first issue: .

> One kind are the MUGS. The opposite of the MUGS are the Spivs – also called wide boys, smart guys, hooligans, louts or racketeers.
> The MUGS are the people who are some use in the world; the people

who do something worth-while for others instead of just grabbing for themselves all the time.

Of course the spivs snigger at that. *They* use the word Mug as an insult. 'Aren't they mugs?' they say about people who believe in living for something bigger than themselves.

That is why someone who gets called a MUG is likely to be a pretty good chap. For one thing, he's got to have guts because he doesn't mind being called a MUG. He *likes* it. He's the sort who will volunteer for a difficult or risky job and say cheerfully, 'Alright, I'll be the Mug'.

Notwithstanding which, *Eagle*'s first issue was a sell-out (more than 900,000 copies), and for the rest of the year it achieved weekly sales of more than 800,000. Hulton soon launched three companion comics: *Girl* in 1951, *Robin* (for under-sevens) in 1953 and *Swift* (for preteens) in 1954. The main man behind this remarkable success story was an Anglican clergyman, Marcus Morris, helped by his assistant Chad Varah (the future founder of the Samaritans) and a brilliant strip cartoonist, Frank Hampson. Morris, the comic's first editor as well as initiator, consciously saw *Eagle* as a riposte to the extraordinarily popular American comics – 'most skilfully and vividly drawn', he conceded, but all too frequently offering content that was 'deplorable, nastily over-violent and obscene, often with undue emphasis on the supernatural and magical as a way of solving problems'. Instead, Morris wanted to use the medium of the strip cartoon 'to convey to the child the right kind of standards, values and attitudes, combined with the necessary amount of excitement and adventure'.[3]

Morris must have been aware of the contrast between what he was trying to do and the extremely popular comics that had been coming out of the austere but far from moralising D. C. Thomson stable in Dundee since before the war.[4] By the early 1950s its comics included *Beano*, *Dandy*, *Hotspur* and *Wizard* (starring the phenomenal athlete Wilson, a more purist figure than *Rover*'s Alf Tupper, 'the Tough of the Track'), with *Topper* following in 1953 and *Beezer* in 1956. The jewel in the Thomson crown was undoubtedly *Beano*, featuring from March 1951 a stand-out star in Dennis the Menace. The Bash Street Kids and Minnie the Minx breezed in soon afterwards. No doubt a child's choice in the end usually came down to a mixture of social class and parental input. *Eagle* provided wholesome adventure, digestible chunks of knowledge and moderately well-disguised moral uplift; *Beano* offered a recognisably urban setting for insatiable naughtiness and an attitude to learning encapsulated by the depiction of 'Softy' Walter (bow tie, private school, ghastly earnest parents) as the invariable anti-hero. Such was *Eagle*'s soaring ascent, in the somewhat anxious moral climate of the early 1950s, that it seemed possible its high-minded formula would better stand the test of time.

Elsewhere in the magazine market, *Woman's Own* was serialising all through the spring of 1950 the reminiscences of Marion Crawford (generally known as 'Crawfie') – a gambit that put half a million on its circulation. Crawfie was the former governess of Elizabeth and Margaret Rose, and her account was also published as a best-selling book. 'I have been reading the Story of the Princesses [in fact called *The Little Princesses*] by Crawfie,' noted Vere Hodgson in May. 'I think the early part about their education is very good, but I think she says too much about the Prince Philip business and Princess Margaret doesn't figure too well.' Indeed she didn't, for Crawfie not only portrayed Margaret Rose in childhood as (in a biographer's apt words) 'spoilt, petulant and mischievous' but implicitly drew the 19-year-old version as 'an exacting, ill-organised and inconsiderate young woman'. Crawfie was never forgiven by the Royal Family, losing her grace-and-favour home and generally being cast into the outer darkness. But after all, what could she have expected? 'She sneaked' was how Margaret in later years reputedly justified the total ostracism.

For the Princess, however, there was a more pressing concern. Peter Townsend – decorated Battle of Britain pilot, married, 16 years older – was equerry to her father; on the basis of a Rolls-Royce Phantom number plate (PM6450), it has been claimed, with some if not total plausibility, that 6 April 1950 was the date on which she and the Group Captain became lovers. Irrespective of that, there were no signs during the rest of 1950 that Crawfie's revelations had diminished Margaret's popularity, especially with the young. 'Is it her sparkle, her youthfulness, her small stature, or the sense of fun she conveys, that makes Her Royal Highness Princess Margaret the most sought-after girl in England?' asked *Picture Post*'s Mima Kerr that summer after several weeks of watching her fulfil engagements. 'And this not only amongst her own set of young people, but amongst all the teenagers who rush to see her in Norfolk and Cornwall, or wherever she goes.' Kerr added, 'In spite of all the elaborate precautions, the general public always has the feeling that Princess Margaret's about to do something unpredictable.'[5] Or, put another way, she had the potential – though the plot had yet to thicken, at least in public – to turn the Royal Family into a soap opera. More than just a precedent, the Crawfie episode revealed the extent of the public's appetite for that type of drama.

The Little Princesses was the book of the season in one sense, but literary historians will always accord that honour to William Cooper's *Scenes from Provincial Life*, published in March. A wonderfully fresh and funny novel, imbued with liberal humanism and as unabashed in its treatment of homosexuality as of pre-marital sex, it was the work of someone who, under his real name of Harry Hoff, made his living as an assistant commissioner with the Civil Service Commission. His background was lower-middle-class – the son of elementary-school teachers in Crewe – and so was that of his hero, Joe Lunn, a young science teacher at a boys' grammar school somewhere in the Midlands, in fact in Leicester. Irreverent and anti-elitist, perceptive about human foibles, profoundly modern in feeling but without any modernist baggage – *Scenes* ought to have won Cooper fame and fortune but only partially did so.

Almost certainly he was ahead of his time, if only by a few years. His book had, the *Times Literary Supplement* thought, 'an original, if not altogether agreeable, flavour', leaving the reader 'with an uncomfortable sensation that reality has been grossly distorted'. The *Spectator*'s reviewer was less critical but similarly uneasy: 'Jaunty in mood and all but dadaistically casual in style, peppered with disarmingly shrewd and truthful observations about life, literature and other matters, *Scenes from Provincial Life* compelled a fair degree of reluctant admiration from me.' An unequivocal admirer was Philip Larkin, who that summer got Kingsley Amis (by now teaching English literature at University College, Swansea) to read it, tactlessly suggesting that it achieved what his friend was striving for in his as yet unfinished novel 'Dixon and Christine'. Amis took umbrage. 'I got hold of *Scenes life* a couple of weeks ago and read it with great attention,' he reported in October. 'I found it, on the whole, *very good*, but not particularly funny ... I liked it rather [for] the exact transcription of an environment.'[6] Still, something may have stuck; Cooper himself would come to think so.

The provincial novel with attitude was quickly followed by the provincial politician with ambition. 'I did not come from a much-travelled family,' Dan Smith (invariably known in his later years as T. Dan Smith) recalled somewhat sardonically about growing up in a ground-floor flat of a Wallsend terrace, near Newcastle. 'A hundred yards for shopping, a couple of hundred yards to the church, made up much of my world. It was a place where the majority of the families who survived the 1914–1918 war were born, reared, worked, married, grew old and died.' Wallsend's main occupation was shipbuilding, but Smith's father was a coal miner. Smith himself, born in 1915, became a painter and decorator when he left school, soon working in Newcastle, but before and during the war, this autodidact devoted most of his energies to the cause of revolutionary socialism (but not the Communist Party), becoming a fluent, locally well-known speaker in such forums as the Market Place at Blyth or the Newcastle Bigg Market.

His politics changed after 1945. Not only did the revolution become an ever more distant prospect each year, but he himself started a painting-and-decorating business that was soon employing up to 200 people. It was probably not long after the local Labour Party had lost control of Newcastle City Council in May 1949, following four years in power, that Smith complained bitterly to a local Labour MP, Arthur Blenkinsop, that pathetically little had been achieved in that time. Blenkinsop challenged him to do better, and, with the MP's help, Smith was accepted, amid considerable misgivings, into the local party and found a winnable ward (Walker, a rundown shipbuilding district of Newcastle). 'I am deeply conscious of the appalling housing conditions which exist in the city and am far from satisfied that anything of note is being done to alleviate these conditions,' he declared in his election manifesto, adding that 'my purpose is to SERVE'. He was duly elected on 11 May 1950, his 35th birthday.

Thirteen days later, he was formally introduced to his fellow-members of the City Council. 'Councillor Smith has shown his ability in public affairs, having been prominent in the youth movement for a considerable period' were the reassuring words of Councillor Renwick. 'He brings with him a spirit of integrity, which is a great thing in this

Council Chamber. I am sure he will be a welcome addition to the Council and will carry out his functions as a councillor in an able and fitting manner.' In his reply, the new man went beyond the customary bromides: 'I hope I will be able to do the job well and that my work will meet with the approval of my fellow-citizens and that in time I will be feared by my opponents.' Smith's first substantive contribution followed in early June. 'I believe so much in equality that if the workers get all they asked for, this issue would not arise,' he asserted in a debate on the proposed abolition of workmen's bus fares:

> If there is one section of the community that is absolutely indispensable it is the working men. I represent the working-class ward of Walker . . . The workers have to travel before eight o'clock in the morning. If you go along Scotswood Road at five o'clock at night you will see them standing in hundreds waiting for buses. The buses are packed, and if they are not run at a profit no buses will ever be run at a profit. It may be only coppers a week, but every sum is made up of coppers.[7]

The end of the 1940s – decade of war and austerity – signalled no immediate passage into the sunlit uplands. 'The blackened, gutted hulks of houses one saw everywhere were the condition towards which the whole city was slowly, inevitably sinking' was how a young South African writer, Dan Jacobson, recalled the London that he got to know after arriving in February 1950:

> The public buildings were filthy, pitted with shrapnel-scars, running with pigeon dung from every coign and eave; eminent statesmen and dead kings of stone looked out upon the world with soot-blackened faces, like coons in a grotesque carnival; bus tickets and torn newspapers blew down the streets or lay in white heaps in the parks; cats bred in the bomb-sites, where people flung old shoes, tin cans, and cardboard boxes; whole suburbs of private houses were peeling, cracking, crazing, their windows unwashed, their steps unswept, their gardens untended; innumerable little cafés reeked of chips frying in stale fat; in the streets that descended the slope to King's Cross old men with beards and old women in canvas shoes wandered about, talking to themselves and

warding off imaginary enemies with ragged arms. As for the rest of the people – how pale they were, what dark clothes they wore, what black homes they came from, how many of them there were swarming in the streets, queuing on the pavements, standing packed on underground escalators.

Altogether, it was a 'decaying, decrepit, sagging, rotten city'.

For those used to the old place, there was the odd sign of things getting better, however. One event in mid-March really got Vere Hodgson going:

> Now we could hardly believe it but last week we had eggs OFF THE RATION. Absolutely remarkable and unheard-of . . . What this means to us only an English housewife can understand. We have been fobbed off with dried eggs and egg powder and lately not even that . . . and at last actually we could beat up two eggs and put them in a cake . . . THE FIRST TIME FOR TEN YEARS.

'It's strange to say "buy an egg" or "buy three eggs" & be able to,' noted Marian Raynham in Surbiton not long afterwards. 'They can be got anywhere just now.' Soap also came off the ration in 1950, but a wide range of foods remained on it, including meat, cheese, fats, sugar and sweets (after the false dawn of 1949), as well as tea. For Grace Golden – 46 years old, utterly lonely, frustrated by her commissions as a commercial artist ('Working on Enid Blyton drawings – feel discouraged as soon as begin,' she noted in July) – it was all part of the general misery, as exemplified on the last Friday in April:

> Woke feeling grim – decide must get new ration book – climb up hill to Ronalds Road to food office to find it was to be had at Central Hall – that appeared to be a Methodist chapel with doors firmly shut – a woman across r^d begins to wave arms at me – at last gather I am to go down a passageway – get wretched thing – have lunch in Express [Dairies] at Highbury Corner.

Even so, there was a striking Gallup poll in May. Asked to compare their present family circumstances with what life had been like as a child, only 25 per cent reckoned they were worse off than their fathers had been, whereas 56 per cent thought they were better off – hardly the march of material progress in irresistible Victorian style but still something.[8]

There was also good news for the country's two or three million motorists. Mollie Panter-Downes may have informed her American readers in late April that 'the doubling of tax on gasoline, which brings the price up to three shillings a gallon, has proved to be the most unpopular item in a generally unpopular budget', but the end of petrol rationing just before the Whitsun weekend a month later graphically revealed the pent-up appetite for unfettered use of the family car. *The Times* urged motorists 'to resist the temptation to say once more, after an interval of ten years, the magic words: Fill her right up!', but the scenes on Whit Monday were chaotic. There were long queues on the main roads out of London, including one 2½ miles long on the road to Worthing; petrol-pump attendants were worked ragged; the car park at Whipsnade Zoo was soon full; and in the evening there was a huge jam on the road from Weston-super-Mare to Bristol. The same month, moreover, saw an equally telling portent. Vladimir Raitz, a Russian émigré who had recently started a company called Horizon Holidays, chartered a Dakota to take 20 holiday-makers to a camp near Calvi in north-west Corsica – reputedly the first British package holiday. For £32 10s they got their airfare, a fortnight under canvas, meals and as much wine as they could drink. 'That was quite a lot of money for the time,' recalled Raitz, 'but compared with a scheduled airfare then of about £70 to Nice, it was definitely a bargain. Our first customers were people like teachers, the middle classes.' So it remained for the next few years, as he ran tours to different Mediterranean resorts unhindered by competition. 'We went to Majorca, Sardinia, Minorca and Benidorm. There was only one hotel at Benidorm then.'[9]

British cooking was also due for some Continental influence. 'When I first came,' the Hungarian-born gastronome Egon Ronay recalled about settling in Britain soon after the war, 'you could eat well in top-class restaurants and hotels, where there were French chefs, but there was nothing in the medium range, apart from Lyons Corner Houses, where you could get a good breakfast. Some of the food was unbelievable, those strange tennis-ball things, Scotch eggs, very badly done.' It was a mediocrity, he believed, driven by class: 'The people who

influenced food at this time had been to public school, where the food
had been not just without interest, but horrifying. So you didn't discuss
food.'

In domestic kitchens, of course, there were all through the 1940s
severely limited ingredients available. 'All winter greens and root
vegetables and hamburgers made of grated potato and oatmeal with
just a little meat' was how the leading cookery writer Marguerite Patten
retrospectively encapsulated that decade's diet. The pages of the
Reading-based *Berkshire Chronicle* suggest, however, that by the early
1950s things were starting to change – and not just in a derationing
sense. Advertisements became rife in 1950 for new types of convenience
food, including the range of Birds Eye 'frosted' foods. 'Don't moan
when summer fruits are over,' declared one, aimed directly at the housewife: 'Birds Eye Quick-Frozen Foods give you garden fresh fruits and
vegetables all the year round – without a refrigerator! And husbands
love them, particularly Birds Eye strawberries, which are sweetened –
and sliced so they're sweet *right through*!' The following year, the
paper's Ladies' Page began to explore Continental cuisine, albeit with
some diffidence and necessary ingenuity: in its Lasagne Casserole, macaroni took the place of lasagne sheets, while cottage cheese made do
for mozzarella.[10]

The person usually credited with hauling British cooking out of the
dark ages is the writer Elizabeth David. *A Book of Mediterranean Food*
appeared in June 1950, three and a bit years after her initial scribblings
in the bleak midwinter of Ross-on-Wye. Complete with an alluring
John Minton dust jacket, David's recipes conjured up an exotic Mediterranean abundance far removed from the realities or even the possibilities
of mid-century Britain. The book was enthusiastically received –
'deserves to become the familiar companion of all who seek uninhibited
excitement in the kitchen', declared the *Observer* – and David quickly
followed it up with the equally evocative and attractive *French Country
Cooking*, published in September 1951.

It is impossible, though, to gauge confidently the true extent of
David's influence. Certainly she wrote extensively, including in the
1950s for *Harper's* and *Vogue*; certainly, as Arabella Boxer has pointed
out, there sprung up in the early 1950s a whole clutch of small London
bistros, such as Le Matelot and La Bicyclette in Pimlico and the

Chanterelle near South Kensington, where 'not only the menu but also the décor owed much to the David books'; and certainly she had her proselytising disciples, most notably George Perry-Smith, whose The Hole in the Wall restaurant opened in Bath in 1952. Yet for all David's elegant prose and, in Boxer's phrase, 'uncompromising intelligence', it is arguable that her influence has been exaggerated. Not only was she far from the most widely read cookery writer – significantly, she seems to have had little or nothing to do with the mass-market women's magazines – but there would be many other factors at work in the gradual post-war emancipation of British cooking and eating, including the spread of foreign travel (not least through National Service), increasing prosperity, and the arrival of Indian and Chinese immigrants.[11] But among those at the very vanguard of the culinary broadening out, David was the totemic figure.

There was one other key mover. Raymond Postgate, son-in-law of the former Labour leader George Lansbury and brother-in-law of the leading socialist intellectual G.D.H. Cole, was a well-known journalist and author in his own right. He was also, in his biographer's words, 'a connoisseur of wine and cookery'. In the late 1940s he decided that the best way to do something about Britain's dreadful reputation for eating out was to recruit a team of volunteers who would offer candid and impartial assessments of the fare being proffered. The first edition of the *Good Food Guide*, under his editorship, duly appeared in the spring of 1951 and sold some 5,000 copies. Perhaps inevitably, the several hundred entries on individual restaurants (barely a handful of which outside London served 'foreign food') comprised recommendations – recommendations that Postgate hoped would stimulate the unrecommended into action. However, while conceding that the shortage of butcher's meat was a genuine problem, he did let fly in his introduction: 'For fifty years now complaints have been made against British cooking, and no improvement has resulted. Indeed, it is quite arguable that worse meals are served today in hotels and restaurants than were in Edwardian days.' From the start, the *Guide* had a pleasingly quirky, readable quality to it ('Preston is a desperate place for anyone who dares to want food after 7.30 p.m.,' observed one volunteer), and that, together with the integrity of the venture, soon won it a considerable reputation. It was also a pioneering case of consumer power – and all the more telling given that its initiator came from the left of the political spectrum.[12]

One aspect of the food revolution is often overlooked: nutrition. Diet records of 4,600 children (across the country) who were four in 1950 revealed the following as a typical day's intake:

Breakfast: Cereals with milk, egg with bread and butter.
Lunch: Lamb chop with potatoes, Brussels sprouts, carrots; followed by rice pudding and tea.
Tea: Bread and butter; jam, cake and tea.
Supper: Glass of milk.

In a 1990s study funded by the Medical Research Council, these records were compared with the results of a similar national study in 1992, again focusing on four-year-olds. The scientists' conclusions were unambiguous: 'The higher amounts of bread, milk and vegetables consumed in 1950 are closer to the healthy eating guidelines of the Nineties. The children's higher calcium intake could have potential benefits for their bone health in later life, while their vegetable consumption may protect them against heart and respiratory disease and some forms of cancer.' There were other plus points for the 1950 diet: fresh vegetables (not fruit juices) as the main source of vitamin C provided the additional nutrients of plant-derived foods; red meat as opposed to poultry (in other words before the rise of chicken as a mass food) was good for iron; and starch rather than sugar as the main source of carbohydrates was more beneficial to gastro-intestinal health. As for the higher calorie intake in 1950 as a result of eating more animal fat, this was almost certainly counteracted by a much more physically energetic lifestyle.[13] It was, overall, a message to gladden any puritan's heart: a shortage of money and of choice was positively beneficial for the children of austerity.

———

There had been three previous tournaments, but the 1950 World Cup, held in Brazil, was the first in which England consented to take part. Scotland also received an invitation but declined it. Advance preparations were negligible, while the party that left London in early June did not even include a doctor. 'It was typical,' recalled one of the players, Tottenham's Eddie Baily. 'There we were going off to a strange country about which we knew very little and there wasn't anyone we could turn to if we were sick or injured. Backward wasn't the word for it.' Missing from the party was England's dominant defender, Neil Franklin. Fed up with his paltry financial rewards under the maximum-wage system then prevailing in English football, he had left his club, Stoke City, at the end of the season and gone to join Santa Fe of Bogotá. The reaction to his move was generally hostile, with much talk of greed and treachery, and he was automatically ineligible for the national team.

It proved a disastrous tournament. Not only did England lose two out of three matches, but one of them was to a footballing minnow, the USA – a 1–0 defeat instantly tagged the shock of the century. In that match, played on 28 June on a rutted and stony pitch at Belo Horizonte, all the luck went against England; it did not help that the team had been picked not by England's manager, the insufficiently combative Walter Winterbottom, but by the Football Association's senior committee member, Arthur Drewry. Tellingly, such was the deep parochialism of the British football world (supporters included) that the whole ill-fated foray received surprisingly muted media attention: the BBC did not cover the matches, while the press was relatively restrained in its treatment of England's humiliation. As for Franklin, his Bogotá venture was a fiasco, but when he returned home later that summer he faced four months' suspension and ostracism by the top clubs. 'Arguably the finest centre-half the England football team ever had', as his obituarist put it, never played for England again.[14]

Even as the shock news came over from Belo Horizonte, England's cricketers were facing an almost equally ignominious defeat. Playing against the West Indies at Lord's, they went into the last day, Thursday the 29th, still needing a mountain of runs. By soon after lunch they had been bowled out, with the West Indies winning by a comprehensive 326 runs – a first victory on English soil. John Arlott, one of the radio commentators on the match, subsequently described what happened next:

A crowd of West Indians rushed on to the field in a final skirmish of
the delight which they had called out from the balcony at the Nursery
End since the beginning of the game. Their happiness was such that no

one in the ground could fail to notice them: it was of such quality that every spectator on the ground must have felt himself their friend. Their 'In, out, in, out, in, out,' their calypsos, their delight in every turn of the game, their applause for players on both sides, were a higher brand of spirits than Lord's has known in modern times. It is one of my major credit marks for the MCC that, faced with all the possible forms which a celebration of victory might take, their only step was to ensure that no portions of the wicket were seized as trophies. Otherwise, these vocal and instrumental supporters were allowed their dance and gallop of triumph.

By one estimate there were only some 30 West Indians – almost all of them soberly dressed – taking part in this outburst of joy, but among them were two celebrated calypsonians who had both come over on the *Empire Windrush* almost exactly two years earlier. One, Lord Kitchener (Aldwyn Roberts), recalled the afternoon long afterwards:

> After we won the match, I took my guitar and I call a few West Indians, and I went around the cricket field, singing. And I had an answering chorus behind me, and we went around the field singing and dancing. That was a song that I made up. So, while we're dancing, up come a policeman and arrested me. And while he was taking me out of the field, the English people boo him, they said, 'Leave him alone! Let him enjoy himself! They won the match, let him enjoy himself.' And he had to let me loose, because he was embarrassed. So I took the crowd with me, singing and dancing, from Lord's, into Piccadilly in the heart of London . . .

The other, Lord Beginner (Egbert Moore), soon afterwards recorded the calypso 'Victory Test Match' – with its infectious chorus about 'those little pals of mine / Ramadhin and Valentine', the two young, hitherto unknown West Indian spinners who between them had destroyed the cream of English batting. 'Hats went in the air,' Beginner sang in the last verse, as he came to the celebrations; he added touchingly, 'People shout and jump without fear.'[15]

There was a heartfelt quality to Arlott's description of the harmonious atmosphere that afternoon at Lord's. Three months earlier, appearing on *Any Questions?* (of which he had been a founder-panellist in October 1948), he had got into serious hot water by describing the pro-apartheid South African government as 'predominantly a Nazi one'. As a result of the ensuing diplomatic reverberations (South Africa was still a member of the Commonwealth), the BBC pulled him from the programme for more than three years.

The panel was thus Arlott-free (but as usual all male) when, later in 1950 in a broadcast from the Guildhall, Gloucester – the programme for many years stuck to a West Country base – its members were asked whether they would 'approve of a coloured person becoming their step-father, brother-in-law or sister-in-law'. First to reply was the recently elected Labour MP Anthony Crosland:

> Certainly the scientists give virtually no evidence of supposing that coloured people are in any way physically, intellectually or in any other way whatsoever, inferior to white people. The fact that they may seem, at any given moment, less well-educated or less quick-witted, or what you will, according to scientists, so far as I can read them, is entirely a matter of education and environment and upbringing and everything else.

Accordingly, his answer was impeccably liberal, as was that of the other politician present, the Tory MP Ted Leather. By contrast, the historian Lord Elton said that he would be 'rather sorry' to see a relation of his making such a marriage, on the grounds that 'you're going to run up against so many difficulties and prejudices in the modern world'. The final panellist was the Dorset countryman Ralph Wightman, recently characterised by Malcolm Muggeridge as 'a standing BBC farmer who appears in many broadcasts to indicate that broadcasting is not the preserve of intellectuals'. As usual, Wightman did not disappoint. 'I would take it further than colour,' he declared. 'If you go to a white foreign race even, you are taking a risk of some sort, in that you're wanting to fit in something which is harder to fit in. I would not like to see a relative of mine marrying a Frenchman or a German.' According to the transcript, 'applause' greeted each of the first three contributions, but for Wightman there was 'laughter'. It only remained for the chairman, the charming, unflappable Freddie Grisewood, to sum up the discussion: 'I think really, in the main, we are agreed.'[16]

How prevalent was racial prejudice – and discrimination – in the early 1950s? Certainly Dan Jacobson, walking along Finchley Road looking for somewhere to live, was struck by how many of the little notices advertising rooms to let included the rubric '"No Coloureds" or even, testifying to some obscure convulsion of the English conscience, "Regret No Coloureds"'. In inner-city Liverpool, John Mays accepted that 'there can be no doubt that a colour bar does exist at employment level, especially for girls and women' but took heart from the fact that there was 'no indication of a colour bar between local children of school age'; while in Cardiff's Bute Town, where there was a not dissimilar concentration of 5,000 or 6,000 black people around the docks, *Picture Post*'s 'Bert' Lloyd found 'the nearest thing to a ghetto we have in this free land', with its inhabitants 'marked off from the rest of the city' not only by 'social barriers' and 'the old Great Western Railway bridge' but also by 'race prejudice'. After quoting a Somali seaman – 'If I go up into town, say to the pictures, why, man, everybody looks at me as if I left some buttons undone' – Lloyd explained how the prejudice all too often operated in practice. For instance, 'Locals applying for jobs outside the dockland area are familiar with the routine treatment: the employer fears his hands will refuse to work alongside a coloured man.' A more academic observer was Michael Banton, who for two years from October 1950 carried out research in Stepney. There he found a fairly high degree of tolerance, but – as he freely admitted – it was an area that over the years had been well used to immigrants of one sort or another.[17]

In any particular situation, it all depended. For example, the management of a Coventry engineering firm, Sterling Metals, came under such union pressure that in 1951 it unequivocally declared at a works conference that 'it was their main desire to recruit white labour'; agreed to segregate white and black gangs; and guaranteed to its white labourers that the Indians in the workforce would not be upgraded. Yet at one suburban golf club (Stanmore in north London), in image the very acme of 19th-hole bigotry, the authorities had stipulated the previous year that, when it came to membership, 'a candidate shall not be refused election merely because of his Race' – though the very fact of the rule suggests that race, in this case probably Jewishness at least as much as blackness, was an issue. Sometimes, of course, it is impossible to tell whether prejudice was at work. When the British middleweight champion Dick Turpin, son of the first black man to settle in Leamington Spa, fought Croydon's Albert Finch at Nottingham ice stadium in April 1950, he knew that a successful defence of his title would give him the Lonsdale Belt to keep and, at least as importantly, a weekly pension of £1 from the British Boxing Board of Control – for life. Turpin knocked his man down twice, but still lost on points.[18]

Fortunately, we have a more systematic assessment of attitudes, carried out by The Social Survey in 1951 with a sample of more than 1,800. 'Providing, of course, that there is plenty of work about,' ran one question, 'do you think that coloured colonials should be allowed to go on coming to this country?' By a smallish margin (46 per cent to 38 per cent) the response was positive. Asked 'Why a coloured person should not find it easy to settle down in this country', 49 per cent identified the colour bar or racial prejudice. As to whether landladies and hoteliers were justified in sometimes shutting the door on non-whites, 46 per cent said they were wrong, 18 per cent said they were right, and 19 per cent said it was a question of circumstances. When it came to personal contact, there was a telling difference between the workplace and the hearth: whereas 69 per cent said that they personally would not mind working with 'a coloured person', only 46 per cent were willing to invite such a person home, and still fewer (30 per cent) could equably contemplate having that person to stay. Those replying in the negative to the prospect of greater intimacy were asked to give their reasons. One extended category was popular – 'they have different habits, customs, different religions, feel they don't belong here; would feel embarrassed in their company, wouldn't get on with them' – as was 'would be afraid of what the neighbours would think, etc'. But the most frequently cited explanation was almost eloquent in its muttered quality: 'Don't know; can't say; just dislike them, etc.'

Overall, the 1951 survey concluded that 'antipathy to coloured people in this country is probably considerable amongst at least one-third of the population', an attitude especially common among the elderly, the poor and those working in low-status occupations; that 'the reactions of another third might be uncertain or unfavourable'; and that, 'even amongst the least antipathetic, who would certainly disapprove of discrimination in theory, there would be some who might not like to go as far as meeting a coloured person socially or letting a room to one if they had one to let'.[19] Every commentator stressed – and would continue to stress – that such prejudice was the result far more of ignorance than of knowledge, but it was still a pretty dismal picture.

Given that the annual level of New Commonwealth (ie black) migration to Britain was running at only about 1,500 during the three years after the *Empire Windrush*, it was unsurprising that race remained a generally low-profile issue. Bishop Barnes of Birmingham, not content with questioning the literal truth of the New Testament, did in December 1950 describe West Indians in Britain as 'a social burden', but this was unusual. Nevertheless, the government did come to two important if negative decisions. The first was to accept the advice of its law officers about the impracticability of legislation against racial discrimination. Although accepting that such legislation 'would satisfy the demands and feelings of coloured people', these officers successfully insisted in January 1951 that it 'would be merely gestural and empty owing to the great difficulty there would be in enforcement'.

The second decision concerned the freedom of entry of colonial subjects as established by the 1948 Nationality Act. Following a report in May 1950 by the Colonial Secretary, James Griffiths, which pointed out that even the fairly limited immigration since the war had caused certain problems (including episodes of civil unrest, as at the Causeway Green Hostel in August 1949), a ministerial committee was established to consider the possibility of limiting 'coloured immigration'. Reporting in January 1951, it recommended that seeking to control numbers would be a mistake – above all on the distinctly imperial rather than domestic grounds that 'the United Kingdom has a special status as the mother country, and freedom to enter and remain in the United Kingdom at will is one of the main practical benefits enjoyed by British subjects, as such'. Or, as one historian, Randall Hansen, persuasively comments, 'The evidence from these deliberations confirms that the attachment of British politicians was fundamentally to the old Commonwealth; new Commonwealth immigrants were accepted, but only in so far as they contributed to a broader structure of subjecthood in which the Dominions' citizens were the key actors.'[20]

Instead, the emphasis of the Colonial Office would continue to be on informal discouragement, principally through applying pressure on the West Indian authorities. And who knew, perhaps the thorny issue would quietly fade away.

The black experience itself in the Britain of the early 1950s was a world away from Whitehall. For E. R. ('Ricky') Braithwaite, a Guyanan with a Cambridge degree but only able to find a teaching job in one of the East End's sink schools, there was a particularly upsetting episode after the death of the mother of his class's only mixed-origin boy. The other children raised money for a wreath, but they all refused to take it to the boy's home – for fear of being seen as fraternising with non-whites. 'It was like a disease, and these children whom I loved without caring about their skins or their backgrounds, they were tainted with the hateful virus which attacked their vision, distorting everything that was not white or English,' Braithwaite recalled in *To Sir, With Love* (1959). 'I turned and walked out of the classroom sick at heart.' Another writer, Sam Selvon, arrived from Trinidad in April 1950 and in time became, in Maya Angelou's words, the 'father of black literature in Britain'. His key novel was *The Lonely Londoners* (1956), describing with humour but also feeling the often bruising, disenchanting immigrant experience in what was becoming London's black quarter – its boundaries comprising the Arch (Marble), the Water (Bayswater), the Gate (Notting Hill) and the Grove (Ladbroke), and its housing conditions almost invariably crowded, squalid and overpriced. Selvon would later be attacked for his excessively male point of view, as 'the boys' searched unflaggingly for the joys of 'white pussy', but in the early 1950s it *was* almost entirely men who came from the Caribbean and settled in the land of the white.[21]

For such it was. And not only white but white indigenous: the 1951 census revealed that a mere 3 per cent of the population had not been born in Britain. Moreover, of that immigrant 3 per cent, the over-whelming majority were white Europeans. These included more than half a million Irish, who undoubtedly suffered from prejudice – notably from landladies reluctant to open their doors to them – but nothing on the scale of the black immigrants at the hands of the insular, reserved, suspicious natives. Crucially, it was a prejudice more covert – and therefore far more anxious-making – than that endured by blacks in, say, the American Deep South. 'The most striking thing about the colour bar in Britain with regard to inter-group relations is its uncertainty,' observed Banton on the basis of his study of relatively tolerant Stepney:

> Some individuals are friendly, some are not, and when a coloured man goes to see an official he never knows quite what sort of reception he will receive. This leads many immigrants to claim that the colour bar is worse in Britain than in the United States; they say that there the discrimination is open and honest, the whites tell you what their policy is and you know what course to take, but in Britain the whites are hypocritical because they will not tell you to your face and 'prejudice is deep in their hearts'.

Most of these black immigrants – usually consigned to unskilled, often rebarbative jobs, whatever their qualifications – proved survivors. Among them was the indomitable figure quoted in the remarkable semi-autobiography, semi-anthology *Journey to an Illusion* by Donald Hinds (who himself did not come over from Jamaica until 1955). This man in 1950 was sharing a basement room (and large bed) in Ladbroke Grove with five other men, until one day their Czech landlord discovered two of the 'black boys' in bed with prostitutes and threw them all out. That evening, the man returned from work to find his possessions scattered in a nearby alleyway. There followed a night of tramping round London:

> In those days police did'n even bother to pick up a black man, because the jail would be a night shelter out of the rain and the cold. That day when I finish work I was feeling so rusty and tired that I drag myself to Charing Cross an' pay a penny an' got into the toilet determined to have a roof over my head that night. I remember that it was a small island man cleaning up the lavatory, I think he was a Bajan. I did'n pay him no mind, I decided that I would curl up on the toilet seat and go off to sleep. I was jus' droppin' off into a sweet sleep when I hear the door breaking down, bam, bam! When I look up the black man climb over the top and see me sleeping on the seat. Man, that Bajan man carry on, you hear. 'Get outa there, man! Is guys like you come to the white

people them country and spoil it up. You should be ashamed of you'self, man. You lettin' the race down, man!' So I come out and just look him over from head to toe and back again and said to him: 'Is not me carrying down the race, boy! You see me come to England goin' around cleaning up people's shit?'[22]

'The new curate seemed quite a nice young man, but what a pity it was that his combinations showed, tucked carelessly into his socks, when he sat down.' Such was the less than multicultural opening sentence of Barbara Pym's debut novel, *Some Tame Gazelle*, published in May 1950. Its atmosphere was, in her biographer's words, 'very much that of 1930s rural churchgoing, something taken for granted, even-tenored, definitely middle of the road', and it won glowing reviews, typified by Antonia White in the *New Statesman* (whose back pages carried considerable literary weight): 'Miss Pym, working in *petit point*, makes each stitch with perfect precision.' For Pym, 37 shortly after its publication, the book's success meant that, while continuing to work at the International African Institute in London, she could with reasonable confidence press on with writing further novels imbued with what Philip Larkin would define as her 'unsensational subject matter and deceptively mild irony'. This was no doubt a relief, all the more so coming only a few months after the magazine *Women and Beauty* had rejected two of her short stories. 'We like your writing very much and you handle the situations most delicately, but in both cases they are only "situations" – not plots,' gently explained its fiction editor, Anita Christopherson. And she went on: 'When we choose our fiction we are rather thinking about pleasing our readers as well as ourselves, and many of them are young romantics, anxious to be caught up in the life of the stories. I think therefore that you are just a shade too objective, too watchful . . .'[23]

Catherine Cookson, six years older than Pym, would never have any difficulty getting her readers caught up in her plots and characters. By the late 1940s she was living in Hastings (where her husband taught maths at the local grammar school) and trying to get over a severe, almost suicidal state of depression, the result in part of a series of miscarriages. At one point she had hoped to adopt a child through a Catholic adoption society, but they struck her off the list on discovering that she had stopped being a practising Catholic. She turned to writing as a form of therapy, and in June 1950 her first novel, *Kate Hannigan*, was published. Based heavily on her own Tyneside childhood – in particular the maze of grim streets between Tyne Dock and East Jarrow – it told the story of a young woman who, like Cookson's mother, conquered the stigma of having an illegitimate child. The book sold well, though not staggeringly so; Cookson's mental health slowly recovered; and, crucially, she had discovered in what would become known as 'Catherine Cookson Country' – usually that of the past – a terrain that could be mined almost endlessly.[24] For her fellow-Geordie, T. Dan Smith, the point of the past was merely to provide lessons for the future, but for Cookson and her faithful readers, the past had – despite or perhaps because of all its horrors – its own all-absorbing authenticity and purpose.

Angus Wilson had not yet published any novels and still had a day job as a librarian in the Reading Room of the British Museum. But in July 1950, only 16 months after his first, very successful collection of short stories (*The Wrong Set and Other Stories*), he brought out a new collection, *Such Darling Dodos*, that made an even bigger impact. As with reviews of Cooper's *Scenes* earlier in the year, admiration for Wilson's robust satire was mixed with a certain discomfort. 'Part-bizarre, part-macabre, part-savage and part-maudlin, there is nothing much like it upon the contemporary scene,' asserted C. P. Snow (himself girding up as a novelist). 'It is rather as though a man of acute sensibility felt left out of the human party, and was surveying it, half-enviously, half-contemptuously, from the corner of the room, determined to strip off the comfortable pretences and show that this party is pretty horrifying after all.' As a result, 'sometimes the effect is too mad to be pleasant'.

Wilson's biographer, Margaret Drabble, claims that the book was an exercise in iconoclasm: he saw the British as self-congratulatory, smug victors in war and proceeded to reveal them to themselves as 'a nation of beggars, snobs, bullies, black-marketeers and hypocrites, ill-dressed, plain, timid, and adventurous only in pursuit of selfish ends'. Was there any humanity in the writing? The critic, poet and sporting journalist Alan Ross thought not, describing Wilson as 'a contemptuous ringmaster' in relation to his characters, who were no more than 'dead corpses'. But for Wilson, Drabble emphasises, there was a larger game afoot: 'questioning all "progressive" principles, be they adopted in the name of liberalism, humanism or socialism', as well as probing issues of 'public and private morality'.[25] It was a big enough agenda.

On the small screen, still a cautious and respectful BBC monopoly, there were as yet virtually no hints of any sociopolitical satire. Even so, the Corporation did in May 1950 (on the same Friday that petrol rationing ended) launch – amid some internal disquiet – a topical discussion programme, *In the News*, with a significantly sharper edge than its *Any Questions?* radio counterpart. By the autumn the programme was going out weekly with a regular panel: Robert (Bob) Boothby, the incorrigibly rebellious Tory MP; Michael Foot, the strongly pro-Bevan left-wing Labour MP; W. J. Brown, the increasingly right-wing journalist who had lost his seat as an independent at the recent election; and A.J.P. Taylor, still a far from well-known Oxford history don. Under the urbane chairmanship of the crime writer and broadcaster Edgar Lustgarten, they produced each week what Grace Wyndham Goldie – a talks producer in the early 1950s and one of the BBC's bolder spirits – recalled as 'a remarkable effervescence of wit, common sense, intellectual honesty and political passion'. It was, of course, too good to last. Even by the end of 1950, a nervous BBC was coming under pressure from the parties to field panellists from the solid, uncontroversial centre of British politics, and although viewing figures remained high (at around half the viewing public), Auntie in the course of 1951 gradually began to insist on panels carefully vetted for balance and acceptability.[26]

But if *In the News* was ahead of its time – arguably by more than half a century – two other new programmes in the summer of 1950 were unmistakably of theirs. 'We see Archie as a boy in his middle teens, naughty but loveable, rather too grown-up for his years, especially where the ladies are concerned, and distinctly cheeky!' envisaged the producer of *Educating Archie*. This radio comedy, scripted in part by Eric Sykes, began on the Light Programme on 6 June and proved such a massive hit that by the end of the year it had won the much-coveted Top Variety Award in the *Daily Mail*'s first-ever National Radio and Television Awards. Archie was a dummy; the ventriloquist Peter Brough was his stepfather; and the original cast featured Max Bygraves ('I've arrived and to prove it I'm here!') as the cockney handyman and

Hattie Jacques as the overweight, excessively amorous Agatha Dingle-body. In the second series the unenviable role of Archie's tutor fell to Tony Hancock ('Flippin' kids!'), who was reputedly so freaked out by the 3-foot dummy – dressed as a schoolboy and with wooden mouth wide open, hanging from a coat hook in Brough's dressing room – that he had recurrent nightmares.[27]

The other new programme was on television: *Andy Pandy*. It was first shown on 11 July – six days after Judy Haines, trying to watch Wimbledon, had noted how 'the Children's Programme, including Prudence, The Kitten, interrupted a set which went to 31–29' – and it was launched against a background of the BBC somewhat self-consciously gearing up its service for children, more than three years after the introduction of the popular puppet Muffin the Mule. A BBC memo earlier in 1950 had set out the objectives:

> Television Children's Hour aims to enrich children's lives and to foster their development by the stimulus and enjoyment of what they see and hear. This aim seems to have several elements:
>   -to entertain and to be liked by the children;
>   -to satisfy the parents that the programme is fostering children's development in ways of which they approve;
>   -to satisfy instructed professional opinion that programmes are soundly conceived and well executed. This refers both to the entertainment value and aesthetic competence, and to the educational and psychological judgement which the programmes will reflect. So far, Television has to some extent not come under the vigilant gaze of psychologists and educationalists.

There could hardly have been a more explicit nod to the enhanced importance of the outside expert.

In the new daily children's service, *Andy Pandy* was to be the programme explicitly targeted at pre-school children, something that had not been done before. Writing in *BBC Quarterly*, the person with overall responsibility for children's programmes, Mary Adams, hoped that its viewers would not just 'watch the movements of a simple puppet, naturalistic in form and expression' but also 'respond to his invitations to join in by clapping, stamping, sitting down, standing up and so forth'.

Poignantly enough, Andy was alone in his basket for the first few weeks, until joined by Teddy and Looby Loo. From the start, there seems to have been something mesmerising about the programme: the all too visible strings; Andy's endearingly jerky walk; his strangely androgynous outfit; and at the end, those plaintive yet reassuring sung words 'Time to go home, time to go home / Andy is waving goodbye, goodbye'. Much depended on Maria Bird, who was both scriptwriter and narrator. 'The techniques of the motherly voice and gaze, the imaging of the insularity of the domestic space, the presentation of a pre-school world of play and nursery rhymes, and the silencing of the characters were all constituted within a discourse concerned with the production of the *mother as supervisor*,' argues one television historian, David Oswell. He adds that 'these techniques, although pleasurable to the child audience, were framed within a particular set of relations which constructed television as safe, maternal, and homely'.

Leaving nothing to chance, the BBC persuaded 300 households (with 459 children aged between two and five) to return questionnaires giving their responses to the early programmes. 'Andy Pandy himself was taken to by most viewers, although it seemed he was as yet not such a popular favourite as Muffin,' noted the subsequent report. 'The most frequent complaint made by the children themselves was that he "couldn't talk".' Overall reaction was broadly if not uniformly positive, with at least a hint of an incipient generation of couch potatoes:

> My children (ages five and three) regard the television as entertainment and are not prepared to get down from their chairs even when invited. They look on Andy as a younger child, to be watched and even tolerated, but not as an equal to be played with.
>
> A little coloured girl watching with us thought that Andy should have a coloured friend to play with.
>
> It seems that slow inconspicuous movements on the screen, unaccompanied by commentary, will quickly lose child's attention.
>
> The most popular song, with all ages, seemed to be 'Andy's hands go up – Andy's hands go down' – and this was often remembered afterwards in play.

The respondents also expressed their attitude to children's television as such. 'One very general argument, which seemed to many parents to be the most important factor, was that children, however young, were almost invariably fascinated by the screen and determined to watch it, so that it was only sensible to offer them something of their own.' From mid-September *Andy Pandy* settled down to every Tuesday (initially at 3.45) and it did not finally leave the screen until the 1970s. Amazingly, only 26 actual black-and-white programmes were ever made; we got to know them well.[28]

On the day before the clown suit's first public outing, the England cricket selectors announced that neither Norman Yardley (the then captain) nor George Mann (a recent captain) would be available to skipper the forthcoming winter tour of Australia. Over the next fortnight, there was intense press speculation about who would get the job. From his influential pulpit in the *Daily Telegraph*, E. W. Swanton reckoned that the two most plausible candidates were Freddie Brown, an amateur, and Tom Dollery, a professional. As it happened, they were the respective captains in the time-honoured annual encounter at Lord's between the Gentlemen (ie the amateurs) and the Players (ie the professionals), starting on 26 July. On the first day, Brown made a superb century, reaching three figures with a straight six into the pavilion. 'The more elderly were reminded of how cricket used to be played,' noted an admiring Swanton, 'and especially how the ball used to be driven before the game's descent, as many would lament, to an age of over-sophistication and a dreary philosophy of safety first.' Next day, Dollery himself scored an admirable century, but within minutes of his declaration and the Gentlemen leaving the field, Brown had been invited to take the side to Australia. Given that there had never yet been a professional captain of England, it was hardly a surprising choice. And, in the eyes of many cricket followers, the appointment was a welcome indication that the amateur spirit of adventure was still alive and well.

Even so, at county level there were clear signs by the 1950 season that – whatever the continuing determination of county committees not to appoint professional captains – the traditional two-class system in the first-class game was only just hanging on. Most of the counties had captains who were either 'shamateurs' (including Brown at Northamptonshire) or, if they could afford to play as genuine amateurs, were far from being worth their place in the side as cricketers. Somerset's Stuart Rogers was an army officer with a disciplinarian streak – but did not bowl and averaged only 25.12 with the bat; Nottinghamshire's William Sime, an Oxford-educated barrister, managed a mere 17.78. The only two professionals in charge were Warwickshire's Dollery and Sussex's James Langridge, the latter after a ferocious pre-season row, as members revolted against the committee's plan to appoint joint captains – both of them amateur, with one in effect a stand-in until the end of the Cambridge term. There was also this season, in early July, an emblematically antediluvian episode at Bristol. The Gloucestershire captain was Basil Allen, an amateur who had captained the county before the war and was determined to uphold the established social order. Coming off the field for an interval, he overheard one of his young professionals, Tom Graveney, say, 'Well played, David' to an opposition batsman, Cambridge University's David Sheppard (the future Bishop of Liverpool). A few minutes later in the pavilion, Allen went over to Sheppard. 'I'm terribly sorry about Graveney's impertinence,' he apologised. 'I think you'll find it won't happen again.'

There was, too, a strongly hierarchical flavour about the composition of the touring party to accompany Brown. In particular, there was the inclusion of three young, palpably inexperienced, Cambridge-educated amateurs: Sheppard and J. G. Dewes had made a pile of runs on a university wicket widely recognised to be a batsman's paradise, while the quick bowler J. J. Warr, likewise still an undergraduate that summer, had bowled well enough but unsensationally, coming 55th in the national averages. Significantly, their county affiliations were respectively Sussex, Middlesex and Middlesex again – socially very acceptable. That winter, for all Brown's gallantry, England lost heavily. Sheppard and Dewes managed 74 runs between them in seven innings; Warr took one wicket for 281 runs. 'Will one ever know what the Selectors were thinking of?' lamented the novelist Rex Warner. And, writing to a moderately sympathetic Australian friend, he reckoned that 'the abolition of the dictatorship of the M.C.C.' was the only thing that might save English cricket.[29]

It was just before Brown presented his calling card at Lord's that *Picture Post* asked the question: 'The Shop round the Corner: Does it Deserve to Survive?' Against a background of 'the small independent shop' – numerically representing up to 90 per cent of retail-trade outlets, albeit little more than half the retail trade's total turnover – coming under increasing pressure from the 'chain stores and multiple shops' that 'had become almost household words', the magazine's Ruth Bowley entered an almost passionate plea for the defence. On the basis of spending several months travelling round Britain and talking to both shopkeepers and their customers, she was convinced that it would represent a huge loss 'if all shopping was centralised', even if it did clip a few points off the cost of living. 'There is an informality about the small shop,' she argued. 'Tired housewives can pop in, dressed in kitchen aprons, men in dungarees call in on their way home from work. One customer I know regularly fetches his newspaper wearing his dressing-gown; another sends his dog. And always there is a welcome for the children, an intelligent interpretation of scribbled shopping lists, and a touching interest in child welfare.' To clinch her point, she quoted the proprietress of a village shop: 'That's the third ice today, Billy. I'll not sell you any more until I hear from your Ma.'

It was not a case that impressed one reader, 'K.P.B.' from London SW15:

Living on a housing estate which is almost entirely served by small shopkeepers, I would emphatically deny the small shopkeepers' right to survive.

Indeed, such services as are rendered by the local butcher vary according to his estimate of the affluence of the customer. It is nauseating to perceive the fawning manner in which prompt and favourable treatment is bestowed on the 'lady' from the mansions surrounding the estate in preference to the housewives from the estate. And the newsagent, the baker, the greengrocer and the cobbler, 'small men' all, behave similarly.

'How different it is,' this reader declared, 'to do business with the multiple stores and the co-operative societies who know nothing of one's social or financial status and dispense their services impartially and with dispatch and civility.'[30]

Unsurprisingly, Bowley did not mention the word 'supermarket'; though the first British usage occurred at least as early as 1943, the term did not become general until the 1950s. Even so, by the late 1940s there were a few pioneers of American-style self-service – and in July

1950, Sainsbury's put down a major marker by opening (in Croydon) its first self-service store. 'Not everyone liked it,' records the obituarist of Alan (later Lord) Sainsbury. 'One customer threw a wire basket at him and a judge's wife in Purley swore violently at him when she saw she was required to do the job of a shop assistant.' It would be many years before 'Q-less shopping' (as Sainsbury's liked to call it) became anything like the norm.

For the time being, the more typical shopping experience was much more like that wonderfully evoked by Margaret Forster (born 1938) in her memoir of growing up in Carlisle. Once a week she and her sister would smarten up, put on clean clothes and with their mother catch a double-decker Ribble bus to go shopping 'up street'. The mother carrying a large leather bag, her daughters flimsy but capacious string bags, they invariably got off at the Town Hall. There were five main staging posts in a wearing process that the young Margaret knew full well was a daughter's duty quite as much as a mother's:

1. **The covered market.** Here the ritual began, as it 'always had done all my mother's life and her mother's before her'. First stop was the butchers' stalls (Cumberland sausage, potted meat, black pudding), followed by the fruit and vegetable stalls. 'Nothing exotic, no pineapples or melons – I hadn't yet seen such fruits – and no fancy foreign vegetables, just huge cabbages and cauliflowers and leeks and onions and millions of potatoes, millions.' Last came the 'butter women', who 'sat behind trestle tables, their butter and cheese arranged in front of them, the butter pats each with an individual crest'. It was invariably cold – stall-holders struggling to weigh things 'with hands wrapped in two pairs of fingerless mittens' – and 'on the many wet days rain would sweep in and trickle down the main cobbled entrance until it became a veritable stream and puddles were hard to avoid'.

2. **Lipton's.** This was the mercifully warm port of call to buy tea and sliced cooked ham, involving 'two different counters in the same shop' and therefore 'two different queues'. During the endless waiting, 'everyone watched to see what others bought and whether any preferential treatment was being given by the assistants'. And when at last one got to the counter, the system of paying was still the time-consuming, pre-1914 method of

'putting the money in cans which whizzed overhead to the central cash desk and then back again with the change wrapped in the bill'.

3. Binn's or Bullough's. Going into either of Carlisle's two prestigious department stores was usually the best bit of the trip. 'We only bought small items there, things my mother knew were the same price every-where. Reels of thread, press-studs, sometimes stationery, never anything expensive. The whole point was just to have a reason for going into Binn's and savouring its graciousness. We never bought even the cheapest item of clothing there.'

4. The Co-op. A large, depressing stone building in Botchergate, with drab-looking goods poorly displayed and poorly lit, this was in her mother's eyes the only place to go for clothes. 'The experience of shop-ping at the Co-op was dismal and there was no joy in our actual essential purchases – vests, knickers, socks and liberty bodices.' Least of all in the bodices, which were 'akin to a corset for the young' but in whose 'protective values against cold' her mother 'placed great faith'.

5. The baker's. This final stop, halfway along Lowther Street, was prin-cipally to buy bread (including 'a special kind of treacle loaf and delicious teacakes'), but occasionally the girls were treated to cream doughnuts or chocolate éclairs 'as a reward for enduring the Co-op'.

Then at last it was time to catch the bus home. 'That was it for another week. We'd been "up street" and my mother was exhausted, mainly with the stress caused by seeing so many things she wanted and couldn't afford to buy.'[31]

———

The summer of 1950 was also holiday time. For Colin Welland, 15 going on 16 and growing up in Newton-le-Willows in Lancashire, it was the opportunity for his first holiday independent of his parents, as he and two mates went to Butlin's in Skegness. 'Butlin's holiday camps were a Valhalla for working-class kids,' he recalled. 'They were just like big schools, really. You had your houses, your discipline, your dining hall, your social activities, competitions – I remember getting to the final of the crown green bowling competition.' In retrospect, he was struck by his naivety. 'For instance, three girls asked us back to their chalet for a drink and we said, "No, thank you, we're not thirsty."' Up the coast from Skegness was Cleethorpes, where another future actor and writer, the 17-year-old Joe Orton (still living with his parents on the Saffron Lane council estate in Leicester), went in August. 'This confirmed all I ever thought about *day trips* and I am certainly not going again in a hurry,' he complained to his diary. 'The tide was out and I was hungry. We couldn't swim and the camp was rotten and Mum played up.' One diarist, Florence Speed, was probably happy enough to be spending August at home in Brixton. 'I was glad I wasn't one of the queued-up holiday-makers,' she reflected after calling in at a 'packed' Victoria station a week or so after Orton's lament. 'The people about to start on holiday displayed no holiday gaiety. Just stood huddled & depressed, & some of them with babies in arms, tired before the journey began.'[32]

Indeed, though one imagines otherwise as one looks at the period photos of the mainly happy, smiling faces on the packed British beaches, life's problems did not go away just because it was the holiday season. The papers of the John Hilton Bureau citizens' advisory service – dealing with up to 5,000 cases weekly – include 'Extracts from Letters' dated the last day of August 1950. Cumulatively they present a grim, if not necessarily representative, picture of mainly domestic misery in a hostile world:

> She would lock herself in the scullery if she couldn't have her own way and then turn on the gas. I was hardened to her after a time and instead of pleading with her I just turned off the gas at the meter.
>
> Since starting my studies I have put some mental strain on myself which is doing my health no good ... They asked me to learn LOGA-RITHMS which I have never even heard of ... I can't see where it is all leading to.
>
> Now my wife never comes into my bedroom to see whether I am dead or alive and my nerves are greatly perturbed by this ordeal ... I have been treated worse than a lodger.
>
> I had to give up my job in insurance and take a job where I could have milk and biscuits at 2-hourly intervals so I took over a public house.

Me and my husband can't understand why we can't get no pension. My husband is no scholar.

The most eloquent, desperate letter was the least punctuated: 'No hope nothing to live for Only rude Man at Assistance Board'.

There was as well – however little spoken about amid the sandcastles or in the problem pages – something else brewing that August, though it did not always command undivided attention. 'The expected birth this week-end of Princess Elizabeth's second baby,' noted Speed on the 13th, 'has pushed Korea into second place in the headlines this Sunday morning.' Princess Anne duly arrived on the Tuesday; the day before, Nella Last in Barrow had another of her conversations with her husband:

I've wondered if he worried about 'outside' affairs. I said today 'it's so worrying to hear so little definite progress of the Americans. A major war seems to be developing under our eyes, as if soon we will see it's not a matter of "principle", a gesture, but an out in the open war between Russia & the rest of the world.' He said impatiently 'you worry too much about what doesn't concern you, & with all your worrying, you cannot alter or help things'.[33]

The Heaviest Burden

'His vital energy, his good looks, his mellifluous voice, his vivid phrase-ology, make him a delight to listen to,' reflected Sir Raymond Streat, chairman of the Cotton Board, after dining with Aneurin Bevan a few weeks before polling day in February 1950. In the ministerial car before dropping Streat off at his club, the conversation turned to the contro-versial centrepiece of Labour's nationalisation plans:

> I talked of steel and said I was convinced it was folly. He spoke of the need for higher output: I said I thought it would all too soon be a case of excess production of steel in the world: he said the State would create outlets for steel by investing in great developments in the colonies and so forth: when I said we had to have surplus income before we could invest capital, his reply was something general and vague about the State being entitled to anticipate returns of investment. I spoke of the psychology of the business world whose technical skills were needed by society and how the steel case might destroy their ability to use their skills by snapping their faith in the future. Here he countered with a spate of eloquence. Steel represented the culmination of phase one of Labour Rule: if Labour blenched at the difficulty and held back, it would show its lack of faith in itself and its doctrine: no, steel must go on, or Labour would lose its very soul.

'I found when I crept into bed that I was frightened,' concluded Streat's graphic account. 'I don't think I particularly want to see him again. No good is done. The experience seems pleasantly stimulating whilst it is taking place, but afterwards you feel you have been in a void where there are no morals or faiths or loves.'

A month later, in early March, Bevan attended his first Cabinet meeting after Labour's disappointing electoral performance. 'Bevan was pugnacious and in a minority of one,' noted another diarist, his fellow-minister Patrick Gordon Walker, about Bevan's insistence that the implementation of steel nationalisation be in the forthcoming King's Speech. 'Morrison spoke strongly of the need for common sense and realism – this was what the country expected. It was no good "dressing up as revolutionaries" and pretending we had a great majority.' The atmosphere, as evoked by Gordon Walker, was palpably uneasy:

> Bevan was very isolated and unpopular.
> Bevin looked ill.
> MPs and Ministers seem to be strongly against Bevan – attributing our setback to 'vermin'.[1]

Bevan did get his way on steel, but otherwise the King's Speech was notably short of substantive content.

With Herbert Morrison for his part continuing to press the case that 'consolidation' should be the order of the day, attention soon turned to a weekend meeting in May (at Beatrice Webb House, Dorking) of the Cabinet, Labour's National Executive Committee and the TUC. 'It is, I think, quite clear that the majority of the electorate are not disposed to accept nationalization for the sake of nationalization,' argued Morrison in a pre-meeting memo pouring scorn on the notion that electors would become enthusiastic about a new nationalisation programme 'if we only bang at them hard enough'. But at Dorking there was stalemate, with Morrison at best winning by default, and it was clear that the question of nationalisation was far from settled.

That autumn, Gallup sounded out public opinion. Only 32 per cent approved of the nationalisation of the steel industry (set for 15 February 1951); in terms of other industries (insurance, chemicals, cement, sugar, meat) where Labour in theory was committed to some form of nationalisation, approval ratings varied between 31 and 22 per cent, with in each case at least one in two disapproving. As for the existing nationalised industries, only health (overwhelmingly) and coal (45 per cent for, 39 per cent against) received approval, with gas and electricity, the railways and road transport all being viewed by a majority as having suffered under nationalisation.[2] These were striking figures, but they did little or nothing to undermine Labour's by now deeply ingrained belief – not only on the left – that public ownership was integral to the party's 'very soul'.

It was in mid-April, a month before Dorking, that the ailing Stafford Cripps presented his last Budget. Explicitly Keynesian, with its stress on fiscal policy as the best way of attaining economic goals, it was understandably viewed as the culmination of the Labour government's shift (in progress since 1947) away from central planning and towards demand management. 'A graveyard of doctrine' was how *The Times* almost gleefully described the party at last learning the lessons of almost five years in government, and Cripps in his speech emphasised his aversion to using 'the violent compulsions that are appropriate to total-itarian planning'.

Even so, despite earlier 'bonfires', there remained on the part of Labour ministers a stubborn attachment to direct economic controls as indispensable to the maintenance of full employment. Only weeks after the budget, the President of the Board of Trade, Harold Wilson, warned his colleagues that there was 'an acute danger of Keynesian ideas dominating our thinking so much that we shall be driven into a Maginot-like dependence on purely financial methods of preventing a depression'. Or, put another way, the arrival of full-flowering Keynes-ianism did not mean that Britain changed overnight from being a significantly controlled economy – whether in terms of building licensing or exchange control or rationing or food subsidies or govern-ment control over raw materials such as coal or import controls. Labour's *instincts*, moreover, remained essentially interventionist. When one moderate junior minister, James Callaghan, made a speech in May accepting that nationalisation should not go beyond the existing fifth of the economy in public ownership, he was at pains to spell out that the other four-fifths could remain in private hands only if it fulfilled stringent, government-ordained requirements in such areas as invest-ment, earnings and the distribution of dividends.[3]

Nor on the other side of the political divide was the Keynesian centre ground unequivocally embraced. One influential Tory, Richard

Law, argued forcibly in his 1950 book *Return from Utopia* that a strong and free economy would remain unattainable so long as exchange controls were still in place, while from that July the bankers and brokers of the City of London found an economic pundit they could trust – and, just as importantly, understand – in the financial journalist Harold Wincott, who began a regular column in the *Financial Times* espousing a passionate pro-market economic liberalism and soon acquired a considerable following. 'Capitalism here is in a parlous state,' he declared in his first piece (entitled 'Rediscovering Capitalism'). 'Some members of the Government abuse it with blind, unreasoning hate; others realise the mischief they have done and are doing but are prevented by the psychological barriers they themselves have built up from putting right past wrongs. The Opposition apologises for capitalism – and steadily emasculates it.'[4]

Generally, the political temperature was surprisingly low during the immediate post-election period. Labour concentrated on nursing its small majority, while the Tories were broadly content to wait on events. Inevitably, the main day-to-day storm clouds concerned the most controversial figure in British politics: Bevan. Justifiably proud of his creation of the NHS and still Minister of Health, he had been engaged since the previous autumn in a determined guerrilla campaign to keep the service free. Prescription charges had been theoretically introduced after devaluation, but he had managed to stop them coming into operation. Now, in the spring of 1950 and in the uncomfortable position of being the principal scapegoat for Labour's electoral near-disaster, he prepared for a more protracted scrap as the issue returned to the fore.

The essence of the case put forward by the Treasury (where Hugh Gaitskell had become Minister of State and was soon effectively deputising for Cripps) was simple: the NHS was continuing dramatically to overshoot its spending estimates and could not be afforded unless charges were introduced – charges which Gaitskell believed to be right in principle as well as financially necessary. Bevan was adamant that the level of NHS spending would soon start to stabilise of its own accord, a view that most historians have endorsed. Whatever the rights and wrongs, the crucial fact was that by the summer, after several months of disputation, two of Labour's outstanding talents were at bitter loggerheads. 'He's nothing, nothing, nothing!' declared Bevan to a colleague about the apparently super-rational Wykehamist whom he could barely bring himself to believe deserved to be a member of the party, while Gaitskell, though genuinely appreciative of his opponent's parliamentary oratory, reckoned him a 'slippery and difficult' customer.[5] The NHS remained, for the time being, free.

None of this had much of a message for Michael Young in Labour's research department, as he continued to explore what he saw as his party's shortcomings in government. At the end of March, he gave a paper entitled 'The British Socialist Way of Life' to a Fabian conference in Oxford. Declaring that it was 'no longer possible to look forward with confidence to steady progress towards the Socialist Commonwealth', and arguing that it had been a serious mistake to concentrate so much during the election on the nationalisation issue, Young suggested an alternative, less dogmatic emphasis:

> In trying to express the basic idea that should underlie our new policy he had been driven to use the word 'brotherhood' for want of a better. His ideal for society was based on the model of the good family, in which the governing principle was that needs should be met by holding all resources available for use where they were needed most . . . The basis of social life was in the family; but the family needed a good deal of outside support if it were not to be in danger of disruption under the impact of modern forces.

'How wealthy do we really *want* to be?' Young asked. And, after rejecting the American model ('not achieving happiness by multiplying people's wants') and stressing the importance of mental as well as physical health, he turned to what, along with the family, would become the key concept of his life's work: 'One essential was to get back for people the sense of community, for which there was no proper basis in the life of modern cities. Those who become isolated in family homes, without close contacts with their neighbours, have no foundation for a satisfactory way of life.' Young concluded with an almost mystical appeal to 'the democratic Socialist way' as the best alternative – in the context of the decline of religion – to the dangers of fascism and Communism: 'A more satisfactory emotional life based on the sense of brotherhood will react to produce a better family life, based on the mutual love of parents and children. On this basis it is possible to build a new religion to fill the void left in men's minds by the collapse of the old beliefs.'

Almost certainly Young by this time was in a mood of growing disenchantment. 'It was obviously impossible to carry through the major proposals in the watered-down but still substantial version of *Let Us Face the Future* [the 1945 manifesto] contained in *Labour Believes in Britain* [the 1949 policy statement], but why nothing was done on such matters as insurance, public buying and consumers' advice, not even committees of enquiry set up, is still a mystery,' he would write in 1953 about the aftermath of 'the pyrrhic victory of 1950, which condemned the government to passivity'. He was especially disappointed by the failure of the government – in particular Wilson at the Board of Trade – to set up a consumer advisory service that would provide comparative testing of products on behalf of the public. The chronology is uncertain, but it seems that Young stopped day-to-day work at the research department in May, though he received party funding to write 'a report on the means of giving ordinary people, whether workers, consumers or citizens, a bigger part in running a socialist democracy'. Later that year, in search of inspiration, he set off on a world tour, encompassing Israel, Australia, New Zealand, India, Pakistan, Malaya and Singapore. He planned to return in 1951 not only to fulfil his commission but also to continue work on the thesis he had already begun at the London School of Economics (LSE) on how Labour and the other parties operated at a local level.[6] He still had, in other words, an essentially *political* orientation, but the signs were clearly visible of a growing impatience with the parameters of conventional politics.

Anthony Crosland, getting used to life in the Commons, was similarly impatient but took some comfort from having been quickly recognised as one of Labour's rising young stars. Barely three months after the election, he was chosen to deliver a reply on the Home Service to what he called 'the unending bellyache of the prophets of woe' – a 'dreary chorus of gloom' pouring forth 'in the City columns of the newspapers, in *The Times* and the *Economist*, in the speeches of company chairmen and Conservative politicians, in broadcasts by orthodox financial experts'. The bulk of his talk was devoted to a sober, authoritative-sounding and predictably positive assessment of the current position, before concluding that, for all the irrationality of some of Labour's inveterate opponents, there was 'no reason why some of us should not remain sane and normal, and admit that a fully-employed economy reaching record levels of production, exports, and capital investment must be in a pretty sound and healthy state'.

That autumn, at another Fabian conference on 'Problems Ahead', Crosland offered his critique of Young's earlier analysis. The two men were friends, but this did not stop Crosland speaking somewhat derisively about Young's 'ideas of groups of extroverts (in shorts) indulging in jolly bouts of brotherly love over glasses of milk'. Overall, though, he fully endorsed Young's thrust that Labour needed to abandon its overly statist ways and instead rediscover the 'moral-cultural-emotional appeal of the William Morris tradition', a tradition that was 'still a perfectly effective Socialist dynamic'. Crosland's mentor, meanwhile, continued to gaze watchfully as well as lovingly upon his protégé. 'Am thinking of Tony, with all his youth and beauty and gaiety and charm and energy and social success and good brains . . . & with his feet on the road of political success now, if he survives to middle age – I weep,' the by now veteran Labour politician Hugh Dalton confided to his diary soon afterwards. 'May he live to reap all the harvest of happiness and achievement which his gifts deserve!'[7]

If there was an equivalent of Crosland in the much larger Tory intake of 1950, it was probably Iain Macleod. Both men were cerebral, charismatic and socially liberal; they had a similarly quixotic, high-handed streak in their respective temperaments; and each was capable of engendering great loyalty from some colleagues, fierce dislike from others. For Macleod, as the son of a Scottish doctor who practised in Yorkshire, it was natural that the social services should become his formative parliamentary speciality. In his maiden speech in March, focusing largely on NHS spending, he sought to identify where Labour's welfare state had taken a wrong turn:

> Today the conception of a minimum standard which held the field of political thought for so long, and in my view should hold it still, is disappearing in favour of an average standard. To an average standard, the old-fashioned virtues of thrift, industry and ability become irrelevant.

The social services today have become a weapon of financial and not of
social policy. This may sound Irish, but it is both true and tragic that, in
a scheme where everyone has priority, it follows that no one has priority.

Macleod was, in other words, questioning the principle of universalism
and instead advocating what would become known as 'selectivity', or
'targeting'.

Later in 1950, he was one of the principal authors and co-editors
of a substantial pamphlet called *One Nation: A Tory Approach to Social
Problems*, according to the title page jointly written by nine new MPs
(including Enoch Powell and Edward Heath, though the latter probably
did not contribute significantly). Despite its consensual, nonadversarial
title, with its deliberate nod to Disraeli, the pamphlet had a surprisingly
hard edge, especially given the probable imminence of the next general
election. The old, pre-1945 themes of sound finance, voluntarism,
charity, efficiency and self-reliance were all invoked; it was claimed
that 'the social well-being of the nation' had 'already been endangered
by the redistribution of wealth'; and a key criterion 'governing the
size of the social services budget' was that 'the good it does must
outweigh the burden which it places on the individual and on industry'.[8]
The pamphlet, published in October, made a considerable impact, and
its authors soon established the One Nation Group as a regular dining
club. Such developments were a clear indication that not all the young
political talent was now going to Labour; they also suggested that the
nature of the post-war welfare state was not yet set in stone.

To the man who in 1950 was poised to emerge, even more than
Bevan, as the conscience of this new dispensation, the concept of selectivity was anathema. That spring saw the publication of *Problems of
Social Policy* by Richard Titmuss – 42, no academic qualifications and
still a relatively little-known figure. The book, an account of the social
services during the war, transformed Titmuss's life. Its most influential
cheerleader was the doyen of British ethical socialists, R. H. Tawney,
who in the course of an ultra-admiring three-page review in the *New
Statesman*, with the author's name misspelled throughout, noted how
'a recurrent theme' was 'the gradual, un-premeditated, emergence from
a morass of obsolescent cant of new conceptions of the social contract'.
Within months, Titmuss was appointed to the LSE's first chair in Social

Administration, the position he would occupy for the rest of his life.

Over the years, there have been many attempts (perhaps stimulated by the absence of a full-length biography) to characterise Titmuss's beliefs and outlook. According to A. H. Halsey, 'his socialism was as English as his patriotism, ethical and non-Marxist, insisting that capitalism was not only economically but socially wasteful, in failing to harness individual altruism to the common good'; Alan Deacon has emphasised Titmuss's essentially moralistic conviction that only if social services were universal would they 'not only redistribute resources but do so in a manner which itself fostered a sense of mutual responsibility'; and Hilary Rose has argued that for Titmuss the key people in bringing about 'the good society' – a society based on the values of equality and community – were to be the enlightened, altruistic middle classes, 'with greatest hope being placed on those whose lives were expressed within public service, whether as officials or professionals'.

There was also fascination with Titmuss the person. One physical description, soon after his death in 1973, evoked an El Greco quality, with 'his great eyes, emaciated face, long body and that indefinable air of what one could only call saintliness'. Yet like most saints, he was not a man altogether at ease with himself. 'In discovering the huge disparities in life chances between those at the bottom and those at the top of the social scale, he was at the same time commenting on his own lack of fortune in not being born at the top,' his daughter, the feminist writer Ann Oakley, has reflected. 'Awareness of class was central to his intellectual perception of society. But it was also constantly felt as an aspect of his own life.' Put another way, Clark's Commercial College, where he had learnt book-keeping at the age of 15, was very different from Dartington (Young) or Highgate (Crosland) or Fettes (Macleod). Unsurprisingly, as Oakley added about Titmuss's far from straightforward relationship with the British establishment, 'you didn't have to be a detective to discern my father's concealed adulation of certain unsocialist institutions'.[9]

———

The Attlee government had two fundamental foreign-policy decisions to take in the summer of 1950. The first concerned Europe. On 9 May the French Foreign Minister, Robert Schuman, publicly unveiled his plan – largely the work of Jean Monnet – for a supranational body under which member states would pool their production of coal and steel. By early June it was clear that Britain was unwilling to participate in what would become in due course the European Coal and Steel Community – the start of 'Europe' as an economic-cum-political project, with the Schuman Plan billed from the outset as 'a first step in the direction of European federation'. Ernest Bevin was still Foreign Secretary; his biographer Alan Bullock has emphasised that his negative response was essentially determined by 'practical arguments such as Western Europe's dependence on American support' and 'the importance to Britain of her position as a world trading power, and as the centre of the Commonwealth'.

It was not a decision with which most of the British political class were inclined to quarrel. Although Edward Heath made a passionate maiden speech arguing that the European cause was one where Britain needed 'to be in at the formative stages so that our influence could be brought to bear', a much more typical Tory attitude was that of Major Harry Legge-Bourke: 'I do not believe that common interests or even common fears are enough; there must also be common sympathies and common characteristics. Whilst those exist in the United Kingdom and in the United States, they do not exist in Europe.' Gut instincts were similar on the Labour benches, where (to his subsequent mortification) a young Roy Jenkins voted against British participation. Some weeks later, Mamaine Koestler was present at a notably cosmopolitan, intellectual dinner party where the line-up included her husband Arthur Koestler, Raymond Aron and Arthur Schlesinger Jr, as well as two of the more cerebral Labour politicians, John Strachey and Richard Crossman:

> Very lively discussion about the isolationist line of the Labour Government, and of the British in general. John and Dick defended this against everybody else; their line is that they'd be delighted to see France, Germany, Italy and Benelux getting together so long as Britain doesn't have to be in, submitting to the authority of shady foreigners and having the welfare state corrupted by immoral inhabitants of non-socialist countries.[10]

The echo of 'socialism in one country' – the old Soviet battle cry – was unmistakable.

'The press, on the whole, approved of the cautious reserve of the British reply,' reported Mollie Panter-Downes in her *The New Yorker* 'Letter from London' on 6 June; she might have cited the still inordinately powerful Beaverbrook papers, which were positively vitriolic about the French initiative ('Let us say No, No, a thousand times No,' screamed the *Sunday Express*). Nor was there any significant enthusiasm from the captains of industry, to judge by the cool response of the Federation of British Industries: with Britain's share of world trade holding up well, there was no appetite for novel solutions to as yet unidentified economic decline. As for the attitude of the man in the street, Herbert Morrison's reaction at the start of June, when told that the French were demanding to know the British position, arguably said it all: 'It's no good. We cannot do it; the Durham miners won't wear it.'[11] An impressionistic assessment no doubt; but the prevailing, deeply entrenched mixture of insularity and 'Britain is best' in society at large hardly suggests that Morrison and his colleagues were acting against the popular will.

The other major foreign-policy decision concerned Korea, after the tanks of Communist North Korea had crossed the 38th parallel on 25 June and proceeded to invade South Korea. The British reaction could hardly have been more instant: not only did Britain at once join with the United States in supporting the UN resolution condemning North Korea's aggression, but within 48 hours the decision had been taken to place the British Pacific Fleet under American command, following President Truman's offer of military aid to the South Koreans. Thereafter, as the Korean War unfolded (including serious Chinese involvement on the side of North Korea), the Anglo-American alliance gave – and was intended to give – every impression of being rock solid.

Such unflinching commitment to a policy of intervention, notwithstanding the undeniable absence of any direct British economic or strategic interest in Korea, inevitably had a profound impact on defence expenditure. As early as August, the three-year estimate for defence spending was increased from £2.3 billion to £3.6 billion, while in January 1951, under continuing American pressure, that figure was raised to £4.7 billion. 'The Prime Minister's defence statement yesterday displayed a greater sense of realism and urgency than the government's critics had expected,' the *Financial Times* grudgingly conceded after this second drastic hike. 'It reflects a determination, at last, to match the vigour of the United States in defending Western security.' The veteran American diplomat Paul Nitze was more generous some 40 years later. 'You can call it hubris or you can call it courage,' he told the historian Peter Hennessy. 'I think we had much to admire the British for [for] what you could call hubris, but which I consider to be breathtaking courage.'

Why did the Attlee government make this huge and arguably irrational commitment? In part because of a mixture of unhappy memories of Labour and appeasement in the 1930s and the haunting fear – persistent since the late 1940s – of Soviet tanks rolling across Western Europe. 'Mr Bevin does not believe that the Russians will venture on aggression against Europe if the European Powers show their determination to fight,' the Foreign Secretary informed his ambassadors in August, ahead of the announcement that National Service was to be extended from 18 months to two years. Memories of appeasement were particularly sharp for Gaitskell, who succeeded Cripps at No. 11 in October and thereafter was primarily responsible for sanctioning, even encouraging, the massive rearmament programme. 'The deep conviction which Hugh had formed in the Munich years played a dominating part in his mind,' his close friend and fellow-minister Douglas Jay recalled. 'He did not make the crude mistake of confusing Stalin or Mao with Hitler. But he did believe that military dictators were usually arbitrary and often expansionist.' Accordingly, 'he became convinced that, as in 1938–40, we must take some deliberate economic risks to defend basic freedoms.'[12]

Even so, the nub of the matter, taking the government and its advisers as a whole, was the nature of the Anglo-American relationship – and in particular the deep British desire to be treated by the Americans as something like equals. 'There could not be a more useful demonstration of the United Kingdom's capacity to act as a world power with the support of the Commonwealth and of its quickness to move when actions rather than words are necessary' was a Foreign Office view of intervention only days after the 38th parallel had been crossed. Not long afterwards, on 17 July, the British ambassador in Washington, Sir Oliver Franks, warned Attlee that the capital was in a mood of such 'emotional overdrive' that the Americans would undoubtedly 'test the quality of the partnership' by the whole-heartedness or otherwise of the British military response. And a week later, he stressed again that any signs of negativity 'could seriously impair the long-term relationship'.

Nevertheless, British intervention in Korea was not only about impressing the Americans; it was also about restraining them. The Americans, reflected Kenneth Younger (Bevin's deputy) in his diary in early August, 'seem to have decided that a war with "the communists" is virtually inevitable and likely to occur relatively soon, say within 3–5 years. They regard all communists alike, no matter what their nationality, and assume that they are all dancing to Moscow's tune and are bound to do so in future . . .' By contrast, the British, 'despite growing pessimism, still give first place to the effort to prevent war. We do not accept it as inevitable . . .' It was in the context of such fears, argues the historian Sean Greenwood on the basis of a close study of the records, that 'the British found themselves sucked into seeking closer collaboration with Washington in order to find out more precisely what American intentions were as well as to douse an over-enthusiasm which might have perilous ramifications'.[13] It was, of course, a strategy based on an illusion about the rewards of sacrifice, but at least it was not held in defiance of more than half a century of evidence showing it to be a chimera.

A bipartisan consensus endorsed the government's approach, as did Florence Speed in Brixton. 'Situation in Korea "grave",' she recorded on 5 July, before going on with what was probably a fairly typical mixture of resignation and pride: 'Reds still having it all their own way. Mr Churchill in a speech yesterday, said, if we do not win in Korea it is the beginning of the Third World War which so many people don't want but think inevitable. It will end I expect in British soldiers replacing the Americans. Britain seems in all wars to carry the heaviest burden.' Soon afterwards, with the first British casualties being announced, the pacifist diarist Frances Partridge, living in Lytton Strachey's old house on the Wiltshire Downs, was struck by how 'a sort of excitement seemed to possess our weekend visitors at the thought of the bravery of soldiers in wartime', one of those visitors being a fellow-member of the Bloomsbury Group, Quentin Bell. 'Talk is quite openly anti-foreign: all Germans are monsters impossible to shake by the hand, the Italians beneath contempt, and the French and Russians as bad as the Germans. Nor is this by any means meant as a joke.'

On 30 July the Prime Minister solemnly broadcast to the nation. 'War creeps nearer and Mr Attlee points out our help in Korea will mean sacrifices,' noted Judy Haines in Chingford that Sunday evening. 'More rationing? and scrambling for food? Oh lor! Better that than bombs.' Predictably, Gallup found in August that no fewer than 78 per cent backed the increased government spending on defence, even though 61 per cent accepted that this would lead to a reduced standard of living. Over the next six months, there remained from the government's point of view an adequate degree of broad-based, patriotic support for the British intervention. 'Our poor boys in Korea with the Americans are getting out of the jam they are in and I hope will reach the coast safely' was how Vere Hodgson put it shortly before Christmas. That, though, was not quite everyone's perspective. After a reference to 'the filthy bomb-drunk Yanks', Kingsley Amis went on in a letter to Philip Larkin early in the New Year: 'Anybody over here now who is not pro-Chink wants his arse filled with celluloid and a match applied to his arse-hairs.'[14] Amis by this time was probably no longer the fervent, card-carrying Communist he had been during the Second World War, but he still broadly held the faith.

The Korean War intensified the Cold War atmosphere. Typical was the reaction in August 1950 of the Archbishop of York, Cyril Garbett, to the Stockholm Peace Petition, endorsed by church leaders in the Communist bloc and demanding a ban on nuclear weapons. 'I am suspicious of the origin and motive of this particular petition,' he told his diocese, 'it is widely believed its promoters are communists or fellow-travellers, if this is so its purpose would be to weaken the resolution of the nation, and to encourage appeasement.' With the Archbishop of Canterbury, Geoffrey Fisher, similarly hostile, clerical support for the petition soon dropped away sharply. That autumn, the government, under pressure from the fiercely anti-Communist TGWU leader Arthur Deakin, considered banning the Communist Party before rejecting the idea as impractical. However, two episodes showed the extent to which freedom of speech was fraying at the edges.

The first concerned *Picture Post*, for which the journalist James Cameron filed a story in September that, accompanied by graphic

Bert Hardy photos, highlighted the ill-treatment of prisoners by the South Koreans. The anti-American implications were too much for the magazine's increasingly right-wing proprietor, Edward Hulton, who not only refused to let the story appear but sacked the long-standing editor, Tom Hopkinson. Thereafter, *Picture Post* never regained the cutting edge that for 12 years had made it such a unique, agenda-setting phenomenon. The other episode was the semi-farcical story of the Second World Peace Congress, due to take place in Sheffield City Hall in November. Between them the government (denouncing it as a Communist front and refusing to issue visas to 'undesirable' delegates) and the local Council managed to prevent it taking place – though some delegates, including Pablo Picasso, did turn up. There were no such problems for the British Society for Cultural Freedom, which met for the first time in January 1951 (two months before the London County Council banned all Communists from its employ) and whose very purpose was to try to counter the influence of Communism. The venue was the Authors' Club, Whitehall, with the poet and critic Stephen Spender in the chair. Just over a year earlier, he had contributed to Richard Crossman's *The God That Failed*, a widely read anthology of intellectuals describing how they had fallen out of love with Communism; now he was poised to emerge as the emblematic, ubiquitous Cold War liberal.[15]

For the Communist Party of Great Britain, the early 1950s were difficult times. In the February 1950 election it managed a pitiful 0.3 per cent of the popular vote, in the process losing its two MPs. And when, a year later, it published *The British Road to Socialism*, the impact was at best muted. 'Its leaden formulas,' observes the biographer of the party's leader, Harry Pollitt, 'did not so much distil the lessons of the British experience as plagiarise those of Eastern Europe.' Or, as one party member subsequently remarked, an apter title would have been *The Russian Road to Socialism, Done into English*. Moreover, the document's claim that the party was now independent from Moscow met for the most part with well-justified scepticism. Indeed, for one member, the writer Mervyn Jones, this was the point at which several years of private doubts came to a head; he left the party after witnessing a draft being changed as a direct result of pressure from Moscow.

Another writer also had her moment of epiphany. 'It is the spring of 1951,' the poet and critic John Jones remembered over half a century later:

> Iris and I are in the Lamb and Flag pub in Oxford. We have finished our game of composing a joint sonnet, writing alternate lines. She looks across the dark silent public bar at a solitary drinker of Guinness and says, 'I want to tell you my ancient mariner tale.' She begins, making no sense to me, with 'Roy Jenkins was right and I was wrong'. Then she plunges into an account of Communist Party organisation . . .

Iris Murdoch was referring to ten years earlier, when her fellow-undergraduate at Oxford had started a Democratic Socialist Club as a breakaway from the Labour Club, which was loyally Stalinist and had Murdoch as chairman. For the young Lionel Blue, himself an Oxford undergraduate by the time of the pub confession, the scales had already fallen. 'Early in 1950, marching in a procession which was bawling the names of Communist leaders, I suddenly asked myself what I was doing in it,' he recalled. 'This wasn't rational. This was idol worship and all the Jew in me revolted. It was cruder juju than poor old Grandma's. I left the procession, dived into an Indo-Pak restaurant and – fortified by two portions of curry – ceased to be a Stalinist/Marxist and never marched for anyone again.'[16]

Lawrence Daly – in his mid-20s, still working down the Glencraig pit in Fife, assiduously selling the *Daily Worker* there every day, recently elected chairman of the Scottish TUC Youth Advisory Council – felt no such qualms about the Communist faith into which he had virtually been born. If anything, the Korean War served to redouble his zeal and sense of certainty. His papers include a letter written to him in October 1950 by James Callaghan, by this time a junior minister at the Admiralty, in reply to Daly's 'long letter', apparently about whether the blame for what Callaghan called 'the present tension' rested with the United States or Russia. 'I am bound to say that I have reached the conclusion, with great regret, that the major responsibility lies with the U.S.S.R. and I disagree with what you say that their attitude has remained unchanged,' wrote Callaghan. 'Is it not clear that Russia has got to the stage now (which I believe to be different from her position in 1945) when everyone in every other country must subordinate his own views to the interests of the U.S.S.R.?' And he cited Russia's build-up of 'the largest submarine fleet that the world has ever seen'.

None of which perturbed young Daly, to judge by his diary soon afterwards:

> *3 November (Friday).* Renée [his middle-class wife] & I set out to listen to 'Venus Observed' – I fell asleep. Then read some of Stalin's 'Leninism'. Renée said play was excellent.
>
> *5 November.* Read some of Joe's 'Marxism & National & Colonial Question' – delightfully sensible.
>
> *6 November.* Went into Cowdenbeath at 4 p.m. for meeting with M. Taylor to discuss work of Party Branch. M. presented powerful analysis of cause of defects in our work – in a blunt & insulting fashion – rightly so.
>
> *9 November.* Tonight I started to read chapter of Marx's 'Capital' & have been delightfully surprised by its readability & wealth of information.
>
> *10 November.* Put bills for Pollitt meeting in canteen & baths [ie at the pit] this morning. As expected baths one was torn down by finishing time. This inevitably happens with Party notices & even TU ones which are suspected of being Communistic. The culprit or culprits must be violently intolerant, probably miserably cowardly, & pitiably ignorant.

Daly was only a spasmodic diarist, and a week later the final entry in this sequence was more personal: 'Lady gave Rannoch [his son] shilling just after we got off the train this morning for being such a well-behaved boy!'[17]

There was an economic as well as an ideological dimension to the war. Here at least, ministers could hardly be accused of going in with their eyes shut. 'Rearmament will compete with exports for our production, and at the same time the rapidly rising price of imported raw materials is causing a further deterioration in the terms of trade,' Bevin and Gaitskell noted solemnly in their October 1950 joint assessment of the financial aspect. 'It will therefore become increasingly difficult to avoid a deficit on the United Kingdom overall balance of payments, which will show itself in a rise in our overseas sterling liabilities.' So it proved: not only did Britain's balance-of-payments situation sharply deteriorate over the next year, but there was also a major stock-piling crisis, in the context of the rapidly rising price of imported raw materials. It did not take long for the conventional wisdom to emerge that Britain's post-war export-led recovery had been halted in its tracks by the decision to intervene in Korea. 'Important sectors of the engineering industries are heavily engaged in defence work when they might otherwise be concentrating their main energies on the export trade,' lamented the Economic Survey in 1953 (by which time the war was drawing to an end). Five years later, Andrew Shonfield, in his survey of post-war economic policy, reckoned that the rearmament programme, by having 'used up all the resources in sight and more', had 'continued to exercise an unfavourable influence on economic development long after the event'.

Economic historians have not, on the whole, much dissented. For Correlli Barnett, this cavalier diversion of resources from exports and investment was graphic testimony to how 'the British governing elite suffered not only from the reflexes of a rich man and a grandee but also from those of a school prefect', in other words high-mindedly trying to set the world to rights. Even Jim Tomlinson, the best-informed, most convincing advocate of the Attlee government across a range of economic issues, concedes that doubling defence expenditure – even before the war comprising 7 per cent of GNP – was 'a reckless gamble'. Significantly, though, a study by Peter Burnham of the war's impact on the British vehicle industry (in particular Leyland Motors) reveals that the 'more astute' sections of the industry (including cars as well as commercial vehicles) were able in the early 1950s 'to increase their industrial infrastructure and secure a high rate of guaranteed profit at the direct expense of the state in a manner which would not have been possible but for rearmament'. And he argues, convincingly, that 'the reasons for long-term decline must be sought in the market structure and practices of firms themselves in addition to looking at the effects of government policy'.[18] The Korean War was, in short, all too easily used as an alibi for more fundamental economic failings.

The more serious, longlasting fall-out from the war was political. At the outset, Bevan and the Labour left were almost unanimously behind the Americans. 'When you are in a world-wide alliance,' Bevan told Younger, 'you can't retreat from it on a single issue.' Moreover, although in Cabinet in early August he criticised the United States for resorting to 'a military defence' against 'Communist encroachment' as opposed to improving 'the social and economic conditions' of threatened countries, Bevan remained during the autumn publicly supportive of the rearmament programme. Certainly he did not voice his doubts at Labour's October conference at Margate, where Panter-Downes described him as looking on the platform 'like a sort of walking Union Jack – crimson face, pugnacious blue eyes, and a thick, silvering thatch of hair'. She also noted how Bevin looked 'tired and oddly shrunken'; how Anthony Crosland was 'alone in courageously pointing out, when rearmament gets going, the problem will be not to reduce the cost of living but to hang on desperately to keep it pegged where it is'; and how 'in the evenings, when the delegates stopped at the various hotel bars to lower a pint before dinner, the regular customers, attended by their glum, well-tailored Scotties and fox terriers, sat sipping their gins with a self-conscious air of being in dubious company'.[19]

Later that month, Cripps at last stood down at No. 11 and was replaced by the obvious choice, Gaitskell. Most senior ministers approved, but Bevan failed to disguise his anger and fired off a letter to Attlee complaining that the appointment was 'a great mistake'. Gaitskell reflected privately on the personal ramifications: 'I suspect that Nye is not so much jealous but humiliated at my being put over him. But HW, and others confirm, is inordinately jealous, though in view of his age [34, ten years younger than Gaitskell] there is really no reason for it. But then one does not look for reasons for jealousy.' It was hardly surprising that Harold Wilson, until recently the coming man in matters economic, should have felt aggrieved. After all, as his biographer Ben Pimlott points out, 'the Chancellorship had been his childhood fantasy'.

Malcolm Muggeridge lunched with the new Chancellor in December and found him 'amiable, and, in his way, intelligent, rather like a certain type of High Church clergyman with a slum parish'. Early in 1951, on 15 January, Bevan set out to Cabinet his profound misgivings about the vastly expanded rearmament programme that Attlee and Gaitskell were now proposing. 'He did not believe that the Soviet Government were relying on a military coup,' recorded the minutes. 'If this was their policy, they would have taken military action before now: he did not believe that they had been deterred from this merely by fear of atomic attack. In his view their main strategy was to force the Western democracies to rearm on a scale which would impair their economies and embitter their peoples.' Two days later, Bevan was moved sideways by Attlee, to the Ministry of Labour; on the 25th, the Cabinet agreed to the programme, despite Gaitskell admitting that such was the shortage of crucial materials – not helped by American stockpiling – that 'there was a danger that the increased defence programme might, in practice, yield less and not more production within the next two years'. Only two ministers (including Wilson) made seriously critical noises, while Bevan stayed largely silent.[20]

'In all this there are personal ambitions and rivalries at work,' reckoned Gaitskell at the start of February. 'HW is clearly ganging up with the Minister of Labour, not that he [ie Wilson] cuts very much ice because one feels that he has no fundamental views of his own.' Even so, Bevan on the 15th still gave his unambiguous public backing to the new programme. 'We do beg that we shall not have all these jeers about the rearmament we are putting under way,' he declared in the Commons. 'We shall carry it out; we shall fulfil our obligation to our friends and Allies.' It was 'one of the most brilliant performances I have ever heard him give,' Gaitskell reflected after Bevan had wound up the defence debate. 'What a tragedy,' he went on, 'that a man with such wonderful talent as an orator and such an interesting mind and fertile imagination should be such a difficult team worker, and some would say even worse – a thoroughly unreliable and disloyal colleague. Will he grow out of this? Will he take on the true qualities that are necessary for leadership? Who can say? Time alone will show.'

Time for once did not dally. On 9 March, after finally persuading an unwilling but failing Bevin to let go of the Foreign Office, Attlee replaced him with Herbert Morrison – almost certainly to Bevan's intense disappointment. Attlee would later claim that Bevan had not wanted the position, but this seems improbable. Certainly, after this third personal setback in barely five months, he was in resigning mood when on the 22nd he listened to Gaitskell explain why, in his forthcoming Budget, the introduction of health charges – specifically, charges on teeth and spectacles – was an indispensable part of paying for the expanded defence programme. Tellingly, Bevan 'found it difficult to believe that the reasons for the proposal were entirely financial in character, since suggestions for a scheme of charges had been put forward persistently for the last three years'. In this he was surely right, for even a broadly sympathetic biographer of Gaitskell concedes of his subject that, following the squalls over health charges the previous year, 'politically he needed to be backed by the Cabinet to assert his ascendancy over Bevan.' It was a tactic that looked likely to work, given that around the table only Wilson joined Bevan in refusing to accept that the principle of a free health service would remain intact despite the introduction of charges. Twelve days later (and exactly a week before the Budget), responding to a heckler at a meeting full of dockers in Bermondsey, Bevan at last came out in public: 'I will not be a member of a Government which imposes charges on the patient.'[21]

A fascinated spectator of the unfolding drama was Anthony Wedgwood Benn, who in November had succeeded Cripps as Labour MP for Bristol South-East. 'I think we were a shade overkeen,' he afterwards explained to the press about the much-reduced majority, 'and started knocking at doors a bit early in the morning when even supporters had no interest in politics.' He let it be known that, as a new MP, it would be necessary for him to lose the stigma of being an intellectual. 'You'd better acquire the stigma before worrying about losing it' was the typically caustic response of Tony Crosland, who had taught him at Oxford. Undeterred, Benn made a well-received maiden speech in February ('South-East Bristol has every reason to be pleased with its new member,' noted Michael Foot in the *Daily Herald*), followed on 9 March, the day of Bevin's resignation, by his first appearance on *Any Questions?*. The programme came from Itchen Grammar School, Southampton, and to read the transcript is to be struck by how the 25-year-old's earnest priggishness was combined with an unmistakable boy-scoutish charm. 'I'm not a bit ashamed to say that we've made lots of mistakes' is how he began an answer about Labour's future nationalisation plans, 'and that we're going to make a lot more, but what I would say, and I'm not a bit ashamed to say, we've profited by experience...'

Benn was already keeping a diary, and the following week he recorded a 'Gala Smoking Concert' held by some 80 Labour MPs in the Smoking Room of the Commons. At one point they sang a ditty (conducted by Callaghan, to the tune of 'John Brown's Body') that owed little to poetry, even less to the political realities of March 1951, and almost everything to a deep, primitive, heartfelt class consciousness:

> We'll make Winston Churchill smoke a Woodbine every day
> We'll make Winston Churchill smoke a Woodbine every day
> We'll make Winston Churchill smoke a Woodbine every day
> When the red revolution comes.[22]

'The awful event of Christmas Day was the stealing of THE CORONATION STONE from Westminster Abbey,' noted Vere Hodgson near the end of 1950. 'The poor Dean has broadcast a heart broken appeal to everyone to help find it. He says he will travel to the ends of the earth to get it back.' She added, 'It seems the Scottish nationalists have taken it. Such nonsense. As if there is not enough trouble in the world. They should go and fight in Korea . . .' Despite the Scottish claim that that country's monarchs had been crowned upon the Stone of Scone since the tenth century, before it had been forcibly removed to England by Edward I in 1296, the bulk of the English press was equally unsympathetic; even the *Manchester Guardian* condemned 'the childish stupidity of these Nationalists, which deserves sharp punishment and no extenuation'. No one was more incensed than the King, who (according to Harold Macmillan's information) had the news kept from him until after his live Christmas Day broadcast, but as soon as he heard wanted to go on the air again to appeal for its return. English public opinion was probably not so different from the royal view of the situation, but Macmillan himself was more relaxed: 'What a strange and delightful interlude in the great world tragedy – a sort of Scottish harlequinade.'

Across the border, embarrassment and gratification seem to have been felt in about equal measure. 'Here, in Scotland, although all reasonable Scots disapprove the act,' observed Randall Philip, Procurator of the Church of Scotland, 'there is considerable satisfaction that, for once, England has realised the existence of its neighbour, and considerable chuckling over the Gilbertian efforts of the police.' These efforts included dragging the Serpentine, closing the Scottish border for the first time in 400 years and much else – all to no avail. It would eventually emerge that the daring theft had been engineered by three male students at Glasgow University and a young Highlands woman who taught domestic science. All four were members of the Covenant movement, demanding that Scotland have its own parliament in Edinburgh. The Covenant had been launched in August 1949 and within a year had collected something like 1.5 million signatures. The Attlee government, accused by the movement of being over-centralising, was unimpressed and gave little ground – a stance fortified in February 1950 by the underwhelming electoral performance of the Scottish Nationalists. 'Despite the miserable showing so far as votes go,' one of its badly defeated candidates, the poet and left-wing controversialist Hugh MacDiarmid (standing under his real name, C. M. Grieve), optimistically reflected soon afterwards, '"it's coming yet for a' that." While not reflected in the voting, the awakened interest in and attention to Scottish affairs of all kinds is most marked everywhere.'[23]

In the event, the much-publicised removal of the Stone proved a significant blow to the Home Rule cause, not only in terms of hardening English opinion. 'The escapade was popular but inappropriate,' observes the Scottish historian Christopher Harvie, 'enhancing emotional nationalism rather than canny moderatism.' Meanwhile, the Stone itself began 1951 in two pieces, following a misadventure as it was prised from under the Coronation Chair. The smaller bit was stowed away in a friendly house in the Midlands; the larger chunk lay equally undetected in a Kent field. Eventually, once the hue and cry had subsided, the two parts were secretly transported to Scotland and put back together by a well-disposed stonemason.

Given the broad degree of satisfaction with the two main pillars of the post-war British settlement – full employment and the welfare state – it was perhaps unsurprising that the movement for Scottish independence or even devolution failed to build up an unstoppable head of steam. The prevailing political conservatism was reinforced by a deep unwillingness to face up to clear signs by the early 1950s that the Scottish economy was facing fundamental problems. The over-reliance on traditional heavy industries had if anything become even more pronounced; Scotland's share of British exports (as measured by value) was declining; and an authoritative report by Alec Cairncross deplored 'the comparative indifference of Scottish industry to new equipment, new knowledge, and new opportunities for development'. A significant source of comfort to those who did contemplate the economic future was the existence since 1943 of the North of Scotland Hydro-Electric Board, charged with developing water power for hoped-for new industrial plants. 'In a way the Hydro Board symbolised the relationship of government and the economy in the 1950s,' comments Harvie. 'Its purposes were vaguely nationalist and vaguely socialist. It served a myth, that of the Highland way of life.'[24] Certainly the Board (chaired for many years by Tom Johnston, wartime Secretary of State for Scotland) was responsible for bringing electricity to many isolated homes. But whether its dams, pylons and power stations were really going to help the socio-economic regeneration of the Highlands was far from clear.

The cause of Welsh nationalism was, by contrast, appreciably less conspicuous in these immediate post-war years. Labour was becoming the ever more dominant party of the Welsh political landscape; Attlee and Morrison adamantly refused to allow Wales to have (like Scotland) its own Secretary of State; the Council for Wales that they did permit to be set up in 1949 was on a wholly advisory basis; and the Welsh language continued its long-term decline, with the 1951 Census revealing not only that barely a quarter of the population (mainly in rural areas) could speak it, but that the adult monoglot Welsh speaker had become a rarity. Instead, even more so than in Scotland, most people looked to the new British settlement to protect their interests – arguably to such an extent that in time '1945' became in Welsh history what '1688' and the Glorious Revolution had for centuries been in English history. This version of the past was one in which Bevan – no Welsh nationalist – would play a heroic, starring role, above all through his creation of the NHS. St David's Day in 2004 was marked by a poll asking the Welsh to nominate their greatest Welsh heroes. There were silver and bronze medals for Tom Jones and Owain Glyndwr; the gold went to the one-time member for Ebbw Vale.[25]

One obdurate, difficult, disagreeable man, himself imbued with a deep detestation of Welsh nationalism, refused from the start to buy into the myth. This was the writer and businessman Charles Horace Jones. Born in Merthyr Tydfil in 1906, Jones had flourished during the war as a self-confessed spiv, and indeed looked exactly like one with his pencil moustache, sleek black hair, invariable cigarette and perpetually sardonic expression. For some years afterwards he ran a crafts business in the town, but gave it up in 1950 to combine writing (including much lampooning doggerel as well as satirical articles and pamphlets) with standing for hours at a time against the lamp-post in Merthyr's high street opposite the jeweller's. There, in the words of an unsympathetic obituarist, 'he would harangue anyone who had the slightest connection with the town's public life, from councillors to lollipop ladies'. Jones, who usually carried a knuckleduster in his pocket, was not a man to cross, but in his malevolent way he offered over the years an acerbic, remarkably sustained commentary on the institutions running post-war Wales and often benefiting handsomely from the new settlement. It was a settlement he saw as inimical to personal initiative and intrinsically liable to foster corruption. He may have had a case. But there remains something rebarbative about the man whose favourite aphorism (among many) is still remembered in Merthyr: 'The best place to bury the hatchet is in your enemy's head.'[26]

12

A Kind of Measuring-Rod

Gladys Langford encountered the welfare state in action on the first Monday in September 1950:

> To Local branch of Nat. Health Insur. to get a new card as I must now pay 3/8 weekly if I want the additional 26/- weekly when I have been 10 years insured. The clerk was a most incompetent person and when she finally accepted the card the L.C.C. had returned to me she said 'We will send you an arrears card as it is one stamp short'. I said 'Oh, I will get a stamp at the P.O. opposite and then it will be stamped to date and save unnecessary labour here and in the Post Office for delivery'. The silly so-and-so refused to let me do this, repeating parrot fashion – 'We will send you an arrears card'!!!![1]

Langford had retired at the end of the summer term after 30 years of teaching, but, with much fortitude amid waves of despair and loneliness, she continued to live at the Woodstock Hotel in Highbury.

Later that month, there appeared in the *British Medical Journal* a report intended to help more people reach retirement age. The co-authors were Richard Doll of the Medical Research Council and the distinguished epidemiologist A. Bradford Hill, together commissioned by the MRC in 1947 to investigate the rising rate of lung cancer. The conventional wisdom was that air pollution was the principal cause, while Doll attributed the rise to the increasing practice of tarring roads. But after extensive interviewing in London hospitals of patients suffering from the disease, he and Hill found that in only two out of 649 cases were they non-smokers. The ensuing report ('Smoking and Carcinoma of the Lung') broke new ground, in Britain anyway, by establishing, albeit with due caution, the link between smoking and lung cancer – at a time when 80 per cent of men and 40 per cent of women smoked. Further research followed almost immediately, including an inquiry into the smoking habits of Britain's 60,000 doctors, but on the part of central government, reliant on tobacco tax for some 16 per cent of its revenue, there was as yet little will to tackle the issue. Smoking, moreover, remained deeply embedded in most people's (or rather, most men's) daily way of life, not least the busy, stressful lives of politicians, civil servants and medical advisers. Doll himself, a 20-a-day man, gave up as soon as the implications of his research became apparent; his reward was to see smoking bans begin to be implemented in the early twenty-first century.[2]

Those who lived and worked amid the nation's collieries certainly knew the scourge of lung disease. 'Oh John, this is a desolate place – like the other side of the moon,' declared Sid Chaplin in July 1950, writing to a friend from Grimethorpe in South Yorkshire. 'These people have lost their souls in trying to escape. Great muck-heaps – great soul-less pits, little scurrying men. They've lost heart . . .' A month later, the ex-Ferryhill miner-novelist, as he was billed by the local paper, was at Coundon in County Durham opening a new sub-branch of Bishop Auckland Library. 'It was a revelation,' he explained about the moment when, growing up in a mining village not far away, he had borrowed from its library D. H. Lawrence's *The Prussian Officer*. 'I discovered then that my life in that little village was worth writing about.' He presented a copy of his new novel, *The Thin Seam*, due to be published in October and, noted the press report, 'set in the familiar surroundings of a Durham mine'.

But before then, Chaplin was back at his day job, working for the National Coal Board's magazine – in which capacity he was soon travelling to the small mining town of New Cumnock in Ayrshire, where on the night of 7 September a sea of mud swept into Knockshinnoch Castle Colliery, sealing off every exit from the mine. Thirteen men died, but 116 were saved in a heroic rescue operation. To the men stuck underground for 48 hours or more, Chaplin paid tribute for 'their discipline in face of many disappointments, their unswerving obedience to their leader, and to the way they faced tribulation with a joke, a quip or a song'; the 'tired and sleepless' officials won praise, too, with 'their minds geared to the job in hand and the timing of every new move almost miraculous'; and he had a special word for the patient, silent crowds of waiting relatives, who 'obeyed the same canon of discipline' as the trapped men. But when in due course a public inquiry was held, the first under nationalisation, *Coal* would have nothing to say about how the NCB successfully managed, like the old owners before them, to evade responsibility.

Chaplin's novel won generally positive reviews from the provincial press but got a stinker from the far more influential *Times Literary Supplement*. It was 'an uneasy marriage between the theological preoccupations now in vogue and a description of eight hours' work in a coal-mine'; and the anonymous reviewer (in fact the Soho literary dandy Julian Maclaren-Ross) was scornful of the way in which 'the self-educated narrator, who occasionally visualizes himself as a latter-day Saint Francis of Assisi, comes at length to identify the rock-face and the underground darkness with the heart of God's mystery'. Altogether the novel was 'pretentious', lacking even 'some idea of the novelist's true function'. But at least the *TLS* reviewed it, unlike the *Spectator, New Statesman* and most of the other weeklies. 'This kind of thing stings,' a bruised Chaplin wrote to his friend John Bate in November: 'Quite honestly, I've come to the conclusion that the literary world is a closed shop, and that I'm an upstart, non-union, and a menace to be frozen out. Duff Cooper brings out a similar novel (form and shape, I mean) and everybody goes daft about it. Why? The novel, by all accounts, is not only weak but positively infantile. But Duff Cooper is part of that rotten world.' Lodging during the working week in the basement of 29 Redcliffe Square in Earl's Court ('every night I settle down in front of a real coal fire to read and write'), Chaplin soon afterwards found out that *Coal* was intending to keep him on after the end of his year's probation. His salary would rise to a handsome £850, and a baby was on the way (his wife and child were still living in County Durham) – altogether it was 'providential'.[3]

One family continued that autumn to semi-obsess the diarists. Vere Hodgson, more critical than most, reflected towards the end of October on the latest royal doings: 'Princess Anne was christened yesterday. There was a picture of Princess Elizabeth in the Telegraph. I like her expression very much. When Princess Margaret settles down and has a family she may improve. I think her speeches are really silly. I know they are written for her, but the patronage in them is nauseating.' Three weeks later, the First Family assembled at the London Palladium for the annual Royal Variety Performance. As ever, there were many leading British acts, including Gracie Fields, Max Wall, Tommy Trinder, Max Bygraves, Frankie Howerd, Billy Cotton and his Band, Flanagan and Allen, Binnie Hale, Nat Jackley and – controversially – Max Miller. The 'Cheekie Chappie' was told by the co-producer, Val Parnell, that he could not do his usual routine, as it might upset the royal party; in the event he not only dipped into his notorious 'blue book' but overran by eight minutes and thereby delayed the appearance of the big American stars Dinah Shore and Jack Benny. 'I'm *British*!' hissed Miller to an upset Parnell in the wings. The royals apparently loved his performance, while the neurotic, ultra-perfectionist Howerd, in unnecessary despair about how his own turn had gone, was comforted by Parnell passing on the King's verdict that he had 'a very nice personality'.[4]

'Testing Intelligence' was the third of eight talks by Sir Cyril Burt on the Home Service that autumn on 'The Study of the Mind'. In it he demonstrated how 'by carefully planned experiments, the psychologists have discovered what kind of problems an average child of such-and-such an age is just able to answer', and how 'this provides them with a kind of measuring-rod for assessing mental abilities. After then declaring that 'our test-results' clearly revealed that 'intelligence is inherited much as stature is inherited', he concluded portentously: 'Obviously, in an ideal community, our aim should be to discover what ration of intelligence Nature has given to each individual child at birth, then to provide him with the appropriate education, and finally to guide him into the career for which he seems to have been marked out'.

Such sentiments carried weight, given that for over three decades Burt had been the country's foremost educational psychologist, first on behalf of the London county Council (LCC) and then (until his recent retirement) at University College London. By 1950 his twin doctrines – of the scientific validity of intelligence testing and of intelligence as derived primarily from hereditary as opposed to environmental factors – had been influential in two key ways: entrenching the orthodoxy that only about 20 per cent of children had the innate intelligence to make them worthy of an academically demanding education; and, in terms of the testing that would determine who those 20 per cent should be, making it largely an IQ test, which he believed was not as susceptible to teaching or coaching as a more traditional exam in the three Rs. In these immediate post-war years, the Burt approach dominated education – not just in the sense of selection for secondary schools but through the ubiquity of streaming for almost all age groups in almost every type of school. After his death in 1971, it would emerge that, from the mid-1950s anyway, he had fabricated at least some of his data on inherited intelligence and the educational implications. 'It seems probable,' concluded Peter Willmott in his judicious 1977 overview of the revelations, 'that British educational policy and practice were influenced by work which was formerly thought to be scientifically authoritative and has now been discredited.'[5]

At the post-war centre of the Burt legacy was, of course, the 11-plus. The Butler Act of 1944 had made secondary education free and universal, but it was the 11-plus that now, for a whole generation, decided who went to grammar schools and who (much more numerous) went to secondary moderns – or, put another way, who were likely to have a prosperous, middle-class future ahead of them and who were not.

Results day could have a cruelty all of its own. 'The school was gathered together and those who had passed were called up to the podium one at a time with their own round of applause,' recalled the newsreader Peter Sissons about Dovedale Primary School in Liverpool, which he attended from 1947 to 1953 with John Lennon and Jimmy Tarbuck. 'The poor sods who had failed were left sitting in the hall – they only realised they had failed because they were not called up.' The authorities were more sensitive at West Dock Avenue Junior School in a working-class district of Hull near the Fish Dock, where one morning Tom Courtenay was called into the staff room by the headmaster:

He was looking very pleased. 'There's something I've got to tell you.' 'What, sir?' My heart was beating fast. 'You've passed your Eleven Plus. You'll be going to the Kingston High School.' How wonderful. 'What about Arthur [his best friend]?' 'No. You and Billy Spencer. Just you two.' Out of a class of fifty. I was beside myself with excitement . . .

'Can I go and tell me mother, sir?' 'Of course you can.' And I ran the very short distance to our house as fast as my legs would carry me. Mother's face shone with delight when I told her, and we hugged and kissed. I had to go back to lessons, of course, though I could scarcely concentrate. Billy and I had been thought the most likely to pass. Three or four other lads had had hopes, however, and looked very disappointed. Arthur didn't seem fazed.

In general, it may well be that most children who failed the exam were unsurprised and took the news with a shrug of the shoulders. But among those for whom it was a major, even traumatic blow were Harry Webb ('that failure permanently ruined my confidence in any kind of written examination,' he recalled as Cliff Richard) and Brian Clough (from a family of nine brought up on a Middlesbrough council estate and, though he tried to pretend it was only football that mattered, the only one to fail). The customary parental reward for passing was a new bike. John Prescott, sitting the exam in his school in South Yorkshire shortly before his family moved to Cheshire, failed, did not get the bike and thereafter never quite forgave the world.[6]

In 1950 just under 20 per cent of 13-year-olds at local authority-maintained schools in England and Wales went to grammars (though with considerable regional variations), the great majority of them single-sex. There was often an awkward rite of passage for the less well-off new boy or girl. 'Our intake sported heaps of blazers and shiny new satchels,' remembered Courtenay. 'Jacketed in homely tweed, I made do with a not even nearly new imitation leather attaché case in which to carry my homework. I thought it was a contemptible object with which to launch my grammar-school career, and it was a difficult thing to hide.' Understandably, some working-class parents, in their anxiety and/or ignorance, went to the opposite extreme. 'They sent me out for my first day at grammar school weighed down with everything the school catalogue said I should have: rugger boots and cricket boots and football boots and the right number of regulation shorts and all that stuff,' recalled Ray Gosling, son of a Northampton factory mechanic. 'I mean they didn't know. The other kids had a right old time laughing at me on that first day, me with me gear, togged out like somebody about to assault Everest. And I felt so ashamed of my parents, and so proud at the same time.'

The 20 years after the war were the heyday of the grammar school. The images from the male version remain particularly strong – the teachers (often Oxbridge-educated) in their long black gowns, the boys in their caps and blazers, the undeviating rigour of the whole perfor-mance – but possibly the best account we have is of Stockport High School for Girls, which the daughter of an engineering draughtsman, Joan Rowlands (later Bakewell), left in 1951 after seven moulding years:

> I was overwhelmed by a body of women resolved to shape and instruct me in their shared world-view. They were a cohort of the army of self-improvement, steeped in the same entrenched, spinsterly values of learning, duty and obedience, tempered with a little laughter when exams weren't too pressing. The school motto set the high-minded tone:

> > Self-reverence, self-knowledge, self-control,
> > These three alone lead life to sovereign power.

> – lines taken from an obscure poem by Tennyson, 'Oenone', which no one could pronounce. The lines were engraved on the four all stained-glass windows along one wall of the assembly hall, and I fretted regularly about what they might mean . . .

> The school was relentlessly competitive and selective. Even within its grammar-school framework we were streamed into A and B classes. (The As did Latin, the Bs domestic science.) The six houses ['named after significant women of achievement'] competed for a silver cup awarded to 'the most deserving house', the winner arrived at by compiling exam results, with netball and tennis tournaments, house drama compe-titions and musical achievements. There were even awards for deportment – for anything that could be marked. We got hooked: it became a way of life – so much so that a gang of friends within the fifth form set up their own ratings system and subject schedules, marking charts, and fines. I know because I was their secretary . . .

> The rules were remorseless, dragooning us in every particular of behaviour. Uniform even meant the same indoor shoes for every pupil;

hair-ribbons had to be navy blue. The school hat had to be worn at all times to and from the school; girls caught without were in trouble. The heaviest burden was the no-talking rule: no talking on the stairs, in the classroom, in the corridors, in assembly – anywhere, in fact, except the playground. We were a silent school, shuffling noiselessly from class to class, to our lunch, to the cloakroom. Each whisper in the corridor, each hint of communication on the stairs was quashed, conduct marks apportioned and lines of Cicero copied out in detention . . .

Among this welter of disapproval – conduct marks, detentions and, finally, a severe talking-to by Miss Lambrick [the headmistress] – physical chastisement was unnecessary. We were cowed long before things became that bad. The cane in the headmistress's room was redundant. When a girl got pregnant – the worst conceivable crime – she was expelled without fuss before she could contaminate the rest of us.

In Stockport as in most other towns or cities, there was considerable prestige attached to the grammar schools, which perhaps more than any other institution set the moral as well as the intellectual standards of the community, especially but not only among the middle class. And almost all their pupils were deeply imbued with a guilt-free sense of belonging to the present and future local elite.[7]

Bakewell's experience was, for all the constraints, broadly positive. It was different for a tailor's son, the future playwright Steven Berkoff, who went to Raines Foundation Grammar School in Stepney in 1948:

The archaic form of punishment was to be given an 'entry' in the teacher's book for some alleged misconduct. After three pencil entries you would have an *ink entry*, which was getting serious, and after three such entries, which could have been accumulated for nothing more than chatting in class, you would be thrashed with a cane by the PT master. I was the first in my class to suffer this humiliation. I was taken in front of the others and told to bend down. I could not believe the ferocity of the first strike across my tender cheeks. My breath was sucked out of me and I burst into a wail, but suffered two more and then sat down on my three stripes. The stripes became quite severe wheals on my backside. Mum was shocked, but thought it was something to do with grammar school discipline. You accepted your punishment since you always did what you were told.

A year or so later, on the Wirral, Glenda Jackson was starting to rebel at West Kirby Grammar School for Girls. 'When I hit puberty at thirteen the genes kicked in and I became seriously uninterested in scholastic subjects,' she recalled. 'I became part of a group of girls who were less academic. There were cupboards in the classrooms and our great joke was to remove the shelves and sit inside. Then the door would be locked and the key hidden and during the course of the lesson rappings and noises would emanate mysteriously . . .' In due course, she fell three subjects short of the necessary six for her School Certificate and left without going to the sixth form. Her parents were working-class; now in her mid-teens she found herself, despite having been to a grammar, working on one of the long mahogany counters of the local Boots Cash Chemist.

This theatrical trio is completed by a young teacher at Exeter Grammar School, telling his father in late 1949 about his experience at the chalkface. The school, he reported, was

> fairly expensive, has most of the mannerisms of a really good school, and is fundamentally sloppy. The boys are like other grammar school boys, the little ones are very brisk and blasé, and the older ones either earnest or faintly hysterical with unused energy and waiting for jobs or conscription. The Common Room was awful, with an invidious atmosphere of comfort and mock responsibility.

The writer was Robert Bolt, who had just started a teaching diploma at Exeter University and whose vivid insights were admittedly the fruit of only a single day's working visit. If he had been there longer, he would no doubt have highlighted also the snobbery that was so pervasive at grammar schools and was arguably their worst feature. It particularly took the form of aping public schools – not least on the playing fields, where rugby tended to be the socially acceptable, officially endorsed winter sport and football as often as not was accorded pariah status. 'Have finished school until April 12th,' noted a relieved Kenneth Preston at Keighley Grammar School, just before Easter 1951. 'The School has had the usual exhortation from Head about not watching football matches.'[8]

If the unique selling proposition of the grammar schools was their adherence to traditional values, the secondary moderns (which in 1950 educated three times as many 13-year-olds) were supposed to be something entirely fresh and different. 'In the idealistic period of the 1940s,' recalled a leading educational sociologist two decades later, 'it was hoped that in the new schools, freed from the constraint of external examinations, there would be the opportunity to develop a new type of education, enjoying parity of esteem with the academic and specialised curriculum of the grammar school, but of a completely different kind.' A curriculum that was 'essentially experimental rather than traditional, general rather than specialised, practical rather than academic' – that was the ambitious aim. It did not work out. Even by the late 1940s, secondary moderns were under pressure to raise their academic game. The labour market was demanding higher levels of skill, and it was already apparent that the notion that the secondary moderns would achieve 'parity of esteem' by being somehow different yet equal cut little ice with the world in general, where the criteria of success turned on external examinations and the provision of specialised courses. 'Before they can hope to attract children of higher ability they must produce results worthy of comparison with those obtained in grammar schools, and they must do this with the children available to the modern schools here and now,' observed one educationist, John Mander, as early as 1948. Three years later, the introduction of the General Certificate of Education (GCE) O level for 16-year-olds – involving a pass standard set appreciably above the pass mark of the old School Certificate – made the chances of obtaining those results significantly less.[9]

Indeed, it was a contest that took place not only on grammar-school terms but on an almost systemically sloping playing field. The intake at secondary moderns comprised 11-plus failures from a predominantly working-class background, with an additional bias towards the semi-skilled and unskilled; the teachers were academically less well qualified than at grammars and were paid less; overall financial resources per pupil head were similarly inferior; the overwhelming majority of pupils left as soon as they could – ie at the end of the term in which they became 15; and the jobs they went to were in general of much lower socio-economic status than those to which grammar-school leavers went in due course. Bravely enough, not everyone threw in the towel. 'There are now no limits of opportunity for the Secondary Modern School, given enough initiative and encouragement,' declared one optimistic headmistress in 1951. 'Prejudice does still remain, and the social value of the selective school is still uppermost in the minds of too many parents. Much has been done, however, to break down this prejudice, and before long it may completely disappear.' John Prescott – five years in the top stream at the Grange Secondary Modern School in Ellesmere Port but leaving without any academic qualifications – would, for one, take some convincing.[10]

In 1994, half a century after the Butler Act, John Hamilton evoked on television his teaching experience at another secondary modern in Cheshire:

Well, I can well remember when we were taking the classes, some of which were not really interested in education at all. And we had in those days just after the war gardens and vegetable patches, because of food growing, and so we used to take these lads out and just tell them to go and plant things like rhubarb, rhubarb was the best, because they couldn't do any damage to rhubarb. We were happy to let them get on with that quietly. The teacher would go off and have his quiet smoke, and not put too much pressure on them to work hard. They were filling in time, as it were, until the end of their school days.

Children realised that they were failures, and that was embedded in their thinking... The teachers too had that sort of limited vision for their pupils. And all that produced a sort of defeatism.

Another young teacher, the future Tory politician Rhodes Boyson (at this stage strongly pro-Labour), went in 1951 to teach English at Ramsbottom Secondary Modern School in Lancashire – 'run-of-the-mill, healthy and cheerful, with no airs and graces and little idea of what it was supposed to achieve'. Several times a week he endured double periods with 4C in a dilapidated laboratory, which 'contained more illiterates, semi-illiterates and lesson resisters than would normally have been found in a whole township'. In his first lesson he tried reading aloud the latest cricket report by Neville Cardus in the *Manchester Guardian*, but 'within seconds, water and gas taps were turned on and all kinds of Olympic wrestling began to take place on the floor'.

Eventually, he gained a measure of control, but at the same time he became increasingly depressed by what he saw as the unwillingness of the school – and indeed of politicians and education officers more generally – to make a real effort to raise academic standards and address the blight of low expectations. 'The secondary modern schools were a government confidence trick which led inevitably to the campaign for comprehensive schools' would be his conclusion some 40 years later. 'They were so general that no one knew what their purpose was.' Clearly, then, there were limits to the new academic zeal of the secondary moderns; just as clearly, there was a lack of focus about any alternative strategy.

Boyson's experiences were mild compared with those of Edward Blishen, who in 1950 started teaching at Archway Secondary Modern School in north London, where he became art master on account of his long hair. Five years later, he published an unflinchingly realistic autobiographical novel, *Roaring Boys* – 'the story,' as the paperback blurb put it, 'of a young teacher who finds himself plunged into a maelstrom of adolescent violence – a naïve idealist shocked by the brutality around him and finally forced to compromise his beliefs.' During Blishen's barely survivable first term, Class 5 were the worst:

> They were a backward third-year class who inhabited a room peculiarly difficult to teach in. The desks were long ones, rising in tiers. This had the effect that most boys were higher than the teacher, who prowled about in a pit below them. It also meant that the larger part of the class was inaccessible, being cosily tucked away in the hinterland of the long desks. Never was the torment of a raw teacher made more possible. I had them for an odd period of English: 'Spelling, perhaps,' the headmaster had said with hurried vagueness. I would stand before them aware only that I had to secure their interest in an accomplishment that plainly was the last in the world they wanted to acquire . . . I would stand before them. That, on the whole, was all I ever did. I taught nothing. It was always half an hour of crazy fury.
>
> My grasp of what was going on was even weaker than with Class 2. All I knew was that when I came through the door they rose and dreadful remarks filled the air.

'Hiya, mister!'

'Here he is, boys. Give him the works!'

'What's this? A teacher?'

'Let's give the bloke a song!'

Then would follow a dizziness of howls and improbable acts.

'All right,' I would shriek, 'I'll give you some very hard arithmetic'.

Boys would rush to the front. 'You'll want paper, sir.' 'Get Mr What's-'is-name some paper.' 'Blackboard, sir?' 'Up with the blackboard for Mr What-d'ye-call-'im.' And I would watch, fulminating uselessly, while a dozen self-selected blackboard erectors struggled with the easel in an ecstasy of mischief that left the Marx Brothers standing. The rest would be at the cupboard, gleefully flinging its contents into mad confusion, snatching at paper until it flew in a snowstorm through the air. 'All stand!' I would yell. And, cheering, they would struggle to their feet; then, shouting 'All sit!' they would crash their bottoms down again on the benches. There were times when I could hardly believe the evidence of my eyes. Were the Police, the Armed Forces, the Government itself, aware that events of this nature could occur in one of the country's schools before a trained teacher on probation?

Remarkably, Blishen stuck it out as a secondary modern teacher until 1959. 'The battle had already been lost outside the school' began his bleak but humane assessment more than three decades later. 'They'd come already hugely discouraged – so discouraged that most of them had not even entertained the idea of making any use of schooling of any ambitious kind at all. Many of them had become by the age of eleven or twelve so tired of the whole grind of schooling. They'd seen so much teaching which seemed to them to be grudging.' Or, as he concluded: 'Most of the boys knew that the system didn't really care about them and wasn't really bothered if they did badly.'[11]

As for parental attitudes, the first systematic study of their preferences in secondary education was undertaken in 1952 by F. M. Martin in south-west Hertfordshire, in effect Watford and its environs. Printing and precision engineering characterised the local economy, with little heavy industry; manual workers made up two-thirds of Martin's sample of 1,446 parents of children eligible for that year's 11-plus. There emerged a clear correlation between class and attitude:

Father's occupational grade	Percentage who		
	Have thought a lot about child's secondary education	Have thought a little about child's secondary education	Have not thought about child's secondary education
Professional	82.7	9.6	7.7
Clerical	70.2	23.1	6.7
Supervisory	62.0	23.2	14.8
Skilled	50.5	27.1	22.3
Unskilled	35.3	30.7	33.9

When it came to preferred types of secondary school, the percentages were also predictable, with 81.7 per cent of parents from the professional category expressing a preference for a grammar school but only 43.4 per cent from the unskilled group; similarly, 70.2 per cent of professionals thought that the move to secondary school would 'make a lot of difference' in their child's life, compared with 40.8 per cent of unskilled parents. Tellingly, of those parents expressing a preference for a grammar school, only 43.5 per cent of professionals were willing to accept a place in a secondary modern, compared with 75.5, 89.4 and 94.7 per cent of supervisory, skilled and unskilled workers respectively.[12]

The obvious alternative was a private, fee-paying school outside the state system. Here Martin found that whereas 49.4 per cent of professionals for whom a grammar school was the first choice were if necessary willing and able to countenance that route, such a course potentially applied to only 1.5 per cent of unskilled workers. By the early 1950s most private schools were fully subscribed – educating some 180,000 out of a total of 5.5 million children – and as ever there was a mixture of motives involved, including socio-cultural as well as economic and educational ones. 'Yafflesmead is rather like home on a larger scale,' Mrs J. R. Luff (living in Haslemere and married to a businessman) explained to *Picture Post* in 1950 about why they had chosen a private school in Kingsley Green, Sussex. 'It is cosy, no long corridors, no bleak classrooms. The children whom Helen [eight] and Andrew [five] meet there, all have the same kind of background and do not have constantly to adjust themselves to different standards.' For the Rev. J. W. Hubbard, who lived in South Walsham near Norwich, sending his 13-year-old son to a boarding school in Harpenden was all about exercising freedom of choice in the best possible cause: 'I want my children to have a "good" education. Not only proper teaching, but also to learn good language, nice manners. As the Junior State schools are run at present, with their overcrowded classrooms, I do not think they can offer a suitable training in all ways as a private school. I'm sure Laurence has a better chance of getting to the university and of becoming a fully developed person if he is educated at St George's.'[13]

Even setting aside the question of private education – obviously feasible only if it could be afforded – the Hertfordshire survey does suggest an appreciably more fatalistic working-class approach to education: taking what was on offer, and in many cases not even contemplating the possibility of anything better. Clearly there were exceptions, perhaps exemplified by Tom Courtenay's mother, who was keenly aware of the advantages – intellectual as much as material – that a grammar-school education potentially offered. Yet at least as typical in the early 1950s may have been the hostile attitude of the bricklayer father of Bill Perks (later Wyman), who abruptly pulled his son out of Beckenham Grammar School shortly before O levels. 'He'd found me a job working for a London bookmaker,' recalled Wyman. 'There was a big future for me there he said, and eventually, with my expertise at figures, he could open his own betting company. I was dumbfounded, but had no say in the matter.' The headmaster tried to get Wyman's father to change his mind, but he was unbending. Having to leave school 'was a bitter blow to my confidence'.

Among most working-class parents of children at secondary moderns, the impatience with education was far more pronounced – an impatience fully shared by their offspring. 'The school-leaving age had been raised to fifteen two years before,' noted Blishen's narrator of his first term's teaching:

This was still a raw issue with most of the boys and their parents. They felt that it amounted to a year's malicious, and probably illegal, detention. Nothing in the syllabus as yet appeared to justify that extra year. And to

justify it to some of these boys would have required some scarcely imag-
inable feat of seduction. We teachers were nothing short of robbers. We
had snatched a year's earnings from their pockets. We had humiliated
them by detaining them in the child's world of school when they should
have been outside, smoking, taking the girls out, leading a man's life . . .

Preventing any further postponement to raising the school-leaving age
(specifically envisaged in the Butler Act) had been Ellen Wilkinson's
great achievement shortly before her death in February 1947, an achievement that had owed much to her impassioned appeal to fellow-ministers
that it was the 'children of working-class parents' who most needed
that extra year of education after the interruptions of wartime. But for
those actual children and their parents, the cheering was – and remained
– strictly muted.[14]

The pioneering survey of how the 1944 Education Act was playing
out in socio-economic practice was conducted by Hilde Himmelweit
in 1951. Her sample comprised more than 700 13- to 14-year-old boys
at grammar and secondary-modern schools in four different districts
of Greater London. In the four grammars, she found that whereas 'the
number of children from upper working-class homes' had 'increased
considerably' since 1944, 'children from lower working-class homes,
despite their numerical superiority in the population as a whole,
continued to be seriously under-represented' – constituting 'only 15
per cent of the grammar school as against 42 per cent of the modern
school sample'. In those grammars, the middle class as a whole took
on average 48 per cent of the places and the working class as a whole
52 per cent (more than two-thirds by the upper working class). In the
four secondary moderns, by contrast, the middle class averaged 20 per
cent of the places, the working class the other 80 per cent.

Himmelweit then demonstrated how the apparent parity between
the middle and working classes at the grammar schools was deceptive
– not only in the obvious sense that the middle class comprised far
fewer than 48 per cent of the overall population and the working class
far more than 52 per cent but also in terms of how the middle-class
boys consistently outperformed the working-class boys academically.
'The results show that, in the teacher's view, the middle-class boy,
taken all round, proves a more satisfactory and rewarding pupil. He

appears to be better mannered, more industrious, more mature and even more popular with the other boys than his working-class co-pupil.' Furthermore, as a correlation, 'Parents' visits [ie to the schools] increased with the social level of the family and decreased with the number of siblings. Middle-class parents were found more frequently to watch plays and sports.' Unsurprisingly, in these grammar schools far more working-class than middle-class boys expressed the wish to leave before going on to the sixth form, often adding that this was what their parents wanted. Yet simultaneously, 78 per cent of the working-class grammar boys, compared with 65 per cent of the middle-class boys, 'regarded their chances of getting on in the world as better than those their fathers had had'.[15] There was, in other words, a marked discrepancy between aspirations and daily conduct. Himmelweit herself refrained from drawing out any ambitious conclusions from her survey, but it was clear that there was still a long way to go before the existing system of secondary education significantly dissolved entrenched class divisions and very different life chances.

Indeed, it was an egalitarian urge that largely lay behind the hardening rank-and-file mood in the Labour Party by the early 1950s in favour of comprehensive education, with a view to abolishing the divide between grammars and secondary moderns. By the summer of 1951, following intensive pressure from the National Association of Labour Teachers, this was official party policy – but it did not mean that most Labour ministers agreed with it. As Minister of Education since early 1947, George Tomlinson had consistently upheld the primacy of the grammar school and did little to encourage those backing the comprehensive or 'multilateral' alternative. With few exceptions, he either blocked, delayed or watered down the various proposals for new comprehensive schools that came across his desk. He was much struck by the way in which support for comprehensives had proved a vote-loser for Labour at the Middlesex County Council elections in 1949; and, as he frankly if privately put it in early 1951, 'the Party are kidding themselves if they think that the comprehensive school has any popular appeal.' Most Labour local authorities, certainly outside Greater London, were similarly cautious. Even in Coventry, which in 1949 came down decisively in favour of comprehensives, the move has been convincingly attributed far less to ideology than to such practical considerations as 'post-war accommodation, overcrowding, the poor quality of the buildings and the demand for secondary school places from the local population'.

Across England and Wales, the overwhelming force in the early 1950s was still with the actual grammars rather than the notional comprehensives, hardly any of which yet existed. The grammars enjoyed enormous prestige, both locally and nationally. There persisted a widespread, understandable belief that they provided a unique – and, since 1944, uniquely accessible – upwards social escalator for the talented and hard-working; there was a desire to give secondary moderns, the other side of the coin, time to prove themselves; the necessarily large size of London's planned comprehensives, involving a roll of more than 2,000 children in each (in order to achieve a viable sixth form) as opposed to the 800 or so of the average grammar, was a major drawback to those indifferent to the egalitarian aspect; and, of course, the Burt-led orthodoxy about intelligence testing still held almost unchallengeable sway.[16]

Inevitably, the challenge of educating a new, post-war generation was much on people's minds. It was certainly on the mind of the writer and journalist Laurence Thompson, who between the autumn of 1950 and the spring of 1951 travelled the country to produce *Portrait of England* – subtitled *News from Somewhere* in homage to William Morris, whose *News from Nowhere* had predicted 1952 as, in Thompson's words, 'the year of revolution from which Utopia sprang'. In London he was told that as many as a quarter of pupils at grammar schools were removed by their parents at 15 in order to enter the labour market; in Manchester he visited several schools; and elsewhere he was told by a chief education officer of how the situation looked on the frontline. 'Ten per cent above average, fifty to sixty per cent average, and the rest can't really benefit from anything we teach them,' declared his battle-hardened witness. 'The proportions will always be the same, and the problem will always be that below-average minority. All we can hope to do is to swing them over into reasonably decent citizens.' One of the schools Thompson visited in Manchester was a primary, where he was shown 'some extempore prayers' written by children due to take the 11-plus at the end of the calendar year. 'Most contained phrases like, "Lord, help me to work quicker and work harder until December comes."'

Generally, Thompson was struck in that city by how the 'clash between what parents want and what educationists think they ought to have' ran 'right through the system'. After depicting, not implausibly, the fairly brutal home environment of many infant-school pupils – 'these children return to a harassed mother, who has perhaps just rushed home from work, to the quick-tempered clout on the ear, the impatient command, the necessity for getting them out of the way, somehow, while mum gets hubby's dinner ready, during which of course she has no time to be interested, as teacher has, in their small achievements' – he went on: 'The result is a mess, and when junior and secondary modern school teachers, with classes much too large, receive these unfortunate hybrids of enlightened education and unenlightened homes, they complain bitterly about "lack of discipline". And yet these children will be, one hopes, just a little more enlightened than their parents.'

Thompson's ruminations, up to this point entirely characteristic of a generation of activators in their unquestioning assumption of a hierarchy of values, culminated when he went to watch the girls of a secondary modern school in a 'mixed' area give a gymnastic display:

> They had the lithe, long-limbed grace which schoolgirls have, and schoolboys have not. They swung from ropes and leapt over horses with a panache and freedom of limb which took my breath away. I found myself thinking, in the gloomy way one does, that in a few years they would be doping themselves with the pictures three times a week in order to endure their stuffy offices and factories; they would be standing packed in buses; suffering the sniggering, furtive, unlovely approach to love in a cold climate; growing old under the burden of children, household duties, fear of war. But does that matter? For an hour they had flowered to perfection. Why must we always want more, more?[17]

'Could you send me a carton of cigarettes?' Vidia (V. S.) Naipaul asked his family in Trinidad soon after his arrival at Oxford in October 1950 to study at University College. 'Everyone here smokes and everyone offers you, and I have fallen back into the habit . . . They are so expensive here.' The next few months were a winter of not always welcome discovery. 'I have eaten potatoes every day of my stay in England, twice a day at Oxford,' he reported from London in December. And in January, back in Oxford:

The English are a queer people. Take it from me. The longer you live in England, the more queer they appear. There is something so orderly, and yet so adventurous about them, so ruttish, so courageous. Take the chaps in the college. The world is crashing about their heads, about all our heads. Is their reaction as emotional as mine? Not a bit. They ignore it for the most part, drink, smoke, and imbibe shocking quantities of tea and coffee, read the newspapers and seem to forget what they have read.

The following month, still in Oxford, the future novelist sounded like a future entrepreneur. 'It is impossible to get rich,' Naipaul grumbled to his family. 'The income taxes are ridiculously high – about nine shillings in the pound after a certain stage, and it probably will go up with this heavy expenditure on re-armament.' After noting that 'everything has a purchase tax,' he concluded: 'For living, this country. For making money, somewhere else.'[18]

Naipaul was fortunate not to be a housewife during this first full winter of the 1950s – a winter of high prices and continuing, even in some cases worsening, shortages. Phyllis Willmott, by this time a young, hard-up mother living in Hackney, reflected in November on the damage being done to the Labour government, which she keenly supported:

I sometimes wonder whether *any* socialists apart from me are registered at our Co-op. 'It's near starvation – no other country in the world puts up with what we do. All the rest have all the meat they want,' I heard someone moaning the other day. And the dreadful thing is that no one took the woman up on what she said. Certainly I didn't. Everyone gave non-committal sighs and grunts. Of course, I should speak up. But why don't I? One reason is because the housewife bit of me finds it hard to defend. I mean, 8d worth of meat! What housewife who has to queue for this can believe she and her other housewives have not got a grievance.

The Ministry of Food had badly messed up over the importation of meat, especially from the Argentine; the result was indeed a desperately inadequate weekly ration, working out at around 4 ounces of beefsteak or 5 ounces of imported lamb chops.

Another housewife, Nella Last in Barrow, recorded her shopping trip on the first Saturday of the New Year:

I wanted a rabbit – I didn't feel like paying the 10d return on the bus to get 2/- worth of meat! I'd rubber Wellingtons, my W.V.S. overcoat and hooded mac on, but the cold seemed to penetrate & every one looked pinched & cold. I paid my grocery order & left one for Monday, & got last week's & this week's eggs – four. There was a really *good* display of meat in the window but no one was interested – tins of gammon ham about I should think 1 lb. were 9/6, & Danish & Dutch 'minced pork in natural juices' at 4/6 & 5/6 for quite a small tin. As one woman remarked 'they don't say any thing of the thick layer of fat, which with the "natural juices" made up more than half of the tin *I* got.' By queuing, I could have got pork sausage for 1/10 a pound, but felt it mightn't agree with either of us. Sausage nowadays seems to contain so *much* fat . . .

Exactly a week later, a third housewife, Judy Haines in Chingford, was also getting fed up. 'I went out after dinner and what a joint!' she recorded. 'The ration is so small it's very difficult to tell what cut it is at the best of times. Argentina seems to be putting a fast one across us, knowing we need her meat, & we'll have no more of it.' She added, 'There's a fuel crisis on, too. *We* have a good supply of coal but let our coke run low as it's off ration & supposed to be plentiful and we're out of it for some time.'

A meat shortage, a fuel crisis, a flu epidemic, a hastily conceived and overambitious rearmament programme having a sharp impact on the consumer: altogether, it was not a happy picture in early 1951. By March it was being reported that as many as 1,700 in a single day were making enquiries about how to emigrate to Canada. But Richard Dimbleby would have none of it. 'I can only speak for myself,' he declared in his staunchly patriotic column in the *Sunday Chronicle*. 'Nothing on earth would ever persuade me to have my home anywhere but in England, where my ancestors have lived ever since they sacked and burned the farms of East Anglia fifteen hundred years ago.'[19]

About the same time, Mass-Observation put the question to the female members of its panel: 'What are your feelings about housework?' Predictably, there was no shortage of replies, from housewives of varying ages and varying degrees of contentment:

I think housework becomes infinitely easier with the right tools. I consider *every* housewife should be able to have a washing machine, a proper wringer, a vacuum cleaner and a refrigerator. Without these tools, a lot of the work is a drudgery and the result is either the woman doggedly keeps on at her work becoming a kind of martyred housewife, or she just skips the lot and a fusty dusty house results. *(37)*

I like Monday least as after a slight relaxation of work on Sunday I find it very hard to get going again on Monday. I dislike washing as I have such a heavy morning and get very tired through standing at the sink. I dislike having my hair damped by steam but refuse to wear any head-covering. Hate the wrinkled appearance of my hands on Monday and usually feel cold. *(40)*

I don't kick against pricks that are unavoidable, but don't pretend I find housework entrancing. *(56)*

The job I like least is 'washing the front' which my mother-in-law insists ought to be done every week – and because I couldn't sit back and see her doing it – I have more or less taken this on altogether – I must admit she does it occasionally if I let it go more than about 10 days. *(25)*

I have a strong sense of beauty and order, and rather enjoy housework. *(59)*

I think housework is an utter waste of time when there are so many more interesting things to be done. *(27)*

Whether she enjoyed it or loathed it, housework was now an inescapable part of life for the servantless and as yet relatively gadgetless average middle-class woman. 'Such a programme for today!' recorded an exhausted Judy Haines on the last Wednesday of March. 'Houseworked like a nigger all morning. Baked during afternoon. Really felt dazed by nightfall.'

Mass-Observation also asked its male panellists how they imagined women felt about housework. 'Women usually really enjoy housework,' replied an industrial chemist, drawing on his experience as an unmarried 28-year-old. 'Those who hate housework are rare.' A married civil servant, 37 and with two boys, was far less sanguine about his wife's attitude: 'I would indeed be a fool if I did not know that she gets fed up to the teeth with it at times living as we do in two rooms and a scullery with no bathroom.' But according to a married police inspector, 48, 'women are keenly jealous of the house – they regard it as their province and to trespass on the preserves is to risk wrath'. Another, higher-profile panellist, Ralph Wightman of *Any Questions?*, would have agreed. Asked during a programme from the Corn Exchange in Plymouth the previous autumn if it was still 'a man's world', his answer was wholly unreconstructed:

> I think that, generally speaking quite seriously, in this country, most woman's work is at home – that's a platitude I know but it is true, and they can make up their minds just how they do the work and when they do it – they usually do it in a most inefficient manner I might say. But – they're the person who decides this is the day for the bedrooms and tomorrow is the day for the washing and next day for the ironing and they fix it and they do it. Whereas, most men, almost all of us, have got to do in our working life precisely what we're told, and that is much less pleasant, much less independence – real independence, and after all, we do earn most of the money anyway, so why shouldn't we have a little relaxation occasionally when we're allowed to escape from this terrific dominance of the home. *(LAUGHTER.)*

A little deserved relaxation, then, for the menfolk – but most Saturday afternoons not for the long-suffering supporters of Accrington Stanley, who in March 1951 took their scarves, mufflers and rattles to Valley Parade and watched their team go down to a 0–7 defeat at the hands of Bradford City. Two injuries reduced the visitors – in what were still pre-substitute days – to nine men. The suffering was not yet over, and the *Accrington Observer* described the match's aftermath:

> The driver pulled his vehicle up, dashed round to the luggage compartment and dragged out the first-aid kit. Swabs were needed to staunch the flow of blood. A few minutes later, he did the same thing, this time because there was an inert passenger in need of revival to consciousness. From a nearby house, a kindly soul produced a cup of hot tea. An ambulance on its way from a battlefront? No, just Accrington Stanley on a routine journey home from yet another heartbreak match in this, the blackest season in the club's history.[20]

The radio remained in the early 1950s a mass medium capable of commanding huge loyalty. 'Listeners welcomed back the Bentley-Nichols-Edwards team with delight, and found the new script and situations as witty, lively and irresistibly amusing as ever,' noted the BBC's audience-research newsletter in November 1950, with the first episode of the new series of *Take It From Here* having been heard by 38 per cent of the adult population. Not long afterwards, a staggering 57 per cent listened to *Variety Cavalcade*, a star-packed programme from the London Palladium celebrating a century of British music hall; no fewer than one in three were listening to *Educating Archie* by the end of its first series; and on Christmas Day, after 62 per cent had heard the King's broadcast at 3 p.m., 'roughly two out of three listeners kept their sets on and nearly all of them heard *Wilfred Pickles' Christmas Party* on the Light Programme' – an eloquent tribute to the pulling power, and centrality in British popular culture, of the star of *Have a Go!*

There was also the immensely popular panel game *Twenty Questions*, each week featuring the Mystery Voice ('and the next object is . . .'). Its regular chairman by early 1951 – by which time the programme was also running on Radio Luxembourg but with a rival line-up – was an irascible, highly knowledgeable former schoolmaster starting to make a name for himself. 'I often wonder if Gilbert Harding *could* be as pompous & "condescending" as he sounds,' reflected Nella Last one Monday evening in March. A fortnight later, she came back to the subject: 'Gilbert Harding was in a less "pompous" mood – why, when I listen to that undoubtedly clever man, do I get the impression that he is a "prisoner" within himself – that he is shy, sensitive, even in his most "cutting" moods? Odd!'[21]

Meanwhile, at 11.00 each weekday morning, *Mrs Dale's Diary* was being listened to by some 13 per cent of adults. 'The Dales are, without a doubt, accepted as typical of an ordinary, suburban, professional family – people who might easily be listeners' neighbours,' purred the BBC's newsletter in October 1950. From the start of 1951, however, they had a rural rival. 'What we need is a farming *Dick Barton*,' a Lincolnshire farmer, Henry Burtt of Dowsby, had declared at a meeting in Birmingham in June 1948 of farmers and Ministry of Agriculture officials – a meeting convened by the producer of agricultural programmes for the BBC Midland Region, Godfrey Baseley, part of whose remit was to encourage small farmers to modernise their methods and thereby increase their output. Baseley took the remark to heart, and almost exactly two years later a pilot week of *The Archers* was successfully broadcast on the Midland Region. The aim, he explained in a memo soon afterwards, was to give an 'accurate' and 'reassuring' picture of country life in Ambridge, drawing 'portraits of typical country people' and 'following them at work and at play and eaves-dropping on the many problems of living that confront country folk in general'. Roughly 15 per cent of each programme would comprise farming advice and information, but there would be sufficient emphasis on entertainment to keep the attention of 'the general listener, i.e. the townsman'.

On New Year's Day 1951, 'an everyday story of country folk', as *The Archers* was invariably billed, began its three-month trial on the Light Programme, rather awkwardly going out only half an hour after Mrs Dale. Even in its first week, however, it attracted audiences double those of *Morning Story*, the programme it had replaced; soon afterwards it was being 'listened to rather more by town than by country dwellers', with as yet only 1.6 per cent of the upper middle class tuning in, as compared to 6 per cent of the working class. The turning point came at Easter, when the programme moved to the choice spot of 6.45 p.m., thereby dislodging (indeed killing off) *Dick Barton* itself; within a week it was being listened to by 10 per cent of the adult population. As with any soap, most people were hooked primarily for human-interest reasons, but almost certainly there was something else going on. 'A gentle relic of Old England, nostalgic, generous, incorruptible and (above all) valiant' was how the BBC publicity machine described the village of Ambridge. 'In other words the sort of British community that the rootless townsman would like to live in and can involve himself in vicariously.'[22]

The BBC itself remained in the early 1950s the starchiest, most paternalistic of organisations. Three weeks after the launch of *The Archers*, it ordained that news bulletins on national radio were henceforth to be read only by men – and what was more, men (including a youngish Robert Dougall) with 'consistent' pronunciation, in other words devoid of a regional accent. 'Experience has shown that a large number of people do not like the news of momentous or serious events to be read by the female voice' was the smooth official explanation for the gender aspect. Even more typical of the BBC's stuffiness was its continuing half-hearted attitude towards television. 'This invasion of our homes must cause something of an upset in family life' was how in symptomatic, authentically Auntie tones the Controller of Scottish Broadcasting, Melville Dinwiddie, would only semi-celebrate in *Radio Times* Scotland's inclusion in March 1952 in the national television service:

> Sound broadcasting as such is upsetting enough when reading and school lessons and other home tasks have to be done, but here is a more intensely absorbing demand on our leisure hours, and families in mid-Scotland will have to make a decision both about getting a receiver and about using it. At the start, viewing will take up much time because of its novelty, but discrimination is essential so that not every evening is spent in a darkened room, the chores of the house and other occupations neglected. We can get too much even of a good thing.

This genuine, high-minded concern about the possible impact of television on family well-being directly echoed fears expressed by the guardians of the nation's spiritual health – foremost among them T. S. Eliot. 'I find only anxiety and apprehension about the social effects of this pastime, and especially about its effect on small children,' he wrote to *The Times* in late 1950 after a visit to America, where television was much more common. One BBC man had already had enough by then of the Corporation's lack of dynamism in relation to the young medium. This was Norman Collins, who on his way to becoming Controller of Television had been a successful publisher and best-selling novelist (*London Belongs To Me*). In October 1950 he resigned: partly in protest against, in his words, 'a vested interest in sound broadcasting' being 'allowed to stand in the way of the most adventurous development of television', and partly because he had come to believe that British television would remain stunted until the BBC was compelled to relinquish its monopoly – a position naturally anathema to the Corporation. There was an opportunistic streak in Collins, and he now devoted his formidable energies to ending that monopoly at the earliest possible moment.[23]

In fact, this was a question already under sustained public scrutiny, in particular through the forum of a government-appointed committee (largely of the great and good, under the chairmanship of Lord Beveridge) that since the summer of 1949 had been considering the future of broadcasting. Reporting on 18 January 1951, its main conclusion was that leaving broadcasting in the hands of a single, public-service, not-for-profit provider remained overall to the public benefit, provided that the BBC made 'steady progress towards greater decentralisation, devolution and diversity'. In effect, Beveridge accepted Lord Reith's argument (advanced in his 1949 autobiography) that only 'the brute force of monopoly' could preserve the BBC's standards, which otherwise would be dragged downwards by commercial competition.

On the day the report appeared, the *Evening Standard* solicited the views of two readers: Geoffrey Schofield (41, a chartered accountant, living in Purley, married with two daughters) and Eva Cornish-Bowden (27, married to an engineer, living in Orpington, two children). Between them they represented what was a fairly evenly divided state of public opinion:

> *Schofield*: At present we don't want competition. Why? I'll tell you. TV is an innovation now. There is no doubt it is going to have an extraordinarily important influence on national life as it progresses. Are we going to develop into a push-button nation when we turn on entertainment at will, or are we going to use this new medium as a basis for increasing and improving the average intelligence of the country?
>
> *Cornish-Bowden*: I bought a television set and I want to be either cleverly entertained or vulgarly entertained. I want to be able to pick my programmes. I feel strongly about that. I want to twiddle the switch of my set and get something I want to see. Not have something I don't want to see pushed on to me.[24]

In terms of the politics, almost everyone knew that the Beveridge line would continue to hold – at least with any certainty – only as long as Labour stayed in power. On the Conservative side there were already significant elements strongly in favour of introducing a commercial rival to the BBC, and plenty of businessmen were well aware that there was serious money to be made if Britain followed the bracing American path.

Whatever the anxieties, there was little real danger of square eyes in the early 1950s. On most weekdays, the single television channel broadcast only from 3.00 to 6.00 p.m. (including *Children's Hour*), followed by two hours of a blank screen (the so-called 'toddler's truce' intended to enable mothers to get their small children to bed), followed by two or so more hours of programmes. There were also major gaps in coverage: wholly inadequate news and current affairs, few meaningful sporting transmissions and virtually no light entertainment (including comedy) as a genre in its own right. *How Do You View?* (starring Terry-Thomas as the smiling, gap-toothed, upper-class cad invariably sporting a cigarette holder) was a partial exception, but its reliance on gags and wisecracks left room for the invention of proper situation comedy. For many people, television was as yet an undiscovered pleasure. 'The great surprise they sprang on me was they have a Television Set,' noted Vere Hodgson after visiting friends over Easter 1951. 'So after a lovely meal Neville just switched it on and behold we saw Picture Page. I DID enjoy it.'

That same day, Florence Speed in Brixton watched the Oxford crew sink in the Boat Race: 'Poor things. We saw it so well on T.V.' But four days later came a cruel blow: 'Fred's T.V. set has had to be taken away for repair. Something has gone wrong with it & Collins' man said they would have to get in touch with Ekco the makers so that he could give no promise about its return.' A keen viewer of *In the News*, Speed thus missed a memorable edition two days afterwards on 30 March. 'It was the occasion of a serious row between A.J.P. Taylor and Michael Foot on the one side and me on the other,' recorded W. J. Brown:

In the show we had much talk from Taylor about the West End restaurants of the rich and their Rolls Royce cars and so on – the sort of stuff I have had from Foot before. I couldn't stand any more of it and said – 'Taylor, you know this is the most disingenuous stuff. You and I have just come from an expensive West End restaurant. We have come in a fine Rolls Royce car. Can't we get away from the Socialism of envy, hatred, malice and all uncharitableness?

'Immediately the show ended,' he added, 'I was attacked with astonishing ferocity by Michael Foot who was livid with rage. He accused
me of bringing in "personal matters" – though he is by far the most
"personal" member of the team.'[25]

At least once a week, the evening's schedule was dominated by a
play, often long enough to leave little time for anything else. The
concept of writing a play specifically for television was unborn, so
invariably it was an adaptation – as often as not of something worthy
rather than necessarily enjoyable – or the rather stilted transmission
of an actual theatrical performance. One Sunday evening in the spring
of 1950, the choice was Eliot's *The Family Reunion*, which received
from the BBC's recently established Television Panel of viewers the
pitiful 'Reaction Index' (running from 1 to 100) of 25, 'the lowest so
far recorded'. That summer, on another Sunday evening, Karel Capek's
The Insect Play picked up a 34, the lowest yet for any play apart from
the Eliot. 'This was a wash out – they all left me viewing on my own,'
complained one Panel member. There was little more appetite by 1951
for the difficult or challenging. 'The play on the first Sunday evening
of the New Year was Christopher Fry's *A Phoenix Too Frequent*,'
noted the viewer-research newsletter. 'With a Reaction Index of 44, it
did not have a much warmer reception than had his earlier play, *The
Lady's Not for Burning*, with 41.' A typical reaction was quoted: 'I
managed to yawn my way through it.' By comparison, a programme
soon afterwards featuring Wilfred Pickles's visit to Stratford-upon-
Avon got an RI of 69, while the Mineworkers' National Amateur
Boxing Championship that spring won an 85. Still, there would be
some encouragement for the Reithians when in early 1952 *The Cocktail
Party* managed a 60. 'T.S. Eliot!' declared a Panel member. 'Prepared
for the worst but pleasantly surprised.'[26]

Eliot and Fry were the two key figures in a new movement – a movement initiated by the latter's *The Lady's Not for Burning*, a huge West
End success in 1949 (featuring Claire Bloom and Richard Burton in
supporting roles). 'In a post-war theatre that had little room for realism,'
noted Michael Billington in his 2005 obituary, 'Fry's medieval setting,
rich verbal conceits and self-puncturing irony delighted audiences, and
the play became the flagship for the revival of poetic drama.' Anthony
Heap, a dedicated first-nighter, was not a fan. Labelling Fry as 'that

current darling of the quasi-highbrows and pseudo intellectuals', he described in his diary in January 1950 attending the premier of Fry's next play, *Venus Observed*: 'As the evening wore laboriously on, it became increasingly apparent that . . . Mr Fry's new blank verse effusion bore a closer resemblance to its predecessor . . . than it did to a play, being equally devoid of genuine dramatic interest.' Gladys Langford, going to the St James's Theatre a day or two later, agreed: 'Oh, what a welter of words! Oh, what an absence of action!' Soon afterwards, Mollie Panter-Downes noted how the play (starring Laurence Olivier) was proving 'a smash box-office hit' despite or perhaps because of receiving 'bemused notices from most of the critics, who professed themselves entranced, though whacked by what it was all about'. She reflected on how the play showed 'all Fry's bewildering, glittering gift for language, unfortunately mixed with a deadly facetiousness that at its worst makes his lines sound like a whimsical comedian's double-talk'.

May saw the West End premier of Eliot's *The Cocktail Party*, which, notwithstanding Heap's hostile verdict – 'Do poets who write plays *have* to be so damnably enigmatic? Or is that just their little joke?' – went on to enjoy a considerable vogue. Early in 1951, some two months after Lawrence Daly had fallen asleep listening to *Venus Observed* on the radio, the *New Statesman*'s perceptive drama critic, T. C. Worsley, sought to contextualise the apparently irresistible rise of verse drama:

What we have seen is the development in the theatre-going public of a new hunger for the fantastic and the romantic, for the expanded vision and the stretched imagination, in short for the larger-than-life. This is easily explainable as a natural reaction from the sense of contraction which pervades at least the lives of the middle classes; and it is still the middle classes who make up the bulk of the theatre-going public.

'If they are finding that they can afford to do less and less,' he concluded with an obligatory sneer at these suburbanites, 'it at least costs no more to please the fantasy with extravagances than to discipline it with dry slices of real life.'[27]

Even so, and whatever the merits or otherwise of this latest fashion, it is difficult to deny the generally sterile, unadventurous state of the

British theatre by the early 1950s. It did not help that the Lord Chamberlain continued to exercise his time-honoured powers of censorship over the precise content of plays. Nor was it helpful that the H. M. Tennent theatrical empire, run from an office at the Globe in Shaftesbury Avenue by Hugh ('Binkie') Beaumont, possessed close to a stranglehold over what was and was not performed in the West End. Beaumont's standards were high, with a penchant for lavishly mounted classic revivals as star vehicles. Typical productions in 1951 included Alec Guinness in *Hamlet*; Laurence Olivier and Vivien Leigh in *Antony and Cleopatra* and *Caesar and Cleopatra* on alternate nights; Gladys Cooper in Noël Coward's *Relative Values*; Celia Johnson and Ralph Richardson in *The Three Sisters*; and John Gielgud and Flora Robson in *The Winter's Tale*. What there was virtually no encouragement for was drama that dealt with contemporary issues. Arguably one of the few playwrights to do so was the immensely popular Terence Rattigan – but only in the sense that his work tapped so deftly into the anxieties and neuroses of the economically straitened post-war middle class. Rattigan himself wrote in 1950 a famous essay denouncing what he called 'the play of ideas' and declaring that 'the best plays are about people and not about things'.[28] It was a proposition that, as 'Binkie' would have agreed, made commercial sense.

If there was one play that epitomised – for good as well as ill – British theatre before the revolution, it was perhaps N. C. Hunter's *Waters of the Moon*. Norman Hunter was a Chekhov-loving retired schoolmaster and obscure playwright; his play, taken up by Beaumont, was set in a shabby-genteel hotel on the edge of Dartmoor, and the first night, with Edith Evans (in evening gowns designed by Hardy Amies), Sybil Thorndike and Wendy Hiller all in leading roles, backed by Donald Sinden as assistant stage manager, was on 19 April 1951 at the Haymarket. An 'enchanting bitter-sweet comedy', thought Heap, 'richly endowed with acutely observed and sympathetically drawn characters'. And, he predicted, 'It is the kind of play that has cast-iron, box-office success written all over it.' The critics were on the whole friendly, with Worsley again on the money. Although finding *Waters* a play unworthy of 'our incomparable Edith Evans', he reckoned that it 'will, all the same, find a large public, the public which so enjoyed Miss Dodie Smith's plays before the war'. He observed that although

Hunter had 'added to the formula some rather crude borrowings from the Russians', his play remained 'essentially a cosy middle-brow, middle-class piece, inhabited by characters by no means unfamiliar in brave old Theatreland' – including 'the maid-of-all-work daughter of the house' (Hiller) and 'a lost relic of the poor, dear upper-middle-classes' (Thorndike).

Worsley and Heap guessed right: the play ran for more than two years and grossed more than £750,000. But for Hunter, despite a couple of reasonable successes later in the fifties, the tide would go out almost as quickly as it had come in, and he died in 1971 a semi-forgotten figure. Seven years later, the Haymarket staged a revival of *Waters*, with Hiller returning to the fray. The theatre management, trying to keep a lid on costs, asked the playwright's Belgian widow Germaine whether it would be acceptable to pay a reduced author's royalty. Germaine, through a spiritual medium, consulted Norman, and Norman replied that it would not.[29]

Their Own Private Domain

'I almost immediately began to cry,' wrote Gladys Langford in north London on the first Monday of April 1951. 'The climbing of steps, the squalor of some of the households, the inability to get a reply & the knowledge that I should have to retread the streets again and again, reduced me to near hysteria.' She was working as a paid volunteer for that month's Census – the first for 20 years and inevitably the source of much relevant data, most especially about housing conditions.

Out of a total of 12.4 million dwellings surveyed in England and Wales, it emerged that 1.9 million had three rooms or less; that 4.8 million had no fixed bath; and that nearly 2.8 million did not provide exclusive use of a lavatory. Overall, in terms of the housing stock, almost 4.7 million (or 38 per cent) of dwellings had been built before 1891, with some 2.5 million of them probably built before 1851. Put another way, the great majority of houses in 1951 without the most basic facilities had been put up by Victorian jerry-builders. The Census, moreover, revealed a significant quantitative as well as qualitative problem: although the official government estimate was that the shortage was around 700,000 dwellings, the most authoritative subsequent working of the data would produce a figure about double that.[1] Of course, it was hardly news that there was a housing problem, but the Census reinforced just how severe that problem was.

Naturally there were major regional variations, even between the large urban areas where most of the substandard housing was concentrated. The following table, derived from the Census, gives the broad picture outside London and Scotland:

Survey Areas	Occupied dwellings with three rooms or less		Households without a fixed bath		Households without exclusive use of a lavatory	
	Number	%	Number	%	Number	%
Tyneside and Sunderland	113,140	42	121,990	42	54,800	19
Durham Coalfield	31,130	40	43,160	54	20,550	26
West Yorkshire	194,000	36	224,590	40	155,230	27
South Yorkshire	38,380	16	114,670	46	34,280	14
East Lancashire	113,990	14	365,080	42	93,170	11
South Lancashire	130,020	10	57,130	49	11,430	10
Liverpool and Bootle	26,140	12	86,350	37	40,000	17
Stoke-on-Trent	7,010	9	41,730	53	10,060	13
Birmingham and The Black Country	66,490	13	210,740	38	111,830	20
South Wales – The Valleys	11,050	6	123,770	66	40,120	21
Survey Areas	731,350	23	1,389,210	43	571,470	19
England and Wales Urban Average	–	16	–	35	–	18

Between the autumn of 1949 and that of 1950, a sociologist, K. C. Wiggans, surveyed living and working conditions in Wallsend, the shipbuilding town near Newcastle upon Tyne from which T. Dan Smith came. Most of the men surveyed lived in the riverside district, consisting 'almost entirely of old houses, many of them condemned and overcrowded'. Wiggans highlighted one man, who 'said that he, and eight others, were occupying a four-roomed upstairs flat, consisting of two bedrooms, a boxroom and a kitchen':

The subject and his wife, a son aged eight, and an unmarried daughter of eighteen slept in one room; a married son, wife and child, aged two, slept and lived in another, whilst a son, aged twenty-one, slept in the kitchen, and an old grandfather had the box room. There was no bath, no hot water, no electric light and the lavatory was down in the backyard. The ceilings and walls of the house were rotten with damp; in wet weather the rain streamed through the roof, with the result that no food could be stored for more than a day or two without going bad.

'A very large proportion of the houses which were visited in this area,' added Wiggans, 'had these particular problems, to a greater or lesser degree.'

Soon afterwards, John R. Townsend visited for the *New Statesman* the 'huge, crazy entanglement of sooty streets sprawling over the southern half of Salford, from Broad Street to the Docks'. Focusing particularly on Hanky Park, the district that had been the setting for Walter Greenwood's *Love on the Dole*, he found 'a fair, perhaps slightly worse than average, specimen of a northern city slum':

> Blackened, crumbling brick, looking as if only its coating of grime held it together; streets so narrow that you need hardly raise your voice to talk to your neighbour across the way; outdoor privies in odorous back entries; dirt everywhere, and no hot water to fight it with; rotting woodwork which doesn't know the touch of fresh paint; walls which often soak up the damp like blotting-paper – in short, nothing really exceptional.

In Salford as a whole, out of the city's 50,000 houses, no fewer than 35,000 were more than 60 years old, with the overwhelming majority having neither bath nor hot water. Would things change? After noting how in 1948 some Salford schoolchildren had been asked to write 'about where they would really like to live', with many expressing 'wild longings to be away from Salford, in reach of the country, the sea, the mountains', Townsend concluded pessimistically: 'As things are shaping at present, it is hardly more than a hope that their children's own children will avoid being born and bred in the back streets.'[2]

The housing situation was even worse in Scotland, where in 1950 it was estimated that around 1.4 million out of a population of some five million were 'denied a reasonable home-life' through having to endure overcrowding, squalor, lack of sanitation and so on. Glasgow above all remained a byword for dreadful housing. The 1951 Census revealed that a staggering 50.8 per cent of the city's stock comprised dwellings of only one or two rooms, compared with 5.5 per cent for Greater London; while in terms of the percentage of population living more than two per room, the respective figures were 24.6 and 1.7. Overall, Glasgow's residential density in 1951 was 163 persons per acre – compared with 48 for Birmingham and 77 for Manchester, both of which English cities thought with good reason that they had major housing problems. Probably nowhere in Glasgow was the squalor greater than in the Hutchesontown district of the Gorbals. There the density was no fewer than 564 persons per acre, with almost 89 per cent of its dwellings (often part of pre-1914 tenements) being of one or two rooms, usually with no bath and frequently with no lavatory of their own. For Glasgow as a whole, it was reckoned by the early 1950s that as many as 600,000 people – well over half the city's population – needed rehousing.[3] It was a daunting (if to some invigorating) statistic.

––––––––––

The majority of housing in the Gorbals was in the hands of private landlords, as in 1951 it was in the case of 51 per cent of the stock in England and Wales (compared with 57 per cent in 1938). Rented housing was, in other words, the largest single sector of the market, and it was a sector in deep, long-term trouble.

'Never receiving any "improvements", never painted, occasionally patched up in the worst places at the demand of the Corporation' – such was the reality in 1950 of the privately rented housing that dominated the Salford slums. For, as Townsend explained:

> Owners say that on the present rents they cannot afford to pay to keep their property fit for habitation, and it is a fact that many of them will give you whole streets of houses for nothing, and ten shillings into the bargain for the trouble of signing the deeds, if you are stupid enough to do so. Some owners have merely disappeared without trace, leaving the rents (and the repairs) to look after themselves until the Corporation steps in.

Soon afterwards, a senior Glasgow housing official confirmed the trend: 'Forty years ago there were many empty houses but few abandoned by their owners. Today there are no empty houses yet many have been abandoned by their owners.'[4]

There were two principal reasons why the private landlord was, in

some cities anyway, in almost headlong retreat. Firstly, a welter of
rent-control legislation, going back to 1915 and involving a freezing
of rent levels from 1939, was indeed a significant deterrent. 'Before
the war, people were willing to pay between one-quarter and one-sixth
of their income on rent,' noted the *Economist*'s Elizabeth Layton in
1951. 'Now they are not so prepared because they have become accustomed to living cheaply in rent-controlled houses and do not appreciate
that, while incomes have increased, rents have lagged behind what is
required to keep old property in repair or to cover the annual outgoings
of new houses.' Undoubtedly at work was an instinctive, widespread
dislike of the private landlord, and this sentiment particularly affected
the second reason for the rented sector's difficulties: namely, government reluctance to help much when it came to making grants for
improvements and repairs. Bevan's 1949 Housing Act did offer the
promise of some assistance, but he was not a minister ever likely to
embrace the landlord as one of his great causes. The hope – at least
on the left – was that sooner rather than later huge swathes of urban
slum clearance would in the process come close to finishing off the
private landlord altogether.

Not all rented housing was wretched, but it does seem that precious
little of it was conducive to the good life. Away from the out-and-out
slum areas, perhaps fairly typical of these immediate post-war years
was the situation in which the Willmotts (Peter, Phyllis and baby son
Lewis) found themselves in the early 1950s. Desperate for somewhere
to live on their own, they landed up in Hackney, occupying (in Phyllis's
words) 'the top two floors of a plain, yellow-brick Victorian house
hemmed in on three sides by streets', including a main road to Dalston
Junction. They had two rooms and a kitchen on the first floor, and a
large room on the floor above, but it was still a pretty dispiriting experience:

> The stairs were meagrely covered with well-worn lino; kitchen, bedroom
> and hall were painted in nondescript shades of beige, and in our sitting-
> room there was a depressing patterned wallpaper of pink and brown ferns.
> The landlord was proud of these decorative features and made it clear
> that he would not permit any changes to them ... We had the use of the
> bath in the kitchen of the ground-floor tenants. We seldom exercised this

right because it was too much trouble to fix a convenient time (and I was afraid of the explosive noises made by the very old geyser). We had to make do with hot water from a gas heater that the landlord allowed us to install over the kitchen sink – at our own expense. There was one shared lavatory on the ground floor, and shared use of the neglected patch of ground that could hardly be called a back garden but could be used to hang out the washing by tenants.

It was much the same for another young family in Swansea. 'It is a ground-floor flat in an ill-built house, rather too small and with no room to put anything,' Kingsley Amis wrote to Philip Larkin in December 1949 from 82 Vivian Road, Sketty, Swansea, which for the previous few weeks had been home for himself, his wife Hilly and two small children, including the infant Martin. 'There are fourteen steps between the front-door and the street, and most of the time I am carrying a pram or a baby up or down them.' Over the next year, the Amis family lived in three other rented places, including two small flats on Mumbles Road, before in early 1951 a small legacy enabled them to buy a house. 'These were primitive places with shared bathrooms and in one case an electric cooker that guaranteed shocks for the user,' notes an Amis biographer; he adds that they were the model for the Lewises' flat in *That Uncertain Feeling* (1955) – a novel in which the Amis-like hero is in a state of perpetual guerrilla warfare with the censorious, small-minded Mrs Davis on the ground floor, where she converts her kitchen door 'into an obstacle as impassable as an anti-tank ditch'.[5]

The growth area in housing by this time was undoubtedly the local-authority sector, a trend strongly encouraged by the Labour government. The figures alone tell the story: 807,000 permanent dwellings were built for local authorities between 1945 and 1951, compared with 180,000 for private owners. And the 1951 Census showed that, in England and Wales, 18 per cent of the housing stock was in the hands of local authorities – an increase of 8 per cent on 1938. As before the war, much of this new public housing was designated for lower-income groups, with councils expected to let it at affordable rents, but Bevan was determined that it should be of sufficient quality to attract the middle class as well in due course. Significantly, his 1949 Housing Act enshrined the long-term provision of local-authority housing for 'all members of the community', not just 'the working classes'. This was not quite such a fanciful aspiration as it would come to seem, given that it has been estimated that in 1953 the average income of council-house tenants was virtually the same as the overall average income – a reflection in part of how most of the real poverty was concentrated in privately owned slums, in part of how predominantly working-class a society Britain remained.[6] And of course, there was for most activators (whether national politicians, local councillors, civil servants, town planners or architects) a powerful urge to put public housing at the heart of the New Jerusalem.

There already existed a flagship for the dream. 'We believe we shall yet see roses growing on Quarry Hill,' a Leeds alderman had declared in March 1938, opening the first section of an estate being built opposite the city's bus station. 'The Housing Committee make the bold claim for this estate that when completed, it will not only be the finest of its kind for wage-earners in this country but also in the world.' Duly finished soon afterwards, the Quarry Hill estate comprised six-storey blocks of flats consciously modelled on the Karl Marx Hof in Vienna, widely known as a paragon of working-class housing. Functioning lifts; the pioneering, French-designed Garchey automatic waste-disposal system; the revolutionary 'Mopin system' of prefabricated blocks of stressed steel and concrete – all were witness to a belief that municipal housing should be the best and the most modern.

But by 1949 there were clear signs of dissatisfaction. 'Quarry Hill Flats, many of its 960 families think, is a grey elephant,' the local press noted somewhat sardonically in September. 'Not exactly a white elephant, for the Corporation Housing Department collects a goodly sum in rents. But untended, neglected, discouraged.' The specific context was a recent manifesto presented to the Housing Committee by the Tenants' Association calling for a range of improvements – especially in terms of open spaces, garden plots and playgrounds – in accordance with the bold promises made at the opening ceremony back in 1938, as well as a variety of other facilities, such as a community centre, a health centre and shops. These proposals were submitted 'as a basis upon which a vast improvement can be made in the condition of the Estate and by which it can become a real community dwelling of which the City can be justly proud'. Later that year, the local authority did bring in dustbins after the much-vaunted Garchey system had broken down, but generally its response to the tenants' initiative was grudging and unimaginative.[7]

Nevertheless, it was almost certainly the case that most people living in Quarry Hill in the late 1940s and for quite a long time afterwards were broadly content to be doing so. And in general, in the tortuous, bittersweet, frequently controversial post-war story of public housing, so much would depend on *external* perceptions – perceptions often at odds with reality. Take Glasgow's Blackhill estate. Built in the 1930s to rehouse slum-dwellers from the city's east end, and set in a hilly area two miles north-east of the city centre, very near a gas plant and chemical works, it never remotely enjoyed flagship status. Here, the process of Glasgow-wide stigmatisation seems to have begun in early 1949, after nine residents had been fatally poisoned by illegal, home-made 'hooch' imbibed during Hogmanay celebrations. It quickly emerged – through a report in a local paper – that the cause was methyl alcohol, stolen by a Blackhill man from the chemical works. Thereafter, as a result of the story spreading across the city by word of mouth, the estate's reputation was indissolubly linked with the episode. So much so that in 1950 one woman, hitherto living in an overcrowded single-end, became a tenant there only with the utmost reluctance. 'There were bad things happening in it that we heard,' she recalled (while still insisting on her anonymity) some 40 years later. 'I'd heard they were running about with knives and hammers and a' this carry-on, and I said, no way am I going there.' She went on:

> We had to take it [the house] because of the room-space, and I was only in it a year when I went away on holiday and closed the house up for a fortnight. And there was nobody touched it. And that's when I realised that it was the name it had got . . . They can all say what they like but I reared, I reared the twins here – they were only thirteen months when I came here and I could put them up beside anybody . . .

In short: 'I came to stay and I found it was entirely different.'[8]

The only stigma that the nation's owner-occupiers – responsible in 1951 for some 31 per cent of the housing stock – had to endure was the almost visceral anti-suburban bias of most progressive thinkers. The popular journalist and broadcaster Godfrey Winn had this stigma in mind when, being driven by his chauffeur along the Kingston bypass in 1951, he came off at Cortlands Corner and turned into Malden Road:

> In a moment, the roar of the traffic was hushed; in a moment, walking between the privet hedge that leads into the cul-de-sac, called Firgrove, I was in the very heart of suburbia, and isn't life there considered by some to be the cemetery of all youthful drama, the burying ground of all ambition, the apotheosis, on the other hand, of all convention? And, in addition, a lonely tomb for all neighbourly and social intercourse.
>
> So the modern school of psychiatrists are never tired of telling us, yet I can only truthfully state myself that my first reaction as I examined the two dozen houses neatly laid out in rows, each with its own well-mown patch of front lawn, its flowering lilacs and laburnums, was that I could think of many far less pleasant places in which to be buried during one's lifetime. Further, that first external impression became only enhanced, and most agreeably so, when I searched behind the façade to meet some of the family units inhabiting this hundred-yard-long road whose houses, built between the wars, originally each cost about a thousand pounds.

Indeed, Winn found in Firgrove an almost suspiciously uniform near-blissful state of contentment, with entirely relaxed and amicable relations between the neighbours. The Peggs, living at number 20, were typical. He was a senior tax inspector who doubled as treasurer of the Green Lane Tennis Club; she was a homemaker ('I can honestly say that I have never envied anyone anything – not even our neighbour's show of tulips this year'); and their grown-up daughter Marion was teaching handicrafts at Wimbledon Art School and saving up for a Baby Morris. Winn joined them for supper, and afterwards there occurred the emblematic moment of his visit:

> The family produced a cable that had just arrived from their son, now married and doing splendidly as an engineer, in Australia. The cable had been sent in birthday greetings to Marion, from Turramurra. Whereupon, I found myself repeating the name aloud, like a mystic invocation – Turramurra, Turramurra – as I asked the three remaining members of

the family whether they were not eager to set forth on a visit to New South Wales themselves, to this far-off place with the strange and challenging name. We take the road to Turramurra.

At once the father answered as though for them all: 'I shall be very happy to spend the rest of *my* days in Firgrove,' he said quietly.

I can understand why now.[9]

———

'The morning's session was dominated by the Housing question,' noted Harold Macmillan in October 1950 during the Tory conference at the Empress Ballroom, Blackpool. 'It is quite obvious that here is something about which everyone feels quite passionately. The delegates reflect not political but human feelings and in their demand for a target of at least 300,000 houses a year, they were really determined as well as excited.' Against the misgivings of most of the front bench (Macmillan excepted), a highly ambitious annual target of 300,000 new houses was duly adopted – over 100,000 more than the current rate, as the Labour government struggled with the economic consequences of first devaluation and then the Korean War. Politically, it was an extremely effective way for the Tories to outflank Labour – but was it a realistic target?

'We can do it,' a foreman ganger, Mr C. Russell, told *Picture Post*. 'I have faith in the present-day worker, but tax on extra work holds him back. It's only natural when beer, cigarettes and cost of living is so high. Some tax-free incentive would do more to increase the rate of building houses than anything else I know.' But a bricklayer, Mr G. Parlour, disagreed: 'If raising this target means forcing the pace and putting one workman against the other, then we are against it. To us free enterprise means the pre-war system of piece-work. We won't have that. Many targets before the war were too high for decent work.'[10] The question of quality was indeed the great imponderable. Bevan had insisted on high minimum standards, including of space – an insistence that inevitably acted as a constraint on the rate of completions. With the Tories committed (initially anyway) to undertaking at least as high a proportion of public housing as Labour, one obvious way of hitting the bewitching 300,000 target would be through a slippage in those standards. Most people, though, simply wanted somewhere half-decent to live.

Meanwhile, as Labour lost the housing initiative, three clear, related trends were becoming apparent by around 1950: the decline (or at best stagnation) of classic '1945-style' town planning and reconstruction; the ever-increasing vogue of the flat; and the rise of the architect and architectural modernism. Between them, these three trends would go a long way towards determining what sort of place Britain was to live in through the 1950s and beyond.

'Well, this Town and Country Planning Act, 1947, hasn't turned the world upside down, has it?' the veteran town planner Sir George Pepler asked rhetorically in the summer of 1949, addressing his colleagues at the Town Planning Institute. 'Perhaps some of us on our more irritable days, discerning the millennium as far off as ever, feel even a touch of the chill hand of despair as we struggle on.' For most of Britain's planners, there was by this time a shared and persistent mood of gloom: not only did the country's continuing economic difficulties severely restrict the implementation of their plans, but so, too, did central government's grant system for local authorities that had acquired land for city-centre redevelopment – a system sufficiently capricious that, in the words of one planning historian, it 'made the local authorities extremely cautious when proceeding with acquisitions, because they had no guarantee that actual redevelopment would follow in the immediate future'. 'Enthusiasm for the reconstruction of our cities and towns is not what it was' was the blunt verdict by January 1951 of one expert, Cyril Dunn, on the government's attitude. As for the local authorities, he saw them as being in the process of 'drifting, sometimes complacently, into compromise schemes'.[11]

The planning cause was not helped by the painfully slow progress being made in the reconstruction of Britain's blitzed provincial cities (such as Portsmouth, Southampton and Bristol), even though this was far less the fault of the planners than of central and local government, each seemingly vying to be more cautious and risk-averse than the other. The major exceptions were Plymouth and Coventry, with the latter continuing to be – as it had since the morning after the bombs rained down in November 1940 – a symbolic beacon of Britain's post-war hopes and aspirations. There, a Labour local authority strongly committed to building a new, modern city centre, complete with a pioneering, mainly pedestrianised shopping precinct, found itself again and again being hampered by a parsimonious central government unconvinced that the local population was as fully behind the plans for Coventry's future as the Council insisted was the case. Nevertheless, even though the outcome was more stuttering progress than the planning visionaries would have wanted, it was not quite stalemate. Crucially, the government did during 1949 at last endorse the plans for both the reconstruction of the central area and the building of a ring road. And by the final day of what had been a traumatic decade, the official local mood was one of optimism. 'As a city and as a community we have pulled ourselves together more than in any year since the war,' asserted the *Coventry Evening Telegraph*. 'The visitor has to search today to find relics of bomb damage, and that cannot be said of any other city which was blitzed. The bombed houses are rebuilt. Paint has removed the post-war shabbiness of our streets.'

J. B. Priestley, visiting 'this mining camp of the motor trade' a few weeks earlier, had already reckoned that something remarkable was under way. Admittedly, he told his Home Service listeners, the slow rate of progress since 1940 in the city centre's reconstruction meant that 'even the very model' was 'beginning to look rather dilapidated and wistful'; yet 'the Fathers of this city and their employees show a spirit that is heartening to the outsider'. Above all, he was struck by Coventry's success at 'trying to create a proud civic spirit':

> Their municipal information bureau is the best I have seen anywhere. When I first looked in, I found a queue of old-age pensioners waiting to receive the fifty free bus tickets they are given every month, to encourage them to get out and about. One old lady, wiping her shoes vigorously at the door, said to me: 'Mustn't dirty this nice place, y'know'. A good sign! . . . Then we had a look at one of the excellent civic restaurants they run in this city, and later at one of the community centres in the suburbs, where there was a fine list of local goings-on . . . Best of all, perhaps, is the job they are doing there to make the schoolchildren understand all the machinery of civic life.

Another visitor, the ineffable, perceptive Godfrey Winn in 1951, also enthused after he had been shown round by the City Architect, Donald Gibson. The city-centre redevelopment that was starting to take shape, the dispersal of noisy, smoky, smelly factories to the outskirts, the eventual creation of 24 'neighbourhoods', each with its own shops, 'village' hall and sports amenities – the whole vision was patiently explained by this planner who, 'with iron-grey hair but the expression of youth', was 'changing the face of the city, and at the same time, through his skilful reshaping, giving his patient new heart and new pride, without destroying her memory or her inbred character'. The two men then reflected:

'All this reminds me of my visit to Stockholm in 1946,' I exclaimed to my guide, as we stood with our backs to Broadgate, beside the green levelling stone, that had been set into the ground as a symbol, also in 1946.

Mr Gibson looked at me in mild surprise through his glasses. 'You can't mean *this*, but instead the models I produced for you of what it will be like *one* day.'

'I'll tell you exactly what I mean. In Stockholm they showed me their wonderful modern buildings and their blocks of workers' flats, with every amenity one could imagine, and in the middle of my admiring them, my interpreter interrupted, a trifle smugly, I thought, to say: "Of course you have very bad slums in England, yes?" I had to agree, though I had a come-back. "When was this built? In 1940. Ah, in 1940, we had other things on our mind."'

'Well, by 1960 you should be able to ask your Swedish friends to visit Coventry and see our shopping precinct. It ought to be finished by then, and will be certainly worth seeing.'

His voice glowed at the prospect. And no wonder. Because there will be no more imaginative shopping centre in the world. In fact, it will be unique, if for only one reason. All traffic down it will be barred. The shops will be on two tiers, and in the centre of the long strip that will run from the back of Broadgate House, there will be flower beds and seats for shoppers to rest their legs, and reminisce about the old days when you had to give up coupons for meat and received but a single meal in return.

'I found myself thinking,' concluded Winn, 'how glad I was that I was seeing it as it was today, with the shoddy market booths, and the inevitable notice displaying Real Nylons, and the haphazard mess of the foundations. What a contrast it would be when the time came at last and how important it was to be patient and believing I reminded myself . . .'[12]

Sadly, this Priestley/Winn portrait of inspiriting civic uplift – based on only fleeting acquaintance – is refuted by the foremost historian of Coventry's post-war reconstruction, Nick Tiratsoo. Instead, he depicts a city that by the late 1940s and early 1950s was increasingly prosperous, including a thriving black market; where its residents and migrant workers were ever more materialistic-cum-individualistic in outlook; where immediate preoccupations, such as housing and entertainment, mattered far more than civic plans that had already taken an age even to start to come to fruition; and where the shallow organisational roots of the ruling local Labour Party were complemented by apathy among the rank and file of the local trade union branches. 'Local people had been moderately interested in reconstruction during periods of the war,' Tiratsoo accepts, 'but afterwards their enthusiasm soon evaporated, despite the best efforts of the Council. Enjoying a good time, when pleasure had been for so long denied, seemed infinitely preferable to joining the earnest discussions of the planners.'

Further evidence of this drift away from the collective – arguably exaggerated even during the war – was provided by the Sociological Survey undertaken by Birmingham University on the Council's behalf from late 1948. In particular, it revealed how tenants on one of Coventry's newly built suburban estates (Canley) had at most only a very limited sense of community or neighbourhood identity. Instead, what they really cared about was their privacy – to such an extent, the researchers concluded that 'residents in the lower income groups may be willing to forego some of the amenities of the house in order to secure these higher standards of privacy'. It was a desire for privacy that extended to their most precious possession. About half the householders on the estate owned a car or a motorbike, reported the local press in March 1951, but 'there is hardly one house on the estate which has a garage'. And it quoted Mrs A. Hackett of 52 Gerard Avenue: 'There are no means of protecting the cars from any mischief-makers. All we can do is throw tarpaulins over them and hope people will have the decency to protect others' property. There is no joy in having a new car if it is going to be exposed to the elements and ruffians to be ruined.'[13]

If Coventry was one exemplar of post-war planning, the other was undoubtedly the New Town, where initial progress was if anything even slower than in the blitzed cities. By the end of 1950, there had been fewer than 500 house completions in the eight new towns on the fringes of London beyond the green belt, with a mere further 2,000 under construction. 'The New Towns project is proceeding mostly on paper' was how one disappointed town-planning expert put it in January 1951, while according to the *Observer* that same month, the prized notion of 'self-contained communities' was already in trouble: 'With the shining exception of Crawley, the New Towns in the London region are already facing a serious unbalance between industry and housing. They are in danger of becoming new dormitory suburbs, and ridiculously remote ones at that.'

Most of the New Town pioneers knew what sort of dwelling they wanted to live in. When in the late summer of 1950 nearly 2,000 London families descended on Crawley New Town to have a look round, the development corporation's chief executive carefully noted their views:

> Amongst these people there was an overwhelming desire to possess a house as distinct from a flat. It was clear that even families which had lived in flats in London wished to get away from the communal staircase and balconies of landings and to have a dwelling with its own front door and large or small piece of garden, according to the individual taste of the tenants in question.

Yet it soon became clear that in the New Towns around London 15 or 20 per cent of the dwellings were to be flats – in other words, not breaking decisively from the prevailing national ratio. These flats included The Lawn, built in Harlow New Town by Frederick Gibberd as Britain's first point block (a type of high-rise narrower than a slab block). 'It's a modest 10 storeys of reinforced concrete structure, faced in different shades of brick and some wholesome beige render' was how an appreciative visitor half a century later would describe this 'gently humane take on a type of building which has since become notorious'. But at the time, Gibberd's Swedish-influenced design caused a considerable stir. 'Is this the beginning of a rational approach to housing?' hopefully asked one architect, Robert Lutyens, son of Edwin.

'We are told of a million dwellings completed, and our hearts sink at the prospect of the semi-detached fallacy indefinitely perpetuated, whereas we hear nothing at all from official quarters of this first triumph of common sense and propriety.' His letter to *The Times* concluded stirringly: 'In Le Corbusier's phrase, instead of parks in cities, let us have more cities in parks to demonstrate our national renaissance.'[14]

As among the Crawley pioneers, so among the populace at large. The finding in 1950 of the Hulton Press's *Patterns of British Life*, based on an extensive national survey, could hardly have been more definite:

> Most people like living in houses rather than flats and they like having a house to themselves. They like their own private domain which can be locked against the outside world and, perhaps as much as anything, they are a nation of garden-lovers. They want space to grow flowers and vegetables and to sit on Sunday afternoons and they want it to be private.

Even so, in outright defiance of such wishes, the pro-flats chorus among many of the nation's activators was starting by the early 1950s to become almost irresistible. Colin Buchanan, of the Ministry of Town and Country Planning, called for more flats to be built in order to increase population densities and thereby save both money and land; Godfrey Winn clearly regarded Stockholm's amenity-stuffed blocks of workers' flats as the very acme of social progress; and the publisher Paul Elek, in an impressionistic account of London depicting the East End as 'this ugly, distorting mirror of humanity' that 'shows only sordidness', saw them as nothing less than potential salvation:

> But new and better-planned blocks of flats go up here and there and a better chance of decent life is given and taken. Ramshackle picturesqueness is replaced by amenities and sanitation, the communal lavatory on one of the landings by bathroom and hot water in every flat, the gutter and dangerous road by garden playground, with fresh grass instead of bare concrete. But it will be a long time before every East End family occupies one of these latest flats, and even then fantastic Whitechapel Road, Commercial Road, and the others will still stand as dreadful monuments to nineteenth and twentieth century muddle and meanness – noise

and dirt, insanitary factory and antiquated workshop mixed up with human habitation, each blighting the other . . .

Those were the very evils that the classic '1945' policy of dispersal and low-density settlement (most notably in New Towns) was intended to alleviate. Why did the pro-flatters so emphatically reject that solution? There were many reasons, including economic, functional and aesthetic ones, yet arguably the most resonant were sociological. Harold Orlans, in his well-researched, mainly critical account of developments at Stevenage New Town, saw the whole debate explicitly in terms of class and well-meaning but fundamentally misguided paternalism:

We have seen no statistics on the subject, but hazard the guess that there are more children per room in working-class flats (and most flat-dwellers are working-class people) than in middle-class houses. It does not follow that these children are any the worse for having been reared in flats, but only that they are different, in some ways, for being working-class, from middle-class children. The implication that their life would be improved if they lived in houses (ie if they lived more as their middle-class critics live) indicates again the bond between the garden city idea and the regnant, puritanical middle-class ideology.

Another activator friend of the urban working class was the prolific architectural writer A. Trystan Edwards. 'If the houses are aligned in friendly streets where the neighbours help one another in their domestic difficulties,' he asserted in *The Times* in 1949, 'people of the lower income groups find it much easier to bring up children than in the frigid social atmosphere of the typical garden suburb.'[15] This was an early sighting of what would later become an immensely influential argument-cum-emotion – one that explicitly identified social virtue and cohesion in living cheek by jowl, even if (an 'even if' not always addressed) the resulting high density in turn meant multistorey blocks of flats replacing all those intimate but irretrievably rundown Victorian houses.

Naturally, the embrace of flats did not take place with uniform speed and fervour. In Lancashire, for instance, there was a continuing attachment to the principle of low-density city redevelopment, with a policy of 'overspill' housing adopted as the means to achieving it. By 1950 significant numbers of Salford people were being decanted to the Worsley overspill estate some seven miles away, while Kirkby was being built to accommodate the residents of overcrowded central Liverpool. It was similar in Newcastle, in that the 1951 Plan involved a commitment to reducing residential densities as the best way of improving housing in the city, though in this case the overspill concomitant, mainly to Longbenton (outside the city's eastern boundary), did involve a higher proportion of multistorey flats than either Worsley or Kirkby did at the same stage. One new Labour councillor wanted more flats in Newcastle itself. 'If returned as your Municipal representative,' T. Dan Smith had promised the electors in the slum-ridden Walker ward in May 1950, 'I would do all in my power to press for the immediate building of suitable modern flats.'[16]

In England's second city there was – at the activator level – a clear, remarkably bipartisan shift towards flats as an acceptable, even intrinsically desirable type of dwelling. By 1950 not only was Birmingham's population rapidly growing, but there was increasingly widespread criticism of the city's low-density, 'cottage' municipal housing estates. Tellingly, the ones built since the war were viewed just as negatively as the pre-war ones – as drab, monotonous, lacking communal facilities and often sited too far from the workplaces of those living in them. Simultaneously, the City Council (Tory since 1949) was, in an effort to quicken the building rate, starting to employ national builders using non-traditional methods (including the use of cranes), which had the potential to undertake far more challenging structures than just two-storey houses. One local architect, seizing the moment, related in the *Birmingham Post* in November 1950 how a recent trip to Holland had convinced him that, in order to provide the requisite accommodation for the city's population along with the desired communal playgrounds and garden areas, 'we must build upwards and not outwards', and that 'those who oppose flats and say "we want houses" must appreciate that "you cannot get a quart into a pint pot".'

Within months, the Birmingham and Five Counties Architectural Association was advocating that multistorey flats should henceforth be built on a significantly larger scale, while even the Birmingham Civic Society argued much the same. By the summer of 1951 the City

Council's House Building Committee had announced that flats would comprise at least a fifth of its 1952 programme, mainly in the central areas but also in the suburbs. Among those inner-city areas were the five publicly acquired redevelopment areas that were going to be cleared of their slums. Across most of the country, slum clearance did not start before the mid-1950s, but in Birmingham the bulldozers were already by 1950 laying waste to the courts and back-to-backs of Duddeston and Nechells, where soon afterwards five lumpy, brick-clad twelve-storey tower blocks began to be constructed. All this in a city where as recently as the late 1940s it had been the unquestioned conventional wisdom that Brummies were not flat-minded, and where, as one observer noted in June 1951, they remained 'understandably suspicious due to ignorance'.[17]

The debate was already over in Sheffield. There, in October 1949, the Housing Committee adopted a plan for flats development (likely to be between four- and six-storey blocks) in the city, with the first scheme to include shops, schools, restaurants, a communal laundry, garages and pram sheds, as well as central heating for the flats themselves. 'Many of the committee's recommendations on design,' reported the local press, 'arose from its recent London and Scandinavian visits.' And the chairman, Alderman Albert Smith (Labour), was quoted: 'Communal restaurants are suggested for the bigger flats, as this form of eating is a very popular social feature in Scandinavia.' The plan then went to the City Council, with the badly rundown Park area (overlooking the railway station) being recommended as the site for the start of this ambitious new policy. One Labour councillor, Alderman C. W. Gascoigne, was unhappy, stating that 'plebiscites up and down the country showed almost 90 per cent in favour of houses as against flats' and that 'houses were infinitely preferable'. But the proposal was approved, and even Gascoigne apparently accepted that it would be uneconomical to build houses in the centre of the city.[18] Such were the beginnings of the Park Hill story – one of the most emblematic in twentieth-century British public housing. During these beginnings, the element of public consultation or involvement seems to have been conspicuous by its absence. Perhaps there was an assumption that the scheme would never actually happen – which, given that nothing did happen for several years, was understandable.

The capital was already on a fast track. 'Everyone who travels about London must have noticed how many new housing schemes are in course of construction,' observed a young architect, Peter Shepheard, in a talk on the Third Programme in December 1950:

> Mainly these are blocks of flats: it is part of London's housing policy to build large blocks of flats first, at a high density of dwellings per acre, in order to house large numbers of families and make room for the houses which will come later . . .
>
> One of these developments, more conspicuous than some others, lies on the north bank of the Thames at Pimlico, between Vauxhall Bridge and Chelsea Bridge. Several tall nine-storey blocks in yellow brick with gaily painted balconies are under construction, and one is finished and occupied. At the river end of the site is a vast round glass tower, 130 feet high, which has puzzled many people, and which in fact encases a huge hot water tank.

He was describing Churchill Gardens. The work of two other young architects, Philip Powell and Hidalgo Moya, this was a vast housing scheme (eventually more than 1,600 dwellings) that largely succeeded in being simultaneously modernist and humane, reflecting their respect for Le Corbusier yet their aversion to monumentality.

Churchill Gardens immediately won a high reputation, not least for the way in which it employed a mixed-development approach to get away from the monotony that beset so many other flats developments. Thus there were the nine-storey blocks of flats but also four-storey maisonettes and even some three-storey terraced houses for large families. It proved a major inspiration. 'For honesty of expression and care in detail there is a lot to be learned from these flats,' declared yet another young architect, Oliver Cox, in the spring of 1951. 'Here, one feels, imagination is based on common sense rather than on a poetic seizure.' He added his hope that the future lay with 'mixed development', which was 'sociologically much better and architecturally more interesting' than the tendency hitherto 'towards the concentration of large flat blocks in central areas and so-called "cottage estates" outside'.[19]

Even as Churchill Gardens triumphed, a new housing era was taking shape at the London County Council.[20] After the sustained attack by architects and their friends on the mediocre quality of most of the London housing being produced by the Valuer's Department, and in the context of continuing criticism of the slow rate of completions, the LCC's Housing Committee decided in December 1949 to return responsibility for housing layout and design to the Architect's Department under Robert Matthew. Brought up in Edinburgh, Matthew much admired that city's tenements and had also been greatly influenced by the modernist teachings of Walter Gropius (founder of the Bauhaus) in favour of high-rise blocks – of about ten storeys – as the best way of combining space, sunlight and greenery on the one hand with an urban, 'townscape' character on the other. In order to achieve social as well as architectural variety, these blocks would (as at Pimlico) be part of mixed-development schemes. With such precepts in mind, Matthew and his deputy Leslie Martin rapidly built up their department during 1950, recruiting many gifted, serious, socially concerned young architects and starting work on several exciting projects. Altogether, it had been a remarkable coup by and on behalf of the architectural profession.

The new balance of power was vividly demonstrated in the autumn of 1950 as the Housing Committee decided what to do about sites available near Putney Heath – sites which two years earlier had been part of the Valuer's undeniably monolithic Putney-Roehampton model, much disparaged (including by local residents) and subsequently put into temporary abeyance. Two competing papers were submitted: by Matthew and by Cyril Walker, the Valuer. Advocating a mixture of four-storey maisonette blocks and much taller point blocks, Matthew put forward two central arguments: 'the monotonous effect of parallel rows of five-storey blocks which would otherwise be necessary to achieve the same density can then be avoided'; and 'the complete vertical standardisation of the point block enables full advantage to be taken of modern reinforced concrete technique'. Walker for his part was adamant that high-rise point blocks, as opposed to the customary 'flatted' four- or five-storey blocks, raised a whole series of practical problems: mothers with small children did not like living at higher levels (as they had already made clear at the eight-storey Woodberry Down estate in Stoke Newington); lifts were vulnerable to power cuts;

there was the extra expense of cleaning staircases and windows; upper floors were colder; and all the flats in a point block would be of an inflexibly uniform size. 'The Committee will appreciate,' declared the defiant Valuer, 'that the erection of 11-storey blocks of the kind proposed is an experiment. Until experience has been gained of the problems of erection and maintenance and of the tenants' reactions it would be unwise to make more than a very limited use of this type.' He lost the vote, and a new estate – to be called Ackroydon, with building due to start in 1952 – went ahead according to Matthew's vision.[21]

It was in a sense an extraordinary situation. By comparison with 20 or 30 years earlier, British modernism was clearly on the retreat, most notably in literature and music; in architecture, however, with its obviously greater potential for social purpose and even social engineering, the reverse was true. At the mid-century point, nevertheless, it was predominantly a *soft*, relatively humanist modernism that (in Coventry as well as in London) held sway. Much turned on attitudes to the definitely non-soft Le Corbusier, whose landmark and intensely polarising block of flats, the Unité d'Habitation, was by this time rising from the ground in Marseilles. Lionel Brett (consultant architect and planner for Hatfield New Town) in late 1949 called the block 'inhumane' and 'frightening', while in the spring of 1950 a major article, 'The Next Step?', by probably the most influential of architectural commentators, J. M. Richards, implicitly rejected Le Corbusier as a relevant figure and instead looked mainly to the example of Scandinavian architects to re-establish 'the human appeal of architecture so that it can perform its traditional cultural role'.

A year later, Matthew's department at the LCC convened a fascinating colloquium to ponder the implications of the most-discussed building since the war. 'Most people with families of any size prefer houses with gardens,' conceded Philip Powell in his formal presentation. 'But the possibility of 20- or 30-storey blocks suggested by the Unité (yet reserved for smaller families), mixed with two- or three-storey compact house-with-garden development, seems to be the only rational approach to high-density planning.' In the ensuing discussion, Oliver Cox (who had joined the department in the autumn of 1950) and others not only argued that Le Corbusier's approach had been needlessly arbitrary, abstract and monumental but also stated flatly that he was 'at fault when he suggests that it is the task of architecture to create a new way of life'. Crucially, however, the meeting as a whole refuted the idea that the Unité was an essay in the monumental; indeed, many speakers testified to the 'humanity' of the scale.[22] In sum, the aesthetically challenged Valuer may have been seen off by the modernists – but among those modernists, the battle of the softs and the hards was only just beginning.

For Frederic Osborn, doughty champion of planned dispersal from the big cities and of low-density, low-level living, it was a battle between two evils. In February 1950 his riposte to the Lutyens vision of 'a 40-storey block of flats in one of the new towns' was typically robust:

> Seeing that a small percentage of people do prefer flats, and, being child-less, can afford higher rents for less space, there is much to be said for building the few flats required in tall towers to diversify the skyline, as in religious ages we built church spires. If that keeps the architects in good heart to do the necessary job of designing functional earth-bound houses for the great majority, both parties may be pleased. On a small scale we may be able to afford imaginative luxuries, but that is the name for them.

The robustness, though, concealed a growing pessimism. 'Here the Modernists stand for multi-storey flats and the Mummyfiers for terrace houses and closed vistas,' Osborn lamented soon afterwards to Lewis Mumford. 'The speculative builder's name is mud; but he stands far nearer to the ordinary man.' Not unpoignantly, he added: 'My dilemma is that I will not join in the popular criticism of planning, with which I greatly sympathise.'

A year later, in April 1951, Osborn found himself countering a savage attack on the planners by the *Economist*. All too conscious that planning's golden hour (roughly 1940–45) had come and gone, he soberly refuted that magazine's central accusation (in effect that the planners had become control freaks) before pinning his hopes for planning's future on greater public involvement. 'Public controversy, especially on issues that genuinely concern the ordinary man and woman, will strengthen planning even if it modifies some of the plans,' he declared. 'The quietest existence, after all, is that of the grave.'[23] But if he really thought that many of his colleagues in the entwined, increasingly professionalised worlds of reconstruction, planning and architecture were going to rally enthusiastically to such a democratic, participative cry, he was – uncharacteristically – deceiving himself.

If there was an apotheosis of 1940s planning, it was Sir Patrick Abercrombie's Clyde Valley Regional Plan, published at full length in late 1949 and enthusiastically greeted by Osborn as a 'superb report – the masterpiece of the Abercrombie series'. It called for almost half of Glasgow's appallingly housed population to be moved outside the city to live instead in healthy, carefully designed, self-supporting new towns beyond the city's green belt. This, for Osborn, was how it was always meant to be.

Sadly for him – and arguably for several hundred thousand Glaswegians – the dream at best only partially materialised. Although one New Town (East Kilbride, situated just a few miles outside the city's boundaries) was under way by the early 1950s, the Glasgow Corporation remained adamant that the city's housing future lay principally within its boundaries. Here, although comprehensive redevelopment of the blighted central areas was still on hold awaiting funding and materials, there was a portentous development in November 1950, when work began on Moss Heights, the city's first high-rise. 'Whether we like it or not – and there is evidence that a great number of Glasgow people do like it – the tenement must continue to house a substantial proportion of the city's population,' declared a bullish *Glasgow Herald* shortly before, though without saying exactly what that evidence was. 'And the 10-storey tenement at Cardonald which will push its way skyward in the coming months will be the forerunner of many more, nearer the heart of the city.'[24]

Another development was in its way equally portentous – one that, in Osborn's eyes, represented an utterly bastardised form of planned dispersal. Determined to counter Abercrombie, and acutely conscious of its hostages-to-fortune slogan ('The Maximum Number of Houses in the Shortest Possible Time'), the Corporation's Housing Department had been pushing ever harder from soon after the war to develop huge housing estates on the city's periphery: well away from the centre but inside the municipal boundaries. The biggest by the late 1940s was Pollok, with a target population of more than 40,000. This was an extraordinary figure, given (to quote Gerry Mooney's study) 'the warnings of the social consequences that large-scale suburban housing estates would produce', and inevitably it had high-density implications. Situated in Glasgow's south-west corner, the estate's origins as a 1930s model garden suburb meant that it had a reasonably large number of cottage-style houses, but during the major expansion after the war, the great bulk of new dwellings were three- or four-storey flat-roof tenements. By 1951 most of the Pollok estate had been completed. It would never be the subject of architectural colloquies, but for good and ill it was already closely mirroring much of the post-war public-housing story.

Pollok's new residents in the late 1940s and early 1950s came mainly from inner-city areas such as Govan or the Gorbals, where they had been living in cheap rented accommodation. Oral recollections more than three decades later, in 1983, evoke something of the momentousness of making the move:

> You had to have your name on the waiting list for years before you were allocated a house. Ours was on the list since 1924. When people applied or were offered a new house the sanitary inspectors came around to make sure there were no bed bugs and that they were good tenants. They visited our house in Hospital Street, Gorbals, to look for bed bugs before we came out to Pollok.
>
> We were eighteen years on the waiting list. The sanitary visited us in the old house before we were moved out here. There was a ballot to see what house you got.
>
> We were on the waiting list for over fourteen years. When you were offered a house you jumped at it.
>
> It was pretty grim and cold when we first arrived in 1947. The gardens were all bare, no street lights and the roads were dirt tracks. But it was great to get away from the smoke of the Gorbals though it took us a while to get used to it out here.

Almost invariably, the single greatest attraction was the dwelling itself, and more often than not the transformed sanitary arrangements:

We moved from a room and kitchen to this four-apartment. It was great to have hot running water and an inside toilet for the first time.

The one thing that stood out was the bathroom. It made a change from having to get washed in an old bathtub.

We were delighted with the new house after living most of our lives in a room and kitchen. The inside toilet was great and the inside bath was well-utilised.

The point bears repeating: these were not picturesque criteria, but to Pollok's newcomers they mattered infinitely more than any planning principle or architectural dogma.

Nevertheless, for all the grateful flushing of indoor toilets and breathing of fresh air, the fact was that living on the periphery soon proved problematic. The 1983 testimony has plenty to say about the early difficulties:

It was a dreadful place at first for social, shopping and recreational facilities, and I know that the lack of proper schools caused considerable aggravation on the part of many people. Some people left the area because of this. Others left simply because there was nothing here and we were paying high rents. We used to go back to the South Side for the pictures and to do the shopping.

There was nothing in the scheme at all. The men missed the pubs the most. People used to go back to the old places all the time to see their friends and visit the old haunts. People who came from Govan took others who came from other areas back with them to the Govan shops. In any case, the shops in the older areas were cheaper than the shops in Pollok and the vans were very expensive.

The vans and the small shops in the area made a fortune. I know that in several cases, the money they made touring Pollok enabled them to buy more expensive shops elsewhere in Glasgow.

All the people settled down well together, although there wasn't the same feelings of community life that we had in the older tenements. Mind you, there was nowhere to meet the other tenants.

People got on okay together but there was no community spirit. By the time you came home from work, if you could get on to a bus that is, there was little time to get ready to go out. That was one of the main problems living so far from the work – it was the time getting there and back.

This general lack of amenities (typified by the poor and expensive bus services) to accompany the new housing can probably be explained, even justified, by the all-out emphasis on getting as many houses and tenements up as quickly as possible, but cumulatively their absence made a big difference to Pollok's chances of becoming a successful estate. Nor overall was it a plus that the Corporation did not allow pubs or bars on its property – a ban going back to 1890 that would last until 1969. There were also some basic failures of planning and design that might otherwise have helped alleviate the often dreary, barrack-like appearance of the flat-roofed, walk-up tenements themselves. The original pre-war layout for the estate (intended for terraced and cottage-type housing) was left largely unaltered; long, unbroken rows of tenements were laid out opposite each other, resulting in parts of the road virtually never seeing the sun; the roads between the tenement blocks were often too narrow; there were no communal gardens; and indeed the main communal facility was the 'midden', or concrete bin-shelter – and even it became, notes Gerry Mooney, 'a point of much criticism as far as the tenement residents were concerned'. All in all, this was a formidable catalogue of defects. But whether the main culprit was undue haste, lack of resources, indifference or just sheer lack of imagination, it is impossible to be sure.

Yet even as the *Govan Press* asserted in September 1950 that 'there are a thousand people living in the Pollok housing scheme who do not want to live there' – which may well have been an underestimate – the plans had been drawn up and completed for similarly vast new estates in Glasgow's three other corners: Drumchapel in the north-west, Castlemilk in the south-east and Easterhouse in the north-east. The very names would in time resonate.[25]

That Dump?

Quarry Hill Experiment was the treat served up to Home Service listeners on the evening of Friday, 6 April 1951. Billed as a 'factual report on thirteen years of community living', it was a judicious and thorough one-hour exploration of how the model estate in Leeds had fared since 1938. A series of critical and perceptive if sometimes buck-passing viewpoints were heard. Accepting that the youth club and social centre had been a failed experiment, the Housing Committee's spokesman declared that 'the rest is with the tenants, the appearance and happiness of the estate depends upon their response and civic pride'. A tenants' spokesman agreed: 'They just don't think of them-selves as a community with community responsibilities.' But an officer of the tenants' association was more inclined to blame the Corporation: 'The people who live in Quarry Hill usually don't know what is going to be done till it *is* done. And so they feel that it's no business of theirs.' All in all, the programme concluded that unless the 'community such as finds itself now in Quarry Hill can adapt itself fully to what is, in many essentials, an un-English way of life', then there was 'a danger that for lack of those very provisions which were to have made community life possible, something of the squalor of the slums may eventually return'. Even so, 'it is something to have attempted such a great experiment' – and 'no one dare deny that the material standard of life in Quarry Hill is as high as any yet provided for what are called "the lower income groups".'

That, no doubt, would have been that – one more worthy radio documentary – but for the fateful, well-meaning contribution of one tenant, Joan Mann: 'Of course, one of the troubles I find is that people look down on me because I live in Quarry Hill. Whenever I mention it, someone is sure to say "What – that dump?" and you can't have pride in a place when people think like that about it.' The term `dump' touched the rawest of nerves. Within days an angry petition had been signed by about a hundred tenants, complaining that the programme had brought Quarry Hill 'into disrepute' and given 'the impression that the intelligence and social standing of its residents are of an extremely low degree'. A protest meeting was called for later in the month.[1]

Sunday the 8th was Census Day, and next morning a young, bound-for-London journalist, Keith Waterhouse, traipsed the streets of Leeds (but probably not around Quarry Hill) with a Census enumerator collecting forms. 'Resentful? Churlish? Not a bit!' declared the talkative official:

> Most people are terrifically bucked at the idea of being counted. They like to feel that the Government knows that they personally do exist, and that the Government is interested in their especial job and the fact that they have to share a bathroom with the people upstairs. They *like* being counted. Mark you, some of them haven't the faintest idea what it's for. One woman asked if it was to do with the voting. Another thinks it's a kind of Gallup Poll, or some thing or other. I didn't bother telling them.

'Everyone on his round of 300 houses gave their information without a murmur,' commented Waterhouse. But the last word went to 'the Census Man', who professed himself 'satisfied' with the whole exercise. 'It has not been good weather for counting heads, but people have been courteous, patient and intelligent. I've had more cups of tea today than I've had in my life before.'

Also on Monday the defeated English cricket team docked at Tilbury. Among the several inexperienced tourists to have disappointed was the 20-year-old Brian Close; his consolation prize was to report back shortly to the Royal Signals at Catterick and complete his National Service. That evening, a touring revue called *Sky High* opened for a week at the Sunderland Empire. Next morning, there was only tepid praise in the local paper for one of its comedy stars – 'I thought Reg

Varney's personality pleasing and warming, but was not so "taken" with some of his comedy' – and no mention of the other, Benny Hill. This was tactful, because Hill's solo spot, successful enough in southern theatres but already in trouble the previous week in Hull, had bombed, culminating in a merciless slow handclap. His confidence shot, he was allowed to stay on for the rest of the week but only as Varney's 'feed'. No such problems that Tuesday evening for Judy Garland, who played two 'triumphant' houses at the London Palladium, complete with 'Clang Clang Clang Went the Trolley'.[2]

Tuesday the 10th was also Budget day – Hugh Gaitskell's first. Among those in a packed Commons (though with Attlee absent, in hospital with a duodenal ulcer) was Ernest Bevin, a sick man recently eased out of the foreign secretaryship. Sitting in the press gallery, Mollie Panter-Downes watched him 'turn his drawn face toward the debonair, carnation-buttonholed Gaitskell, already like the ghost of a grand old trade-union Labour movement, hovering on the edge of the banquet of the brainy new order that has met the workers via the London School of Economics rather than via the hard-life school of the poor'. Another observer of the scene, from across the floor, was Harold Macmillan. 'It was like a very good lecture to a Working Man's Club,' he thought, before summarising the main aspects of a fiscal package designed to meet the spiralling costs of rearmament: '6d more on income tax; 50% instead of 30% on distribution profits; double the purchase tax on motor-cars; 4d more on petrol'. Gaitskell also proposed that, in Macmillan's words, 'the patient shd pay half the cost of the spectacles and half the cost of the dentures supplied at present gratis' – at which point, unrecorded by Macmillan, a muffled cry of 'Shame!' was heard from Jennie Lee, standing next to her husband behind the Speaker's chair. Aneurin Bevan himself, 'red in the face and breathing like an angry bull' according to another Tory diarist ('Chips' Channon), walked out as soon as Gaitskell ended that passage. 'What will Bevan do?' Macmillan asked himself. He added that his expectation was that Bevan would not resign.

Gaitskell's Budget was overall moderately well received, but Gladys Langford spoke for most people after most Budgets in the immediate post-war period when she noted gloomily, 'Oh, dear! What a THIN time lies ahead.' With the Westminster atmosphere at its most febrile, the Parliamentary Labour Party met on Wednesday morning. There, Bevan duly attacked the NHS charges but announced to applause that he had 'decided not to take a certain course' – which most observers took to mean that he would not be resigning over the issue. 'Bevan Gives Way On Health Charges' was the confident headline of the *Daily Telegraph* next day. Labour's youngest MP, Anthony Wedgwood Benn, was among those speaking at the meeting. 'I welcomed the budget,' he recorded in his diary. 'On this question of "principle" of a free health service, it is nonsense. There are many national scandals it would be costly to correct. This is not a question of principle, but to the contrary, it is a practical matter.' He also noted how during his speech a half-asleep Bevin had woken up, looked at the speaker and asked, 'Who is that boy?' And how, told who it was, the weary titan had said, 'Nice boy, nice boy.'[3]

Another nice, Oxford-educated boy was sampling the delights of the British seaside. 'I am writing this from Blackpool,' V. S. Naipaul reported back home next day. 'It is a big machine made to extort money from the people on holiday, full of fortune-tellers, gypsies, all named Lee, and all claiming to be the only Gypsy Lee on the front – eating places and amusement shops.' Just up the coast, almost all attention that Wednesday was on the latest news from Fartown, Huddersfield. Barrow's rugby-league club had on Saturday drawn 14–14 with Leeds in the cup semi-final at the cavernous Odsal stadium, Bradford; today, with no floodlights available, the replay was scheduled for a 5.30 kick-off. The outcome was 28–13 to Willie Horne's team. 'Well done, gallant warriors of Craven Park!' exalted the *Barrow News*. 'The great exploits of its Rugby team have brought joy and honour to the town, and Barrow is proud of them.'

But not everyone saw the bright side, as Nella Last, herself this side of the moon, found out on Thursday:

> I was talking to a shopkeeper today, & he was a bit gloomy about all the money taken out of Barrow already by the Rugby ... In the paper it said 40,000 went to Odsal & 4,000 to Huddersfield for the replay. They couldn't do it at less than £1 a head on the average – and tonight the fare to Wembley was announced – 54/6, & in another column is announced 10,000 tickets for Wembley Stadium would be allotted

tomorrow! With little or no overtime being worked in the Yard at present, if people *do* flock to Wembley, it stands to reason some one or something will suffer!

There were indeed troubles at the Barrow Shipyard, where for three months the engineers and coppersmiths had imposed a ban on overtime and piecework, but the previous Saturday, even as most Barrovians were flocking to Bradford, that had not stopped the Barrow Shipyard Band competing at Bolton in the North Western Area Brass Band Championship, albeit to finish unplaced after being unluckily drawn to play first.[4]

That same Saturday, the day after the Quarry Hill radio programme, a listener living elsewhere in Leeds had walked through the estate, and on Friday the 13th his or her unflattering description, under the name 'Sightseer', appeared in the local press and raised the controversy up a further notch: '"Dump" is a correct expression to apply to the condition of the estate itself . . . The Quarry Hill perspective is one of dirty, ugly concrete, equally ugly and none-too-good tar macadam, bare, clay earth, combining to create an appearance of monstrous desolation. It is evident there is unrest among the people who live there.' 'Sightseer' was especially affronted by walking through 'the arch facing the Headrow' and being 'greeted around the corner with a display of rubbish around a large and disreputable rubbish box' – something which 'I do not think would have been tolerated in the old Quarry Hill!' Perhaps 'Sightseer' should have been accompanied by Anthony Crosland. 'Is extreme tidiness a virtue or a vice?' the *Any Questions?* team was asked that evening in Frome, shortly after the rising Labour star had entered a stout defence of Gaitskell's Budget. 'It's the most disgusting vice,' he answered. 'It's on a par with being a vegetarian, with not smoking, not drinking. (*Laughter.*) I feel more strongly about this than I can possibly express to you. I'm perfectly speechless with the strength of my feeling on this subject.'

Next day, Saturday the 14th, Gladys Langford was not much more enthusiastic than 'Sightseer' when, motivated by a desire to see the preparations for the imminent Festival of Britain, she went to the Embankment: 'WHAT a muddle! Hideous buildings in a sea of mud!' The Festival would never be seen by Ernest Bevin, still occupying the

Foreign Secretary's official residence at Carlton Gardens. That afternoon, reading official papers in bed (in his capacity as Lord Privy Seal),
he had a final heart attack and died – 'the key to his red box', according
to his biographer, 'still clutched in his hand'. If the weather had not
been so bitingly cold, he would have been at Wembley to see England
lose 3–2 at home to Scotland after playing most of the game with ten
men following Wilf Mannion's early injury. 'All right, we lost the
British Football Championship,' began Desmond Hackett's typically
bombastic match report in the *Daily Express*, 'but, by jove! we found
something that has been missing around English Soccer for years –
that good old fighting spirit.'[5]

In the Commons on Monday tributes were duly paid to Bevin –
including one by Herbert Morrison, deputising for the still-hospitalised
Attlee and speaking, according to Macmillan, 'very clumsily and inar-
tistically' – but far more people were interested in that evening's *Twenty
Questions*, partly to find out whether Gilbert Harding was going to
be even shorter-tempered than in recent weeks. Among them was Nella
Last. 'Quite the worst of a few bad 20 Questions since Gilbert Harding
assumed the post as Quizmaster,' she noted afterwards. 'He didn't
sound sober to me, horrid pompous man. How Richard Dimbleby
keeps as patient as he does – or Jack Train swallow the sneering way
he is addressed some times, beats me.' Next morning, the press went
to town, reporting how the microphone had been accidentally on as
Harding, introducing his team to the studio audience, had said testily,
'This is the last time we shall have this nonsense', and also how he had
ended the programme with a barely coherent monologue: 'Well, there
is a hectic evening for you. I have four successes, the team has had
six, which seems all right. I have nothing more to say whatever
except that they done one thing in 18 and, one thing or another, and
after all you have been listening, and if you have not it serves you
right.' The BBC announced that day that he was to 'rest by agreement'
from the programme. But he still had to go to Edinburgh to record
his final *Round Britain Quiz* in the current series, and at King's
Cross 'burly, red-faced, bachelor Harding, nearing 44' spoke briefly
to the press: 'I've persuaded my sister to come with me, because I
don't want to be alone just now.'[6]

In Scotland itself, there was the formal opening on Tuesday

afternoon of the new primary school in Muirshiel Crescent, Pollok, built from prefabricated timber units specially imported from Austria. 'The people who were responsible for planning Pollok and other districts had made insufficient provision for the schooling of the children,' conceded Bailie E. J. Donaldson, Convenor of Education, but 'it was hoped that by September approximately 18 temporary schools with 90 classrooms to accommodate 4,000 children would be completed in Pollok.' The big event of the day, however, was back in London. Since the 9th the trial had been taking place at the Old Bailey of seven unofficial dockers' leaders, charged with offences under Order 1305, a wartime regulation designed to prevent industrial disputes. For several months there had been widespread unofficial strike action by dockers on the Mersey and in London, and the prosecution – brought by the Attorney-General, Sir Hartley Shawcross – was a clear attempt to break the unofficial movement. After a summing up by the Lord Chief Justice, the implacable Lord Goddard, that emphasised that 'strikes intended to overawe courts or juries are illegal', the jury on the 17th was considering its verdict. Outside, several thousand dockers waited for hours, among them Jack Dash. 'Things seemed to be going very slowly, the lads were getting edgy and restless,' he recalled:

So we decided to break into song. It's amazing what meaning you can put into such songs as *Rule Britannia, Sons of the Sea*, and *Land of Hope and Glory* if you're in the right combative mood, and there was a moving rendering of *Kevin Barry* from some of the Irishmen present. Now, I don't know if we were being too patriotic, or if we were disturbing the office staffs in the adjacent buildings, but quite suddenly, up from the direction of Snow Hill Police Station, our tuneful chants were interrupted by a clip-clop, clip-clop, and sure enough, there were the Cossacks – the mounted police – trotting towards us.

The patriotic singing took on a greater fervour and volume. With skilful horsemanship, the Cossacks began to manoeuvre us from the middle of the road to the pavement; then one over-zealous chap rode his horse into the pavement and hemmed a group of men against the wall. A police helmet went flying. Out came the batons, and it looked for a moment as if a major conflict was about to start.

Law and order, however, was just about restored and eventually the jury reached its verdict, acquitting the seven of the charges under Order 1305, though finding them guilty of a lesser offence according to the terms of the National Dock Labour Scheme. Released on bail, pending sentence, the leaders were carried away shoulder-high. Effectively killing Order 1305 and re-establishing the unfettered right to withdraw labour, the outcome was, according to Dash in 1969, 'the most important post-war victory for the trade union movement'.[7]

The next two days revealed Shawcross the pragmatist: first he withdrew the prosecution against the seven; then he announced that no action would be taken against the four young Scots who had stolen the recently surrendered Coronation Stone, on the grounds that it was best to avoid creating martyrs. Meanwhile, 'The Dockers' K.C.', as he had been dubbed many years earlier, was cremated at 1 pm on Wednesday. 'Trekked to Golders Green for Bevin's funeral,' recorded Gladys Langford. 'Recognised Hore Belisha, Churchill, Morrison & Aneurin Bevan. The last reclined in a lovely car. They "do themselves well" these Labour M.P.s.' Half an hour later, the BBC circumspectly played gramophone records instead of repeating Monday's memorable edition of *Twenty Questions*. But for another, less temperamental star, there could never be enough repeats. 'Girls tore themselves away from buckets, spades and earth,' noted Judy Haines in Chingford on Thursday, 'for Andy Pandy – a film of Tuesday's performance.'

Two days later, there was one of the period's far from infrequent railway accidents, in this case involving a 'Soccer Special' on the way to the Scottish Cup Final at Hampden Park, Glasgow. Three died and 68 were injured, as 'once-gay tartan scarves, tam-o'-shanters and football favours hung grotesquely among the twisted steel and splintered woodwork'. But the match went ahead – no one seems to have doubted that it would – and Celtic beat Motherwell 1–0 in front of the usual 134,000. Down south there was another cup final – the Amateur Cup Final, played at Wembley and attended by a crowd of (astonishing as it now seems) 100,000. Pegasus, formed only three years earlier as a combined Oxford and Cambridge Universities side, defeated the north-east's Bishop Auckland 2–1 with a performance admired by the quality press for its almost Continental-style fluency. According to Geoffrey Green, the football correspondent of *The Times* who wrote with such romantic flair that he made many upper-middle-class readers take the game even half-seriously for the first time, it was an outcome that had 'perhaps satisfied the desires of a sentimental majority'. The indefatigable Gladys Langford, though, chose the theatre that Saturday, going to the Haymarket to see *Waters of the Moon*. 'People in the gallery,' she noted, 'roared at Wendy Hiller "Speak up!" which must have been very disconcerting.'[8]

Over the weekend, it emerged that Bevan had, after much prevarication, at last decided to resign. 'The Budget, in my view, is wrongly conceived in that it fails to apportion fairly the burdens of expenditure as between different social classes,' he wrote on Saturday afternoon to Attlee (still in St Mary's). Significantly, he broadened his case: 'It is wrong because it is based upon a scale of military expenditure, in the coming year, which is physically unobtainable, without grave extravagance in its spending.' Then in the Commons on Monday he made a resignation statement perhaps best evoked by Macmillan's diary:

> Bevan's 'apologia' was certainly novel in manner, if not in matter. It was a violent castigation of his colleagues, delivered with incredible asperity, not to say malice. Up to a certain point it was well done; but he lost the House at the end. Members were shocked by his explanation of why he agreed to the 1/- contribution towards prescription and the 25,000 cut in house-building last year. He had only agreed because he knew these measures were impracticable and could not in fact be carried out. He out-manoeuvred – not to say, 'double-crossed' his colleagues.

'The Socialists,' added Macmillan, 'are very angry at his "disloyalty" – which threatens their own seats and pockets. But really they agree with his sentiments.'

Next morning, at a special meeting of the PLP, Bevan gave an even more intemperate performance. According to Hugh Dalton, he was 'sweating & shouting & seemed on the edge of a nervous breakdown'; both Dalton and a colleague found the egocentricity (at one point Bevan referred to '*my* Health Service') unpleasantly reminiscent of Oswald Mosley. In her next *The New Yorker* letter, Mollie Panter-Downes summed up the conventional wisdom about Bevan's post-resignation future when she observed that some of those who had seen him as a potential Prime Minister 'now suspect that he is less a statesman, thinking of England in the round, than a politician, thinking in terms of a game of politics with Englishmen, played with distorting Welsh violence'. For Attlee, writing to his brother a week after Bevan's resignation (and shortly after leaving hospital), there was as usual little more to be said: 'The Bevan business is a nuisance. The real wonder is that we kept him reasonably straight for so long. But with this and Ernie's death I did not have as restful time as I should have liked.'[9]

On the same day as Bevan's resignation statement, two other ministers resigned: Harold Wilson (President of the Board of Trade) and John Freeman (Under-Secretary at the Ministry of Supply). Wilson's resignation statement on the Tuesday was far more impressive than Bevan's but the tag now given to him by Hugh Dalton, that he was 'Nye's little dog', soon stuck. Indeed, *The Times* had already noted how 'this second resignation appears to be treated by the Government and the Labour Party as a matter of no great consequence', while the *Manchester Guardian* observed that 'a certain superiority of manner in debate has not helped his popularity.' Raymond Streat, who over recent years had got to know Wilson quite well, reflected soon afterwards on what for him, as for most people, was an unexpected turn of events:

> I knew he was pally with Bevan of late. Why he should turn that way baffles me. Surely Wilson's natural role was that of the intellectual professional politician in the Socialist party. How he could possibly see himself in the class of emotional socialists or in a clique of intrigues and power gamblers within the party I cannot imagine. Latterly he had begun to fancy himself as a negotiator – high office had begun to go to his head. I am sorry in a way. Wilson is from many aspects a thoroughly nice young man. He has brains and can work fast and well.

'I think now,' Streat prophesied, 'he will become just a political jobber and adventurer.'

It is pretty clear in retrospect that the motives of all three main protagonists – Gaitskell, Bevan and Wilson – were the usual mix of the pure and the impure. Gaitskell's more critical biographer, Brian Brivati, emphasises his consistency over the issue of NHS spending and his determination that the NHS 'would be managed like any other part of the state and subject to the control of the Treasury', but at the same time he 'might also have seen his chance to take a commanding lead at the head of his generation of Labour Ministers'. John Campbell, Bevan's non-hagiographical biographer, sees ego rather than political ambition as such at work, arguing that – whatever the probably superior intrinsic merits of Bevan's entirely sincere case in relation to both NHS financing and the unrealistically ambitious rearmament programme – he went 'catastrophically wrong' by 'getting the matter out of perspective, by overplaying his hand so self-indulgently, by losing his temper and abusing his colleagues [notably Cabinet on the 19th], and ultimately in allowing himself to be persuaded [above all by his wife and Michael Foot] to resign, against the better judgement of his cooler friends'. As for Wilson, his biographer Ben Pimlott does not deny his 'bitter determination, if possible, to block Gaitskell's path' or his ambition for high office should Bevan become leader after an electoral defeat for Labour, but he also notes Wilson's growing and genuine fascination with Bevan and his left-wing politics, as well as his equally genuine 'shrewd assessment of the likely impact of defence spending on the economy'.

For all three in April 1951, transcending the immediate verdicts on the resignation drama, there remained everything to play for. 'It is really a fight for the soul of the Labour Party,' remarked Gaitskell at one point as it unfolded. And soon after, he reflected, 'Who will win it? No one can say as yet. I'm afraid that if Bevan does we shall be out of power for years and years.'[10]

On the evening of Wilson's resignation, John Arlott took the *Twenty Questions* chair in place of Harding and had, according to the *Daily Express* anyway, a bit of a nightmare:

> Arlott was a stonewaller. When he did try to help he overdid it. Often he omitted to give the number of questions. That is a major error in this radio parlour game. It is vital to keep up the excitement.
>
> His attempts at humour were heavy-handed. His crosstalk with the team sounded forced rather than fluent . . .

Kenneth Preston in Keighley did not listen, but the next evening, in stream-of-consciousness mood, he was stationed by his trusty wireless:

I am at present listening to an international boxing contest [at Haringay] between Don Cockell (Great Britain) and Freddie Beshore (United States) much to Kath's [his wife's] disgust. Harold Wilson has now resigned and duly given his reason in Parliament. Sir Hartley Shawcross (another clever devil) has been made President of the Board of Trade and [Alf] Robens has been made Minister of Labour. Parliament is now discussing the proposed charges [in the event carried easily enough] for false teeth and spectacles. It seems as though a General Election is nearer now than it was. There does not seem to be much prospect of a knock-out in this fight. The American seems to be so tough that Cockell seems to be banging away at a wall. However much the Englishman hits him he still comes on. The Englishman has won on points. We have no fire tonight and now it is not very warm. It would be a good idea to go to bed before we become any colder. The U.N. forces are still having to give ground in Korea. It is being said in America that now that Bevan has gone on one side and [General] MacArthur on theirs that there is prospect of a greater measure of co-operation between the two countries than there was before. At long last an agreement on meat has been signed with Argentina and now Webb [Minister of Food] is having to pay more than he would have had to pay if he had accepted Argentina's previous offer.

'I think I am going to have a look at my "Dead Souls" now before I get off to bed,' he added. 'It really is a most amazing book.'

Two evenings later, on Thursday the 26th, the special meeting convened by the Quarry Hill Flats Tenants' Association at last took place at the estate's social centre. A local reporter recorded some lively exchanges:

Mrs Dove, a tenant and member of the Association, said, in her opinion, that the flats were rapidly becoming a slum and was glad that the broadcast had roused the tenants into taking action.

Then a gentleman stood up and said that the flats were 'dumps' – in every respect. 'I do not want to live here at all' he said. ('Then get out' came from the back of the hall.)

'The broadcast was in very bad taste,' cried a lady at the front, 'and gave a disgraceful impression of our homes.'

'The damage is already done,' – another was on his feet, 'and the only thing that we can do now is to prove that it was totally wrong.'

'And how are we going to do that?' shouted a man from the back corner.

'By demanding a public apology from the B.B.C.'

'And do you really think you'll get it?' another chap added with a that's-what-you-think snigger.

By this time the meeting was in unroar . . .

Eventually, the proposal to demand a public apology from the programme's producer was defeated by 33 votes to 16. Fatalism, it seemed, ruled. 'Will the interest caused by the broadcast remain with the tenants so that the effect will prove beneficial in its outcome?' wondered the not unfriendly reporter. 'Or are they content to remain the inhabitants of a "dump"?'[11]

On Saturday the 28th there was as usual a full Football League programme (Accrington Stanley going down to the only goal at Hartlepool), but the nation's attention was firmly fixed on the Cup Final at Wembley, where Blackpool were due to play Newcastle United. 'This has come to be regarded as "the Matthews final",' wrote Geoffrey Green in *The Times* that morning. 'One cannot expect this supreme player to last for ever, and this may well be his last chance to procure the only prize – a cupwinner's medal – that has escaped him in a wonderful career. The whole country, except the north-eastern corner, of course, wishes him success.' Stanley Matthews was now 36, and this was the second Cup Final since the war to be billed as the Blackpool right winger's last chance.

That afternoon, the familiar, deeply reassuring pre-match rituals were enacted – the Band of the Coldstream Guards, the community singing (starting with 'Abide With Me'), the presentation of the teams to a heavily overcoated King George – before the game began. The first half was scoreless, despite what Green in his match report described as 'the uncontrolled lonely brilliance of Matthews', but early in the second half, with the match now being watched by television viewers as well as the 100,000 in the stadium, Newcastle's centre forward, Jackie Milburn, scored twice in five minutes. 'There was a violent pounding on my back as someone beat a victory tattoo,' was how a spectator standing among Geordies in the three-bob 'H' pen described the reaction to the second goal, 'and the harsh crack of the rattles merged with a mighty outburst which seemed to shake the arena and call a tune from the empty beer bottles lying about my feet.' It only remained for the Magpies to play out time, which they comfortably did.

Afterwards, Joe Harvey and his men climbed up to the Royal Box to receive the Cup and their winners' medals. There was a special moment for Jack Fairbrother – the Newcastle goalkeeper whom the Football Association had unsuccessfully urged to wear a baseball cap, apparently because a cloth cap was too working-class. Grinning as he passed Princess Margaret, he was greeted with, 'A lovely day for you!' Meanwhile, Matthews, in Green's words, 'slipped quietly from the scene'.[12]

Afterword

It had been an extraordinarily hard six years since the end of the war – in some ways even harder than the years of the war itself. The end was at last in sight of a long, long period of more or less unremitting austerity. Few adults who had lived through the 1940s would readily forgo the prospect of a little more ease, a little more comfort. A new world was slowly taking shape, but for most of these adults what mattered far more was the creation and maintenance of a safe, secure home life – in any home that could be found. 'The Safe Way to Safety whenever and wherever infection threatens in your own home' ran the reassuring message in the spring of 1951 from the makers of Dettol. 'Such deep, safe, soapy suds!' was the unique selling proposition of New Rinso. 'If it's safe in water, it's safe in Lux.'[1] For the children of the 1950s, there would be – for better or worse – no escape from the tough, tender, purifying embrace of family Britain.

Notes

Abbreviations

Abrams	Mark Abrams Papers (Churchill Archives Centre, Churchill College, Cambridge)
BBC WA	BBC Written Archives (Caversham)
Brown	Diary of W. J. Brown (Department of Documents, Imperial War Museum)
Chaplin	Sid Chaplin Papers (Special Collections, University of Newcastle upon Tyne)
Daly	Lawrence Daly Papers (Modern Records Centre, University of Warwick)
Fabian	Fabian Society Papers (British Library of Political and Economic Science)
Ferguson	Diary of Colin Ferguson (Glasgow City Archives)
Ford	Diary of Erica Ford (Ealing Local History Centre)
Gaitskell	Philip M. Williams (ed), *The Diary of Hugh Gaitskell, 1945–56* (1983)
Golden	Diary of Grace Golden (Museum of London)
Haines	Diary of Alice (Judy) Haines (Special Collections, University of Sussex)
Headlam	Stuart Ball (ed), *Parliament and Politics in the Age of Churchill and Attlee: The Headlam Diaries 1935–1951* (Cambridge, 1999)
Heap	Diary of Anthony Heap (London Metropolitan Archives)
Hodgson	Diary of Vere Hodgson (held by Veronica Bowater, literary executor)
King	Diary of Mary King (Birmingham City Archives)
Langford	Diary of Gladys Langford (Islington Local History Centre)
Lewis	Diary of Frank Lewis (Glamorgan Record Office)
Loftus	Diary of Ernest Loftus (Thurrock Museum)
M-O A	Mass-Observation Archive (Special Collections, University of Sussex)
Osborn	Michael Hughes (ed), *The Letters of Lewis Mumford and Frederic J. Osborn* (Bath, 1971)
Preston	Diary of Kenneth Preston (Bradford Archives)
Raynham	Diary of Marian Raynham (Special Collections, University of Sussex)
St John	Diary of Henry St John (Ealing Local History Centre)
Speed	Diary of Florence Speed (Department of Documents, Imperial War Museum)
Streat	Marguerite Dupree (ed), *Lancashire and Whitehall: The Diary of Sir Raymond Streat: Volume Two, 1939–57* (Manchester, 1987)
Uttin	Diary of Rose Uttin (Department of Documents, Imperial War Museum)
Willmott	Diary of Phyllis Willmott

All books are published in London unless otherwise stated.

A World to Build

1 Waiting for Something to Happen

1. M-O A, FR 2263.
2. Heap, 8 May 1945; *Independent on Sunday*, 11 Jul 1999; Langford, 8 May 1945; Harold Nicolson, *Diaries and Letters, 1939–1945* (1967), p 456; M-O A, FR 2263.
3. Nicolson, *Diaries and Letters*, p 457; Langford, 8 May 1945; Vera Brittain, *Wartime Chronicle* (1989), p 265; Heap, 8 May 1945; Langford, 8 May 1945; BBC WA, R9/9/9 – LR/3470; Lewis, 8 May 1945.
4. M-O A, FR 2263; Ursula Vaughan Williams, *R.V.W.* (1964), p 262; Cecil Beaton, *The Happy Years* (1972), p 38; diary of Joan Waley, 8 May 1945; Haines, 8 May 1945.
5. Streat, p 259; Loftus, 8 May 1945; David Rayvern Allen, *Arlott* (1994), p 78; James Lees-Milne, *Prophesying Peace* (1984), p 187; M-O A, TC 49/1/C.
6. *Nella Last's War* (Bristol, 1981), p 280; BBC WA, R9/9/9 – LR/3470; Lewis, 8 May 1945.
7. Joan Wyndham, *Love is Blue* (1986), pp 177–8; *The Noël Coward Diaries* (1982), p 29; Heap, 8 May 1945.
8. M-O A, FR 2263; Ferguson, 9 May 1945; King, 8 May 1945; Streat, p 260; Haines, 8 May 1945.
9. *Hereford Times*, 12 May 1945; *Midland Counties Express*, 12 May 1945; M-O A, FR 2263.
10. Langford, 9 May 1945; St John, 8–9 May 1945; *The Journals of Denton Welch* (1984), p 191.
11. Lees-Milne, p 188; *The Second World War Diary of Hugh Dalton* (1986), p 858; recollections of Michael Burns; Langford, 9 May 1945; Lewis, 9 May 1945; Heap, 9 May 1945; *Fifty Years On* (Radio 4, 23 May 1995); Heap, 9 May 1945.
12. Kenneth Tynan, *Letters* (1994), pp 70–71; M-O A, FR 2263.

2 Broad Vistas and All That

1. The main source for this paragraph is A. H. Halsey (ed), *Twentieth-Century British Social Trends* (Basingstoke, 2000).
2. *Picture Post*, 4 Jan 1941.
3. Richard Bradford, *Lucky Him* (2001), p 52.
4. F.W.S. Craig (ed), *British General Election Manifestos* (1975), pp 123–31; Asa Briggs, *Michael Young* (Basingstoke, 2001), p 69.
5. *Times Literary Supplement*, 14 Jan 2000.
6. John Vaizey, *In Breach of Promise* (1983), p 141; John Singleton, 'Labour, the Conservatives and Nationalisation', in Robert Millward and John Singleton (eds), *The Political Economy of Nationalisation in Britain, 1920–1950* (Cambridge, 1995), p 17.

7. Alan Deacon and Jonathan Bradshaw, *Reserved for the Poor* (Oxford, 1983), p 42; Nicholas Timmins, *The Five Giants* (2001), p 47; Jane Lewis, *Women in Britain since 1945* (Oxford, 1992), p 21; Jeffrey Weeks, *Sex, Politics and Society* (Harlow, 1989), p 232; *New Statesman*, 6 Feb 1998 (Raymond Plant). Generally on the Beveridge Report, see: Rodney Lowe, *The Welfare State in Britain since 1945* (Basingstoke, 1999), chap 6.1; Timmins, chaps 1–3.

8. Ralf Dahrendorf, *LSE* (Oxford, 1995), p 385; Jim Kincaid, 'Richard Titmuss 1907–73', in Paul Barker (ed), *Founders of the Welfare State* (1984), pp 114–20; Charles Webster, 'Investigating Inequalities in Health before Black', *Contemporary British History* (Autumn 2002), p 86; John E. Pater, *The Making of the National Health Service* (1981), p 78; *Guardian*, 20 May 1994 (Paul Addison).

9. *Times Educational Supplement*, 24 Jul 1943; Gary McCulloch, *Philosophers and Kings* (Cambridge, 1991), p 61; *TES*, 24 Jul 1943.

10. *Financial News*, 22 Jan 1934; Paul Oliver et al, *Dunroamin* (1981), pp 34–7, 46; George Orwell, *Coming up for Air* (Penguin edn, 1962), pp 13, 16; Thomas Sharp, *Town Planning* (1940), pp vii, 54, 57, 109; *Independent*, 19 Feb 2001; *Architectural Review* (Apr 1943), p 86; Gordon E. Cherry, *Urban Change and Planning* (Henley-on-Thames, 1972), p 163; Harold Wilson, *The Governance of Britain* (1976), p 54.

11. F. J. Osborn, 'Space Standards in Planning', in Gilbert and Elizabeth Glen McAllister, *Homes, Towns and Countryside* (1945), p 101.

12. Lionel Esher, *A Broken Wave* (1981), p 31; Patrick Dunleavy, *The Politics of Mass Housing in Britain, 1945–1975* (Oxford, 1981), p 54; *Picture Post*, 4 Jan 1941; *Architectural Review* (May 1942), p 128; Sharp, *Town Planning*, pp 76, 78.

13. Peter Hall, *Cities of Tomorrow* (Oxford, 2002), p 236; Arnold Whittick, *F.J.O.* (1987), p 74; Nicholas Bullock, 'Plans for Post-war Housing in the UK', *Planning Perspectives* (Jan 1987), pp 82, 78; Nick Tiratsoo et al, *Urban Reconstruction in Britain and Japan, 1945–1955* (Luton, 2002), p 6.

14. Junichi Hasegawa, *Replanning the Blitzed City Centre* (Buckingham, 1992), pp 50–52, 77–9; Hasegawa, 'The Reconstruction of Portsmouth in the 1940s', *Contemporary British History* (Spring 2000), pp 49–50; Nick Tiratsoo, 'Labour and the Reconstruction of Hull, 1945–51', in Tiratsoo (ed), *The Attlee Years* (1991), pp 127–31.

15. Gordon E. Cherry, 'Lessons from the Past', *Planning History*, 11/3 (1989), pp 3–7; Tiratsoo et al, *Urban Reconstruction*, p 5; Cherry, 'Lessons', p 5; Brian Chalkley, 'The Plan for the City Centre', in Mark Brayshay (ed), *Post-war Plymouth* (Plymouth, 1983), pp 17–18, 27–8, 30.

16. *Architectural Review* (Jan 1941), pp 31–2; Hasegawa, *Replanning*, p 32; Nick Tiratsoo, *Reconstruction, Affluence and Labour Politics: Coventry 1945–60* (1990), p 13; Tiratsoo et al, *Urban Reconstruction*, p 17. In general on the reconstruction plans for Coventry, see: Tiratsoo, *Reconstruction, Affluence and Labour Politics*, chap 2.

17. *Picture Post*, 4 Jan 1941; Steven Fielding et al, *'England Arise!'* (Manchester, 1995), pp 81–2.

18. Jeremy Nuttall, '"Psychological Socialist", "Militant Moderate": Evan Durbin and the Politics of Synthesis', *Labour History Review* (Aug 2003), pp 238, 241, 243; Stephen Brooke, 'Evan Durbin: Reassessing a Labour "Revisionist"', in *Twentieth Century British History*, 7/1 (1996), p 34; E.F.M. Durbin, *The Politics of Democratic Socialism* (1940), pp 330–31; Jim Tomlinson, 'Planning: Debate and Policy in the

1940s', *Twentieth Century British History*, 3/2 (1992), p 164. In general on Durbin, in addition to the above, see: Elizabeth Durbin, *New Jerusalems* (1985).

19. *Architectural Review* (Feb 1942), p 40; James Lansdale Hodson, *The Sea and the Land* (1945), p 303; Deacon and Bradshaw, *Reserved for the Poor*, pp 32–4.

20. *The Collected Essays, Journalism and Letters of George Orwell, Volume II* (1968), p 104; M-O A, TC 2/2/J; Vere Hodgson, *Few Eggs and No Oranges* (Persephone edn, 1999), p 334; Mass-Observation, 'Social Security and Parliament', *Political Quarterly* (Jul–Sept 1943), pp 249, 246–7; John Jacobs, 'December 1942: Beveridge Observed', in John Jacobs (ed), *Beveridge 1942–1992* (1992), pp 21–2; Tony Mason and Peter Thompson, '"Reflections on a Revolution"?', in Tiratsoo, *Attlee Years*, p 57; Robert J. Wybrow, *Britain Speaks Out, 1937–87* (Basingstoke, 1989), p 16; BBC WA, R9/9/9 – LR/3163.

21. M-O A, FR 1162.

22. José Harris, 'Did British Workers Want the Welfare State?', in Jay Winter (ed), *The Working Class in Modern British History* (Cambridge, 1983), p 214; Jacobs, 'December 1942', p 21; M-O, 'Social Security', p 253.

23. George H. Gallup (ed), *The Gallup International Public Opinion Polls: Great Britain 1937–1975, Volume One* (New York, 1976), p 75; *Express and Star*, 22 Nov 1943.

24. Hodson, *Sea*, pp 303, 348; Steven Fielding, 'What Did "The People" Want?', *Historical Journal*, 35/3 (1992), pp 627–8; Jacobs, 'December 1942', p 30.

25. Wybrow, *Britain Speaks Out*, p 16; Singleton, 'Labour', pp 21–2; Rodney Lowe, 'The Second World War, Consensus, and the Foundation of the Welfare State', *Twentieth Century British History*, 1/2 (1990), p 175; *The Collected Essays, Journalism and Letters of George Orwell, Volume III* (1968), p 226.

26. Mass-Observation, *The Journey Home* (1944), pp 42, 96, 105, 109–10; M-O A, TC 3/1/F.

27. M-O A, FR 1162.

28. *Architectural Review* (Nov 1941), p 148; Naoki Motouchi and Nick Tiratsoo, 'Max Lock, Middlesbrough, and a Forgotten Tradition in British Post-war Planning', *Planning History* (2004), pp 17–20; *Journal of the Town Planning Institute* (Nov–Dec 1945), pp 1–5.

29. *Architectural Review* (Apr 1943), p 88; Hasegawa, *Replanning*, pp 80–84; Peter J. Larkham, 'Rebuilding the Industrial Town', *Urban History* (Dec 2002), pp 401–2.

30. *Coventry Standard*, 1 Mar 1941; Hasegawa, *Replanning*, p 39; *Coventry Evening Telegraph*, 15/19/21 Dec 1944; Mason and Thompson, 'Reflections', pp 63–4.

31. Mass-Observation, 'Some Psychological Factors in Home Building', *Town and Country Planning* (Spring 1943), pp 8–9; Mass-Observation, *People's Homes* (1943), pp 4–5, 219, 226; *Architectural Review* (Nov 1943), p 144.

32. Mass-Observation, *People's Homes*, p xix; Mrs M. Pleydell-Bouverie, *Daily Mail Book of Britain's Post-War Homes* (1944), pp 19–20; R. E. Pahl, *Divisions of Labour* (Oxford, 1984), pp 321–2; Nick Tiratsoo, 'The Reconstruction of Blitzed British Cities, 1945–55', *Contemporary British History* (Spring 2000), p 39.

33. Tiratsoo, 'Blitzed', p 38; Mark Clapson, *Invincible Green Suburbs, Brave New Towns* (Manchester, 1998), p 58; The Social Survey, *Furniture* (1945), pp 20–21.

34. F. J. Osborn, *New Towns After the War* (1942), p 13; *Picture Post*, 18 Jan 1941.

35. Mass-Observation, *People's Homes*, pp xxiii, 226; Bullock, 'Plans', pp 78, 80; Pleydell-Bouverie, p 19.

36. Dennis Chapman, *A Social Survey of Middlesbrough* (1945–6), pt II, pp 1, 3, 12; pt II, pp 9–10; pt III, pp 14, 24–32; pt IV, pp 1–5, 16.

37. Mason and Thompson, 'Reflections', pp 56–7; Lowe, 'Consensus', pp 177–8; Nicholas Joicey, 'A Paperback Guide to Progress', *Twentieth Century British History* 4/1 (1993), pp 41–4; Harold Nicolson, *Diaries and Letters, 1939–1945* (1967), p 465; *New Society*, 25 Apr 1963; Ross McKibbin, *Classes and Cultures* (Oxford, 1998), pp 527–8; *Picture Post*, 18 Jan 1941; Adrian Smith, 'The Fall and Fall of the Third *Daily Herald*, 1930–64', in Peter Catterall et al (eds), *Northcliffe's Legacy* (2000), pp 179–80.

38. Lesley A. Hall, *Sex, Gender and Social Change in Britain since 1880* (Basingstoke, 2000), pp 139–40; Eliot Slater and Moya Woodside, *Patterns of Marriage* (1951), pp 82–3, 249–54.

3 Oh Wonderful People of Britain!

1. *The Diaries of Sir Robert Bruce Lockhart, Volume Two* (1980), pp 439–40; Langford, 22 May 1945; Haines, 16/19/26 May 1945; St John, 1 Jun 1945; Loftus, 7 Jun 1945.

2. Edmund Wilson, *The Forties* (New York, 1983), p 107; Eric Parker, *Surrey* (1947), pp 105–9; *Author* (Winter 1996), p 137; The Rev. W. Awdry, *The Three Railway Engines* (1967), p 40; *Guardian*, 7 Jun 1995; *Letters for a Life: The Selected Letters and Diaries of Benjamin Britten, 1913–1976, Volume Two* (1991), p 1252.

3. St John, 14 Jun 1945; Keith Waterhouse, *City Lights* (1994), p 170; Humphrey Carpenter, *Dennis Potter* (1998), pp 27–32.

4. Michael Foot, *Aneurin Bevan, Volume I* (Granada edn, 1975), pp 503–4; Edward Pearce, *Denis Healey* (2002), p 54; Austin Mitchell, *Election '45* (1995), p 20.

5. Martin Gilbert, *'Never Despair': Winston S. Churchill, 1945–1965* (1988), pp 32, 49; Haines, 4/5 Jun 1945; Robert Rhodes James, *Bob Boothby* (1991), p 330; Ursula Bloom, *Trilogy* (1954), pp 167–8; Thelma Cazalet-Keir, *From the Wings* (1967), p 124; *Times Literary Supplement*, 9 Jul 2004 (Angus Calder); *News of the World*, 1 Jul 1945; Paul Addison, 'Churchill and the Price of Victory', in Nick Tiratsoo (ed), *From Blitz to Blair* (1997), p 74.

6. Julian Amery, *Approach March* (1973), p 438; Hugh Thomas, *John Strachey* (1973), p 223; *Spectator*, 15 Mar 2003 (Antonia Fraser); John Campbell, *Margaret Thatcher, Volume One* (2000), p 53; *Among You Taking Notes... The Wartime Diary of Naomi Mitchison* (1985), p 327; Anne Perkins, *Red Queen* (2003), p 78; Simon Hoggart and David Leigh, *Michael Foot* (1981), pp 90–91; Chaplin, 7/3/1, 8 Jul 1945; *Tottenham and Edmonton Weekly Herald*, 22/29 Jun 1945.

7. *Luton News*, 21/28 Jun 1945, 5 Jul 1945.

8. Lord Elwyn-Jones, *In My Time* (1983), p 84; Mitchell, *Election '45*, p 44; Nina Bawden, *In My Own Time* (1994), p 77.

9. M-O A, FR 2270A; Mass-Observation, 'Post-Mortem on Voting at the Election', *Quarterly Review* (Jan 1946), p 59; *The Complete Works of George Orwell, Volume 17* (1998), p 192; Wilson, *The Forties*, pp 109–10; Tony Mason and Peter Thompson, '"Reflections on a Revolution"?', in Nick Tiratsoo (ed), *The Attlee Years* (1991), p 64.

10. *Manchester Guardian*, 4 Jul 1945; Langford, 5 Jul 1945; *The Correspondence of H. G. Wells:, Volume 4* (1998), p 523; *Independent*, 30 Jun 2003; Mitchell, *Election '45*,

p 78; Loftus, 5 Jul 1945; St John, 5 Jul 1945; Ferguson, 5 Jul 1945; *News of the World*, 8 Jul 1945; Pathe Newsreel, circa 10 Jul 1945.

11. *News of the World*, 8 Jul 1945; *Nella Last's War* (Bristol, 1981), p 293; James Hinton, 'Militant Housewives', *History Workshop* (Autumn 1994), p 132; Haines, 14 Jul 1945; *Selected Letters of André Gide and Dorothy Bussy* (Oxford, 1983), p 243; *Tottenham and Edmonton Weekly Herald*, 20 Jul 1945.

12. Brown, 2/4, 12 Jul 1945; Osborn, p 88; M-O A, FR 2270B.

13. David Kynaston, *The City of London, Volume III* (1999), pp 508–9; M-O A, FR 2270A.

14. *Lockhart*, p 473; Kenneth O. Morgan, 'Wales since 1945', in Trevor Herbert and Gareth Elwyn Jones (eds), *Post-War Wales* (Cardiff, 1995), p 10; Mitchison, *Among You*, pp 334–5; Selina Hastings, *Evelyn Waugh* (1994), p 495; Walter Allen, *As I Walked Down New Grub Street* (1981), pp 103–4.

15. Tony Benn, *Years of Hope* (1994), p 91; Francis Beckett, *Clem Attlee* (1997), p 198; William Harrington and Peter Young, *The 1945 Revolution* (1978), p 192.

16. A.J.P. Taylor, *Beaverbrook* (1972), p 568; Anthony Howard, '"We Are The Masters Now"', in Michael Sissons and Philip French (eds), *Age of Austerity* (Oxford, 1986), p 3; James Agate, *Ego 8* (1946), p 184.

17. Loftus, 26 Jul 1945; King, 26 Jul 1945; Heap, 27 Jul 1945; *Nella Last's War*, p 298; Haines, 26 Jul 1945; Harrington and Young, *1945*, p 189; Michael Ignatieff, *Isaiah Berlin* (1998), p 134; Peter J. Conradi, *Iris Murdoch* (2001), p 211; Dylan Thomas, *The Collected Letters* (2000), p 624; *The Nightfisherman: Selected Letters of W. S. Graham* (Manchester, 1999), p 51.

18. Pamela Street, *Arthur Bryant* (1979), p 132; John Gale, *Clean Young Englishman* (1988), p 84; *The Noël Coward Diaries* (1982), p 36.

19. Gilbert, *'Never Despair'*, pp 113, 115; Mark Garnett, *Alport* (1999), p 66; *Horizon* (Sept 1945), p 149; *The Collected Essays, Journalism and Letters of George Orwell, Volume III* (1968), pp 446–7.

20. Retrospective explanations include: Henry Pelling, 'The 1945 General Election Reconsidered', *Historical Journal*, 23/2 (1980), pp 399–414; Gary McCulloch, 'Labour, the Left, and the British General Election of 1945', *Journal of British Studies* (Oct 1985), pp 465–89; Geoffrey K. Fry, 'A Reconsideration of the British General Election of 1935 and the Electoral Revolution of 1945', *History* (Feb 1991), pp 43–55; Steven Fielding, 'What Did "The People" Want?', *Historical Journal*, 35/3 (1992), pp 623–39; Stephen Brooke, 'The Labour Party and the 1945 General Election', *Contemporary Record* (Summer 1995), pp 1–21; Michael David Kandiah, 'The Conservative Party and the 1945 General Election', *Contemporary Record* (Summer 1995), pp 22–47.

21. Kandiah, 'Conservative Party', p 106.

22. *Orwell, Volume III*, pp 447–8; *The Times*, 15 Dec 1990; Uttin, 29 Jul 1945.

23. John K. Walton, *Blackpool* (Edinburgh, 1998), p 139; Heap, 29 Jul 1945; *Radio Times*, 27 Jul 1945; Harold Nicolson, *The Later Years, 1945–1962: Diaries and Letters, Volume III* (1968), p 30; Christopher Mayhew, *Time to Explain* (1987), p 88; Gaitskell, p 7.

24. Brown, 1/15, 2 Aug 1945; Lord Taylor of Mansfield, *Uphill All The Way* (1972), p 138; *Lockhart*, p 477; Richard Rose, 'Class and Party Divisions', *Sociology* (May 1968), p 131.

25. *News Chronicle*, 7 Aug 1945; *Radio Times*, 3 Aug 1945; Norris McWhirter, *Ross* (1976), pp 59–60; Heap, 6 Aug 1945.

26. BBC WA, Home Service, 6 Aug 1945; Bloom, *Trilogy*, p 159; Elizabeth Longford, *The Pebbled Shore* (1986), p 226; Joan Wyndham, *Love is Blue* (1986), p 189; Canon L. John Collins, *Faith under Fire* (1966), pp 98–9.

27. Martin Stannard, *Evelyn Waugh: No Abiding City, 1939–1966* (1992), p 151; *Joyce & Ginnie: The Letters of Joyce Grenfell and Virginia Graham* (1997), p 134; *Noël Coward Diaries*, p 37; Frances Spalding, *Vanessa Bell* (1983), p 328; *Letters of J.R.R. Tolkien* (1981), p 116; Ferguson, 8 Aug 1945; Langford, 7 Aug 1945.

28. St John, 7/9 Aug 1945; *Nella Last's War*, pp 302–4.

29. Langford, 14 Aug 1945; *Nella Last's War*, p 305–6; Loftus, 14/15 Aug 1945; *Merthyr Express*, 18 Aug 1945.

30. Headlam, p 475; Haines, 15–16 Aug 1945; Uttin, 15 Aug 1945; Langford, 15 Aug 1945; Heap, 15 Aug 1945.

31. Osborn, pp 92, 95; *Grantham Journal*, 17 Aug 1945.

4 We're So Short of Everything

1. *Tribune*, 14/28 Dec 1945. On the tour itself, see: Ronald Kowalski and Dilwyn Porter, 'Political Football', *International Journal of the History of Sport* (Aug 1997), pp 100–21.

2. *Accrington Observer*, 8/12 Jan 1946; Rogan Taylor and Andrew Ward, *Kicking and Screaming* (1995), p 60; Andrew Ward, *Armed with a Football* (Oxford, 1994), pp 2–9; Heap, 4 Oct 1945; Ford, 21 Sept 1945; Joanna Bourke, *Working-Class Cultures in Britain 1890–1960* (1994), p 186; Ted Kavanagh, *Tommy Handley* (1949), pp 199–200; King, 29 Apr 1946; Kevin Brownlow, *David Lean* (1996), p 203. On *ITMA*, see also Denis Gifford, *The Golden Age of Radio* (1985), p 134; John Gross, *A Double Thread* (2001), p 79.

3. William Glock, *Notes in Advance* (Oxford, 1991), p 40; *Independent*, 4 Aug 1995 (Bryan Robertson); Golden, 12 Mar 1946; Bryan Appleyard, *The Pleasures of Peace* (1989), p 56; *Tatler*, 7 Nov 1945; *Chips: The Diaries of Sir Henry Channon* (1967), p 414.

4. Barry Turner and Tony Rennell, *When Daddy Came Home* (1995), pp 61, 95, 100.

5. Elizabeth Wilson, *Only Halfway to Paradise* (1980), p 22; Jane Lewis, *Women in Britain since 1945* (Oxford, 1992), p 17; Cynthia L. White, *Women's Magazines, 1693–1968* (1970), pp 135–6; *Guardian*, 8 Nov 1999; Janice Winship, 'Nation Before Family', in *Formations of Nation and People* (1984), p 196; Haines, 3 Mar 1946; Heap, 21 Mar 1946; James Lansdale Hodson, *The Way Things Are* (1947), p 278.

6. *The Times*, 18 Dec 2003; *Independent*, 16 Feb 1989; *The Times*, 23 Oct 2000; *Independent*, 26 Oct 2000.

7. Muriel Bowmer Papers (Department of Documents, Imperial War Museum), vol 5, fols 1099, 1118; Barbara Pym, *A Very Private Eye* (1984), p 249; *The New Yorker*, 1 Dec 1945; George Beardmore, *Civilians at War* (1984), p 200; Gerard Mooney, 'Living on the Periphery' (PhD, University of Glasgow, 1988), p 218.

8. M-O A, TC 1/9/B; Brenda Vale, *Prefabs* (1995), p 171; *Pilot Papers* (Nov 1946), pp 28–38.

9. *The New Yorker*, 1 Sept 1945; Bowmer, fol 1090; Heap, 31 Dec 1945.

10. M-O A, FR 2291; Langford, 3 Nov 1945; St John, 8 Nov 1945; King, 9 Nov 1945; Aidan Crawley, *Leap Before You Look* (1988), p 213; Streat, p 325.

11. Haines, 15 Jan 1946; Hinton, pp 132–4; M-O A, TC 67/6/A; Raynham, 13–15 Mar 1946, 2 Apr 1946.

12. Ina Zweiniger-Bargielowska, *Austerity in Britain* (Oxford, 2000), pp 125–6; *The New Yorker*, 9 Mar 1946; Speed, 7/10–11/26 Apr 1946.

13. Sylvia Townsend Warner, *Letters* (1982), p 91; Peter Stead, 'Barry Since 1939', in Donald Moore (ed), *Barry* (Barry Island, 1985), p 450; Quentin Crisp, *The Naked Civil Servant* (Fontana edn, 1977), p 173.

14. John Hilton Bureau Papers (Special Collections, University of Sussex), Box 3, Administrative Files, 28 Sept 1945; *The New Yorker*, 17 Nov 1945; Rupert Croft-Cooke, *The Dogs of Peace* (1973), p 22; Hodgson, 29 Apr 1946; M-O A, D 5353, 5 Sept 1945; Zweiniger-Bargielowska, *Austerity*, chap 4 (incl pp 161, 172); *The New Yorker*, 5 Jan 1946.

15. Bill Naughton, 'The Spiv', *Pilot Papers* (Jan 1946), pp 99–108; Hodson, *Way*, p 159; Turner and Rennell, *Daddy*, p 46.

16. Loftus, 23 Oct 1945; Hodson, *Way*, p 206; Brown, 1/15, 16 Dec 1945; David Hughes, 'The Spivs', in Michael Sissons and Philip French (eds), *Age of Austerity* (Oxford, 1986), p 85; *New Yorker*, 6 Apr 1946; Turner and Rennell, *Daddy*, p 157.

17. Hodson, *Way*, pp 119–20; Reg Green, *National Heroes* (1997), p 144; *New Yorker*, 27 Jul 1946; David Rayvern Allen, *E. W. Swanton: A Celebration* (2000), p 87; Michael Marshall, *Gentlemen and Players* (1987), pp 140–41; *Wisden Cricketers' Almanack, 1947* (1947), pp 193, 412; Lesley A. Hall, *Sex, Gender and Social Change in Britain since 1880* (Basingstoke, 2000), p 147; Nick Tiratsoo, *Reconstruction, Affluence and Labour Politics* (1990), p 50; M-O A, TC 58/1/I.

18. Speed, 6 Aug 1946; M-O A, TC 49/2/C; *Joyce & Ginnie: The Letters of Joyce Grenfell and Virginia Graham* (1997), p 143; Raynham, 8 Jun 1946; M-O A, TC 49/2/C.

19. Asa Briggs, *The History of Broadcasting in the United Kingdom, Volume IV* (Oxford, 1979), pp 197–8, 716, 201.

20. *Coventry Evening Telegraph*, 29 Jun 1946; Hinton, p 135; Haines, 19/20 Jul 1946; Golden, 22 Jul 1946; Speed, 26 Jul 1946; M-O A, TC 67/6/D.

21. Speed, 7/13 Jun 1946; Langford, 19 Aug 1946.

22. Mollie Panter-Downes, *One Fine Day* (Virago edn, 1985), p 174; Angela Thirkell, *Private Enterprise* (1947), pp 188–9; David Pryce-Jones, 'Towards the Cocktail Party', in Sissons and French, *Austerity*, p 203.

23. *Sunday Pictorial*, 7/21 Jul 1946; James Hinton, 'Self-help and Socialism', *History Workshop* (Spring 1988), pp 100–26; *Pilot Papers* (Nov 1946), pp 16–17, 21; *Evening Standard*, 13 Sept 1946.

24. BBC WA, *Woman's Hour*, 7 Nov 1946; Briggs, p 56; Haines, 12 Nov 1946; BBC WA, R9/9/10 – LR/6869.

25. Fay Weldon, *Auto da Fay* (2002), pp 154–5; M-O A, FR 2429A; Hodgson, 24 Nov 1946; Speed, 10 Oct 1946; Langford, 8 Dec 1946; Haines, 19 Dec 1946.

26. Speed, 5 Dec 1946; St John, 15 Dec 1946; Hodson, *Way*, p 299; Mass-Observation, *Puzzled People* (1947), pp 21–2, 42, 51–2, 65, 77, 83–4, 120, 122.

27. Ferdynand Zweig, *Labour, Life and Poverty* (1949), pp 7, 58–64, 127–30, 134–6, 146–7, 152, 154–6, 175.

5 Constructively Revolutionary

1. *Spectator*, 20 Sept 2003 (Raymond Carr); Fabian, G 49/10.
2. Chaplin, 7/3/1, 21 Feb 1946, 12 Jun 1946; *Durham Chronicle*, 21 Feb 1947.
3. Daly, 302/5/8, 302/4/1, 6 Jan 1946, 302/3/1, 23 Feb 1947; *Guardian*, 24 Aug 1979.
4. Heap, 8 Sept 1945; Ben Pimlott, *Hugh Dalton* (1985), p 434; *Like It Was: The Diaries of Malcolm Muggeridge* (1981), p 204; Mervyn Jones, *Michael Foot* (1994), p 141; Kenneth O. Morgan, *Callaghan* (Oxford, 1997), p 60; *New Statesman*, 2 Nov 1946.
5. Brown, 1/15, 14 Feb 1946; Brian Brivati, introduction to Alan Bullock, *Ernest Bevin* (2002), p xiii; Peter Weiler, 'Britain and the First Cold War', *Twentieth Century British History*, 9/1 (1998), pp 127–38; *The Collected Essays, Journalism and Letters of George Orwell, Volume IV* (1968), p 222; Alan Bullock, *Ernest Bevin, Foreign Secretary, 1945–1951* (Oxford, 1983), p 221; *Chips: The Diaries of Sir Henry Channon* (1967), pp 411–12; *The New Yorker*, 20 October 1945; *Tatler*, 5 Dec 1945.
6. Langford, 24 May 1946; Margaret Gowing, *Britain and Atomic Energy, 1945–1952: Volume I* (1974), p 184; Peter Hennessy, *Whitehall* (Pimlico edn, 2001), p 713.
7. Robert Skidelsky, *John Maynard Keynes, Volume Three* (2000), p 470; Bernard Donoughue and G. W. Jones, *Herbert Morrison* (1973), p 353; Richard Toye, '"The Gentlemen in Whitehall" Reconsidered', *Labour History Review* (Aug 2002), pp 197–9.
8. Alec Cairncross, *Years of Recovery* (1985), p 303; Kenneth O. Morgan, *Labour in Power, 1945–1951* (Oxford, 1984), pp 130, 135; Glen O'Hara, 'British Economic and Social Planning, 1959–1970' (PhD, University of London, 2002), pp 4–5.
9. Donoughue and Jones, *Herbert Morrison*, p 354; Stephen Brooke, 'Problems of "Socialist Planning"', *Historical Journal*, 34/3 (1991), p 692; Richard Toye, 'Gosplanners versus Thermostatters', *Contemporary British History* (Winter 2000), p 93.
10. J. D. Tomlinson, 'The Iron Quadrilateral', *Journal of British Studies* (Jan 1995), p 100; Elizabeth Durbin, *New Jerusalems* (1985), p 74; Jim Tomlinson, 'Attlee's Inheritance and the Financial System', *Financial History Review* (1994), p 145; Nicholas Davenport, *Memoirs of a City Radical* (1974), pp 72, 149.
11. Martin Francis, 'Economics and Ethics', *Twentieth Century British History*, 6/2 (1995), pp 240–41; James Lansdale Hodson, *The Way Things Are* (1947), p 135; *Hansard*, 6 May 1946, cols 604–5.
12. *The Times*, 28 Oct 1946; Manny Shinwell, *Lead With The Left* (1981), p 136; Geoffrey Goodman, 'The Role of Industrial Correspondents', in Alan Campbell et al (eds), *British Trade Unions and Industrial Politics, Volume One* (Aldershot, 1999), p 27; Hodson, *Way*, p 174; Tom Driberg, 'Swaff' (1974), p 223; Michael Young, *Labour's Plan for Plenty* (1947), p 80.

6 Farewell Squalor

1. *The Times*, 30 May 1946; *Financial Times*, 23 Apr 1946; Correlli Barnett, *The Audit of War* (Pan edn, 1996), p 276; Jim Tomlinson, 'Welfare and the Economy', *Twentieth Century British History*, 6/2 (1995), p 219; Tomlinson, 'Why So Austere?', *Journal of Social Policy* (Jan 1998), p 64.
2. Barnett, *Audit*, p 304; Julian Le Grand, *Motivation, Agency and Public Policy* (Oxford, 2003), p 7.

3. Charles Webster, 'Birth of a Dream', in Geoffrey Goodman (ed), *The State of the Nation* (1997), p 120.

4. Rudolf Klein, *The New Politics of the NHS* (1995), pp 26, 17, 20; David Widgery, *The National Health* (1988), p 25; Bruce Cardew, 'The Family Doctor', in James Farndale (ed), *Trends in the National Health Service* (Oxford, 1964), p 157; Wellcome Library for the History and Understanding of Medicine, Archives, GP/7/A.6; Rodney Lowe, *The Welfare State in Britain since 1945* (Basingstoke, 1999), p 176; John Campbell, *Nye Bevan* (1997), p 179; Michael Foot, *Aneurin Bevan, Volume 2* (1973), p 155.

5. Nicholas Timmins, *The Five Giants* (2001), pp 135–6; Joan C. Brown, 'Poverty in Post-war Britain', in James Obelkevich and Peter Catterall (eds), *Understanding Post-war British Society* (1994), p 117; Alan Deacon and Jonathan Bradshaw, *Reserved for the Poor* (Oxford, 1983), p 47.

6. Tomlinson, 'Austere', pp 67–73; David Vincent, *Poor Citizens* (Harlow, 1991), pp 128–9.

7. Andrew Saint, *Towards a Social Architecture* (1987), p 239; Betty D. Vernon, *Ellen Wilkinson* (1982), p 217; Gary McCulloch and Liz Sobell, 'Towards a Social History of the Secondary Modern Schools', *History of Education* (Sept 1994), p 279; Michael Young, *Labour's Plan for Plenty* (1947), p 117; P. J. Kemeny, 'Dualism in Secondary Technical Education', *British Journal of Sociology* (Mar 1970), p 86; D. W. Dean, 'Planning for a Post-war Generation', *History of Education* (Jun 1986), p 107; Barnett, *Audit*, p 302.

8. Brian Simon, *Education and the Social Order, 1940–1990* (1991), pp 104–6; Alan Kerckhoff et al, *Going Comprehensive in England and Wales* (1996), pp 18–19; Vernon, *Ellen Wilkinson*, pp 6–7; Howard Glennerster, *British Social Policy since 1945* (Oxford, 1995), p 62; Martin Francis, '"Not Reformed Capitalism, But … Democratic Socialism"', in Harriet Jones and Michael Kandiah (eds), *The Myth of Consensus* (Basingstoke, 1996), p 43; Ross McKibbin, *Classes and Cultures* (Oxford, 1998), p 234.

9. John Colville, *The Fringes of Power, Volume Two* (Sceptre edn, 1987), p 262; *The Times*, 29 Jun 1946; Dean, 'Planning', p 114; McKibbin, *Classes*, p 246.

10. Fred Grundy and Richard M. Titmuss, *Report on Luton* (Luton, 1945), p 66; Alison Ravetz, 'Housing the People', in Jim Fyrth (ed), *Labour's Promised Land?* (1995), pp 161–2; *Sunday Pictorial*, 21 Jul 1946.

11. Brian Lund, *Housing Problems and Housing Policy* (Harlow, 1996), p 41; Timmins, *Five Giants*, p 145; Steven Fielding et al, *'England Arise!'* (Manchester, 1995), pp 103–4.

12. Bertram Hutchinson, *Willesden and the New Towns* (1947), pts III, VII; *The Times*, 7 Mar 1946; Patrick Dunleavy, *The Politics of Mass Housing in Britain, 1945–1975* (Oxford, 1981), p 229.

13. Nigel Warburton, *Ernö Goldfinger* (2004), pp 126–9; Osborn, p 102; *Coventry Standard*, 31 Aug 1946; J. M. Richards, *The Castles on the Ground* (1946), p 13; Richards, *Memoirs of an Unjust Fella* (1980), p 188; John Betjeman, *Coming Home* (1997), pp 198–9.

14. Garry Philipson, *Aycliffe and Peterlee New Towns* (Cambridge, 1988), p 28; James Landsdale Hodson, *The Way Things Are* (1947), pp 282–3.

15. Andrew Homer, 'Creating New Communities', *Contemporary British History*

(Spring 2000), pp 65–70; Meryl Aldridge, *The British New Towns* (1979), p 33; Colin Ward, *New Town, Home Town* (Stevenage, 1980), pp 10–11; Bob Mullan, *Stevenage Ltd* (1980), p 42.

16. M-O A, FR 2375; Harold Orlans, *Stevenage* (1952), pp 63–7; Jack Balchin, *First New Town* (Stevenage, 1980), pp 10–11; Mullan, *Stevenage Ltd* p 42.

17. Elain Harwood, 'The Road to Subtopia', in Andrew Saint (ed), *London Suburbs* (1999), p 133; Saint, *Social Architecture*, p 58. See also Andrew Blowers, 'London's Out-county Estates', *Town and Country Planning* (Sept 1973), pp 409–14.

18. Simon Berry and Hamish Whyte (eds), *Glasgow Observed* (Edinburgh, 1987), p 234; N. R. Fyfe, 'Contested Visions of a Modern City', *Environment and Planning A*, 28/3 (1996), p 393; Miles Glendinning, '"Public Building"', *Planning History*, 14/3 (1992), p 15.

19. Nick Tiratsoo et al, *Urban Reconstruction in Britain and Japan, 1945–55* (Luton, 2002), pp 40–41; John J. Parkinson-Bailey, *Manchester* (Manchester, 2000), p 189; Percy Johnson-Marshall, *Rebuilding Cities* (Edinburgh, 1966), p 294; Alison Ravetz, *Remaking Cities* (1980), p 24; Peter Mandler, 'New Towns for Old', in Becky Conekin et al (eds), *Moments of Modernity* (1999), p 214; Peter J. Larkham, 'The Place of Urban Conservation in the UK Reconstruction Plans of 1942–1952', *Planning Perspectives* (Jul 2003), pp 295–324.

20. Larkham, 'Place', p 303; David Kynaston, *The City of London, Volume IV* (2001), p 128; Junichi Hasegawa, *Replanning the Blitzed City Centre* (Buckingham, 1992), p 120.

21. *Coventry Evening Telegraph*, 10/13/19 Oct 1945; Phil Hubbard et al, 'Contesting the Modern City', *Planning Perspectives* (Oct 2003), p 388.

22. Tiratsoo et al, *Urban Reconstruction*, p 11; Ravetz, *Remaking*, pp 39, 66; Arnold Whittick, *F.J.O.* (1987), p 91; J. B. Cullingworth, *Town and Country Planning in England and Wales* (1964), p 269; Headlam, pp 505–6; *The Times*, 1 Jul 1948.

23. Edmund Dell, *A Strange Eventful History* (1999), p 74; Alun Howkins, *The Death of Rural England* (2003), p 147; Scott Newton and Dilwyn Porter, *Modernisation Frustrated* (1988), p 117; *Financial Times*, 16 Feb 1991 (Andrew St George); *Independent*, 23 Oct 1999 (Duff Hart-Davis).

7 Glad to Sit at Home

1. Streat, p 310; Anthony Howard, '"We Are The Masters Now"', in Michael Sissons and Philip French (eds), *Age of Austerity* (Oxford, 1986), p 16; James Lees-Milne, *Caves of Ice* (Faber edn, 1984), pp 38, 46; *Independent*, 16 Dec 1991; David Kynaston, *The City of London, Volume IV* (2001), pp 8–9, 19, 24; Ralph Miliband, *Parliamentary Socialism* (1972), p 291.

2. James Lansdale Hodson, *The Way Things Are* (1947), p 309; Martin Daunton, *Just Taxes* (Cambridge, 2002), p 221; Kenneth O. Morgan, *Labour in Power, 1945–1951* (Oxford, 1984), p 185.

3. *The Collected Essays, Journalism and Letters of George Orwell, Volume II* (1968), p 99; *The Complete Works of George Orwell, Volume 16* (1998), p 425; *The Collected*

Essays, Journalism and Letters of George Orwell, Volume IV (1968), pp 220–21; Kenneth O. Morgan, *The People's Peace* (Oxford, 1990), p 108; Osborn, p 108; John Littlewood, *North Hants Golf Club Centenary History, 1904–2004* (Droitwich, 2004), p 65.

4. David Cannadine, *In Churchill's Shadow* (2002), p 236; Lees-Milne, *Caves*, p 94; J. B. Priestley, *Letter to a Returning Serviceman* (1945), p 31; Steven Fielding et al, *'England Arise!'* (Manchester, 1995), pp 137–8.

5. Fielding et al, *'England Arise!'*, pp 139, 152–4; Richard Weight, *Patriots* (2002), pp 185, 190.

6. *Radio Times*, 27 Sept 1946; Fielding et al, *'England Arise!'*, p 147; *Radio Times*, 27 Sept 1946; BBC WA, R9/9/11 – LR/47/1778, 6 Nov 1947; BBC WA, R9/9/11 – LR/47/161, 3 Feb 1947; BBC WA, R9/9/12 – LR/48/596, 16 Apr 1948; *Listener*, 30 Jan 1947; Asa Briggs, *The History of Broadcasting in the United Kingdom, Volume IV* (Oxford, 1979), p 82.

7. Priestley, *Letter*, p 30; Raphael Samuel, 'The Lost World of British Communism', *New Left Review* (Nov/Dec 1985), p 8; Osborn, p 133; Fielding et al, *'England Arise!'*, chap 5.

8. Bertram Hutchinson, *Willesden and the New Towns* (1947), pt IV; *Planning*, 15 Aug 1947, p 72; M-O A, TC 53/2/A; *Listener*, 23 Oct 1947.

9. Dilwyn Porter, 'The Attlee Years Reassessed', *Contemporary European History*, 4/1 (1994), p 98; Sagittarius, *Let Cowards Flinch* (1947), p 24; Speed, 14 Oct 1946.

8 Christ It's Bleeding Cold

1. Hodgson, 1 Jan 1947; William Ashworth, *The History of the British Coal Industry, Volume 5* (Oxford, 1986), pp 6, 3; Bill Jones et al, '"Going from Darkness to the Light"', *Llafur*, 7/1 (1996), pp 103–8; *Durham Chronicle*, 10 Jan 1947; *Coal Magazine* (Jan 1949), p 7.

2. Ferdynand Zweig, *Men in the Pits* (1948), pp 10, 15, 108–11, 142–3.

3. Jones et al, '"Going"', pp 100, 104; Ina Zweiniger-Bargielowska, 'South Wales Miners' Attitudes towards Nationalisation', *Llafur*, 6/3 (1994), pp 73–4, 76; Peter Ackers and Jonathan Payne, 'Before the Storm', *Social History* (May 2002), pp 193–4.

4. W. R. Garside, *The Durham Miners, 1919–1960* (1971), p 395; Mark Tookey, 'Three's a Crowd?', *Twentieth Century British History*, 12/4 (2001), pp 500, 504–5, 495; Gaitskell, pp 28–30; Alex J. Robertson, *The Bleak Midwinter* (Manchester, 1987), p 73.

5. Heap, 22 Jan 1947; Speed, 24–5/28–30 Jan 1947; SWCC (South Wales Coalfield Collection at Archives, University of Wales Swansea), Oakdale Navigation Lodge minutes, MNA/NUM/L/59/A23; James Lees-Milne, *Caves of Ice* (Faber edn, 1984), p 131.

6. *London Magazine* (Aug 1956), pp 45–7; John Lehmann, *The Ample Proposition* (1966), pp 30, 70.

7. Lewis, 3 Feb 1947; King, 3/5 Feb 1947; James Lansdale Hodson, *The Way Things Are* (1947), pp 313, 316; King, 7 Feb 1947; *Financial Times*, 8 Feb 1947; Ferguson, 9 Feb 1947; Hodgson, 9 Feb 1947; Lees-Milne, *Caves*, p 134.

8. Robertson, *Bleak Midwinter*, pp 18, 21, 95–6; Jones et al, '"Going"', pp 101, 108;

SWCC, Penalta Lodge records, MNA/NUM/L/63/D50; Zweig, *Pits*, pp 17–18.

9. *The Letters of Kingsley Amis* (2000), p 116; David Kynaston, *The City of London, Volume IV* (2001), p 18; Speed, 10/18 Feb 1947; Haines, 13 Feb 1947; Langford, 14/16/22 Feb 1947; Heap, 19 Feb 1947; Lewis, 14/19 Feb 1947.

10. M-O A, TC 68/5/B; Robertson, *Bleak Midwinter*, p 116.

11. Roy Hattersley, *A Yorkshire Boyhood* (1983), p 135; Bill Wyman, *Stone Alone* (1990), p 47; John Coldstream, *Dirk Bogarde* (2004), pp 162–7; Artemis Cooper, *Writing at the Kitchen Table* (1999), pp 131–2.

12. Robertson, *Bleak Midwinter*, pp 117–18; Hodgson, 3 Mar 1947; Langford, 10 Mar 1947.

13. Ford, 18 Mar 1947; Susan Cooper, 'Snoek Piquante', in Michael Sissons and Philip French (eds), *Age of Austerity* (Oxford, 1986), p 37; Robertson, *Bleak Midwinter*, pp 122–5; Steven Fielding et al, *'England Arise!'* (Manchester, 1995), pp 161–2; M-O A, TC 25/17/F; *Times*, 19 Mar 1947.

14. Robertson, *Bleak Midwinter*, p 158; Pearson Phillips, 'The New Look', in Sissons and French, *Age of Austerity*, p 127.

15. Zweig, *Pits*, pp 11, 155–60; Roy Mason, *Paying the Price* (1999), p 42.

16. See the stimulating, persuasive analysis in Ackers and Payne, 'Before the Storm', pp 184–209.

17. M-O A, FR 3007.

9 Our Prestige at Stake

1. M-O A, TC 3/3/C; Mary Abbott, *Family Affairs* (2003), p 111; *News Chronicle*, 15 Apr 1948.

2. Hodgson, 10 Mar 1947; M-O A, TC 1/9/F; Janice Winship, 'Nation Before Family', in *Formations of Nations and People* (1984), pp 197–8.

3. M-O A, TC 85/7/B; Geoffrey Thomas, *Women and Industry* (1948), pp 1, 4; Phyllis Willmott, *Joys and Sorrows* (1995), pp 21–2; Willmott, 18 Jul 1947; *The Times*, 22 Sept 1988, *Independent*, 23 Sept 1988; Sue Aspinall, 'Women, Realism and Reality in British Films, 1943–53', in James Curran and Vincent Porter (eds), *British Cinema History* (1983), p 286.

4. M-O A, FR 2537.

5. Phyllis G. Allen, 'Evening Activities in the Home', *Sociological Review* (1951), Section 7, pp 1–15; BBC WA, R9/9/12–LR/48/1261; Anthony Adamthwaite, '"Nation Shall Speak Unto Nation"', *Contemporary Record* (Winter 1993), pp 558–9.

6. BBC WA, R9/21; Haines, 26 Jul 1947, 9 Aug 1947, 11/13/16 Sept 1947, 4 Oct 1947; Ford, 9–10/12/29 Feb 1948, 1/15 Mar 1948; BBC WA, R9/9/12–LR/48/1219.

7. *Radio Times*, 11 Apr 1947; *Independent*, 1 Jun 1990 (Sowerbutts obituary); M-O A, TC 53/2/D; Helena Barrett and John Phillips, *Suburban Style* (1987), p 186; Jenny Uglow, *A Little History of British Gardening* (2004), p 286.

8. *Daily Express*, 10/12 May 1947; Neville Cardus, *Cardus in the Covers* (1978), p 106; *Independent*, 31 Oct 2003; *Daily Telegraph*, 16 Dec 1991 (Arlott obituary); *Pilot Papers* (Dec 1947), p 75.

9. Patrick Slater, *The Demand for Holidays in 1947 and 1948* (The Social Survey, 1948), p 2; M-O A, TC 58/2/F; Chaplin, 7/3/1, 18 Jun 1947.

10. Brown, 1/16, 7 May 1947; Langford, 12 Aug 1947; Colin Ward and Dennis Hardy, *Goodnight Campers!* (1986), p 110; M-O A, TC 58/2/G.
11. Chris Bryant, *Glenda Jackson* (1999), pp 9–10; Bill Wyman, *Stone Alone* (1990), pp 48–9; Brian Simon, *Education and the Social Order, 1940–1990* (1991), p 108; L. S. Hearnshaw, *Cyril Burt* (1979), p 118; Nirmala Rao, 'Labour and Education', *Contemporary British History* (Summer 2002), p 113.

10 The Whole World is Full of Permits

1. Kenneth O. Morgan, *Labour in Power, 1945–1951* (Oxford, 1984), pp 253–4; Giles Radice, *Friends and Rivals* (2002), p 64; Edward Pearce, *Denis Healey* (2002), p 76.
2. Adrian Turner, *Robert Bolt* (1998), p 69; Mervyn Jones, *Chances* (1987), p 114; Steve Parsons, 'British "McCarthyism" and the Intellectuals', in Jim Fyrth (ed), *Labour's Promised Land?* (1995), pp 227–31; Phillip Deery, '"The Secret Battalion"', *Contemporary British History* (Winter 1999), p 20.
3. Bernard Donoughue and G. W. Jones, *Herbert Morrison* (1973), p 403; Morgan, *Labour*, p 121; *Coventry Evening Telegraph*, 17 May 1948; Asa Briggs, *Michael Young* (Basingstoke, 2001), pp 81–2; Gaitskell, p 72.
4. James Lees-Milne, *Caves of Ice* (Faber edn, 1984), p 192; M-O A, TC 25/17/I; M-O A, D 5353, 10 Aug 1947; Kenneth Harris, *Attlee* (1982), p 346; Lees-Milne, *Caves*, p 197; John Fforde, *The Bank of England and Public Policy, 1941–1958* (Cambridge, 1992), p 157.
5. *Wisden Cricketers' Almanack, 1948* (1948), p 227; *Financial Times*, 21 Aug 1947; Speed, 28 Aug 1947; Lees-Milne, *Caves*, p 208; St John, 28 Aug 1947.
6. For a helpful overview of the whole question of planning vis-à-vis Keynesianism in 1947/8, see: Jim Tomlinson, *Democratic Socialism and Economic Policy* (Cambridge, 1997), chap 10.
7. Stephen Brooke, 'Problems of "Socialist Planning"', *Historical Journal*, 34/3 (1991), pp 687–702; Chris Wrigley, 'Trade Union Development 1945–79', in Wrigley (ed), *A History of British Industrial Relations, 1939–1979* (Cheltenham, 1996), p 77; *New Statesman*, 18 Oct 1947; Nick Tiratsoo, 'Labour and the Reconstruction of Hull, 1945–51', in Tiratsoo (ed), *The Attlee Years* (1991), p 137.
8. *Coventry Evening Telegraph*, 9 Jun 1947, 22 May 1948.
9. Patrick Dunleavy, *The Politics of Mass Housing in Britain, 1945–1975* (Oxford, 1981), p 260; *Manchester Guardian*, 19 Apr 1948; Steen Eiler Rasmussen, *London* (1948), p 426; *Journal of the Town Planning Institute* (Jul–Aug 1948), p 151; James Lansdale Hodson, *Thunder in the Heavens* (1950), p 105.
10. J. B. Priestley, *The Linden Tree* (1948), pp 62–3; Vincent Brome, *Aneurin Bevan* (1953), pp 1–3.
11. Tony Benn, *Years of Hope* (1994), pp 125–7; *Horizon* (Jul 1947), p 1; *The Letters of Sidney and Beatrice Webb, Volume III* (Cambridge, 1978), p 465; Philip M. Williams, *Hugh Gaitskell* (1979), p 141.
12. Steven Fielding et al, *'England Arise!'* (Manchester, 1995), p 172; Jeremy Nuttall, '"Psychological Socialist", "Militant Moderate"', *Labour History Review* (Aug 2003), pp 247–8; Stephen Brooke, 'Evan Durbin', *Twentieth Century British History* 7/1 (1996), p 51.

13. Streat, pp 414, 419; Ben Pimlott, *Harold Wilson* (1992), p 111; David Howell, 'Wilson and History', *Twentieth Century British History*, 4/2 (1993), p 180.

14. This account of the Conservative Party's post-1945 remaking of policy owes much to Harriet Jones, '"New Conservatism?"', in Becky Conekin et al (eds), *Moments of Modernity* (1999), pp 171–88.

15. Bertrand de Jouvenel, *Problems of Socialist England* (1949), p 23; Margaret Thatcher, *The Path to Power* (1995), p 48; *My Dear Max: The Letters of Brendan Bracken to Lord Beaverbrook, 1925–1958* (1990), p 58; Conservative Party, *The Industrial Charter* (popular edn, 1947), p 4; *Spectator*, 16 May 1947, 10 Oct 1947; *The Times*, 3 Oct 1947. Also for the Brighton conference, see: Anthony Howard, *RAB* (1987), pp 156–7.

16. Jones, '"New Conservatism?"', pp 177–8, 187; Reginald Maudling, *Memoirs* (1978), p 45; Scott Kelly, 'Ministers Matter', *Contemporary British History* (Winter 2000), pp 38–9; Headlam, p 526.

17. M-O A, FR 2516; Lees-Milne, *Caves*, p 241.

11 Ain't She Lovely?

1. John Barnes, *Ahead of His Age* (1979), pp 402, 410; W. R. Matthews, *Memories and Meanings* (1969), p 310; *Sunday Pictorial*, 19/26 Oct 1947; *The Times*, 16 Sept 1972.

2. *Sunday Pictorial*, 12 Jan 1947; Robert Lacey, *Majesty* (Sphere edn, 1978), p 200; *Times*, 15 Nov 1997; Speed, 10 Jul 1947; Philip Ziegler, *Crown and People* (1978), pp 82–3; James Lees-Milne, *Caves of Ice* (Faber edn, 1984), p 246; James Lansdale Hodson, *Thunder in the Heavens* (1950), pp 61–2; Nick Clarke, *The Shadow of a Nation* (2003), p 19; Headlam, p 533; Golden, 28 Nov 1947; Hodgson, 18 Jan 1948.

3. Gaitskell, p 62; *Daring to Hope: The Diaries and Letters of Violet Bonham Carter, 1946–1969* (2000), p 46; Streat, pp 444–5; Harold Nicolson, *The Later Years, 1945–1962: Diaries and Letters, Volume III* (1968), pp 142–3, 148.

4. Nick Tiratsoo, 'Popular Politics, Affluence and the Labour Party in the 1950s', in Anthony Gorst et al (eds), *Contemporary British History, 1931–1961* (1991), p 53; Uttin, 2 Dec 1947; Speed, 18 Sept 1947, 13 Oct 1947; Lees-Milne, *Caves*, p 239; Susan Cooper, 'Snoek Piquante', in Michael Sissons and Philip French (eds), *Age of Austerity* (Oxford, 1986), p 40; *Listener*, 3 Jun 1948.

5. *Daily Express*, 16 Apr 1947; BBC WA, *Woman's Hour*, 14 Oct 1947; King, 22 May 1948; Martin Westlake, *Kinnock* (2001), p 16; Heap, 17 Oct 1947; Golden, 13 Jan 1948.

6. *News Chronicle*, 19 Apr 1948; *The New Yorker*, 19 Jun 1948; *The Selected Letters of Tennessee Williams, Volume II* (2006), p 198; Raynham, 2 Jul 1947; Melanie Tebbutt, *Women's Talk?* (Aldershot, 1995), p 74; *Punch*, 15/22/29 Oct 1947, 5/12 Nov 1947; *British Medical Journal*, 29 Nov 1947; Ina Zweiniger-Bargielowska, *Austerity in Britain* (Oxford, 2000), pp 222–3.

7. Enid Palmer letters (Department of Documents, Imperial War Museum), 4/14/16/24 Apr 1948; Ina Zweiniger-Bargielowska, 'Consensus and Consumption', in Harriet Jones and Michael Kandiah (eds), *The Myth of Consensus* (Basingstoke, 1996), pp 89, 95; Richard Hoggart, *The Uses of Literacy* (1957), p 37.

8. Christina Hardyment, *Slice of Life* (1995), p 31; Hodson, *Thunder*, p 66; *Barnsley*

Chronicle, 13 Dec 1947; M-O A, Directives for Jan 1948, Replies; Preston, 19 Feb 1948; M-O A, Directives for Jan 1948, Replies; *Spivs' Gazette*, Mar 1948. In general on the black market, in addition to Zweiniger-Bargielowska, *Austerity in Britain*, chap 4, see: Edward Smithies, *The Black Economy in England since 1914* (Dublin, 1984); Mark Roodhouse, 'Popular Morality and the Black Market in Britain, 1939–55', in Frank Trentmann and Flemming Just, *Food and Conflict in Europe in the Age of the Two World Wars* (Basingstoke, 2006).

9. Kathryn A. Morrison, *English Shops and Shopping* (New Haven, 2003), pp 239, 275, 276; David Powell, *Counter Revolution* (1991), p 66; *Store* (Feb 1948), p 20; *Co-operative News*, 17 Jan 1948, 13 Mar 1948; *Dictionary of Business Biography, Volume 3* (1985), pp 475–9.

10. *Vogue* (Oct 1947), p 37; Pearson Phillips, 'The New Look', in Sissons and French (eds), *Age of Austerity*, pp 129–30, 132–4; *The New Yorker*, 24 Jan 1948; Langford, 24 Apr 1948; Golden, 28 Apr 1948; Theo Aronson, *Princess Margaret* (1997), pp 106–7; M-O A, FR 3095.

11. Angela Partington, 'The Days of the New Look', in Jim Fyrth (ed), *Labour's Promised Land?* (1995), p 252; *Independent*, 14 Jan 2002; Carolyn Steedman, *Landscape for a Good Woman* (1986), pp 12, 28.

12. Ina Zweiniger-Bargielowska, 'Rationing, Austerity and the Conservative Party Recovery after 1945', *Historical Journal*, 37/1 (1994), p 180; Roy Lewis and Angus Maude, *The English Middle Classes* (1949), pp 213–14; *Economist*, 3 Jan 1948; *Listener*, 3 Jun 1948.

13. *The Diaries of Evelyn Waugh* (1976), p 689; C. R. Perry, 'In Search of H.V. Morton,' *Twentieth Century British History*, 10/3 (1999), p 453; David Kynaston, *The City of London, Volume IV* (2001), pp 24–5; John Brophy, *The Mind's Eye* (1949), pp 64–5.

14. Hodson, *Thunder*, pp 16, 29, 83, 216; John Turner, 'A Land Fit for Tories to Live In', *Contemporary European History*, 4/2 (1995), p 193; *New Statesman*, 12 Jun 1948; Langford, 2 May 1947.

15. Frances Partridge, *Everything to Lose* (1985), p 57; Denis Gifford, *The Golden Age of Radio* (1985), p 179; Terry Hallett, *Bristol's Forgotten Empire* (Westbury, 2000), p 155; *The Kenneth Williams Diaries* (1993), pp 20–21; *Aldershot News*, 6 Feb 1948; Roger Lewis, *The Life and Death of Peter Sellers* (1994), p 108; *Daily Express*, 7 May 1948.

16. *Accrington Observer*, 14/17 Feb 1948; Rogan Taylor and Andrew Ward, *Kicking and Screaming* (1995), p 37.

17. Hodson, *Thunder*, p 116; Preston, 9 Apr 1948; Gaitskell, p 69.

18. Langford, 19 Jun 1947; *Daily Telegraph*, 1 Aug 2002 (Higgins obituary); *Horizon* (Dec 1947), p 300; *News Chronicle*, 24 May 1948; Brown, 1/16, 18 Feb 1948; Richard Davenport-Hines, *The Pursuit of Oblivion* (2001), p 298.

19. Headlam, pp 552–3; Kenneth O. Morgan, *Callaghan* (Oxford, 1997), p 85; *Sunday Pictorial*, 18 Apr 1948; Langford, 4 May 1948; *News Chronicle*, 24 May 1948; Fenton Bresler, *Lord Goddard* (1977), p 182; Hartley Shawcross, *Life Sentence* (1995), p 168.

20. David Renton, 'Not Just Economics but Politics as Well', *Labour History Review* (Summer 2000), p 174; Richard Weight, *Patriots* (2002), p 83; Kynaston, *City*, p 223.

21. K. L. Little, *Negroes in Britain* (1948), p 243; Anthony H. Richmond, *Colour*

Prejudice in Britain (1954), pp 76–7; E. R. Braithwaite, *To Sir, With Love* (1959), pp 36–49; G. K. Evans, *Public Opinion on Colonial Affairs* (The Social Survey, Jun 1948), pp ii–iv.

22. Kathleen Paul, 'The Politics of Citizenship in Post-War Britain', *Contemporary Record* (Winter 1992), pp 464, 467; Clive Harris, 'Post-war Migration and the Industrial Reserve Army', in Winston James and Clive Harris (eds), *Inside Babylon* (1993), pp 21–2.

23. Randall Hansen, 'The Politics of Citizenship in 1940s Britain', *Twentieth Century British History*, 10/1 (1999), pp 87–8.

24. David Watson, 'Research Note', *Historical Studies in Industrial Relations* (Mar 1996), p 157; *Hansard*, 8 Jun 1948, col 1851; Harris, 'Migration', pp 23, 24–5; Hansen, 'Politics', p 90; Paul, 'Politics of Citizenship', p 456.

25. *Star*, 22 Jun 1948; Mike Phillips and Trevor Phillips, *Windrush* (1998), pp 66, 70; *Clapham Observer*, 2/9 Jul 1948.

12 A Change in the Terms of Struggle

1. BBC WA, *Woman's Hour*, 22/29 Jun 1948.

2. *British Medical Journal*, 16 Nov 1946, 28 Dec 1946; Langford, 6 May 1948; Michael Coveney, *The World According to Mike Leigh* (1996), p 41; *Star*, 26 Jun 1948.

3. Tom Wildy, 'The Social and Economic Publicity and Propaganda of the Labour Governments of 1945–51', *Contemporary Record* (Summer 1992), pp 45–71; *Falkirk Herald*, 3 Jul 1948; *New Statesman*, 3 Jul 1948; *Punch*, 30 Jun 1948; Janice Winship, 'Nation Before Family', in *Formations of Nations and People* (1984), p 201; *Vogue* (Jul 1948), p 53.

4. *Tablet*, 4 Jul 1998 (Clifford Longley); Steven Fielding et al, *'England Arise!'* (Manchester, 1995), p 172; Raynham, 27 Apr 1948; Hodgson, 4 Jul 1948; *Liverpool Daily Post*, 1 Jul 1948.

5. Phyllis Willmott, *Joys and Sorrows* (1995), pp 42, 64, 66; J.W.B. Douglas and J. M. Blomfield, *Children Under Five* (1958), pp 45–51, 57, 69, 99.

6. Wildy, 'Publicity and Propaganda', pp 64–5; *The Times*, 5 Jul 1948; Preston, 5 Jul 1948.

7. *Daily Mirror*, 5 Jul 1948; *The Times*, 5 Jul 1948; *Manchester Guardian*, 5 Jul 1948; Heap, 5 Jul 1948; diary of Cyril Leach (at Harrow Local History Centre), 5 Jul 1948.

8. *Star*, 5 Jul 1948; *Lancashire Daily Post*, 5 Jul 1948; *The Times*, 23 Jun 1998; M-O A, D5353, 5 Jul 1948.

Smoke in the Valley

1 What Do You Say?

1. *Daily Mirror*, 30 Jul 1948; *The Times*, 30 Jul 1948; *Picture Post*, 14 Aug 1948; *Daily Telegraph*, 3 Feb 1999 (Dearlove letter); *The Times*, 2 Aug 1948; Andrea Murphy, *From the Empire to the Rialto* (Birkenhead, 1995), pp 131–49; David Rayvern Allen, *Arlott* (1994), p 136. On Wooderson, see *Independent*, 29 Dec 2006, for obituary by Steven Downes, who quotes the Queen's remark to an official at Wembley Stadium: 'Of course, we couldn't have had poor little Sydney.'

2. M-O A, D 5353, 14 Aug 1948; BBC WA, R9/12/3, 14 Aug 1948; *Sporting Life*, 19 Aug 1948; *Spectator*, 26 Mar 2005 (Frank Keating); St John, 28 Aug 1948.

3. *The Times*, 8 Sept 1948; Gaitskell, p 84; *Scarborough Evening News*, 10 Jun 1948; Norman Wisdom, *My Turn* (2002), pp 140–41; *Independent*, 29 Oct 1998 (Paul Vallely).

2 Oh, For a Little Extra Butter!

1. M-O A, Directives for Oct/Nov 1948, replies from A–B file (men), A–C file (women); Heap, 30 Jul 1948; *The New Yorker*, 18 Sept 1948; Ferguson, 22 Mar 1949.

2. Ben Pimlott, *Harold Wilson* (1992), pp 124–9; *Picture Post*, 1 Jan 1949; *Daring to Hope: The Diaries and Letters of Violet Bonham Carter, 1946–1969* (2000), p 65; Langford, 21 Nov 1948; *Picture Post*, 1 Jan 1949; Hodgson, 20 Mar 1949; *Coventry Evening Telegraph*, 30 Mar 1949; *New Yorker*, 9 Apr 1949; Haines, 25 Apr 1949; Abrams, Box 63 ('Ministry of Food Surveys, 1941–64' file); Uttin, 3 Sept 1949.

3. John Gross, 'The Lynskey Tribunal', in Michael Sissons and Philip French (eds), *Age of Austerity* (Oxford, 1986), pp 245–63; *New Yorker*, 12 Feb 1949; *Picture Post*, 12 Feb 1949; Langford, 28 Dec 1948; *Joyce & Ginnie: The Letters of Joyce Grenfell and Virginia Graham* (1997), pp 157–8; *Daily Telegraph*, 18 Apr 1995, *Independent*, 19 Apr 1995 (English obituaries).

4. *Daily Express*, 26/28 Oct 1948; *The Times*, 27 Oct 1948, 8 Nov 1948; Channel 4, *Classic British Cars*, 13 Apr 1999.

5. Hodgson, 12 Dec 1948; Theo Aronson, *Princess Margaret* (1997), p 110; *Middlesbrough Evening Gazette*, 20 Aug 1948; *Coventry Evening Standard*, 27 Apr 1949; James Lees-Milne, *Midway on the Waves* (Faber edn, 1987), pp 91, 196; *Picture Post*, 27 Nov 1948; Preston, 15 Nov 1948; Heap, 15 Nov 1948, 16 Dec 1948; Harold Nicolson, *The Later Years, 1945–1962: Diaries and Letters, Volume III* (1968), p 157.

6. *Picturegoer*, 18 Dec 1948; Heap, 11 Dec 1948; Christine Geraghty, *British Cinema in the Fifties* (2000), pp 136–8; Charles Barr, *Ealing Studios* (1977), p 77; Hodgson, 6 Feb 1949; Sue Harper and Vincent Porter, *Weeping in the Cinema in 1950* (Brighton, 1995); story confirmed by Joan Bakewell.

7. *Sunday Pictorial*, 20 Feb 1949; BBC WA, R9/74/1, Aug 1949; M-O A, FR 3106; David Oswell, *Television, Childhood and the Home* (Oxford, 2002), pp 87–92.

8. Raynham, 17/20/23/30 Sept 1948; Ted Kavanagh, *Tommy Handley* (1949), pp 251–2; *Daily Mail*, 10 Jan 1949; M-O A, D 5353, 9 Jan 1949; M-O A, Bulletins, New Series No 32, Feb 1950.

9. Frank Muir and Denis Norden Archive (Special Collections, University of Sussex), Box 3, *Take It From Here* scripts, second series, 'Winslow Boy'; Heap, 10 Jan 1949; Preston, 10 Jan 1949; Raynham, 9 Jan 1949; M-O A, D 5353, 9 Jan 1949; Hodgson, 16 Jan 1949; M-O A, Bulletins, New Series No 32, Feb 1950.

10. Kavanagh, *Tommy Handley*, pp 9, 16; Hodgson, 16 Jan 1949; M-O A, Bulletins, New Series No 32, Feb 1950.

11. BBC WA, R34/259; Graham McCann, *Frankie Howerd* (2004), pp 87–8.

12. Isaiah Berlin, *Flourishing: Letters 1928–1946* (2004), p 304; *Vogue* (Jul 1948), p 44; *The Letters of Kingsley Amis* (2000), p 186; Kingsley Amis, *Memoirs* (1991), pp 102–4; *The Letters of Ruth Draper, 1920–1956* (1979), p 310; Lees-Milne, *Midway*, pp 71, 116, 207.

13. Peter Hall, *Making an Exhibition of Myself* (1993), pp 54–5; F. R. Leavis, *The Great*

Tradition (Peregrine edn, 1962), p 10; John Gross, *The Rise and Fall of the Man of Letters* (1969), pp 270, 281; T. S. Eliot, *Notes towards the Definition of Culture* (1948), pp 31, 48, 99, 101-2, 106-7, 108; Brian Simon, *Education and the Social Order, 1940-1990* (1991), pp 126-9.

14. Ronald Reagan, *My Early Life* (1981), pp 208-10; Edmund Morris, *Dutch* (1999), pp 270-71; Rev. Oliver Leonard Willmott, *The Parish Notes of Loders, Dottery and Askerswell, Volume 1* (Shrewsbury, 1996), Jan-Mar 1949.

15. *The Complete Works of George Orwell, Volume 19* (1998), pp 435-44; Godfrey Hodgson, 'The Steel Debates', in Sissons and French (eds), *Age of Austerity*, p 297; Headlam, p 568.

16. Michael Foot, *Aneurin Bevan, Volume 2* (1973), pp 259-61; John Campbell, *Nye Bevan* (1997), pp 206-7.

17. Kenneth O. Morgan, *Labour in Power, 1945-1951* (Oxford, 1984), pp 126-7; Laurie Dennett, *A Sense of Security* (Cambridge, 1998), pp 295-301; Ron Noon, 'Goodbye, Mr Cube', *History Today* (Oct 2001), pp 40-41; *Sunday Pictorial*, 23 Jan 1949; *Tribune*, 28 Jan 1949.

18. Michael Young, *Small Man, Big World* (republished in *Social Science as Innovator – Michael Young* [Cambridge, MA, 1983]), pp 196-7, 205-8; *Tribune*, 11 Mar 1949; Dartington Hall Trust Archive, LKE/G/35, 6 Jul 1948, 14 Dec 1948; Phyllis Willmott, *Joys and Sorrows* (1995), pp 102, 135-6; Keith Jefferys, *Anthony Crosland* (2000), pp 29-30; Michael Young, *The Chipped White Cups of Dover* (1960), p 16. For a helpful overview, setting Young and Crosland in context, see: Martin Francis, 'Economics and Ethics', *Twentieth Century British History*, 6/2 (1995), pp 220-43.

19. *New Statesman*, 11 Sept 1948.

3 Jolly Good as a Whole

1. *The Times*, 30 Mar 1999 (Alan Hamilton); *Picture Post*, 10 Sept 1949; David Cannadine, *The Decline and Fall of the British Aristocracy* (1990), pp 646, 639-40; *West London Chronicle*, 13 May 1949; Janet Street-Porter, *Baggage* (2004), pp 29-32; W.F.F. Kemsley and David Ginsburg, *Consumer Expenditure Series: Expenditure on Laundries, Dyeing and Cleaning, Mending and Alterations and Shoe Repairing Services* (The Social Survey, Aug 1949), p 18; Hoover, *The Official Opening of the Factory of Hoover, Limited at Pentrebach, Merthyr Tydfil, Tuesday October 12th 1948* (Merthyr Tydfil, 1948), pp 44-5.

2. Channel 4, *Pennies from Bevan*, 14 Jun 1998; Philip M. Williams, *Hugh Gaitskell* (1979), p 211; *The New Yorker*, 8 Jan 1949; *Guardian*, 25 Jun 1998 (Susannah Frankel); *Journal of the John Hilton Bureau* (Special Collections, University of Sussex, Box 12), 14 Jan 1949; *The New Yorker*, 8 Jan 1949; John Campbell, *Nye Bevan* (1997), pp 180, 181; Headlam, p 574.

3. *British Medical Journal*, 19 Feb 1949; Campbell, p 182; Jim Tomlinson, 'Welfare and the Economy', *Twentieth Century British History*, 6/2 (1995), pp 210-11; M-O A, TC 13/4/C; M-O A, Bulletins, New Series No 48, Dec 1952/Jan 1953; *The Kenneth Williams Diaries* (1993), p 41.

4. For a valuable corrective, see: Nicholas Bullock, 'Re-assessing the Post-War Housing Achievement: The Impact of War-damage Repairs on the New Housing Programme in London', *Twentieth Century British History*, 16/3 (2005), pp 256-82.

5. Malden & Coombe Old People's Welfare Association, *The Reason for Old People's Week* (Malden, 1949); Cliff Richard, *Which One's Cliff?* (Coronet edn, 1981), p 23; Peter Hall, *Cities of Tomorrow* (Oxford, 2002), p 240; *The New Yorker*, 24 Jul 1948; *Picture Post*, 22 Jan 1949.

6. *Coventry Evening Telegraph*, 27 Apr 1949; *Town and Country Planning* (Spring 1949), pp 38–9; Osborn, p 179; *Architects' Journal*, 10 Mar 1949, 26 May 1949; *Lewisham Journal*, 18 Mar 1949. For a more detailed 'housing versus architecture' overview, see: Nicholas Bullock, *Building the Post-War World* (2002), pp 206–16.

7. Hodgson, 1 May 1949; Roger Berthoud, *The Life of Henry Moore* (1987), pp 217–18; Langford, 29/30 Apr 1949; M-O A, FR 3120.

8. *Daily Telegraph*, 27 Mar 1996 (Snagge obituary); Valerie A. Tedder, *Post War Blues* (Leicester, 1999), p 55; *Guardian*, 23 Dec 1997, *Independent*, 31 Dec 1997 (Woodcock obituaries); *Wisden Cricketers' Almanack, 1950* (1950), p 241; *Spectator*, 19 Jun 2004 (Frank Keating).

9. Langford, 24 Jun 1949. This reading of *Passport to Pimlico* owes much to Charles Barr, *Ealing Studios* (1977), pp 95–107, and Andy Medhurst, 'Myths of Consensus and Fables of Escape', in Jim Fyrth (ed), *Labour's Promised Land?* (1995), pp 295–6.

10. James Lansdale Hodson, *Thunder in the Heavens* (1950), p 159; *The New Yorker*, 12 Feb 1949; *Weston Mercury*, 28 May 1949; *Picture Post*, 4/25 Jun 1949; *The Private Diaries of Sydney Moseley* (1960), p 472.

11. Gordon Johnston, 'Writing and Publishing the Cold War', *Twentieth Century British History*, 12/4 (2002), p 451; *The Collected Essays, Journalism and Letters of George Orwell, Volume IV* (1968), p 564; Robert Hewison, *In Anger* (1988), p 28; Osbert Lancaster, *Signs of the Times* (1961), p 49; Arthur Hearnden, *Red Robert* (1984), p 253; Hodgson, 10 Jul 1949; *Sunday Pictorial*, 10 Jul 1949. On the politics of the 1949 dock strike, see also Phillip Deery, '"The Secret Battalion"', *Contemporary British History* (Winter 1999), pp 3–6.

12. Steve Parsons, 'British "McCarthyism" and the Intellectuals', in Fyrth, *Labour's Promised Land?*, pp 230–34, 238; Hewison, *In Anger*, pp 28–30; Anthony Howard, *Crossman* (1990), pp 150–51.

13. Mervyn Jones, *Chances* (1987), pp 116–18; *The Times for Lochgelly, Bowhill, Dundonald, Glencraig and Lochore*, 12 May 1949; *Daily Herald*, 14 May 1949; A. J. Davies, *To Build a New Jerusalem* (1992), pp 180–82; Willie Thompson, 'British Communists in the Cold War, 1947–52', *Contemporary British History* (Autumn 2001), p 121; J. D. Bernal, 'The Biological Controversy in the Soviet Union and Its Implications', *Modern Quarterly* (Summer 1949), pp 203–17; *Times Literary Supplement*, 20 Aug 1999 (Christopher Hitchens); William Gallacher, *The Case for Communism* (1949), front cover, pp 134–5. In general on Communist Party culture in the 1940s and 1950s, see the wonderfully vivid essays in Raphael Samuel, *The Lost World of British Communism* (2006).

14. Doris Lessing, *Walking in the Shade* (1997), pp 3–5; Radio 4, *Fifty Years On*, 7 Aug 2002; Doris Lessing, *In Pursuit of the English* (Sphere edn, 1968), pp 37–9, 112; Carole Klein, *Doris Lessing*, pp 126–7; Hewison, *In Anger*, p 33.

15. Lessing, *Walking*, pp 12–13; H. D. Willcock, *Report on Juvenile Delinquency* (1949), p 48; Clive Harris, 'Post-war Migration and the Industrial Reserve Army', in Winston James and Clive Harris (eds), *Inside Babylon* (1993), pp 27–8; D. W. Dean,

'Coping with Colonial Immigration, the Cold War and Colonial Policy', *Immigrants & Minorities* (Nov 1987), p 326; Harold Nicolson, *The Later Years, 1945–1962: Diaries and Letters, Volume III* (1968), p 169.

16. Michael Banton, *White and Coloured* (1959), p 157; Julia Drake, 'From "Colour Blind" to "Colour Bar"', in Lawrence Black et al, *Consensus or Coercion?* (Cheltenham, 2001), p 86; *Picture Post*, 2/16 Jul 1949; *Birmingham Gazette*, 10/11 Aug 1949.

17. *The Political Diary of Hugh Dalton, 1918–40, 1945–60* (1986), p 450; *The New Yorker*, 10 Sept 1949.

18. Philip Ziegler, *Wilson* (1993), pp 73–6; Alec Cairncross, *Living with the Century* (Fife, 1998), p 136; 'Witness Seminar: 1949 Devaluation', *Contemporary Record* (Winter 1991), p 495; Milton Gilbert, *Quest for World Monetary Order* (New York, 1980), p 53.

19. *Listener*, 22 Sept 1949; *Like It Was: The Diaries of Malcolm Muggeridge* (1981), p 351; Hodgson, 18 Sept 1949; Preston, 18 Sept 1949; Langford, 18 Sept 1949; *The New Yorker*, 1 Oct 1949; *Daily Telegraph*, 1 Mar 2003 (Robert Philip); *Speedway World*, 24 Aug 1949; *Daily Mirror*, 23 Sept 1949.

4 A Decent Way of Life

1. M-O A, D 5353, 14 Oct 1949; *Nottingham Journal*, 17 Oct 1949; Alan Sillitoe, *The Loneliness of the Long-Distance Runner* (Pan edn, 1961), pp 111, 114; Graham McCann, *Frankie Howerd* (2004), p 93.

2. Raynham, 22 Oct 1949; *Listener*, 27 Oct 1949; Haines, 24 Oct 1949; Robert J. Wybrow, *Britain Speaks Out, 1937–87* (Basingstoke, 1989), p 28; Heap, 25 Oct 1949; *Picture Post*, 22 Oct 1949, 12 Nov 1949; Barbara Pym Papers (Bodleian Library, Oxford), 40, fol 23; St John, 22 Nov 1949; Olga Cannon and J.R.L. Anderson, *The Road from Wigan Pier* (1973), p 106.

3. Channel 4, *Children of the Iron Lung*, 21 Sept 2000; Geoffrey Rivett, *From Cradle to Grave* (1997), p 58; *Independent*, 28 Mar 2000 (Dury obituary); Julian Critchley, *A Bag of Boiled Sweets* (1994), p 38; Haines, 22/23 Nov 1949; Barbara Stoney, *Enid Blyton* (1974), p 159; Denis Gifford, *The Golden Age of Radio* (1985), p 156; BBC WA, R9/74/1, Mar 1950.

4. *Listener*, 15 Dec 1949; *Sunday Mercury*, 11/18 Dec 1949; *Birmingham News*, 17 Dec 1949; Asa Briggs, *Sound and Vision* (Oxford, 1995), p 221; BBC WA, R9/74/1, R9/4, 20 Feb 1950; Haines, 9 Jan 1950.

5. Speed, 1 Jan 1950; Dartington Hall Trust Archive, LKE/G/35, 4 Jan 1950; Douglas Jay, *Change and Fortune* (1980), pp 192–3.

6. David Hughes, 'The Spivs', in Michael Sissons and Philip French (eds), *Age of Austerity* (Oxford, 1986), p 74; *The Times*, 19/27 Jan 1950; D. J. Taylor, *Orwell* (2003), pp 7–9; Ludovic Kennedy, *Ten Rillington Place* (Panther edn, 1971), pp 227–8.

7. Andy Medhurst, 'Myths of Consensus and Fables of Escape', in Jim Fyrth (ed), *Labour's Promised Land?* (1995), p 300; Charles Barr, *Ealing Studios* (1977), pp 90–91; Charles Barr, 'The National Health', in Ian MacKillop and Neil Sinyard (eds), *British Cinema of the 1950s* (Manchester, 2003), p 68; *Woman's Own*, 16 Mar 1950; Langford, 27 Jan 1950; Golden, 2 Jun 1950; Heap, 25 Feb 1950; Sue Harper

and Vincent Porter, *Weeping in the Cinema in 1950* (Brighton, 1995), pp 10–11; McCann, *Frankie Howerd*, p 96.

8. Ted Willis, *Evening All* (1991), pp 70–72; John Barron Mays, 'A Study of the Police Division', *British Journal of Delinquency* (Jan 1953), pp 187, 189; Barbara Weinberger, *The Best Police in the World* (Aldershot, 1995), pp 41–4, 72–3.

9. Geoffrey Gorer, *Exploring English Character* (1955), pp 213–21.

10. Heap, 22 Mar 1950; Hodgson, 2 Apr 1950; BBC WA, R9/13/27; Susan Sydney-Smith, *Beyond Dixon of Dock Green* (2002), p 98; T. Ferguson and J. Cunnison, *In Their Early Twenties* (1956), p 73; John Barron Mays, *Growing Up in the City* (Liverpool, 1954), pp 21–2, 32, 190.

11. Abigail Wills, 'Delinquency, Masculinity and Citizenship in England 1950–1970', *Past and Present* (May 2005), pp 157–60; H. D. Willcock, *Report on Juvenile Delinquency* (1949), pp 92–7.

12. Langford, 1 Jun 1949; Willcock, *Report*, pp 21, 37; R.F.L. Logan and E. M. Goldberg, 'Rising Eighteen in a London Suburb', *British Journal of Sociology* (Dec 1953), pp 323–45.

13. Joanna Bourke, *Working-Class Cultures in Britain, 1890–1960* (1994), p 182; Tom Hickman, *The Call-Up* (2004), pp 10–11; Kathleen Tynan, *The Life of Kenneth Tynan* (1987), p 77; Tony Richardson, *Long Distance Runner* (1993), pp 38–9; Stephen Martin, 'Your Country Needs You', *Oral History* (Autumn 1997), pp 70–72.

14. Mary Abbott, *Family Affairs* (2003), p 107; Dannie Abse, *A Poet in the Family* (1974), pp 146–7; Adrian Walker, *Six Campaigns* (1993), p 4; William Osgerby, '"One for the Money, Two for the Show"' (PhD, University of Sussex, 1992), pp 177, 90.

15. Trevor Royle, *The Best Years of Their Lives* (1997), pp 84–5, 88; Bill Williamson, *The Temper of the Times* (Oxford, 1990), pp 95–7; T. Ferguson and J. Cunnison, 'The Impact of National Service', *British Journal of Sociology* (Dec 1959), p 286; Arthur Marwick, *Britain in Our Century* (1984), p 153; Sidney R. Campion, *The World of Colin Wilson* (1962), pp 42–3.

16. Liz Stanley, *Sex Surveyed, 1949–1994* (1995), pp, 87, 97, 111, 123–4, 132–4, 137–40, 155, 166. For a trenchant critique of the sexing up of 'Little Kinsey' in an October 2005 BBC television documentary, see: Norman Dennis, 'Propaganda or Public Service Broadcasting?', *Civitas Review* (Feb 2006), pp 1–13.

17. Gorer, *Exploring*, pp 86–7, 93, 96–7, 98–114,.

18. Jeffrey Weeks, *Coming Out* (1990), pp 158–9; *Independent*, 22 Dec 2001 (Philip Hoare); *Woman's Own*, 11 May 1950; John Coldstream, *Dirk Bogarde* (2004), p 194.

19. Mark Abrams, 'Social Trends and Electoral Behaviour', *British Journal of Sociology* (Sept 1962), pp 240–41; M-O A, Directives for Aug 1949, Replies (Women A–M).

20. Martin Francis, '"Not Reformed Capitalism, But … Democratic Socialism"', in Harriet Jones and Michael Kandiah (eds), *The Myth of Consensus* (Basingstoke, 1996), p 43; Headlam, pp 615–16; Matthew Hilton, 'Michael Young and the Consumer Movement', *Contemporary British History* (Sept 2005), p 312; *Independent*, 3 Jul 1997 (Young interview); Speed, 25 Jan 1950; Conservative Party, *This Is The Road* (1950), pp 1–4.

21. *Financial Times*, 14 Mar 1992 (David Butler); Lewis Baston, *Reggie* (Stroud, 2004), p 71; H. G. Nicholas, *The British General Election of 1950* (1951), p 126; BBC WA, R9/13/37; *The New Yorker*, 4 Mar 1950.

22. Mervyn Jones, *Michael Foot* (1994), pp 167–71; Baston, *Reggie*, pp 73–4; Robert Shepherd, *Iain Macleod* (1994), p 58; Simon Heffer, *Like a Roman* (1998), pp 132–3; Robert Shepherd, *Enoch Powell* (1996), pp 79–81; John Campbell, *Edward Heath* (1993), p 67; Campbell, *Margaret Thatcher, Volume One* (2000), p 80; Crosland Papers (British Library of Political and Economic Science), 16/1, 3/9 Feb 1950.

23. Headlam, p 619; Lord Hill of Luton, *Both Sides of the Hill* (1964), p 126; Bruce Belfrage, *One Man in His Time* (1951), p 214; Haines, 15 Feb 1950.

24. Harold Macmillan, *Tides of Fortune* (1969), p 312; Mark Benney et al, *How People Vote* (1956), pp 129–30, 155–6, 159; Mass-Observation, *Voters' Choice* (1950), p 5; Steven Fielding et al, *'England Arise!'* (Manchester, 1995), p 193; M-O A, TC 76/4/E.

25. Nicholas, *General Election*, pp 107–8, 127–8; Benney et al, *How People Vote*, p 160; Bourke, *Working-Class Cultures*, p 189; M-O A, D 5353, 4 Feb 1950; *Listener*, 23 Feb 1950; Hill, p 128; Preston, 14 Feb 1950; Hodgson, 18 Feb 1950.

26. Stuart Laing, *Representations of Working-Class Life, 1957–1964* (Basingstoke, 1986), p 7; Nicholas, *General Election*, p 126; Martin Gilbert, *'Never Despair'* (1988), pp 510-11; Harold Nicolson, *The Later Years, 1945–1962: Diaries and Letters, Volume III* (1968), p 186; Francis Beckett, *Clem Attlee* (1997), p 279; *Voters' Choice*, pp 8–9; *Listener*, 23 Feb 1950.

27. McCann, *Frankie Howerd*, p 65; Cliff Goodwin, *When the Wind Changed* (1999), p 111; Fenton Bresler, *Lord Goddard* (1977), p 206; *Independent*, 11 Jun 2003 (Robert Verkaik); Raynham, 10–19 Feb 1950; *Independent*, 23 Aug 2001 (Steve Connor); BBC WA, R9/74/1, Apr 1950.

28. Gaitskell, p 162; Fielding et al, *'England Arise!'*, p 191; Headlam, p 616; Nicholas, *General Election*, p 284; M-O A, TC 76/4/E.

29. M-O A, TC 76/4/J; *The New Yorker*, 4 Mar 1950; Goodwin, *Wind*, p 111; *Like It Was: The Diaries of Malcolm Muggeridge* (1981), p 380; *The Diaries of Cynthia Gladwyn* (1995), p 118; Haines, 23 Feb 1950; John Fowles, *The Journals, Volume I* (2003), p 19; BBC WA, R9/74/1, Apr 1950.

30. Nicolson, *Later Years*, p 187; Langford, 24 Feb 1950; *The New Yorker*, 4 Mar 1950; Haines, 24 Feb 1950; BBC WA, R9/74/1, Apr 1950.

31. Hodgson, 25 Feb 1950; Raynham, 24 Feb 1950; *Economist*, 4 Mar 1950; Nicolson, *Later Years*, p 188; M-O A, D 5353, 24 Feb 1950; M-O A, TC 76/4/A.

32. *Socialist Commentary* (Apr 1950), p 88; Mark Benney and Phyllis Geiss, 'Social Class and Politics in Greenwich', *British Journal of Sociology* (Dec 1950), p 323.

Part Two

5 A Negative of Snowflakes

1. Laurence Thompson, *Portrait of England* (1952), p 65; West Midland Group, *Conurbation* (1948), pp 100–103, 16.

2. Roland Quinault, 'Britain 1950', *History Today* (Apr 2001), p 16; G. C. Allen, *The Structure of Industry in Britain* (1961), p 11; *The Times*, 9 Jan 1995; Peter Pagnamenta and Richard Overy, *All Our Working Lives* (1984), p 20; Clara H. Greed, *Women and Planning* (1994), pp 126–9.

3. *Picture Post*, 21 Oct 1950; Stewart Dalton, *Crashing Steel* (Barnsley, 1999), pp 6–7; Thompson, *Portrait*, p 245; Michael Blakemore, *Arguments with England* (2004),

pp 75–6; *Manchester Evening Chronicle*, 12/16 Oct 1951; *Sunday Times*, 7 Nov 2004 (Hunter Davies).

4. James Lees-Milne, *Caves of Ice* (Faber edn, 1984), p 211; Blakemore, *Arguments*, p 75; *The New Yorker*, 25 Dec 1948; Michael Bond, *Bears & Forebears* (1996), p 119; West Midland Group, *Conurbation*, pp 113–15; *Listener*, 27 Sept 1951; Meredith Veldman, *Fantasy, the Bomb, and the Greening of Britain* (Cambridge, 1994), pp 208–9, 273–99.

5. Colin G. Pooley and Jean Turnbull, 'Commuting, Transport and Urban Form', *Urban History* (Dec 2000), pp 366–7; Gordon E. Cherry, *Town Planning in Britain since 1900* (Oxford, 1996), p 160; Peter Cain's recollection of growing up in Bolton.

6. *Illustrated London News*, 10 Jan 1948; H. C. Casserley, *The Observer's Book of British Steam Locomotives* (1974), pp 176–7; Paul Vaughan, *Exciting Times in the Accounts Department* (1995), pp 3–4.

7. Peter Bailey, 'Jazz at the Spirella', in Becky Conekin et al (eds), *Moments of Modernity* (1999), p 23; *Planning*, 17 Oct 1949, p 115; Margaret Hanson et al, *The Inner Circle* (Stroud, 2002).

6 Part of the Machinery

1. Seán Damer, *'Last Exit to Blackhill'* (Glasgow, 1992), p 39; Ian Jack, *Before the Oil Ran Out* (1987), pp 1–3.

2. This paragraph is based on: Ross McKibbin, *Classes and Cultures* (Oxford, 1998), pp 106–11; David C. Marsh, *The Changing Social Structure of England and Wales, 1871–1961* (1965), pp 130–53; Sidney Pollard, *The Development of the British Economy* (1983), pp 264–5.

3. Ferdynand Zweig, *The British Worker* (1952), p 203.

4. Nigel Watson, *The Celestial Glass Bottle Company* (Cambridge, 1991), pp 36–8; Alan Sillitoe, *Saturday Night and Sunday Morning* (1958), pp 23, 31; Arthur J. McIvor, *A History of Work in Britain, 1880–1950* (Basingstoke, 2001), pp 242–3; Willmott, Oct 1948; Peter Pagnamenta and Richard Overy, *All Our Working Lives* (1984), p 14.

5. *Illustrated London News*, 30 Aug 1947; McKibbin, *Classes*, p 118; McIvor, *History of Work*, p 245; *News Chronicle*, 21 Dec 1949; Duncan Gallie, 'The Labour Force', in A. H. Halsey (ed), *Twentieth-Century British Social Trends* (Basingstoke, 2000), pp 303, 306; Derek H. Aldcroft and Michael J. Oliver, *Trade Unions and the Economy* (Aldershot, 2000), p 71; William Ashworth, *The History of the British Coal Industry, Volume 5* (Oxford, 1986), p 556; Ferguson, 31 Oct 1950.

6. Geoffrey Tweedale, *Magic Mineral to Killer Dust* (Oxford, 2001), pp 106, 184, 286; Laurence Thompson, *Portrait of England* (1952), p 121; Ashworth, *History*, pp 565–7; Ronald Johnston and Arthur McIvor, '"Dust to Dust"', *Oral History* (Autumn 2001), p 53.

7. Zweig, *British Worker*, pp 115–16.

8. David Lascelles, *Other People's Money* (2005), p 19; David Kynaston, *Cazenove & Co* (1991), p 167; John Griffiths, '"Give my Regards to Uncle Billy ..."', *Business History* (Oct 1995), pp 33–5; Adrian Smith, 'Cars, Cricket and Alf Smith', *International Journal of the History of Sport* (Mar 2002), p 144; Steve Humphries and John Taylor, *The Making of Modern London, 1945–85* (1986), p 12. In general on Alfred Herbert, see: John McG. Davies, 'A Twentieth Century Paternalist', in Bill

Lancaster and Tony Mason (eds), *Life and Labour in a Twentieth Century City* (Coventry, 1986?), pp 98–132; Ken Grainger, 'Management Control and Labour Quiescence', in Michael Terry and P. K. Edwards (eds), *Shopfloor Politics and Job Controls* (Oxford, 1988), pp 84–115.

9. *Merthyr Express*, 3 Jul 1948; *Independent*, 8 Apr 2000 (Martin Kelner); Valerie A. Tedder, *Post War Blues* (Leicester, 1999), pp 98–9.

10. Elizabeth Roberts, *Women and Families* (Oxford, 1995), pp 12, 119–20; Margaret Black, 'Clerical Workers in the 1950s and 1960s', *Oral History* (Spring 1994), p 54; Ferdynand Zweig, *Women's Life and Labour* (1952), p 103; Joanna Bourke, *Working-Class Cultures in Britain, 1890–1960* (1994), p 129.

11. Elizabeth Wilson, *Only Halfway to Paradise* (1980), p 46; Lascelles, *Other People's Money*, p 97; Patricia Hollis, *Jennie Lee* (Oxford, 1997), p 156; Simon Gunn and Rachel Bell, *Middle Classes* (2002), p 156; John Betjeman, *Collected Poems* (2001), p 181.

12. Lascelles, *Other People's Money*, p 98; Sue Bruley, 'Sorters, Pressers, Pipers and Packers', *Oral History* (Spring 1997), pp 79–81; McKibbin, *Classes*, p 133.

13. Pearl Jephcott, *Rising Twenty* (1948), pp 72–4; Zweig, *Women's Life*, pp 9, 11–12, 17–18, 22, 29, 34–6, 161–2.

14. Zweig, *British Worker*, chaps 9–10.

15. Geoffrey Tweedale, *Steel City* (Oxford, 1995), p 314; Stewart Dalton, *Crashing Steel* (Barnsley, 1999), p 7; McIvor, *Work*, p 249; *Spectator*, 23 Apr 2005 (interview with Field); Ferguson, 28 Aug 1950; *The Times*, 9 May 1997 (interview with Field).

16. Watson, *Celestial Glass*, p 39; Norman Dennis et al, *Coal is Our Life* (Tavistock Publications edn, 1969), pp 29–30; *News Chronicle*, 21 Dec 1949; Abrams, Box 65 ('Esso Surveys, 1952–3' file); Zweig, *British Worker*, pp 100–101.

17. Norah M. Davies, 'Attitudes to Work', *British Journal of Psychology* (Mar 1948), pp 110–17, 131, 126–7; Charlie Mayo, 'King's Cross Rail Diary, 1952–3' (Archives, Ruskin College, Oxford, Ms 54).

7 Stiff and Rigid and Unadaptable

1. *Picture Post*, 5 Nov 1949; *Listener*, 19 Jan 1950; *The New Yorker*, 21 May 1949; *Daily Telegraph*, 6 Nov 1999 (John Keegan); *Listener*, 19 Jan 1950.

2. *Times Literary Supplement*, 26 Oct 2001; Correlli Barnett, *The Lost Victory* (Pan edn, 1996), pp 3–5, 28–9, 52–5, 92, 111–12. For the case that the sterling area's economic consequences for Britain were not necessarily adverse, see: Catherine Schenk, *Britain and the Sterling Area* (1994).

3. Barnett, *Lost Victory*, pp 350, 347; Rodney Lowe, 'The Second World War, Consensus and the Foundation of the Welfare State', *Twentieth Century British History*, 1/2 (1990), p 172; Jim Tomlinson, 'Welfare and the Economy', *Twentieth Century British History*, 6/2 (1995), pp 194–219.

4. Information from Lord Howe of Aberavon; S. N. Broadberry and N.F.R. Crafts, 'British Economic Policy and Industrial Performance in the Early Post-War Period', *Business History* (Oct 1996), p 77; Helen Mercer, 'Anti-monopoly Policy', in Mercer et al (eds), *Labour Governments and Private Industry* (Edinburgh, 1992), p 55.

5. Dave Russell, *Looking North* (Manchester, 2004), p 59; Preston, 3 Jul 1949; *Isis*, 23 May 1951; *Independent on Sunday*, 4 Jun 1995 (Hazell interview).

6. David Lascelles, *Other People's Money* (2005), chap 4; David Kynaston, *The City of London, Volume IV* (2001), p 54; Lascelles, p 6; Kynaston, *City*, pp 159, 168.

7. Geoffrey Owen, *From Empire to Europe* (1999), chap 15; Kynaston, *City*, p 52.

8. Kynaston, *City*, p 53; David Kynaston, *Siegmund Warburg* (2002), p 39; Streat, p 556; Gaitskell, p 227.

9. Barnett, *Lost Victory*, pp 183–4; Kynaston, *City*, pp 9–10; Peter Clarke, *The Cripps Version* (2002), p 488; Mercer et al, *Labour Governments*, p 6.

10. Barnett, *Lost Victory*, pp 183–4; Samuel Brittan, *Steering the Economy* (Penguin edn, 1971), p 69; Roy Denman, *The Mandarin's Tale* (2002), pp 19, 23; *Times Literary Supplement*, 9 Jun 2006.

11. J. D. Tomlinson, 'The Iron Quadrilateral', *Journal of British Studies* (Jan 1995), pp 107–9; Gaitskell, p 79; Jim Tomlinson, *Democratic Socialism and Economic Policy* (Cambridge, 1997), pp 119–20; Michael Burrage, 'Nationalisation and the Professional Ideal', *Sociology* (May 1973), pp 263–6; Martin Chick, *Industrial Policy in Britain, 1945–1951* (Cambridge, 1998), chap 5; *Financial Times*, 18 Apr 2001 (John Kay).

12. *Socialist Commentary* (Feb 1950), p 30; Correlli Barnett, *The Verdict of Peace* (2001), pp 285–9.

13. Broadberry and Crafts, 'Economic Policy', p 70; Roy Lewis and Angus Maude, *Professional People* (1952); Owen, *From Empire*, pp 419–21; *Dictionary of Business Biography, Volume 3* (1985), pp 690–93.

14. Owen, *From Empire*, pp 189–90; *Financial Times*, 1 Mar 1991 (McDonald obituary); *Daily Telegraph*, 2 Mar 2001 (Bamford obituary); *Independent*, 4 Sept 2001 (Hamlyn obituary); *Dictionary of Business Biography, Volume 4* (1985), pp 689–93.

15. Papers of Lord Hinton of Bankside (Institution of Mechanical Engineers), A.3, p 242. In general on Portal, see: Denis Richards, *Portal of Hungerford* (1977); *Dictionary of Business Biography, Volume 4* (1985), pp 759–62 (entry by Geoffrey Tweedale).

16. Nick Tiratsoo, '"Cinderellas at the Ball"', *Contemporary British History* (Autumn 1999), pp 105–20; Tiratsoo, 'Limits of Americanisation', in Becky Conekin et al (eds), *Moments of Modernity* (1999), p 110; Maurice Zinkin, 'The Unilever Years III', in Charles Wilson (ed), *Geoffrey Heyworth* (1985), p 27; Alec Cairncross, *Living with the Century* (Fife, 1998), p 182; D. C. Coleman, *Courtaulds, Volume III* (Oxford, 1980), pp 12–38.

17. Derek H. Aldcroft and Michael J. Oliver, *Trade Unions and the Economy* (Aldershot, 2000), pp 46, 90; Richard Hyman, 'Praetorians and Proletarians', in Jim Fyrth (ed), *Labour's High Noon* (1993), p 166.

18. *Economic Journal* (Dec 1949), p 509; Robert Taylor, *The TUC* (Basingstoke, 2000), pp 104–21; Noel Whiteside, 'Industrial Relations and Social Welfare, 1945–79', in Chris Wrigley (ed), *A History of British Industrial Relations, 1939–1979* (Cheltenham, 1996), p 111.

19. David Howell, '"Shut Your Gob!"', in Alan Campbell et al (eds), *British Trade Unions and Industrial Politics, Volume One* (Aldershot, 1999), pp 122–3; John Callaghan, 'Industrial Militancy, 1945–79', *Twentieth Century British History*, 15/4 (2004), pp 388–401; *The Times*, 14 Apr 1953 (labour correspondent).

20. Allan Flanders, *Trade Unions* (1952), pp 78–9; William Brown, 'The High Tide of Consensus', *Historical Studies in Industrial Relations* (Sept 1997), pp 135–49.

21. Ferdynand Zweig, *The British Worker* (1952), pp 180, 185; Taylor, *TUC*, p 103; Joseph Goldstein, *The Government of British Trade Unions* (1953), pp 9, 239, 269; Flanders, *Trade Unions*, pp 57–8.
22. Ferdynand Zweig, *Women's Life and Labour* (1952), pp 126, 129–30; Chris Wrigley, 'Trade Union Development, 1945–79', in idem (ed), *History*, p 65; Pearl Jephcott, *Rising Twenty* (1948), pp 121–2.
23. Brown, 'High Tide', pp 141, 144; Zweig, *British Worker*, pp 175–6.

8 Too High a Price

1. Roger Middleton, *The British Economy since 1945* (Basingstoke, 2000), p 119; BBC WA, *Any Questions?*, 2 Mar 1951; *New Statesman*, 24 Nov 2003 (Gerald Crompton); *Sunday Times*, 12 Aug 2001 (Corelli Barnett); Charles Loft, 'The Beeching Myth', *History Today* (Aug 2004), p 39; Correlli Barnett, *The Lost Victory* (Pan edn, 1996), pp 265–6; Correlli Barnett, *The Verdict of Peace* (2001), p 138.
2. Barnett, *Verdict*, p 464, 465; Roger Fieldhouse, 'Education and Training for the Workforce', in Jim Fyrth (ed), *Labour's High Noon* (1993), pp 98–100, 107–8; Brian Simon, *Education and the Social Order, 1940–1990* (1991), p 91; Kevin McCormick, 'Elite Ideologies and Manipulation in Higher Education', *Sociological Review* (Feb 1982), pp 59–60.
3. Martin Daunton, *Just Taxes* (Cambridge, 2002), pp 221, 227; R. C. Whiting, 'Income Tax, The Working Class and Party Politics, 1948–52', *Twentieth Century British History*, 8/2 (1977), pp 202–3, 216; Geoffrey Thomas, *Incentives in Industry* (1953), p 24.
4. Helen Mercer, 'Anti-monopoly Policy', in Mercer et al (eds), *Labour Governments and Private Industry* (Edinburgh, 1992), p 57; Peter Bird, *The First Food Empire* (Chichester, 2000), p 239; Geoffrey Tweedale, *Steel City* (Oxford, 1995), p 330.
5. Ferdynand Zweig, *Productivity and Trade Unions* (Oxford, 1951), pp 16–25; S. N. Broadberry and N.F.R. Crafts, 'The Post-War Settlement', *Business History* (Apr 1998), p 75. For an antidote to the Broadberry/Crafts stress on the seriousness and pervasiveness of the problem, see: Nick Tiratsoo and Jim Tomlinson, 'Restrictive Practices on the Shopfloor in Britain, 1945–60', *Business History* (Apr 1994), pp 65–84.
6. David Kynaston, *The Financial Times* (1988), p 298; Norman Tebbit, *Upwardly Mobile* (1988), p 15.
7. *Daily Mirror*, 30 Sept 1949.
8. Nick Tiratsoo, 'Limits of Americanisation', in Becky Conekin et al, *Moments of Modernity* (1999), pp 96–113; Ian Clark, *Governance, the State, Regulation and Industrial Relations* (2000), chap 6.
9. M-O A, Directives for Aug 1950, Replies (Men A–E); *Listener*, 2 Feb 1950; Charles Barr, *Ealing Studios* (1977), pp 159–64, 166–70.

9 Proper Bloody Products

1. Gaitskell, p 121; Simon Courtauld, *To Convey Intelligence* (1999), pp 17–18. See also Michael Richardson, *The Durham Miners' Gala* (Derby, 2001).

2. Gaitskell, pp 60, 89, 93; *Dictionary of Business Biography, Volume 3* (1985), pp 255–60 (entry by Jenny Davenport).

3. *Coal Magazine* (Jan 1949), p 7; William Warren Haynes, *Nationalization in Practice* (1953), pp 140–41; Neil K. Buxton, *The Economic Development of the British Coal Industry* (1978), pp 234–5; *Listener*, 23 Nov 1950.

4. *Coal Magazine* (Jan 1949), p 7; Paul Routledge, *Scargill* (1993), pp 27–8; Michael P. Jackson, *The Price of Coal* (1974), p 81; William Ashworth, *The History of the British Coal Industry, Volume 5* (Oxford, 1986), p 169; Stanislas Wellisz, 'Strikes in Coal-Mining', *British Journal of Sociology* (Dec 1953), pp 346–66; *Observer*, 3 Aug 1952.

5. Jackson, *Price*, p 95; Norman Dennis et al, *Coal is Our Life* (Tavistock Publications edn, 1969), pp 14, 75–6, 78–83, 97–112; Ferdynand Zweig, *The British Worker* (1952), pp 34, 104; Routledge, *Scargill*, pp 21–2.

6. *Picture Post*, 28 Feb 1948.

7. Jim Phillips, 'The Postwar Political Consensus and Industrial Unrest in the Docks, 1945–55', *Twentieth Century British History*, 6/3 (1995), p 304.

8. Correlli Barnett, *The Verdict of Peace* (2001), pp 251, 255; *The Times*, 8 Jul 1949; Correlli Barnett, *The Lost Victory* (Pan edn, 1996), pp 270–71; Fred Lindup, 'Unofficial Militancy in the Royal Group of Docks, 1945–67', *Oral History* (Autumn 1983), pp 21–33; Peter Turnbull, 'Dock Strikes and the Demise of the Dockers' "Occupational Culture"', *Sociological Review* (May 1992), p 295; *Dictionary of Labour Biography, Volume IX* (Basingstoke, 1993), pp 59–63 (entry by Daniel Ballard and David E. Martin); *Independent*, 9 Jun 1989 (Dash obituary).

9. Phillips, 'Political Consensus', p 305; Peter Turnbull et al, 'Persistent Militants and Quiescent Comrades', *Sociological Review* (Nov 1996), pp 708–9; Ballard and Martin, *Dictionary of Labour*, p 60; Colin J. Davis, 'New York City and London, 1945–1960', in Sam Davies et al (eds), *Dock Workers* (Aldershot, 2000), pp 223–4.

10. University of Liverpool (Department of Social Science), *The Dock Worker* (Liverpool, 1954), pp 56, 66, 68, 89–90, 125–6, 140, 174, 176–8, 185, 189, 202.

11. *The Times*, 27 Oct 1948; *Financial Times*, 28 Oct 1948; *Listener*, 11 Nov 1948; Roy Church, *The Rise and Decline of the British Motor Industry* (Basingstoke, 1994), p 44; James Foreman-Peck et al, *The British Motor Industry* (Manchester, 1995), p 94; Political & Economic Planning, *Motor Vehicles* (1950), pp 36–40; Peter J. S. Dunnett, *The Decline of the British Motor Industry* (1980), pp 36–40.

12. Political & Economic Planning, *Motor Vehicles*, pp 28–9; David Burgess-Wise, *Ford at Dagenham* (Derby, 2002?), pp 99, 102, 118; Graham Turner, *The Car Makers* (Penguin edn, 1964), p 35; Geoffrey Owen, *From Empire to Europe* (1999), p 219; *Dictionary of Business Biography, Volume 3* (1985) (entry by David Burgess-Wise); Barnett, *Lost Victory*, pp 332–6.

13. Burgess-Wise, *Business Biography*, p 169; Dave Lyddon, 'The Car Industry, 1945–79', in Chris Wrigley (ed), *A History of British Industrial Relations, 1939–1979* (Cheltenham, 1996), p 194; Peter Pagnamenta and Richard Overy, *All Our Working Lives* (1984), p 225; Huw Beynon, *Working for Ford* (Pelican edn, 1984), p 54; Steve Humphries and John Taylor, *The Making of Modern London, 1945–1985* (1986), p 11; Turner, *Car Makers*, pp 130–35. In general on Ford, see also Steven Tolliday, 'Ford and "Fordism" in Postwar Britain', in Tolliday and Jonathan Zeitlin (eds), *The Power to Manage?* (1991), pp 81–114.

14. Len Holden, *Vauxhall Motors and the Luton Economy, 1900–2002* (Woodbridge, 2003), p 57, chap 6; H. A. Turner et al, *Labour Relations in the Motor Industry* (1967), p 347; Lyddon, 'Car Industry', pp 197–8.

15. Roy Church, 'Deconstructing Nuffield', *Economic History Review* (Aug 1996), pp 561–83; Church, *Rise and Decline*, p 79; Graham Turner, *The Leyland Papers* (1971), pp 92–4; Barnett, *Verdict*, pp 387–8; Steven Tolliday, 'Government, Employers and Shop Floor Organization in the British Motor Industry' in Tolliday and Jonathan Zeitlin (eds), *Shop Floor Bargaining and the State* (Cambridge, 1985), pp 108, 118; Les Gurl Papers (Archives, Ruskin College, Oxford), 57/1.

16. Mark Singlehurst and Kevin Wilkins, *Coventry Car Factories* (Coventry, 1995), p 12; David Thoms and Tom Donnelly, *The Coventry Motor Industry* (Aldershot, 2000), pp 128, 136; John Salmon, 'Wage Strategy, Redundancy and Shop Stewards in the Coventry Motor Industry', in Michael Terry and P. K. Edwards (eds), *Shopfloor Politics and Job Controls* (Oxford, 1988), p 189; Laurence Thompson, *Portrait of England* (1952), p 79.

17. Jack Jones, *Union Man* (1986), p 123; Steven Tolliday, 'High Tide and After', in Bill Lancaster and Tony Mason (eds), *Life and Labour in a Twentieth-Century City* (Coventry, 1986?), pp 209–10, 215–16; Paul Thompson, 'Playing at Being Skilled Men', *Social History* (Jan 1988), pp 56–64.

18. Thoms and Donnelly, *Coventry*, pp 157–8; Tolliday, 'High Tide', pp 210–12.

19. Thompson, 'Playing', pp 61, 68–9; Barnett, *Lost Victory*, pp 388–90; Pagnamenta and Overy, *Working Lives*, p 229; Martin Adeney, *The Motor Makers* (1988), p 206. For a different perspective on Standard in the Black era, see: Nick Tiratsoo, 'The Motor Car Industry', in Helen Mercer et al (eds), *Labour Governments and Private Industry* (Edinburgh, 1992), pp 170–80.

20. Barnett, *Verdict*, p 389; Holden, *Vauxhall*, p 57; Turner, *Leyland*, p 90; *The Times*, 23 Aug 1999 (Gerald Palmer obituary); Steve Jefferys, 'The Changing Face of Conflict', in Terry and Edwards, *Shopfloor Politics*, pp 61–6; Salmon, 'Wage Strategy', p 194; *Dictionary of Business Biography, Volume 3* (1985), p 858 (entry by Richard Overy); *Dictionary of Labour Biography, Volume IX* (Basingstoke, 1993), p 79 (entry by Alistair Tough); John McIlroy, '"Every Factory Our Fortress"', *Historical Studies in Industrial Relations* (Autumn 2001), pp 81–2; Etheridge Papers (Modern Records Centre, University of Warwick), 202/S/J/8/7, 202/S/J/8/5.

10 Andy Is Waving Goodbye

1. *The Times*, 21 Mar 1996, *Independent*, 22 Mar 1996 (Barry Appleby obituaries); Colin MacInnes, *English, Half English* (1986), p 41.

2. *Picture Post*, 14 Apr 1950.

3. Marcus Morris, *The Best of Eagle* (1977), pp 3, 65. See also Sally Morris and Jan Hallwood, *Living with Eagles* (1998).

4. *The Times*, 31 Dec 1988 (John Bryant); *Independent*, 1 Apr 1996 (Jim White). See also Denis Gifford, *The British Comic Catalogue, 1874–1974* (1975).

5. Nick Clarke, *The Shadow of a Nation* (2003), pp 51–2; Hodgson, 14 May 1950; Theo Aronson, *Princess Margaret* (1997), p 113; *Times Literary Supplement*, 4 Oct 1996 (Anthony Howard); *Daily Mail*, 11 Feb 2002; *Picture Post*, 12 Aug 1950.

6. *Times Literary Supplement*, 24 Mar 1950; *Spectator*, 7 Apr 1950; Humphrey Carpenter, *The Angry Young Men* (2002), p 50. For a subtle and convincing

reappraisal of Cooper, see: D. J. Taylor, 'Behind the Scenes', *Times Literary Supplement*, 9 Jun 2006.

7. Dan Smith, *An Autobiography* (Newcastle upon Tyne, 1970), pp 1–33; *Proceedings of the Council of the City and County of Newcastle upon Tyne for 1950–1951* (Newcastle upon Tyne, 1951), pp 16–17, 96. In the absence of a biography of Smith, see also the special issue of *North East Labour History* (1994, Bulletin no 28).

8. Dan Jacobson, 'Time of Arrival', in Ian Hamilton (ed), *The Penguin Book of Twentieth-Century Essays* (1999), p 300; Hodgson, 19 Mar 1950; Raynham, 1 May 1950; Golden, 26 Apr 1950, 16 Jul 1950; Robert J. Wybrow, *Britain Speaks Out, 1937–87* (Basingstoke, 1989), p 29.

9. *The New Yorker*, 29 Apr 1950; Reader's Digest, *Yesterday's Britain* (1998), pp 204–5; *Guardian*, 27 Dec 1990 (Raitz interview).

10. *Independent*, 11 Nov 1989 (Ronay interview); *Independent*, 9 Sept 2000 (Patten interview); Stuart Hylton, *Reading in the 1950s* (Stroud, 1997), pp 9, 23.

11. *Observer*, 18 Jun 1950; *Times Literary Supplement*, 26 Nov 1999 (Arabella Boxer); *Guardian*, 24 Apr 2004 (Ian Jack). In general on David, see: Artemis Cooper, *Writing at the Kitchen Table* (1999).

12. *Dictionary of Labour Biography, Volume II* (1974), pp 304–11 (entry by Margaret Cole); Raymond Postgate (ed), *The Good Food Guide, 1951–1952* (1951), pp 7, 132; *Independent*, 8 Jul 1989 (Anthony Howard). See also Clarke, *Shadow*, pp 135–6.

13. *Independent*, 30 Nov 1999 (Steve Connor).

14. *Independent*, 30 May 1998 (Eddie Baily interview), 10 Feb 1996 (Neil Franklin obituary by Ivan Ponting). See also: Stephen Wagg, *The Football World* (Brighton, 1984), p 85; Rogan Taylor and Andrew Ward, *Kicking and Screaming* (1995), chap 8.

15. Vijay P. Kumar, *Cricket Lovely Cricket* (New York, 2000), p 124; Mike Phillips and Trevor Phillips, *Windrush* (1998), pp 101, 103; *London Is The Place For Me* (CD) (2002).

16. David Rayvern Allen, *Arlott* (1994), pp 145–53; BBC WA, *Any Questions?*, 8 Dec 1950; *Like It Was: The Diaries of Malcolm Muggeridge* (1981), p 401.

17. Jacobson, 'Time of Arrival', p 301; John Barron Mays, *Growing Up in the City* (Liverpool, 1954), p 43; *Picture Post*, 22 Apr 1950; Michael Banton, *The Coloured Quarter* (1955), pp 182–9.

18. Steven Tolliday, 'High Tide and After', in Bill Lancaster and Tony Mason (eds), *Life and Labour in a Twentieth-Century City* (Coventry, 1986?), p 207; Richard Holt, *Stanmore Golf Club, 1893–1993* (Stanmore, 1993), p 63; *The Times*, 9 Jul 1990, *Independent*, 10 Jul 1990 (obituaries of Dick Turpin).

19. Michael Banton, 'The Influence of Colonial Status upon Black-White Relations in England, 1948–58', *Sociology* (Nov 1983), pp 549–55.

20. Kathleen Paul, *Whitewashing Britain* (Ithaca, 1997), p 132; John Barnes, *Ahead of His Age* (1979), p 427; D. W. Dean, 'Coping with Colonial Immigration, the Cold War and Colonial Policy', *Immigrants & Minorities* (Nov 1987), pp 324–5; Randall Hansen, 'The Politics of Citizenship in 1940s Britain', *Twentieth Century British History*, 10/1 (1999), pp 91–3.

21. *Guardian*, 23 Jul 2005 (Caryl Phillips), 22 Jun 1995 (Maya Jaggi).

22. Roland Quinault, 'Britain 1950', *History Today* (Apr 2001), p 17; Banton, *Coloured Quarter*, p 190; Donald Hinds, *Journey to an Illusion* (1966), pp 60–61.

23. Barbara Pym, *Some Tame Gazelle* (Grafton Books edn, 1981), p 5; Hazel Holt, *A Lot to Ask* (1990), p 151; *New Statesman*, 1 Jul 1950; *The Dictionary of National Biography: 1971–1980* (Oxford, 1986), p 695 (entry by Philip Larkin); Barbara Pym Papers (Bodleian Library, Oxford), 163/1, fol 10.

24. Cliff Goodwin, *To Be A Lady* (1995), pp 156–8; *The Times*, 12 Jun 1998 (Cookson obituary). See also Robert Colls, 'Cookson, Chaplin and Common', in K.D.M. Snell (ed), *The Regional Novel in Britain and Ireland, 1800–1990* (Cambridge, 1998), pp 164–200.

25. Margaret Drabble, *Angus Wilson* (1995), pp 167–74.

26. This paragraph is based on: Adam Sisman, *A.J.P. Taylor* (1994), pp 196–7; Mervyn Jones, *Michael Foot* (1994), pp 177–8; Asa Briggs, *Sound and Vision* (Oxford, 1995), pp 548–51; Kathleen Burk, *Troublemaker* (New Haven, 2000), pp 383–6.

27. *Independent*, 7 Jun 1999 (Brough obituary); Cliff Goodwin, *When the Wind Changed* (1999), pp 128–31.

28. Haines, 5 Jul 1950; David Oswell, *Television, Childhood and the Home* (Oxford, 2002), pp 56, 63, 64; Hilary Kingsley and Geoff Tibballs, *Box of Delights* (1989), p 13; BBC WA, R9/13/51.

29. E. W. Swanton, *Sort of a Cricket Person* (1972), p 172; Swanton, *As I Said at the Time* (1983), p 308; *Wisden Cricketers' Almanack, 1951* (1951), p 276; Stephen Wagg, '"Time Gentlemen Please"', in Adrian Smith and Dilwyn Porter (eds), *Amateurs and Professionals – Post-War British Sport* (2000), pp 31–59; Rex Warner and Lyle Blair, *Ashes to Ashes* (1951), pp 29, 101.

30. *Picture Post*, 15/29 Jul 1950.

31. *Independent*, 14 May 1996 (Malcolm Hornsby), 26 Oct 1998 (Lord Sainsbury obituary by Robert Butler); Reader's Digest, *Yesterday's Britain*, p 205; Margaret Forster, *Hidden Lives* (1995), pp 165–9.

32. *Independent*, 26 Jun 1993 (Colin Welland); Joe Orton Papers (Special Collections, University of Leicester), 1/20/1, 10 Aug 1950; Speed, 19 Aug 1950.

33. John Hilton Bureau Papers (Special Collections, University of Sussex), Box 12: Journal 1949–54, 'Extracts from Letters', 31 Aug 1950; Speed, 13 Aug 1950; M-O A, D 5353, 14 Aug 1950.

11 The Heaviest Burden

1. Streat, pp 528–30; Patrick Gordon Walker, *Political Diaries, 1932–1971* (1992), p 187.

2. Bernard Donoughue and G. W. Jones, *Herbert Morrison* (2001), p 456; Mervyn Jones, *Michael Foot* (1994), p 179; Robert J. Wybrow, *Britain Speaks Out, 1937–87* (Basingstoke, 1989), p 29.

3. Kenneth Harris, *Attlee* (1982), p 452; Peter Clarke, *The Cripps Version* (2002), pp 496–7; Neil Rollings, '"Poor Mr Butskell"', *Twentieth Century British History*, 5/2 (1994), pp 189–95; Glen O'Hara, 'British Economic and Social Planning, 1959–1970' (PhD, University of London, 2002), p 6; Kenneth O. Morgan, *Callaghan* (Oxford, 1997), pp 106–7.

4. Scott Kelly, 'Ministers Matter', *Contemporary British History* (Winter 2000), pp 39–40; *Financial Times*, 11 Jul 1950.

5. Brian Brivati, *Hugh Gaitskell* (1996), p 116; Philip M. Williams, *Hugh Gaitskell* (1979), p 214.

6. Fabian, G 50/3; *Political Quarterly* (Jan–Mar 1953), p 103; Matthew Hilton, 'The Fable of the Sheep', *Past & Present* (Aug 2002), pp 234–5; Martin Francis, 'Economics and Ethics', *Twentieth Century British History*, 6/2 (1995), p 240; Asa Briggs, *Michael Young* (Basingstoke, 2001), p 99.

7. *Listener*, 8 Jun 1950; Francis, 'Economics and Ethics', p 239; Susan Crosland, *Tony Crosland* (1982), p 54.

8. Robert Shepherd, *Iain Macleod* (1994), pp 59–61; Robert Walsha, 'The One Nation Group', *Twentieth Century British History*, 11/2 (2000), pp 193–4; Iain Macleod and Angus Maude (eds), *One Nation* (1950), pp 18, 90.

9. *New Statesman*, 22 Apr 1950; A. H. Halsey, *No Discouragement* (1996), p 218; Alan Deacon, 'Richard Titmuss', *Journal of Social Policy* (Apr 1993), pp 236–7; Hilary Rose, 'Rereading Titmuss', *Journal of Social Policy* (Oct 1981), pp 480–81; Margaret Gowing, 'Richard Morris Titmuss', in *Proceedings of the British Academy* (1975), p 428; David Reisman, *Richard Titmuss* (Basingstoke, 2001), pp 22–3. See also Ann Oakley, *Man and Wife* (1996), a remarkable portrait of her parents' early years.

10. Ben Pimlott, *Hugh Dalton* (1985), p 580; Alan Bullock, *Ernest Bevin: Foreign Secretary, 1945–1951* (Oxford, 1983), p 782; John Campbell, *Edward Heath* (1993), p 76; Edward Pearce, *Denis Healey* (2002), p 141; Mamaine Koestler, *Living with Koestler* (1985), p 159.

11. *The New Yorker*, 17 Jun 1950; *New Statesman*, 10 Jun 1950; Alan McKinley et al, 'Reluctant Europeans?', *Business History* (Oct 2000), p 96; Edmund Dell, *A Strange Eventful History* (1999), p 188.

12. David Kynaston, *The Financial Times* (1988), p 230; Peter Hennessy, *Never Again* (1992), p 410; Bullock, *Ernest Bevin*, p 799; David Marquand, *The Progressive Dilemma* (1999), p 125.

13. Correlli Barnett, *The Verdict of Peace* (2001), pp 16, 24, 26; Sean Greenwood, '"A War We Don't Want"', *Contemporary British History* (Winter 2003), pp 1–24.

14. Speed, 5 Jul 1950; Frances Partridge, *Everything to Lose* (1985), p 123; Haines, 30 Jul 1950; Wybrow, *Britain Speaks*, p 29; Hodgson, 10 Dec 1950; *The Letters of Kingsley Amis* (2000), p 252.

15. Dianne Kirby, 'Ecclesiastical McCarthyism', *Contemporary British History* (Jun 2005), pp 191–3; James Cameron, *Point of Departure* (Panther edn, 1985), pp 145–9; Bill Moore, *Cold War in Sheffield* (Sheffield, 1990); Steve Parsons, 'British "McCarthyism" and the Intellectuals', in Jim Fyrth (ed), *Labour's Promised Land?* (1995), p 240; Hugh Wilford, '"Unwitting Assets?"', *Twentieth Century British History*, 11/1 (2000), p 47; *Independent*, 18 Jul 1995 (Spender obituary by Peter Porter).

16. Kevin Morgan, *Harry Pollitt* (Manchester, 1993), p 169; Mervyn Jones, *Chances* (1987), pp 117–18; *Times Literary Supplement*, 5 Oct 2001 (John Jones); Lionel Blue, *My Affair with Christianity* (1998), p 19.

17. Daly, 302/3/2, 31 Oct 1950, 302/5/2, 3–17 Nov 1950.

18. Barnett, *Verdict*, p 33; Samuel Brittan, *Steering the Economy* (Penguin edn, 1971), p 184; Andrew Shonfield, *British Economic Policy since the War* (1958), p 56; Barnett, *Verdict*, p 35; Jim Tomlinson, *Democratic Socialism and Economic Policy* (Cambridge, 1997), p 234; Peter Burnham, 'Rearming for the Korean War', *Contemporary Record* (Autumn 1995), pp 343–67.

19. John Campbell, *Nye Bevan* (1997), p 220; *The New Yorker*, 21 Oct 1950.
20. Williams, *Hugh Gaitskell*, p 238; Gaitskell, p 216; Ben Pimlott, *Harold Wilson* (1992), p 157; *Like It Was: The Diaries of Malcolm Muggeridge* (1981), p 421; Campbell, *Bevan*, pp 225–6.
21. Gaitskell, pp 233, 237–8; Williams, *Hugh Gaitskell*, p 248; Campbell, *Bevan*, p 233; Brivati, *Hugh Gaitskell*, p 117; Campbell, *Bevan*, p 233.
22. *Daily Express*, 1 Jan 1951; Crosland, *Crosland*, p 52; Jad Adams, *Tony Benn* (1992), p 74; BBC WA, *Any Questions?*, 9 Mar 1951; Tony Benn, *Years of Hope* (1994), p 145.
23. Hodgson, Christmas 1950; Richard Weight, *Patriots* (2002), p 133; *The Macmillan Diaries: The Cabinet Years, 1950–1957* (2003), pp 38–40; *The Journal of Sir Randall Philip* (Edinburgh, 1998), p 199; *The Times*, 2 Apr 2004 (Gavin Vernon obituary); *The Letters of Hugh MacDiarmid* (1984), p 269.
24. Christopher Harvie, *Scotland and Nationalism* (1998), pp 120–23, 171; Richard J. Finlay, *Modern Scotland, 1914–2000* (2004), pp 203–21.
25. Janet Davies, 'The Welsh Language', in Trevor Herbert and Gareth Elwyn Jones (eds), *Post-War Wales* (Cardiff, 1995), p 55; *Spectator*, 22 May 2004 (Hywel Williams).
26. *Independent*, 18 Sept 1998 (Jones obituary by Meic Stephens). For a somewhat kindlier assessment, see obituary in *Daily Telegraph*, 15 Sept 1998.

12 A Kind of Measuring-Rod

1. Langford, 4 Sept 1950.
2. This paragraph is based on: Matthew Hilton, *Smoking in British Popular Culture, 1800–2000* (Basingstoke, 2000), pp 179–80; *Independent*, 3 Aug 2000 (Jeremy Laurance); Virginia Berridge, 'Post-war Smoking Policy in the UK and the Redefinition of Public Health', *Twentieth Century British History*, 14/1 (2003), pp 64–6; *Observer*, 24 Apr 2005 (Simon Garfield).
3. Chaplin, 7/3/1, 24 Jul 1950, 23 Nov 1950, 22 Dec 1950; *Northern Despatch*, 29 Aug 1950; *Coal* (Oct 1950), pp 10–17; *Times Literary Supplement*, 13 Oct 1950. For a penetrating assessment of Chaplin at this time, see also Robert Colls, 'Cookson, Chaplin and Common', in K.D.M. Snell (ed), *The Regional Novel in Britain and Ireland, 1800–1990* (Cambridge, 1998), pp 164–200.
4. Hodgson, 22 Oct 1950; Max Wall, *The Fool on the Hill* (1975), pp 192–3, 249–50; Graham McCann, *Frankie Howerd* (2004), p 110.
5. *Listener*, 16 Nov 1950; Peter Willmott, 'Integrity in Social Science – The Upshot of a Scandal', *International Social Science Journal*, 29/2 (1977), p 335. In general on Burt's influence and legacy, see: L. S. Hearnshaw, *Cyril Burt* (1979); Robin Pedley, *The Comprehensive School* (Penguin edn, 1969), pp 35–6; John Vaizey, *In Breach of Promise* (1983), p 117; Brian Simon, *Education and the Social Order, 1940–1990* (1991), pp 157–9.
6. *The Times*, 1 Jul 2000; Tom Courtenay, *Dear Tom* (2000), pp 76–7; Cliff Richard, *Which One's Cliff?* (Coronet edn, 1981), p 31; *Independent*, 21 Sept 2004 (Clough obituary); Colin Brown, *Fighting Talk* (1997), pp 34–6.
7. Brian Simon, 'The Tory Government and Education, 1951–60', *History of Education* (Dec 1985), p 295; Courtenay, *Dear Tom*, p 92; *TV Times*, 14 Dec 1974; Joan Bakewell, *The Centre of the Bed* (2003), pp 62, 66–7; Peter Stead, 'Barry since 1939', in Donald Moore (ed), *Barry* (Barry Island, 1985), pp 458–61.

8. Steven Berkoff, *Free Association* (1996), p 11; Chris Bryant, *Glenda Jackson* (1999), pp 13, 16; Adrian Turner, *Robert Bolt* (1998), p 69; Preston, 21 Mar 1951.

9. *Sociological Review* (Nov 1963), p 380 (Olive Banks); Olive Banks, *Parity and Prestige in English Secondary Education* (1955), p 216; Nicholas Timmins, *The Five Giants* (2001), pp 153–4.

10. William Taylor, *The Secondary Modern School* (1963), pp 12–13; *Socialist Commentary* (Sept 1951), p 214; Brown, *Fighting Talk*, p 35.

11. BBC 2, *The New Jerusalem: A Place in the Class*, 2 Jul 1995; Rhodes Boyson, *Speaking My Mind* (1995), pp 43–7; Edward Blishen, *Roaring Boys* (Panther edn, 1966), back cover, pp 20–21; BBC 2, *From Butler to Baker*, 11 Jan 1994.

12. F. W. Martin, 'An Inquiry into Parents' Preferences in Secondary Education', in D. V. Glass (ed), *Social Mobility in Britain* (1954), chapt 7.

13. Ibid, p 171; *Picture Post*, 28 Jan 1950.

14. Bill Wyman, *Stone Alone* (1990), p 55; Blishen, *Roaring Boys*, p 15; Simon, *Education*, p 99.

15. H. T. Himmelweit, 'Social Status and Secondary Education since the 1944 Act', in Glass, *Social Mobility*, pp 141–59.

16. D. W. Dean, 'Planning for a Postwar Generation', *History of Education* (Jun 1986), p 101; Robert G. Burgess, 'Changing Concepts of Secondary Education', in Bill Lancaster and Tony Mason (eds), *Life and Labour in a Twentieth-Century City* (Coventry, 1986?), p 298; Ross McKibbin, *Classes and Cultures* (Oxford, 1998), p 235.

17. Laurence Thompson, *Portrait of England* (1952), pp 7, 190–94.

18. V. S. Naipaul, *Letters Between a Father and Son* (1999), pp 28, 45, 63–5.

19. Phyllis Willmott, *Joys and Sorrows* (1995), p 128; M-O A, D 5353, 6 Jan 1951; Haines, 13 Jan 1951; *Sunday Chronicle*, 11 Mar 1951.

20. M-O A, Directives for Mar–Apr 1951, Replies (Women F–N); Haines, 28 Mar 1951; M-O A, Directives for Mar–Apr 1951, Replies (Men); BBC WA, *Any Questions?*, 29 Sept 1950; Phil Walley, *Accrington Stanley Football Club* (Stroud, 2001), p 31.

21. BBC WA, R9/74/1, Nov 1950–Feb 1951; Denis Gifford, *The Golden Age of Radio* (1985), p 295; M-O A, D 5353, 5/19 Mar 1951.

22. BBC WA, R9/74/1, May 1951, Oct 1950; William Smethurst, *The Archers* (1996), p 12; Asa Briggs, *Sound and Vision* (Oxford, 1995), p 99; BBC WA, R9/74/1, Feb–Mar 1951, May 1951; Richard Weight, *Patriots* (2002), p 159.

23. *The Times*, 23 Jan 1951; John Caughie, *Television Drama* (Oxford, 2000), p 36; *Times Literary Supplement*, 1 Oct 1999 (Mick Hume); Briggs, *Sound and Vision*, pp 416–19.

24. Briggs, *Sound and Vision*, pp 345, 40; *Evening Standard*, 19 Jan 1951.

25. Caughie, *Television*, pp 33–4; Peter Goddard, '"Hancock's Half-Hour"', in John Corner (ed), *Popular Television in Britain* (1991), p 76; Mark Lewisohn, *Radio Times Guide to TV Comedy* (2003), pp 389, 754; Hodgson, 1 Apr 1951; Speed, 24/28 Mar 1951; Brown, 1/16, 2 Apr 1951.

26. Caughie, *Television Drama*, pp 37–41; BBC WA, R9/4, 12 Feb–11 Mar 1950, R9/19/1, Jun 1950, Feb 1951, Mar 1951, May 1951, Mar 1952.

27. *Guardian*, 4 Jul 2005; Heap, 18 Jan 1950; Langford, 21 Jan 1950; *The New Yorker*, 11 Feb 1950; Heap, 3 May 1950; Robert Hewison, *In Anger* (1986), p 81.

28. Dominic Shellard, '1950–54', in Shellard (ed), *British Theatre in the 1950s* (Sheffield, 2000), pp 28–40; Richard Huggett, *Binkie Beaumont* (1989), p 424; Christopher Innes,

'Terence Rattigan', in Shellard, *British Theatre*, pp 53–63; *New Statesman*, 4 Mar 1950.
29. Heap, 19 Apr 1951; *New Statesman*, 28 Apr 1951; Huggett, *Binkie Beaumont*, p 428; Charles Duff, *The Lost Summer* (1995), p 125.

13 Their Own Private Domain

1. Langford, 2 Apr 1951; F. T. Burnett and Sheila F. Scott, 'A Survey of Housing Conditions in the Urban Areas of England and Wales', *Sociological Review* (Mar 1962), pp 36–8; F. J. McCulloch, 'Housing Policy', *Sociological Review* (Mar 1961), p 105.
2. Burnett and Scott, 'Survey', p 42; K. C. Wiggans, 'Job and Health in a Shipyard Town', *Sociological Review* (1952), Section Five, p 2; *New Statesman*, 2 Dec 1950.
3. *New Statesman*, 22 Jul 1950; T. Brennan, *Reshaping a City* (Glasgow, 1959), pp 20–21; Andrew Gibb, *Glasgow* (Beckenham, 1983), p 161; Ronald Smith, *The Gorbals* (Glasgow, 1999), p 15.
4. Alan Holmans, 'Housing', in A. H. Halsey (ed), *Twentieth-Century British Social Trends* (Basingstoke, 2000), p 487; *New Statesman*, 2 Dec 1950; Miles Horsey, *Tenements and Towers* (Edinburgh, 1990), p 27.
5. Elizabeth Layton, 'The Economics of Housing', *Town Planning Review* (Apr 1951), p 9; Jim Yelling, 'Public Policy, Urban Renewal and Property Ownership, 1945–55', *Urban History* (May 1995), pp 50–54; Phyllis Willmott, *Joys and Sorrows* (1995), pp 123–4; *The Letters of Kingsley Amis* (2000), p 222; Richard Bradford, *Lucky Him* (2001), p 126; Kingsley Amis, *That Uncertain Feeling* (Penguin edn, 1985), p 103.
6. Patrick Nuttgens, *The Home Front* (1989), p 67; Holmans, 'Housing', p 487; Harriet Jones, '"This is Magnificent!"', *Contemporary British History* (Spring 2000), p 102; Brian Lund, *Housing Problems and Housing Policy* (Harlow, 1996), p 121.
7. Peter Mitchell, *Memento Mori* (Otley, 1990), pp 8 (preface by Bernard Crick), 42, 66; *Yorkshire Observer*, 26 September 1949; Alison Ravetz, *Model Estate* (1974), pp 226–9.
8. Seán Damer, *'Last Exit to Blackhill'* (Glasgow, 1992), pp 32–9.
9. Godfrey Winn, *This Fair Country* (1951), pp 109–17.
10. *The Macmillan Diaries: The Cabinet Years, 1950–1957* (2003), pp 23–4; *Picture Post*, 2 Dec 1950.
11. *Journal of the Town Planning Institute* (Sept–Oct 1949), p 232; Junichi Hasegawa, *Replanning the Blitzed City Centre* (Buckingham, 1992), pp 108–9; *Observer*, 28 Jan 1951.
12. Nick Tiratsoo, *Reconstruction, Affluence and Labour Politics* (1990), chap 4; *Coventry Evening Telegraph*, 31 Dec 1949; *Listener*, 1 Dec 1949; Winn, *This Fair Country*, pp 221–3.
13. Nick Tiratsoo, 'Coventry', in Tiratsoo et al (eds), *Urban Reconstruction in Britain and Japan, 1945–1955* (Luton, 2002), pp 24–5; Tiratsoo, *Reconstruction*, p 57; *Coventry Standard*, 16 Mar 1951.
14. *New Society*, 8 Feb 1979 (Gordon Cherry); *Evening Standard*, 15 Jan 1951; *Observer*, 28 Jan 1951; C.A.C. Turner, 'Houses and Flats at Crawley', *Town and Country Planning* (Feb 1951), p 83; Harold Orlans, *Stevenage* (1952), pp 120–21; *Daily Telegraph*, 26 Apr 2003 (Keith Miller); *The Times*, 7 Feb 1950.

15. Nick Tiratsoo, 'The Reconstruction of Blitzed British Cities, 1945–55', *Contemporary British History* (Spring 2000), p 40; C. D. Buchanan and D. H. Crompton, 'Residential Density and Cost of Development', *Town and Country Planning* (Dec 1950), pp 514–18; Winn, *This Fair Country*, p 222; Paul Elek, *This Other London* (1951), pp 52–3; Orlans, *Stevenage*, p 106; *The Times*, 25 Jun 1949.

16. Peter Shapely et al, 'Civic Culture and Housing Policy in Manchester, 1945–79', *Twentieth Century British History*, 15/4 (2004), pp 417–20; *Manchester Guardian*, 3 Mar 1950; David Byrne, 'The Reconstruction of Newcastle', in Robert Colls and Bill Lancaster (eds), *Newcastle upon Tyne* (Chichester, 2001), p 343; Benwell Community Project, *Slums on the Drawing Board* (Newcastle upon Tyne, 1978), p 8; Dan Smith, *An Autobiography* (Newcastle upon Tyne, 1970), p 33.

17. Anthony Sutcliffe and Roger Smith, *Birmingham, 1939–1970* (1974), pp 428–9, 431; Anthony Sutcliffe, 'A Century of Flats in Birmingham, 1875–1973' in Sutcliffe (ed), *Multi-Storey Living* (1974), p 200; Herbert Jackson, 'Birmingham's Planning Problems', *Town and Country Planning* (Jun 1951), pp 221, 281–2; Sutcliffe, 'Century', p 200; Gordon E. Cherry, *Birmingham* (Chichester, 1994), p 170; Miles Glendinning and Stefan Muthesius, *Tower Block* (New Haven, 1994), p 167.

18. *Sheffield Telegraph*, 30 Sept 1949, 6 Oct 1949.

19. *Listener*, 21 Dec 1950, 10 May 1951. In general on Churchill Gardens, see: Nigel Glendinning, 'Art and Architecture for the People?', in Jim Fyrth (ed), *Labour's Promised Land?* (1995), pp 278–9; Nicholas Bullock, *Building the Post-War World* (2002), pp 85–6.

20. On Matthew and his department's takeover at the LCC, see: Miles Glendinning, 'Teamwork or Masterwork?', *Architectural History* (2003), pp 311–12; Nicholas Bullock, 'Ideals, Priorities and Harsh Realities', *Planning Perspectives* (Jan 1994), pp 97–8; Nuttgens, *Home Front*, pp 68–9.

21. Nicholas Day, 'The Role of the Architect in Post-War State Housing' (PhD, University of Warwick, 1988), pp 257–8.

22. Bryan Appleyard, *The Pleasures of Peace* (1989), pp 26–7; Lionel Brett, 'Post-War Flats in Britain', *Architectural Review* (Nov 1949), p 315; Bullock, *Building*, pp 57–8; *Architectural Review* (May 1951), p 299.

23. *The Times*, 13 Feb 1950; Osborn, p 185; *Town and Country Planning* (Apr 1951), pp 151–2.

24. *Spectator*, 27 Jan 1950; Frank Worsdall, *The Tenement* (Edinburgh, 1979), p 145.

25. Seán Damer, *Glasgow* (1990), p 189; Gerard Mooney, 'Living on the Periphery' (PhD, University of Glasgow, 1988), pp 220, 229–32, 240–51, 253; Thomas A. Markus, 'Comprehensive Development and Housing, 1945–75', in Peter Reed (ed), *Glasgow* (Edinburgh, 1993), p 153.

14 That Dump?

1. Alison Ravetz, *Model Estate* (1974), pp 134, 135; Peter Mitchell, *Memento Mori* (Otley, 1990), p 84; *Yorkshire Evening Post*, 17 Apr 1951.

2. *Yorkshire Evening Post*, 9 Apr 1951; *Sunderland Echo*, 10 Apr 1951; Mark Lewisohn, *Funny, Peculiar* (2002), pp 176–7; *Daily Mirror*, 10 Apr 1951.

3. *The New Yorker*, 28 Apr 1951; *The Macmillan Diaries: The Cabinet Years, 1950–*

57 (2003), pp 62–3; Philip M. Williams, *Hugh Gaitskell* (1979), pp 255–6; Langford, 10 Apr 1951; John Campbell, *Nye Bevan* (1997), p 238; Tony Benn, *Years of Hope* (1994), pp 147–8.

4. V. S. Naipaul, *Letters Between a Father and Son* (1999), p 85; *Barrow News*, 14 Apr 1951; M-O A, D 5353, 12 Apr 1951.

5. *Yorkshire Evening Post*, 13 Apr 1951; BBC WA, *Any Questions?*, 13 Apr 1951; Langford, 14 Apr 1951; Alan Bullock, *Ernest Bevin: Foreign Secretary, 1945–1951* (Oxford, 1983), p 835; *Daily Express*, 16 Apr 1951.

6. *Macmillan Diaries*, p 64; M-O A, D 5353, 16 Apr 1951; *Daily Mirror*, 17 Apr 1951; *Daily Express*, 17/18 Apr 1951.

7. *Govan Press*, 20 Apr 1951; *Daily Mirror*, 18 Apr 1951; Jack Dash, *Good Morning, Brothers!* (1969), pp 86–7. In general on the case of 'the Seven', see: Jim Phillips, 'The Postwar Political Consensus and Industrial Unrest in the Docks, 1945–55', *Twentieth Century British History*, 6/3 (1995), pp 309–10; Nina Fishman, '"A Vital Element in British Industrial Relations"', *Historical Studies in Industrial Relations* (Autumn 1999), pp 70–71.

8. Langford, 18 Apr 1951; Haines, 19 Apr 1951; *News of the World*, 22 Apr 1951; Dilwyn Porter, 'Amateur Football in Britain, 1948–63: The Pegasus Phenomenon', in Adrian Smith and Dilwyn Porter (eds), *Amateurs and Professionals in Post-War British Sport* (2000), pp 1–30; *The Times*, 23 Apr 1951; Langford, 21 Apr 1951.

9. Kenneth Harris, *Attlee* (1982), pp 477, 480; *Macmillan Diaries*, p 66; Campbell, *Nye Bevan*, pp 244–5; *The New Yorker*, 19 May 1951.

10. Ben Pimlott, *Harold Wilson* (1992), pp 162, 168; Streat, p 579; Brian Brivati, *Hugh Gaitskell* (1996), p 117; Campbell, *Nye Bevan*, p 250; Gaitskell, p 257.

11. *Daily Express*, 24 Apr 1951; Preston, 24 Apr 1951; *Leeds Guardian*, 27 Apr 1951.

12. *The Times*, 28/30 Apr 1951; *Newcastle Journal*, 30 Apr 1951; Mike Kirkup (ed), *Charlie Crowe's Newcastle United Scrapbook* (Seaham, 2001), pp 35, 37; *The Times*, 30 Apr 1951.

Afterword

1. *Woman*, 5 May 1951.

Acknowledgements

I am grateful to the following for kindly allowing me to reproduce copyright material: Evelyn Abrams (Mark Abrams); Dannie Abse (*Farewell to the Twentieth Century*, Pimlico, 2001); Gillon Aitken Associates (Copyright © V. S. Naipaul 1951, Copyright © V. S. Naipaul 1999); Pat Arlott (John Arlott); Ouida V. Ascroft (Florence Speed); Don Bachardy (Christopher Isherwood): Lady Diana Baer (Mollie Panter-Downes); Joan Bakewell; Stuart Ball; Michael Banton; Correlli Barnett; BBC Written Archives Centre; Prue Bellak (Julian Critchley); Tony Benn; Birmingham City Archives (Mary King); Michael Blakemore; Michael Bloch (James Lees-Milne); The Robert Bolt Estate; Mark Bostridge and Rebecca Williams (Vera Brittain's literary executors, for quotations from her *Wartime Chronicle*); Veronica Bowater (Vere Hodgson); Lady Florette Boyson (Sir Rhodes Boyson); E. R. Braithwaite; British Library of Political and Economic Science (Crosland papers); Robin Bruce Lockhart (Sir Robert Bruce Lockhart); Sue Bruley; Michael Burns; John Campbell; Rene and Michael Chaplin (Sid Chaplin); Jonathan Clowes Ltd (*Letters* Copyright © 2001 Kingsley Amis, *Memoirs* © 1991 Kingsley Amis, on behalf of the Literary Estate of Kingsley Amis; Copyright © 1998 Doris Lessing, © 1961 Doris Lessing, © 2002 Doris Lessing, on behalf of Doris Lessing); The Estate of Cyril Connolly (extracts from *Horizon* magazine, copyright © 1945, 1947 Cyril Connolly, reproduced by permission of the Estate of Cyril Connolly, c/o Rogers Coleridge & White Ltd, 20 Powis Mews, London W11 1JN); Curtis Brown Group Ltd (on behalf of the Estate of Pamela Hansford Johnson, copyright © Pamela Hansford Johnson 1948); Renée Daly (Lawrence Daly); Seán Damer; The Dartington Hall Trust

Archive; Hunter Davies; Norman Dennis; Faber and Faber Ltd (Steven Berkoff, *Autobiography*; T. S. Eliot, *Notes towards the Definition of Culture*); Fabian Society; Margaret Fenton (Frederic Osborn); Annemarie Flanders (Allan Flanders); Howard Ford (Erica Ford); Margaret Forster; Enid Grant (Enid Palmer); Rachel Gross (Geoffrey Gorer); Sir Peter Hall; Bill Hamilton, Literary Executor of the Estate of the late Sonia Brownell Orwell, and Secker and Warburg Ltd (extracts from the published writings of George Orwell, copyright © George Orwell); Lord Hattersley; Trustees of HM Book Trust (Harold Macmillan); Pamela Hendicott (Judy Haines); David Higham Associates (Arthur Bryant, John Lehmann, Malcolm Muggeridge, Dylan Thomas); Donald Hinds (*Journey to an Illusion*); Hazel Holt (Barbara Pym); Steve Humphries (*The Making of Modern London, 1945–1985*); Institution of Mechanical Engineers (Lord Hinton of Bankside); Islington Local History Centre (Gladys Langford); Ian Jack (*Before the Oil Ran Out*, Secker & Warburg, 1987); Dan Jacobson; Jackie Jones (Mervyn Jones); Lynn Jones (Lynn Creedy); P. J. Kavanagh (Ted Kavanagh); Dora L. Kneebone (Rose Uttin); Lawrence & Wishart (Jack Dash, *Good Morning, Brothers!*); Sir Michael Levey (John Brophy); Alison Light (Estate of Raphael Samuel, for extract from *The Lost World of British Communism*, Verso, 2006); Liverpool University Press (John Barron Mays); Arthur McIvor; Trustees of the Mass-Observation Archive; Gerry Mooney; Jane Moser (Joan Waley); Jamie Muir and Denis Norden (Frank Muir and Denis Norden Archive); John Murray Ltd ('Business Girls' by John Betjeman, from *Collected Poems*, copyright © The Estate of John Betjeman); News International Archive and Record Office (Papers of the John Hilton Bureau); Juliet Nicolson (Harold Nicolson); Jill Norman (Elizabeth David); The Joe Orton Estate; Peter Pagnamenta; Angela Partington; The Estate of Frances Partridge (extracts from *Everything to Lose*, copyright © 1985 Frances Partridge, first published in 1985 by Victor Gollancz, reproduced by permission of the Estate of Frances Partridge, c/o Rogers Coleridge & White, 20 Powis Mews, London W11 1JN); PFD (extracts from *The Sea and the Land*, copyright © Estate of James Lansdale Hodson 1945, *The Way Things Are*, copyright © Estate of James Lansdale Hodson 1948, and *Thunder in the Heavens*, copyright © Estate of James Lansdale Hodson 1950, on behalf of the author's Estate; extracts from *The Kenneth Williams Diaries*, copyright © The Estate of Kenneth Williams 1994, on behalf of the author's Estate; extracts from *Love is Blue*, copyright © Joan Wyndham 1986); Mike and Trevor Phillips (*Windrush*); Allan Preston (Kenneth Preston); The Random House Group Ltd (*Dear Tom: Letters from Home* by Tom Courtenay, published Doubleday); Alison Ravetz; Marian Ray and Robin Raynham (Marian Raynham); Basil Streat (Sir Raymond Streat); Valerie Tedder; Paul Thompson; Barry Turner (*When Daddy Came Home* by Barry Turner and Tony Rennell); Graham Turner; Geoffrey Tweedale; Roxana and Matthew Tynan (*Letters of Kenneth Tynan*); UCL Library Services, Special Collections (Hugh Gaitskell); University of Wales Swansea, Library & Information Services (South Wales Coalfield Collection); Nigel Watson; Seymour J. Weissman (Evan Durbin); The Wellcome Library for the History and Understanding of Medicine; Phyllis Willmott; Colin Wilson; Bill Wyman; Emma and Toby Young (Michael Young); Ina Zweiniger-Bargielowska.

I am indebted, in many different ways, to archivists, librarians, fellow-historians, friends and relatives. They include: Sarah Aitchison; Helen Arkwright; Martin Banham; Nicola Beauman; Elizabeth Bennett; Piers Brendon; Sophie Bridges; Steve Bunker; Peter Cain; Terry Carney; Mark Clapson; Nigel Cochrane; Rob Colls; Fiona Courage; Heather Creaton; Seán Damer; Patric Dickinson; Marguerite Dupree; Joy Eldridge; Amanda Engineer; Angela Eserin; Alexandra Eveleigh; Robert Frost; Andrew George; Elizabeth Hennessy; Len Holden; David and Val Horsfield; Bill and Gisela Hunt; Caroline Jacob; Harriet Jones; Jacqueline Kavanagh; Bill Lancaster; Valerie Moyses; Jonathan Oates; Erin O'Neill; Stanley Page; Anne Perkins; Andrew Riley; Simon Robbins; Richard Roberts; Richard Saville; Dennis Sherer; Dorothy Sheridan; Emma Shipley; Adrian Smith; John Stevens; David Taylor; Richard Temple; Deborah Thom; Alistair Tough; Jenny Uglow; John Wakefield; Andy Ward; David Warren; Tracy Weston; Yvonne Widger; Melanie Wood; Christine Woodland.

Since 2001 I have been a visiting professor at Kingston University, where I have enjoyed the company and stimulation of Gail Cunningham and her colleagues in the Faculty of Art and Social Sciences.

The following people kindly read all or part of the various drafts: Julian Birkett; Brian Brivati; Mike Burns; Juliet Gardiner; John Gross; Lucy Kynaston; James Lappin; David Loffman; Sara and Steve Marsh; Glen O'Hara; Dil Porter; Harry Ricketts; Phyllis Willmott. I owe much to their comments, encouragement and often salutary sense of perspective.

My greatest debt, of course, is to those who have been most intimately involved in this project: Amanda Howard for transcribing my tapes; Andrea Belloli for her copy-editing; Libby Willis and Patric Dickinson for reading the proofs; Douglas Matthews for compiling the index; my agent Deborah Rogers and her assistant Hannah Westland; my editor Bill Swainson and his colleagues at Bloomsbury, including Nick Humphrey for his help with pictures and Emily Sweet for putting the book to bed; and, above all, Lucy, Laurie, George and Michael at home. Their belief in me and what I am trying to do has made all the difference.

New Malden, autumn 2006

Picture Credits

VE Day celebrations in Lambert Square, Coxlodge, Newcastle upon Tyne (*NCJ Media Ltd*)

The Tory candidate addresses an election meeting in Bethnal Green, June 1945. Photograph by Kurt Hutton (*Picture Post, Getty Images*)

Aneurin Bevan in Ebbw Vale during the 1945 election. Photograph by Ian Smith (*Time and Life, Getty Images*)

The Haymarket, Sheffield, 1946 (*Local Studies Department, Sheffield Central Library*)

Museum steps, Liverpool, 1946. Photograph by E. Chambré Hardman (*NT/E. Chambré Hardman Collection*)

Mrs Francis, Christmas Street, off the Old Kent Road, 1946. Photograph by Charles Hewitt (*Picture Post, Getty Images*)

The Gorbals, Glasgow, 1948. Photograph by Bert Hardy (*Picture Post, Getty Images*)

'Mr Browning's Winning Team': West Sussex, 1947. Photograph by Marjorie Baker (*Henfield Parish Council*)

England versus South Africa at Lord's, June 1947 (*Reproduced from John Arlott's* Vintage Summer: 1947)

Margate, June 1948. Photograph by Chris Ware (*Picture Post, Getty Images*)

Holidaymakers outside Waterloo station, July 1948. Photograph by James Wilds (*Topham Picture Library*)

Elephant and Castle, December 1948. Photograph by Bert Hardy (*Picture Post, Getty Images*)

Mrs Lilian Chandler and the President of the Board of Trade (Harold Wilson) discuss the housewife's plight, December 1948. Photograph by Bert Hardy (*Picture Post, Getty Images*)

Durham Miners' Gala, 23 July 1949 (*Gilesgate Archive (M. Richardson)*)

Reading the small ads, London, 1950 (*The Museum of London*)

Blackpool, 1949. Photograph by John Gay (*English Heritage, National Monuments Record/heritage-images*)

The *Ark Royal*, Birkenhead, 1950. Photograph by E. Chambré Hardman (*NT/E. Chambré Hardman Collection*)

The Pool of London, autumn 1949. Photograph by Bert Hardy (*Picture Post, Getty Images*)

The car dealers of Warren Street, autumn 1949. Photograph by Charles Hewitt (*Picture Post, Getty Images*)

The victorious Newcastle team returns from the 1951 Cup Final (*NCJ Media Ltd*)

Index

Aaronovitch, Sam, 342
Abdy, Sir Robert ('Bertie'), 175
Abercrombie, Sir Patrick, 34–5,
  163–4, 331, 615; *Town and
  Country Planning*, 35–6
Aberdeen: team policing, 362
Abrams, Mark, 337, 368, 377, 425
Abse, Dannie, 371
Accrington Stanley football club,
  94, 265, 582
Acton Society Trust, 444, 475
Adams, Mary, 526
Advisory Council for Science
  Policy, 462
*Advisory Handbook for the
  Redevelopment of Central
  Areas*, 165
Agate, James, 76
agriculture: and planning, 169–70
Agriculture Act (1947), 169–70
Alexander, Albert Victor (*later
  Earl*), 433
Alexander, Norah, 258
Alexandra Palace, London, 117
Allen, Basil, 529
Allen, Walter, 74
Alport, Cub, 78
Alston, Rex, 217, 278
Amalgamated Engineering Union
  (AEU), 499
Amery, Julian (*later Baron*), 66
Amethyst, HMS, 341
Amis, (Sir) Kingsley: membership
  of Communist Party, 133; on
  cold winter (1946–7), 196; on
  Lord David Cecil, 311; reads
  Cooper's *Scenes from Provincial
  Life*, 507; on Korean War,
  548; homes in Swansea, 597;
  That Uncertain Feeling, 597;
  Who Else Is Rank?, 21
Anderson, Cliff, 202
Andersson, Arne, 82
Andy Pandy (TV programme),
  526–8, 626
Angelou, Maya, 521
Anglo-American Council for
  Productivity, 467

Anne, Princess: birth, 534;
  christening, 562
anti-Semitism, 270
Antiquis, Alec de, 267
Any Questions? (radio
  programme), 460, 516, 525,
  555, 623
Appleby, Barry and Dobs, 503
apprenticeships, 461
Approved Schools Gazette, 367
Archer, Lola, 338
Archers, The (radio programme),
  584
Architects' Journal, 332–3
Architectural Review, 33, 47, 158,
  332
architecture: and post-war plans,
  28–9, 31, 232; and modernism,
  157–8, 613; *see also* housing;
  town planning
Aris, Stephen, 504
Arlott, John, 10, 217, 293, 515–17,
  629
Armand, Louis, 461
armed forces: indifference to poli-
  tics, 44
Army Bureau of Current Affairs
  (ABCA), 39, 44, 176
Arnold, Matthew, 175
Aron, Raymond, 544
art: modern, 96, 334; encouraged,
  176
Arts Council, 175–6
asbestos: as health hazard, 411
Ashton, T., 269
Association of Parents of
  Backward Children (*later
  National Society for Mentally
  Handicapped Children; then
  MENCAP*), 100–1
atomic bomb, 82–5; *see also*
  nuclear weapons
Atomic Energy Research Estab-
  lishment, Harwell, 386–7
Attenborough, Richard (*later
  Baron*), 154, 372
Attlee, Clement (*later* 1st Earl):
  favours continuation of coalition

government, 63; election
  campaign and victory (1945),
  65–6, 75; premiership, 75–6;
  attends Potsdam Conference,
  78; announces peace with
  Japan, 86–7; speech encouraging work, 99; criticised for
  post–war conditions, 115; and
  foreign policy, 134, 543; and
  welfare provision, 144;
  schooling, 153; on national
  ownership of land, 169;
  moderate programme, 180–1;
  Shinwell and, 189; radio broadcasts, 201, 227, 284, 383, 385–6;
  advised to replace ministers,
  202; constraints on Communist
  Party members, 224; austere
  economic measures, 226–7,
  229; and Durbin, 236; on
  capital punishment, 268; and
  Commonwealth immigrants,
  275–6; public view of, 316–17;
  announces expenditure cuts,
  353; announces 1950 election,
  358; in general election (1950),
  383, 385; and redistribution of
  parliamentary seats, 392; on
  Britain's overseas commitments, 433; lacks experience of
  industry, 442; addresses
  Durham Miners' Gala, 470;
  and Korean War, 546, 548;
  rearmament programme, 553;
  transfers Bevan to Ministry of
  Labour, 554; rejects Scottish
  and Welsh nationalism, 557–8;
  duodenal ulcer, 621; and
  Bevan's resignation, 627–8
Austin motor company, 497–9
'Autolycus' *see* Landells, Walter
Awdry, Rev. William: *The Three
  Railway Engines*, 62
Ayres, Ruby M., 211

Bailey, David, 259
Bailey, McDonald, 346
Bailey, Peter, 403

Baily, Eddie, 515
Bainbridge, (Dame) Beryl, 6
Bajak, Brenda, 98
Bakewell, Joan (née Rowlands), 304, 566–7
balance-of-payments: crisis (1949), 348; and effect of Korean War, 552
Balfour of Burleigh, George John Gordon Bruce, 7th Baron, 438
Ballard, J. G., 171
Bamford, Joseph, 448
bananas: reintroduced, 107
Bank of England: nationalised, 139, 238; creation of sterling area, 434; relations with industry, 439
banks and banking: employees, 412, 417; clearing, 438; investment and capital raising, 439–40
Banton, Michael, 518, 522
Baring, Evelyn, 196
Barings Brothers (firm), 440
Barker, Eric, 306
Barker, Theo, 448
Barnes, Ernest William, Bishop of Birmingham: on West Indians in Britain, 520; The Rise of Christianity, 242–3
Barnett, Cedric, 439
Barnett, Correlli, 144–5, 151, 432, 441–3, 446–7, 461, 490–1, 552; The Lost Victory, 432–3, 435
Barrow-in-Furness: rugby league team, 622–3; shipbuilding, 623
Bartlett, Sir Charles, 448
Bartók, Béla, 96
Baseley, Godfrey, 584
Bassey, (Dame) Shirley, 271
Bate, John, 131, 562
Bateson, F. W., 311
Bath, Henry Frederick Thynne, 6th Marquess of, 325
Bawden, Nina, 68
BBC Quarterly, 357
Beano (comic), 505
Beardmore, George, 101
Beaton, (Sir) Cecil, 9, 310
Beaumont, Hugh ('Binkie'), 590
Beaverbrook, William Maxwell Aitken, 1st Baron: and 1945 election result, 76, 78; and Conservative Party aspirations, 238
Beek, Harmsen Van Der, 356
'Beginner, Lord' see Moore, Egbert
Belcher, John, 299
Belfrage, Bruce, 382, 391
Bell, Quentin, 547
Bell, Vanessa, 84
Benn, Anthony Wedgwood, 75, 234, 555, 622
Bennett, Miss A., 269
Bennett, Alan, 17
Bennett, Nigel, 114
Benney, Mark, 382, 392
Benny, Jack, 563
Bentley, Dick, 307, 583
Berkoff, Steven, 567
Berlin, (Sir) Isaiah, 77, 310

Bernal, John Desmond, 343
Berry, Les, 114
Beshore, Freddie (boxer), 630
Betjeman, (Sir) John: favours suburbs, 158; A Few Late Chrysanthemums, 416; 'What Would Wren Have Built Today?', 29
Bevan, Aneurin: welcomes 1945 election, 64; popular criticism of, 110; disfavours worker control, 141; character and appearance, 145, 535; inaugurates and runs National Health Service, 145–8, 279, 285, 558; supports National Assistance Act, 148–9; housing policy, 154–6, 330, 601; supports nationalisation of steel, 225–6, 535–6; defines democratic socialism, 233; hatred of Tory Party, 284; speech on social services, 284; speech at 1949 Labour Party conference, 318–19; on demands on National Health Service, 327; and cost of National Health Service, 328–9, 629; lives with in-laws, 381; on Churchill's proposed summit meeting with USSR, 385; attacked in 1950 election campaign, 392; attacks stockbrokers, 467; reforms dock labour, 480; walks out of Gaitskell's 1951 budget, 521; Streat on, 535; defends free NHS, 538, 554–5; attitude to United States, 542–3; criticises Gaitskell's appointment as Chancellor, 553; on rearmament programme, 553–4; moved to Ministry of Labour, 554; resigns, 555, 627–30; revered in Wales, 558; Housing Act (1949), 596–7; attacks NHS charges, 622
Bevan, Eddie, 188
Bevan, M. A., 273
Beveridge, Sir William (later Baron): Report on social security (1942), 21, 24–6, 40–1, 43, 148–9; and town planning, 30–1; stands as Liberal candidate (1945), 66–7; and costs of National Health Service, 327; on future of broadcasting, 586
Bevin, Ernest: as Minister of Labour, 22, 452; favours continuation of coalition government, 63; character and influence as Foreign Secretary, 134–5, 222; on British nuclear weapons, 136; Violet Bonham Carter meets, 298; and devaluation of pound, 349; on Britain's world role, 433; trade unionism, 452; background as docker, 479; opposes joining Europe, 544; and Soviet

potential aggression, 546; on rearmament for Korean War, 551; Morrison succeeds as Foreign Secretary, 554; hears Gaitskell's first budget, 621–2; death and cremation, 623–4, 626, 629
bicycles, 403
'Big Bang' theory, 388
Billington, Michael, 588
Bird, Maria, 527
Birds Eye (food company), 512
Birley, Robert, 340
Birmingham: victory celebrations, 13, 17–18; industrial conditions, 397–8; 'Inner Circle' bus route, 404; motor manufacturing, 496–7; housing, 609–10
Black Country, 397–8
Black, Sir John, 493, 496
black market, 111–12, 119, 253–5, 299–300, 605
Blackhill estate, Glasgow, 599
Blackpool, 217
blacks (negroes): as immigrants, 270–5; and race riots, 292; attitudes to, 345–7, 517–22
Blakemore, Michael, 399, 401
Blandford, John Spencer-Churchill, Marquess of ('Sunny'), 294, 301
Blankers-Koen, Fanny, 292
Blenkinsop, Arthur, 508
Bligh, Jasmine, 116
Blishen, Edward: Roaring Boys, 571–2, 574
Bloom, Claire, 588
Bloom, Ursula, 83
Blue Lamp, The (film), 359–61, 364
Blue, Lionel, 550
Blundell, Margaret, 52–3, 56
Blunt, Anthony, 334
Blyton, Enid, 356
Boat Race (Oxford and Cambridge), 113, 335, 587
Bogarde, (Sir) Dirk, 199, 360, 361, 377
Bolt, Robert, 213, 568
Bolton, (Sir) George, 441
Bondfield, Margaret, 98
Bonham Carter, Mark (later Baron), 245
Bonham Carter, Lady Violet, 245, 298
Boothby, Robert (later Baron), 65, 82, 525
Botting, A. E., 352
Boult, Sir Adrian, 176
Boulting, Roy and John, 154, 371
Bournville Village, Birmingham, 30
Bowen, Elizabeth, 171
Bowlby, John, 38, 129–30; Forty-four Juvenile Thieves, 98
Bowley, Ruth, 338–9, 530
Bowmer, Muriel, 101, 103
Boxer, Arabella, 512–13
boxing (sport), 202, 336, 519
Boyson, (Sir) Rhodes, 570–1
Bracken, Brendan (later Viscount), 238

Braddock, Bessie, 149, 257
Bradman, Don, 278, 293
Braithwaite, Eustace R. ('Ricky'), 271–2, 521
Braithwaite, Sir John, 439
Brazil: 1950 World Cup, 514
bread: quality and quantity, 108; rationed, 117–18, 121; de-rationed, 297
Brett, Lionel (later 4th Viscount Esher), 613
Bridges, Sir Edward, 443
Brief Encounter (film), 95, 99
Briggs, Asa (later Baron), 459
Brighton: squatting, 72
Bristol: town planning, 35, 48, 165–6, 602
Bristol Empire (theatre), 264
Britain: conditions in 1945, 19–20; currency convertibility, 134; decline as world power, 135, 433–5; independent nuclear deterrent, 136; resistance to European membership, 544–5; in Korean War, 545–8
Britain Can Make It exhibition (1946), 124
British Broadcasting Corporation (BBC): and victory celebrations, 10; post-war programme reforms, 81, 123–4; resumes television broadcasts, 116; London Listening Panel, 124, 388; inaugurates Third Programme, 176; bans discussion of contemporary debates, 212; popular programmes, 293, 583–4; Variety Programmes Policy Guide ('The Green Book'), 309–10; opens Sutton Coldfield TV transmitter, 357; Television Panel, 358; aloofness from 1950 election campaign, 380; reports 1950 election results, 390; and social issues, 525; children's programmes, 526–7; conservatism and paternalism, 584; monopoly questioned, 585–7
British Housewives' League, 71, 106, 117
British Institute of Management, 447
British Medical Association: on effect of food shortage, 107; attitude to National Health Service, 147, 279–80
British Nationality Act (1948), 273
British Railways, 403
British Road to Socialism, The (Communist Party publication), 549
British Society for Cultural Freedom, 549
Brittain, Vera, 7
Britten, Benjamin (later Baron): Peter Grimes (opera), 62
Brivati, Brian, 628
Broderick, James, & Co., 207
Brome, Vincent, 233–4

Brook Street Bureau, 100
Brophy, John, 261
Brough, Peter, 525
Brown, Freddie, 528–9
Brown, George (later Baron George-Brown), 81
Brown, Dr Graham, 67–8
Brown, W. J., 72, 81, 112, 122, 134, 218, 268, 525, 587
Browne, E. H., 473–4
Bruce Lockhart, Sir Robert see Lockhart, Sir Robert Bruce
Bruce, Robert, 163–4
Bruley, Sue, 418
Bryant, (Sir) Arthur, 77
Buchanan, Colin, 607
Bullock, Alan (later Baron), 224, 544
Burnham, Peter, 546
Burns, Michael, 17
Burrows, Sir Richard, 471
Burt, Sir Cyril, 563–4, 577
Burton, Richard, 588
Burtt, Henry, 583
buses, 403–4
business schools, 450
Bussy, Dorothy, 72
Butler, Frank, 215–16
Butler, Richard Austen ('Rab'): Education Act (1944), 21, 27–8, 150, 152, 313, 564, 575; and Conservative defeat (1945), 78; chairs policy review committee, 238–40
Butlin, (Sir) Billy, 218; holiday camps, 218–20, 267, 532
by-elections, 118
Bygraves, Max, 525
Bywaters, Harry, 95

Cable and Wireless: nationalised, 139
Cairncross, (Sir) Alec, 137, 349, 450, 558
Callaghan, James (later Baron), 74, 133, 269, 453, 537, 550, 556
Calman, Mel, 371
Cameron, James, 548
Campbell, John, 318–19, 629
Camrose, William Ewert Berry, 1st Viscount, 389
Canada: emigration to, 580
cancer see lung cancer
Cannon, Les and Olga, 354
Capek, Karel: The Insect Play, 588
capital punishment, 267–9
capitalism, 436–7, 538
Cardiff: blacks in, 271, 518
Cardus, (Sir) Neville, 216
Carlisle, 400
Carr, (Sir) Raymond, 129
cartels, 464
Carter, G., 347
Castle, Barbara (later Baroness), 66, 68, 74, 133, 416
Catholic Church: opposes National Health Service, 282
Catton, H. A., 357
Cecil, Lord David, 310–11
Census (1951), 592–3, 597, 619

Central Electricity Generating Board (CEGB), 446
Chamberlain, Neville, 193
Chambers, (Sir) Paul, 463
Chandler, Godfrey, 412
Chandler, Lilian, 298–9
Channon, Sir Henry ('Chips'), 97, 135, 621
Chaplin, Sid, 46, 66, 131, 186, 217, 472–4, 561; The Leaping Lad, 131, 472; The Thin Seam, 561–2
Chapman, Dennis, 53–5, 158
Charles, Prince of Wales: birth, 302–3
Cherry, Gordon, 35
children: mentally handicapped, 100–1; delinquent, 113; and maternal efficiency, 283; stories and radio programmes, 356; effect of Dick Barton on, 364–5; television programmes, 526–8
Christie, (Dame) Agatha, 211
Christie, John Reginald Halliday, 359
Christopherson, Anita, 523
church attendance, 125
Church of England: doctrines and belief, 242–3
Churchill Gardens, Pimlico, 611
Churchill, Randolph, 84, 380
Churchill, Sarah, 241
Churchill, (Sir) Winston: and victory celebrations, 7, 10, 12; wartime coalition government, 22, 63; and welfare proposals, 25; disparages town planning, 31; dissolves coalition and calls election (July 1945), 64; election campaign and defeat (1945), 64–5, 67, 70–1, 73, 76, 78–80; in Parliament, 81; promises new homes, 102; and Conservative policy review, 238–9, 241; condemns proposed nationalisation of iron and steel, 317; criticises Picasso, 334; in general election (1950), 383, 385, 391; on Korean War, 547
cigarettes: availability, 248, 297
cinema, 95, 304, 336–7, 359–60
citizenship, 273–4
City of London: as financial centre, 434, 438, 440; traditions and standards, 438–9, 441
Civil Aviation Bill (1946), 140
civil service: administrative qualities, 443–4; senior, 443; and nationalisation, 444
Clark, Dr Alistair, 327
Clark, Petula, 218, 303
Clarke, C. W.: Farewell Squalor, 159
Clarke, John, 244
class (social): and infant mortality, 26; and egalitarianism, 40–1; and post-war changes, 43–4; conflicts, 55–7; cultural

class (social) (*cont.*)
preferences, 56; reaction to rationing, 118–19; and social changes, 120; snobbery and prejudices, 174–5, 263; and management, 446–7; *see also* elitism; middle class; working class

Clegg, Hugh, 455

Close, Brian, 336, 620

closed shop *see* restrictive practices

clothes: rationed, 121–2, 251; restrictions, 248–9; rationing eased and ended, 297–8; *see also* fashion

Clough, Brian, 565

Clyde Valley Regional Plan, 163, 615

coal: burning and pollution, 401; as power source, 401–3; industry management, 471–3, 476–7; imported, 475; accidents and deaths, 561–2; *see also* National Coal Board

Coal (magazine), 562

coal mines: working conditions, 2–4; nationalised, 185–8, 203, 473–4; lifestyle and attitudes of miners, 186–9, 195–6, 203–5, 475–8; and fuel crisis (1947), 194–9; strikes, 203, 474–5; and diseases, 410

Cobbett, William, 174

Cobbold, Cameron Fromanteel (*later* 1st Baron; 'Kim'), 441

Cockell, Don (boxer), 630

co-habitation, 206

Cohen, (Sir) Jack, 256

Cold War: beginnings, 223–4; intensifies, 313, 340; and anti-communism, 341; and Korean War, 548

Cole, G.D.H., 43, 131

Coleman, Donald, 451

Collins, Rev. John, Dean of Oriel, 84

Collins, Norman, 357, 585

Colston, Charles, 326

Colville, Sir John (Jock), 153

comic books (children's), 504–6

Commons, House of: Labour Party sings 'Red Flag' in, 81–2; debates abolition of capital punishment, 268; *see also* Lords, House of

Communism: Truman denounces, 222; diminishing intellectual appeal, 313; blamed for dock strike, 340; antipathy to, 341; adherents, 342–3; in trade unions, 454–6; in coal mines, 474; and Stockholm Peace Petition, 548; and Second World Peace Conference, 549

Communist Party of Great Britain, 132–3, 223–4, 342, 454, 498, 549–51

community sense, 178–9

Companies Act (1948), 436

company directors, 446

competition, 460, 464, 468

Comprehensive Development areas (CDAs), 168

Comprehensive School, The (1948 report), 221

Compton, Denis, 216, 227–8

Compton-Burnett, (Dame) Ivy, 311

Comyns, Joan, 354

Connolly, Cyril, 78, 234, 267

Conservative Party: accepts national health service, 26; election defeat (1945), 76–80; policy review, 238–41; election fund, 261–2; Bevan expresses hatred of, 284; in general election (1950), 377–81, 384–5, 390–1; and social services, 542; Conference, Blackpool (1950), 601

consumer-advisory service, 379

convertibility (of sterling), 226, 228–30

Cooke, Alistair, 71

cooking: improvements, 511–14

Cookson, (Dame) Catherine, 523–4

Cooper, Alfred Duff (*later* 1st Viscount Norwich), 562

Cooper, William (i.e. Harry Hoff): *Scenes from Metropolitan Life*, 443, 524; *Scenes from Provincial Life*, 507–8, 524

Co-operative stores, 256

Cornish-Bowden, Eva, 586

Coronation Stone (Stone of Scone): stolen, 556–7

corporal punishment, 364

Costello, Elvis, 327

country houses: opened to public, 325

County of London Plan (1943), 34, 159

Courtauld, Samuel, 451

Courtaulds (textile manufacturers), 451

Courtenay, (Sir) Tom, 564

Coventry: town planning, 36–7, 49, 164, 166–7, 230–1, 332; wartime revival, 49–50; in election campaign (1945), 69–70; housing, 331; motor manufacturing, 492–6; reconstruction, 602–6, 613

Coward, (Sir) Noël, 12, 78, 84, 121

Cowley, Oxford, 490–2

Cox, Oliver, 611, 613

Craigie, Jill, 66, 629

Crawford, Marion ('Crawfie'): *The Little Princesses*, 506–7

Crawley, Aidan, 105

Crawley New Town, 606–7

Creedy, Lynn, 285

cricket: Test matches, 60, 82, 114, 216–18, 278, 293, 520, 528–9; amateur–professional distinction, 113–14, 528–9; Eton–Harrow match, 113; radio commentaries, 216–17, 278; West Indian victory over England (1950), 515; England team, 528

crime: rates, 112–13, 267–8, 364; thefts, 252; and punishment, 267, 364; *see also* juvenile delinquency

Criminal Justice Bill (1948), 268

Cripps, Sir Stafford: on dropping of atom-bomb, 84; on central economic planning, 138, 298; opposes workers' control, 140; as Minister of Economic Affairs, 228; as Chancellor of Exchequer, 229; severe economic measures, 248–9; imposes capital levy, 262; on diminishing gold reserves, 347; cuts imports, 348; illness, 348; devalues pound, 349–51, 384; opposes market economy, 350; on budget and general election (1950), 358; entertaining, 388; qualities, 442; and trade unions, 453; criticises Standard Vanguard car, 496; final budget (1950), 537; Gaitskell succeeds as Chancellor, 546, 553; Benn succeeds as MP, 555

Crisp, Quentin: *The Naked Civil Servant*, 109

Critchley, (Sir) Julian, 355

Crockett, Bob, 188

Croft-Cooke, Rupert, 110

Crosland, Charles Anthony Raven: political ambitions and principles, 323–4, 381; wins parliamentary seat (1950), 391; on managers' privileged backgrounds, 496; liberal views on race, 517; broadcasts on current political situation, 540–1; on rearmament and living costs, 553; deflates Benn, 555; mocks tidiness, 623

Crossman, Richard, 74, 81, 342, 544; *The God That Failed* (anthology), 549; *Keep Left* (with Michael Foot and Ian Mikardo), 222

Crothers, Marjorie, 355

Crowther, Geoffrey (*later* Baron), 431–2, 468

culture: encouragement of, 176–8; class differences, 264, 266–7; and elitism, 311–14

Cunard, Maud Alice (Emerald), Lady, 97

Cunard, Nancy, 275–6

Cutler, Marion, 123, 278–9

Cynthia and Gladys (jugglers), 264

Czechoslovakia: Communist coup (1948), 222–3

Dagenham, Essex, 486–9

Daily Dozen, The (radio programme), 70

Daily Express: opposes National Health Service, 280; the Gambols cartoons in, 503

Daily Herald: class appeal, 56; Post-war Homes Exhibition (1945), 72; supports Labour, 317

Daily Mail: Ideal Home Exhibition, 207

Daily Mirror: popularity, 56; condemns *Woman's Hour*, 124; on social security, 285

Daily Worker: premises, 157–8

Dain, Dr Guy, 279

Dalby, W. Barrington, 72

Dalkeith, Walter Francis John Montagu Douglas Scott, Earl of, 301

Dalton, Hugh: and Michael Young, 16, 22; as Chancellor of Exchequer, 81, 135, 139, 172, 229, 248; and American Loan, 133; resigns, 228–9; suspends convertibility, 228; on cigarette smoking, 248; and Anthony Crosland, 323, 541; on dollar crisis, 347; recalls women to work, 409; qualities, 442; on Hyndley, 472; on Bevan's resignation, 627; on Harold Wilson, 628

Dalton, Stewart, 399, 423

Daly, Lawrence, 132–3, 342, 550–1, 589

dance halls, 95

Dartington Hall, Devon, 322

Dash, Jack, 481–3, 625

Davenport, Nicholas, 442

David, Elizabeth, 199, 512–13

Davies, Clement, 174

Davies, Hunter, 400

Davis, Norah M., 426–7

Davison, Giles, 504

Deacon, Alan, 543

Deakin, Arthur, 229, 341, 452–4, 456, 548

Dearlove, Jack, 291

death penalty *see* capital punishment

defence expenditure, 546, 552

de Freitas, (Sir) Geoffrey, 153

Dell, Ethel M., 211

demobilisation (from armed services), 97

democracy: Michael Young on, 321

Denman, (Sir) Roy, 443

Dennis, Joe, 409

Dennis, Norman and others: *Coal Is Our Life*, 476

Dent, Harold, 28

dentistry: and National Health Service, 327–8

Derry & Toms (store), 261

detergents, 299

devaluation (of sterling), 348–51, 434

Development Councils, 138

Dewes, J. G., 529

Dick Barton (radio programme), 364–5, 583–4

Dickens, Charles, 211

diet, 250, 252; children's, 514; *see also* food; rationing

Dimbleby, Richard: describes victory celebrations, 11; television commentaries, 117; radio programmes, 212; and Tate & Lyle anti-nationalisation campaign, 319–20; defends living in England, 580; on *Twenty Questions*, 624

Dinwiddie, Melville, 585

Dior, Christian, 257

divorce, 58, 97, 206–7, 374

docks and dockers, 478–85; *see also* strikes

doctors: attitude to National Health Service, 279–80

Doll, (Sir) Richard, 560–1

Dollery, Tom, 528–9

Donaldson, Bailie E. J., 625

Dors, Diana, 303

Dougall, Robert, 584

Dowler, Arthur, 264

Drabble, Margaret, 524–5

Draper, Ruth, 311

Drewry, Arthur, 515

Driberg, Tom, 141

Drogheda, Charles Garrett Moore, 11th Earl of, 466

Dudley Committee: *The Design of Dwellings* (1944), 34, 53

Dunn, Cyril, 602

Durbin, Evan: background and character, 38; economic ideas, 38–9, 67; in 1945 election campaign, 70, 74; attends Dalton dinner party, 81; on human wickedness, 130–1; advocates economic planning, 138, 229; on British non-acceptance of socialism, 235–6; drowned, 295; *The Politics of Democratic Socialism*, 38

Durham Miners' Gala, 470–1

Dury, Ian, 354

Eagle (comic), 504–6

Ealing Studios: films, 336, 469

Easington Colliery, Durham, 471

East Kilbride New Town, 615

Economic Affairs, Ministry of, 228

economic planning, 22–3, 136–42, 537–8

Economist (magazine): on town planners, 614

economy (British): systemic weakness, 431–8

Ede, James Chuter, 268

Edelman, Maurice, 283

Eden, Sir Anthony (*later* 1st Earl of Avon), 239

Edinburgh: redevelopment plan, 165

Educating Archie (radio programme), 525–6, 583

education: reform proposals, 27–9, 576–8; under Labour government, 150–3; T. S. Eliot on, 313–14; and social ideals, 314; and intelligence testing, 564; private, 574; and social class, 574–6; *see also* schools; training and education

Education Act (1944; 'Butler Act'), 21, 27–8, 150, 152, 313, 564, 575

Edwards, A. Trystan, 608

Edwards, Herbert E., 166

Edwards, Jimmy, 307, 583

Electrical Trades Union, 454, 456

Elek, Paul, 607

Eliot, T. S.: on effects of television, 585; *The Cocktail Party*, 588–9; *The Family Reunion*, 588; *Notes Towards a Definition of Culture*, 312–14

elitism, 311–14

Elizabeth, Princess (*later* Queen): and victory celebrations, 12; comment on hat, 117; visits Coventry, 231; marriage, 243–5; Marion Crawford's account of, 506; children, 534; appearance, 562

Elizabeth, Queen of George VI, 245–6

Elmhirst, Leonard and Dorothy, 322–3, 358

Elton, Godfrey, 1st Baron, 517

Elwyn-Jones, Baron, 68

emigration, 249, 260–1, 580

Empire Windrush (ship), 274–5, 292, 346, 520

employment *see* work

Engineering Employers Federation, 493

English, Arthur, 300

environment, 399–401

'Establishment', 174

Etheridge, Richard (Dick), 498–9

Europe: union movement, 544–5

European Coal and Steel Community, 544

Evans, Dame Edith, 590

Evans, Lincoln, 225

Evans, Timothy, 359

Evening Standard, 260

exchange controls, 436

Exeter, 165

exports: increase in, 432; market for, 435; *see also* trade (overseas)

Fabian Society, 129, 322–3

Fairbrother, Jack, 632

Falkirk Herald, 280

Family Allowances Act (1946), 148

family life, 97–100, 534–5

Family Welfare Association, 283

farming: productivity, 169; and radio programmes, 583–4

fashion, 257–60

Faulkner, Hugh, 147

Fayers, E. S., 93

Feather, Victor, 487

Featherstone ('Ashton'), Yorkshire, 476–7

Federation of British Industries, 464, 545

Ferguson, Colin, 13, 71, 84, 193–4, 298, 410, 424

Ferguson, Thomas, 365

Festival of Britain (1951), 623

Field, Frank, 424

Field, Sid, 264, 386
Fielding, Steven, 179
films see cinema
finance: management, 437–40
Financial Times: on welfare and productivity, 143; on fuel crisis (1947), 193; on convertibility crisis, 228; restrictive practices, 466; Wincott writes for, 538
Finch, Albert, 519
Fisher, Geoffrey, Archbishop of Canterbury, 84, 242–3, 548
Flanders, Allan, 454–7; *The System of Industrial Relations in Great Britain* (ed. with Hugh Clegg), 455, 458
flats see housing
Fleming Report (on public schools, 1944), 27, 153
floods (1947), 201
Florence, P. Sargant, 51
food: shortages and rationing, 19, 103–8, 115, 119, 121–2, 298–9, 579–80; and dock strike (1945), 104; and black market, 111–12; low quality, 247, 250; convenience, 512; see also bread; cooking; diet; rationing
Foot, Michael: elected to Parliament in 1945 election, 66, 74; meets wife, 66; opposes US loan, 133; on health of post-1947 children, 250; attacks Priestley as defeatist, 320; retains Parliamentary seat in 1950 election, 380, 391; on Arthur Deakin, 452; addresses Durham Miners' Gala, 470; on panel of *In the News*, 525, 587–8; praises Benn, 555; and Bevan's resignation, 629; *Keep Left* (with Richard Crossman and Ian Mikardo), 222
football (soccer): post-war resumption, 93–4, 113, 216, 352; radio commentaries, 124; and mid-week ban (1937), 201; Great Britain v. Rest of Europe match (1947), 215–16; 1948–9 season begins, 294; Cup Final (1949), 335–6; World Cup (1950), 514–15; Cup Final (1951), 531–2; scorned at grammar schools, 568; Scotland win over England (1951), 624; Amateur Cup Final (1951), 626; Scottish Cup Final (1951), 626; and violence, 626
football pools, 219
Ford, Erica, 94, 200–1, 213
Ford, Ernest, 36
Ford motor company, 408, 486–8, 497
Forshaw, J. H., 34
Forster, E. M.: *Howards End*, 140, 162
Forster, Margaret, 531
Fowles, John, 390
France: railways, 461

Franklin, Neil, 515
Franks, Sir Oliver, 438, 546
Freeman, John, 81, 172, 628
Freeman, Sir Wilfrid, 451
Fry, Christopher: *The Lady's Not for Burning*, 588; *A Phoenix Too Frequent*, 588; *Venus Observed*, 589
Fry, Maxwell, 32, 34n, 52
Fryd, Judy, 100–1
FT 30-Share Index, 439
Fuchs, Klaus, 386–7
fuel, 402
fuel crisis (1947), 193–200

Gaitskell, Hugh: attends Dalton dinner party, 81; on Shinwell, 189; dispute with Bevan over nationalisation, 226; on non-socialist views of electorate, 235; on Princess Elizabeth, 245; visits Butlin's holiday camp, 267; tribute to Durbin, 295; and management of economy, 349; on Cripps's dinner party, 388; disparages Cobbold, 441; on dealings with civil servants, 444; on Durham Miners' Gala, 470; criticises National Coal Board, 471; dispute with Bevan over charges for NHS, 538–9, 554–5; succeeds Cripps as Chancellor, 546, 553; supports rearmament, 546, 553–4; on trade balance, 551; view of Bevan, 554; presents first budget (1951), 621–3; and management of National Health Service, 628; and Party conflicts, 628–9
Gale, John, 78
Gallacher, Willie: *The Case for Communism*, 343
Gallup polls: on continuing austerity, 246; on desire to emigrate, 249; on black market, 254; on death penalty, 267, 269; on housing shortage, 330; on Attlee's austerity measures, 353; on 1950 general election, 388; on nationalisation programme, 536; on support for defence spending, 548
gambling: by miners, 186–7
Gambols, the (cartoon figures), 503–4
Garbett, Cyril, Archbishop of York, 548
garden cities, 31, 33, 159, 174
gardening, 214–15
Garland, Judy, 621
Garland, Sam, 190
Garland, W. H., 276
Garrad, Laurel, 354
Gascoigne, Alderman C. W. (of Sheffield), 610
General Certificate of Education (GCE), 569

General Elections: (1945), 64–70, 73–9; (1950), 358, 377–93, 503
George V, King: Nicolson writes life, 246
George VI, King: broadcasts victory address, 10–11, 14; and Coventry rebuilding plans, 37; and Labour election victory (1945), 75; attends FA Cup Finals, 94, 631; attends opening of 1948 Olympic Games, 291; anger at theft of Coronation Stone, 556
Germany: motor manufacturing, 485, 490, 497
Gibberd, (Sir) Frederick, 606
Gibson, Donald, 36–7, 49, 164, 166–7, 331, 603–4
Gibson, George, 299
Gide, André, 72
Giles, Carl Ronald (cartoonist), 82, 301, 503
Gisborn, Valerie, 336, 414
Gladstone, William Ewart, 229, 237
Gladwyn, Cynthia, Lady, 390
Glasgow: victory celebrations, 13; town planning, 31, 163–4; housing, 102, 594–5, 599, 615–18; and Clyde Valley Regional Plan, 615
Glass, Dorrie, 167
Glendenning, Raymond, 72
Glendinning, Miles, 164
Glock, William, 96
Goddard, Rayner, Baron, 269, 335, 359, 625
Golden, Grace, 118, 196, 245, 249, 258, 361, 510
Goldfinger, Ernö, 33, 157–8
Goldie, Grace Wyndham, 525
Goldstein, Joseph, 456–7
Gollancz, (Sir) Victor, 84
Good Food Guide, The, 513
Goodman, Geoffrey, 141
Gordon, J. C. Lee, 158
Gordon Walker, Patrick (later Baron), 536
Gorer, Geoffrey, 362–4, 375–6
Gosling, Ray, 565
Gould, Jessie, 249
government ministries: created, 22
Gowing, Margaret, 135
Graham, Virginia, 116
Graham, W. S., 72
Grand National (steeplechase), 113, 335
Gratwick, P. J., 451
Graveney, Tom, 529
Great Expectations (film), 95
Greater London Plan (1945), 32
green belt, 32
Green, Geoffrey, 626, 631–2
Greene, Graham, 74–5
Greenwood, Sean, 547
Greenwood, Walter, 400; *Love on the Dole*, 594
Grenfell, Joyce, 84, 115–16, 300
Grew, Celia, 167
greyhound racing, 201

Grieve, Mary, 208
Griffin, Cardinal Bernard, Archbishop of Westminster, 282
Griffiths, George, 81–2
Griffiths, James, 148–9, 520
Grisewood, Freddie, 117, 517
Gropius, Walter, 612
Gross, John, 313
Guinea Pig, The (film), 154
Gurl, Les, 491–2

Hackett, Mrs A. (of Coventry), 605
Hackett, Desmond, 624
Hägg, Gunder, 82
Haileybury school, 153
Haines, Alice ('Judy'): and victory celebrations, 9–10, 14, 87; on Korean War, 54; entertainment, 60; on Churchill's anti-Socialist speech, 65; on return of street lights, 71; and Labour victory (1945), 77; on women working, 99; on shortages, 105, 117, 197, 580–2; on Woman's Hour, 124; birth of child, 125; acquires and watches TV, 213, 358, 526; on end of sweet rationing, 299; on Attlee's expenditure cuts, 353; acquires double pushchair, 356; supports Labour in 1950 election, 382, 390–1; on housework, 581; on TV watching, 626
Haley, Sir William, 176, 357
Hall, (Sir) Peter, 312
Hall, (Sir) Robert, 463
Hall, Ruth B., 242
Halliburton, Horace, 347
Halsey, A. H., 543
Hamer, Harold, 367
Hamilton, John, 570
Hamlyn, Paul (later Baron), 448
Hamm, Jeffrey, 270
Hampson, Frank, 505
Hanbury-Williams, John, 451
Hancock, Tony, 386, 389, 526
Handley, Tommy, 95, 306–9
Hanks, Reginald, 490
Hanley, Jimmy, 361
Hanley, Thomas, 111–12
Hansen, Randall, 273, 520
Harben, Philip, 212
Harding, Gilbert, 583, 624, 629
Hardstaff, R., 256
Hardwicke, (Sir) Cedric, 9
Hardy, Barbara, 301
Hardy, Bert, 549
Harlow New Town, 606
Harris, E. (Coventry housewife), 117
Harris, Wilson, 75
Harrison, Kathleen, 218
Harrisson, Tom: on popular expectations, 42–3; on British apathy, 124; on Third Programme, 177; 'Propaganda for Town Planning' (lecture), 46–7; see also Mass-Observation

Harrod, (Sir) Roy, 416, 466
Hart-Davis, Richard, 172
Harvey, Joe, 632
Harvie, Christopher, 557
Hasty Heart, The (film), 314
Hatfield New Town, 613
Hattersley, Roy (later Baron), 199
Have a Go! (radio programme), 123, 352, 583
Hayek, Friedrich August von: The Road to Serfdom, 22, 39
Haynes, William Warren: Nationalization in Practice, 473
Hazell, Quinton, 437
Headlam, Sir Cuthbert: on state opening of 1945 Parliament, 87; on town and country planning, 168; on Conservative economic policy, 240; on death penalty, 268; on nationalisation of steel, 317; on cost of National Health Service, 328; and Conservative election campaign (1950), 379, 381, 388
Healey, Denis (later Baron), 64, 74; Cards on the Table, 222
health: inequitable provision, 20–1; see also National Health Service
Heap, Anthony (and Marjorie): and victory celebrations, 6–7, 12–13, 17; on continuation of controls, 77; on radio programmes, 81; visits cinema, 82, 303, 361; on entertainments, 94; on women working, 99; on shortages, 104; anti-Americanism, 133; on fluorescent lighting, 189; on severe winter, 197; buys suit, 248; on social security, 285; on relaxing of clothes rationing, 297; on ITMA, 308; on Attlee expenditure cuts, 353; on criminal violence, 364; playgoing, 588–91
Hearne, Richard ('Mr Pastry'), 212
Heath, (Sir) Edward, 381, 391, 542, 544
Heath, Ted (band leader), 95
Hennessy, Sir Patrick, 486, 487
Hennessy, Peter, 546
Henriques, Fernando, 476
Henriques, Robert, 460
Henry Hall's Guest Night (radio programme), 293
Herbert, (Sir) Alan P., 281
Herbert, Sir Alfred, 413
Here Come the Huggetts (film), 303–4
Hewison, Robert, 341
Hibberd, Stuart, 11
Hickey, William (Daily Express columnist), 141
Hill, A. Bradford, 560
Hill, Benny, 212, 621
Hill, Dr Charles, 381, 383–5
Hiller, Wendy, 590–1, 627
Himmelweit, Hilde, 575–6

Hinds, Donald: Journey to an Illusion, 522
Hinton, Christopher (later Baron), 449
Hiroshima, 83, 85
Hitler, Adolf, 15, 21, 80
Hodgkinson, George, 231
Hodgson, Vere: on anti-authority feelings, 110; on nationalisation of mines, 185; on severe winter, 194, 200; at Ideal Home Exhibition, 207; sees Princess Elizabeth's wedding presents, 245; on introduction of National Health Service, 282; longs for extra butter, 299; on Princess Margaret's rumoured engagement, 301; on Scott of the Antarctic (film), 304; on Tommy Handley's death, 308–9; applauds Munnings's attack on Picasso, 334; on Cripps's devaluation of pound, 350; fear of mugging, 364; praises Charles Hill's broadcast, 384; on 1950 election result, 391; reads Marion Crawford's Little Princesses, 506; on de-rationing of eggs, 510; on Korean War, 548; on theft of Coronation Stone, 556; on Princess Anne's christening, 562; on TV ownership, 587
Hodson, James Lansdale: and reforms, 39; on servicemen's indifference to politics, 44; on women working, 100; on general dishonesty, 111; on Boat Race, 113; on church-going, 125; on unpopularity of nationalisation, 140; on Durham pit village, 159; on bitterness among well-to-do, 172; on mining conditions, 188; on severe winter, 194; on state of nation, 232; on appeal of royal family, 244; on spivs, 252; on middle-class politics, 262–3; on Zweig's findings, 266
Hogg, Quintin (Baron Hailsham), 274
Hoggart, Richard, 252
Holden, (Sir) Charles, 165
Holford, William (later Baron), 165
Holiday Camp (film), 218, 303
holiday camps, 217–20, 532
holidays, 114–15, 217; package, 511; day trips, 533
Holidays with Pay Act (1938), 217
Holland-Martin, 'Ruby', 228
Hollies, Eric, 293
Holloway, Stanley, 337
Homes for London exhibition (1949), 332
homosexuality, 376–7
Hopkinson, (Sir) Tom, 549
Horizon Holidays, 511
Horne, Willie, 622

Horner, Arthur, 470, 474
horse racing, 113, 293, 335
Housewives' Choice (radio programme), 293
Housewives' League *see* British Housewives' League
housework, 207–8, 580–2
housing: shortage and inadequacy, 20, 72, 101–2, 122, 248, 317, 330–1, 594–6; controversy over provision of flats, 34–5, 53, 89, 103, 157, 331–3, 602, 606–14; individual requirements and preferences, 50–2; exhibitions, 72–3; and squatting, 72, 122, 156; buying and renting, 101; prefabricated, 102, 122–3, 155, 248; local authority building, 154–8, 597–9; public–private provision, 154–7; design, 157–9; and New Towns, 159; building, 332–3, 592; in 1951 Census, 592–5, 597; in Scotland, 594; landlord controlled, 595–6; discussed at 1950 Conservative Party conference, 601; standards, 601–2; *see also* town planning
Housing Act (1949), 596
How Do You View? (TV programme), 587
Howard, Ebenezer, 159; *Tomorrow: A Peaceful Path to Real Reform*, 31
Howell, David, 237
Howerd, Frankie, 212, 310, 353, 361, 563
Howgill, R.J.F., 380
Hoyle, (Sir) Fred, 387–8
Hubback, Eva, 98
Hubbard, Rev. J. W., 574
Huggett family (fictional), 218, 303
Huggetts Abroad, The (film), 303
Hull, 230
Hulton, Sir Edward, 549
Hulton Press, 504–5, 607
Humber Pullman motor car, 496
Hume, David, 145
Hume, Donald, 358–9
Hunot, Peter, 102–3
Hunt, Peter, 370
Hunt, William Holman, 96
Hunter, Germaine, 591
Hunter, Norman C.: *Waters of the Moon*, 590–1
Hurst, Margery, 100
Hutton, Graham, 260
Huxley, Marjorie, 247
Hyde, Ryan, 326
Hyndley, John Scott Hindley, Viscount, 185, 472

Ideal Home Exhibition, 207
Illustrated London News (magazine), 402, 409
immigration, 270–7, 520–2
In the News (TV programme), 525, 587

incentives, 460, 462–4
income tax, 111, 463, 579
India: independence, 135
Industrial Charter, The (Conservative Party review, 1947), 238–41
Industrial and Commercial Finance Corporation (ICFC), 439–40
industry: manufacturing, 398–9; and environment, 399–400; workforce, 405–9; diseases and accidents, 410–11; paternalism in, 413–14; export markets, 435; cultural bias against, 436–7; management, 446–51
infant mortality, 26
inflation: and wage restraint, 229
intelligence tests, 563–4, 577
Irish: as immigrants, 270, 521
Iron and Steel Corporation, 317
iron and steel industry: nationalisation delayed, 224–6, 317, 535–6; and price-fixing, 464; productivity, 467
Isaacs, George, 274
Isherwood, Christopher, 190–2
Issigonis, Alec, 301, 491
ITMA (*It's That Man Again*; radio programme), 95, 123, 306, 308–9
Ivimey, Alan, 123

Jack, Harry, 405–6
Jackson, C.M.J., 431
Jackson, Glenda, 220, 568
Jacob, Naomi, 211
Jacobson, Dan, 509, 518
Jacques, Hattie, 306, 526
Jacques, John, 256
James, Eric: *An Essay on the Content of Education*, 314
Japan: atom-bombed, 82–3; surrenders, 86–7
Jay, Douglas (*later* Baron): and management of economy, 349; and 1950 election result, 388; on Gaitskell's militancy, 546; *The Socialist Case*, 136
JCB excavators, 448
Jenkins, Roy (*later* Baron), 64, 74, 550
'Jennifer' *see* Kenward, Betty
Jephcott, Pearl, 324, 458; *Rising Twenty*, 418
Jews: prejudice against, 270
John Hilton Bureau, 327, 533
Johnson, Hewlett, Dean of Canterbury, 340
Johnson, Pamela Hansford: *A Summer to Decide*, 341
Johnson-Marshall, Percy, 165
Johnson-Marshall, Stirrat, 150
Johnston, Tom, 558
Jones, Arthur Creech, 274–5
Jones, Charles Horace, 559
Jones, George, 333
Jones, Jack, 493
Jones, John, 550

Jones, Mervyn, 223, 342, 549
Jones, Sydney T., 194, 196
Jones, Tom, 558
Jones, Wally, 484
Joseph, Sir Keith (*later* Baron), 436
Jouvenel, Bertrand de, 238
juvenile delinquency, 364–8

Katzin, Olga ('Sagittarius'), 180, 230
Kavanagh, Ted, 306, 308
Kay, John, 445
Keating, Frank, 336
Kee, Robert, 346–7
Keele University, 462
Kelly, Flight Sergeant, 83
Kelly, George, 387
Kent, Jean, 325
Kenward, Betty ('Jennifer'), 96, 135
Kerr, Evelyn S., 377
Kerr, Mima, 506–7
Kerrigan, Peter, 482
Keynes, John Maynard, Baron: economic reforms, 22–3, 537; chairs Arts Council, 176; resists equal opportunity for women, 416; on overseas liabilities, 433; on British assumption of wealth, 434; and City short-termism, 440
Kind Hearts and Coronets (film), 336–7
King, Mary, 14, 76, 95, 105, 193, 248
Kingswood, Norah, 281
Kinnock, Neil (*later* Baron), 248
Kipling, Rudyard, 45
Kitchener, Lord (calypso singer) *see* Roberts, Aldwyn
Klein, Rudolf, 146
Knock, Colin, 172
Knockshinnoch Castle Colliery, Ayrshire, 561
Koestler, Arthur and Mamaine, 544
Korean War (1950–3), 534, 545–52, 630

Labour Believes in Britain (policy statement), 318, 540
Labour, Ministry of: and Commonwealth immigrants, 272, 274
Labour Party: manifesto (April 1945), 21–2; nationalisation programme, 21, 24, 45, 139–42, 224–5, 317–18, 536–7; and economic planning, 24, 136–7, 141, 537, 541; discontinues coalition government, 63–4; election campaign and victory (1945), 67–71, 73–80; forms government (1945), 81; social background of MPs, 82; in by-elections, 118–19; Clause Four of constitution, 141; and social welfare, 143, 148; housing policy, 155; middle-

class disenchantment with, 171–3, 198; limited social reforms, 173–4; and official-dom, 192; attacked by Communist Party, 223; and convertibility crisis, 226–8; and socialist ideals, 234–5, 320–1, 323–4, 539–41; class and cultural attitudes, 267; Orwell assesses achievements, 316–17; annual conference (Blackpool, 1949), 318; and general election (1950), 377–8, 381, 384–5, 388–93; condemns monopolies, 436; and trade unions, 453; and competition, 464; attitude to united Europe, 544; supports participation in Korean War, 546; favours comprehensive education, 576

labour relations, 473–96; see also restrictive practices; strikes (industrial)

Lambert, Gavin, 360
Lambert, Joan, 208
Lancaster, (Sir) Osbert, 30, 340, 503
land ownership, 169
Landau, Alfreda, 71
Landells, Walter ('Autolycus'), 73
Laner, Allen, 192
Langford, Gladys: and victory celebrations, 6–8, 15, 17; enter-tainment, 60; and hostility to Churchill, 70; on victory over Japan, 85–6, 88; on shortages, 105, 197; sense of alienation, 119; on buying in Woolworths, 125; disparages Empire Day, 135; on thaw after great freeze, 200; comments on films, 218, 337, 361; on New Look, 258; on rise of workers, 262–3; on violent crime, 267, 269; on NHS doctors, 280; on dreariness, 298; on spivs, 300; on Munnings's attack on Picasso, 334; on Cripps's announcement of devaluation of pound, 350; on child delin-quency, 368; in 1950 election, 390; on bureaucracy of welfare state, 560; playgoing, 589, 627; works for Census, 592; on Gaitskell's Budget, 621; on preparations for Festival of Britain, 623; attends Bevin's funeral, 626

Langridge, James, 529
Larkham, Peter, 165
Larkin, Philip: on war, 16; and Amis's complaint of cold in Oxford, 196; and Amis's view of Lord David Cecil, 311; admires William Cooper, 507; on Barbara Pym, 523; and Amis's comments on Korean War, 548; and Amis's home in Swansea, 597

Lascelles, Sir Alan ('Tommy'), 26, 244

Laski, Harold, 67, 69, 75
Last, Nella: and victory celebra-tions, 11; and queuing, 71; and Labour victory (1945), 77; outings, 85–6, 286; and victory over Japan, 86–7; on black market, 111; disparages Attlee, 227; shopping, 293; on death of Tommy Handley, 307–8; on Wilfred Pickles, 352; and political broadcasting, 383; on 1950 election result, 391–2; on Korean War, 534; on Barrow-in-Furness, 622

launderettes, 325–6
Laurie, Dr J.G., 280
Law, Richard: Return from Utopia, 537–8
Lawrence, D. H., 38; The Prussian Officer, 561
Lawton, Tommy, 215–16, 265, 352
Laxell, Leslie, 448
Layton, Elizabeth, 596
Leach, Cyril, 285
Leach, (Sir) Edmund, 26
lead poisoning, 410
Lean, (Sir) David, 95
Leather, Ted, 517
Leavis, F. R.: The Great Tradition, 312–13
Le Corbusier (Charles Édouard Jeanneret), 32, 611, 613; City of Tomorrow, 164
Lee, Jennie (later Baroness), 381, 416, 621
Lee, Peter, 159
Leeds: housing programme, 598–9; see also Quarry Hill estate
Lees-Milne, James: on victory celebrations, 10, 16; on Labour legislation, 171; on National Trust policy, 175; on severe winter (1946–7), 190, 194; on Attlee's economic measures, 226–8; on Churchill's optimism, 241; on marriage of Princess Elizabeth, 244; on poor quality of food, 247; on Princess Margaret, 302; elitism, 311–12; on industrial landscape, 401
Legge-Bourke, Major Harry, 544
Le Grand, Julian, 145
Lehmann, John, 192, 234
Leigh, Dr Abe, 280
Leigh, Mike, 280
leisure, 175–8; among young people, 368; see also holidays; reading; sport
Lend-Lease: ends, 103, 133
Lennon, John, 327, 564
Lessing, Doris, 344–5
Let Us Face the Future (Labour Party manifesto, 1945), 21–2, 24, 540
Let Us Win Through Together (Labour Party manifesto, 1950), 378
Letchworth, Hertfordshire, 31

Levenshulme Palace, Manchester, 192
Lever Brothers (company), 413
Leverhulme, William Lever, 1st Viscount, 413
Levin, Bernard, 77
Levy, Benn, 223
Lewis, Eileen, 121
Lewis, Frank, 8, 12, 17, 193, 197
Lewis, Roy and Angus Maude: Professional People, 447
Leyland Motors, 552
Liberal Party: in 1950 election, 388, 391
libraries (public), 210
life expectancy, 20
Linford, Ron, 413
Listen with Mother (radio programme), 356
Listener (magazine), 356–7
Liston, Dr R. P., 280
literature: and criticism, 211–13; and provincial novel, 507–8; successful fiction, 523–4
Liverpool: housing needs, 609
Liverpool Daily Post, 282
living standards, 337–9
Lloyd, A. L. ('Bert'), 399, 518
Lloyd George, David, 229, 401
local government: and health service, 146–7; and poor relief, 149; and housing provision, 154–5, 157–8, 597–9, 602
Lock, Max, 35, 47
Lockhart, Sir Robert Bruce, 60, 73–4
Loders and Dottery, Dorset, 315–16
Loftus, Ernest, 10, 61, 70, 76, 86, 112
London: and 1945 victory celebrations, 5–13, 17, 87–8; town planning, 31; Victory Parade (June 1946), 115–16; satellite towns and out-county estates, 161–2; in severe winter (1946–7), 190–1; housing, 332–3, 611; fog, 315n, 401; dockworkers, 481–3; conditions, 509–10; restu-rants, 512–13; blacks in, 521
London, City of: redevelopment plans, 165–6
London County Council: and town planning, 34–5, 162; builds flats and houses, 331–2, 612–13
London Palladium (theatre), 264
Longbridge, 497–9
Longford, Elizabeth, Countess of, 83
Longford, Francis Aungier Pakenham, 7th Earl of, 66, 130
Longleat (estate), Wiltshire, 325
Lord Chamberlain: censorship, 590
Lord, Leonard (later Baron), 497–9
Lords, House of: powers, 173–4; rejects suspension of death penalty, 269; see also Commons, House of

Loss, Joe, 95
Lovelock, Irene, 71
Lowe, Rodney, 147
Lowther, Sir William, 141
Lucie-Smith, Edward, 371
Luff, Mrs J. R., 573
lung cancer, 560–1
Lustgarten, Edgar, 525
Luton, 489; 1945 election campaign, 67–8
Lutyens, Robert, 606, 614
Lyons, (Sir) William, 492
Lysenko, Trofim, 343
Lyttelton, Humphrey, 12
Lyttelton, Oliver (later 1st Viscount Chandos), 240

Macartney, John, 301
Macaulay, (Dame) Rose, 177
McCallum, R. B., 100
McCann, Graham, 386
McCarthy, Senator Joseph, 341
McCrindle, Alex, 224
MacDiarmid, Hugh (i.e. C. M. Grieve), 557
McDonald, Daniel, 448
MacDonald, Ramsay, 38, 138
Mace, Dr David, 109
MacGregor, Sue, 344
MacInnes, Colin, 503
McIvor, Arthur J., 408
Maclaren-Ross, Julian, 562
Macleod, Iain, 381, 391, 541–2
Macmillan, Harold (later 1st Earl of Stockton): loses seat in 1945 election, 79; and Conservative Party policy reforms, 240; on election campaign (1950), 382, 388; 1950 election victory, 391; and theft of Coronation Stone, 556; on housing, 601; on Gaitskell's 1951 budget, 621; on Morrison's tribute to Bevin, 624; on Bevan's resignation statement, 627; The Middle Way, 24, 240
MacPherson, Stewart, 11
Maggie, The (film), 469
Mais, S.P.B., 437
Mallalieu, J.P.W. ('Curly'), 470–1
Mallon, Jimmy, 346
managers and management, 444–51, 467
Manchester: redevelopment plan, 164–5, 231; Levenshulme Palace, 192–3; education, 577
Manchester Guardian: disparages state welfare, 285
Manley, Dorothy, 292
Mann, George, 528
Mannion, Wilf, 216, 294, 624
Manzoni, Herbert, 231
Margaret Rose, Princess: and victory celebrations, 12; manner, 245; wears New Look, 258; at opening of Olympic Games (1948), 291; rumoured engagement to Marquess of Blandford, 294,

301; character and manner, 301–2; at ITMA broadcast, 306; Marion Crawford's account of, 506; and Peter Townsend, 506; popularity, 506–7; Vere Hodgson on, 563; at 1951 Cup Final, 632
Mark, John, 291
Marks & Spencer stores, 256
marriage: and class, 56–9; and demobilised husbands, 97–8; breakdowns, 109; and unmarried couples, 206; and extramarital relations, 374–6; and working women, 418; see also family life
Marriage Guidance Council, 109
MARS (Modern Architectural Research Group), 32, 36
Marshall Aid (for European reconstruction), 222
Marshall, Howard, 11
Martin, F. M., 572–3
Martin, (Sir) Leslie, 333, 612
Martin, Mortimer, 276
Martin, Stephen, 370
Mason, Roy (later Baron), 204
Mass-Observation: on 1945 victory celebrations, 5, 9–10, 13, 15, 18; on post-war changes and expectations, 40–2, 45–6; on Beveridge Report, 41; on town planning, 50; and election campaign (1945), 69, 73; on food shortage, 106; on Victory Parade (1946), 116; and bread rationing, 118; on religious belief and observance, 126; on nationalisation, 187, 204; on fuel crisis (1947), 198; on Attlee's radio broadcast, 201; on unmarried couples, 206; on reading habits, 210; on holiday camps, 218; and Labour Party cuts, 227; on Conservative Party's Industrial Charter, 240; on religious attitudes, 242; on black market, 253–4; on New Look, 258; on current inconveniences, 296; on weeping at cinema, 304, 361; on television, 305; on National Health Service, 329; and public reaction to paintings, 335; on attitudes to blacks, 345; on juvenile delinquency, 367; on sexual morality, 373–5; and general election (1950), 378, 382, 388–9, 392; on housework, 580–1

Mathew, Francis, 466
Mathew, Sir Theobald, 376
Matisse, Henri: exhibition (1945), 96; Munnings denounces, 334
Matthew, (Sir) Robert, 163, 333, 612–13
Matthews, Joy, 17–18
Matthews, (Sir) Stanley, 215–16, 265–6, 631–2

Maudling, Reginald, 74, 239, 379, 381, 391
Mayhew, Christopher (later Baron), 81
Mayo, Charlie, 428–9
Mays, John, 361–2, 365–6
means-testing, 149
meat: shortages, 579–80, 630
Medhurst, Andy, 360
Medical Research Council, 560
Melson, Alf, 478
Messer, Sir Frederick, 148
Meynell, Sir Francis, 207
Midbank Chronicle (Midland Bank staff magazine), 417
middle class: and housing, 156; disenchantment with Labour government, 171–3; effect of Attlee administration on, 181; reading, 210; sense of deprivation, 260–3; role and social value, 262; and Mrs Dale's Diary, 263–4; living standard decline, 337–9; and austerity measures, 354; and education, 575–6
Middlesbrough: town plan, 47, 54, 158; community study, 53–5
Mikardo, Ian, 68; Keep Left (with Richard Crossman and Michael Foot), 222
Milburn, Jackie, 631
Miller, Max, 310, 414, 563
Mills, Freddie, 336
Mills, (Sir) John, 304
Miners' Charter (1946), 189
Minogue, Kenneth, 22
Minton, John, 512
Mitchison, Gilbert Richard, 66, 74
Mitchison, Naomi, 66, 163
Mitford, Nancy: Love in a Cold Climate, 376
Mitten, Charlie, 265–6
Modern Homes Exhibition, Dorland Hall, London (1946), 102
Moffat, Abe, 474
Monarch gramophones, 448
Monnet, Jean, 544
monopolies, 436, 464
Monopolies Commission, 464
Monserrat, Nicholas, 44
Mooney, Gerry, 616, 618
Moore, Egbert ('Lord Beginner'), 516
Moore, Henry, 334–5
Moore, John, 170
morale: and post-war disenchantment, 109–10, 121, 124, 252
More, Kenneth, 199
Morgan Grenfell (firm), 440
Morgan, Kenneth, 137, 173
Morning Story (radio programme), 584
Morris, Marcus, 505
Morris Minor motor car, 301, 491
Morris Motors, 490–2, 497

Morris, William, 31; *News from Nowhere*, 577

Morrison, Herbert (*later* Baron): on social idealism, 37; and 1945 election result, 75; on economic planning, 136–7; and nationalisation, 139; disfavours worker control, 141; advocates local control of hospitals, 146; opposes House of Lords reform, 174; opposes steel nationalisation, 225; replaced by Cripps as planner, 228; class prejudices, 262; and authorship of *Labour Believes in Britain*, 318; opens block of flats in Lewisham, 333; and general election (1950), 358, 378, 383; on management of nationalised industries, 444; on incentives, 462; addresses Durham Miners' Gala, 470; caution on steel nationalisation, 536; on resistance to joining Europe, 545; succeeds Bevin as Foreign Secretary, 554; rejects Welsh nationalism, 558; *Socialisation and Transport*, 24

Morrison, Kathryn, 256

Morton, H. V., 260

Moscow Dynamo (football club), 93

Moseley, Sydney, 339

Mosley, Simon, 244

motor cars: models and supply, 301; numbers, 402; industry, 485–98, 552; and petrol tax, 510; ownership, 605

Motor Show, Earls Court (1948), 301

Mott, Police Inspector, 361

Mountbatten, Admiral of the Fleet Louis, 1st Earl, 243

Moya, Hidalgo, 611

Mr Cube (Tate & Lyle cartoon character), 319

Mrs Dale's Diary (radio programme), 263–4, 306, 583

Muffin the Mule (TV puppet), 526–7

Muggeridge, Malcolm, 133, 350, 389, 517, 553

Muir, Frank, 307, 309

Mullard Valve Company, 417

Mumford, Lewis, 178, 332, 614

Munnings, Sir Alfred, 334–5

Murdoch, (Dame) Iris, 77, 129, 133, 550

Muriel, Ernest, 261

Murray Hill, Diana, 122

music, popular, 202

Music While You Work (radio programme), 420

Nagasaki, 84

Naipaul, (Sir) Vidia S., 437, 578–9, 622

Nash, Heddle, 95

National Assistance Act (1948), 148

National Association of Labour Teachers, 151, 221, 576

National Coal Board (NCB): miners' leaders reject Shinwell's offer of seat on board, 141; established, 185; relations with miners, 189, 203–4, 475; and working conditions, 410; management, 471–4, 475; and mining accidents, 562; *Plan for Coal*, 473–4

National Council of Social Service, 35

national debt, 20

National Dock Labour Scheme (NDLS), 480, 482–4, 626

National Farmers' Union, 169

National Health Service: proposed by Beveridge, 26–7, 41; free, universal access, 27; public reaction to, 44–5, 282, 329–30; Labour enthusiasm for, 143; operation and management, 145–8; comes into force, 278–83; costs, 327–9; demand for services, 327–8; and silicosis, 410; Bevan defends free principle, 538–9, 554; charges introduced, 538, 554–5, 621–2; Macleod's critique of, 541–2

National Insurance Act (1946), 148–9

National Insurance Scheme, 278–81

National Investment Council, 138–9

National Parks, 414

National Service, 369–73

National Trust, 174–6

National Union of Mineworkers (NUM), 188–9, 453, 474

National Velvet (film), 82

nationalisation: Labour proposals for, 21, 24, 45, 535–7; Macmillan supports, 24; Churchill condemns, 65; programme, 139–42, 224–6, 317–18, 535–7; worker participation rejected, 140–1; coal mines, 185–6, 472–3; steel industry, 224–6, 317, 535–6; management weaknesses, 444–5; public attitudes to, 536–7

nationalism: in Scotland and Wales, 556–8

Nationality Act (1948), 520

New Cumnock, Ayrshire, 561

New Look (fashion), 257–60

New Statesman (weekly magazine): supports National Insurance scheme, 281

New Towns, 159–63, 230, 321, 606, 608

New Towns Act (1946), 160

Newcastle upon Tyne: industry, 399; T. Dan Smith in, 508–9; housing, 609

newspapers: class appeal, 56; reading, 210; restrictive practices, 466

Nicholas, Herbert, 380, 384

Nicholas, R., 164

Nicholls, Audrey, 94

Nicholls, Dandy, 199

Nichols, Joy, 307, 583

Nicolson, (Sir) Harold: on victory celebrations, 6–7; on class resentment, 55; on Harold Wilson, 81; and convertibility crisis, 226; reluctant socialism, 227; writes life of George V, 246; on appeal of royal family, 303; on influx of West Indians, 346; on Churchill's proposed summit meeting with USSR, 385; and general election results (1950), 390–1

Nixon, David, 295

Noble, Phyllis *see* Willmott, Phyllis

Noel-Baker, Philip, 401

Norden, Christine, 209

Norden, Denis, 307, 309

Norman, Montagu, 1st Baron, 270

North Atlantic Treaty Organisation (NATO), 340

North of Scotland Hydro-Electric Board, 558

Northover, A. R., 414

Norwich, 165

Norwood, Sir Cyril, 28; Report (on education, 1943), 27–8, 38, 150

nuclear weapons: Britain develops and possesses, 136; *see also* atomic bomb

Nuffield, William Morris, Viscount, 301, 490–2

nylon stockings, 125, 297

Oakdale Colliery, South Wales, 190

Oakley, Ann, 543

O'Gorman, Dave and Joe, 264

Olivier, Laurence (*later* Baron), 589

Olympic Games, London (1948), 291

One Nation: A Tory Approach to Social Problems (pamphlet), 542

One Nation Group (Conservatives), 542

O'Neil, T., 269

'Open the Door, Richard' (popular song), 202

opera, 62

Orton, Joe, 533

Orwell, George: on cravenness of left, 38; on popular apathy, 45; and election campaign and result (1945), 69, 79–80; attacks professional football, 93; on Bevin's popularity, 134; on lack of social revolution under Labour, 173–4; on Labour's achievements, 316–17; death and funeral, 359; *Coming up for Air*, 30; *The Lion and the Unicorn*, 40, 173; *Nineteen Eighty-Four*, 316, 339

Osborn, (Sir) Frederic: as advocate of town and country planning, 32–3; on Abercrombie, 34, 615; dislike of high-rise flats, 52, 89, 332, 614; on squatters, 72; on political temper in Britain, 89; on dispersal and satellite towns, 158, 614; serves on Reith Committee, 160; on public control and private ownership, 168; on garden cities, 174; and communal life, 178; *Overture to Planning*, 33

Oswell, David, 527

Out of the Blue (variety show), 295

Owen, (Sir) Geoffrey, 447–8

Owen Glyndwr, 458

Oxford: Cutteslowe walls, 55; redevelopment plan, 165

Page, Philip, 13

Pakenham, Frank *see* Longford, 7th Earl of

Palmer, Enid, 250–2

Panter-Downes, Mollie: contributes 'Letter from London' to *The New Yorker*, 101, 297; on housing, 101, 331; on effects of ending Lend-Lease, 103; on poor bread quality, 108; on popular disquiet over peace, 109–10; on shortages, 111, 297; on lack of servants, 113; on admiration for Bevin, 135; on return of petrol ration, 249; on women's clothes, 257; on Belcher affair, 299; on National Health Service, 327–8; on middle-class life, 338; and dollar crisis, 348, 350–1; and general election (1950), 380, 389–90; on London fog, 401; on British economy, 432; on petrol tax, 511; and British caution over Europe, 545; describes Bevan, 553; on Christopher Fry's *Venus Observed*, 589; on ailing Bevin, 621; on Bevan's post-resignation future, 627; *One Fine Day*, 120

Park Hill estate, Sheffield, 610

Parker, Eric, 61

Parkinson, Hargreaves, 466

Parlour, G., 601

Parnell, Val, 563

Partington, Angela, 258

Partridge, Frances, 263, 547

Passfield, Baron *see* Webb, Sidney

Passport to Pimlico (film), 337

Patten, Marguerite, 124, 512

Patterns of British Life (Hulton Press publication), 607

Pay As You Earn (PAYE), 463

pay bargaining, 453

Paynter, Will, 474

Penguin New Writing, 192

Penguin Specials (publisher's series), 55

pensions (old age), 148

People's Homes (Mass-Observation survey), 50, 53

Pepler, Sir George, 602

Percy Report (on local technical colleges, 1945), 462

Perkins, Frank, 440

Perry, Percival Lea Dewhurst Perry, 1st Baron, 486

Perry-Smith, George, 513

Peterlee, County Durham, 159

Petre, Captain, 113

petrol: ration, 249; taxed, 511

Philip, Prince, Duke of Edinburgh, 243–4, 303

Philip, (Sir) Randall, 556

Phillips, Al, 202

Picasso, Pablo: exhibition (1945), 96; Munnings condemns, 334; attends Second World Peace Congress, 549

Pickles, Wilfred, 123, 352, 583, 588

Picture Post (magazine): 'Plan for Britain' (1941), 20, 37; on housing, 52; on plight of middle class, 338–9; on cost of living, 353; on dockers, 478–9; on small independent shops, 529; bans Korean War prisoners story, 548–9

Pierrepoint, Albert, 267, 359

Piggott, Lester, 293–4

Pilkington, Alastair, 448–9

Pilkington Bros Ltd (glass manufacturers), 449

Pilkington, Councillor S. T., 265

Pimlott, Ben, 237, 553, 629

Piper, John, 158

Pleydell-Bouverie, Mrs Michael, 51, 53

Plowden, Sir Edwin, 349

Plymouth: town planning, 35–6, 165, 602

police: depicted in *The Blue Lamp*, 359–61; methods, 362; public attitude to, 362–4

polio, 354–5

Political and Economic Planning (PEP), 39

Pollitt, Harry, 223, 549, 551

Pollok estate, Glasgow: housing, 616–18; schools, 625

Polson, Gordon, 464

polytechnics, 462

Pontin's holiday camps, 218

Port Sunlight, near Liverpool, 413, 450

Portal, Charles Frederick Algernon, 1st Viscount, 449, 451

Porter, Dilwyn, 180

Portsmouth: redevelopment plan, 164, 602

Postgate, Raymond, 479, 513

Potsdam conference (1945), 78

Potter, Dennis, 63

pound *see* sterling (currency)

Pound, Frank, 417

Powell, Anthony, 359

Powell, Enoch, 381, 391, 542

Powell, Glan, 188

Powell, Michael and Emeric Pressburger, 209

Powell, (Sir) Philip, 611, 613

Power Without Glory (play), 199

Prescott, John, 565, 570

Preston, Kenneth, 254, 266, 284, 308, 350, 384, 437, 568, 629

Price, Cliff, 188

Price, Tommy, 351

prices, 247, 353, 579; controls, 110–11; fixing, 436, 464

Priestley, J. B.: on leisure and social activities, 175, 177, 180–1; on English privacy, 178; on political control of lives, 320; Charles Hill criticises, 384; visits rebuilt Coventry, 603, 605; *The Linden Tree*, 232; 'When Work is Over', 37

Private's Progress (film), 372

production controls, 111

productivity, 467

Profumo, John, 66, 74

Pryce-Jones, David, 121

public corporations, 22–3

public houses (pubs), 128

Punch (magazine), 249

Putney Heath: housing development, 612

Puzzled People (M-O investigation), 126

Pyke, Magnus, 250

Pym, Barbara, 101, 354; *Some Tame Gazelle*, 523

Quarry Hill estate, Leeds, 598–9, 619, 623, 630–1

Quarry Hill Experiment (radio programme), 619, 630–1

race: and immigration, 267, 271–4, 520–1; riots and disturbances, 292; attitudes to, 345–7, 517–22

radio: popular programmes, 95, 352–3; popularity, 211–12, 306, 583–4

Rae, John, 80

railways, 402–3, 428, 460–1

Raitz, Vladimir, 511

Raleigh bicycle manufacturers, 407

Ramelson, Bert, 474

Rank, J. Arthur (*later* Baron), 74

Raphael, Frederic, 270

Rasmussen, Steen Eiler: *London: The Unique City*, 231–2

rationing: post-war, 19, 103, 246–7, 251–2, 293, 579; relaxed, 510, 512

Rattigan, (Sir) Terence, 590

Ravetz, Alison, 155, 168

Raynham, Marian, 107–16, 249, 282, 306, 308, 353, 387, 391, 510

reading, 210–11, 266; *see also* literature

Readman, Alison, 100
Reagan, Ronald, 314–15, 401
Rebuilding Britain (National Gallery exhibition, 1943), 31, 48
Red Shoes, The (film), 209
Reeves, Wendy, 97
Reid, Sir Charles, 471
Reith, John, Baron: Committee (on New Towns, 1946), 160; on role of BBC, 586
religion: belief and church attendance, 125–6; controversies over, 242
resale-price maintenance, 464
Research Services Ltd., 425
restaurants: and eating out, 247; bistro-type, 512–13
restrictive practices, 460, 465–7, 475, 479–84, 487, 495; *see also* strikes
Revie, Don, 336
Reynolds, Sir Joshua, 334
Richard, (Sir) Cliff (born Harry Webb), 330, 565
Richards, J. M., 47, 332–3, 335, 613; *The Castles on the Ground*, 158
Richardson, (Sir) Albert, 171
Richardson, Tony, 370
Richmond, Anthony, 271
Ridealgh, Mabel, 257–8
Rillington Place, Notting Hill, 359
roads, 461
Robens, Alf (later Baron), 630
Roberts, Aldwyn ('Lord Kitchener'), 276, 515
Roberts, Alderman Alfred, 90
Roberts, Dr Ffrangcon, 328
Roberts, Margaret *see* Thatcher, Margaret
Robertson, Sir Dennis, 452
Robin (comic), 505
Robinson Family, The (radio programme), 263
Rock, Jane, 63
Rogers, Stuart, 529
Ronay, Egon, 511
Ronson, H., 269
Rootes Group (motor manufacturers), 492–3, 496
Rootes, (Sir) Reginald, 493
Rootes, William (later Baron), 493
Rose, Sonny, 202
Ross, Alan, 524
Rothermere, Anne Geraldine, Viscountess (later Fleming), 74, 135
Rothermere, Esmond Cecil Harmsworth, 2nd Viscount, 135
Round Britain Quiz (radio programme), 624
Rover motor company, 496–7
Royal Academy: Summer Show (1949), 334–5
Royal Command films, 304
Royal Commission on the Taxation of Incomes and Profits (1952), 463

royal family: public attitude to, 231, 243–6, 301–2; attends Royal Variety Performance, 563
Royal Variety Performance, 563
Royle, Trevor, 372
Rubinstein, William D., 432
Rudé, George, 341
rugby league, 622
Russell, C., 601
Russell-Smith, Enid, 145
Russia *see* Soviet Russia
Rutherford, Margaret, 337

Sackville-West, Vita, 65, 226, 346
Sadd, Sir Clarence, 172
'Sagittarius' *see* Katzin, Olga
Sainsbury, Alan (later Baron), 531
Saint, Andrew, 162
St John, Henry: background, 15–16; lacks interest in public events, 16; on shortages, 61, 228; visits Windmill Theatre, 63; on train journey, 70; on public lavatory graffiti, 85; buys costly sandwich, 105; church attendance, 125; seeks accommodation in London, 294–5; grumbling, 295, 354
St Thomas' Hospital, London, 283
Salford: housing, 594–5, 609
Salisbury: redevelopment plan, 165
Salomon, Walter, 270
Samuel, Raphael, 177
Saraband for Dead Lovers (radio programme), 293
Sargent, Sir Malcolm, 291
Saturday Night Theatre (radio programme), 293
Saunders, Edith, 123
Scargill, Arthur, 478
Schlesinger, Arthur, Jr, 544
Schofield, Geoffrey, 586
schools: public, 27, 153, 174, 446; secondary, 28, 150–2, 221, 569–74; comprehensive, 152–3, 221, 576–7; grammar, 220, 314, 564–9, 575–7; and recruitment to management, 446; technical and vocational, 461–2; and 11-plus examination, 564–5; and GCE O level, 569; leaving age raised, 574–5; and social class, 574–6; *see also* education
Schumacher, E. F. (Fritz), 401–2
Schuman, Robert, 543–4
science: policy and training, 462
Scotland: nationalists steal Coronation Stone, 556–7; economic difficulties, 557–8; television in, 585; housing, 594
Scott of the Antarctic (film), 304, 361
Sellers, Peter, 264
Selvon, Sam: *The Lonely Londoners*, 521
servants: shortage, 113
Setty, Stanley, 358–9

sex: before marriage, 206, 375–6; attitudes and morality, 373–6
Sharp, Thomas, 3, 30, 48, 165
Shawcross, Sir Hartley (later Baron), 171, 269, 625, 630
Shearer, Moira, 209
Sheffield: industry, 399, 423; and price-fixing, 464; housing and flat development, 610
Shepheard, Peter, 611
Sheppard, David, 529
Sherman, Vincent, 315
Shinwell, Emanuel (later Baron), 141, 189, 193–5, 198, 262
shipbuilding, 450
Shonfield, (Sir) Andrew, 552
shopping: self-service, 256, 531; small independent shops and chain stores, 529–32; and shortages, 579–80
Shore, Dinah, 563
Sight and Sound (magazine), 360
silicosis, 410
Silkin, Lewis, 89, 160–2, 165, 168, 232
Sillitoe, Alan, 352; *Saturday Night and Sunday Morning*, 407–8
Silverman, Sydney, 268
Silvey, R.J.E., 212
Sime, William, 529
Simon, Brian, 341
Simon of Wythenshawe, Shena D., Lady: *Three Schools or One?*, 221
Sinden, (Sir) Donald, 590
Sissons, Peter, 564
Sky High (revue), 620
Slater, Eliot and Moya Woodside: *Patterns of Marriage*, 56–8
Slaughter, Clifford, 476
slums, 20; clearance, 610
Smith, Alderman Albert (of Sheffield), 610
Smith, Sir Ben, 106
Smith, Dodie, 590
Smith, D. R., 346
Smith, T. Dan, 508–9, 524, 593, 609
Smithers, Sir Waldron, 239
smoking: as cause of lung cancer, 560–1; prevalence, 578
Smuts, Field Marshal Jan Christian, 176
Snagge, John, 308, 335
snoek (South African fish), 247–8
Snow, Charles P. (later Baron), 524
soap, 299
Sobell, Michael, 448
social groups, 179
social security: and Beveridge Report proposals, 21, 25–6; Labour programme, 148–50; as state responsibility, 149–50, 285
social services: Labour's programme for, 143–4; introduced, 284; Macleod on, 541–2
Social Survey (1951): on race attitudes, 519–21
socialism: Churchill attacks, 64–5; goals and ideals, 129–30, 232–5;

socialism (cont.)
  and equality of opportunity,
  152; and officialdom, 192;
  Harold Nicolson on, 227;
  Bevan on, 233, 318–19; as
  Labour ideal, 234–5, 320–1,
  323–4, 539–41; Foot defends,
  320; Michael Young on, 322,
  539; Charles Hill attacks, 384;
  Titmuss on, 542–3; see also
  Labour Party
Society of Motor Manufacturers
  and Traders, 485
Society of Women Housing
  Managers, 52, 231
Soil Association, 169
Solomons, Jack, 72
Southampton: reconstruction plan,
  602
Soviet Russia: popular attitudes to,
  133; Bevin's mistrust of, 134–5;
  expansionist threat, 222–4; US
  hostility to, 222; and British
  Communists, 342–3; aggres-
  siveness, 546; Callaghan
  criticises, 550–1
Spark, (Dame) Muriel, 326
spectacles: free on National
  Health, 327
Spectator (magazine): on proposed
  National Health Service, 27; on
  Conservative policy, 238–9; in
  1950 general election, 385
Speed, Florence: on food waste,
  108; and 1946 Victory Parade,
  115; on shortages, 119, 228;
  on poor food quality, 125;
  meets angry worker, 181; on
  severe winter, 190; on shopping, 196–8; on Princess
  Elizabeth's engagement, 243;
  on snoek, 247; on pre-election
  de-rationing, 358; on 1950
  Conservative manifesto, 379;
  stays at home for holiday,
  533; and Korean War, 534;
  watches Boat Race, 587
speedway (sport), 351
Spence, James, 98
Spender, (Sir) Stephen, 549
spivs, 111–12, 119, 227, 253, 255,
  264, 300
Spivs' Gazette, 255
sport, 93, 113; midweek ban, 201;
  see also individual sports
Spry, Constance, 215, 244
squatting and squatters, 72, 122–3,
  156
Stalin, Josef: at Potsdam conference, 78; supported by British
  Communist Party, 223, 342;
  and Churchill's proposed
  summit meeting, 385
Standard Motors (later Triumph),
  492–6
Stanley, Sydney, 300
Stanmore golf club, 518
Stark, Graham, 264
Steedman, Carolyn: Landscape for
  a Good Woman, 259–60

steel see iron and steel industry
sterling (currency): convertibility
  crisis, 226, 228, 434; and
  diminishing gold reserves,
  347–8; devaluation, 348–51;
  area created, 434–5
Sterling Metals, Coventry, 518
Stevenage New Town, 159, 161–2,
  608
Stewart, Patrick, 70
Stock Exchange: and 1945 election,
  73
Stockholm: town planning, 604,
  607
Stockholm Peace Petition, 548
Stockport High School for Girls,
  566–7
Stoke Lacy, Herefordshire, 14
Stoke Newington: Woodberry
  Down estate, 612
Stone of Scone see Coronation
  Stone
Strachey, John, 66, 117, 544
Strauss, George, 485
Streat, Sir Raymond, 10, 105, 171,
  237, 245, 441–2, 535, 628
Street, A. G., 214–15
Street-Porter, Janet (née Bull),
  326
Streeter, Fred, 214
strikes (industrial): dockers'
  (October 1945), 104–5; (July
  1949), 340, 480; (1951), 625;
  coalminers' (1947–50), 203,
  474; (1893), 477; working
  days lost through dockers,
  480; at Ford works, 487; court
  trial (1951), 625–6; see also
  labour relations; restrictive
  practices
Stubbins, Albert, 216
suburbs, 30, 32, 158, 600–1; and
  gardening, 214–15
Sunday Pictorial (newspaper), 121,
  304, 340
supply-side economics, 460
Sutton Coldfield: television transmitter, 357
Swaffer, Hannen, 67
Swanton, E. W., 114, 217, 528
sweets: de-rationed, 299
Swift (comic), 505
Sykes, Eric, 353, 525

Take It From Here (radio
  programme), 307, 309, 583
Tarbuck, Jimmy, 564
Tarran, Capt. A. E., 269
Tate & Lyle sugar company:
  opposes nationalisation, 319;
  paternalism, 413
Tawney, Richard Henry, 130, 542
taxation, 173, 462; see also income
  tax
Taylor, A.J.P., 177, 525, 587
Taylor, D. J., 444
Taylor, Elizabeth, 82
Tebbit, Norman (later Baron),
  466
telecommunications, 460–1

television: resumes service, 116;
  broadcasts Victory Parade,
  117; BBC indifference to,
  212–13, 585; early programmes
  and viewers, 212–14; lack of
  news bulletins, 212; increase
  in viewers and programmes,
  304–5, 356–7; children's
  programmes, 526–8;
  commercial, 586–7; range of
  programmes, 586–8
Temple, William, Archbishop of
  Canterbury: Christianity and
  the Social Order, 55
Tennent, H. M. (theatre agency),
  590
Terry-Thomas (i.e. Thomas Terry
  Hoare Stevens), 587
Tesco stores, 256
Tewson, Vincent, 453
Thatcher, Margaret, Baroness (née
  Roberts), 66, 181, 238, 381, 391
theatre: popularity, 94–5;
  encouraged, 176; in Bristol,
  264; variety, 264–5; poetic
  drama, 588–9; censorship,
  590; West End, 590–1
Third Programme (BBC radio),
  176–7
Thirkell, Angela: and hostility to
  Labour government, 172;
  Private Enterprise, 120–1
This Is The Road (Conservative
  Party manifesto), 379
Thomas, Dylan: narrates When
  We Build Again, 30; on
  Labour election victory
  (1945), 77; broadcasts on
  Third Programme, 177; writes
  to John Arlott, 216–17
Thomas, Geoffrey: Incentives in
  Industry, 463
Thompson, E. P., 342
Thompson, Laurence, 399, 410,
  492; Portrait of England, 577–8
Thompson, Paul, 493–6
Thompson, Peter, 179
Thomson, D. C. (publishers), 505
Thorn, Jules, 448
Thorndike, (Dame) Sybil, 242,
  590–1
Thurston, P. G., 242
Times, The: favours National
  Health Service, 143; on town
  planning, 168; on social secu-
  rity, 285; on The Blue Lamp,
  360; on exchange controls,
  436
Times Educational Supplement: on
  educational reform, 27–8
Times Literary Supplement, 562
Tiratsoo, Nick, 179, 605
Titfield Thunderbolt, The (film),
  468
Titmuss, Richard, 26, 55, 543;
  Problems of Social Policy, 40,
  542; Report on Luton, 154
Tolkien, J.R.R., 84
Tomlinson, George, 151, 221, 576
Tomlinson, Jim, 138, 144, 149, 552

Town and Country Planning Acts: (1944), 31; (1947), 602

Town and Country Planning (magazine), 332

Town and Country Planning, Ministry of: established, 30–1

town planning: wartime schemes, 28–34, 46–9; and community feeling, 53–5, 231; and New Towns, 159–63; post-war redevelopment schemes, 160–8; restrained by convertibility crisis, 230; decline, 602–8, 614; *see also* housing

Townsend, John R., 594–5

Townsend, Group Captain Peter, 506

trade (overseas), 432, 464–5, 551–2

trade unions: and worker control, 140–1; status and membership, 452–3, 456; and pay bargaining, 453–4, 459; and communists, 454–6; weaknesses, 455–9; and shop stewards, 457; and women, 457–8; and economy, 458–9; rules and customs, 459; in motor industry, 491–2, 498–9; *see also* labour relations; restrictive practices; strikes

Trades Union Congress: accepts wage restraint, 229, 453

Train, Jack, 624

training and education, 460–1

trams, 403

transport: means of, 402–3; and supply-side economics, 460–1; *see also* railways; roads

Transport and General Workers' Union (TGWU), 229–30, 452, 456

Tribune (magazine), 320, 322

Tribute to the King (radio programme), 10

Trinder, Tommy, 11–12

Troop, Freddie, 496

Truman, Harry S.: announces dropping of atomic bomb, 82; anti-Soviet stance, 222; and Korean War, 545

Tunney, Hubert, 185

Turnbull, Peter, 483

Turner & Newall (asbestos manufacturer), 411

Turner, Graham, 488–9

Turner, Sir Samuel, 411

Turpin, Dick (boxer), 276, 519

Tweedale, Geoffrey, 411

Twenty Questions (radio programme), 583, 624, 629

Tynan, Kenneth, 17, 370

Uglow, Jenny, 215

unemployment, 45, 57, 435; *see also* work

United States of America: discontinues Lend-Lease, 103, 133; British attitudes to, 133, 467–8; loan to Britain, 133; foreign policy, 222–3; and convertibility

of sterling, 226; Britain's dollar reserves reduced, 228; anticommunism in, 341; and sterling area, 434; productivity, 467; and Korean War, 545–7; relations with Britain, 546

universities: increase in numbers, 462

Uttin, Rose, 81, 88, 197, 246, 299

Vaizey, John (*later* Baron), 23

Vanguard motor car (Standard), 496

Varah, Chad, 505

Variety Bandbox (radio programme), 300, 352, 361

Variety Cavalcade (radio programme), 583

Varney, Reg, 620–1

Vaughan, Paul, 403

Vaughan Williams, Adeline, 9

Vaughan Williams, Ralph, 304

Vauxhall motor company, 489–90

VE Day (8 May 1945), 5–18

venereal diseases, 114

Vic Oliver Introduces (TV programme), 358

Victory Parade (radio broadcast), 11–12

Vincent, David, 149

VJ Day (15th August 1945), 86–9

Vogue (magazine), 257, 282

Volkswagen motor company, 490, 495, 497

Vote for Huggett (film), 303

voters: views and attitudes, 382–3

wages: restraints, 229–30, 452, 454; gender differentials, 415–17

Wales: coal mines and miners, 187, 190, 194–6; nationalist movement, 558

Waley, Joan, 9

Walker, Cyril, 163, 612

Walker, Mrs M., 357

Walker, Patrick Gordon *see* Gordon Walker, Patrick

Walkey, Mrs N.E., 339

Wallace, Billy, 301

Wallace, Edgar, 211

Waller, Madge, 42

Wallsend, near Newcastle, 593

Wanchove, Averill, 275–6

War Factory (Mass-Observation study), 44

Warbey, William, 67–8, 75

Warburg, Frederick, 339

Warburg, (Sir) Siegmund, 441

Ward, Edmund, 62

Waring, Peter, 116

Warner, Jack (actor), 218, 303, 359, 361

Warner, Jack (Hollywood film producer), 315

Warner, Rex, 529

Warner, Sylvia Townsend, 109

Warner's holiday camps, 218

Warnes, Stanley, 188

Warr, J. J., 529

Warwick, 165

washing machines, 326

Waterhouse, Keith, 63, 619

Waterlogged Spa (radio programme), 306

Waters of the Moon (play), 627

Waugh, Evelyn: on 1945 election result, 74; on Randolph Churchill, 84; disparages Picasso, 96; resists emigration to Ireland, 260; *Brideshead Revisited*, 62

weather: severe winter (1946–7), 189–200, 202

Weaver, Denis, 439

Webb, Beatrice (*later* Lady Passfield), 323–4, 342

Webb, Maurice, 630

Webb, Sidney (*later* Baron Passfield), 235, 323–4, 342

Week-End Book, The, 207

Welch, Denton, 16

Weldon, Fay (Franklin Birkinshaw), 124

welfare state: and Beveridge Report proposals, 21, 26; public attitudes to, 43; Labour programme for, 143–5; effect on middle class, 173; introduced, 283–5; Ronald Reagan on, 315; economic cost, 435

Welland, Colin, 532

Wellisz, Stanislas, 474

Wells, H. G., 70

Welsh language, 558

Welwyn Garden City, Hertfordshire, 31

Wembley: Olympic Games (1948), 291

West Indians: immigrants, 271, 273–6, 346, 520–1; cricket team and supporters, 515–16

When We Build Again (documentary film), 30

Whisky Galore! (film), 336

White, Antonia, 523

White, Freddy, 334

White, Jack, 202

Whitham, Basil, 167

Whittaker, Mary, 248

Widgery, David, 147

Wiener, Martin J.: *English Culture and the Decline of the Industrial Spirit, 1850–1980*, 436–7

Wiggans, K. C., 593–4

Wightman, Ralph, 12, 214–15, 517, 582

Wiles, Sir Harold, 273

Wilkinson, Ellen, 150–2, 155, 193, 575

Willcock, H. D., 367–8

Willesden: housing survey, 156–7

Williams, Kenneth, 264, 330

Williams, Philip, 392

Williams, Raymond, 340

Williams, Tennessee, 249

Williams, Tom, 169

Williams-Ellis, Sir Clough, 29

Willink, Henry, 26–9

Willis, Ted (*later* Baron), 361

Willmott, Rev. Oliver, 315–16
Willmott, Peter, 323, 564, 596
Willmott, Phyllis (née Noble), 209, 283, 323, 408–9, 579, 596
Wills, Abigail, 367
Wilmot, Harold, 347
Wilson, (Sir) Angus, 524–5
Wilson, Colin, 373
Wilson, Edmund, 61, 69
Wilson, Harold (later Baron): and Labour government (1945), 81; background and career, 236–7; debates with Mrs Chandler, 298–9; relaxes controls on goods, 298; and management of economy, 349, 537; and consumer needs, 540; jealousy of Gaitskell, 553–4; criticises rearmament programme, 554; defends free National Health Service, 555; resigns (1951), 628–30; admires Bevan, 628–9
Wimbledon: tennis championships, 113
Wimpey (acrobat), 264
Wincott, Harold, 538
Windmill Theatre, London, 63
Winn, Godfrey, 218, 600, 603–5, 607
Winterbottom, Walter, 515
winters: severe ('big freeze', 1946–7), 189–200, 202
wireless see radio
Wisden's Cricketers' Almanack, 114
Wisdom, Norman, 264–5, 285
Withers, Audrey, 282
Wodehouse, (Sir) Pelham G., 325
Wolstenholme, Kenneth, 124
Wolverhampton: town planning, 48
Woman's Hour (radio programme), 123, 278
Woman's Own (magazine): praises The Blue Lamp, 361; and Dirk Bogarde's romantic ideals, 377; serialises Marion Crawford, 506

women: and Beveridge Report, 25; home requirements, 51; indifference to politics, 58, 324; status, 98–100; working, 99–100, 208–9, 406, 409, 415–21; and housekeeping, 207–8, 580–2; and clothes, 249, 251, 257–9; car driving, 301; and trade unions, 457–8; BBC bans as news readers, 584–5; see also marriage
Women and Beauty (magazine), 523
Women and Industry (Social Survey study), 418
Woodcock, Bruce, 72, 336
Wooderson, Sydney, 82, 291
Woodhams, Martin, 357
Woolton, Frederick James Marquis, 1st Earl of, 261
Worcester, 165
work: occupations and conditions, 405–15, 422–5; and paternalism, 413; and job-satisfaction, 423–9; and earnings, 425–6; hours, 425; see also women
Workers' Education Association (WEA), 176
Workers' Playtime (radio programme), 110
working class: militancy, 44; indifference to politics, 57–8, 127; attitudes and characteristics, 127–8, 263–4; and political radicalism, 131–2; effect of Labour government on, 181–2; reading habits, 210–11; sexual morality, 375; and 1950 general election, 393; transport, 402–4; occupations and conditions, 405–9, 412; and industrial diseases, 410–12; and works outings, 414–15; attitude to education, 574–6; see also class (social)
World Peace Conference, Second (1950), 549
World Speedway Championship (1949), 351

Worsley, T. C., 589–91
Worth, Squadron Leader, 66
Wright, Billy, 335
Wyatt, Woodrow (later Baron), 81
Wyman, Bill (born Bill Perks), 199, 220, 574
Wyndham, Joan, 12, 83

Yardley, Norman, 278, 528
Young, Michael (later Baron): lunch with Dalton, 16, 23; background, 22; drafts Labour Party manifesto (1945), 22, 130; on ten-year plan for future of socialism, 130, 232; favours nationalisation, 225; political change of heart, 323, 540–1; Willmott praises, 323; commitment to Labour Party, 324; and law reform, 324; writes Labour's 1950 election programme, 324, 358, 379; 'The British Socialist Way of Life' (paper), 539–41; Labour's Plan for Plenty, 141, 151; Small Man, Big World, 320–3
Younger, Kenneth, 547
youth: and National Service, 269–73; behaviour, 368–9

Zinkin, Maurice, 450
Zweig, Ferdynand: interviews workers, 127–8, 266, 366; on coalminers, 186–7, 195, 203–4, 477; on manual and office worker differences, 406; on inhumanity in industry, 411; on trade unions, 456, 458–9; on restrictive practices, 465; The British Worker, 422–6; Women's Life and Labour, 419–21, 457–8
Zweiniger-Bargielowska, Ina, 111, 187, 260

A NOTE ON THE AUTHOR

David Kynaston was born in Aldershot in 1951. He has been a professional historian since 1973 and has written fifteen books, including *The City of London* (1994–2001), a widely acclaimed four-volume history, and *WG's Birthday Party*, an account of the Gentleman v. Players match at Lord's in July 1898. He is currently a visiting professor at Kingston University.

ALSO AVAILABLE BY DAVID KYNASTON
FAMILY BRITAIN

Family Britain brilliantly continues David Kynaston's groundbreaking history of post-war Britain with a vivid portrait of the 1950s, a time when Britain was starting to move away from the hardships of austerity. Great national events jostle alongside everything that gave 1950s Britain its distinctive flavor from Butlin's holiday camps, Kenwood food mixers and *Hancock's Half-Hour* to Ekco television sets, skiffle and teddy boys. An astonishing array of vivid, intimate and unselfconscious voices drive the narrative, punctuated by the appearance of such well-known figures as Doris Lessing (joining and later leaving the Communist Party), John Arlott (sticking up on *Any Questions?* for the rights of homosexuals) and *Tiger's* Roy of the Rovers (making his debut for Melchester). *Family Britain* offers an unrivalled perspective on Britain during seven momentous years.

✳

'I could quote forever from this magnificent book. Professor Kynaston is the most entertaining historian alive'
PHILIP HENSHER, SPECTATOR

'An outstanding history evokes Fifties' Britain in all its conservatism, idealism and lost innocence ... Plenty of historians have written about it before. But none have captured it better or with more human sympathy than David Kynaston, in this deeply researched, richly detailed and very moving book. *****'
DAILY TELEGRAPH

'Evocative and hugely appealing ... On almost every page there is an arresting detail, statistic or quotation'
SUNDAY TIMES

✳

ISBN: 978 0 7475 8385 1 · HARDBACK · £25.00

ORDER YOUR COPY: BY PHONE +44 (0)1256 302 699; BY EMAIL: DIRECT@MACMILLAN.CO.UK
DELIVERY IS USUALLY 3–5 WORKING DAYS. FREE POSTAGE AND PACKAGING FOR ORDERS OVER £20.

ONLINE: WWW.BLOOMSBURY.COM/BOOKSHOP
PRICES AND AVAILABILITY SUBJECT TO CHANGE WITHOUT NOTICE.

WWW.BLOOMSBURY.COM/DAVIDKYNASTON

B L O O M S B U R Y